Psychological Testing
Principles, Applications, and Issues

ROBERT M. KAPLAN
DENNIS P. SACCUZZO
San Diego State University

BROOKS/COLE PUBLISHING COMPANY
Monterey, California

Consulting Editor: *Lawrence S. Wrightsman*

Brooks/Cole Publishing Company
A Division of Wadsworth, Inc.

Printed in the United States of America

10 9 8 7 6 5 4 3

Library of Congress Cataloging in Publication Data

Kaplan, Robert M.
  Psychological testing.

  Includes index.
    1. Psychological tests.   I. Saccuzzo,
Dennis P., date–   . II. Title. [DNLM:
1. Psychological tests—Methods.   BF 176
K17p]
BF176.K36   150'.28'7   81-38461
ISBN 0-8185-0494-3   AACR2

Cover Photo: *Courtesy of Art Kane, The Image Bank West*

Subject Editor: *C. Deborah Laughton*
Manuscript Editor: *Pamela Fisher*
Production Editor: *Marlene Thom*
Interior Design: *Otto Speck*
Cover Design: *Debbie Wunsch*
Illustrations: *Art by Ayxa*
Typesetting: *Thompson Type, San Diego, California*

To Cathie and Lorraine

Preface

Psychology is a broad, exciting field. Psychologists today work in a variety of settings, including everything from schools and clinics to biochemistry laboratories and industrial settings. Despite this diversity two common themes link all psychologists: all study behavior, and all depend to some extent on its measurement. This book concerns a particular type of measurement, psychological tests, that measure characteristics pertaining to all aspects of behavior in human beings.

This book resulted from the mutual interests of both authors. As active participants in the development and use of psychological tests, we became disheartened because far too many undergraduate college students view psychological testing courses as boring and unrelated to their goals or career interests. In contrast, we view psychological testing as an exciting field. It is rich in the history of psychology, yet it is constantly in flux because of challenges, new developments, and controversies. A book on testing should encourage, not dampen, a student's interest. Thus we provide an overview of the many facets of psychological tests and measurement principles in a style that will appeal to the contemporary college student.

To understand all the applications and issues in psychological testing, the student must learn some basic principles. Because this requires some knowledge of introductory statistics, some reviewing and a careful reading of Part 1 will pave the way for an understanding of the applications of tests discussed in Part 2. Part 3 examines the issues now shaping the future of testing. Such issues include test anxiety, test bias, and the interface between testing and the law. The very future of applied psychology may depend on the ability of psychologists to face these challenging issues.

Throughout the book there is a series of focused discussions and focused examples. These sections are designed to illustrate the material in the book through example or to provide a more detailed discussion of a particular issue. There are also some technical boxes that are used to demonstrate technical material such as statistical calculations.

Students today often prefer informal discussions and personally relevant examples. Consequently we decided to use models from a variety of fields and to write in an informal style to maximize interest. However, testing is a serious and complicated field in which there are major disagreements among scholars and experts of the highest level. Therefore, we have treated these aspects of testing with more formal discussion and detailed referencing.

Many people helped us in our goals for this book, and we thank them all. Major sections of the manuscript were reviewed by more than 150 students who made countless suggestions for revision. Cathy Sullivan read and critiqued the entire manuscript twice. Jerry Sattler assisted by reading several chapters and providing valuable consultation. Connie Toevs provided a variety of important services from finding current references to typing and proofreading.

Very special thanks go to Rick Jacobs of Pennsylvania State University and R. J. Rankin of the University of Oregon, who carefully read and evaluated several drafts of the book. The many insightful comments of the following reviewers are also gratefully acknowledged: Paul J. Danielson, University of Arizona; James Jaccard, Purdue University; Patricia Mitchell, Middle Tennessee State University; Robert Rumery, Illinois State University; Gilbert Sax, University of Washington; L. Robert Sorensen, California Polytechnic State University; and Wesley C. Zaynor, Kent State University. Tim Connor of the San Diego County Counsel's Office provided a very careful analysis of Chapter 21, "Testing and the Law." As an attorney he was able to find specific problems in wording and substance.

The Brooks/Cole Publishing editors also deserve to be commended. They have been actively involved in all stages of the writing and production processes. When Todd Lueders, our initial editor, left, Debbie Laughton kept the project going without interruption. Then Marlene Thom, production editor, continued to provide top-notch and highly professional assistance. Last, but far from least, we thank our academic editor, Larry Wrightsman of the University of Kansas. Professor Wrightsman went beyond the call of duty with his unwavering support, limitless encouragement, and immaculate attention to countless details.

This preface would not be complete without special acknowledgment of our wives and families, who lived through the ordeal of this project. Lorraine Saccuzzo read, edited, and typed major portions of the manuscript. Cathie Atkins (Kaplan) reviewed many chapters and suggested countless changes.

Robert M. Kaplan
Dennis P. Saccuzzo

Contents in Brief

Contents in Detail

Chapter 15 Structured Personality Tests   312

Chapter 16 Tests for Choosing Careers   339

Chapter 22 The Future of Psychological Testing   492

Psychological Testing
Principles, Applications, and Issues

PART

1

PRINCIPLES

CHAPTER

1

Introduction

Learning objectives

When you have completed this chapter, you should be able to do the following:

1. *Define the terms* psychological test *and* psychological testing.
2. *Distinguish between an individual test and a group test.*
3. *Define the terms* achievement, aptitude, *and* intelligence *and identify a concept that can encompass all of these terms.*
4. *Distinguish between ability tests and personality tests.*
5. *Define the phrase* structured personality test.
6. *Explain how structured personality tests differ from projective personality tests.*
7. *Explain what a normative or standardization sample is and why such a sample is important.*
8. *Identify one of the major differences between the Wechsler-Bellevue intelligence scale and the Stanford-Binet intelligence scale.*
9. *Identify the major developments in the history of psychological testing.*
10. *Explain the relevance of psychological tests in contemporary society.*

If you were asked to identify the ten most important topics in psychology, psychological testing would certainly be considered for your list. If the restriction was added that your list include only the ten most important controversial applications of psychological knowledge to practical human problems, then psychological testing would certainly be included.

Psychological tests permeate our society. Few Americans over the age of 6 have escaped at least some form of contact with psychological tests. They have found their way into primary and secondary schools, institutions of higher education, professional. training programs, business and industry, the military, clinical settings, and just about everywhere. Despite their widespread use, psychological tests are highly controversial, with social, political, and economic ramifications. Society at large as well as professionals involved with psychological tests (for example, psychiatrists, social workers, educators, and psychologists) seem to have a deep ambivalence toward psychological tests.

I. PSYCHOLOGICAL TESTING

You are probably already familiar with some of the more elementary concepts of psychological testing. For the sake of clarity, however, it is important to begin with definitions of even the most basic terms so that you will know how they are used in this textbook.

A. *What a test is*

Every schoolchild has had experience with tests. A *test* is a measurement device. A spelling test, for example, measures how well someone spells or the extent to which someone has mastered or learned to spell a specific list of words. At some point during the next few weeks it is likely that your instructor will want to measure the extent to which you have mastered the material of this textbook. To accomplish this, your instructor may give you a test.

B. *Psychological test defined*

A *psychological test* is a device for measuring characteristics of human beings that pertain to behavior. There are many types of behavior. An *overt* behavior is an observable activity of an individual. Some psychological tests attempt to measure the extent to which a human being might engage in or "emit" a particular overt behavior or whether the individual is even able to so emit. Other tests measure the extent to which a person has previously engaged in some overt behavior. Behavior can also be *covert*. This behavior takes place within an individual and cannot be observed. For example, your feelings and thoughts are types of covert behavior. Some tests attempt to measure such behavior. Thus, psychological tests measure past, present, or future behavior.

In measuring past behavior a psychological test attempts to evaluate or ascertain (that is, measure) what the individual has already done. When an instructor gives a test on the material from a textbook, to a large extent he or she is evaluating the student's prior overt and covert behavior—namely, how much the student has studied. In measuring present behavior a psychological test attempts to determine current functioning. For example, in addition to evaluating past behavior, a test on the material in a textbook also measures how much the student can recall and can understand at the time of testing. Finally, a test may attempt to predict future behavior, forecasting the chances or "probability" that you may emit a certain behavior or whether you are capable of it. For example, a test may help estimate the probability that you can complete an advanced professional degree program.

C.   *Types of tests*

Just as there are many types of behavior, so there are many types of tests. Tests that can only be given to one person at a time are known as *individual tests*. The situation involved in an individual test is similar to that in individual psychotherapy. The "examiner" or "test administrator" (that is, the person giving the test) gives the test to only one person at a time, just as in individual psychotherapy when only one person is seen at one time. A *group test*, by contrast, can be administered to more than one person at a time by a single examiner, as when your instructor gives everyone in the class a test at the same time.

There are special tests to measure certain types of behavior. One type of behavior can be referred to as *human ability*, or behavior that reflects either what a person has learned or the person's capacity to emit a specific behavior. A test that measures what you have already learned about psychology, for example, is an ability test. A test that measures how well you might be able to complete a doctoral program in psychology is also an ability test.

Consistent with current formulations (Anastasi, 1980), the definition of human ability used in this text does not make fine distinctions among various types of human ability. However, to get a better idea of the meaning of human ability, it is helpful to look at how previous experts have defined it. Historically, many experts involved in the measurement of human ability distinguished among achievement, aptitude, and intelligence. *Achievement* is a term that has commonly been used to refer to previous learning. A test that measures or evaluates how many words you can spell correctly is referred to as a spelling achievement test. *Aptitude*, by contrast, is a term that has commonly been used to refer to the potential for learning a specific skill. Whereas a spelling achievement test measures how many words you already know how to spell, a spelling aptitude test measures how many words you might be able to spell given a certain amount of training, education, and experience. Your music aptitude, for example, refers in part to how well you might be able to learn to play a musical instrument given a certain number of lessons. Intelligence, in turn, has traditionally been distinguished from achievement and aptitude. *Intelligence* is a term that has commonly been used to refer to a person's general potential, independent of prior learning. When you say a person is "smart," you are probably referring to intelligence. When a father scolds his daughter because she has not done as well in school as she is capable of doing, presumably he is saying that she has not used her intelligence (potential) to achieve (that is, acquire new knowledge).

The distinctions among achievement, aptitude, and intelligence, however, are all but meaningless because all three are highly interrelated (Coleman & Cureton, 1954; Kelley, 1927, pp. 193–209). Attempts to separate prior learning from potential for learning, for example, have not been successful. There is a considerable overlap among achievement, aptitude, and intelligence tests. In view of this overlap, all three concepts are encompassed by the term *human ability* (see Carroll & Horn, 1981).

Although achievement, aptitude, and intelligence can all be encompassed under the concept of human ability, there is a clear-cut distinction between ability tests and personality tests. Whereas ability tests are related to capacity or potential, *personality tests* are related to the overt and covert dispositions of the individual—for example, the tendency that a person will show a particular behavior or response in any given situation. Remaining isolated from others, for instance, does not require any special skill or ability, but some people prefer or are disposed to remain thus isolated. This is their typical behavior. Personality tests measure typical behavior.

There are several types of personality tests. In Chapter 15, for example, you will learn about structured (that is, objective) personality tests. *Structured personality tests* provide a statement, usually of the "self-report" variety (for example, "I like rock and roll music"), and require the subject to choose between two or more alternative responses such as "True" or "False." Most group tests used to measure how well you have mastered assigned material in your college courses are of the structured variety. Students, for example, often distinguish between structured, or objective, tests and essay tests. Structured tests require you to recall or recognize something, whereas essay tests require you to produce something spontaneously.

In contrast to structured tests, but like essay tests, projective personality tests are unstructured. A *projective personality test* is one in which the stimulus (test materials) and/or required response are ambiguous. For example, in a projective test known as the Rorschach inkblot test, the stimulus is an inkblot. Furthermore, rather than being asked to choose among alternative responses as in the structured personality tests, the individual is asked to provide a spontaneous response. The inkblot is presented to the subject, who is asked "What might this be?" The general idea behind projective tests is that when a person interprets an ambiguous stimulus, the person's interpretation of that stimulus will reflect his or her unique characteristics. (See Chapter 17.)

D. *Psychological testing defined*

Psychological testing is a term that refers to the "use" of psychological tests. It refers to all the possible uses, applications, and underlying concepts of psychological tests. Anyone who creates or in any way makes use of a psychological test is engaging in psychological testing, which is what this textbook is all about.

II. PLAN FOR THE BOOK

This book is divided into three parts: *principles*, *applications*, and *issues*. Together, these sections provide an extensive coverage of psychological testing from the most basic ideas through some of the most complex. Basic ideas and events are introduced early and stressed throughout so that newly acquired knowledge is reinforced through practice. In covering principles, applications, and issues our intent has been to provide not only the *who's* of psychological testing but also the *how's* and *why's* of major developments in the field. We also address the important concern of many students—relevance—by examining the diverse uses of tests and resulting data.

A. *Principles of psychological testing*

By *principles of psychological testing* we mean the basic concepts and fundamental ideas that underlie all psychological tests. These are covered in Part 1 of the text. There are some basic statistical concepts, for example, that provide the foundation for understanding psychological tests. These concepts are presented in Chapters 2 and 3. Chapters 4 and 5 cover two of the most fundamental concepts of psychological tests, reliability and validity. *Reliability* refers to the dependability of psychological tests. As you will learn, there are many ways a test can be dependable (that is, reliable). For example, test results may be reliable over time, which means that when the same test is given twice within any given time interval the results tend to be the same or highly similar. In Chapter 4 you will learn about the different types of reliability. *Validity* is a term that refers to the meaning of test results. More specifically, validity refers to what is being measured by a psychological test. If research findings suggest that a particular test does in fact measure human ability, we say there is evidence for the validity of the measure of human ability. When we ask the question "What does this psychological test measure?", we are essentially asking "For what inferences is this test valid?"

Another principle or fundamental idea of psychological testing concerns how a test is created or constructed. The principles of test construction are covered in Chapter 6. Chapter 7 covers the selection of psychological tests and presents the basic knowledge one needs to have in selecting tests for specific purposes. The act of giving a test is known as *test administration*. Some tests are easy to administer, but others must be administered in a highly specific way. Chapter 8, the final chapter of Part 1, covers the basic fundamentals of administering a psychological test.

B. *Applications of psychological testing*

Whereas the focus of Part 1 is on principles of testing, Part 2 is on applications. Here we provide a detailed analysis of many of the most popular tests and how they are used or applied. Chapter 9 provides an overview of the essential terms and concepts that relate to the application of psychological tests. After this overview, Chapter 10 discusses interview techniques. An *interview* is a method of gathering information by conversations or direct questions. Not only has the interview traditionally been among the major techniques of gathering information in psychology in general, but interview data also provide an important complement to psychological test results.

Chapters 11, 12, and 13 cover individual tests of human ability. As you will learn, there are a wide variety of fine psychological tests of human ability. In Chapter 14 group tests of human ability are discussed. Chapters 15 through 18 cover the basic personality tests. Chapter 15 is on structured personality tests. Chapter 16 covers the so-called interests tests, which measure behavior relevant to such factors as occupational preferences. Chapter 17 covers projective personality tests. In Chapter 18 we will find many of the newly developed alternatives to the more traditional tests covered in Chapters 15, 16, and 17.

Taken together, Chapters 15 through 18 provide an in-depth coverage of the most widely used and newly developed personality tests. These chapters not only provide descriptive information, but also delve into the ideas underlying the various tests.

C. *Issues of psychological testing*

Beyond principles and applications, there are many social and theoretical issues related to testing (Haney, 1981). These issues have become especially important in the 1980s (Gordon & Terrell, 1981) and cannot be overlooked in a comprehensive coverage of psychological tests. Part 3, the last section of the book, covers many of these issues. As a compromise between breadth and depth of coverage, we decided to focus on a comprehensive discussion of those issues that have particular importance in the current professional, social, and political environment.

Chapter 19 reviews the research on test anxiety, which is one of the major factors causing decreases in test performance in academic settings. The next two chapters cover particularly sensitive controversies. Chapter 20, for example, examines the issue of test bias, one of the most controversial issues in the field today (Cole, 1981). Psychological tests have been accused of being discriminatory or biased against certain groups. Chapter 20 takes a careful look at both sides of this delicate controversy. Because of charges of bias and other problems, psychological testing is increasingly coming under the scrutiny of the law (Bersoff, 1981). Thus, the issue of test bias is related to legal issues. This relationship between testing and the law is examined in Chapter 21. In Chapter 22 a general overview of other major issues that are presently shaping the future of psychological testing in America is provided (for example, see Korchin & Schuldberg, 1981). From our review of the issues, we speculate on what the future holds for psychological testing.

III. HISTORICAL PERSPECTIVE

Having given you an overview of the plan of the book, we will now briefly provide the historical context to give you a perspective. Consistent with our plan to proceed from the more basic concepts to the more complex ones and to reintroduce critical concepts to enhance learning, our historical discussion will touch on some of the material presented earlier in this chapter.

A. Early antecedents

It is common to think of testing as both a recent and an American development. Indeed, most of the major developments in testing have occurred in this century, and a good number of them have taken place in the United States. The origins of testing, however, are neither recent nor American. Historians have obtained evidence that the ancient Chinese had a relatively sophisticated civil service testing program more than 4000 years ago (DuBois, 1966, 1970). Oral examinations were given every third year in China, and their results were used for work evaluations and promotion decisions.

By the time of the Han Dynasty (206 B.C. to 220 A.D.), the use of *test batteries* (a group of tests used in conjunction) was quite common. These early tests related to such diverse topics as civil law, military affairs, agriculture, revenue, and geography. Tests had become quite well developed by the time of the Ming Dynasty (1368–1644 A.D.). During this period, there was a national multistage testing program that involved local and regional testing centers equipped with special testing booths. Those who had done well on the tests at the local level went on to provincial capitals for more extensive essay examinations. After this second testing, those with the highest test scores (best results) went on to the nation's capital for a final round of examinations. Only those who passed this third set of tests were eligible for public office.

The Western world most likely learned about testing programs through exposure to the Chinese. Reports by British missionaries and diplomats encouraged the English East India Company to copy the Chinese system in 1832 as a method for selecting employees for overseas duty. Testing programs worked well for the company, and so the British government adopted a similar system of testing for its civil service in 1855. Following the British endorsement of a Civil Service Testing System, the French and the German governments followed suit. In 1883 the American government established the American Civil Service Commission, which developed and administered competitive examinations for certain governmental jobs. The impetus of the testing movement in the Western world grew rapidly around this time (Parkinson, 1957; Wiggins, 1973).

B. *Charles Darwin and individual differences*

Perhaps the most basic concept underlying psychological testing pertains to the concept of individual differences. No two snowflakes are identical, and no two fingerprints are the same. Similarly, no two people are exactly alike in ability and typical behavior. Psychological tests are specifically designed to measure these individual differences among people.

Although human beings realized long ago that individuals differ, developing tools for measuring such differences, as you will see, is no easy matter. To develop a measuring device, we must understand what we want to measure. An important step toward understanding individual differences came with the publication of Charles Darwin's highly influential *Origin of the Species* in 1859. According to Darwin's theory, higher forms of life evolved on this planet partially because of differences among individual forms of life within a species or type of animal. Briefly, given that individual members of a species differ, some will possess characteristics that are more adaptive or successful than those possessed by others. Darwin also believed that those with the best or most adaptive characteristics will survive at the expense of those who are less fit, and the survivors then pass their characteristics on to the next generation. Through this process, he claimed, life has evolved to its presently complex and incredibly intelligent levels.

A relative of Darwin, Sir Francis Galton, soon began applying Darwin's theories to the study of human individual differences. Given the concepts of survival of the fittest and of individual differences, Galton set out to show that some humans possessed characteristics that made them more fit than other humans, a theory he articulated in his book *Hereditary Genius*, published in 1869. Galton (1883) subsequently began a series of experimental studies to document the validity of his position. He concentrated on demonstrating that individual differences existed in human sensory and motor functioning, such as reaction time, visual acuity, and physical strength. In so doing, Galton initiated a search for knowledge concerning human individual differences, which is now one of the most important domains of scientific psychology.

Galton's work was extended by American psychologist James McKeen Cattell, who coined the term *mental test* (Cattell, 1890). Cattell's doctoral dissertation was based on Galton's work concerning individual differences in reaction time. In continuing Galton's exploration of human individual differences and introducing the term *mental test*, Cattell perpetrated and stimulated the forces that ultimately led to the development of modern psychological tests. Galton's influence on Cattell is clearly revealed in the latter's statement that Galton is "the greatest man whom I have ever known" (Cattell, 1930, p. 116).

Intellectual and professional curiosity alone, however, did not provide sufficient conditions for the creation of modern psychological tests. Although individual differences may be among the pillars that underlie psychological tests, modern tests were born in response to important needs. One such need centered on the problem of classification and identification of the mentally and emotionally handicapped. One of the earliest tests resembling present-day procedures, the Seguin Form Board (Seguin, 1866), was developed in an effort to educate and evaluate the mentally retarded. Similarly, Kraepelin (1912) devised a series of examinations or tests for evaluating emotionally impaired persons.

The first major breakthrough in the creation of modern psychological tests came at the turn of the 20th century. The French minister of public instruction appointed a commission to study ways of identifying intellectually subnormal individuals in order to provide them with appropriate educational experiences. One member of that commission was Alfred Binet. Working in conjunction with French physician T. Simon, Binet developed the first major general intelligence test, which contained 30 items of increasing difficulty. Binet's early effort launched the first systematic attempt to evaluate individual differences in human intelligence. (See Chapter 11.)

C. The evolution of intelligence tests

The history and evolution of Binet's intelligence test is instructive. The first version of the test, known as the Binet-Simon Scale, was published in 1905. As stated above, this instrument contained 30 items of increasing difficulty and was designed to identify intellectually subnormal individuals. Like all well-constructed tests, the Binet-Simon Scale of 1905 was augmented by a comparison sample. (A comparison sample is sometimes referred to as a normative or standardization sample.) Binet's standardization sample consisted of 50 children who had been given the test under *standard conditions*—that is, with precisely the same instructions and format. In obtaining this standardization sample the authors of the Binet test now had something with which they could compare the results from any new subject. Without such a comparison group the meaning of scores would have been difficult, if not impossible, to evaluate. However, by knowing such things as the number of correct responses found on the average in the standardization sample, it was at least possible to state whether a new subject was below or above it (for example, see Green, 1981).

It is easy to understand the importance of a standardization sample. However, the importance of obtaining a standardization sample that represents the population from which new people are tested has sometimes been ignored or overlooked by test users. For example, if the standardization sample consisted of 50 White males from wealthy families, then the meaning of the score of a Black female child from a poverty-stricken family could not be easily or fairly evaluated. Nevertheless, comparisons of this kind are not all that uncommon.

Binet was aware of the importance of a standardization sample. Indeed, one facet in the evolution of the Binet test has been an attempt to increase the size and representativeness of the standardization or comparison sample. A *representative sample* is one that comprises individuals similar to those for whom the test is to be used. When the test is used for the general population, a representative sample must be one that reflects all segments of the population.

By 1908 the Binet-Simon Scale had been substantially improved. It was revised to include nearly twice as many items (59) as the 1905 scale. Of even more significance, the size of the standardization sample was increased to more than 200. The 1908 Binet-Simon Scale also introduced the historically significant concept of mental age. A child's mental age was determined by the test. In simplified terms you might try to think of mental age as a measurement of a child's performance on the test relative to other children of a particular age group. If a child's test performance equaled that of the average 8-year-old, for example, then his or her mental age would be 8. That is, in terms of the abilities measured by the test, this child could be viewed as having a similar level of ability as the average 8-year-old. The actual or chronological age of the child could be 4 or 12, but in terms of test performance the child functions at the same level as the average 8-year-old. The mental age concept was one of the most important contributions of the revised 1908 Binet-Simon Scale.

The Binet-Simon Scale was revised again in 1911, but that revision contained only minor improvements. By this time, however, the idea of intelligence testing had swept across the world and was especially entrenched in the United States. By 1916 L. M. Terman of Stanford University revised the Binet test for use in America. (There had been earlier American versions, which will be discussed in Chapter 11.) Terman's revision, known as the Stanford-Binet Intelligence Scale (Terman, 1916) was the only American version of the Binet test that flourished. It was characteristic of one of the most important trends in testing—the drive toward better and better tests.

Terman's 1916 revision of the Binet-Simon Scale contained numerous improvements. The standardization sample was increased to include 1000 persons, original items were revised, and many new items were added. Terman's 1916 Stanford-Binet Intelligence Scale added respectability and momentum to the newly developing testing movement, which began in the United States around World War I in response to the demand for a quick, efficient way of evaluating the emotional and intellectual functioning of thousands of military recruits.

The Binet test was an individual test. World War I, however, created a demand for large-scale group testing, because there was a shortage of trained personnel who could evaluate the huge influx of military recruits in terms of ability and emotional functioning. Therefore, shortly after the United States became actively involved in World War I, the Army requested the assistance of Robert Yerkes, who was the president of the American Psychological Association (see Yerkes, 1921). Yerkes headed a committee of distinguished psychologists, who soon developed group tests of human abilities: the Army Alpha and the

Army Beta. The Army Alpha was a structured ability test that required reading ability. The Army Beta, by contrast, was designed to measure the intelligence of illiterate adults.

World War I saw the widespread development of group tests, in which many people could be simultaneously tested. Also about this time the scope of testing was broadened to include tests of achievement, aptitude, interest, and personality. As previously indicated, however, achievement, aptitude, and intelligence tests overlapped considerably; the distinctions proved to be illusory. (Measures of personality have a separate history and will be discussed in a subsequent section.) It is noteworthy, however, that the 1916 Stanford-Binet Intelligence Scale appeared at a time of strong demand and high optimism and faith in the potential of measuring human behavior through psychological tests. World War I and the creation of group tests then added momentum to the testing movement. Shortly after the appearance of the 1916 Stanford-Binet Intelligence Scale and the Army Alpha test, schools, colleges, and industry began using tests. It appeared to many that this new phenomenon, the psychological test, held the key to the solution of the problems emerging from the rapid expansion of technology and population growth characteristic of modern-day societies.

The period following World War I saw an astonishing growth in testing, both in terms of number and types of tests. By 1921 the Rorschach inkblot projective personality test was introduced, and an increasing number of psychologists began finding employment opportunities outside the academic setting in the applied area of administering and interpreting tests.

For every movement, however, there is a countermovement, and the testing movement in the United States was no exception. Critics soon became vocal enough to dampen enthusiasm and to place even the most optimistic advocates of tests on the defensive. Little by little the limitations, weaknesses, and problems with existing tests were noted by researchers, who demanded nothing short of the highest possible standards. One of the most systematic, persistent, and organized attacks on tests by psychologists was directed at the so-called structured personality tests. However, no test was safe from criticism, not even the Stanford-Binet, which had been a landmark in the testing field. Thus, although tests were used between the two world wars, and many new tests were developed, the accuracy and utility of tests remained under heavy fire.

Just prior to the outbreak of World War II in Europe, however, tests began to enjoy a renewed level of respectability. The knowledge and experience of the previous two decades began to manifest themselves in new and improved tests. By 1937 the Stanford-Binet was revised again. Among the many improvements was the inclusion of a normative (standardization or comparison) sample of more than 3000 individuals. No other individual intelligence test before or since has had a larger standardization sample. Only the group tests, such as the Scholastic Aptitude Test (SAT), which can be administered on a mass scale, have larger normative samples.

Only two years after the 1937 revision of the Stanford-Binet test, David Wechsler published the first version of the Wechsler intelligence scales (see Chapter 12), the Wechsler-Bellevue Intelligence Scale (W-B) (Wechsler, 1939). The Wechsler-Bellevue scale contained several interesting innovations in intelligence testing. Unlike the Stanford-Binet test, which produced only a single score (the so-called IQ or intelligence quotient), Wechsler's test yielded several scores, permitting an analysis of an individual's pattern or combination of abilities. Among the various scores produced by the Wechsler test was the performance IQ. As you will see, performance tests do not require a verbal response.

Thus, intelligence can be evaluated in a context that is as free as possible from verbal or language skills. The Stanford-Binet test had long been criticized because of its emphasis on language and verbal skills. With its verbal emphasis, the Binet test was inappropriate for many individuals (especially those who are nonverbal or illiterate). In addition, there are few people, if any, who believe that language or verbal skills play an exclusive role in human intelligence. Wechsler's inclusion of a nonverbal (performance) scale thus helped overcome some of the weaknesses of the Binet test that stemmed from its heavy verbal emphasis. (Performance scales and other important concepts in intelligence testing will be formally defined in Chapter 12, which covers the various forms of the Wechsler intelligence scales.)

D. *Personality tests: 1920 – 1940*

During the period immediately preceding and following World War II personality tests began to blossom. Whereas intelligence tests attempted to measure ability or potential, personality tests attempted to measure presumably stable characteristics or traits that theoretically underlie behavior. A *trait* can be defined as an enduring or persistent characteristic of an individual that is independent of situations. For example, it can be argued that some people are optimistic and some pessimistic. Optimistic people remain optimistic regardless of whether things are going well. A pessimist, by contrast, is always looking at the negative side of things. Optimism and pessimism can thus be viewed as traits. They are relatively enduring characteristics of an individual that manifest themselves across a wide variety of situations. They are characteristics of the individual that are brought into a situation. One of the basic goals of traditional personality tests is to measure traits. As you will learn, however, the notion of traits has important limitations (see Chapter 22).

The earliest personality tests were structured paper-and-pencil group tests. These tests provided multiple choice and true/false questions that could be mass (group) administered. Because they provide a high degree of structure (that is, a definite stimulus and specific alternative responses that can be unequivocally scored), these paper-pencil group personality tests are often referred to as objective or structured personality tests. The first structured personality test, the

Woodworth Personal Data Sheet, was developed during World War I and was published in final form just after the war.

As indicated earlier, the motivation underlying the development of the first personality test was the need for a method of screening military recruits. The history of testing indicates that tests such as the Binet or Woodworth were created by necessity to meet unique challenges. However, like the early ability tests, the first structured personality test was simple by today's standards. Interpretation of results from the Woodworth test depended on the now-discredited assumption that the content of an item could be accepted at face value. If the person marked "yes" to the statement "I have a good appetite," then it was assumed that he or she had a good appetite. As logical as this assumption seems, experience has shown that it is often false. In addition to problems with honesty, the person responding to the question may not interpret the meaning of "good appetite" in the same way as the test administrator. (There are other problems with tests like the Woodworth, and these are discussed in Chapter 15.)

The introduction of the Woodworth test was enthusiastically followed by the creation of a variety of structured personality tests, all of which assumed the accuracy of a test response. However, just as ability tests such as the Binet had been scrutinized, analyzed, and criticized by researchers, so were the initial structured personality tests. Indeed, the criticism of structured personality tests that relied on face value alone became so intense that they were nearly driven out of existence. What followed was the development of new tests based on more modern concepts that revitalized the use of structured personality tests (see Chapter 15). Thus, after an initial surge of interest and optimism during most of the 1920s, structured personality tests declined in usage by the late 1930s and into the early 1940s. Following World War II, however, personality tests based on fewer or different assumptions were introduced, rescuing the structured personality test concept.

During the brief but dramatic rise and fall of structured personality tests based on assumed accuracy, interest in projective tests began to grow. In contrast to structured personality tests that, in general, provide a relatively unambiguous test stimulus and specific alternative responses, projective personality tests provide an ambiguous stimulus. Furthermore, in a projective test the response requirements are unclear. Scoring of projective tests is often subjective.

Unlike the early structured personality tests, interest in the projective Rorschach inkblot test grew slowly. The rationale for the Rorschach test was first published by Herman Rorschach of Switzerland in 1921. However, several years passed before the Rorschach was introduced into the United States by David Levy. The first Rorschach doctoral dissertation conducted in U.S. universities was not completed until 1932, when Sam Beck, Levy's student, decided to scientifically investigate the properties of the Rorschach test. Although initial interest in the Rorschach test was lukewarm at best, its attractiveness progressed rapidly following Beck's work, despite numerous obstacles that took the form of suspicion, doubt, and criticism from the scientific community.

Adding to the momentum for the acceptance and use of projective tests was the development of the Thematic Apperception Test (TAT) by Henry Murray and Christina Morgan in 1935. Whereas the Rorschach test contained completely ambiguous inkblot stimuli, the TAT was a bit more structured. Its stimuli consists of ambiguous pictures depicting a variety of scenes and situations, such as a boy sitting in front of a table with a violin on it. Unlike the Rorschach test, which asks the subject to explain what the inkblot might be, the TAT requires the subject to make up a story about the ambiguous scene. The TAT purports to measure human needs and thus to ascertain individual differences in factors that underlie human behavior. (In Chapter 17 you will learn more about projective tests in general and about the Rorschach and the TAT in particular.)

E.   *The emergence of new approaches to personality testing*

The popularity of the two most important projective personality tests, the Rorschach and TAT, grew rapidly by the late 1930s and early 1940s, perhaps because of disillusionment with structured personality tests (Dahlstrom, 1969a). However, many psychologists seem to have a deeply ingrained suspicion of projective tests, especially the Rorschach, so projective tests were far from universally accepted.

In 1943 the development of the Minnesota Multiphasic Personality Inventory (MMPI) began a new era for structured personality tests. The idea behind the MMPI, although not new, helped revolutionize structured personality tests. The problem with early structured personality tests, like the Woodworth, was that these tests made far too many assumptions that subsequent scientific investigations failed to substantiate. The authors of the MMPI, by contrast, argued that the meaning of a test response must be determined by empirical research. The MMPI is currently the most widely used and referenced personality test in existence. Its emphasis on the need for empirical data in determining the meaning of test results has stimulated the development of a large body of knowledge.

Like other major tests that have appeared in the 20th century, the MMPI was met with initial enthusiasm and followed by disillusionment as weaknesses were revealed and became glaringly apparent. However, because of the large number of research studies that add insights to the meaning of its scores, the MMPI has enjoyed substantial popularity and support from the scientific as well as the professional community. In 1957 the California Psychological Inventory (CPI) was developed within the context of the same commitment to empirical research as the MMPI. (As you will see in Chapter 15, both the MMPI and CPI contain significant problems.)

Just about the time that the MMPI appeared, personality tests based on the statistical procedure called *factor analysis* began to emerge. Factor analysis is a method for finding the minimum number of concepts or factors to account for a large number of variables. We may say a person is outgoing, is gregarious, seeks company, is talkative, and enjoys relating to others. However, these descriptive adjectives contain a certain amount of redundancy or overlap. A factor analysis can identify the extent of this overlap. For example, a factor analysis of the above adjectives might reveal that they all can be accounted for or subsumed by a single concept (or factor): extroversion.

The first serious attempt to employ factor analytic techniques in the development of a structured personality test was made by J. P. Guilford in the early 1940s. By the end of that decade R. B. Cattell introduced the Sixteen Personality Factor Questionnaire (16 PF) which, to this day, remains one of the most well-constructed structured personality tests and an important example of a test developed with the aid of factor analysis. (Factor analytic structured tests are also discussed in Chapter 15.)

F. *The period of rapid changes in the status of testing*

The 1940s saw not only the emergence of a whole new technology in psychological testing, but also the growth and emergence of applied aspects of psychology. The role and significance of tests used in World War I were reaffirmed in World War II. By this time the government had become interested in encouraging the continued development of applied psychological technology. As a result, considerble federal funding was funneled through the Veterans Administration in order to provide paid, supervised training experiences for clinically oriented psychologists. By 1949 formal university training standards were developed and accepted, and clinical psychology was born. Other applied branches of psychology—such as industrial psychology, counseling psychology, educational psychology, and school psychology—soon began to blossom.

One of the major functions of the applied psychologist was psychological testing. The Shakow et al. (1947) report (whose recommendations provided the foundation for the formal training standards in clinical psychology), specified that psychological testing was one of the unique functions of the clinical psychologist and recommended that testing methods only be taught to doctoral psychology students. A position paper of the American Psychological Association published about seven years later (APA, 1954) reinforced the specification that testing belongs to the clinical psychologist by its formal declaration that the psychologist would conduct psychotherapy only in "true" collaboration with physicians. Thus, testing but not psychotherapy could be conducted independently by a psychologist. Indeed, as long as psychologists assumed the role of tester they played a complementary, but often secondary or subservient, role to the medical practitioners. The medical profession could have made clinical psychology's emergence difficult but did not, because as tester the psychologist could be an aid to the physician. Therefore, the late 1940s and early 1950s saw the use of tests as the major function of the clinical psychologist (Shaffer, 1953).

For better or worse, depending on your perspective, the government's efforts to stimulate the development of applied aspects of psychology, especially clinical psychology, were extremely successful. Hundreds of highly talented and creative young people were attracted to clinical and other applied areas of psychology. These individuals, who were to utilize tests and other psychological techniques in the solution of practical human problems, were uniquely trained as scientific practitioners of the principles, empirical foundations, and applications of the science of psychology.

Soon the highly talented group of post-World War II psychologists began rejecting the secondary role relative to the medical profession that was inherent in the testing situation as practiced in the 1940s and 1950s (Lewandowski & Saccuzzo, 1976). Many of these early clinical practitioners, armed with rather powerful knowledge from scientific psychology, must have felt like second-rate citizens when compared to physicians. Unable to engage in the independent practice of psychotherapy, some psychologists perhaps sensed they were being treated like technicians whose purpose was to serve the medical profession. Psychologists then began to reject a secondary role to the medical profession.

Many psychologists, furthermore, apparently associated tests with a secondary relationship to the medical profession and thus rejected tests right along with this secondary role (Lewandowski & Saccuzzo, 1976). At the same time, the potentially intrusive nature of tests and fears of misuse of tests began creating suspicion, distrust, and contempt for tests among the public. Attacks on testing came from within the profession of psychology and also from sources external to the profession. These attacks intensified and multiplied so fast that many psychologists jettisoned all ties to the traditional tests developed during the first half of this century, and testing again underwent a sharp decline in status in the late 1950s that persisted into the 1970s (see Holt, 1967).

G. *The current environment*

Most things seem to go through cycles, and psychological testing is no exception. Although the attacks and efforts to impose restrictions on tests continue unabated, a new interest in psychological testing has emerged in the 1980s. Some psychologists, for example, have developed entirely new approaches. As in the past, psychological testing remains one of the most important yet controversial topics within psychology. If you are a psychology major, a thorough, up-to-date knowledge of the material in this text will be one of the most important aspects of your education. No matter what your specialty within psychology, you will find the basic principles discussed in the early chapters of this book invaluable.

If you are among those who are interested in using psychological techniques in an applied setting, then the information contained in the chapters ahead is of great significance. Deep in the historical roots of psychology and through the present, psychological tests have been among the most important instruments of the psychologist in general and of those who apply psychology in particular.

Testing is indeed one of the essential elements of psychology. Not all psychologists use tests, and some psychologists are against them. Yet all areas of psychology depend upon measurement. In fact, all areas of psychology depend upon knowledge gained in research studies in which measurements are taken. The meaning and dependability of these measurements are unmistakably among the most crucial foundations of research in psychology. An understanding of the basic principles of measurement is necessary for the effective study of any area of human behavior.

The use of specific psychological tests is one of the basic skills of the applied psychologist. In clinical settings, for example, testing is the unique function of the psychologist. Psychotherapy is often performed by psychiatrists, social workers, nurses, and even untrained volunteers. It is the psychologists, however, who administer and evaluate the results of psychological tests. Thus, training in psychological testing is one of the psychologist's most distinguishing marks. In industrial and educational psychology, knowledge of psychological testing is also one of the most important distinguishing skills the psychologist brings to the job.

In today's complex society the relevance of the principles, applications, and issues of psychological testing extends far beyond the field of psychology. Therefore, even if you do not plan to become a psychologist, you are very likely to encounter psychological tests at some time in the future. Attorneys, physicians, social workers, business managers, educators, and many other professionals are frequently confronted with reports based on psychological tests. To make adequate use of information based on psychological tests, you need the kind of knowledge that is presented in this book.

Even if you enter a profession or occupation with little relevance to psychological testing, the principles, applications, and issues of psychological testing will be of interest to you. The lives of you and your family are likely to be touched someday by psychological tests. The more you know about psychological tests, the better able you will be to insure that your encounters with them will be positive. With attacks on tests and threats to prohibit or greatly limit their use, you have a responsibility to yourself and to society to know as much as you can about psychological tests. The future of testing may very well depend upon you and people like you. The more you know about testing, the better able you will be to base your decisions on facts and to insure that tests are used for the most beneficial and constructive purposes.

Tests have probably never been as important as they are in our contemporary society. To illustrate our point, let us consider just one type of testing—academic aptitude. Each year more than 2.5 million individuals take tests so that schools can have some evidence of their academic suitability, and the testing process begins early in the person's life. Prestigious presecondary schools require a test that is taken by more than 16,000 children each year. When these students become adolescents and want to get into college preparatory schools, about 20,000 take a screening examination. Very few students who want to go to a four-year college can avoid taking a college entrance test. The Scholastic Aptitude Test alone is given to more than 1.8 million high school students each year. Another 100,000 high school seniors take other tests in order to gain advanced placement in college.

These figures do not include the 75,000 persons who take a special test for admission to business school or the 120,000 persons who take a law school admission test. We have not even mentioned tests for graduate school, medical school, dental school, and others. Millions of tests are given each year. The results of these tests are used to make very important decisions because they are sources of information about human characteristics. They are, without doubt, extremely important, and they influence the lives of countless members of our society.

IV. SUMMARY

The history of testing in America has been brief but intense. Although tests have always been available, psychological testing is very much a product of modern society with its unprecedented technology, population growth, and unique problems. Because tests have played a role in solving the challenges posed by developments in modern times, they have also played a role in modern U.S. history. You should realize, however, that despite all the recent advances in the theory and technique of psychological testing, there are still many unsolved technical problems and hotly debated social, political, and economic issues. Nevertheless, the prevalence of tests in our society, despite strong opposition, indicates that although they are far from perfect, psychological tests must be fulfilling some important need in the decision-making process that permeates all facets of society. Because decisions must be made, with or without the aid of psychological tests, tests will flourish until a better or more objective way of making decisions emerges.

The modern history of psychological tests shows that they have evolved in a complicated environment in which hostile and facilitative forces have interacted to produce a balance characterized by innovation and a continual quest for better methods. One interesting thing about tests is that people seem to find it hard to remain neutral about them. If you are not in favor of them, then you probably have some reservations about them. We ask that you maintain a flexible, open mind before forming an opinion. No matter what your attitude toward them, however, the study of psychological tests can be a most rewarding educational experience. After reading this text, if you know enough to form your own independent judgment of psychological testing, then this book has accomplished its goal.

2

Norms and Basic Statistics for Testing

Learning objectives

When you have completed this chapter, you should be able to do the following:

1. *Discuss three properties of scales of measurement.*
2. *Determine why properties of scales are important in the field of measurement.*
3. *Tell why methods are available for displaying distributions of scores.*
4. *Explain why the stem-and-leaf-display approach has advantages over traditional frequency distributions as a method for summarizing data.*
5. *Describe the mean and the standard deviation.*
6. *Define a z score and how it is used.*
7. *Relate the concepts of mean and standard deviation and z score to the concept of a standard normal distribution.*
8. *Define quartiles, deciles, and stanines and explain how they are used.*
9. *Tell how norms are created.*
10. *Relate the notion of tracking to the establishment of norms.*

We use numbers as a basic way of communicating: our money system requires the understanding and manipulation of numbers, we estimate how long it will take us to do things, we count, we express our evaluations of things on scales, and so on. Think about how many times you use numbers in an average day. There is no way of avoiding them.

One of the advantages of number systems is that they allow us to manipulate numbers without changing the qualities they represent. Through sets of well-defined rules we can use numbers to learn more about the world. Tests are devices used to translate observations of behavior into numbers. The outcome of a test is almost always represented as a score, and much of this book is about what scores mean. This chapter reviews some basic rules that are used to evaluate number systems. These rules and number systems will be our partners in learning about human behavior.

If you have had a course in basic psychological statistics, this chapter will help you review the basic concepts from your statistics course. If additional review is needed, you should reread your introductory statistics book. Most introductory statistics books cover the information in this chapter. If you have not had a course in statistics, this chapter will provide you with some of the information needed for understanding other chapters in this book.

I. WHY WE NEED STATISTICS

Modern psychology has advanced beyond centuries of speculation about human "nature" through its commitments to the scientific method. Scientific study requires systematic observations and an estimation of the extent to which our observations could have been influenced by chance alone. Statistical methods serve two important purposes in our quest for scientific understanding.

First, they help us describe things. Numbers provide convenient summaries and allow us to evaluate some observations relative to others. For example, if you get a score of 54 on a psychology examination, you probably want to know what the 54 means. Is it lower than the average score, or is it about the same? Knowing the answer can make the feedback you get from your examination more meaningful. Should you discover that the 54 puts you in the top 5% of the class, you might assume you have a good chance for an "A." If it puts you in the bottom 5%, you will feel differently.

Secondly, we can use statistics to make inferences, which are logical deductions about things that cannot be observed directly. For example, we do not know how many people watched a particular television movie unless we ask everyone. However, if we use scientific sample surveys, we can make an inference about the percentage of people who saw the film. Data gathering and analysis might be considered analogous to criminal investigation and prosecution (Tukey, 1977). The first step is the detective work of gathering and displaying clues. This is what Harvard statistician John Tukey calls *exploratory data analysis.* Then there is a period of *confirmatory data analysis,* when the clues are evaluated against rigid statistical rules. This latter phase is like the work done by the judges and juries.

Some students have an aversion to numbers and anything mathematical. If you are one of these people, you are not alone. Feeling uneasy about statistics is common not only among students but even among some professional psychologists. However, it is widely believed that statistics and the basic principles of measurement are at the center of the modern science of psychology. Scientific statements are usually based on careful study, and such systematic study requires some numerical analysis.

This chapter will review both descriptive and inferential statistics. *Descriptive statistics* are methods used in providing a concise description of a collection of quantitative information. *Inferential statistics* are methods used in making inferences from observations of a small group of people known as a *sample* to a larger group of individuals known as a *population*. Typically the psychologist wants to make statements about the larger group, but it is not possible to make all the necessary observations. Instead, observations are made on a relatively small group of subjects (sample), and inferential statistics is used to estimate the characteristics of the larger group.

Among the topics covered in this chapter are scales of measurement, the frequency distribution, the percentile distribution, stem-and-leaf displays, the mean, the standard deviation, and norms.

II. SCALES OF MEASUREMENT

Measurement requires the application of rules for assigning numbers to objects. The rules are the specific procedures used in transforming qualities of attributes into numbers (Nunnally, 1978). For example, to rate the quality of wines, the wine taster must be given a specific set of rules. The wine might be rated on a 10-point rating scale, in which 1 means extremely bad and 10 is for extremely good. To assign the numbers, the system of rules must be clearly defined. The basic feature of such systems is the scale of measurement. For example, to measure the height of your classmates you might use the scale of inches; to measure their weight, you might use the scale of pounds.

Of course, in psychology we do not have clearly acknowledged and widely accepted scales of measurement. Nevertheless, we do have numerous systems by which we assign numbers. Indeed, the study of measurement systems is what this book is about. Before we consider any specific scale of measurement, it is important to consider general properties of measurement scales.

A. *Properties of scales*

There are three important properties that make scales of measurement different from one another: magnitude, equal intervals, and absolute 0.

Magnitude.   Magnitude is the property of "moreness." A scale has the property of magnitude if we can say that one instance of the attribute represents more, less, or equal amounts of the quantity of interest than another instance of the attribute (McCall, 1980). On a scale of height, for example, if we can say that John is taller than Fred, then the scale has the property of magnitude. An example of a scale that does not have the property of magnitude is when a gym coach assigns numbers to teams in a league for identification (Team 1, Team 2, and so forth). Here the numbers are used only to label the teams, so the property of magnitude is not achieved. If the coach were to rank order the teams by the number of games they won, then the new numbering system (games won) would have the property of magnitude.

Equal intervals.   The concept of equal intervals is a little more complex. A scale has the property of equal intervals if the difference between two points at any place on the scale has the same meaning as the difference between two other points that differ by the same number of scale units. For example, the difference between inch 2 and inch 4 on a ruler means the same as the difference between inch 10 and inch 12. The difference is exactly 2 inches in each case.

As simple as this concept seems, it is very rare to find good evidence that a psychological test has the property of equal intervals. For example, the difference between IQs of 45 and 50 does not mean the same thing as the difference between IQs of 105 and 110. Although each of these differences is 5 points ($50-45=5$ and $110-105=5$), the 5 points at one level do not mean the same thing as 5 points at a higher level. When a scale has the property of equal intervals, the relationship between the measured units and some outcome can be described by a straight line or a linear equation in the form of $Y=a+bx$. This equation tells us that as we increase in equal units on our scale, there are equal increases in the meaningful correlates of our units. For example, Figure 2-1 shows the hypothetical relationship between scores on a test of manual dexterity and ratings of artwork. Notice that the relationship is not a straight line. By examining the points of the figure you will see that at some points the relationship is approximately linear: increases in manual dexterity are associated with increases in ratings of artwork. Then the relationship becomes nonlinear. The figure shows that after a manual dexterity score of about 5, greater increases in dexterity are needed to produce smaller increases in ratings of the quality of the artwork.

Absolute 0.   An absolute 0 is obtained when nothing at all exists of the property being measured. For example, if you are measuring heart rate and observe that your patient has a rate of 0 and has died, you would conclude that there is no heart rate at all. For many psychological qualities it is extremely difficult, if not impossible, to define an absolute 0 point. For example, if we are measuring shyness on a rating scale with points 0 through 10, it is hard to say

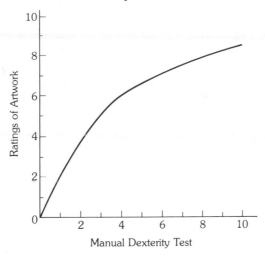

Figure 2-1. Hypothetical relationship between ratings of artwork and manual dexterity. In some ranges of the scale, the relationship is more direct than it is in others.

that 0 means the person is not shy at all (McCall, 1980). Table 2-1 defines four scales of measurement based on the properties we have just discussed.

TABLE 2-1 Scales of measurement and their properties

		Property	
Type of Scale	Magnitude	Equal Interval	Absolute 0
Nominal	No	No	No
Ordinal	Yes	No	No
Interval	Yes	Yes	No
Ratio	Yes	Yes	Yes

B. Types of scales

Table 2-1 shows that a *nominal scale* does not have the property of magnitude, equal intervals, or absolute 0. Nominal scales are really not scales at all; their only purpose is to name objects. For example, the numbers on the backs of football players' uniforms are nominal in nature. In social science research, it has been common to label groups in sample surveys with numbers (such as 1=White, 2=Black, and 3=Mexican-American). However, when these numbers have been attached to categories, analysis using standard statistical procedures is not usually advisable. On the scale above for ethnic groups, a mean of 1.87 would have no meaning.[1]

[1]This is not to say that sophisticated statistical analysis is not possible when the data are nominal. Indeed, several new and exciting developments in data analysis allow extensive and detailed inquiry with nominal data (see Goodman, 1972; Gokhale & Kullback, 1978).

A scale with the property of magnitude but not the property of equal intervals or the property of absolute 0 is known as an *ordinal scale*. An ordinal scale allows us to rank individuals or objects but not to say anything about the meaning of the differences between the ranks. If you were to rank order the members of your class in terms of their height, you would have an ordinal scale. Note that you would do this without concern for the differences between the ranks. For example, if Fred were the tallest, Susan the second tallest, and George the third tallest, you would assign them the ranks 1, 2, and 3, respectively. You would not give any consideration to the fact that Fred is 8 inches taller than Susan, but Susan is only 2 inches taller than George.

For most problems in psychology we do not have the precision to measure the exact differences between intervals. So most often we use ordinal scales of measurement. For example, IQ tests (see Chapter 11) do not have the property of equal intervals or absolute 0, but do have the property of magnitude. If they had the property of equal intervals, the difference between an IQ of 70 and one of 90 should have the same meaning as the difference between an IQ of 125 and one of 145. Because it does not, the scale can only be considered ordinal. Furthermore, there is no point on the scale at which there is no intelligence at all. Thus, the scale does not have the property of an absolute 0.

When a scale has the property of magnitude and equal intervals but not the property of an absolute 0, we refer to it as an *interval scale*. The most common example of an interval scale is the measurement of temperature in degrees of Fahrenheit. This temperature scale clearly has the property of magnitude since 35°F is warmer than 32°F, 65°F is warmer than 64°F, and so on. Also, the difference between 90°F and 80°F is equal to a similar difference of 10° at any point on the scale. However, on the Fahrenheit scale temperature does not have the property of an absolute 0. If it did, the 0 point would be more meaningful. As it is, 0 on the Fahrenheit scale does not have a particular meaning. Freezing occurs at 32°F, and boiling of water occurs at 212°F. Because the scale does not have an absolute 0, it is not possible to make statements in terms of ratios. A temperature of 22°F is not twice as hot as 11°F, and a temperature of 70°F is not twice as hot as one of 35°F.

The Celsius scale of temperature is also an interval rather than a ratio scale. Although 0 represents freezing on the Celsius scale, the 0 is still not an absolute 0. Remember that absolute 0 is a point at which nothing of the property being measured exists. Even on the Celsius scale of temperature there is still plenty of room on the thermometer below 0. When the temperature goes below freezing, some aspect of heat is still being measured.

A scale that has all three properties (magnitude, equal intervals, and absolute 0) is called a *ratio scale*. To continue our example with the scales of temperature, a ratio scale is one that has the properties of the Fahrenheit scale and the Celsius scale but also includes a meaningful 0 point. Physicists and chemists tell us that there is a point at which all molecular activity ceases. This is the point of absolute 0. The Kelvin scale of temperature is an example of a scale that includes the absolute 0 point and is thus an example of a ratio scale. There are some examples of ratio scales in the numbers we see on a regular basis. For example, consider the number of yards gained by running backs on professional football teams. Zero yards actually means that the player has gained no yards at all. If one player has gained 1000 yards and another has gained only 500, then we can say that the first athlete has gained twice as many yards as the second.

Another example is speed of travel. For instance, 0 mph (miles per hour) is the point at which there is no speed at all. If you are driving onto a highway at 30 mph and you increase your speed to 60 when you get in lane, it is appropriate to say you have doubled your speed.

III. DISTRIBUTIONS

A single test score will mean more if we relate it to other test scores. A distribution of scores summarizes the scores for a group of individuals. Theoretical distributions show the probabilities of obtaining a distribution by chance. In testing, there are many ways of recording a distribution of scores.

A. *Frequency distributions*

The *frequency distribution* is a simple way of displaying data from tests. It is a technique for systematically displaying scores on a variable or a measure to reflect how frequently each value was obtained. With a frequency distribution we define all the possible scores and determine how many people obtain each of these scores. Usually when we make a frequency distribution, scores are arranged on the horizontal axis from the lowest to the highest value. The vertical axis is used to record how many times each of the values on the horizontal axis is observed. For most distributions of test scores we will find that the frequency distribution is approximately *bell shaped*. A bell-shaped distribution will have the greatest frequency of scores toward the center of the distribution, and the frequency of the values decreases as the values become greater or less than the value in the center of the distribution.

Figure 2-2 shows a frequency distribution of 1000 observations that takes on values between 61 and 90. Notice that the most frequent observations are the ones toward the center of the distribution around 75 and 76. As we look more toward the extremes of the distribution we find a systematic decline in the frequency with which we observe the scores. For example, we find that the score of 71 is observed less frequently than the score of 72, which is observed less frequently than the score of 73, and so on. Similarly, the score of 73 is observed more frequently than the score of 79, which is noted more often than the score of 80, and so forth.

This neat symmetric relationship will not be characteristic of all sets of scores. But it will occur frequently enough in practice for us to devote special

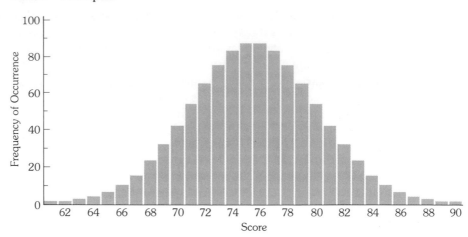

Figure 2-2. Normal distribution of 1000 observations.

attention to it. In the section on the normal distribution we will explain this concept in a little more detail.

Figure 2-3 gives an example of a frequency distribution from actual observations. This graph shows the number of points scored in 448 professional football games played during the 1978 NFL (National Football League) season. The number 448 results because each of 28 teams played 16 regular season games. Looking at the figure we find an approximately bell-shaped distribution.

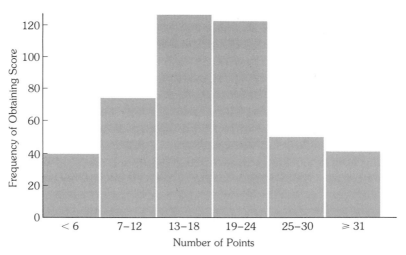

Figure 2-3. In the 1978 NFL season there were 448 games. For each game there were two scores, or one score for each of two teams (for example, Chargers 34, Raiders 21). When the number of points are aggregated into six-point blocks, the distribution of scoring is approximately normal.

Another way of looking at the same set of football scores is to present them in a *frequency polygon*. Here points are placed on a graph to represent the frequencies of observations in the different categories. Then lines are used to connect the frequencies.

Whenever you draw a frequency distribution or a frequency polygon you must decide on the width of the *class interval*. The class interval is the unit for the horizontal axis. For example, in Figures 2-3 and 2-4 the class interval is 6. The demarcations along the *x* axis increase in 6-point intervals as we move along it. The 6-point class interval is used because the nature of football scoring (a touchdown = 6 points, a field goal = 3, and so on) makes certain scores unlikely. Thus the 6-point interval gives a clear picture.

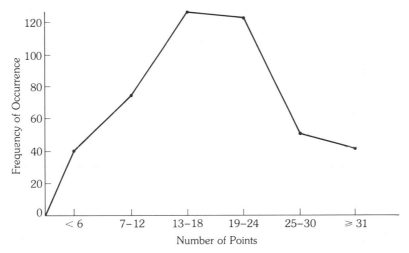

Figure 2-4. Frequency polygon for the same data displayed in **Figure 2-3.**

(Optional)

B. *Exploratory data analysis*

A common practice in the use of tests is to look at the distribution of scores. Distributions and their characteristics are central in testing because each point on the distribution represents a person we are concerned about. Recently Tukey (1977) introduced a new set of simple procedures to help test users understand characteristics of performance by simply looking at a distribution of scores. He calls this process *exploratory data analysis*. He differentiates exploratory data analysis from *confirmatory data analysis,* the process by which we make inferences and test hypotheses. Exploratory data analysis should precede any confirmatory analysis. Among other things, it is a process by which we learn about the data and determine whether there is anything strange about it.

Tukey regards exploratory data analysis as statistical detective work: the task is to find and reveal clues about the data. Once the clues have been obtained it is the work of the "statistical judicial system" to make decisions about the evidence. Thus the statistical courts use the methods of confirmatory data analysis such as analysis of variance, *t* tests, and correlations. One type of exploratory data analysis is the *stem-and-leaf display*. This technique is relatively new, and you may not find it in some introductory statistics books. However, it is fun to use and gives a good picture of your data.

Stem-and-leaf displays. A stem-and-leaf display is a method for creating a frequency distribution that retains most of the information about the original numbers. Usually the *x* axis of a frequency distribution is horizontal. In the stem-and-leaf display the frequency distribution leans on its side, with a vertical *x* axis. An example of a stem-and-leaf display is given at the end of this section.

To create a stem-and-leaf display, you will have to become familiar with some terminology. In the language of exploratory data analysis, a *batch* is a collection of data or one group of data. The stem-and-leaf display was created as a method for displaying and organizing a batch of data. It was intended for use by people who did not necessarily have an extensive background in statistics. Some of the basics are discussed in Focused Discussion 2-1. We can only offer a brief overview of exploratory data analysis here. For those who wish to learn more about this new topic, we suggest J. W. Tukey's *Exploratory Data Analysis* (1977).

■ FOCUSED DISCUSSION 2-1 EXPLORATORY DATA ANALYSIS

To get acquainted with exploratory data analysis, you should perform the following operations for a set or batch of data. The new terms associated with this technique will be defined as they are introduced.

1. Find the depth of the median (or 50th percentile), where *n* is the number of cases in the batch.

$$\text{Depth of median} = \frac{n+1}{2}$$

2. Find the depth of the hinge (round odd quarters to nearer integer). By *depth* we mean the number of cases from the top or the bottom of the distribution that the score is found.

$$\text{Depth of hinge} = \frac{\text{Depth of median} + 1}{2}$$

In each stem-and-leaf display a 5-point summary is provided. The components of the summary and the symbols associated with them are as follows:

Symbol	Term	Definition
↑	Maximum value	Largest score in batch.
uh	Upper hinge	Point marking the upper quartile. This can be found by counting down from the maximum value the number of cases for the depth of the hinge.
m	Median or middle value	The second quartile or the median. The median is found by counting down from the maximum value the number of scores equal to the depth of the median.
lh	Lower hinge	The score associated with the first quartile. It can be found by counting down from the median the number of scores associated with the depth of the hinge or counting up from the lowest score the number of cases equal to the depth of the hinge.
↓	Minimum value	Lowest score in batch.

An example at the end of this section (on page 34) shows a stem-and-leaf display.

How to make a stem-and-leaf display

To make a stem-and-leaf display, you will need to go through the following steps.

1. Display your batch of numbers. The following batch is from the nutrition scores of protein foods as reported by M. F. Jacobson in *Nutrition Scoreboard* (New York: Avon Books, 1975).

    Liver sausage (2 oz) 104; chicken breast (2.7 oz) 62; tuna fish, packed in oil (3 oz) 55; round steak, very lean (3 oz) 53; turkey meat (3 oz) 52; sockeye salmon, canned (3 oz) 48; pork chop, lean (1.7 oz) 47; hamburger, lean (3 oz) 46; veal cutlet (3 oz) 45; round steak, lean and fat (3 oz) 43; lamb chop, lean, roasted (2.5 oz) 43; soybeans, cooked (.5 cup) 41; cod, broiled (3 oz) 40; flounder, baked (3 oz) 38; eggs (2 oz) 36; roast ham, lean and fat (3 oz) 35; hamburger, regular (3 oz) 34; pot roast, lean and fat (3 oz) 33; navy beans (.5 cup) 32; Alpo dog food, fortified (3 oz) 30; pork chop, lean and fat (1.7 oz) 29; salami (2 oz) 27; pork sausage (2 oz) 27; drumstick, chicken, fried (1.3 oz) 26; lentils, cooked (.5 cup) 24; shrimp (1.5 oz) 24; ham, boiled and sliced (2 oz) 22; sirloin steak, lean and fat (3 oz) 19; McDonald's small hamburger (1.6 oz) 18; peanut butter (2 tb) 17; hot dog, pure beef (1) 6; spam (3 oz) 4; bacon (3 slices) 4; bologna (2 oz) 2.

2. Remove or ignore decimal points, and truncate the numbers so that there are only two digits. The remaining right number is the unit for the stem-and-leaf display. For example, in this case the unit is ones.

3. For each of your two-digit numbers, the left number is the stem. Make a column listing all of the stems:

```
                        10
                         9
                         8
                         7
                         6
                         5
                         4
                         3
                         2
                         1
                         0
```

4. The number in the units position will be the leaf on the display. For each number, find the appropriate stem and add the leaf to the display.

```
        10 |
         9 |
         8 |
         7 |
         6 | 2        for the number 62
         5 |
         4 |
         3 |
         2 |
         1 | 9        for the number 19
         0 |
```

5. Be sure to list the value of a unit when you complete the rest of the display. In this example the unit is ones. Also, we have added another column in order to describe some of the items with high and low values.

Unit Equals ones

Stem	Leaf	Item
10	4	Liver sausage
9		
8		
7		
6	2	Chicken breast
5	532	Tuna, lean round steak, turkey
4	87654320	
3	8654320	
2	9776442	
1	987	
0	6442	Hot dog, spam, bacon, bologna

Special problems in stem-and-leaf displays

Sometimes it is difficult to create a stem-and-leaf display because there are too many stems or too many leaves. However, there are easy solutions to these problems.

1. Too few stems. When this occurs all of the leaves will pile up, and it will be hard to

get a good idea of the nature of the distribution. For example, examine the stem-and-leaf display for this batch of nutrition values for bread, rice, pasta, and crackers.

   Bread: Rye bread, American (2 slices) 29; whole wheat bread (2 slices) 26; pumpernickel bread (2 slices) 26; white bread, enriched (2 slices) 22; hamburger or hot dog bun (1 slice) 18; white bread, not enriched (2 slices) 12.

   Rice: Brown rice (.5 cup) 22; parboiled rice (.5 cup) 17; white rice, enriched (.5 cup) 16; instant rice, enriched (.5 cup) 14.

   Pasta: Egg noodles, enriched (.9 cup) 28; elbow macaroni, enriched (.75 cup); spaghetti, enriched (.75 cup) 26.

   Crackers: Triscuit crackers (4) 9; Saltines (4) 8.

The solution to this problem is to spread the stem-and-leaf display by dividing the stems. In the above example, each stem is divided into two stems—one for leaves 5 and above and one for leaves 4 and below.

	2·	966866
	2	22
Example:	1·	876
	1	24
	0·	98
	0	

Sometimes it is even desirable to divide each stem into five stems.

2*	98
2s	666
2f	
2t	22
2	
1*	8
1s	76
1f	4
1t	2
1	
0*	98
0s	
0f	
0t	
0	

   * for leaves of eight and nine
   s for leaves of six and seven
   f for leaves of four and five
   t for leaves of two and three
     for leaves of zero and one

2. Too many stems. When this happens, each stem will have hardly any leaves. This would have been the case for the stem-and-leaf display on page 34 if the unit had been thousands. This problem can sometimes be avoided by truncating at a different point to create a display with ten times fewer stems. When you do this, remember that the unit is now ten times larger.

An example of a stem-and-leaf display

Stem-and-leaf display for how your state ranks in pay. The data give average 1978 pay for 50 states plus District of Columbia: Alabama $10,919; Alaska $20,487; Arizona $11,426; Arkansas $9,785; California $12,891; Colorado $11,882; Connecticut $12,552; Delaware $12,976; District of Columbia $16,145; Florida $10,613; Georgia $10,813; Hawaii $11,634; Idaho $10,687; Illinois $13,693; Indiana $12,378; Iowa $11,027; Kansas $10,846; Kentucky $11,468; Louisiana $11,681; Maine $9,743; Maryland $12,111; Massachusetts $11,711; Michigan $14,622; Minnesota $11,802; Mississippi $9,568; Missouri $11,652; Montana $10,668; Nebraska $10,336; Nevada $12,064; New Hampshire $10,467; New Jersey $12,962; New Mexico $10,844; New York $13,427; North Carolina $10,166; North Dakota $10,315; Ohio $13,025; Oklahoma $11,254; Oregon $12,202; Pennsylvania $12,238; Rhode Island $10,524; South Carolina $10,038; South Dakota $9,368; Tennessee $10,695; Texas $11,911; Utah $11,242; Vermont $10,111; Virginia $11,240; Washington $13,185; West Virginia $12,174; Wisconsin $11,731; Wyoming $12,430.

Unit Equals $100

Stem Equals $1000		State
20	4	Alaska
19		
18		
17		
16	1	District of Columbia
15		
14	6	Michigan
13	6410	
12•	9985	
12	4322110	
11•	98877666	
11	442220	
10•	9888766665	
10	433110	
9•	75	Arkansas, Mississippi
9	3	South Dakota

Note: • signifies thousands unit greater than 5; states with extremely low average incomes and high average incomes are labeled. (*From* U.S. News and World Report, *January 14, 1980, p. 7.*)

The authors thank Dr. M. Robin Di Matteo of the University of California, Riverside, for providing step-by-step instructions for stem-and-leaf display construction.

(End of Optional Section)

C. *Relative performance*

The easiest way to order a group of individuals is to rank them on a defined attribute. If we were to rank a group of skiers according to their race performance on a particular day at Aspen, Colorado, we would assign the skier with the fastest time rank 1, the skier with the second fastest time rank 2, and so on. The difficulty with this kind of ranking system is that it does not consider the number of people who were ranked. If you finish 24th in a foot race, the meaning of your rank of 24 will differ depending on the number of people in the race. If the race were only among the 25 people in your gym class, finishing 24th would suggest that you are a slow runner. On the other hand, if you finished 24th in the 1981 San Francisco Bay to Breakers run, which had nearly 30,000 entrants, your performance would probably be considered very good.

Percentile ranks are used to replace simple ranks when it is necessary to systematically consider how many scores there are in a group. A percentile rank expresses the proportion of scores that fall *below* a particular score. To calculate a percentile rank you need only follow these simple steps:

1. Determine how many people obtained a score below the score of interest.
2. Determine how many people were in the group.
3. Divide the number of people below (Step 1) by the number of people in the group (Step 2).
4. Multiply the result of this division (Step 3) by 100.

The formula is $B/N \times 100$ = percentile rank, where B = number of scores below or less than the score of interest and N = total number of scores. This means that you form a ratio of the number of people below the score and the number of scores. Because there will always be either fewer or the same number of cases in the numerator (top half) of the equation as there are in the denominator, this ratio will always be less than or equal to 1. To get rid of the decimal points we multiply by 100.

As an example, let us consider the runner who finishes 24th out of 25 students in a gym class. To obtain the percentile rank we divide 1 (the number of people finishing behind the person of interest) by 25 (the number of scores in the group). This gives us 1/25, or .04. Then we multiply this result by 100 to obtain the percentile rank, which is 4. This rank tells us the runner is in the 4th percentile.

In the 1981 Bay to Breakers example, if you had finished 24th, then the number of people who were behind you would be 29,976. Dividing this by the number of entrants we have 29,976/30,000 = .9992. If we multiply by 100, we will get the percentile rank, which is 99.92. This tells us that finishing 24th in the Bay to Breakers foot race is exceptionally good. A runner finishing 24th would be in the 99.92th percentile.

D.   *Things to be aware of when using percentages*

Although percentile ranks are easy to compute and interpret by most people, there are a few occasions in which some get confused. People may confuse percentile rank with the percentage of items correct. In giving feedback about test performance this is easily avoided by explaining briefly what the percentile rank means. For a person with a percentile rank of 67 on the Graduate Record Examination, for example, you might explain that the person had performed better than 67% (or 67 out of every 100 people) of the national sample on which the test was validated.

When reporting percentile ranks it is important to report two essential bits of information. First, you should always describe the group the percentile ranks are calculated for. Finishing in the 22nd percentile in the Boston Marathon is more of an accomplishment than finishing in the 22nd percentile of the San Diego Marathon, because the former restricts entry to persons who have done well (running 26 miles in less than 2 hours and 50 minutes for men under age 40) in another marathon race. Second, you must always report how many people the percentiles were based on. For example, are you in the 22nd percentile of a group of 50 runners, 500 runners, or 5000 runners?

Using percentiles is only the first step in using numerical systems to describe test scores. In the following sections we will cover the mean and the standard deviation. Then we will discuss standardized scores, which can be used to relate scores back to a percentile distribution in a more sophisticated way.

IV.   DESCRIBING DISTRIBUTIONS

A.   *Mean*

Statistics are used to summarize data. If you consider a set of scores, the mass of information will be too much to interpret all at once. That is why we need certain numerical conveniences to help summarize the information. The mean is simply the average score. An example of the set of scores that could be summarized is shown in Table 2-2. These scores are the number of games won by various football teams during the 1978 NFL football season. We refer to each score as a variable, which we signify as X. A variable is a score that takes on different values. The number of games won is a variable, because different teams won different numbers of games.

The arithmetic average score in a distribution is called the *mean*. To calculate the mean, we total the scores and divide by the number of cases. Usually we signify the number of cases by N. The capital Greek letter sigma (Σ) means summation. Thus the formula for the mean that we signify as $\bar{X}$ is

$$\bar{X} = \frac{\Sigma X}{N}$$

In words, this formula says total the scores and divide by the number of cases that you totaled. An example is given in the table.

TABLE 2-2 Number of games won by professional football teams during the 1978 season

Team	Games won
AMERICAN CONFERENCE	
East Division	
New England	11
Miami	11
New York Jets	8
Buffalo	5
Baltimore	5
Central Division	
Pittsburgh	14
Houston	10
Cleveland	8
Cincinnati	4
West Division	
Denver	10
Oakland	9
Seattle	9
San Diego	9
Kansas City	4
NATIONAL CONFERENCE	
East Division	
Dallas	12
Philadelphia	9
Washington	8
St. Louis	6
New York Giants	6
Central Division	
Minnesota	8
Green Bay	8
Detroit	7
Chicago	7
Tampa Bay	5
West Division	
Los Angeles	12
Atlanta	9
New Orleans	7
San Francisco	2
	$\Sigma X = 223$

To find the mean, perform the following steps: (1) Obtain ΣX or the sum of the scores: $\Sigma X = 11+11+8+ \cdots +7+2 = 223$. (2) Find N or the number of scores: $N = 28$. (3) Divide ΣX by N: $\Sigma X/N = 223/28 = 7.96$.

Note: There were 16 games during the season. Ordinarily the mean would be 8, because half the games during a season are won and the other half are lost (averaged over teams). However, in 1978 there was one tie, which caused the mean to be slightly lower than 8.

B. *Standard deviation*

Although it is very informative to know the mean of a group of scores, the mean does not give us all the desired information about the group of scores. As an illustration, look at the following two sets of numbers.

Set 1	Set 2
4	2
4	4
4	6
4	1
4	4
4	7

Calculate the mean of the first set. You should get 4. Now what is the mean of the second set? If you calculate correctly, you should get 4 again. In other words, two distributions of scores that appear very different may give you the same mean. Therefore, it is important to consider other characteristics of the distribution of scores besides the mean.

The variation we would like to consider here is similar to the average deviation around the mean. One way to do this is to subtract the mean from each score $(X-\bar{X})$. Statisticians often signify this with a lowercase x $[x=(X-\bar{X})]$. Then we total the deviations. Try this for the data in Table 2-2. Did you get 0? You should have, and this is not an unusual example. In fact, the sum of the deviations around the mean will always equal 0. However, we do have an alternative: we can square all of the deviations around the mean in order to get rid of any negative signs. Then we can obtain the average squared deviation around the mean, which is known as the *variance*. The formula for the variance is

$$\sigma^2 = \frac{\Sigma(X-\bar{X})^2}{N}$$

where $(X-\bar{X})$ is the deviation of a score from the mean. The variance is a very useful statistic and is commonly used in data analysis. The variance, however, shows our variable in squared deviations around the mean rather than in deviations around the mean. In words, the variance is the average squared deviation around the mean. In order to get it back into the units that will make sense to us, all we need to do is to take the square root of the variance. The square root of the variance is the *standard deviation* (σ), and it is represented by the following formula:

$$\sigma = \sqrt{\frac{\Sigma(X-\bar{X})^2}{N}}$$

In words, the standard deviation is the square root of the average squared deviation around the mean. Although the standard deviation is not technically equal to the average deviation, it will give you an approximation of how much the scores deviate from the mean (on the average). The variance and the standard deviation have many advantages because of their mathematical prop- erties. For example, knowing the standard deviation of a normally distributed batch of data allows us to make precise statements about the distribution. The formulas presented above are for the variance and the standard deviation of a population. That is why we use the lowercase Greek sigma (σ and σ^2). Most often we use the standard deviation for a sample to estimate the standard deviation in a population. When we do, we replace the Greek σ with the Roman letter S. Also, we divide by $N-1$ rather than N:

$$S = \sqrt{\frac{\Sigma(X-\bar{X})^2}{N-1}}$$

In calculating the standard deviation, it is often easier to use the raw score equivalent formula, which is

$$S = \sqrt{\frac{\Sigma X^2 - \frac{(\Sigma X)^2}{N}}{N-1}}$$

This calculation can also be done automatically by some minicalculators.

C. Z score

One of the problems with means and standard deviations is that they do not have clear meanings to us. For example, if the mean of some set of scores is 57.6, it still does not convey all of the information we would like. There are other metrics designed for a more direct interpretation. The z score is a transformation of data into standardized units that are easier for psychologists to interpret. A z score is the difference between a score and the mean divided by the standard deviation. In other words, a z score is the deviation of a score X from the mean in standard deviation units. If a score is equal to the mean, its z score will be 0. For example, suppose the score and the mean are both 6 (6−6=0), and 0 divided by anything is still 0. If the score is larger than the mean, the z score will be positive; if the score is less than the mean, the z score will be negative.

Let us try a few examples. The formula for a z score is

$$z = \frac{X - \bar{X}}{S}$$

Suppose that $X = 6$, the mean $\bar{X}=3$, and the standard deviation (S) also equals 3. The z score will equal 1 because, plugging these values into the formula, $(6-3)/3=3/3=1$. This means that the score 6 differs from the mean about as much as scores differ from the mean on the average (1 standard deviation).

Let us try one more. Suppose $X=4$ and the mean is equal to 5.75. The standard deviation is equal to 2.11. What is the z score? By our calculations it is $-.83$: $(4-5.75)/2.11=-1.75/2.11=-.83$. In other words, this means that the score we observed (4) is .83 standard deviations below the average score. Or it means that the score is below the mean, but its difference from the mean is slightly less than that by which scores differ from the mean on the average. Some other examples are shown in Table 2-3.

TABLE 2-3 The calculation of mean, standard deviation, and z scores

Name	Test Score (X)	X²
Carla	70	4,900
Fred	85	7,225
Monica	92	8,464
Andrew	65	4,225
James	83	6,889
Diana	98	9,604
Marcel	75	5,625
Sean	90	8,100
Jennie	60	3,600
Amanda	78	6,084
	$\Sigma X=796$	$\Sigma X^2=64,716$

$$\bar{X}=\frac{\Sigma X}{N}=\frac{796}{10}=79.60$$

$$S=\sqrt{\frac{\Sigma X^2-\frac{(\Sigma X)^2}{N}}{N-1}}=\sqrt{\frac{64,716-\frac{(796)^2}{10}}{10-1}}=12.27$$

$$\text{Monica's } z \text{ score}=\frac{X-\bar{X}}{S}=\frac{92-79.6}{12.267}=1.01$$

$$\text{Marcel's } z \text{ score}=\frac{X-\bar{X}}{S}=\frac{75-79.6}{12.267}=-.37$$

$$\text{Jennie's } z \text{ score}=\frac{X-\bar{X}}{S}=\frac{60-79.6}{12.267}=-1.60$$

D. Standard normal distribution

Next we will discuss the standard normal distribution, because it is of central importance to statistics and to psychological testing. First you should participate in a short exercise. Take any coin and flip it 10 times. Now repeat this exercise of 10 coin flips 25 times. As you are doing this, record the number of heads you observe in each group of 10 flips. When you are done, make a frequency distribution showing how many times you observed 1 head in your 10 flips, 2 heads, 3 heads, and so on.

Your frequency distribution might look like the example shown in Figure 2-5. The most frequently observed event occurs when you observe about equal numbers of 5 heads and 5 tails. As you go toward the 10 heads and 0 tails or 10 tails and 0 heads, then events are observed with less frequency. For example,

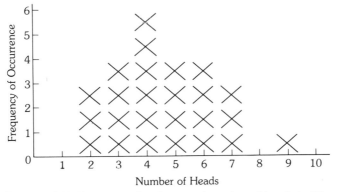

Figure 2-5. Frequency distribution of number of heads in 25 sets of 10 flips.

there were no occasions in which fewer than 2 heads were observed and only 1 occasion in which more than 8 heads were observed. This is very much what we would expect from the laws of probability. On the average we would expect half of the flips to show heads and half to show tails if heads and tails are equally probable events. However, although it is still possible to observe a long string of heads or tails, it is improbable. In other words, we will sometimes observe that the coin comes up heads in 9 out of 10 flips. The likelihood that this will happen, however, is quite small.

Figure 2-6 shows the theoretical distribution of heads in an infinite number

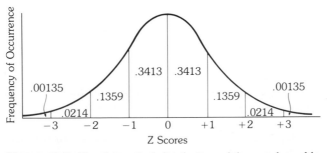

Figure 2-6. The theoretical distribution of the number of heads obtained in an infinite number of coin flips.

of flips of the coin. This figure might look a little like the distribution you obtained from your coin-flipping experience or the distribution shown in Figure 2-5. Actually this is the normal distribution or what is known as a *symmetrical binomial probability distribution*. It is defined precisely by the equation

$$Y = \frac{N}{\sigma\sqrt{2\pi}} \, e^{-(X-\mu)/2\sigma^2}$$

Where Y = height of curve for particular values of X
π = pi or a constant of 22/7 or 3.1416
e = a natural logarithm = 2.7183
N = number of cases on which observations were made
    (thus the total area under the curve will equal N)
μ = the mean of the distribution
σ = the standard deviation of the distribution

On most occasions we refer to units on the x axis of the normal distribution in z score units. Any variable transformed into z score units will take on special properties. First, z scores have a mean of 0 and a standard deviation of 1. If you think about this for a minute, you should be able to reason out why this is true. You might remember that the sum of the deviations around the mean is always equal to 0. The top part of the z score equation is just the deviation around the mean, while the bottom part is a constant (S). Thus, the mean of z scores can be expressed as

$$\frac{\frac{1}{s}\Sigma(X-\bar{X})}{N} \quad \text{or} \quad \frac{\Sigma z}{N}$$

Because $\Sigma(X-\bar{X})$ will always equal 0, the mean of z scores will always be 0. In Figure 2-6 the standardized or z score units are marked on the x axis. The numbers under the curve are the percentages of cases we would expect to observe in this area. For example, we see that 34.13% of the cases fall between the mean and 1 standard deviation above the mean. Do not forget that 50% of the cases fall below the mean. Putting these two bits of information together, we can conclude that if a score is 1 standard deviation above the mean, then it is at about the 84th percentile (50+34.13=84.13 to be exact). A score that is 1 standard deviation below the mean would be at about the 16th percentile (50−34.13=15.87). Thus, we can use what we have learned about means, standard deviations, z scores, and the normal curve to transform raw scores, which have very little meaning to us, into percentile scores, which are easier to interpret. These methods can be used whenever the distribution of scores is normal. Methods for abnormal distributions will not be covered.

Going back and forth between percentages and *z* scores. Appendix 1 at the back of the book is a table that relates z scores to percentages.

For any z score you can use this table to find the percentage of cases that fall below it. The z scores are listed in the column labeled z scores, and the percentages are listed in the other columns. First, suppose we have a z score of 1.0. Find this value in the z score column. Now go over to the percentile column and find the value adjacent to the z of 1.0. You will notice that the value is 84.13. This means that when a z score is 1.0, 84.13% of the cases fall below that point.

Now try to find the percentage of cases that would fall below a z score of 1.19. If you are using the table correctly, you should obtain 88.30. Now try −.75. The first hint you should be aware of is that this is a negative z score, so the percentage of cases falling below should be less than 50. Looking up the z score of .75 in the table, we find that 22.66% of the cases fall below this z score.

We can turn the process around. Instead of using z scores to find the percentiles, we can use the percentiles to find the corresponding z scores. To do this we need only look in the table under percentiles and find the corresponding z score. For example, suppose we wish to find the z score associated with the 90th percentile. We look at the table and find that the value closest to the 90th percentile is 89.97, which lies adjacent to the z score of 1.28. This tells us that persons obtaining z scores greater than 1.28 are above the 90th percentile in the distribution.

An example close to home.   One of the difficulties in grading students is that performance is usually rated in terms of raw scores, such as the number of items a person gets correct on an examination. You are probably familiar with the experience of having a test returned to you with some number at the top which makes little sense to you. For instance, the professor comes into class and hands you your test with a 72 on the top of the paper. Then you must wait patiently while he or she draws the distribution on the board and attempts to put your 72 into some category that you understand, such as B+.

An alternative way of doing things would be to give you feedback about your performance as a z score. To do this your professor would just subtract the average score (mean) from your score and divide by the standard deviation. If your z score was positive, you would immediately know that your score was above average; if it were negative, you would know your performance was below average.

Suppose that your professor tells you in advance that you will be graded on a curve system, according to the following rigid system. If you are in the top 15% of the class, you will get an "A" (85th percentile or above); between the 60th and the 84th percentile, you will get a "B"; between the 20th and the 59th percentile, you will get a "C"; between the 6th and the 19th percentile, you will get a "D"; and in the 5th percentile or below, you will not pass. Using Appendix 1, you should be able to find the z scores associated with each of these cutoff points. Try it on your own, and then consult Table 2-4 to see if you are correct.

TABLE 2-4 z score cutoffs for a grading system

Grade	Percentiles	z Score Cutoff
A	85–100	1.04
B	60–84	.25
C	20–59	−.84
D	6–19	−1.56
F	0–5	Less than −1.56

Looking at Table 2-4 you should be able to determine what your grade would be in this class on the basis of your z score. If your z score is 1.04 or greater, you would receive an "A." If it were greater than .25 but less than 1.04, you would get a "B," and so on. This system does rest on the assumption that the scores are normally distributed.

Now let us try an example that puts a few of the concepts together. Suppose that you get a 60 on a social psychology examination. You learned in class that the mean for the test was 55.70 and that the standard deviation was 6.08. If your professor uses the same grading system that we just described, what would your grade be?

To solve this problem we must first find your z score. The formula for a z score is

$$z = \frac{X - \bar{X}}{S}$$

So your z score would be

$$z = \frac{60 - 55.70}{6.08} = \frac{4.30}{6.08} = .707$$

Looking at Table 2-4, we find that .707 is greater than .25, which is the cutoff for a "B" but less than 1.04, which is the cutoff for an "A." Now let us find your exact standing in the class. To do this we will need to look again at Appendix 1. Because the table only gives z scores to the second decimal, we will round .707 to .71. Looking at the appendix, we find that 76.11% of the cases fall below a z score of .71. This means that you would be in approximately the 76th percentile or that you would have performed better on this examination than approximately 76 out of every 100 students.

E. McCall's T

There are a variety of other systems by which we can transform raw scores in order to give them more intuitive meaning. One system was established quite some time ago by W. A. McCall (1939), who originally intended to develop a system to derive equal units on mental quantities. He suggested that a random sample of 12-year-olds be tested and that distribution of their scores be obtained. Then percentile equivalents were to be assigned to each raw score, showing the percentile rank in the group for the persons obtaining that raw score. After this had been accomplished the mean of the distribution would be set at 50, to correspond with the 50th percentile. In McCall's system the standard deviation was set at 10.

In effect, what McCall generated was a system that is exactly the same as standard scores (z scores), except the mean in McCall's system is 50 rather than 0 and the standard deviation is 10 rather than 1. Indeed, a z score can be transformed to a T score by applying the linear transformation

$$T=10z+50$$

In words, you can get from a z score to McCall's T by multiplying the z score by 10 and adding 50. It should be noted that McCall did not originally intend to create an alternative to the z score. Rather he wanted to obtain one set of scores that could then be applied in other situations without restandardizing the entire set of numbers.

As many people have pointed out (for example, Angoff, 1971), there is nothing magical about the mean of 50 and the standard deviation of 10. It is a simple matter to create systems such as standard scores with any mean and standard deviation you would like. If you want to say that you got a score 1000 points higher than a person who was 1 standard deviation below you, you could devise a system with, say, a mean of 100,000 and a standard deviation of 1000. If you had calculated z scores for this distribution of scores, you would obtain this with the transformation

$$NS \text{ (for New Score)} = 1000z + 100,000$$

If fact, you can create any system desired. To do it, just multiply the z score by whatever you would like the standard deviation of your distribution to be and then add the number you would like for the mean of your new distribution.

An example of a test that was developed using standardized scores is the Scholastic Aptitude Test (SAT). When this test (which you may have taken to be admitted to college) was created in 1941, the developers decided to make the mean score 500 and the standard deviation 100. Thus they multiplied the z scores for those who took the test in 1941 by 100 and added 500. Since the test has been in use, the basic scoring system has not been changed.

F. *Quartiles and deciles*

The terms *quartiles* and *deciles* are frequently used when tests and test results are discussed. These two terms refer to divisions of the percentile scale into groups. The quartile system divides the percentage scale into four groups, while the decile system divides the scale into ten groups.

Quartiles are points that divide the frequency distribution into equal fourths. The 1st quartile is the 25th percentile, the 2nd quartile is the median or the 50th percentile, and the 3rd quartile is the 75th percentile. These are abbreviated Q_1, Q_2, and Q_3, respectively. One-quarter of the cases will fall below Q_1, one-half will fall below Q_2, and three-quarters will fall below Q_3. The interquartile range is the interval of scores bounded by the 25th and 75th percentiles. In other words, the interquartile range is bounded by the range of scores that represents the middle 50% of the distribution.

Deciles are similar to quartiles except that they use points that mark 10% rather than 25% intervals. Thus, the top decile, or D_9, is the point at which 90% of the cases fall below. The next decile (D_8) marks the 80th percentile, and so forth.

Another system was developed in the U.S. Air Force during World War II and is known as the *stanine system*. This system converts any set of scores into a transformed scale, which ranges from 1 to 9. Actually the term *stanine* comes from "standard nine." The scale is standardized to have a mean of 5 and a standard deviation of approximately 2. It has been suggested that stanines have computational advantages because they require only one column on a computer card (Anastasi, 1976). Table 2-5 shows how percentile scores are converted into stanines.

TABLE 2-5 Transformation of percentile scores into stanines

Percentage of Cases	Percentiles	Stanines
4	1–4	1
7	5–11	2
12	12–23	3
17	24–40	4
20	41–60	5
17	61–77	6
12	78–89	7
7	90–96	8
4	97–100	9

As you can see in Table 2-5, for every 100 scores, the lowest 4 (or bottom 4% of the cases) fall in the first stanine. The next 7 (or 7% of the cases) fall into the second stanine, and so on. Finally, the top 4 cases fall into the top stanine. Using what you have learned about z scores and the standard normal distribution, you should be able to figure out the stanine for a score if you know the mean and the standard deviation of the distribution the score comes from. For example, suppose that Igor received a 48 on his chemistry midterm. The mean in Igor's class was 42.6, and the standard deviation was 3.6. First we must find Igor's z score. We do this by using the formula

$$z = \frac{X - \bar{X}}{S} \qquad \text{so} \qquad z = \frac{48 - 42.6}{3.6} = 1.50$$

Now we need to transform Igor's z score into his percentile rank. To do this we use Appendix 1 in the back of the book. The appendix shows that a z score of 1.5 is in approximately the 93rd percentile (middle column) and falls in the 8th stanine.

Actually you would rarely go through all these steps to find a stanine. There are easier ways of doing this, and there are computer programs that do it automatically. However, working out stanines the long way will help you become familiar with a variety of concepts covered in this chapter. The concepts include (1) standard scores, (2) means, (3) standard deviations, and (4) percentiles.

Let us review the five steps to go from raw scores to stanines:

1. Find the mean of the raw scores.
2. Find the standard deviation of raw scores.
3. Transform raw scores to z scores.
4. Transform z scores to percentiles (using Appendix 1).
5. Use Table 2-5 to convert percentiles into stanines.

Remember, in practice you probably would use a computer program to obtain the stanines. Exercise in computing stanines the long way is intended to give you practice with some of the concepts we have covered.

Technical Box 2-1

Many authors have contested the U.S. Air Force stanine system because it does not have a standard deviation of exactly 2. In 1958, Henry Kaiser of the University of California at Berkeley revised the stanine system by introducing minor modifications in the percentile cutoffs. In Kaiser's revised system the standard deviation is exactly 2.

In addition to the stanine scale, similar systems have been proposed. For example, one early variant was the Sten scale, which had 5 units above and 5 units below the mean on a 10-point scale (Canfield, 1951). The most recent addition has been the c scale (Guilford & Fruchter, 1973), which has 11 points and a standard deviation of 2.

V. NORMS

Norms refer to the performance by a defined group on a particular test. There are many ways to express norms, and we have discussed some of these under the headings of z scores, percentiles, means, and the like. The norms for a test are based on the distribution of scores obtained by some defined sample of individuals. The mean is a norm, and the 50th percentile is a norm. Norms are used to give information about performance relative to what is expected.

Much has been written about norms and their inadequacies. Much of this material will be discussed in later chapters in relation to particular tests. In this section we will only cover the highlights. Whenever you see a norm for a test you should always ask how it was established. Norms are obtained by administering the test to a sample of people and obtaining the distribution of scores for that group.

For example, you might develop a measure of anxiety associated with taking tests in college. After establishing some psychometric properties for the test, it would be administered to normative groups of college students. The scores for these groups of college students might then serve as the norms. For example, it might be found that for the normative groups of students, the average score was 19. Then, when your friend Alice comes to take the test and obtains a score of 24, the psychologist using the test might conclude that Alice is above the average in test anxiety.

The SAT, as indicated earlier, has norms. The test was administered to thousands of high school seniors from all over the United States. By creating distributions of scores for this normative group, it was possible to obtain a distribution to provide meaning for particular categories of scores. For example, in the national sample, a person who scored 650 on the verbal portion of the SAT was at the 93rd percentile of high school seniors. However, if you took the test after 1941 and scored 650, it did not mean that you were at the 93rd percentile of the people who took the test when you did. Rather it meant that you would have been at the 93rd percentile if you had been in the group the test had been standardized upon. However, if the normative group was a representative sample of the group to which you belonged (and there is every reason to believe it is), then it is reasonable to assume that you were in approximately the 93rd percentile of your own group.[2]

A. Age-related norms

Certain tests have different normative groups for particular age groups. Most IQ tests are of this sort. We will talk about IQ tests in more detail in Chapter 11. When the Stanford-Binet IQ test was originally created, distributions of the performance of random samples of children were obtained for various age groups. When applying an IQ test, the tester's task is to determine the mental

[2]Based on the *American Testing Program Guide* for 1979–1981.

age of the person being tested. This is accomplished through various exercises that help locate the age level norm at which a child is performing.

B. Tracking

One of the most common uses of age-related norms is for growth charts used by pediatricians. Consider the question "Is my son tall or short?" The answer will usually depend on a comparison of your son to other boys of the same age. Your son would be very tall if he stood 5 ft. at age 8 but very short if he were only 5 ft. at age 18. Thus the comparison is usually with persons of the same age group.

Beyond this rather obvious type of age-related comparison, child experts have discovered that children at the same age level tend to go through different growth patterns. Children who are small infants often remain small and continue to grow at a slower pace. Pediatricians must know more about a child than just age. They must know what percentile the child is in within a given age category. For a variety of physical characteristics, children tend to stay at about their same percentile level relative to other children in their age group as they grow older. This tendency to stay at about the same level relative to one's peers is known as *tracking*. Height and weight are good examples of physical characteristics that track. Figures 2-7 and 2-8 show the expected rates of growth for boys and girls in terms of height and weight. Notice that the children who were the largest babies tended to remain the largest as they got older.

A pediatrician would use the chart to determine the expected course of growth for a child. For example, if a 3-month-old boy came into the office and weighed 13.2 lb. (6 kilos), the doctor would locate the child as the center line on the bottom half of Figure 2-7. By age 36 months the child would be expected to weigh just under 33 lb. The tracking charts are very useful to doctors because they help determine whether the child is going through some unusual growth pattern. A boy who weighed 13 lb. at age 3 months might come under scrutiny if at age 36 months he weighed only 28 lb. This might be normal for 3-year-olds in a different track, but for the child who started out larger, the doctor might want to examine him more closely to determine why the child did not stay in his track.

Although the tracking system has worked well for medicine, it has stirred considerable controversy when it has been applied to education. Some people believe that there is an analogy between the rates of physical growth and the rates of intellectual growth. Just as there are some slow growers who eventually will be shorter adults, some researchers believe that there are slow learners who will eventually know less as adults. Furthermore, it has been suggested that the rate at which children learn differs. Thus, children are separated early in their educational careers and placed in classrooms to correspond with these different tracks. A good many educators have attacked the tracking system because it unfairly discriminates against some children.

Because psychological tests are used to place children in these tracks, the

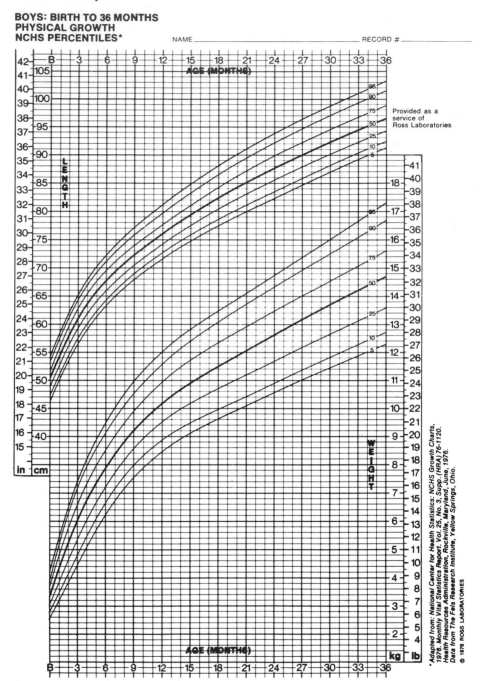

Figure 2-7. Tracking chart for boys' physical growth from birth to 36 months. (*Adapted from the National Center for Health Statistics: NCHS Growth Charts. Health Resources Administration, Rockville, Maryland, June, 1976.*)

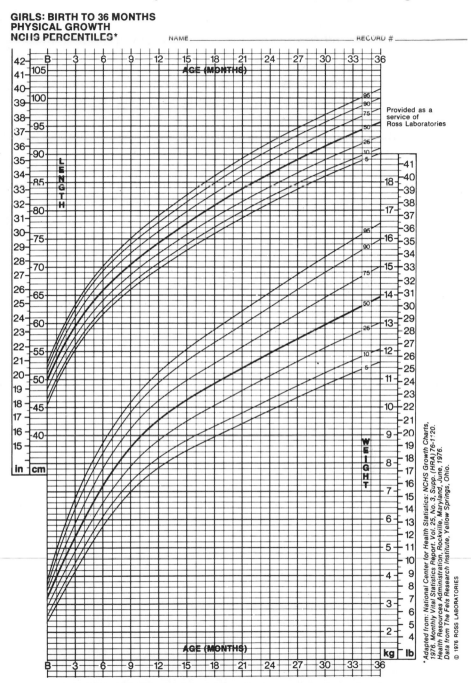

Figure 2-8. Tracking chart for girls' physical growth from birth to 36 months. (*Adapted from the National Center for Health Statistics: NCHS Growth Charts. Health Resources Administration, Rockville, Maryland, June, 1976.*)

tests have come under severe scrutiny and attack. We will return to this controversy in Chapter 20.

C. *Criterion-referenced tests*

The purpose of establishing norms for a test is to determine how a test taker does in comparison to others. A test that compares each person to a norm is called *norm referenced*. This use of tests has been objected to by many because it forces competition among people. Young children exposed to many norm-referenced tests as early as elementary school get caught up in a never-ending battle to perform better than average. In addition to the function of ranking people according to performance, tests can also play an important role in the identification of problems and in suggesting new directions for individualized programs of instruction. During the last decade there has been a growing interest in tests that are used to determine whether students know specific information. These tests do not compare students with one another—they compare each student's performance with a criterion or an expected level of performance (Linn, 1980).

A criterion-referenced test is one that describes the specific types of skills, tasks, or knowledge that the test taker can demonstrate. For example, a criterion-referenced test might include items testing skill in addition, subtraction, multiplication, long division, and short division. The results of the test might demonstrate that a particular child can add, subtract, and multiply but has difficulty with both long and short division. The results of the test would not be used to make comparisons between the child and other members of his or her class. Instead, they would be used to design an individualized program of instruction that focuses on division. Thus, the criterion-referenced testing movement emphasizes the diagnostic use of tests. The tests are diagnostic in the sense that they can be used to identify problems that can be remedied.

VI. SUMMARY

In this chapter we discussed some basic rules for translating observations of behavior and mental processes into numbers. The use of number systems is important for all scientific exercises in order to gain precision. Measures of psychological processes are represented by one of four types of scale. A *nominal scale* is a system that simply assigns numbers to categories. This type of scale has none of the properties of a numbered scale. An *ordinal scale* has the property of magnitude and allows us to rank objects, but it does not have the property of equal intervals or an absolute 0. An *interval scale* can describe the distances between objects because it has the property of equal intervals in addition to the property of magnitude. The *ratio scale* has an absolute 0 in addition to equal intervals and magnitude. Any mathematical operation is permissible with a ratio scale.

In order to make sense out of test scores we have to examine the score for an individual, relative to the scores of others. To do this requires that we create a *distribution* of test scores. There are several ways of displaying the distribution of scores, including *frequency distributions, frequency polygons,* and *stem-and-leaf displays*. We also need statistics to describe the distribution. The *mean* is the average score, the *variance* is the averaged squared deviation around the mean score, and the *standard deviation* is the square root of the variance. Using these statistics we can tell a lot about a particular score by relating it to characteristics of a well-known probability distribution known as the *standard normal distribution*.

Norms are used to relate a score to a particular distribution for a subgroup of a population. For example, norms are used to describe where a child is on some measure relative to other children of the same age. In contrast, criterion-referenced tests are used to document specific skills rather than to compare people. In summary, this chapter reviewed basic statistical methods for describing scores on one variable. In Chapter 3 we will discuss statistical methods for showing the relationship between two or more variables.

Correlation and Regression

Learning objectives

When you have completed this chapter, you should be able to do the following:

1. *Express the extent to which two measures are associated.*
2. *Explain what a scatter diagram is and how it is used.*
3. *Define a positive correlation and a negative correlation.*
4. *Discuss some of the differences between correlation and regression.*
5. *Tell how a regression line describes the relationship between two variables.*
6. *Discuss under what circumstances you would use the point biserial correlation, the phi coefficient, or the tetrachoric correlation.*
7. *Outline the procedure you would use to predict one score from the linear combination of several scores.*
8. *Explain factor analysis and how it is used.*

A banner headline in an issue of the *National Enquirer* read "FOOD CAUSES MOST MARRIAGE PROBLEMS." The article inside the magazine talked about "Startling Results of Studies by Doctors and Marriage Counselors." Actually the headline was not based on any systematic study. Rather, it used the opinions of some physicians and marriage counselors who felt that high blood sugar is related to low energy level, which in turn causes marital unhappiness.

Unfortunately, the *National Enquirer* did not report enough data for us to make an evaluation of the hypothesis. However, we feel comfortable concluding that an association between diet and divorce has not been established. Before we are willing to accept the magazine's conclusion we must ask many questions.

This chapter focuses on one of the many issues raised in the report—the level of association between variables.[1]

The *Enquirer* tells us that diet and unhappiness are associated, but it does not tell us to what extent. Is the association greater than we would expect by chance? Is it a strong or a weak association?

Lots of things seem to be related. For example, life stress is associated with heart disease, training is associated with good performance in athletics, overeating is associated with indigestion. People are always telling us that things are associated. For some events the association is obvious. For example, the angle of the sun in the sky and the time of day are associated in a very predictable way. This is because time was designed to be used in relation to the angle of the sun in the sky. Other associations are less obvious. The association between performing well on the Scholastic Aptitude Test and obtaining good grades in college is one example.

Sometimes we do not know whether these events are meaningfully associated with one another. If we do conclude that events are associated in some fundamental way, it is important to have a precise index of the degree. This chapter will discuss statistical procedures that allow us to make precise estimates of the degree to which variables are associated. These methods are very important, and we will refer to them frequently in the remainder of this book. The indexes of association used most frequently in testing are correlation, regression, and multiple regression. Before moving ahead with the methods for calculating correlation and regression, you should be aware that this chapter is a little more technically oriented than most of the others in this book. Thus, it may require that you read it slowly—particularly if it has been a while since you had a statistics course. Comprehending this material, however, should pay off, because correlation and regression are at the heart of the testing field. If you know how to interpret correlational data, it should make you a wiser consumer of test information and should also help you evaluate information in fields out of testing and psychology.

I. THE SCATTER DIAGRAM

Before presenting the measures of association, we will look at visual displays of the relationship between variables. In the last chapter we concentrated

---

[1]There were many other problems with the *Enquirer* report. The observation was based on the clinical experiences of some health practitioners who found that many couples who came in for counseling had poor diets. One major oversight was that there was no control group of people who were not having marriage problems. We do not know from the study whether couples having problems have poor diets in greater proportions than people in general. Another problem is that neither diet nor marital happiness was measured in a systematic way. Thus we are left with subjective opinions about the levels of these variables. Finally, we do not know the direction of causation: does diet cause unhappiness or does unhappiness cause poor diet. Another possibility is that some other problem (such as stress) may cause both poor diet and unhappiness.

on univariate distributions of scores. These involve only one variable—or each person may have one score. This chapter will consider statistical methods for studying bivariate distributions, which have two scores for each individual. For example, when we study the relations between test scores and classroom performance, we are dealing with a bivariate distribution. Each of several persons has a score on the test and a score for classroom performance. Averaged over individuals, we seek to learn whether these two variables are associated.

A scatter diagram is a picture of the relationship between two variables. An example of a scatter diagram is shown in Figure 3-1. The axes in the figure

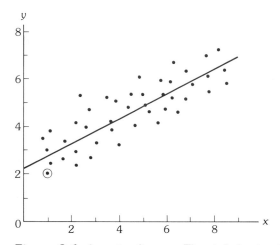

Figure 3-1. A scatter diagram. The circled point shows a person who had a score of 1 on X and of 2 on Y (see the text). The line expresses the regression that describes the best linear relationship between X and Y.

represent scales for two variables. Values of X are shown on the horizontal axis, and the vertical axis is for the values of Y. Each point on the scatter diagram shows where a particular individual scored on both X and Y. For example, one person had a score of 1 on X and a score of 2 on Y. This point is circled in the figure. It can be located if we find 1 on the x axis and go straight up to where there is a point at the level of 2 on the y axis. Each point summarizes the scores for X and Y for one individual. As you can see, the figure presents a lot of information. Each point represents the performance of one person who has been assessed on two measures.

The next sections will present methods for summarizing the information in the scatter diagrams by finding the straight line that comes closer to more points than any other. One of the reasons that it is important to examine the scatter diagram is because the relationships between X and Y are not always best described by a straight line. For example, the relationship shown in Figure 3-2 is probably best described by a curved line. The methods of linear correlation or linear regression, which are presented in this chapter, are not appropriate for describing nonlinear relationships as illustrated in Figure 3-2.

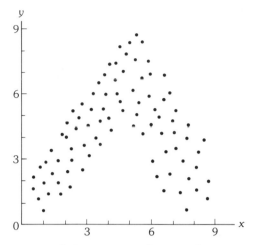

Figure 3-2. A scatter diagram showing a nonlinear relationship. Linear regression and linear correlation may not be appropriate to describe this type of relationship.

II. CORRELATION

In correlational analysis we ask if two variables *covary*. In other words, does Y get larger whenever X gets larger? For example, does the patient feel dizzier when we increase the dosage of the drug? Do people get more diseases when they are under more stress? Correlational analysis is designed primarily to examine linear relationships between variables. Although we can use correlational techniques to study nonlinear relationships, that is beyond the scope of this book.[2]

A *correlation coefficient* is a mathematical index used to describe the direction and magnitude of the relationship. Figure 3-3 shows three different types of relationships between variables. The first section of the figure demonstrates a *positive correlation*. This means that higher scores on Y are associated with higher scores on X and lower scores on Y are associated with lower scores on X. The second section shows *negative correlation*. When there is a negative correlation, higher scores on Y are associated with lower scores on X and lower scores on Y are associated with higher scores on X. This might describe the relationship between taking barbiturates and amount of activity. The higher the drug dosage, the less active patients will be. The third portion of Figure 3-3 shows *no correlation* or a situation in which the variables are not related. Here

[2]Readers interested in methods for studying nonlinear relationships should review McNemar (1969).

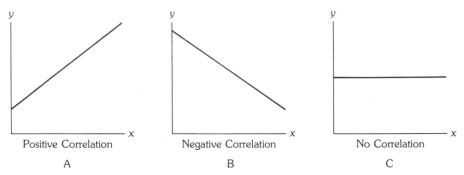

Figure 3-3. Three hypothetical relationships. Section A shows a positive correlation, Section B shows a negative correlation, and Section C shows no correlation.

scores on X do not give us information about scores on Y. An example of this sort of relationship would be the lack of correlation between shoe size and IQ.

There are a variety of ways to calculate a coefficient of correlation. All involve pairs of observations: for each observation on one variable, there is an observation on one other variable for the same person.[3] Table 3-1 shows a set of observations on two variables arranged in ordered pairs. The observations are the number of games won and the average number of points scored by 28 teams in the National Football League during the 16 regular season games of the 1978 NFL football season. There are many ways to calculate a correlation coefficient, and these methods are all mathematically equivalent. Before we present methods for calculating the correlation coefficient, we will first discuss regression. Regression is the basic method upon which correlation is based.

TABLE 3-1 Average points scored per game and number of games won by ten teams during the 1978 NFL season

Team	X Games Won	Y Points*	XY	X²	Y²
Pittsburgh	14	22	308	196	484
Los Angeles	12	20	240	144	400
New England	11	22	242	121	484
Houston	10	18	180	100	324
Philadelphia	9	17	153	81	289
Detroit	8	18	144	64	324
Chicago	7	16	112	49	256
St. Louis	6	15	90	36	225
Kansas City	4	15	60	16	225
San Francisco	2	14	28	4	196
	$\Sigma X=83$	$\Sigma Y=177$	$\Sigma XY=1557$	$\Sigma X^2=811$	$\Sigma Y^2=3207$

*Rounded to the nearest whole point.

[3]The pairs of scores do not always need to be for a person. They might also be for a group, an institution, a team, and so on.

III. REGRESSION

A. *The regression line*

The regression line is the best-fitting straight line through a set of points in a scatter diagram. It is found by using the principle of least squares. This principle minimizes the squared deviation around the regression line.

The mean is the point of least squares for any single variable. This means that the sum of the squared deviations around the mean will be smaller than it will be at any other point. The regression line is the running mean or line of least squares in two dimensions or in the space created by two variables. Consider the situation shown in the scatter diagram in Figure 3-1. For each level of X (or point on the X scale) there is a distribution of scores on Y. In other words, we could find a mean of Y when X is 3 and another mean of Y when X is 4 and so on. The least squares method in regression finds the straight line that comes as close to as many of these Y means as possible. In other words, it is the line at which the squared deviations around the line are at a minimum.

The formula for a regression line is

$$Y' = a + bX \leftarrow \quad \text{Raw score or actual value of } X$$

Predicted value of Y   intercept   Regression coefficient

$$y' = mx + b$$

In order to use the regression equation we must define some of the terms. The term on the left of the equation is Y'. This is the predicted value of Y. When we create the equation we use observed values of Y and X. The equation is the result of the least squares procedure and shows the best available relationship between X and Y. When the equation is available we can take a score on X and plug it into the formula. What results is a predicted value of Y.

The most important term in the equation is the regression coefficient or b. The regression coefficient is the ratio of a covariance to a variance. However, it can also be expressed as the ratio of the sums of squares for the covariance to the sums of squares for X. It can be calculated by the following formula:

$$b = \frac{N(\Sigma XY) - (\Sigma X)(\Sigma Y)}{N \Sigma X^2 - (\Sigma X)^2}$$

The slope describes how much change is expected in Y each time X increases by one unit. For example, Figure 3-4 shows a regression line with a slope of .67. In this figure the difference between 1 and 2 in units of X is associated with an expected difference of .67 in units of Y (for X=1, Y=2.67 and for X=2, Y=3.34; 3.34−2.67=.67). The regression coefficient is some-

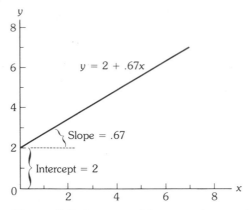

Figure 3-4. A picture of the regression equation. The slope is the amount of increase on the Y axis divided by the range of scores on the X axis. The intercept is the value of Y when X is 0.

times expressed in different notation. For example, the Greek β is often used for a population estimate of the regression coefficient.

The intercept a is the value of Y when X is 0. In other words, it is the point at which the regression line crosses the Y axis. This is shown in Figure 3-4. It is easy to find the intercept once we know what the regression coefficient is. To do this we use the following formula:

$$a = \bar{Y} - b\bar{X}$$

An example showing how to calculate a regression equation is given in Technical Box 3-1. Whether or not you become proficient at calculating regression equations, you should learn to interpret them in order to be a good consumer of research information.

Technical Box 3-1 Calculation of a Regression Equation (Data from Table 3-1)
Formulas:

$$b = \frac{N(\Sigma XY) - (\Sigma X)(\Sigma Y)}{N\Sigma X^2 - (\Sigma X)^2}$$

$$a = \bar{Y} - b\bar{X}$$

Steps
1. Find N by counting the number of paired observations.
$$N = 10$$
2. Find ΣX by summing the X scores.
$$14 + 12 + 11 + \cdots + 2 = 83$$

3. Find ΣY by summing the Y scores.
$$22+20+22+ \cdots +14=177$$
4. Find ΣX^2. Square each X score, and then add them up.
$$196+144+121+ \cdots +4=811$$
5. Find ΣY^2. Square each Y score, and then add them up.
$$484+400+484+ \cdots +196=3207$$
6. Find ΣXY. For each pair of observations multiply X by Y. Then add up the products.
$$(14\times22)+(12\times20)+(11\times22) \mid \cdots +(2\times14)-$$
$$308+240+242+ \cdots +28=1557$$
7. Find $(\Sigma X)^2$ by squaring the result of Step 2.
$$83^2=6889$$
8. Find $(\Sigma Y)^2$ by squaring the result of Step 3.
$$177^2=31,329$$
9. Find $N\Sigma XY$ by multiplying the results of Steps 1 and 6.
$$10\times1557=15,570$$
10. Find $(\Sigma X)(\Sigma Y)$ by multiplying the results of Steps 2 and 3.
$$83\times177=14,691$$
11. Find $N\Sigma XY-(\Sigma X)(\Sigma Y)$ by subtracting the results of Step 10 from the results of Step 9.
$$15,570-14,691=879$$
12. Find $N\Sigma X^2$ by multiplying the results of Steps 1 and 4.
$$10\times811=8110$$
13. Find $N\Sigma X^2-(\Sigma X)^2$ by subtracting the results of Step 7 from those of Step 12.
$$8110-6889=1221$$
14. Find b by dividing the results of Step 11 by those of Step 13.
$$\frac{879}{1221}=.72$$
15. Find $\bar{X}$ by dividing Step 2 by Step 1.
$$\frac{83}{10}=8.30$$
16. Find $\bar{Y}$ by dividing Step 3 by Step 1.
$$\frac{177}{10}=17.70$$
17. Find $b\bar{X}$ by multiplying Step 14 by Step 15.
$$.72\times8.3=5.98$$
18. Find a by subtracting the results of Step 17 from Step 16.
$$17.70-5.98=11.72$$
19. The resultant regression equation is
$$Y=a+bX$$
$$=11.72+(.72)X$$

Correlation is a special case of regression in which the scores for both variables are in standardized or z units. Having the scores in z units is a nice convenience because it eliminates the need to find the intercept. In correlation the intercept will always be 0. Furthermore, the slope in correlation will be easier

Technical Box 3-2 Calculation of a Correlation Coefficient (Data from Table 3-1)

Steps

1. Find N by counting the number of paired observations.
$$N=10$$

2. Find ΣX by summing the X scores.
$$14+12+11+\cdots+2=83$$

3. Find ΣY by summing the Y scores.
$$22+20+22+\cdots+14=177$$

4. Find ΣX^2. Square each X score, and then add them up.
$$196+144+121+\cdots+4=811$$

5. Find ΣY^2. Square each Y score, and then add them up.
$$484+400+484+\cdots+196=3207$$

6. Find ΣXY. For each pair of observations multiply X by Y. Then add up the products.
$$(14\times22)+(12\times20)+(11\times22)+\cdots+(2\times14)$$
$$=308+240+242+\cdots+28=1557$$

7. Find $(\Sigma X)^2$ by squaring the result of Step 2.
$$83^2=6889$$

8. Find $(\Sigma Y)^2$ by squaring the result of Step 3.
$$177^2=31{,}329$$

9. Find $N\Sigma XY$ by multiplying the results of Steps 1 and 6.
$$10\times1557=15{,}570$$

10. Find $(\Sigma X)(\Sigma Y)$ by multiplying the results of Steps 2 and 3.
$$83\times177=14{,}691$$

11. Find $N\Sigma XY-(\Sigma X)(\Sigma Y)$ by subtracting the results of Step 10 from the results of Step 9.
$$15{,}570-14{,}691=879$$

12. Find $N\Sigma X^2$ by multiplying the results of Steps 1 and 4.
$$10\times811=8110$$

13. Find $N\Sigma X^2-(\Sigma X)^2$ by subtracting the results of Step 7 from Step 12.
$$8110-6889=1221$$

14. Find $N\Sigma Y^2$ by multiplying the results of Steps 1 and 5.
$$10\times3207=32{,}070$$

15. Find $N\Sigma Y^2-(\Sigma Y)^2$ by subtracting the results of Step 8 from Step 14.
$$32{,}070-31{,}329=741$$

16. Find $\sqrt{\left[N\Sigma X^2-(\Sigma X)^2\right]\left[N\Sigma Y^2-(\Sigma Y)^2\right]}$ by multiplying Steps 13 and 15 and then taking the square root of the product.
$$\sqrt{1221\times741}=\sqrt{904{,}761}=951.19$$

17. Find $r=\dfrac{N\Sigma XY-(\Sigma X)(\Sigma Y)}{\sqrt{\left[N\Sigma X^2-(\Sigma X)^2\right]\left[N\Sigma Y^2-(\Sigma Y)^2\right]}}$ by dividing the results of Step 11 by Step 16.
$$\frac{879}{951.19}=.92$$

to interpret because it is in a standardized unit. An example of how to calculate a correlation coefficient for the data in Table 3-1 is given in Technical Box 3-2. You can find computational examples in almost any introductory statistics book. In the calculation of the correlation coefficient, we can bypass the step of changing all of the scores into z units. This gets done as part of the calculation process. You may notice that Steps 1 through 13 are identical for calculating regression (Box 3-1) and the correlation (Box 3-2). Technical Box 3-3 shows how to calculate a correlation coefficient for the same data using the SPSS computer program. Technical Box 3-4 gives a theoretical discussion of correlation and regression.

Technical Box 3-3   Using the SPSS Computer Program to do Correlation

Most university computer centers have the SPSS computer program. Few psychologists still calculate correlations by hand, as illustrated in Box 3-2. Rather they take advantage of high-speed computers that can perform the calculations rapidly and accurately. Following is an example of how to calculate the correlation in Table 3-1 with the SPSS computer program. It is convenient to divide this task into the following steps.

Steps

1. Punch the data on IBM cards or make a disk file. In the first two columns put a unique ID number for each team. If you had 10 teams, the first card would be 01 and the last would be 10. In columns 4 and 5 punch the data for games won, and in columns 7 and 8 punch the data for average points scored. Each card will represent the data for one team. Be sure to leave columns 3 and 6 blank.
2. Find out from your local computer center how to execute the SPSS program. This will be a little different at each university or college. The cards used to execute the program are called JCL for Job Control Language. Your local computer consultant can tell you how to prepare them.
3. Set up a deck as follows:

   (JCL Cards)

Column 1	Column 16
RUN NAME	SAMPLE PEARSON CORRELATION
VARIABLE LIST	ID WINS POINTS
INPUT MEDIUM	CARD
INPUT FORMAT	FREEFIELD
NO OF CASES	10
PEARSON CORR	WINS WITH POINTS
READ INPUT DATA	
(place your data cards here)	
FINISH	
/*	

4. Submit your deck, and see how you do. Remember, a computer cannot read spelling errors. Be very careful in your preparation of the deck.
5. If you would like a scatter diagram of your data, replace the PEARSON CORR card with

   SCATTERGRAM   WINS WITH POINTS

The Pearson Product Moment correlation coefficient, which is illustrated in Technical Box 3-3, is a ratio used to determine the degree of variation in one variable that can be estimated from knowledge about variation in the other variable. The correlation coefficient can take on any value between -1.0 and 1.0.

As you can see from Technical Boxes 3-1 and 3-2, the calculation of the correlation coefficient and the regression equation can be a long and difficult process. You may be able to avoid the many computational steps by using a calculator. There are many inexpensive pocket calculators preprogrammed for correlation and regression. When you go to buy a calculator it would be worthwhile to hunt for one with these functions.

Technical Box 3-4 A More Theoretical Discussion of Correlation and Regression

The difference between correlation and regression is analogous to that between standardized scores and raw scores. In correlation we look at the relationship between variables when each one is transformed into standardized scores. In Chapter 2 standardized or z scores were defined as $(X-\bar{X})/s$. In correlation, both variables are in z scores, so they both have a mean of 0. In other words, the mean for the two variables will always be the same. As a result of this convenience, the intercept will always be 0 (when X is 0, Y is also 0) and will drop out of the equation. The resulting equation for translating X into Y then becomes $Y=rX$. In other words, the predicted value of Y will equal X times the correlation between X and Y. If the correlation between X and Y is .80 and the standardized (z) score for the X variable is 1.0, the predicted value of Y would be .80. Unless there is a perfect (1.0 or -1.0) correlation, scores on y will be predicted to be closer to the Y mean than scores on X. A correlation of .80 means that the prediction for Y is 80% as far from the mean as the observation for X. A correlation of .50 would mean that the predicted distance between the mean of Y and the predicted Y is half of the distance between the associated X and the mean of X.

One of the positive benefits of using the correlation coefficient is that it has a reciprocal nature. The correlation between X and Y will always be the same as the correlation between Y and X. For example, if the correlation between drug dosage and activity is .68, the correlation between activity and drug dosage will also be .68. Regression is used to transform scores on one variable into estimated scores on the other. We often use regression to predict raw scores on Y on the basis of raw scores on X. For instance, we might seek an equation to predict grade point average on the basis of Scholastic Aptitude Test score. Because regression uses the raw units of the variables, the reciprocal property does not hold. The coefficient describing the regression of X on Y is usually not the same as the coefficient describing the regression of Y on X.

The term *regression* was first employed in 1885 by an extraordinary British intellectual named Sir Francis Galton, whom we discussed in Chapter 1.

Galton was fond of describing social and political changes that occur over successive generations. He noted that extraordinarily tall men tended to have sons who were a little shorter than they and that unusually small men tended to have sons closer to the average height (but still shorter than average). Over the course of time, individuals with all sorts of unusual characteristics tended to produce offspring who were closer to the average. Galton thought of this as regression toward mediocrity. This idea became the basis for a statistical procedure used to describe how scores tend to regress toward the mean. If a person had been extreme on X, regression would predict that they would be less extreme on Y. Karl Pearson developed the first statistical models of correlation and regression in the late 19th century.

Statistical definition of regression

Regression analysis is used to show how change in one set of scores is related to change in another set of scores. In psychological testing we often use regression to determine whether changes in test scores are related to changes in performance. Do people who score higher on tests of manual dexterity perform better in dental school? Can IQ score measured during high school predict monetary income 20 years later? Regression analysis and related correlational methods tell us the degree to which these variables are linearly related. In addition, it gives us an equation that can be used to estimate scores on a criterion (such as dental school grades) on the basis of scores on a predictor (such as manual dexterity).

In Chapter 2 we introduced the concept of variance. You might remember that the variance was defined as the average squared deviation around the mean. We used the term *sum of squares* for the sum of squared deviations around the mean. Symbolically this was

$$\Sigma(X-\bar{X})^2$$

The variance was the sum of squares divided by $N-1$. The formula for this is

$$S_x^2 = \frac{\Sigma(X-\bar{X})^2}{N-1}$$

We also gave some formulas for the variance of raw scores. The variance of X could be calculated from raw scores using the formula

$$S_x^2 = \frac{\Sigma X^2 - \frac{(\Sigma X)^2}{N}}{N-1}$$

If there were another variable, Y, we could calculate the variance using a similar formula:

$$S_Y^2 = \frac{\Sigma Y^2 - \frac{(\Sigma Y)^2}{N}}{N-1}$$

To calculate regression we need a term for the *covariance*. This tells us how much two measures covary or vary together. In order to understand covariance let's look at the extreme case of the relationship between two identical sets of scores. In this case there will be a perfect association. We know that we can create a new score which exactly repeats the scores on any one variable. If we created this new twin variable, it would covary perfectly with the original variable. Regression analysis attempts to determine how similar the covariance between two variables is by dividing the covariance by the average variance from each variable.

To calculate the covariance we need to find the sum of cross products which is defined as

$$\Sigma_{XY} = \Sigma(X - \bar{X})(Y - \bar{Y})$$

and the raw score formula which is often used for calculation is:

$$\Sigma_{XY} = \Sigma XY - \frac{(\Sigma X)(\Sigma Y)}{N}$$

The covariance is the sum of cross products divided by $N - 1$.

Now look at the similarity of the formula for the covariance and the formula for the variance. This might be easier if we put them side by side:

$$S^2_{XY} = \frac{\Sigma XY - \frac{(\Sigma X)(\Sigma Y)}{N}}{N - 1} \qquad S^2_X = \frac{\Sigma X^2 - \frac{(\Sigma X)^2}{N}}{N - 1}$$

Try substituting X for Y in the formula for the covariance. You should get

$$\frac{\Sigma XX - \frac{(\Sigma X)(\Sigma X)}{N}}{N - 1}$$

If you replace ΣXX with ΣX^2 and $(\Sigma X)(\Sigma X)$ with $(\Sigma X)^2$ you will see the relationship between variance and covariance.

$$\frac{\Sigma X^2 - \frac{(\Sigma X)^2}{N}}{N - 1}$$

In regression analysis we examine the ratio of the covariance to the average of the variances for the two separate measures. This gives us an estimate of how much variance in one variable we can determine by knowing about the variation in the other variable.

B. How to interpret a regression plot

Regression plots are pictures that show the relationship between variables. A common use of regression in testing is to determine the criterion validity, or the relationship between a test score and the criterion (see Chapter 5). The problems we deal with in studies of criterion validity require us to predict some criterion score on the basis of a predictor or test score. Suppose that you want to build a test to predict how enjoyable someone will turn out to be as a date. If you selected your dates randomly and had no information about them in advance, you might be best off just using normative information.

You might expect that the distribution of enjoyableness of dates is normal. Some people are just not fun for you to go out with at all whereas others are exceptionally enjoyable. However, the great majority of the people are some fun but not excessively so and fall between these two extremes. Figure 3-5 shows what a frequency distribution for enjoyableness of dates might look like. As you can see in the graph, the highest point, which shows where dates are most frequently classified, is where the average date would be.

If you had no other way of predicting how much you would like your dates, the safest prediction would be to pick this middle level of enjoyableness because it is the one observed most frequently. This is called *normative* because it uses information gained from representative groups. Knowing nothing else about an individual, we can make an educated guess that a person will be average in enjoyableness because past experience has demonstrated that the mean or average score is also the one observed most frequently. In other words, knowing about the average date gives you some information about what to expect from a particular date. But it is doubtful that you would really want to choose dates this way. You probably would rather use other information such as the person's educational background, attitudes, and hobbies to predict whether that person would be enjoyable for you to spend an evening with.

Most people do employ some system to help them make important personal choices. These systems, however, are never perfect. Thus you are left with

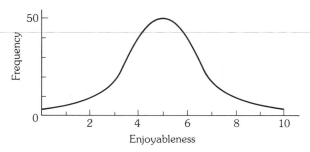

Figure 3-5. Hypothetical distribution of the enjoyableness of dates. Few dates are extremely unenjoyable or extremely enjoyable. The greatest number fall about in the middle.

something which is not perfect but still better than just using normative information. In regression studies we develop equations that help us describe more
precisely where tests fall between being perfect predictors and being no better
than just using the normative information. This is done by graphing the relationship between test scores and the criterion. Then a mathematical procedure is
used to find the straight line that comes as close to as many of the points as
possible.

   Figure 3-6 shows the points on a hypothetical dating desirability scale and
the enjoyableness of dates. The line through the points is the one that minimizes
the squared distance between the line and the data points. In other words, the
line is the one straight line that summarizes more about the relationship between
dating desirability and enjoyableness than any other straight line.

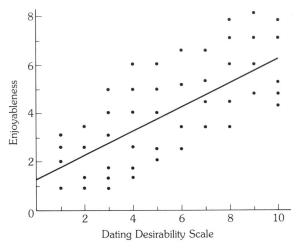

Figure 3-6. Hypothetical relationship between dating desirability and the
enjoyableness of dates. Each point summarizes the dating desirability score
and the enjoyableness rating for a single subject. The line was derived from a
mathematical procedure to come as close to as many points as possible.

   Figure 3-7 shows the hypothetical relationship between a test and a criterion. Using this figure you should be able to find the predicted value on the
criterion variable by knowing the score on the test or the predictor. Here is how
you would read the graph. First pick a particular score on the test, say 8. Find 8
on the axis of the graph above the label "Test Score" (horizontal axis). Now
draw a line straight up until you hit the slanted line on the graph. This is the
regression line. Now make a 90° angle left turn and draw another pencil line until
it hits the other axis of the graph, which is labeled "Criterion Score." The dashed
line in Figure 3-8 shows the course you should have taken. Now read the
number on the criterion axis where your line has stopped. This score of 7.4 on

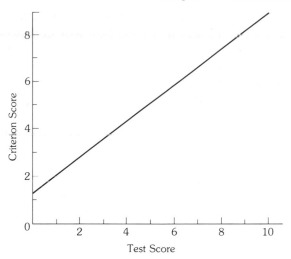

Figure 3-7. Predicted relationship between a test score and a criterion.

the criterion variable is the score you would have expected to obtain on the basis of information you gained by using the test.

Notice that the line in Figure 3-8 is not at a 45° angle and that the two variables were measured in the same units. If it were a 45° angle, the test would be a perfect (or close to perfect) forecaster of the criterion. However, this is almost never the case in practice. Now do the same exercise you did for the test score of 8 with test scores from the extremes of the distributions. Try the scores 0 and 10. If you use these you will find that the score of 10 for the test gives you a

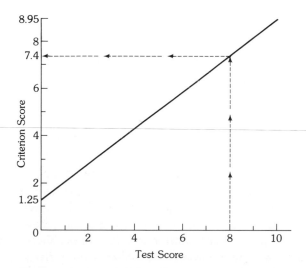

Figure 3-8. The dotted line shows how you should have obtained a predicted criterion score of 7.4 from the test score of 8.

criterion score of 8.95, and the test score of 0 gives you a criterion score of 1.25. Notice how far apart 0 and 10 are on the test. Now look at how far apart 1.25 and 8.95 are on the criterion. You will see that using the test as a predictor is not as good as perfect prediction, but it is still better than using the normative information. If we had used only the normative information, we would have predicted that all scores would be the average score on the criterion. And if there were perfect prediction, the distances between 1.25 and 8.95 on the criterion would have been the same as the distances between 0 and 10 on the test.

Figure 3-9 shows what a variety of different regression slopes looks like. Notice that the higher the standardized regression coefficient, the steeper the line appears. Now look at the regression line with a slope of 0. This one is parallel to the axis for the test score and perpendicular to the line for the criterion. A regression line like this shows that the test score tells us nothing about the criterion beyond the consensus information.

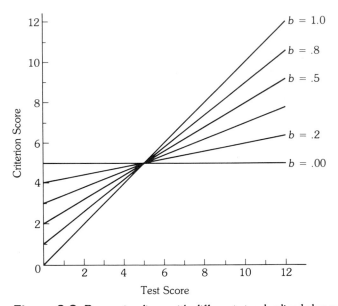

Figure 3-9. Regression lines with different standardized slopes.

Try an example. Take a test score of 11. Just as you did before, make a pencil line straight up from this score until you hit the regression line for a slope of 0. Now move the line at a 90° angle to the left until you hit the "Criterion Score" axis. The score should be 5. Now do the same thing for a test score of 3. Did you get the same predicted criterion score? You should have. In fact, any test score will give you the same predicted criterion score. And that score always will be the average score on the criterion. The slope of 0 tells you that the test and the criterion are unrelated and that your best bet under these circumstances will be to predict the average score on the criterion.

Take some time and try finding the predicted score on the criterion for test scores of 11 and 3. Do it for several of the different slopes shown in Figure 3-9. Notice that the steeper the slope of the regression line, the farther apart the predicted scores on the criterion. Table 3-2 shows the predicted scores for all of the different slopes. You can use it to check your answers.

When the regression lines have slopes of 0 or nearly 0, it is best not to take any chances in forecasting the criterion. Instead you should depend on the normative information and guess the mean of Y. As the slope becomes steeper, the more prepared we are to take some chances and estimate that there will be differences in criterion scores.

It is instructive to think about Figure 3-9 as we reflect on the meaning of psychological tests. For example, if the SAT has a slope of .5 for predicting grades in college, this would mean that the SAT performance relationship is defined by the line labeled "b=.5" in Figure 3-9. Using this sort of information college administrators can forecast that there will be some slight differences in college performance which might be predicted from the SAT. However, because the slope is not steep, their predictions are somewhere between perfect prediction and what they would get if they used the consensus information. We will talk more about the meaning of these relationships in Chapters 5 and 7.

TABLE 3-2   Expected criterion scores for two test scores when predicted from regression lines with different slopes

Test Score	Slope	Predicted Criterion Score
11	1.0	11.00
3	1.0	3.00
11	.8	9.80
3	.8	3.40
11	.5	8.00
3	.5	4.00
11	.2	6.20
3	.2	4.60
11	.00	5.00
3	.00	5.00

IV.   OTHER CORRELATION COEFFICIENTS

The Pearson Product Moment correlation is only one of many types of correlation coefficients. It is the one most commonly used because most often we want to find the correlation between two continuous variables. Continuous variables can take on any values over a range of values. Height, weight, and intelligence are examples of continuous variables. However, there are situations where we want to find the correlations between variables which are scaled in other ways.

Spearman's rho is a method of correlation that is used to find the association between two sets of ranks. The rho coefficient is easy to calculate and is often used when the individuals in a sample can be ranked on two variables but their actual scores are not known.

There is a whole family of correlation coefficients that involves dichotomous variables, which have only two levels. Some dichotomous variables are called "true dichotomous" because they naturally form two categories. For example, sex is a true dichotomous variable and has the two levels male and female. Other dichotomous variables are called "artificial dichotomous" because there was originally an underlying continuous scale which was forced into a dichotomy. Passing or failing a bar examination might be an example of an artificial dichotomy. Actually, many scores can be obtained, but the examiners decide only to consider pass or fail. The types of correlation coefficients used to find the relationship between dichotomous and continuous variables are shown in Table 3-3.

TABLE 3-3 Appropriate correlation coefficients for relationships between dichotomous and continuous variables*

		Variable X		
		Continuous	Artificial dichotomous	True dichotomous
Variable y	Continuous	Pearson r	Biserial r	Point biserial r
	Artificial dichotomous	Biserial r	Tetrachoric r	Phi
	True dichotomous	Point biserial r	Phi	Phi

*The entries in the table suggest which type of correlation coefficient is appropriate given the characteristics of the two variables. For example, if variable Y is continuous and variable X is true dichotomous, you would use the point biserial correlation.

The *biserial correlation* is used to express the relationship between a continuous variable and an artificial dichotomous variable. For example, the biserial correlation might be used to assess the relationship between passing or failing the bar examination (artificial dichotomous variable) and grade point average in law school (continuous variable). If the dichotomous variable had been "true" (such as sex), we would use the *point biserial correlation*. For instance, the point biserial correlation would be used to find the relationship between sex and grade point average. When both variables are dichotomous and at least one of the dichotomies is "true," the association between them can be estimated using the *phi coefficient*. For example, the relationship between passing or failing the bar examination and sex (male or female) could be estimated using the phi coefficient. If both of the dichotomous variables are artificial, we might employ a special correlation coefficient known as the *tetrachoric correlation*. Among these special correlation coefficients, the point biserial, phi, and Spearman's rho coefficients are probably used most often. The formulas for calculating these types of correlation are given in Technical Box 3-5.

Technical Box 3-5 Formulas for Spearman's Rho, the Point Biserial Correlation, and the Phi Coefficient

Spearman's Rho
Formula:

$$\rho = 1 - \frac{6 \Sigma d_i^2}{N^3 - N}$$

Where ρ = rho

d_i = a subject's rank order on variable 2 minus his/her rank order
  on variable 1

N = number of paired ranks

When used: To find the association between pairs of observations, each expressed in
  ranks.

Point Biserial Correlation
Formula:

$$r_{pbis} = \left[\frac{\bar{Y}_1 - \bar{Y}}{S_y} \right] \sqrt{\frac{P_x}{(1 - P_x)}}$$

Where r_{pbis} = the point biserial correlation coefficient

X = a true dichotomous (two-choice) variable

Y = a continuous (multilevel) variable

$\bar{Y}_1$ = the mean of Y for subjects having a "plus" score on X

$\bar{Y}$ = the mean of Y for all subjects

S_y = the standard deviation for Y scores

P_x = the proportion of subjects giving a "plus" score on X

When used: To find the association between a dichotomous (two-choice) variable
  and a continuous variable. For the true dichotomous variable, one of
  the two choices is arbitrarily designated as a "plus" response.

Phi Coefficient
Formula:

$$\phi = \frac{P_c - P_x P_y}{\sqrt{P_x (1 - P_x) P_y (1 - P_y)}}$$

Where ϕ = the phi coefficient

P_c = the percentage in the "plus" category for both variables

P_x = the percentage in the "plus" category for the first variable

P_y = the percentage in the "plus" category for the second variable

When used: To find the association between two dichotomous (two category) variables. A dichotomous variable might be "yes-no" or "on-off." In each case one of the two choices is arbitrarily chosen as a "plus" response. When using phi, one of the variables must be a "true" dichotomy (if both were "artificial" the tetrachoric correlation would be more appropriate).

V.   TERMS AND ISSUES IN THE USE OF CORRELATION

When you use correlation or read studies that report correlational analysis, you will need to know the terminology. Some of the terms and issues you should be familiar with include *residual, standard error of estimate, coefficient of determination, coefficient of alienation, shrinkage, cross validation, correlation causation problem,* and *third variable.* Following are brief discussions of these terms and concepts.

Residual. A regression equation gives a predicted value of Y' for each value of X. In addition to these predicted values, there are observed values of Y. The difference between the predicted and the observed values is called the *residual.* Symbolically the residual is defined as $Y - Y'$.

In regression analysis the residuals have certain properties. One important property is that the sum of the residuals will always equal 0, $[\Sigma(Y-Y')=0]$. In addition, the sum of the squared residuals will be the smallest value according to the principle of least squares $[\Sigma(Y-Y')^2=\text{smallest value}]$.

Standard Error of Estimate. Once we have obtained the residuals we can find their standard deviation. However, in creating the regression equation, two constants (a and b) have been found. Thus we must use two degrees of freedom rather than one, as is usually the case in finding the standard deviation. The standard deviation of the residuals is known as the *standard error of estimate,* which is defined as

$$S_{yx} = \sqrt{\frac{\Sigma(Y-Y')^2}{N-2}}$$

The standard error of estimate is a measure of accuracy of prediction. Prediction is most accurate when the standard error of estimate is relatively small. As it becomes larger, the prediction becomes less accurate.

Coefficient of Determination. The correlation coefficient squared is known as the *coefficient of determination.* This value tells us the percentage of total variation in scores on Y that we know as a function of our information about X. For example, if the correlation between the SAT and performance in the first year of college is .40, the coefficient of determination would be .16. This means that we could explain 16% of the variation in first-year college performance as a function of knowing SAT scores.

Coefficient of Alienation. The *coefficient of alienation* is a measure of non-association between two variables. This is calculated as $\sqrt{1-r^2}$ or the square root of $1-$coefficient of determination. For the SAT example, the coefficient of alienation would be $\sqrt{1-.16}=\sqrt{.84}=.92$. This means that there is a high degree of nonassociation between the SAT and college performance.

Shrinkage. Many times a regression equation is created on one group of subjects and then used to predict the performance of another group. One of the problems with regression analysis is that it takes advantage of chance relationships within a particular population of subjects. Thus, there is a tendency to overestimate the relationship, particularly if the sample of subjects is small. *Shrinkage* is the amount of decrease observed when a regression equation is created for one population and then applied to another. Formulas are available to estimate the amount of shrinkage to expect given characteristics of the variance, covariance, and sample size (Lord, 1950; McNemar, 1969; Uhl & Eisenberg, 1970).

An example of shrinkage might be when a regression equation is developed to predict first-year college grade-point average on the basis of the Scholastic Aptitude Test. Although the percentage of variance in grade-point average might be fairly high for the original group, we can expect to account for a smaller percentage of the variance when the equation is used to predict grade-point average in the next year's class. This decrease in the percentage of variance accounted for is the shrinkage.

Cross Validation. The best way to insure that proper inferences are being made is to use the regression equation to predict performance in a group of subjects other than the ones upon which the equation was created. Then a standard error of estimate can be obtained for the relationship between the values predicted by the equation and those observed. This process is known as *cross validation*.

The Correlation-Causation Problem. Just because two variables are correlated, it does not necessarily mean that one has caused the other. For example, because there is a correlation between the number of hours spent viewing television and aggressive behavior, it does not mean that excessive viewing of television causes aggression. This relationship could mean that an aggressive child might prefer to watch a lot of television.

Third Variable Explanation. In the example of television and aggression there are other possible explanations for the observed relationship between viewing and aggressive behavior. One is that some third variable causes both excessive viewing of television and aggressive behavior. For example, poor social adjustment might explain both. Thus the apparent relationship between viewing and aggression actually might be the result of some variable that is not included in the analysis and may be unknown. We usually refer to this external influence as a *third variable*.

■ FOCUSED EXAMPLE 3-1 THE DANGER OF INFERRING CAUSATION FROM CORRELATION

A recent article published in a newspaper supplement discussed the stressfulness of a variety of occupations. A total of 130 job categories were rated for stressfulness by examining Tennessee hospital and death records for evidence of stress-related diseases such as heart attacks, ulcers, arthritis, and mental disorders. The 12 highest and the 12 lowest were as follows:

Most stressful	*Least stressful*
1. Unskilled laborer	1. Clothing sewer
2. Secretary	2. Garment checker
3. Assembly-line inspector	3. Stock clerk
4. Clinical lab technician	4. Skilled craftsperson
5. Office manager	5. Housekeeper
6. Foreperson	6. Farm laborer
7. Manager/administrator	7. Heavy-equipment operator
8. Waitress/waiter	8. Freight handler
9. Factory machine operator	9. Child-care worker
10. Farm owner	10. Factory package wrapper
11. Miner	11. College professor
12. House painter	12. Personnel worker

The article advises readers who want to remain healthy to avoid the "most stressful" job categories.

However, the evidence may not warrant the authors' advice. Although it is quite possible that diseases are associated with particular occupations, this does not necessarily mean that holding the jobs causes the illnesses. There are a variety of other explanations. For example, people with the propensity for heart attacks and ulcers might be more likely to select jobs as unskilled laborers or secretaries. Thus the direction of causation might be that health condition causes job selection rather than the reverse. Another possibility is a third variable explanation. Some other factor might cause the apparent relationship between job and health. For example, the income level might cause both life stress and illness. It is well known that poor people have lower health status than wealthy people. It is possible that impoverished conditions might cause a person to accept certain jobs and also to have more diseases.

These three possible explanations are diagrammed on the following page. An arrow shows a causal connection.

Economic Status
↙ ↘

Job → Illness | Job ← Illness | Job   Illness

Job causes illness | Tendency toward illness causes people to choose certain jobs | Economic status (third variable) causes job selection and illness

In this example we are *not* ruling out the possibility that job causes health condition. In fact, it is quite plausible. However, because the nature of the evidence is correlational, it cannot be said with certainty that job causes illness.

(Optional)

VI. MULTIVARIATE ANALYSIS

Multivariate analysis considers the relationship between combinations of three or more variables. For example, the prediction of success in the first year of college from the linear combination of SAT verbal and SAT quantitative scores would be a problem for multivariate analysis. However, the field of multivariate analysis is a technical one, and it requires an understanding of linear and matrix algebra. Therefore, a detailed discussion of multivariate analysis is beyond the scope of this book.

On the other hand, multivariate analysis is common to the testing field. It will be important for you to have a general idea of what the different methods entail. This section will familiarize you with some of the multivariate analysis terminology. It should help you identify the situations in which some of the different multivariate methods are used. Several references are available in case you would like to learn more about the technical details (Cooley & Lohnes, 1971; Harris, 1975; Kaplan & Litrownik, 1977; Kerlinger & Pedhazur, 1973; Cohen & Cohen, 1975; Kleinbaum & Kupper, 1978; Timm, 1975; Wiggins, 1973).

A. *General approach*

Multivariate methods have advantages for the study of behavior because they permit us to examine the relationships among many variables. The correlational techniques we have presented thus far in the chapter only describe the relationship between two variables. For example, they might consider only the relationship between stress and illness. In order to more fully understand the causes of illness, we need to consider many potential factors in addition to stress. Multivariate analysis allows us to study the relationship between many predictors and an outcome. In addition, the methods allow us to study the relationship among the predictors.

Multivariate methods differ in the number and kind of predictor variables they utilize. They are the same in that they all transform groups of variables into linear combinations. A linear combination of variables is a weighted composite of the original variables. The weighting system combines the variables in order to achieve some goal. The different multivariate techniques differ according to the goal they are trying to achieve.

A linear combination of variables looks like this:

$$Y' = a + b_1X_1 + b_2X_2 + b_3X_3 + \cdots + b_kX_k$$

where Y' is the predicted value of Y, a is a constant, X_1 to X_k are variables and there are k such variables, and the b's are regression coefficients. If you feel anxious about such a complex-looking equation, there is no need to panic. Actually, this equation describes something similar to what was presented in the section on regression. The difference is that instead of relating Y to X, we are now dealing with a linear combination of X's. The whole right side of the equation creates a new composite variable by transforming a set of predictor variables.

B. *An example using multiple regression*

Variables that are "important" in this combination will be associated with larger regression coefficients. An example using multiple regression might help illustrate this concept. Suppose we want to predict success in law school from three variables: undergraduate grade point average (GPA), rating by former professors, and age. This type of multivariate analysis is called *multiple regression*, and the goal of the analysis is to find the linear combination of the three variables that provides the best prediction of law school success. We find the correlation between the criterion (law school GPA) with some composite of the predictors (undergraduate GPA plus professor rating plus age). The combination of the three predictors, however, is not just the sum of the three scores. Instead, we program the computer to find a specific way of adding the predictors together that will make the correlation between the composite and the criterion as high as possible. A weighted composite might look something like this:

Law school GPA=.8 (z scores of undergraduate GPA)+.24 (z scores of professor ratings)+.03 (z scores for age)

This example suggests that undergraduate GPA is given more weight in the prediction of law school GPA than the other variables. The undergraduate GPA is multiplied by .80, while the other variables are multiplied by much smaller coefficients. Age is multiplied by only .03, which is very close to no contribution. Because any number multiplied by 0 will be 0, you can see that age will almost drop out of the equation. This is because .03 times any z score for age will give a number that is nearly 0 and, in effect, we would just be adding 0 to the composite.

The reason for using z scores for the three predictors is that the coefficients in the linear composite will be greatly affected by the range of values taken on by the variables. GPA is measured on a scale from 0 to 4.0, while the range in age might be 21 to 70. In order to compare the coefficients to one another we need to transform all of the variables into similar units. This is accomplished by using z scores (see Chapter 2). When the variables are expressed in z units, the coefficients or weights for the variables are known as *standardized regression coefficients* (sometimes called B's and betas). There are also some cases in which we want to use the variables in their natural units. For example, we sometimes want to find an equation we can use to estimate someone's predicted level of success on the basis of personal characteristics, and we do not want to bother changing these characteristics into z units. When we do this, the weights in the model are called *raw regression coefficients* (sometimes called b's).

Before moving on, we should caution you about interpreting regression coefficients. In addition to being a reflection of the relationship between a particular variable and the criterion, the coefficients are affected by the relationship among the predictor variables. You need to be very careful when the predictor variables are highly correlated with one another. Two predictor variables that are highly correlated with the criterion will not *both* receive large regression coefficients if they are highly correlated with one another.

For example, suppose that undergraduate GPA and professor's ratings are both highly correlated with law school GPA. However, these two predictors also are highly correlated with one another. In effect, the two measures seem to be of the same thing (which would not be surprising because the professors assigned the grades). So professor's rating may get a lower regression coefficient because some of its predictive power is already taken into consideration through its association with undergraduate GPA. We can only be confident in interpreting regression coefficients when the predictor variables do not overlap. They may do so when the predictors are uncorrelated.

C. *Discriminant analysis*

Multiple regression is appropriate when the criterion variable is continuous. However, there are many cases in testing when the criterion is a set of categories. For example, we often want to know the linear combination of variables that differentiates passing from failing. When the task is to find the linear combination of variables that provides a maximum discrimination between categories, the appropriate multivariate method is discriminant analysis. An example of discriminant analysis might involve attempts to determine whether a set of measures predicts success or failure on a particular performance evaluation. Many tests had been given previously, and discriminant analysis is used to find the linear combination of these tests which best separates success from failure. Sometimes we want to determine the categorization into more than two categories. To accomplish this we use *multiple discriminant analysis*.

Discriminant analysis has many advantages in the field of test construction. For example, one approach to test construction is to identify two groups of people which represent two distinct categories on some trait. For example, two groups of children might be classified as "language disabled" and "normal." Then a variety of items would be presented, and discriminant analysis would be employed to find the linear combination of items that best accounts for differences between the impaired and the nonimpaired children. By use of this information, new tests could be developed to help diagnose language impairment. Furthermore, learning about the differences between impaired and nonimpaired children might provide insight into the nature of the problem and eventually lead to better treatments.

D. Factor analysis

Discriminant analysis and multiple regression analysis are techniques that find linear combinations of variables which maximize the prediction of some criterion. Factor analysis is used to study the interrelationships among a set of variables without reference to a criterion. Factor analysis might best be thought of as a data reduction technique. When we have responses to a large number of items or a large number of tests, it is often desirable to reduce all this information down into two more manageable chunks. Earlier we presented a two-dimensional scatter diagram. The task in correlation was to find the best-fitting line through the space created by these two dimensions. As we add more variables in multivariate analysis, we increase the number of dimensions. For example, a three-dimensional plot is shown in Figure 3-10. You can use your imagination to

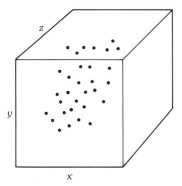

Figure 3-10. Three-dimensional scatter plot. A three-dimensional scatter plot might be represented by this box. In addition to plotting points on the X and Y axes, we must also locate them with relevance to a third Z axis. Although it is hard to show more than two dimensions on a flat page, you can think of a three-dimensional figure as a box.

visualize what a larger set of dimensions would look like. Some people claim they can visualize more than three dimensions, while others feel they can not. In any case, consider that points are plotted in the space created in these many dimensions.

In factor analysis we first create a matrix that shows the correlation between every variable with every other variable. Then we find the linear combinations of the variables that describe as much of the interrelationships between the variables as possible. These linear combinations of the variables are called *principal components*, and the goal in creating them is to describe as much of the association between the variables as possible. We can find as many principal components as there are variables. However, each principal component is extracted according to mathematical rules that make it independent or uncorrelated with all of the other principal components. The first component will be the most successful in describing the variation among the variables, and each succeeding component will be somewhat less successful. Thus, we often decide to examine only a few components that account for larger proportions of the variation. The principal components are factors.

Once the linear combinations or principal components have been found, we can find the correlation between the original items and the factors. These correlations are called *factor loadings*. The expression "item 7 loaded highly on factor *1*" means there was a high correlation between item 7 and the first principal component. By examining which variables load highly on each factor, you can help determine the meaning for the factors. Focused Example 3-2 shows how the meaning of various factors in a scale on interpersonal trust were evaluated.

Factor analysis is a complex and technical method, and there are many options the user must learn about. For example, users frequently use methods that help them get a clearer picture of the meaning of the components by transforming the variables in a way that pushes the factor loadings toward the high or the low extreme. These transformation methods involve rotating the axes in the space created by the factors and have therefore been labeled methods of *rotation*. There are many options for methods of rotation, and there are other options about the characteristics of the matrix that originally is entered into the analysis. If you are interested, there are several books that discuss factor analysis methods in great detail, including H. H. Harmon's *Modern Factor Analysis* (1967) and R. L. Gorsuch's *Factor Analysis* (1974).

■ FOCUSED EXAMPLE 3-2   THE FACTORS OF TRUST

Rotter (1967) described a scale for the measurement of interpersonal trust. Trust was defined as "an expectancy held by an individual or a group that the word, promise, verbal or written statement of another individual or group can be relied upon" (p. 651). However, since the publication of the original trust article, several authors have reported that trust seems to be composed of several independent factors (Chun & Campbell, 1974; Kaplan, 1973; Wright & Tedeschi, 1975). The method used to draw these conclusions was factor analysis. In each case the items were given to a large group of people and the results were subjected to factor analysis. This procedure reduced the many items down to a smaller number of factors. The factors are linear combinations of the original items. Then item loadings, which are the correlations of the original items with the factors, were studied in order to name the factors. Table 3-4 shows the loadings of the items upon three of the factors (from Kaplan, 1973).

TABLE 3-4 Loadings of trust scale items on three largest factors

Item no.	Item	Loading factor I	II	III
A.	**Items with high loadings on institutional factor**			
4.	This country has a dark future unless we can attract better people into politics.	−.67	−.12	−.06
5.	Fear of social disgrace or punishment rather than conscience prevents most people from breaking the law.	−.54	.02	−.06
13.	The United Nations will never be an effective force in keeping world peace.	−.41	.09	−.21
16.	The judiciary is a place where we can all get unbiased treatment.	.37	.23	.00
19.	Most people would be horrified if they knew how much news the public hears and sees is distorted.	−.69	.18	.28
21.	Most elected public officials are really sincere in their campaign promises.	.44	.17	−.02
24.	Even though we have reports in newspapers, radio, and TV, it is hard to get objective accounts of public events.	−.67	−.08	.00
28.	If we really knew what was going on in international politics, the public would have more reason to be more frightened than it now seems to be.	−.49	.01	.24
33.	Many major national sports contests are fixed in one way or another.	−.55	−.04	.28
B.	**Items with high loadings on sincerity factor**			
1.	Hypocrisy is on the increase in our society.	.09	−.52	.08
12.	Most students in school would not cheat even if they were sure of getting away with it.	.29	.45	.07
27.	Most experts can be relied upon to tell the truth about the limits of their knowledge.	.20	.66	.20
34.	Most idealists are sincere and usually practice what they preach.	.12	.62	−.20
38.	Most repair persons will not overcharge even if they think you are ignorant of their specialty.	.11	.48	−.35
44.	Most people answer public opinion polls honestly.	.04	.58	.16
C.	**Items with high loadings on caution factor**			
2.	In dealing with strangers one is better off being cautious until they have provided evidence that they are trustworthy.	−.22	−.03	.74
7.	Using the honor system of not having a teacher present during examinations would probably result in increased cheating.	.13	.08	.45
32.	In these competitive times you have to be alert or someone is likely to take advantage of you.	−.12	−.01	.53
42.	A large share of the accident claims filed against insurance companies are phony.	−.07	−.14	.57

Adapted from "A New Scale for the Measurement of Interpersonal Trust," by J. B. Rotter. In *Journal of Personality*, 1967, 35, 651–665.

Once the factor loadings have been obtained, the researcher must attempt to name the factors by examining which items load highly upon them. In this case an item was used to help interpret a factor if its item loading on the factor was greater than .35 or less than −.35. In the Kaplan study (1973), three factors of trust were found.

Factor I: Institutional trust. This represented trust toward major social agents in society. It included items regarding competence of politicians such as "This country has a dark future unless we can attract better people into politics" (−.67). Many of the items conveyed misrepresentation of public events by either the government or the mass media. For example, some items with high loadings included "Most people would be horrified if they knew how much news the public hears and sees is distorted" (−.69) and "Even though we have reports in newspapers, radio, and T.V., it is hard to get an objective account of public events" (−.67).

Factor II: Sincerity. Items loading highly on sincerity tended to focus on the perceived sincerity of others. These items include "Most idealists are sincere and usually practice what they preach" (.62) and "Most people answer public opinion polls honestly" (.58). Nearly all the items with high loadings on the second factor began with the word "Most." Because of this loose wording, it would be possible for people to agree with the items because they believe in the sincerity of *most* people in a given group but still feel little trust for the group because of a few "rotten eggs." Thus, a woman could believe most car repairers are sincere but still service her own car because she fears victimization by overcharging.

Factor III: Caution. This contained items that expressed fear that some people will take advantage of others. For example, items stated that "In dealing with strangers one is better off to be cautious until they have provided evidence that they are trustworthy" (.74) and "In these competitive times you have to be alert or someone is likely to take advantage of you" (.53). Note that caution appears to be independent of perceived sincerity.

The data imply that generalized trust may be composed of several dimensions. The trust scale may prove to be a valuable tool for clinicians and researchers. Their purposes may be better served, however, if they focus on specific components of trust rather than the generalized case.

(End of Optional Section)

VII. SUMMARY

This chapter began with a discussion of a claim made in the *National Enquirer* that poor diet causes marital problems. Actually there was no specific evidence that diet *causes* the problems—only that diet and marital difficulties are associated. However, the *Enquirer* failed to specify the exact strength of the association. The rest of the chapter was designed to help you be more specific than the *Enquirer* article was by learning to specify associations with precise mathematical indexes known as *correlation coefficients*.

First we presented pictures of the association between two variables, which are called *scatter diagrams*. Second we presented a method for finding a linear equation to describe the relationship between two variables. This regression method uses the data in raw units. The results of regression analysis are two constants: a *slope* describing the degree of relatedness between the variables and an *intercept* giving the value of the Y variable when the X variable is 0. When both of the variables are in standardized or z units, the intercept is always 0, and it drops out of the equation. In this unique situation we solve for only one constant, which is r or the *correlation coefficient*.

When using correlational methods we must take many things into consideration. For example, correlation does not mean the same thing as causation. In the case of the *Enquirer* article the observed correlation between diet and problems in marriage may mean that diet causes the personal difficulties. However, it may also mean that marriage problems cause poor eating habits or that some *third variable* causes both diet habits and marital problems. In addition to the difficulties associated with causation, we must always consider the strength of the correlational relationship. The *coefficient of determination* describes the percentage of variation in one variable which is known on the basis of its association with another variable. The *coefficient of alienation* is the percentage of variation which is not known from information about the other variable.

The field of *multivariate analysis* involves a complicated but important set of methods for studying the relationships among many variables. *Multiple regression* is a multivariate method for studying the relationship between one criterion variable and two or more predictor variables. A similar method known as *discriminant analysis* is used to study the relationship between a categorical criterion and two or more predictors. *Factor analysis* is another multivariate method for reducing a large set of variables down into a smaller set of composite variables.

Correlational methods are the most commonly used statistical techniques in the testing field. The concepts presented in this overview will be referred to throughout the remainder of this book.

CHAPTER

4

Reliability

Learning objectives

When you have completed this chapter, you should be able to do the following:

1. *Tell what measurement error is and how it interferes with scientific studies in psychology.*
2. *Given that reliability is the ratio of true variability to observed variability, explain what this tells us about a test with a reliability of .30, .60, or .90.*
3. *Relate how test-retest reliability is assessed.*
4. *Explain the difference between test-retest reliability estimates and split-half reliability estimates.*
5. *Discuss how the split-half method underestimates the reliability of a short test and what can be done to correct this problem.*
6. *Know the easiest way to find average reliability.*
7. *Define a coefficient alpha and tell how it differs from other methods of estimating reliability.*
8. *Discuss how high a reliability coefficient must be before you would be willing to say the test is "reliable enough."*
9. *Explain what can be done to increase the reliability of a test.*
10. *Tell how the reliability of behavioral observations is assessed.*

Howard Cosell mumbled into the microphone as Philadelphia Phillie shortstop Larry Bowa entered the batter's box: "His batting average is only 261, but this kid is a 300 hitter." With this comment Cosell indicated a discrepancy between Bowa's current batting average and his true ability, a common occurrence in the measurement of many different human abilities. For example, after

85

an examination students sometimes feel that, although they know the material, the actual questions did not allow them to display their real knowledge. And actors sometimes complain that the five-minute sample of their performance in an audition is not an adequate measure of their talents.

Discrepancies between true ability and measurement of ability constitute errors of measurement. In psychological testing we do not attach a negative connotation to the word *error*. It does not imply that a mistake has been made. Rather we acknowledge that there always will be some inaccuracy or error in our measurements. Our task is to find out the magnitude of this error and to develop ways to minimize it. This chapter is about the conceptualization and assessment of measurement error. We call the chapter *Reliability* because tests that are relatively free of measurement error are deemed to be reliable. Tests that have relatively greater measurement error are considered to be unreliable.

I.   HISTORY AND THEORY OF RELIABILITY

A.   *Conceptualization of error*

Students majoring in physical science have chosen to study phenomena that are relatively easy to calibrate. Many physical qualities are simple to measure, and the instrumentation used to measure them is quite precise. If you want to measure the width of this book, for example, you need only apply a measuring stick and record the number of inches or centimeters.

In psychology we have many problems that make the measurement task more difficult. First, we rarely are interested in measuring simple qualities such as width. Instead, we usually go after more complex traits such as intelligence or aggressiveness. These attributes cannot be seen or touched. Furthermore, there are no rigid yardsticks that can be used to measure such characteristics. Instead we are forced to use "rubber yardsticks," which may stretch to overestimate our measurements on some occasions and shrink to give underestimates on others (Nunnally, 1978). A builder might not be able to get by with a rubber yardstick, and psychologists must assess their measuring instruments to determine how much rubber is in them. A psychologist attempting to understand human behavior on the basis of very unreliable tests might be like a carpenter trying to build a house with a rubber measuring tape that never recorded the same length for the same piece of board.

As you will learn from this chapter, the theory of measurement error is very well developed within psychology. As a result we are very sophisticated about the assessment of reliability and are concerned that our measurements be dependable. This is not to say that measurement error is unique to psychology. In fact, serious measurement error is known to occur in most physical, social, and biological sciences. For example, measures of the gross national product (economics) and blood pressure (medicine) are known to be less reliable than well-constructed psychological tests. However, the concern with reliability has been a particular obsession for psychologists. This is evidence of the advanced scientific status of psychology.

B. Spearman's early studies

Psychology owes its advanced development of reliability assessment to the early work of British psychologist Charles Spearman. The basic notion of sampling error was introduced almost 250 years ago (DeMoivre, 1733), and the product moment correlation (see Chapter 3) was developed by Karl Pearson and published in 1896 (Pearson, 1896). Reliability theory puts these two concepts together in the context of measurement. Spearman, who was a contemporary of Pearson, actually worked out most of the basics of contemporary reliability theory and published his work in a 1904 article entitled "The Proof and Measurement of Association Between Two Things." Because the British Journal of Psychology did not begin until 1907, Spearman was forced to publish his work in the American Journal of Psychology. Spearman's work was absorbed quickly in the United States. The article was published in the January issue and came to the attention of measurement pioneer Edward L. Thorndike, who that very year was writing the first edition of Introduction to the Theory of Mental and Social Measurements (Thorndike, 1904).

Thorndike's book, although an early 20th-century work, is remarkably sophisticated, even by contemporary standards (Stanley, 1971). Since 1904 many developments on both sides of the Atlantic Ocean have led to further refinements in the assessment of reliability. Most important among these is a 1937 article by Kuder and Richardson, in which several new reliability coefficients were introduced. Later Cronbach and his colleagues (Cronbach et al., 1972) made a major advance by developing methods for evaluating many sources of error in behavioral research.

C. Basics of test score theory

The classical test score theory assumes that each person has a true score that would be obtained if there were no errors in measurement. However, because our measuring instruments are imperfect, the score we observe for each person may differ from the person's true ability or characteristic. The difference between the true score and the score we observe results from measurement error. In symbolic representation, we can say that the observed score (X) is composed of two components, a true score (T) and an error component (E):

$$X = T + E$$

$$\nearrow \qquad \uparrow \qquad \nwarrow$$

Observed   True   Error
score   score

Or we can say that the difference between the score we obtain and the score we are really interested in is equal to the error of measurement:

$$X - T = E$$

A major assumption in classical test theory is that errors of measurement are random. Although systematic errors are acknowledged in most measurement problems they are less likely to force an investigator to make the wrong conclusions. A carpenter who always misreads a tape measure by 2 inches (or makes a systematic error of 2 inches) would still be able to cut boards to be the same length. Using the rubber-yardstick analogy, we would say that this carpenter works with a ruler that is always stretched to be 2 inches too long. Classical test theory deals with the rubber-yardstick problems in which the ruler stretches and contracts in a random way.

Using a random rubber yardstick we would not get the same score on each measurement. Instead we would get a distribution of scores like that shown in Figure 4-1. Each observed score in the distribution would be composed of two

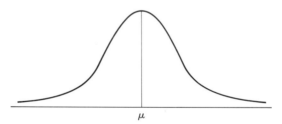

μ

Figure 4-1. Distribution of observed scores for repeated testing of the same person. The mean of the distribution is the estimated true score, and the dispersion represents the distribution of random errors.

components: a true score component (T) and an error component (E). Basic sampling theory tells us that the distribution of random errors would be bell-shaped. Thus the center of the distribution should represent the true score, and the dispersion around the mean of the distribution should display the distribution of sampling errors. This tells us that any one application of the rubber yardstick may or may not tell us the true score. But through repeated applications we would be able to estimate the true score by finding the mean of the observations.

Figure 4-2 shows three different distributions. In the first distribution there is great dispersion around the true score. In this case you might not want to depend on a single observation, because it might be quite far from the true score. The third section in Figure 4-2 displays a situation in which the dispersion around the true score is very small. In this case most of the observations actually are very close to the true score, and it might be more accurate to draw conclusions on the basis of fewer observations.

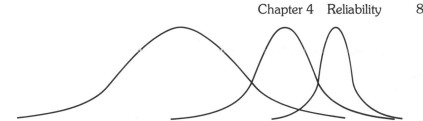

Figure 4-2. Three distributions of observed scores. The left distribution is one in which error is the greatest, and the right distribution has the least error.

The dispersions or distributions around the true score in Figures 4-1 and 4-2 tell us how much error there is in the measure. Classical test theory assumes that the true score for an individual will not change with repeated applications of the same test. Because of random error, however, repeated applications of the same test can produce different scores. The reason is that random error is responsible for the distribution of scores shown in Figures 4-1 and 4-2. Theoretically, the standard deviation of the distribution of errors for each person tells us about the magnitude of measurement error. Although this theory only deals with the distribution of errors for a single person, we usually assume that the distribution of random errors will be the same for all persons. Thus classical test theory uses the standard deviation of errors as the basic measure of error. Usually we call this the *standard error of measurement* and describe it symbolically as:

$$\sigma_{meas}$$

The rubber-yardstick analogy may be useful in helping you understand this concept. Suppose that you have a table that is 30 inches high. If you were to measure the height of the table using a steel yardstick, you probably would always find it to be the same height: 30 inches. However, now you try to measure the table with the rubber yardstick. The first time you try the stick has stretched and you record 28 inches. The next time you discover the stick has shrunk, and it gives you 32 inches for the height of the table. Now we are in trouble because repeated applications of the yardstick will not always give us the same information about the height of the table.

However, there is one way out of this situation. If we assume that the yardstick stretches and shrinks in a random fashion, then we can say that the distribution of scores given by the yardstick will be normal. Most scores will be close to the actual or true score, and we would expect scores that are greatly different from the true score to occur less frequently. Thus it would be rare to observe a score as low as 5 inches or as high as 55 inches. The mean of the distribution of scores from repeated applications of the rubber yardstick would be an estimate of the true height of the table. The standard deviation would be the standard error of measurement. Remember from Chapter 3 that the standard deviation tells us something about the average deviation around the mean.

The standard error of measurement tells us, on the average, how much a score varies from the true score.

II. MODELS OF RELIABILITY

Federal government guidelines require that a test be reliable before it can be used to make employment decisions. This is a very wise procedure, and in this section we hope to justify the need for high standards of reliability. Most reliability coefficients are correlations. However, it is sometimes more useful to define reliability as its mathematically equivalent ratio. It can be shown that the reliability coefficient is the ratio of the variance of the true score of a test to the variance of the observed score:

$$R = \frac{\sigma_T^2}{\sigma_X^2}$$

Where R = the theoretical reliability of the test
   σ_{T^2} = the variance of the true score
   σ_{X^2} = the variance of the observed score
We have used the Greek σ squared instead of S squared to symbolize the variance because the equation describes theoretical values in a population rather than those actually obtained from a sample. The ratio of true score variance to observed score variance can be thought of as a percentage. In this case it is the percentage of the observed variation (σ_{X^2}) that is attributable to variation in the true score. If we subtract this ratio from 1.0, we will have the percentage of variation attributable to random error.

Consider the situation in which the reliability is estimated to be .60. This tells us that 60% of the variation is associated with true variation between people who took the test. The remaining 40% of the variation is random. Suppose you are given a test that will be used to select people for a particular job and the reliability of the test is .40. When the employer gets the test back and begins comparing applicants, 40% of the variation or difference between the people will be explained by real differences between people, and 60% must be ascribed to random or chance factors. Now you can see why the government needed to insist on high standards of reliability.

In Chapter 5 we will discuss validity and show how the meaning of a test comes to be defined by demonstrating correlations between the test and other variables. Attempting to define the validity of a test will be a futile effort if the test is not reliable. Theoretically, a test should not correlate more highly with any other variable than it correlates with itself. The maximum validity coefficient (R_{12max}) between two variables is equal to the square root of the product of their reliabilities. Or $R_{12max} = \sqrt{R_{11}R_{22}}$, where R_{11} and R_{22} are the reliabilities for the two variables.

Because validity coefficients are not usually expected to be exceptionally high, it is possible that a modest correlation between the true scores on two traits would be missed if the test for each of the traits was not highly reliable. Table 4-1 shows the maximum validity you would expect to find given various levels of reliability for two tests. Sometimes it is not possible to demonstrate that a reliable test has meaning. In other words, it is possible to have reliability without validity. However, it is logically impossible to demonstrate that an unreliable test is valid.

TABLE 4-1 How reliability affects validity*

Reliability of test	Reliability of criterion	Maximum validity (correlation)
1.0	1.0	1.00
.8	1.0	.89
.6	1.0	.77
.4	1.0	.63
.2	1.0	.45
.0	1.0	.00
1.0	.5	.71
.8	.5	.63
.6	.5	.55
.4	.5	.45
.2	.5	.32
.0	.5	.00
1.0	.0	.00
.8	.0	.00
.6	.0	.00
.4	.0	.00
.2	.0	.00
.0	.0	.00

*The first column shows the reliability of the test. The second column displays the reliability of the validity criterion. The numbers in the third column are the maximum theoretical correlations between tests, given the reliability of the measures.

A. Sources of error

There may be many reasons why an observed score is different from a true score. There may be situational factors such as loud noises in the room while the test is being administered. The room may be too hot, or it may be too cold. The health status of the test takers also could affect test scores. For example, you may know how hard it is to do well on an examination when you have a cold or are just feeling depressed. Reliability assessment deals with these factors indirectly by using time sampling. Here the test is given at different points in time. Each test administration is considered an independent sample. The most common use of time sampling is *test-retest reliability*. With this method the same group of people is tested at two different points in time with the same test. Then the correlation between these two samples is used as an estimate of reliability. The test-retest method is best suited for time-related sources of error. Time-related error is only one of many sources of error, and reliability theory is better equipped to evaluate errors that are internal underrepresentation. Studies that evaluate internal problems in a test are best understood in terms of a *domain sampling model* (see section D). Methods are available to assess each of these types of errors.

B.   *Time sampling: Test-retest method*

Test-retest reliability estimates are used to evaluate the error associated with administering a test at two different points in time. This type of analysis is only of value if we are measuring "traits" or characteristics of individuals that are not believed to change over time. We usually assume that an intelligence test measures a general ability that is not transient. Therefore, if we administer an IQ test at two points in time and get different scores, it might be concluded that the lack of correspondence is due to random measurement error. Usually we do not assume that a person got smarter or less so.

Some tests might not be appropriate for test-retest evaluation because they measure some characteristic that is constantly changing. In Chapter 17 we discuss the Rorschach inkblot test and note that its value seems to be to tell the clinician how the client is functioning at a particular point in time. Thus differences between Rorschach scores at two points in time could reflect one of two things: (1) there may have been a change in the true score being measured or (2) there may have been measurement error. This tells us that the test-retest method is appropriate only for the measurement of stable traits.

Test-retest reliability is relatively easy to evaluate. All you need to do is administer the same test on two well-specified occasions and then find the correlation between scores from the two administrations. Using the correlational methods we presented in Chapter 3, you should have little difficulty calculating the correlation between the two test administrations to estimate test-retest reliability.

As is often the case, you will need to consider many other details in addition to the methods for calculating the test-retest reliability coefficient. Being a good consumer and user of the information gained from these mechanical exercises will require some careful thought. One thing you always should consider is the possibility of a *carry-over effect*. This effect occurs when the first testing session influences scores on the second one. This will happen when test takers can remember their answers from the first time they took the test. Suppose we ask someone the trivia question "Who were the next-door neighbors in the old television program 'I Love Lucy'"? Then we ask the same question two days later. Response on the second occasion might be influenced by having been asked the question only two days earlier. When there are carry-over effects, the test-retest correlation usually will overestimate the true reliability.[1]

---

[1]Carry-over problems are only of concern when the changes over time are random. In cases where the changes are systematic, carry-over effects do not harm the reliability. An example of a systematic carry over would be when everyone improved exactly 5 points. In this case no new *variability* would occur. Random carry-over effects occur when the changes are not predictable from earlier scores.

A similar problem is what is known as the *practice effect*. Some skills improve with practice. Thus when the test is given a second time, test takers score better because they have sharpened their skills by having taken the test the first time. Asking people trivia questions about old television programs might stimulate them to think more about the old shows or may actually give them some of the information. This sometimes happens on tests of manual dexterity: experience taking the test can improve dexterity skills. As a result, scores on the second administration usually will be higher than they had been on the first administration.

Because of these problems the time interval between testing sessions must be selected and evaluated carefully. If the two administrations of the test are very close in time, there is a greater risk of carry-over and practice effects. However, as the time between testing sessions increases many other factors intervene and serve as possible alternative explanations of the differences between scores on the two testing sessions. For example, if a test is given to children at ages 4 and 5 and the scores for the two administrations of the test correlate .43, we are left with several alternative explanations. The low correlation might mean (1) that the test has poor reliability, (2) that children change on this characteristic between ages 4 and 5, or (3) that some combination of low reliability and change in the children is responsible for the .43 correlation. Most test-retest evaluations do not allow us to choose among these alternatives.

When you find a retest correlation in a test manual, you should pay careful attention to the interval between the two testing sessions. A well-evaluated test will have many retest correlations associated with different time intervals between testing sessions. Most often you will want to be assured that the test is reliable over the time interval of your own study. You also should consider what events occur between the original testing and the retest. For example, activities such as reading a book, participating in a course of study, or watching a TV documentary can alter the test-retest reliability estimate.

Sometimes, poor test-retest correlations do not mean that a test is unreliable; instead, they suggest that the characteristic under study has changed. One of the problems with classical test theory is that it assumes that behavioral dispositions are constant over time. For example, if I am an aggressive person, it is assumed that I will be aggressive all of the time. However, some authors have suggested that important behavioral characteristics, such as motivation, fluctuate over the course of time. In classical test theory these variations are assumed to be error. However, advanced theories of motivation predict these variations, and test theorists have been challenged to develop models to account for these systematic variations (Atkinson, 1981).

C. *Error associated with the use of particular items*

Another concern in building a reliable test is that the test scores not represent any one particular set of items. If you are making a test for some particular characteristic, you might choose many different items to represent this construct. For example, if you are developing a test to determine spelling ability, there are many different words that could be chosen for inclusion in the spelling test. One form of reliability analysis is to determine the error variance attributable to the selection of one particular set of items. *Parallel test forms* reliability is used for this purpose.

Parallel test forms reliability is used to compare two equivalent forms of a test. Two forms of a test are constructed according to the same rules, but the two forms have different items. The term *parallel forms* is used because the tests are constructed the same way and should measure the same attribute. The two forms are parallel because they use different items. However, the rules used to select items of a particular difficulty level are the same.

When two forms of the test are available, it is possible to compare performance on one form versus the other. Some textbooks refer to this process as *equivalent forms reliability*, whereas others simply call it *parallel forms*. Sometimes the two forms are administered to the same group of people on the same day. The Pearson Product Moment correlation coefficient (see Chapter 3) is used as an estimate of the reliability. When both forms of the test are given on the same day, the only sources of variation are random error and the difference between the forms of the test. (The order of administration is usually counterbalanced to avoid practice effects.) Sometimes the two forms of the test are given at different points in time. In this case error associated with time sampling also is included in the estimate of reliability.

The use of two parallel or equivalent forms of a test provides one of the most rigorous assessments of reliability commonly in use. Unfortunately, the use of parallel forms occurs in practice less often than is desirable. Often test developers find it burdensome to develop two forms of the same test, and practical constraints make it difficult to retest the same group of individuals on a second occasion. Instead, many test developers prefer to estimate the reliability based on a single form of the same test.

D. *The domain sampling model*

The domain sampling model considers the problems of using a limited number of items to represent some larger domain. For example, suppose we want to evaluate your spelling ability. In order to accomplish this the best technique would be to systematically go through an English dictionary, have you spell each word, and determine the percentage you spell correctly. However, it is unlikely that you would have time available for this. Instead we need to find a way to evaluate your spelling without having you spell every word. To accomplish this evaluation we use a sample of words. Remember that what we are really attempting to evaluate is how *well* you can spell, which would be determined by your percentage correct if you had been given all of the words in the English language. This percentage would be your "true score." Our task in reliability analysis is to estimate how much error we will make by using the score from the shorter test as an estimate of your true ability.

Theoretically this model conceptualizes reliability as the correlation between the observed score on the shorter test and the long-run true score. The measurement we consider in the domain-sampling model is the error introduced by using a sample of items (or words in this case) rather than the entire domain.[2] As the sample gets larger, it will be more and more representative of the domain. As a result, the larger the number of items, the higher the reliability. We will show you exactly how larger numbers of items increase reliability in a later section of this chapter.

When tests are constructed, each item is a sample of the ability or behavior under study. Long tests have many such samples, and short tests have very few. However, we assume that each item is an equal representation of the studied ability.

Reliability can be estimated from the correlation of the observed test score with the true score.[3] This would be easy to find if we could obtain true scores. However, finding the true scores is not practical and rarely possible. In the example presented above, finding the true score would involve testing people on all of the words in the English language.

Because true scores are not available, our only alternative is to estimate what they would be. Under the assumption that items are randomly drawn from a given domain, each test or group of items should yield an unbiased estimate of the true score. Because of sampling error, however, different random samples of items might give different estimates of the true score. The distribution of these estimates should be random and normally distributed. If we create many tests by sampling from the same domain, we should get a normal distribution of unbiased estimates of the true score. In order to estimate reliability we can create many *randomly parallel tests* by drawing repeated random samples of items from the same domain. In the spelling test example, we would draw several different lists of words randomly from the dictionary and would consider each of these samples to be an unbiased test of spelling ability. Then we would find the correlation between each of these tests with all of the other tests. The correlations then would be averaged.[4]

In practice we rarely develop randomly parallel tests because test items seldom are selected at random. In fact, the items usually are selected for a particular purpose. However, the same general strategy is often used to select items for the different parallel forms of the test. Selecting the items by this nonrandom process does not greatly affect estimates of reliability. Another problem is that it is uncommon in practice to have more than two forms of a test. Instead of evaluating the average correlation between a test and all of its

---

[2]The term *domain* is used to describe a very large collection of items. Some authors prefer the term *universe* or *population* to describe the same concept (Nunnally, 1978).

[3]As Allen and Yen (1979) point out, there are at least six alternative interpretations of the reliability coefficient. The one interpretation we offer here is the one most commonly used.

[4]Technically it is inappropriate to average correlation coefficients. The appropriate method is to use Fisher's *r* to *z'* transformation to convert the correlations into approximate *z* scores. Then the *z'* scores are averaged, and the mean *z'* is transformed back into a correlation (McNemar, 1967).

randomly parallel forms, we typically evaluate the correlation between the test and the one other form we have created. As a result the estimates of reliability often used in practice may be less dependable than desired.

Technical Box 4-1 The Unbiased Estimate of Reliability

Test theorists have demonstrated mathematically that an unbiased estimate of the reliability of a test is given by the square root of the average correlation between a test and all other randomly parallel tests from the domain. Symbolically,

$$r_{1t} = \sqrt{\overline{r}_{1j}}$$

Where 1 = scores on Test 1

     t = the true score for the ability of interest

     $\overline{r}_{1j}$ = the average correlation between Test 1 and all other randomly
            parallel tests.

As we learned in Chapter 3, product moment correlation coefficients always take on values between -1 and 1. When we are estimating reliability the correlation almost always will be positive. When a number is less than 1.0, its square root always will be larger than itself. Thus the correlation between two randomly parallel tests will be smaller than the estimated correlation between one of the tests and the true score according to the formula. For example, if the correlation between two randomly parallel tests is .64, the estimated reliability of the test will be $\sqrt{.64}$=.80. This is built into the estimation of reliability, because it would be impossible for a test to correlate more highly with any other test than it would correlate with its own true score. Thus the correlation between two randomly parallel tests would be expected to be less than the correlation of either test with the true score.

In practice we do not always have two forms of a test. More often we are stuck with only one test form. Under these circumstances we must estimate the reliability for this single group of items. There are different methods for assessing the different sources of variation within a single test. One method is to evaluate the *internal consistency* of the test by dividing it into subcomponents. Another method is to examine the error variance that might be introduced by readministering the test at different points in time. This is known as the *test-retest method* (see section B above).

Internal consistency: the split-half method. In split-half reliability, a test is given and divided into halves that are scored separately. We then compare the results of one half of the test with the results of the other. The two halves of the test can be created in a variety of different ways. If the test is long, the best method is to randomly divide the items into two halves. However, for ease in computing scores for the different halves, some people prefer to calculate a score for the first half of the items and another score for the second half.

Although it is convenient, this method can cause problems when items on the second half of the test are more difficult than items on the first half. If the test gets progressively more difficult, you might be better advised to use the *odd-even* system, whereby a subscore is obtained for the odd-numbered items in the test and another subscore is found for the even-numbered items.

To estimate the reliability of the test we *could* find the correlation between the two halves. However, this would be an underestimate because each subtest is only half as long as the full test. As we discussed earlier, test scores gain reliability as the number of items increases. An estimate of reliability based on two "half tests" would be deflated because each half would be less reliable than the whole test. The correlation between the two halves of the test would be a reasonable estimate of the reliability of half of the test. In order to correct for *half-length*, the Spearman-Brown formula can be applied. It allows you to estimate what the correlation between the two halves would have been if each half had been the length of the whole test:

$$R = \frac{2r}{1+r}$$

Where R is the estimated correlation between two halves of the test if each had had the total number of items and r is the correlation between the two halves of the test.[5] For example, suppose the correlation between two halves of a test was .70. According to the formula, the estimated reliability would be

$$R = \frac{2(.70)}{1+.70} = \frac{1.40}{1.70} = .82$$

The effect of using the Spearman-Brown formula is to increase the estimate of reliability. The left-hand column in Table 4-2 shows several estimates of

TABLE 4-2 Estimates of split-half reliability before and after correction for half-length using the Spearman-Brown formula

Before correction	After correction	Amount of change
.05	.09	.04
.15	.26	.11
.25	.40	.15
.35	.52	.17
.45	.62	.17
.55	.71	.16
.65	.79	.14
.75	.86	.11
.85	.92	.07
.95	.97	.02

[5]There are different forms of the estimation formula, as will be shown later in the chapter.

reliability that are not corrected using the Spearman-Brown procedure. The middle column of the table shows the same values after they have been corrected. The third (right-hand) column shows the amount of change the correction introduces. As you can see, the Spearman-Brown procedure has a substantial effect, particularly in the middle ranges of the scale.

There are some circumstances in which the Spearman-Brown correction is not advisable. One of these is when the two halves of the test have unequal variances. Under the circumstances in which the halves do not appear to be equivalent, Cronbach's (1951) coefficient alpha (α) can be used. The alpha coefficient, which is a general reliability coefficient, will provide the lowest estimate of reliability that can be expected. If alpha is very high, you might assume that the reliability of the test is acceptable. What this means is that the lowest boundary of reliability is still very high—the reliability will not drop below alpha. An alpha level that is low, on the other hand, gives you less information. Because the alpha coefficient only marks the lower bound for the reliability, the actual reliability may still be high. Thus, if the variances for the two halves of the test are unequal, coefficient alpha can be used to confirm that a test has substantial reliability. However, it cannot tell us that a test is unreliable. The formula for coefficient alpha is

$$\alpha = \frac{2\left[\sigma_x^2 - (\sigma_{y1}^2 + \sigma_{y2}^2)\right]}{\sigma_x^2}$$

Where α = the coefficient alpha for estimating split-half reliability
    σ_x^2 = the variance for scores on the whole test
σ_{y1}^2 , σ_{y2}^2 = the variances for the two separate halves of the test

When the variances for the two halves of the test are equal, the Spearman-Brown coefficient and coefficient alpha will give the same results. Under other specific circumstances, both procedures may underestimate the true reliability (see Allen & Yen, 1979).

General measures of internal consistency.   In addition to the split-half technique, there are many other methods for estimating the internal consistency of a test. Many years ago Kuder and Richardson (1937) greatly advanced reliability assessment by developing methods for evaluating reliability within a single administration of a test, but their approach does not depend on some arbitrary splitting of the test into halves.

Decisions about how to split tests into halves cause many potential problems for split-half reliability. The two halves of the test may have different variances. For example, the split-half method also requires that each half of the test must be scored separately, and this can create additional work. The Kuder-Richardson technique avoids these problems, because it is a general method that simultaneously considers all of the possible ways of splitting the items.

Technical Box 4-2 Using Coefficient Alpha to Estimate Split-Half Reliability When the Variances for the Two Halves of the Test Are Unequal

Formula: $R = \dfrac{2[S_x^2 - (S_{y1}^2 + S_{y2}^2)]}{S_x^2}$

Data: $S_x^2 = 11.5$

$S_{y1}^2 = 4.5$

$S_{y2}^2 = 3.2$

Steps

1. Find the variance for the whole test.

$$S_x^2 = 11.5$$

2. Add together the variances for the two halves of the test.

$$S_{y1}^2 = 4.5 \qquad S_{y2}^2 = 3.2 \qquad 4.5 + 3.2 = 7.7$$

3. Find $S_x^2 - (S_{y1}^2 + S_{y2}^2)$ by subtracting the results of Step 2 from those of Step 1.

$$11.5 - 7.7 = 3.8$$

4. Find $2[S_x^2 - (S_{y1}^2 + S_{y2}^2)]$ by multiplying the results of Step 3 times 2.

$$2(3.8) = 7.6$$

5. Find alpha by dividing the results of Step 4 by Step 1.

$$\frac{7.6}{11.5} = .66$$

KR20. The formula for calculating the reliability of a test in which the items are scored 0 or 1 (usually for right or wrong) is known as the *KR20* or *KR 20*. The formula came to be labeled this way because it was the 20th formula presented in the famous article by Kuder and Richardson (the K and R are obtained from the authors' initials).

The formula is

$$KR_{20} = R = \frac{N}{N-1}\left(\frac{S^2 - \Sigma pq}{S^2}\right)$$

Where KR_{20} = the reliability estimate (R)

S^2 = the variance of the total test score

p = the proportion of people getting each item correct (this is found separately for each individual item)

q = the proportion of people getting each item incorrect. For each item q will equal $1-p$.

N = the number of items on the test

Σpq = the sum of the products of p times q for each item on the test

Although we will not go through the mathematical derivations of the KR_{20}, studying the components of the formula may give you a better understanding of how it works. First you will recognize the term S^2 from Chapter 2. This is the variance of the test scores. The variance term appears twice in the formula: once on the top of the right portion in the equation and once on the bottom of the right portion. The other term in the right portion is Σpq. This is the sum of the proportion of people passing each item times the proportion of people failing each individual item. It can be shown that the product pq is the variance for an individual item. Thus Σpq is the sum of the individual item variances.

Now let's think about conditions that would make the term on the right side of the equation either large or small. First consider the situation in which the variance (S^2) is equal to the sum of the variances of the individual items. Symbolically this would be $S^2 = \Sigma pq$. In this case the right-hand term in the formula would be 0 and, as a result, the estimate of reliability would be 0. This tells us that in order to have nonzero reliability, the variance for the total test score must be greater than the sum of the variances for the individual items. This will only happen when the items are measuring the same thing.

The only situation that will make the sum of the item variance less than the total test score variance is when there is *covariance* between the items. Covariance occurs when the items are correlated with one another. The greater the covariance, the smaller the Σpq term will be. When the items covary they can be assumed to measure the same general trait, and the reliability for the test will be high. As Σpq approaches 0, the right side of the equation approaches 1.0. The other factor in the formula is an adjustment for the number of items in the test. This will allow the estimate of reliability to be higher for longer tests.

In addition to the KR_{20}, Kuder and Richardson presented a special case of the reliability formula that does not require the calculation of the p's and q's for every item. Instead, an approximation of the sum of the pq products is used, and this approximation is the mean test score. This was the next formula presented in the famous Kuder-Richardson article and was labeled Formula 21. Thus it has become known as the KR_{21}. The KR_{21} procedure rests on several important assumptions. The most important is that all of the items are of equal difficulty or that the average difficulty level is 50%. Difficulty is defined as the percentage of test takers passing the item. In practice these assumptions are rarely met, and it is usually found that the KR_{21} formula provides an underestimate of split-half reliability:

$$KR_{21} = \frac{N}{N-1} \left[1 - \frac{\overline{X}(1 - \frac{\overline{X}}{N})}{S^2} \right]$$

where all terms are as previously defined.

Technical Box 4-3   The Calculation of Reliability Using KR_{20}

Formula: $KR_{20} = \dfrac{N}{N-1} \left(\dfrac{S^2 - \Sigma pq}{S^2} \right)$

Data: NS = number of test takers = 50

$\qquad N$ = number of items = 6

$\qquad S^2$ = variance (Step 6) = 2.8

Item	Number of test takers responding correctly	p (from Step 2)	q (from Step 3)	pq (from Step 4)
1	12	.24	.76	.18
2	41	.82	.18	.15
3	18	.36	.64	.23
4	29	.58	.42	.24
5	30	.60	.40	.24
6	47	.94	.06	.06

$\qquad\qquad\qquad\qquad\qquad\qquad\qquad\qquad\qquad\qquad\qquad\qquad\qquad \Sigma pq = 1.10$
$\qquad\qquad\qquad\qquad\qquad\qquad\qquad\qquad\qquad\qquad\qquad\qquad\qquad$ (from Step 5)

Steps

1. Determine the number of test takers NS.

$$NS = 50$$

2. Find p by dividing the number of people responding correctly to each item by the number of people taking the test (Step 1). This is the level of difficulty.

$$\frac{12}{50} = .24 \qquad \frac{41}{50} = .82 \qquad \bullet\bullet\bullet$$

3. Find q for each item by subtracting p (the result of Step 2) from 1.0. This gives the proportion responding incorrectly to each item.

$$1.0 - .24 = .76 \qquad 1.0 - .82 = .18 \qquad \bullet\bullet\bullet$$

4. Find pq for each item by multiplying the results of Steps 2 and 3.

$$(.24)(.76) = .18 \qquad (.82)(.18) = .15 \qquad \bullet\bullet\bullet$$

5. Find Σpq by summing the results of Step 4 over the N items.

$$.18+.15+.23+.24+.24+.06=1.1$$

6. Find S^2 which is the variance for the test scores. To do this you will need the scores for each individual in the group. The formula for the variance is

$$S^2 = \frac{\Sigma X^2 - \left[\frac{(\Sigma X)^2}{NS}\right]}{NS-1}$$

In this example $S^2 = 2.8$.

7. Find $S^2 - \Sigma pq$ by subtracting the results of Step 5 from Step 6.

$$2.8 - 1.1 = 1.7$$

8. Find $(S^2 - \Sigma pq)/S^2$ by dividing the results of Step 7 by Step 6.

$$\frac{1.7}{2.8} = .607$$

9. Find N or the number of the number of items.

$$N=6$$

10. Find $N/(N-1)$ by dividing the results of Step 9 by Step 9 minus 1.

$$\frac{6}{5} = 1.2$$

11. Find KR_{20} by multiplying the results of Steps 9 and 10.

$$(1.2)\ (.607) = .73$$

Alpha. Mathematical proofs have demonstrated that the KR_{20} formula will give the same estimate of reliability that would be obtained if you took the mean of the split-half reliability estimates obtained by dividing the test in all possible ways (Cronbach, 1951). You can see that the Kuder-Richardson procedure is very general and usually will be more valuable than a split-half estimate of internal consistency. However, there are still cases in which the KR_{20} formula will not be appropriate for evaluation of internal consistency. These situations occur when a test has items that are not scored as "right" or "wrong." The KR_{20} formula requires that you find the proportion of people who got each item "correct."

There are many types of tests for which there are no right or wrong answers. This is typically the case for personality and attitude scales. For example, on an attitude questionnaire, you might be presented with a statement such as "I believe extramarital sexual intercourse is immoral." You must indicate whether you strongly disagree, disagree, are neutral, agree, or strongly agree. None of these choices is incorrect, and none of these is correct. Rather, your response indicates where you stand on the continuum between agreement and disagreement. In order to extend the Kuder-Richardson method for use with this sort of item, Cronbach developed a formula that could be used to estimate the internal consistency of tests where the items are not scored as 0 or 1 (right or wrong). In doing so, Cronbach developed a more general reliability estimate which he called coefficient alpha or α. The formula for coefficient alpha is[6]:

$$R = \alpha = \left(\frac{N}{N-1} \right) \left(\frac{S^2 - \Sigma S_i^2}{S^2} \right)$$

As you may notice, this looks very similar to the KR_{20} formula. The only difference is that Σpq has been replaced by ΣS_i^2. This new term, S_i^2, is for the variance of the individual items. The summation sign, Σ, informs us that we are to sum the individual item variances. S^2 is for the variance of the total test score. The only real difference is the way the variance of the items is expressed. Actually coefficient alpha is a more general reliability coefficent than KR_{20} because S_i^2 can describe the variance of items whether or not they are in a right-wrong format. Thus coefficient alpha is the most general case of internal consistency reliability.

All of the measures of internal consistency evaluate the extent to which the different items on a test measure the same ability or trait. They all will give low estimates of reliability if the test is designed to measure several traits. Using the domain sampling model, we define a domain that represents a single trait or characteristic, and each item is an individual sample of this general characteristic. When the items do not measure the same characteristic, the test will not be internally consistent.

One popular method for dealing with the situation in which a test apparently measures several different characteristics is to perform factor analysis (see Chapter 3). This can be used to divide the items into subgroups, each internally consistent. However, the subgroups of items will not be related to one another.

---

[6]You may recall the discussion of coefficient alpha in the section on internal consistency. Although the formula on this page appears different, it is mathematically equivalent to the first one.

Factor analysis can help a test constructor build a test which has submeasures for several different traits. When factor analysis is used correctly, these subtests will be internally consistent (highly reliable) and independent of one another. For example, factor analysis might be used to divide a group of items on interpersonal communication into two subgroups. One might be assertiveness items and the other subgroup might be aggressiveness items. The reliability of the aggressiveness and the assertiveness subscales might be quite high. However, the correlation between assertiveness and aggressiveness scores would be quite low. The nature of the factor analysis method insures these characteristics. Thus factor analysis is of great value in the process of test construction.

E. *Reliability of a difference score*

There are some applications of psychological testing when you will need to calculate a *difference score,* which is created by subtracting one test score from another. This might be the difference between performance at two points in time—for example, when you test a group of children before and after they have experienced a special training program. Or it may be the difference between measures of two different abilities. This might occur when you want to know whether a child is doing better in reading than in math. Whenever comparisons between two different attributes are being made (such as reading versus math), it is necessary to make the comparison in z or standardized units (see Chapter 2).

Difference scores create a host of problems that make them more difficult to work with than single scores. In order to understand the problems, we must refer back to the definition of an observed score as composed of both true score (T) and error (E). In a difference score the E or error portion is expected to be larger because it absorbs error from both of the scores used to create the difference score. Furthermore, the T or true score portion might be expected to be smaller because whatever is common to both measures will be canceled out when the difference score is created. As a result of these two factors, the reliability of a difference score is expected to be lower than the reliability of either score on which it is based. If two tests measure exactly the same trait, the score representing the difference between them will be expected to have a reliability of 0.

As was previously mentioned, it is most convenient to find difference scores by first creating z scores for each measure and, second, finding the difference between them (Score 2 – Score 1). The reliability of scores that represent the difference between two standard scores (or z scores) is given the formula

$$R = \frac{\frac{1}{2}(r_{11} + r_{22}) - r_{12}}{1 - r_{12}}$$

where r_{11} = the reliability of the first measure
r_{22} = the reliability of the second measure
r_{12} = the correlation between the first and the second measures

Using this formula you can calculate the reliability of a difference score for any two tests for which the reliabilities and the correlation between them are known. For example, suppose that the correlation between two measures is .70 and the reliabilities of the two measures are .90 and .70, respectively. The reliability of difference between these two measures is

$$R = \frac{\frac{1}{2}(.90+.70)-.70}{1-.70}$$

$$= \frac{.10}{.30}$$

$$= .33$$

As this example demonstrates, the reliability of the difference score between tests with reliabilities as high as .90 and .70 is only .33. The situation in which the reliability of the difference score is lower than the average reliabilities of the two initial measures is not unusual. In fact, this will occur in all cases except when the correlation between the two tests is 0.

The low reliability of a difference score should be a matter of concern to the practicing psychologist and education researcher. Because of their poor re-liabilities, difference scores cannot be depended upon for making interpretations of patterns. For example, it may be difficult to draw the conclusion that a patient is more depressed than schizophrenic on the basis of an MMPI (see Chapter 15) profile showing a lower depression than schizophrenia score. Any differences between these two scales must be interpreted cautiously because the reliability of the score representing the difference between the two scales can be expected to be low. The difficulties associated with using difference scores have been well studied. In a widely cited article, Cronbach and Furby (1970) demonstrated that there are many pitfalls associated with the use of difference scores to measure change. For example, it appears impossible to make a meaningful interpretation of the difference between scores on the same children that are taken at the beginning and at the end of a school year. Measuring the "change" that occurred during that school year requires the use of sophisticated experimental designs in which children are randomly assigned to experimental and control conditions.

F.   *Reliability of criterion-referenced tests*

Variations of the methods for assessing the reliability of randomly parallel tests have been developed specifically for criterion-referenced tests (Millman, 1979). One procedure requires two equal-length samples of items to be ran-domly drawn from the same domain (Lord, 1978). There also is a technique that can be used to evaluate the reliability of a criterion-referenced test made up of only one sample of items (Subkoviak, 1980). If you are interested in estimating the reliability of a criterion-referenced test, excellent tables that outline the steps can be found in an article by Millman (1979).

III.   USING RELIABILITY INFORMATION

Now that you have learned about reliability theory, and methods for estimating reliability, it will be worthwhile to review some practical aspects of reliability assessment. Different levels of reliability are required for different situations.

A.   *How reliable is reliable?*

People often ask how high a reliability coefficient must be before it is "high enough." The answer depends on the use of the test. It has been suggested that reliability estimates in the range of .70 to .80 are good enough for most purposes in basic research. In many research studies we only attempt to gain approximate estimates of whether two variables are related. In a research setting it may be appropriate to estimate what the correlation between two variables would have been if the measures had been more reliable. If the results look promising, it then may be appropriate to spend the extra time and money necessary to make the research instruments more reliable. It even has been argued that it would be a waste of time and effort to refine research instruments beyond a reliability of .90. Although the higher reliability is desirable, it may not be worthwhile in terms of the added burden and costs (Nunnally, 1978).

In clinical settings high reliability is extremely important. When tests are used to make important decisions about someone's future you must be certain to minimize any error in classification. Thus a test with a reliability of .90 might not be good enough. For a test used to make a decision affecting some person's future you should attempt to find a test with a reliability greater than .95.

B.   *What to do about low reliability*

Many test constructors want their tests to be used in applied settings, but analysis reveals that the test reliability is inadequate. Fortunately, psychometric theory does offer some options. Two of the most common approaches are to increase the length of the test and to throw out items that run down the reliability. Another procedure is to estimate what the true correlation would have been if the test did not have measurement error.

Increase the number of items.   According to the domain sampling model, each item in a test is an independent sample of the trait or ability being measured. The larger the sample, the more likely it is that the test will be representative of the true characteristic. Using the domain sampling model, the reliability of a test increases as the number of items increases. Thus one way to increase the reliability of a test is to increase the number of items.

A medical example will help clarify why longer tests are more reliable. Suppose that you go to the doctor with indigestion. It is in your best interest for the doctor to make a reliable judgment about the etiology of your problem. How comfortable would you feel if the doctor asked only one question to provide a diagnosis? You probably would feel more comfortable if the doctor asked numerous questions. In general, people feel that the more information a doctor obtains by asking questions and performing tests, the more reliable the diagnosis will be. This same situation applies to psychological tests.

A decision to increase the number of items might result in a long and costly process. When new items are added, the test must be reevaluated, and it may turn out to be below an acceptable level of reliability. In addition, adding new items can be very costly and can make a test so long that few people would be able to sit through it. Fortunately, there are procedures that can be used to estimate how many items will have to be added in order to bring a test up to an acceptable level of reliability. This is accomplished by applying the Spearman-Brown prophecy formula. In the section on split-half reliability, we introduced the Spearman-Brown formula. This application requires a different form.

The Prophecy Formula. The prophecy formula for estimating how long a test must be in order to achieve a desired level of reliability is another case of the general Spearman-Brown method for estimating reliability. Algebraic manipulations of the general formula can be used to turn it around and solve for the length needed for any desired level of reliability. The formula is

$$N = \frac{r_d(1-r_o)}{r_o(1-r_d)}$$

Where N = the number of tests of the current version's length that would be needed to have a test of the desired level of reliability

r_d = the desired level of reliability

r_o = the observed level of reliability based on the current version of the test

Consider an example in which a 20-item test had a reliability of .76. We would like to bring the reliability up to .85. Putting these numbers into the prophecy formula, we get

$$N = \frac{.85\,(1-.76)}{.76\,(1-.85)} = \frac{.204}{.114} = 1.79$$

These calculations tell us that we would need 1.79 tests the length of the current 20-item test to bring the reliability up to the desired level. In order to find the number of items that would be required for the test, we must multiply the number of items on the current test by N from the preceding formula. In the example, this would give $20 \times 1.79 = 35.8$. So the test would have to be expanded from 20 to about 36 items in order to achieve the desired reliability of

.85. This assumes that the added items come from the same pool as the original items and that they have the same psychometric properties.

The decision to expand a test from 20 to 36 items must depend upon economic and practical considerations. The test developer first must ask whether the increase in reliability is worth the extra time, effort, and expense required to achieve this goal. If the test is to be used for personal decisions it may be dangerous to ignore any effort that will enhance the reliability of the test. On the other hand, if the test is only to be used to get an idea of whether two variables are associated, the expense of extending it may not be worth the effort and cost.

When the prophecy formula is used, certain assumptions are made that may or may not be valid. One of these assumptions is that the probability of error in items added to the test is the same as that for the original items in the test. However, there may be some occasions in which adding many items would bring about new sources of error. For instance, if the test becomes very long, fatigue might begin to become a major source of error.

As an example of a situation in which it may not be worthwhile to attempt to bring up the reliability of a test, consider a 40-item test that has a reliability of .50. We would like to bring the reliability up to .90. Using the prophecy formula we get

$$N = \frac{.90\,(1-.50)}{.50\,(1-.90)} = \frac{.90\,(.50)}{.50\,(.10)} = \frac{.45}{.05} = 9$$

These figures tell us that the test would have to be nine times its present length in order to have a projected reliability of .90: $9 \times 40 = 360$ items long. Creating a test 360 items long would be very expensive, and validating it would require a considerable time investment for both test constructors and test takers. Beyond these problems, there might be new sources of error in the 360-item test that would not have been a problem for the shorter measure. For example, many errors may occur on the longer test simply because people get tired and bored during the long process of answering 360 questions. There is no way of taking these factors into account using the prophecy formula.

Factor and item analysis.   The reliability of a test is dependent on all of the items being measures of the same underlying characteristic. Although we always intend to create tests in this way, it often happens that some items which are not measures of this same construct get included. Leaving these items in the test will serve to reduce the reliability. The reliability estimates we have discussed in this chapter depend on high intercorrelations among the items. In order to assure that the items are measuring the same thing, two approaches are suggested. One is to perform factor analysis (see Chapter 3 and also Gorsuch, 1974; Nunnally, 1978; Harman, 1967). Tests will be most reliable if they are *unidimensional*. This means that one factor should account for considerably more of the variance than any other factor. Items that do not load on this factor might be considered for elimination.

Another related approach is to examine the correlation between each item and the total score for the test. This is a form of item analysis (see Chapter 6) and often is called *discriminability analysis*. When the correlation between performance on a single item and the total test score is low, the item is probably measuring something different than other items on the test. It also might mean that the item is so easy or so hard that people do not differ in their response to it. In either case, the low correlation indicates that the item serves to drag down the estimate of reliability and that it would be worthwhile to exclude it.

Correlation for attenuation.   Low reliability is a real problem in psychological research and practice because it reduces the chances of finding significant correlations between measures. We know that if a test is unreliable, information obtained with it can be of little or no value. Thus we say that potential correlations are *attenuated* or diminished by measurement error.

Fortunately, measurement theory does allow us to estimate what the correlation between two measures would have been if they had not been measured with error. These methods "correct" for the attenuation in the correlations caused by the measurement error. In order to use the methods one need know only the reliabilities of two tests and the correlation between them. The correction for attenuation is

$$\hat{r}_{12} = \frac{r_{12}}{\sqrt{r_{11}r_{22}}}$$

Where $\hat{r}_{12}$=the estimated true correlation between Tests 1 and 2
  r_{12}=the observed correlation between Tests 1 and 2
  r_{11}=the reliability of Test 1
  r_{22}=the reliability of Test 2

Suppose, for example, that a test of manual dexterity and a test of general athletic skill were correlated .34; the reliabilities of the tests were .75 and .82 for the dexterity and the athletic skill tests, respectively. The estimated true correlation between athletic ability and manual dexterity would be

$$\frac{.34}{\sqrt{(.75)(.82)}} = \frac{.34}{\sqrt{.615}} = \frac{.34}{.78} = .44$$

As the example shows, the estimated correlation increases from .34 to .44 when the correction is used.

Sometimes one measure meets an acceptable standard of reliability but the other one does not. In this case we would want to correct for the attenuation caused only by the one unreliable test. To do this we use the formula

$$\hat{r}_{12} = \frac{r_{12}}{\sqrt{r_{11}}}$$

Where $\hat{r}_{12}$=the estimated true correlation

r_{12}=the observed correlation

r_{11}=the reliability of the variable that does not meet our standard of reliability

For example, suppose we want to estimate the correlation between manual dexterity and grade point average in dental school. The reliability of the manual dexterity test is .75, which is not acceptable to us, but dental school GPA is assumed to be measured without error. Using the fallible manual dexterity test, we observed the correlation to be .53. Plugging these numbers into the formula we get

$$\frac{.53}{\sqrt{.75}} = \frac{.53}{.87} = .61$$

This informs us that correcting for the attenuation caused by the manual dexterity test increased our observed correlation from .53 to .61.

IV.   RELIABILITY IN BEHAVIORAL OBSERVATION STUDIES

Psychologists with behavioral orientations usually prefer not to use psychological tests. Instead they favor the direct observation of behavior. To measure aggression, for example, they would record the number of times a child hits or kicks another child. Observers would tabulate the number of observable responses in each category. Thus there would be a score for "hits," another score for "kicks," and so on.

Some people feel that behavioral observation systems are so simple that they are free from psychometric problems. Unfortunately, this is not the case. In practice the reliability of behavioral observation systems is frequently a problem. Unreliability in behavioral observation results from discrepancies between true scores and the scores recorded by the observer. For example, there may be a difference between the actual number of times a child hits or kicks another one and the number of behaviors the observer reports for these categories. There may be many reasons for these discrepancies. For instance, errors commonly occur when an observer misses certain events or when time sampling is done. Because it is sometimes impossible to continuously monitor behavior, it is common to take samples of behavior at certain time intervals. Under these circumstances, sampling error must be considered.

Sources of error introduced by time sampling error are similar to sampling items from a large domain. When each time sample is thought of as an "item," these problems can be handled using sampling theory and methods such as alpha reliability.

The problem of error associated with different observers, however, presents some unique difficulties. In order to assess these problems we need to estimate the reliability of the observers. There are at least three different ways this can be done.

The most common method for evaluating the reliability of observers is to record the percentage of times two or more observers agree. Unfortunately, this method is not the best one for at least two reasons. First, percentage agreement does not take into consideration the level of agreement that would be expected by chance alone. For instance, if two observers are recording whether a particular behavior either occurred or did not, they would have a 50% likelihood of agreeing by chance alone. Thus a method for assessing reliability of judges should include an adjustment for level of agreement to be expected by chance. Second, percentages are not appropriate for mathematical manipulation. It is not technically appropriate to average percentages. Indexes like standardized or z scores are manipulable and are better suited for the task of reliability assessment.

After reviewing several approaches, Hartmann (1977) concluded that the kappa statistic is best suited for assessing the level of agreement among several observers. The kappa statistic was introduced by Cohen (1960) as a measure of agreement between two judges who each rate a set of objects using nominal scales. The method was extended by Fliess (1971) to consider the agreement between any number of observers. The calculation of kappa is beyond the scope of this presentation. Interested readers can find the procedures in Fliess (1971). An approximation of the coefficient for the agreement between two observers is given by the phi coefficient, which was discussed in Chapter 3.

Technical Box 4-4   Using the SPSS Program to Calculate Reliability

The SPSS computer program can be used to calculate most of the estimates of reliability discussed in this chapter. You will need to consult the program write-up in order to get the program to work for your particular data set. However, once you are familiar with the program and with the different forms of reliability, you should have little difficulty making the computer perform the complex calculations. Here are a few examples.

1. *Test-Retest Reliability*. In order to perform test-retest reliability you need to create a data file that includes the test scores for the two points in time. You might call these

variables TIME1 and TIME2. Use one card for each person, and have the two scores separated by a blank space on each card. To estimate the reliability you need only find the correlation between the test scores obtained at the two points in time. An example deck set up for a group of 100 people might be as follows:

(Insert the SPSS job control cards specific to your local computer center.)

```
RUN NAME              TEST-RETEST RELIABILITY
VARIABLE LIST         TEST1  TEST2
INPUT FORMAT          FREEFIELD
N OF CASES            100
INPUT MEDIUM          CARD
PEARSON CORR          TEST1 WITH TEST2
STATISTICS            ALL
READ INPUT DATA

(Data cards go here.)

FINISH

/ *
```

The result will be a computer printout showing the correlation between test scores obtained at two different test administration sessions. This correlation coefficient can be used as the estimate of test-retest reliability.

2. *Split-Half Reliability*. To calculate split-half reliability with the SPSS program you need to have scores for the two halves of the test. These can be found by using the COMPUTE facility in SPSS.

Suppose a test has ten items and these are to be identified as V1, V2 . . ., V10. The SPSS program can be used to score the test and to estimate the subscores for each half. The test is scored using the RECODE statements. Each item is recoded so that a correct response is given a score of 1 and an incorrect response is given a score of 0. In the following example a ten-item multiple choice test was given to 35 people. The test was scored, and the items were divided into odd and even subtests. Then the correlation between the two subtests was estimated. The correct choices for the items are as follows:

Item	Choice
1 (V1)	3
2 (V2)	2
3 (V3)	1
4 (V4)	3
5 (V5)	1
6 (V6)	2
7 (V7)	4
8 (V8)	1
9 (V9)	2
10 (V10)	4

The deck setup might be

(Insert the SPSS job control cards for your local computer center.)

```
RUN NAME             SPLIT HALF RELIABILITY      These cards re-
VARIABLE LIST        V1 TO V10                   code the raw
INPUT FORMAT         FREEFIELD                   multiple re-
N OF CASES           35                          sponses so that
INPUT MEDIUM         CARD                        a correct re-
RECODE               V3 V5 V8 (2,3,4=0)          sponse is
RECODE               V2 V6 V9 (1,3,4=0)(2=1)     scored 1 and
RECODE               V1 V4 (1,2,4=0) (3=1)       an incorrect
RECODE               V7 V10 (1,2,3=0) (4=1)      response is
COMPUTE              ODD=V1+V3+V5+V7+V9           scored 0.
COMPUTE              EVEN=V2+V4+V6+V8+V10         These cards
PEARSON CORR         ODD WITH EVEN               calculate the
STATISTICS           ALL                         odd/even sub-
READ INPUT DATA                                  scale scores.
                                                 This card asks
(Data cards go here.)                            for the corre-
                                                 lation that
FINISH                                           will be used
                                                 to estimate the
/ *                                              reliability.
```

Remember that the correlation you get back from the computer will not be adjusted for half-length. In order to get the estimate of reliability, you must plug the odd-even correlation into the formula for half length (see page 97).

3. *Alpha Reliability*. Version 7 of SPSS includes a special subprogram for reliability. This new addition to SPSS is very valuable because it can be used to calculate all kinds of reliability coefficients. Following is an example of a deck setup to estimate coefficient alpha for a group of ten items on a personality test. In this case there is no right or wrong response for the items. Actually the reliability subprogram of SPSS is very adaptable, and it is capable of performing most types of reliability analyses discussed in this chapter. An example of a deck setup for calculating the alpha coefficient for items that are not scored right or wrong follows. In this example there are ten items that we have symbolized as V1 to V10. There would be one card for each of 60 test takers, and responses for the ten items would be on a single card for each subject and separated by blank spaces.

(Insert the SPSS job control cards for your local computer center.)

```
RUN NAME             COEFFICIENT ALPHA FOR 10 ITEMS
VARIABLE LIST        V1 TO V10
INPUT FORMAT         FREEFIELD
N OF CASES           60
INPUT MEDIUM         CARD
RELIABILITY          VARIABLES=V1 TO V10 / MODEL=ALPHA
                     SCALE(NOSPLIT)=V1 TO V10 /
OPTIONS              1,3
STATISTICS           ALL
READ INPUT DATA

(Put the data cards here.)

FINISH
/ *
```

V. SUMMARY

Measurement error is common in all fields of science. Psychological and educational specialists, however, have devoted a great deal of time and study to measurement error and its effects. Tests that are relatively free of measurement error are considered to be reliable, and tests that contain relatively great measurement error are considered to be unreliable. The basics of contemporary theories and methods of reliability were worked out in the early part of this century by Charles Spearman. Test score and reliability theories have gone through continual refinements.

When we evaluate reliability we first must specify the source of measurement error we are trying to evaluate. If we are concerned about errors that result from the test being given at different points in time, we might consider the test-retest method in which test scores obtained at two different points in time are correlated. On other occasions we are concerned about errors that arise because we have selected a small sample of items to represent a larger conceptual domain. To evaluate this type of measurement error we would use a method assessing the internal consistency of the test, such as the split-half method. The KR_{20} and alpha methods are general methods for estimating the internal consistency of a test.

The standard of reliability for a test depends on the situation in which the test will be used. In some research settings it may not be worth the extra time and money required to bring a test up to an exceptionally high level of reliability. On the other hand, very strict standards for reliability are required when a test is to be used for making decisions that will affect people's lives. When a test has unacceptably low reliability, the test constructor might wish to boost the reliability by increasing the test length or by using factor analysis to divide the test into homogeneous subgroups of items. In research settings it is sometimes possible to deal with the problem of low reliability by estimating what the correlation between tests would have been if there had been no measurement error. This procedure is called *correction for attenuation*.

Recently there has been an increased interest in evaluating the reliability of behavioral observations. The percentage of items observers agree upon is not the best index of reliability for these studies because it does not take into consideration how much agreement is to be expected by chance alone. Correlation-like indexes such as kappa or phi are better suited to estimate reliability in these behavioral studies.

Reliability is one of the basic foundations of behavioral research. If a test is not reliable, it will not be possible to demonstrate that it has any meaning. In the next chapter we will focus on how the meaning of tests is defined.

5

Validity

Learning objectives

When you have completed this chapter, you should be able to do the following:

1. Determine the relationship between establishing test validity and the use of the scientific method.
2. Explain why it is inappropriate to refer to so-called "face validity" as a form of validity.
3. List the categories of validity recognized in the booklet Standards for Educational and Psychological Tests.
4. Tell how the strategy for establishing content validity differs from that used to obtain evidence for other types of validity.
5. Discuss the difference between predictive and concurrent criterion validity.
6. Relate the concept of coefficient of determination (from Chapter 3) to the interpretation of the validity coefficient in criterion validity.
7. Tell how to interpret the results of a test that, for example, had a validity coefficient of .35 for predicting success on a particular job.
8. List some of the issues that should be taken into consideration when interpreting a validity coefficient.
9. Know when construct validation is appropriate.
10. Select some hypothetical construct and then describe how you would go about developing a measure for it.

The case of Willie Griggs was argued before the U.S. Supreme Court in October 1970. Griggs and 12 other Black laborers were employees of the Dan River Steam Station of the Duke Power Company in Draper, North Carolina.

Griggs and the others involved in the lawsuit were classified as laborers by the company, and their primary work assignment was sweeping and cleaning. The men would have preferred to be promoted to the next highest classification level, which was coal handler. However, the company required a passing score on a general intelligence test in order to assign this promotion. Of the 95 employees at the power station, 14 were Black. Among the 14 Black workers, 13 were assigned to sweeping and cleaning duties. The major obstacle for the men moving up in the company was their performance on the test.

Because the test appeared to render ineligible a much higher proportion of Black employees, the power company was sued for engaging in a discriminatory employment practice. The central issue in the lawsuit was the meaning of the test scores. The power company managers argued that using the test "would improve the overall quality of the work force." They suggested that they did not intend to discriminate on the basis of race and that the test helped them find employees who were most capable.

In the course of the court battle, the power company was required to show why the test had meaning for the particular jobs within their establishment. In other words, the company had to prove that the test had a specific meaning for particular jobs such as laborer or coal handler. On hearing the arguments, the Supreme Court decided that the tests were unrelated to measuring job capability. They ruled that the tests served as "built-in headwinds" for minority groups and had no meaning for the purpose of hiring or promoting workers to the classification of coal handler.

As a result of the *Griggs v. Duke Power* decision employers have been forced to provide evidence that a test used for selection of employees or for promotion purposes has a specific meaning. In the field of testing we refer to this meaning as *validity*. The meaning of a test is defined by very specific evidence, and there are very specific methods used to acquire this information. The meaning of a test is established by this evidence and not by the word of a psychologist. Just as in a legal court proceeding, a psychologist must obey specific rules of evidence in establishing that a test has a particular meaning for a specific purpose. In this chapter we will review the rules of evidence most frequently employed. Some of the court cases similar to the one involving Willie Griggs will be discussed in Chapter 21.

I. LEARNING TO ASK ABOUT THE VALIDITY EVIDENCE

Psychologists and other professionals continually attempt to convince the public that their discipline is meaningful. In the case of psychological tests certain segments of the public may have been convinced to become overly trusting. After you read this chapter we hope that you will be able to determine when test results are meaningful and when they are questionable.

A. The definition of validity

Validity can be defined as the agreement between a test score or measure and the quality it is believed to measure. Over the years psychologists have created many subcategories of validity, and different definitions of validity began to blossom. In time it became hard to determine whether psychologists who referred to different types of validity were really talking about something different. Validity defined the meaning of tests and measures—yet the term *validity* itself was beginning to lose its own meaning. In 1974 a joint committee of the American Psychological Association, the American Educational Research Association, and the National Council on Measurement in Education published a booklet entitled *Standards for Educational and Psychological Tests* (1974). We will refer to this booklet frequently because it provides a sensible set of guidelines for psychological tests that have won approval by the major professional groups.

The joint committee set aside numerous other definitions of validity and instead classified types of validity under three major headings: *content, criterion,* and *construct.* Other textbooks may use other headings for validity, but these all can be subsumed under the three categories suggested by the joint committee. For example, what has been called *concurrent* validity and *predictive* validity are really subcategories of *criterion validity*. *Empirical* validity and *statistical* validity also are synonyms for *criterion validity*. *Convergent* validity and *discriminant* validity are really types of evidence for *construct validity*. *Trait* validity and *factorial* validity sometimes also are considered synonyms for *construct validity*.

B. Nature of evidence

Obtaining data in validity studies is like gathering evidence for a court trial. Some psychologists have made the analogy between psychological inquiry and the legal system. One of the similarities is that we always begin by assuming that there is no reason to believe a measure is valid. Evidence for validity comes from showing the association between the test and other variables. The rules strictly forbid saying there is a relationship without some proof. This is similar to the legal notion of innocent until proven guilty. Proof of guilt must be persuasive. In a similar manner, we must have convincing proof that there is a relationship between two variables before we are justified in touting the connection.

II. TYPES OF VALIDITY

The Joint Committee on Educational and Psychological Tests discussed three types of validity: content, criterion, and construct. Each of these will be discussed below. In addition, we will comment on what some people call *face validity*. The joint committee refused to recognize face validity as a legitimate category because it is not technically a form of validity. However, the term needs to be mentioned because it is commonly used in the testing literature.

A. *Face validity*

Face validity is the mere appearance that a measure has validity. Sometimes psychologists report exactly what they observe and do not try to generalize. When they do, they are depending on face validity. They assume that the measures have meaning themselves and that no other generalizations are necessary. In many behavioral studies this level of validity is just fine. For example, if you are interested in bar-pressing behavior in rats and observe the bar press, no generalizations are necessary. The observed bar-press response is exactly what you want to talk about. Indeed, the face validity is all that is needed to make the point. On the other hand, implying that the bar-press response means something—for instance, that it is predictive of later feeding behavior—requires some evidence that feeding is really predictable from bar pressing.

In other words, you are now using bar pressing as a real basis for inference, and so you will need real validity evidence. We are not suggesting that face validity is unimportant. In many settings it is crucial to have a test that "looks like" it is valid. These appearances can help motivate test takers because they can see that the test is relevant. For example, suppose you had developed a test to screen applicants for a training program in accounting. Items that asked about balance sheets and ledgers might make the applicants more motivated than items about fuel consumption. However, both types of items might be testing the same arithmetic reasoning skill. We often say a test has face validity if the items are reasonably related to the perceived purpose of the test.

B. *Content validity*

How many times have you studied for an examination and known almost everything? Yet the professor is able to come up with some strange items that do not seem to represent the content of the course. If this has happened you may have encountered a test with poor content validity. A test or measure possesses content validity to the extent that it provides an adequate representation of the conceptual domain it is designed to cover. For example, if you are being tested on the first six chapters of this book, the test you take is content valid to the extent that the items on the test adequately represent the information in the chapters.

Traditionally content validity has been of greatest concern in educational testing. If you have a test in history, the concern has been that scores on the test represent your comprehension of the history you are expected to know. Many factors can limit performance on history tests and therefore make the professor's inferences about your knowledge less valid on the basis of your score. These factors could include characteristics of the items (such as vocabulary some students will not understand) or the sampling of items (such as selection of items that do not represent the information the test is supposed to evaluate).

It is difficult to separate content validity from other types of validity. In fact, many psychologists have commented that the boundaries between content and other forms of validity are not clearly defined (Campbell, 1976; Dunnette & Borman, 1979; Dunnette, 1976; Tenopyr, 1977; Ebel, 1977; Messick, 1975). However, there are some unique features of the content validation strategy. Aside from face validity, content validity is the only type of validity for which the evidence is logical rather than statistical. Actually content validation involves inferences about the test scores (Tenopyr, 1977). In content validation we attempt to determine whether the test has been constructed adequately. For example, we ask if the items were chosen to be a fair sample of the content area. Establishing the content validity of a test requires good logic, intuitive skills, and perseverance. The test constructor must be careful and willing to continually revise the items.

■ FOCUSED EXAMPLE 5-1   CHALLENGING THE PROFESSOR

Most professors have had the experience of having the content validity of their tests challenged. The challenge is usually by a student who complains that "your test did not give me an opportunity to demonstrate what I know" or "you assigned Chapters 1 through 5, but nearly all of the items came from Chapters 1 and 2—how can you evaluate whether we know anything about the other material we were supposed to read?" In the process of creating good and fair tests, the professors should continually face this sort of questioning and attempt to create tests that will not evoke legitimate criticism. Good judgment is always required in test development: we can never get around the need for rational judgment (Ebel, 1977).

It is often the case that test scores reflect many factors in addition to what we assume the test should measure. For example, your professor may assume that your score on a psychology examination represents the proportion of items you know how to answer correctly. However, it may be that you knew how to answer many more of the items correctly but that other factors have interfered. For example, many students do poorly on tests because of anxiety (see Chapter 19) or reading problems. A slow reader may get a low score on an examination because he or she did not have adequate time to read through all of the questions. Thus content validity must consider all of the other factors that might influence performance. These considerations are necessary in order to make accurate generalizations about what the test score really means. Chapter 8 will present a more detailed discussion of this problem.

C.   *Criterion validity*

Folklore includes stories about fortune-tellers who can look into crystal balls and see the future. Much to our dismay, we do not believe that anyone has been able to manufacture a crystal ball that really tells exactly what the future will hold.

Instead of turning to fortune-tellers with crystal balls, people who need to know about the future have frequently turned to psychologists. We want to know how well someone will do on a job or which students we should select for our graduate program or who is most likely to get a serious disease. The problem is that, while we want to know how well someone will do in the future, we need that information now. We depend on psychological tests to forecast future behavior.

The assessment of criterion validity tells us just how good the tests are in serving these predictive purposes. A measure achieves criterion validity to the extent that it corresponds to an accurate measure of interest. The reason for assessing criterion validity is that the test or measure is to serve as a "stand in" for the measure we are really interested in.

Predictive and concurrent validity.   The forecasting function of tests is actually a type or form of criterion validity that is known as *predictive validity*. Predictive validity is used for the purpose of forecasting. For example, the SAT has predictive validity as a college admissions test if it accurately forecasts how well high school students will do in their college studies. The SAT, including its quantitative and verbal subtests, is the predictor variable, and the college grade point average is the criterion. The purpose of the test is to predict the likelihood of succeeding on the criterion—that is, achieving a high grade point average in college. A valid test for this purpose would make the task of college admissions committees much easier, because they would have some feeling in advance about which students would succeed. Unfortunately, many tests do not have exceptionally impressive prediction records, and we must search continually for better ways to predict outcomes.

Another type of criterion validity is *concurrent validity*. Studies of concurrent validity assess the simultaneous relationship between the test and the criterion. For example, we often look at the relationship between an employment screening test and performance on the job. The measures are actually taken at the same point in time, because the test is designed to predict how well the person will do right away. In the case of employment screening tests, a person might have to be hired in order to evaluate how well he or she would do on the criterion of job performance. Studies on concurrent validity are used to estimate how well the person will do on the job if he or she were hired now.

Job samples provide a good example of the use of concurrent validity. Industrial psychologists often have to select employees on the basis of limited information. One method that has gained in popularity in recent years is to test the potential employees on a sample of behaviors that are representative of the tasks that will be required of them. For example, Campion (1972) found that the most effective way to select maintenance mechanics was to obtain samples of mechanical work. Because these samples were shown to correlate well with performance on the job, the samples alone could be used for selection and screening of applicants. Impressive results support the use of work samples for selecting employees in a variety of areas, including motor skills (Asher & Sciarrino, 1974) and work in the petroleum industry (Dunnette, 1972).

■ **FOCUSED EXAMPLE 5-2 PREDICTION OF HEART DISEASE FROM PERSONALITY**

In a best-selling book, *Type A Behavior and Your Heart*, Friedman and Rosenman (1974) argued that certain individuals maintain a lifestyle into which stress is practically built. These people were designated as Type A. The typical Type A personality is a hard-driving, competitive individual whose calendar shows something scheduled for every hour of the day. These Type A individuals are much more likely to develop heart disease than Type B individuals, who are more relaxed and less likely to invite stressful situations.

The Type A and Type B individuals are assessed by a *standardized stress interview*. During this interview a subject is asked approximately 25 questions about his or her ambitions, sense of time urgency, competitiveness, and feelings of hostility. Those who become classified as Type A tend to exhibit certain specific responses during the interview. Behaviorally they speak rapidly, anticipate what is going to be said next, and breathe heavily during conversation. In addition, they are compulsive about getting things done, have few other interests outside of their jobs, and believe they can overcome any obstacle. People who become classified as Type B exhibit little time urgency, although they may sometimes feel under pressure, but are more relaxed and less in a hurry. In general, Type B personalities are described as less hurried, less easily aroused to anger, and more relaxed.

On the basis of the standardized stress interview, Jenkins, Rosenman and Zyzanski (1972) created a self-administered form of the questionnaire that can be used to classify people into personality patterns A and B. Examples of the items in this questionnaire include the following[1]:

1. Has your spouse or friend ever told you that you eat too fast? A pattern A response is "yes, often," and pattern B responses are "yes, once or twice" or "no, no one has told me this."
2. How would your spouse (or closest friend) rate you? Pattern A responses are "definitely hard-driving and competitive" and "probably hard-driving and competitive," and B responses are "probably relaxed and easy going" and "definitely relaxed and easy going."
3. How would your spouse (or best friend) rate your general level of activity? An A response is "too active, needs to slow down," and B responses are "too slow, should be more active" and "about average, is busy much of the time."

[1]The scoring of the questionnaire is somewhat complex. It was derived by optimal scaling and discriminant function equations. The items have been reproduced by permission from the Jenkins Activity Survey. Copyright © 1979, 1966, 1965 by the Psychological Corporation. All Rights Reserved.

---

4. Do you ever set deadlines or quotas for yourself at work or at home? An A response is "yes, once per week or more often," and B responses are "no" and "yes, but only occasionally."

Without some linkage to other information, these questions have little meaning. However, studies have shown that responses to these questions are helpful in predicting who will eventually get heart disease (predictive validity) and who will have beginning signs of heart disease now (concurrent validity).

First let us consider the predictive value of the A-B category scales. One important study assessed 3154 men for the A-B behavior patterns and a variety of other heart attack risk factors in 1960 and 1961. Then the men were followed to determine who eventually developed heart disease during the next eight to nine years. The results of the study demonstrated that the men who were classified as Type A in 1960 and 1961 were nearly twice as likely to develop new cases of coronary heart disease during the next eight and a half years. Out of nearly 1500 men classified as Type A, 178 developed demonstrable clinical evidence (as assessed by two heart specialists who did not know which personality type the tests showed the men to be). In comparison, only 79 of a comparably sized group of Type B men developed the disease. Among men who did develop coronary heart disease, those who had been classified as Type A eight or nine years earlier were five times as likely to have a second heart attack (Rosenman, Brand, Jenkins, Friedman, Straus, & Wurm, 1975).

The data, then, do indicate that the screening tests which classify people into Type A and Type B personalities can serve as an imperfect crystal ball. Although they are far from perfect in predicting who will develop heart disease, they do give some significant information in advance.

In addition to the predictive validity of the Type A-B classification measures, other studies have established the concurrent validity of the measures. In heart disease, classic studies have established certain factors that are associated with increased risk of heart disease. A variety of studies have demonstrated that Type A personalities are associated with many of these risk patterns. For example, Type A behavior has been shown to be related to artherosclerosis or narrowing of a major artery feeding into the heart (Blumenthal, Williams, Kong, Thompson, Jenkins, & Rosenman, 1975; Zyzanski, Jenkins, Ryan, Flessas, & Everist, 1976). Other studies have shown that Type A's have higher levels of serum cholesterol (Blumenthal et al., 1975) and higher fasting triglyceride levels (Friedman, Rosenman, & Byers, 1964). Although about as many Type B's smoke as Type A's, the Type A individuals consume more cigarettes per day (Rosenman & Friedman, 1974). Furthermore, Type A individuals respond with more intensity to stressful situations (Glass, 1977). All of these factors are associated with increased likelihood of future heart disease. In summary, the measures that categorize people into Type A and B are meaningful because they have been shown to relate to criteria that are important to us. They have some predictive validity because the classification can forecast which people are more likely to develop heart disease, and they have some concurrent validity because they relate to specific current behavioral and biochemical indicators associated with the chances of developing heart disease.

Another use of concurrent validity occurs when a person might not know how he or she would respond to the criterion measure. For example, the Strong-Campbell Interest Inventory (SCII) uses patterns of interest among persons who are satisfied with their careers as criteria (Campbell, 1977). Then the patterns of interest for people taking the tests are matched to these criteria for various occupations.

Validity coefficient.   The relationship between a test and a criterion is usually expressed as a correlation. This correlation is called a *validity coefficient*, and it tells the extent to which the test is valid for making statements about the criterion.

Not all validity coefficients are the same value, and there are no hard and fast rules about how large the coefficient must be in order to be meaningful. In practice it is rare to see a validity coefficient larger than .60, and validity coefficients in the range of .30 to .40 are commonly considered high. A coefficient is statistically significant if the chances of obtaining its value by chance alone are quite small: usually less than 5 in 100. For example, suppose that the SAT had a validity coefficient of .40 for predicting grade point average at a particular West Coast university. Because this coefficient is likely to be statistically significant, we can say that the SAT score tells us more about how well people will do in college than we would know by chance.

There are many reasons why college students differ from one another in their academic performance. You probably could easily list a dozen. Because there are so many factors that contribute to college performance, it would be too much to expect that the SAT could explain all of the variation. The question we must ask is "How much of the variation in college performance will we be able to predict on the basis of SAT scores?"

The validity coefficient squared is the percentage of variation in the criterion that we can expect to know in advance because of our knowledge of the test scores. Thus we will know .40 squared or 16% of the variation in college performance because of the information we have from the SAT test. The remainder of the variation in college performance is actually the greater proportion: 84% of the total variation is still unexplained. In other words, when students arrive at college, most of the reasons why they perform differently will still be a mystery to college administrators and professors.

However, if school officials have used the SAT to select the students, they did so to learn about 16% of the variation between students that could be predicted before any students were admitted. It is important to realize that accounting for small percentages of the variance in some criterion under different circumstances is very useful for people making decisions. Obviously college administrators feel that the small bit of information they get from SAT scores aids them in selecting the right students for their institution.

■ FOCUSED EXAMPLE 5-3 NADER'S RAID ON THE EDUCATIONAL TESTING SERVICE

Ralph Nader, an aggressive attorney and consumer advocate, has earned a solid reputation over the years for his attacks on giant corporations, including automobile manufacturers and food producers. The Nader approach is to "expose" the public to the misdeeds of the corporations. Early in 1980 Nader released the results of his six-year investigation of the Educational Testing Service—America's largest test producer. At the time the report was released, Nader called a press conference and exclaimed "What this report makes clear is that ETS's claims to measure aptitude and predict success are false and unsubstantiated and can be described as a specialized kind of fraud."

What Nader disputed was the predictive validity of ETS tests such as the SAT and the GRE. The data used by Nader and his team of researchers were no different from that used by the ETS officials. However, the way Nader chose to interpret the data was very different. ETS has consistently reported that the SAT, for example, accounts for a small but significant percentage of the variance in first-year college grade point average. However, Nader did not interpret the results in terms of percentage of variance as typically explained in the field of psychometrics. Instead, he reported the percentage of cases the test successfully predicted according to his own criteria. On the basis of this approach he concluded that the test only predicted successfully in 12% of the cases (still within range of the 16% of the variance estimate frequently given by ETS). However, Nader's calculations were not based on an appropriate statistical model (Kaplan, in press).

On the basis of his interpretation of the data, Nader suggested that there should be more regulation of the testing industry. Referring to ETS, he explained "They have assumed a rare kind of corporate power, the power to change the way people think about their own potential, and through the passive acceptance of their test scores by admissions officers, to decide who will be granted and who will be denied access to education and career opportunities." (From *APA Monitor*, 1980, *11* (2), 1–7.)

It is clear that Nader uncovered an important problem. Yet it is not certain that the Educational Testing Service deserves all of the blame. ETS does put out its own guidelines for the use of the SAT and other tests. These booklets, which are designed to be read by college admissions officers, clearly acknowledge the limitations of the tests. For example, college administrators are told that the test accounts for a small but significant percentage of the variation in college performance and are advised to look at other criteria in addition to test scores. Thus much of the problem lies with the admissions committees and with college administrators who passively accept SAT scores as the ultimate predictor of college performance. Those administrators who know how to interpret the evidence for predictive validity do not make the sort of error Nader warned about.

There are many circumstances in which using a test may not be worth the effort if it only contributes a few percentage points to the understanding of variation in a criterion. Actually low validity coefficients (.30 to .40) sometimes can be very useful even though they may explain only about 10% of the variation in the criterion. For example, Dunnette (1967) demonstrated how a simple questionnaire used for military screening could save taxpayers $4 million every month even though the validity was not remarkably high. (And this analysis was done before the days of high inflation. If it had been done today, the estimated savings would be far more!) There also are some circumstances in which a validity coefficient of .30 or .40 means almost nothing. In Chapter 7 we will show how validity coefficients are translated into specific decision models and how industrial psychologists use information about test validity to save money.

Evaluating validity coefficients. In order to be an informed consumer of information about tests, you should learn to review carefully any information offered by a test developer. Not all validity coefficients of .40 will have the same meaning. Thus there are a few things you should watch out for in evaluating this information. We will cover some of these issues here and go into more depth on this topic in Chapter 7.

In their booklet on *Standards for Educational and Psychological Tests*, the joint committee of the American Psychological Association, The American Educational Research Association, and the National Council on Measurement in Education (1974) list several things to be concerned about when interpreting validity coefficients. Here are some of their recommendations.

Look For Changes in the Cause of Relationships. You should always be aware that the conditions of a validity study are never exactly reproduced. For example, if you are taking the Graduate Record Examination (GRE) in order to gain admission to graduate school, the conditions under which you take the test may not be exactly the same as those in the studies that established the validity of the GRE. Many things may change, including the way grades are assigned in graduate school and the population taking the test.

The logic of criterion validation presumes that the causes of the relationship between the test and the criterion will still be in effect after the test is in use. In most circumstances this will be the case. Yet there may be circumstances in which the relationship changes. For example, a test might be used and shown to be valid for selecting supervisors in industry. However, the validity study may have been done at a time when all of the employees were male. The test may be valid to select supervisors for male employees. Later the company might have hired female employees, and the test may no longer be valid for selecting supervisors, because it may not take into consideration the abilities necessary to supervise a sexually mixed group of employees.

What Does the Criterion Mean? Another element to look out for when evaluating validity coefficients is the meaning of the criterion. Criterion validity studies mean nothing at all unless the criterion is valid. Some test constructors attempt to correlate their tests with other tests with unknown validity. A meaning-less group of items that correlates well with another meaningless group of items is still meaningless.

For applied research the criterion should relate specifically to the use of the test. The intent of the SAT is to predict performance in college, and so the appropriate criterion is grade point average, which is a measure of college performance. If any other inferences are to be made on the basis of the SAT, additional evidence to support these inferences is required. For example, if you want to say that the SAT tells you something about adaptability, evidence must be obtained on the relationship between SAT and some measure of adaptability.

Review of the Subject Population in the Validity Study. Another reason to be cautious of validity coefficients is that the validity study might have been done on a population not representative of that to which inferences will be made. For example, there is some debate about whether the validity coefficients for intelli-gence tests that are based primarily on samples of White students are accurate when they are used to test Black students (Thorndike, 1971; Temp, 1971; Cleary, 1968; Sattler, 1979). We will review this problem in detail in Chapter 20.

When tests are used in industrial settings, validity studies can be seriously jeopardized by attrition. Those who do poorly on the job drop out or get fired and are not available to be studied when it comes time to do the job assessment. If there was a group that did well on the test but failed on the job, it might not be represented and could be systematically eliminated from the study because the workers were already off the job by the time the assessment came around.

Be Sure the Sample Size Was Adequate. Another problem to look out for is a validity coefficient based on a very small number of cases. Sometimes a proper validity study cannot be done because there are too few people to study. A common practice is to do a small validity study with the people you have around. Unfortunately, a small study can be quite misleading. A correlation obtained from a small sample cannot be depended upon as can a correlation obtained from a large sample. This is particularly true for multiple correlation and multiple regression. The smaller the sample, the more likely the correlation will capitalize on chance variation in the data. Thus a validity coefficient based on a small sample may have a greater tendency to be artificially inflated.

A good validity study will present some evidence for *cross validation*. A cross validation study assesses how well the test actually does in forecasting for an independent group of subjects. In other words, the initial validity study assesses the relationship between the test and the criterion whereas a cross validation study checks how well this relationship holds for an independent group of subjects. The larger the sample size in the initial study, the better the likelihood that the relationship will cross validate.[2]

----

[2]Correct cross-validation methodology requires that the raw score weights from the original sample be applied to the validation sample. The use of standard score or standardized weights is not appropriate because the means and standard deviations for the validation sample may be different from those in the original sample (Dorans & Drasgow, 1980).

Never Confuse the Criterion with the Predictor. At the university where we work one department had a certain cutoff score on the Graduate Record Examination that it required students to meet before they could be admitted to the program. Occasionally the department would admit a student to the program but would require the student to meet the minimum GRE score before it would confer a degree. The logic behind this policy represents a clear misunderstanding of the test and its purpose.

In this case the GRE is the predictor and success in graduate school is the criterion. The only reason for using the test in the first place is to help select students who have the highest probability of success in the program. Many students in this program already had succeeded on the criterion (success in the program). Before the university would acknowledge that the students indeed had succeeded, they had to go back and demonstrate that they would have been predicted to do well on the criterion. This reflects a clear confusion between predictor and criterion.

This example also demonstrates that the GRE is not a valid predictor of success among those provisionally accepted into this program. Indeed, most of the students who were given provisional admission because of low GRE scores succeeded by completing the program. The only reason for using the test is to *forecast* who is likely to finish. When the students succeed in completing the requirements for their degrees, there would no longer be any need for the test. This calls into question the rationale for using the test at all.

Check for Restricted Range on Both Predictor and Criterion. A variable has a "restricted range" if all scores for that variable fall very close together. For example, if we look at the grade point averages of graduate students in Ph.D. programs, they tend to fall within a limited range of the scale—usually above 3.5 (on a 4-point scale). The problem this creates is that correlation depends upon variability. If all the people in your class have a grade point average of 4.0, it would not be possible to predict *variability* in graduate school grade point average. Correlation requires that there be variability in both the predictor and the criterion.

One of the major problems with the GRE is that it does not correlate well with graduate school grade point average. Ingram (1980) did a detailed review of studies on the value of the GRE as a predictor of success in graduate school. He found that among all of the published studies, the verbal portion of the GRE significantly predicted graduate school grade point average in only 25% of the studies and the quantitative portion predicted this same criterion in only 12.5% of the studies.

There are at least three explanations for Ingram's findings. First, the GRE may not be a valid test for selecting graduate students. Second, those students who are admitted to graduate school represent such a restricted range of ability that it is not possible to find significant correlations. Those students with low GRE scores are never admitted to graduate school and, therefore, never get into the study. Third, grades in graduate school often represent a restricted range. Once admitted, students in graduate programs are usually given all A's and B's. A grade of C usually is considered a failing grade.

■ **FOCUSED EXAMPLE 5-4   WALTER MISCHEL'S ATTACK ON TESTS**

A scientific field requires sharp criticism in order to clarify issues and to redefine itself. In the late 1960s Stanford psychologist Walter Mischel published a major attack on the use of psychological tests (Mischel, 1968). There has now been enough time for the field to digest the criticism and to answer some of the affront by refining its methods and by striving for a science of assessment that would not lend itself to such criticism.

Among the many ideas discussed in Mischel's book is the value of the notion of a trait. Many psychological tests are designed to determine the extent to which individuals possess traits that characterize them throughout their lives. Are they intelligent? Are they assertive? Are they authoritarian? Mischel pointed out that trait measures do poorly at predicting how someone will behave in a particular situation. A high score on an authoritarianism scale, for example, might not predict whether someone will act in an authoritarian fashion when given the choice.

On the basis of paper-and-pencil tests we often forecast how people will behave in particular situations. However, such tests often are validated against other paper-and-pencil measures rather than against valid measures of the behaviors we are interested in.

Mischel used research on the authoritarianism scale as an illustration of this point. In the early 1950s a group of social scientists from the University of California described an "authoritarian personality" as someone holding an implicit antidemocratic ideology which, among other things, advocated political and economic conservatism, antagonism to out-group members (such as racial minorities), unbounded patriotism, and a reverence for power (Adorno et al., 1950).

The morality of the authoritarian personality is exemplified by some of the statements he or she endorses (see Table 5-1). These items are called the fascistic or F scale.

The authoritarian person is clearly a strong believer in law and order, but this person also advocates values that supposedly are part of one's personal conscience, such as strong belief in the perfection of the "American Way." The overall profile of the authoritarian person is not very flattering, though. It emerges as a rigid, power-oriented, crusty, right-winger.

The social scientists who built the authoritarianism scale did their work well. In hundreds of studies they demonstrated that the F scale was related to a plethora of other interesting personal characteristics including cooperation in psychological experiments, intent to reenlist in the military, IQ, prejudice, and Presidential voting preferences (Titus and Hollander, 1957). Some of these studies actually demonstrated that the correlations between the F scale and the other tests or behaviors were quite high. However, closer inspection of this research suggested that the highest correlations were found in comparisons between the F scale and very similar paper-and-pencil questionnaires. For example, it was shown that the F scale correlated between .74 and .85 with questionnaires that asked about negative characteristics of

Jews such as the likelihood they were "intrusive," "seclusive," or "offensive" (Adorno et al., 1950).

The problem was that it was more difficult to demonstrate that the F scale was predictive of anything except responses to other questionnaires. Studies did not demonstrate that the F scale really predicted how people behaved (Mischel, 1968).

TABLE 5-1   Typical Statements Endorsed by Authoritarians*

Obedience and respect for authority are the most important virtues children should learn.

Young people sometimes get rebellious ideas, but as they grow up they ought to get over them and settle down.

Every person should have complete faith in some supernatural power whose decisions he or she obeys without question.

When a person has a problem or worry, it is best not to think about it but to keep busy with more cheerful things.

Nowadays, when so many different kinds of people move around and mix together so much, a person has to be careful not to catch an infection or disease from them.

Wars and social troubles may someday be ended by an earthquake or flood that will destroy the whole world.

People are divided into two distinct classes: the weak and the strong.

Homosexuals are hardly better than criminals and ought to be severely punished.

The wild sex life of the old Greeks and Romans was tame compared to some of the goings-on in this country, even in places where people might least expect it.

Certain religious sects that refuse to salute the flag should be forced to conform to such patriotic action or else be abolished.

America may not be perfect, but the "American Way" has brought us as close as human beings can get to a perfect society.

*Adapted from Adorno et al., 1950.

A validity study that demonstrates that a test has a high correlation with another test is meaningless unless the other test has some established meaning. Correlations between two tests, both with unknown validity, tell us only that something which does not have any established meaning is related to something else with no established meaning.

Although criterion validity is very common in psychological and educational research, there are some instances in which it simply does not apply. By definition the criterion must be a superior, more accurate measure of the phenomenon if it is to serve as a verifying norm. If a criterion exists, only greater practicality or less expense justifies the use of concurrent measures as proxies or substitutes for the criterion. If the criterion is not a superior measure, then failure of correspondence by any new measure may be a defect in the criterion itself. For example, studies on the validity of measures of general health have been hindered because a clear criterion of health has never been defined (Kaplan et al., 1976). The development of a health index helped define the meaning of the term *health*. Often work on a psychological test involves the simultaneous development of a concept and the instrumentation to measure the concept. This cannot be accomplished by criterion validity studies. Instead we need a more involved approach known as *construct validation*.

D. *Construct validity*

Before 1950 most social scientists considered only criterion and content forms of validity. By the mid-1950s investigators concluded that no clear criteria existed for most of the social and psychological characteristics they wanted to measure. Developing a measure of intelligence, for example, was difficult because no one could say for certain what intelligence was. Criterion validity studies would require that a specific criterion of intelligence be established against which the tests could be compared. The problem was that there was no criterion for intelligence. Intelligence is actually a hypothetical construct we cannot touch or feel.

In contemporary psychology we often want to measure intelligence, love, curiosity, or mental health. All these are constructs that are not clearly defined, and there is no established criterion against which we can compare the accuracy of our test. These are the truly challenging problems in measurement.

Construct validity is established through a series of activities in which a researcher simultaneously defines some construct and develops the instrumentation to measure it. This process is required when "no criterion or universe of content is accepted as entirely adequate to define the quality to be measured" (Cronbach & Meehl, 1955, page 282). Construct validation involves assembling evidence about what a test really means. This is done by showing the relationship between a test and other tests and measures. Each time a relationship is demonstrated, one additional bit of meaning can be attached to the test. Over a series of studies, the meaning of the test gradually begins to take shape. Construct validation is an ongoing process, similar to amassing support for a complex scientific theory. No single set of observations provides crucial or critical evidence. Yet over time many observations gradually clarify what the test means.

■ FOCUSED EXAMPLE 5-5   THE MEANING OF LOVE

An interesting example of construct validation comes from the work of Zick Rubin (1970, 1973), who noted that love has been one of the most discussed issues of all time. Throughout history, men and women have written and sung about love more than any other topic. The index to *Bartlett's Familiar Quotations* shows that references to love are second only to citations to "man" (with "love" cited 769 times and "man" cited 843 times). All of this preoccupation with love, however, has not led to a better understanding of the true meaning of "love." Perhaps it is something we can feel but not necessarily understand well enough to describe in a definite way.

A few years ago there was a famous trial in Los Angeles in which singer

Mischelle Triola Marvin sued actor Lee Marvin for half of his earnings while the couple lived together. A big issue in the trial was the couple's unmarried status during the period in which the earnings occurred. During the trial, Lee's attorney questioned the actor about the extent to which he loved Mischelle while they lived together. Unfortunately, there is no scale on which the actor could rate his love. If he had been asked his height, he could have used the scale of inches. But love? How could he put that into a number? However, the actor did resort to a gas-tank analogy. He said his love for the singer was like when you are driving your car and you look over at your gas gauge and find it "about half full." That is about how much he loved Mischelle— about a half tank. If there had been a measure of love, he would not have needed to use such a crude analogy (Rubin, 1979).

The first step in the development of Rubin's love scale was to create a list of items that represented all the different things people might call love. This was not an easy task, because all of us have different romantic ideals. In order to create a measure of love, Rubin had to condense conventional wisdom about loving and liking into sets of statements to which people could respond on a scale. The scale would present statements, and subjects could respond by indicating the extent to which they agreed or disagreed on a 5-point scale (where 1 is for strong disagreement and 5 is for strong agreement).

Collecting the statements or any other original set of items for construct validation is not easy, because you never know which items eventually will be relevant to the construct you are attempting to measure. Building the love scale was particularly tough in this regard. In order to prepare his measure, Rubin read extensively about love.

Elizabeth Barrett Browning wrote "How do I love thee? Let me count the ways." Indeed, after reading the many diverse views of love, Rubin hardly knew where to begin counting. Because this was a study in construct validity, however, it was important that Rubin considered counting. Construct validity requires that there be content validity. Content validity in turn requires that the domain of inference (in this case love) be fully represented by the items. All of the ways that love is defined by different people must be included in this collection.

Rubin began his study by condensing conventional wisdom about loving and liking into sets of statements that people could respond to on a scale ranging from disagreement to agreement. Some of the items were intended to measure love, while others were supposed to tap liking. Next he gave the pool of items to 198 students from the University of Michigan. Each of the items had a blank in which a name could be filled in. The students responded to the questions twice, one time filling in the name of their lover and another time filling in the name of a friend. Then the items were subjected to factor analysis. This is a method for reducing a large number of items or variables into smaller and more manageable composites of items called factors (see Chapter 4).

In the love scale three factors were obtained: (1) attachment (for example, "If I were lonely, my first thoughts would be to seek _____ out"), (2) caring ("If _____ were feeling bad, my first duty would be to cheer him/her up"), and (3) intimacy ("I feel that I can confide in _____ about virtually everything"). The items on the liking scale focused on favorable aspects of the other person along such dimensions as adjustment, maturity, good judgment, and intelligence.

The data from these scales were subjected to several statistical procedures that helped to discriminate between responses of lovers and friends and eventually led to the establishment of two measures (a love scale and a liking scale). Now that measures of liking and loving were available, it was necessary to determine whether they were really measuring what they were supposed to. One study, using dating couples, suggested that loving and liking were not necessarily related. There was a modest relationship between scores on the two scales, which was weaker for women than for men. This suggested, especially for women, that it is possible to love someone whom you may not particularly like.

There are several indications that the love scale really was measuring "love." For example, men and women scored higher on the love scale when they filled in the names of their lovers than when they filled in the name of a same-sex friend. There also was a substantial correlation between love scale scores and estimates of the likelihood of marriage. The greater the love score, the more probable marriage was considered to be.

Finally, some of the dating couples were separated into strong love (high love scores) or weak love (low love scores) groups. From behind a one-way mirror the researchers noted how much eye contact the lovers had with one another. Strong lovers, it was observed, spent more time simply gazing into one another's eyes than did weak lovers. When paired with a strong opposite-sex lover from another couple, mutual eye contact was no greater than it was for people who were weak lovers.

In summary, Rubin began his study of love with neither a clear definition of love nor a method of measuring it. Through a series of structured exercises he gradually came to have a better grasp of the construct. For example, he discovered that lovers mark some items differently than couples who are just friends. He also discovered that "love" may have at least three independent components. Once the basic scale was developed, each new application defined a new meaning. For instance, one study showed that the scale predicts how much time lovers will spend gazing into each other's eyes. Thus in future applications of the love scale we would expect couples who score as strong lovers (for one another) to spend more time in mutual gaze.

Several years ago Campbell and Fiske (1959) introduced an important set of logical considerations for developing tests with construct validity. They distinguished between two types of evidence that are essential for a meaningful test. These forms of evidence are convergent and discriminant. In order to argue that a test has meaning, a test constructor is advised to be armed with as much evidence as possible for these two types of validity. Below we will present the basic logic of the Campbell and Fiske approach. For those who desire a more detailed presentation, the 1959 reference is recommended.

Convergent evidence. *Convergent evidence* for validity is obtained when a measure correlates well with other tests that are believed to measure the same construct. This sort of evidence shows that measures of the same construct "converge" or narrow in on the same thing. In many ways convergent evidence for construct validity is like criterion validity. In each case scores on the test are related to scores on some other measure. In the case of convergent evidence for construct validity, however, there is no criterion to define what you are attempting to measure. Criterion validity is fine for situations in which you are attempting to predict performance on a particular variable—such as success in graduate school. Here the task is well defined, and all you need to do is to find the items that are good predictors of this graduate school criterion. In construct validity there is no well-defined criterion, and the meaning of the test comes to be defined by the variables it can be shown to be associated with.

An example of the need to obtain construct validation evidence comes from studies by Kaplan, Bush, and Berry (1976), who attempted to define and measure the construct *health*. Health is a complex concept involving many facets. Because of the complexity of the health concept, no single measure can serve as the criterion against which a measure of health can be assessed. This situation requires studies in construct validation. Some of the construct validation studies were used to demonstrate the convergent validity of the measure of health the authors call a *health index*.

Convergent evidence is obtained in one of two ways. The first is by showing that a test measures the same things as other tests used for the same purpose. The second is by demonstrating specific relationships that could be expected if the test is really doing its job. Studies on the health index included both types of evidence. In demonstrating the meaning of the health index the authors continually asked themselves "If we were really measuring health, what relationships would we expect to observe between the health index and other measures?" The simplest relationship is between health index scores and the way people rate their own health status. This relationship was strong and clearly showed that the index captured some of the same information individuals used to evaluate their own health. However, a good measure must go beyond this simple bit of validity evidence because self-ratings are unreliable. If they were not, we would use self-perceived health status as the index of health because it is easier than using the health index.

However, in construct validity no single variable can serve as the criterion. Thus other studies were used to show a variety of other relationships. For example, it was shown that people who scored as less healthy on the health index also tended to report more symptoms and chronic medical conditions. It also was hypothesized that health status would be related to age, and it was observed that these two variables were indeed systematically related. Older persons in the sample tended to be lower in health status.

The researchers also evaluated specific hypotheses that were advanced on the basis of some theoretical notion about the construct. In the health index studies the authors reasoned "If the index really measures health, then we would expect that people who score low on the measure should visit doctors more often." A study confirmed that they do indeed, and this provided evidence for one more inference. Also, certain groups (such as disabled persons) should have lower average scores on the index than other groups (such as nondisabled persons). Again, a study confirmed this hypothesis (Kaplan, Bush, & Berry, 1976). Thus in a series of studies the number of meanings that could be given to the health index was gradually expanded. Yet convergent validity does not comprise all of the evidence that is necessary to argue for the meaning or construct validity of a psychological test or measure. We also must have discriminant evidence for construct validity.

Discriminant evidence.   Science can be very conservative. It confronts scientists with difficult questions such as "Why should we believe your theory if we already have a theory that seems to say about the same thing?" An eager scientist may answer this question by arguing that his or her theory is distinctive and better. In testing we have a similar dilemma. Why should we create a new test if there is already one available to do the job? Thus one type of evidence a person needs in test validation is proof that the test measures something unique. For example, if a health index measures the same thing as self-rated health, number of symptoms, and number of chronic medical conditions, why do we need it in addition to all these other measures? The answer is that the measure taps something other than the tests used in the convergent validity studies. This demonstration of uniqueness is called *discriminant evidence*.

By providing evidence that a test measures something different from other tests we also provide evidence that we are measuring some unique construct. Calling an old construct by a new name always should be avoided. Discriminant evidence indicates that the measure does not represent a construct other than the one for which it is devised.

As this discussion implies, construct validity actually subsumes all the activities used in other types of validation studies. In construct validation, for example, content validation is an essential step. Furthermore, convergent and discriminant studies actually correlate the tests with many different criteria. Thus there is a similarity between construct and criterion validity. Some psychologists argue that construct validity actually is the only major category of validity that need concern us and that others might be thought of as subcategories of construct validity (Messick, 1975, 1980; Tenopyr, 1977). According to testing pioneer Lee Cronbach, it may not be appropriate to continue to divide validity into three parts. Cronbach maintains, "All validation is one, and in a sense all is construct validation" (Cronbach, 1980, page 99).

The procedures for establishing the validity of a criterion-referenced test are quite similar to those for studying the validity of any other test. As you may recall from Chapter 2, criterion-referenced tests have items designed to match certain specific instructional objectives. For example, if the objective for some educational program is for children to be able to list 75% of the countries in Europe, the criterion-referenced test could ask that the countries be listed. If the children listed 75% of the countries, they would pass the test. They would be evaluated against this specific criterion rather than on the basis of how they perform relative to other students. Validity studies for the criterion-referenced tests would compare scores on the test to scores on other measures that are believed to be related to the test. Some specific procedures for evaluating the validity of a criterion-referenced test have been discussed by some authors in more technical articles (see Cronbach, 1971; Hambleton, 1980; Millman, 1974).

III. SUMMARY

Validity is a basic idea in measurement and in the science of psychology. Although we have emphasized the validity of psychological tests, the ideas we discussed apply equally to all measures. To make any inference a good scientist must have substantiating data.

Once a test is "validated" many psychologists mistakenly think it can be used for all purposes. The mistake here is that tests are used to support many different inferences. Actually, there should be as many validity studies as there are inferences about the scores (Cronbach, 1971). Anytime we claim a test score means something different, we need a new validity study. Validity really refers to the things that are said on the basis of the test scores and not to the tests themselves (Tenopyr, 1977).

This suggests that acquiring evidence about the meaning of tests should be an ongoing process. The more a test or a measure is used, the more we learn about what it means. According to two well-known applied psychologists, "Test users should never feel that they know enough about the behavioral meaning of their selection methods" (Dunnette & Borman, 1979, page 484).

6

Building a Test

Learning objectives

When you have completed this chapter, you should be able to do the following:

1. Describe two types of item formats commonly used in objective classroom examinations.
2. Know whether or not you should guess on a multiple-choice examination when you are not sure of the correct answer.
3. Explain the types of measurement problems the Likert format is used for.
4. Discuss what sorts of problems you might encounter if you used a 10-point category scale to rate the abilities of a group of similar individuals.
5. Set the level of item difficulty needed for a test that discriminates well between individuals.
6. Describe the process of assessing item discriminability.
7. Define an item characteristic curve and tell how it is used.
8. Draw an item characteristic curve for an item that discriminates well at high levels of performance but not at low levels.
9. Explain how item characteristic curves can be used to find items that are unfair to students who "overstudied."
10. Discuss some of the limitations of item analysis for tests designed to find specific learning problems.

At this point in your studies you are probably an experienced test taker. Over the years you have had experience taking numerous tests. Most of these have been classroom exercises. However, you also have been exposed to standardized tests such as the SAT or the IOWA Achievement Test.

As an experienced test taker, you also may have become an experienced test critic. After taking a test most students are willing to render an opinion: to judge whether it was a fair test or a good test. When you feel that the test was bad, you might ask yourself "How could the test have been better?" In this chapter we will give some of the basics for creating test items. In the next chapter we will discuss how to choose and use published tests.

I. ITEM WRITING

When a professor announces that there will be a test, one of the first questions is "What kind of test?" Will it be a true-false test, a multiple-choice test, an essay test, or a test in which one must fill in the blanks? Not all tests are in the same format. As you will learn in Part Two of this book, personality and intelligence tests require all sorts of different responses. After defining the objectives and purpose of the test, the next question faced by the test constructor is the type of response he or she wants to require. In part this choice will be determined by the purpose of the test. For example, if it is a test that requires right or wrong answers, the task will usually be true-false, multiple choice, matching, or essay.

A. *Item formats*

The type of test you probably have experienced most is one in which you are given credit for a specific response. In classroom situations credit is often given for selection of the "correct" alternative for each test item and only one alternative is scored as correct. True-false and multiple-choice examinations use this system. Similar formats are used for many other purposes, such as evaluating attitudes, determining knowledge about traffic laws, or deciding whether someone has characteristics associated with a particular health condition. The simplest test of this type uses a dichotomous format.

The dichotomous format.   The dichotomous format offers two alternatives for each item. Usually a point is given for selection of only one of the alternatives. The most common example of this format is the true-false examination. This test presents students with a series of statements. The student's task is to determine which statements are true and which are false. There are many virtues of the true-false test including ease of construction and ease of scoring, but the method has also become popular because a teacher can easily construct a test by copying lines out of a textbook. The lines that are copied verbatim are designated as "true." Other statements are doctored, so they are no longer true.

The advantages of true-false items include their obvious simplicity, ease of administration, and quick scoring. However, there also are disadvantages. For example, true-false items encourage students to memorize material, and it is often possible for students to perform well on a test covering material they do not really understand. Another problem is that the probability of getting any item correct by chance alone is 50%. Thus, in order for a true-false test to be reliable, it requires many items.

The dichotomous format is not unique to true-false or educational tests. Many personality tests require responses in a dichotomous format. This may be true-false, or it may be in some other two-choice format such as yes-no. Personality test constructors often prefer this type of format because it requires absolute judgment. For example, in response to an item such as "I often worry about my sexual performance," persons are not allowed to be ambivalent—they must respond true or false. Dichotomous items have many advantages for personality tests with many subscales. One is that it makes the scoring of the subscales easy. All that is necessary is to count the number of items a person endorses from each subscale.

Although the true-false format is popular in educational tests, it is not used as frequently as the multiple-choice test, which represents the polychotomous format.

The polychotomous format.   The polychotomous format is similar to the dichotomous format except that each item has more than two alternatives. Typically a point is given for the selection of one of the alternatives, and no point is given for selecting any other choice. The multiple-choice examination is the polychotomous format you have encountered most often because it is a popular method of measuring academic performance in large classes. Multiple-choice tests are easy to score, and the probability of obtaining a correct response by chance is lower than it is for true-false items. A major advantage of this format is that it takes very little time for test takers to respond to a particular item because they do not have to write. Thus the test can cover a large amount of information in a relatively short period of time.

When taking a multiple-choice examination your task is to determine which of several alternatives is "correct." All choices that are not correct are called *distractors*. As we will demonstrate in the section on item analysis, the choice of distractors is very important.

Because most students are familiar with multiple-choice tests and related formats such as matching, there is no need to elaborate on their description. However, it is worthwhile to consider some of the issues in the construction and scoring of multiple-choice tests. One question is "How many distractors should a test have?"

Psychometric theory suggests that the items will be more reliable if there are a large number of distractors. In other words, adding more distractors should increase the reliability of the items. This problem has been studied by a number of psychometricians, and there is general agreement about the results of the calculations. However, in practice adding distractors may not actually increase the reliability because it is difficult to find *good* ones. The reliability of an item is not enhanced by distractors that are never selected. Studies have shown that it actually is rare to find items for which more than three or four distractors operate efficiently. Ineffective distractors actually may hurt the reliability of the test because they are time consuming to read and can limit the number of items that can be included in a test. After a careful review of the distractor problem, Wesman (1971) concluded that item writers should try to find three or four good distractors for each item. They are an essential ingredient of good items.

Another issue is the scoring of multiple-choice examinations. Suppose you bring your roommate to your sociology test and he or she fills out an answer sheet without reading the items. Will your roommate get any items correct? The answer is yes—by chance alone. If each item has four choices, the test taker would be expected to get 25% correct. If the items had three choices, a 33.33% correct rate would be expected. Because some answers are "correct" simply by the luck of guessing, a correction for guessing is sometimes used. The formula to correct for guessing is

$$\text{Correction} = R - \frac{W}{n-1}$$

Where R = the number of right responses
  W = the number of wrong responses
  n = the number of choices for each item

Omitted responses are not included—they provide neither credit nor penalty. For example, suppose that your roommate randomly filled out the answer sheet to your sociology test. The test had 100 items, each with four choices. By chance his or her expected score would be 25 correct. Let's assume that he or she got exactly that (if the test was filled out randomly, we might not get exactly 25, which is the average random score). The expected score corrected for guessing would be

$$R - \frac{W}{n-1} = 25 - \frac{75}{4-1} = 25 - \frac{75}{3} = 25 - 25 = 0$$

In other words, when the correction for guessing is applied, the expected score is 0.

A question frequently asked by students is "Should I guess on multiple-choice items when I don't know the answer?" The answer depends on how the test will be scored. If a correction for guessing is not used, the best advice is "guess away." By guessing you have a chance of getting the item correct. You do not have this chance if you do not attempt it. However, if a correction for guessing is used, random guessing will do you no good. Some speeded tests are scored so that the correction for the guessing formula includes only the items that were attempted. That is, those which were not attempted are not counted either right or wrong. In this case random guessing and leaving the items blank each has the same expected effect.

How about cases when you don't know the right answer but are able to eliminate one or two of the alternatives? How many times have you had it down to two alternatives, but couldn't figure out which of the two was correct? In this case it is advisable to guess. The correction formula assumes that you are equally likely to respond to each of the four categories. For a four-choice item it would estimate your chance of getting the item correct by chance alone to be one in four. However, if you can eliminate two alternatives, the chances are actually one in two. This gives you a slight advantage over the correction formula.

True-false and multiple-choice formats are common to educational and achievement tests in which each item has one correct and one or more incorrect alternatives. Similar formats are found on personality tests in which a yes or a no response might indicate that a person either has or does not have a particular trait. For example, frequently used personality inventories such as the Minnesota Multiphasic Personality Inventory (MMPI) or the California Psychological Inventory (CPI) present subjects with a long list of statements to which one responds either yes or no (see Chapter 15).

Other personality and attitude measures do not deem any response "right." Rather, they attempt to quantify characteristics of the response. These formats include the Likert format, the category scale, and the Q-sort.

The Likert format.   One popular format for attitude and personality scales requires that a respondent indicate the degree of agreement with a particular attitudinal question. This technique is called the *Likert format* because it was used as part of Likert's (1932) method of attitude scale construction. A scale using the Likert format would consist of a series of items, such as "I am afraid of heights." Instead of giving a yes or no reply, five alternatives are offered: strongly disagree, disagree, neutral, agree, and strongly agree. This format is very popular in attitude measurement. For example, it is possible to determine the extent to which people endorse statements such as "The government should not regulate private business."

Responses in Likert format can be subjected to factor analysis. This makes it possible to find groups of items that go together. A similar technique that uses a greater number of choices is the category scale.

The category format.   Ten-point rating scales have become so commonplace that a Hollywood movie was named "10." When asked for an evaluation of many things, people are requested to rate them on a 10-point scale. The scale need not have exactly 10 points—it can have either more or fewer categories. Rating scales of this sort are called *category scales*.

Although the 10-point scale is very common to psychological research and to everyday conversation, there is still controversy about when and how it should be used. We recently encountered a college basketball coach who rates the quality of upcoming high school players on a 10-point rating scale. It is assumed that this rating provides a reliable estimate of the players' abilities. However, experiments have shown that responses to items on 10-point scales are affected by the groupings of the items being rated. For example, if coaches are asked to rate the abilities of a group of 20 very talented players, they may tend to make fine distinctions among them and use many of the categories on the 10-point scale. A particular player who is rated as a 6 when he is on a team with many outstanding players might be rated as a 9 if he were judged along with a group of poorly coordinated players (Parducci, 1968, 1982). When given a group of objects to rate, subjects have a tendency to spread their responses evenly across the 10 categories (Stevens, 1966).

Recent experiments have shown that this problem can be avoided if the endpoints of the scale are very clearly defined and the subjects are frequently reminded of the definitions of the endpoints. For example, instead of asking coaches to rate the ability of basketball players on a 10-point scale, they would be shown films of what was meant by 10 and other films of what was meant by 1. Under these circumstances, the subjects are less likely to offer a response that is affected by other stimuli in the group (Kaplan & Ernst, 1980).

People often ask "Why use a 10-point scale instead of a 13-point scale or a 43-point scale?" As it turns out, this has been a matter of considerable study. Some have argued that the optimal number of points is around 7 (Symonds, 1924), whereas others have suggested that the optimal number of categories should be three times this number (Champney & Marshall, 1939). As is often the case, the number of categories required depends on the fineness of the discrimination subjects are willing to make. If the subjects are unconcerned about something, they will not make fine discriminations, and a scale with just a few categories will do about as well as a scale that has many. However, when people are very involved with some issue, they will tend to use a greater number of categories. For most rating tasks, however, a 10-point scale seems to provide enough discrimination. Anderson (1976) has found that a 10-point scale provides substantial discrimination between objects for a wide variety of stimuli.

Checklists and Q-sorts.   One format common in personality measurement is the adjective checklist (Gough, 1960). With this method a subject is given a long list of adjectives and asked to indicate whether each one is characteristic of himself or herself. Adjective checklists can be used for describing either oneself or someone else. For example, in one study at the University of California at Berkeley raters checked the traits they thought were characteristic of a group of 40 graduate students. Half these students had been designated by their instructors as exceptional in originality, and the other half had been characterized as low in originality. The results demonstrated that the adjectives

■ FOCUSED EXAMPLE 6-1 THE EFFECT OF CONTEXT ON VALUE RATINGS

The numbers we assign when using rating scales are sometimes influenced by the context or the background against which objects are rated. In one experiment college students were asked to rate how immoral they believed certain acts to be. The students were divided into two groups. One group rated the items in the top list (see below) and the other group rated the items in the bottom list. There were 12 items in each list, but the top list typically represented "mild" actions, and the bottom list typically represented more severe actions. The figures to the right represent average ratings by a large number of college students. If you study the two lists, you will discover that six items are included on both lists. However, these items are judged more leniently when they are included with items on the bottom list. This experiment shows that the numbers we assign when using rating scales are affected by context (Parducci, 1968).

Registering in a hotel under a false name.	1.68
Bawling out servants publicly.*	2.64
Contributing money to a cause in which you do not believe in order to escape criticism.	3.03
Keeping a dime you find in a telephone booth.	1.08
Publishing under your own name an investigation originated and carried out without remuneration by a graduate student working under you.*	3.95
Failing to pay your bus fare when the conductor overlooks you.	2.36
Playing poker on Sunday.	1.17
Failing to put back in the water lobsters that are shorter than the legal limit.*	2.22
Cheating at solitaire.	1.53
Fishing without a license.	2.27
Habitually borrowing small sums of money from friends and failing to return them.*	2.93
Stealing towels from a hotel.	2.58
Stealing a loaf of bread from a store when you are starving.	1.79
Poisoning a neighbor's dog whose barking bothers you.*	4.19
Lying about your whereabouts to protect a friend's reputation.	1.60
Wearing shorts on the street where it is illegal.	1.59
Pocketing the tip which the previous customer left for the waitress.*	3.32
Getting your own way by playing on people's sympathies.	2.90
Using guns on striking workers.	3.82
Bawling out servants publicly.*	2.39
Stealing ten dollars from an impecunious acquaintance.	3.79
Selling to a hospital milk from diseased cattle.	4.51
Publishing under your own name an investigation originated and carried out without remuneration by a graduate student working under you.*	3.47
Spreading rumors that an acquaintance is a sexual pervert.	3.91
Having a sane person committed to a mental hospital in order to get rid of him.	4.46
Failing to put back in the water lobsters that are shorter than the legal limit.*	1.82

Having sexual relations with a sibling (brother or sister).	3.72
Putting your deformed child in the circus.	3.81
Habitually borrowing small sums of money from friends and failing to return them.*	2.37
Having incestuous relations with your parent.	3.88
Murdering your mother without justification or provocation.	4.79
Poisoning a neighbor's dog whose barking bothers you.*	3.65
Testifying falsely against someone for pay.	4.07
Teaching adolescents to become dope addicts.	4.51
Pocketing the tip which the previous customer left for the waitress.*	2.46
Sending another person to take a civil service exam for you.	3.39

(From "The Relativism of Absolute Judgments," by A. Parducci. In *Scientific American*, 1968, *219* (6), 84–90. Reprinted by permission.)

Items followed by an * appear on both lists.

chosen to describe members of these two groups differed. The highly original students were characterized most often by the traits "adventurous," "alert," "curious," "quiet," "imaginative," and "fair-minded." In contrast, the low originality students were seen as "confused," "conventional," "defensive," "polished," "prejudiced," and "suggestible."

The adjective checklist requires subjects to endorse or not endorse self-descriptive adjectives, and it only allows these two choices. A similar technique known as the Q-sort increases the number of categories. The Q-sort can be used to describe oneself or to provide ratings of others (Stephenson, 1953). With this technique a subject is given statements and asked to sort them into nine piles. For example, Block (1961) gave observers 100 statements about personal characteristics. The statements were sorted into piles indicating the degree to which they appeared to be accurate about some particular person. If you were using this method you might be asked to rate your roommate. You would be given a set of 100 cards. Each card would have a statement on it, such as the following:

Has a wide range of interests.
Is productive; gets things done.
Is self-dramatizing; is histrionic.
Is overreactive to minor frustrations; is irritable.
Seeks reassurance from others.
Appears to have a high degree of intellectual capacity.
Is basically anxious.

If a statement really hit home, you would place it in Pile 9. Those that were not at all descriptive would be placed in Pile 1. Most of the cards are usually placed in

Piles 4, 5, and 6. The frequency of items placed in each of the categories usually looks like a bell-shaped curve (see Figure 6-1). The items that end up in the extreme categories usually say something interesting about the person.

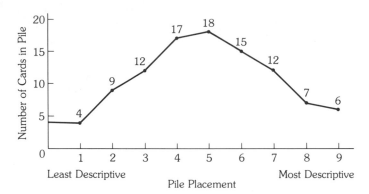

Figure 6-1. The California Q-sort. The number of items distributed in the nine piles of the California Q-sort approaches a normal distribution.

B. *Other possibilities*

The formats for items we have discussed are only a few of the many possibilities. If you are interested in learning more about item writing and item formats, you might check some classic references (Guilford, 1954; Edwards, 1957; Torgerson, 1958).

Unfortunately, there is no simple formula for item writing. Several people have studied the issue carefully and have contributed many useful suggestions (Ebel, 1972; Stanley & Hopkins, 1972; Sax, 1980; Wesman, 1971). If you need to write test items, you should consult these sources. However, writing good items remains an art rather than a science. There is no substitute for using precise language, knowing the subject matter, being familiar with the level of examinees, and using your imagination (Wesman, 1971). Once the items are written and they have been administered, there are item analysis techniques that can be used to evaluate them.

II. ITEM ANALYSIS

A good test has good items. But what are good items? How many times have you been in a class in which students launched a full-scale battle over particular items in a multiple-choice test? Good tests with good items are hard to create. Doing them well requires careful attention to the principles of test construction. *Item analysis* is a general term for a set of methods used to evaluate test items. It is one of the most important aspects of test construction. Although there are many techniques of item analysis, the basic methods involve assessment of item difficulty and item discriminability.

A. *Item difficulty*

For a test measuring achievement or ability, item difficulty is defined by the number of people who get a particular item correct. For example, if 84% of the people taking a particular test get Item 24 correct, the difficulty level for that item is .84. Some people have suggested that these proportions are not really indicators of item "difficulty" but rather that they measure item "easyness." The higher the proportion of people getting the item correct, the easier the item (Allen & Yen, 1979).

How hard should items be in a good test? This depends on the uses of the test and the types of items. The first thing a test constructor needs to determine is the probability that an item can be answered correctly by chance alone. A true-false item could be answered correctly half of the time if people just guessed randomly. Thus a true-false item with a difficulty level of .50 would not be a good item. A multiple-choice item with four alternatives could be answered correctly 25% of the time. Therefore, we would require item difficulty greater than 25% for an item to be reasonable in this context. Other obvious limits are the extremes of the scale. An item that is answered correctly by 100% of the respondents is of little value in a test because it does not discriminate between individuals.

The optimum difficulty level for items is usually about halfway between 100% of the respondents getting the item correct and the level of success expected by chance alone. Thus the optimum difficulty level for a four-choice multiple-choice item is about .625. To arrive at this value we take the 100% success level (1.00) and subtract from it the chance performance level (.25). Then we divide by 2 to find the halfway point and add this value to the expected chance level. The steps are outlined below.

Step 1. Find the half of the difference between 100% success and chance performance.

$$\frac{1.00-.25}{2}=\frac{.75}{2}=.375$$

Step 2. Add this value to the probability of performing correctly by chance.

chance performance
↓
$$.375+.25=.625$$
↑   ↑
midway point   optimum item difficulty

In most tests we do not want to have all of the items of equal difficulty. Instead, it is preferable to have items that represent a variety of difficulty levels.

This is important because a good test will discriminate at a variety of different levels. For example, if a professor wants to determine how much students in the class have studied, he or she would like to discriminate between students who have not studied at all and those who have studied just a little. Furthermore, the professor might want to discriminate between students who have studied just a little and those who have studied a fair amount. Finally, he or she might want to distinguish those students who have studied more than average from those who have worked and studied exceptionally hard. In other words, the professor needs to make a variety of different discriminations. In order to accomplish this, items at many different levels of difficulty are required.

For most tests, items in the difficulty range of .30 to .70 tend to maximize the information about the differences between individuals. However, some tests require a concentration of more difficult items. For example, if a test is to be used to select medical students and only a small number of qualified applicants can be accepted, a test with more difficult items will make finer discriminations. Conversely, a test used to select students for educable mentally retarded classes should have a greater concentration of easier items in order to make fine discriminations between individuals who ordinarily do not perform well on tests (Allen & Yen, 1979). In constructing a good test you also must give some consideration to human factors. For example, items answered correctly by all students will have poor psychometric qualities, but they may help the morale of the students who take the test. A few easier items may help keep test anxiety in check, which in turn adds to the reliability of the test.

Item difficulty is only one way test items can be evaluated. Another way is to examine the relationship between performance on particular items and performance on the whole test. This is known as discriminability.

B. *Discriminability*

In the last section we discussed analysis of item difficulty. These procedures are used to determine the proportion of people who succeed on a particular item. Another way to examine the value of items is to ask "Who gets this item correct?" Assessment of item discriminability is used to determine whether the people who have done well on particular items have done well on the whole test. There are a variety of ways to evaluate the discriminability of test items.

The extreme group method.   The easiest way is to compare people who have done very well with others who have done very poorly on a test. For example, you might find the students with test scores in the top 25% and those in the bottom 25% of the class. Then you can find the proportion of people in the higher group and the proportion of people in the lower group who got each item correct. The difference between these proportions is the discrimination index. Technical Box 6-1 demonstrates this method.

Technical Box 6-1   Finding the Item Discrimination Index by Using the Extreme Group Method

Step 1. Identify a group of students which has done well on the test—for example, those in the 67th percentile and above. Also identify a group which has done poorly—for example, those in the 33rd percentile and below.

Step 2. Find the proportion of students in the high group and the proportion of students in the low group that got each item correct.

Step 3. For each item subtract the proportion of correct responses for the low group from the proportion of correct responses for the high group. This gives the item discrimination index (d_i).

Example:

Item number	Proportion correct for students in the top third of class (P_t)	Proportion correct for students in the bottom third of class (P_b)	Discriminability index ($d_i = P_t - P_b$)
1	.89	.34	.55
2	.76	.36	.40
3	.97	.45	.52
4	.98	.95	.03
5	.56	.74	−.18

In this example Items 1, 2, and 3 appear to discriminate reasonably well. Item 4 does not discriminate well because it is too easy. On this item the level of success is high for both groups. Item 5 appears to be a bad item because it is a "negative discriminator." This sometimes happens on multiple-choice examinations when overprepared students find some reason to disqualify the response keyed as "correct."

The point-biserial method.   Another way to examine the discriminability of items is to find the correlation between performance on the item and performance on the total test. You might remember from Chapter 3 that the correlation between a dichotomous (two-category) variable and a continuous variable is called a *point-biserial correlation*. The point-biserial correlation between an item and a total test score is

$$r_{pbis} = \left[\frac{\bar{Y}_1 - \bar{Y}}{S_y}\right] \cdot \sqrt{\frac{P_x}{(1-P_x)}}$$

Where r_{pbis} = the point-biserial correlation or index of discriminability

$\bar{Y}_1$ = the mean score on the test for those who got Item 1 correct

$\bar{Y}$=the mean score on the test for all persons

S_y=the standard deviation of the exam scores for all persons

P_x=the proportion of persons getting the item correct (from Allen & Yen, 1979)

For example, suppose that 58% of the students in a psychology class gave the correct response to Item 15 on their midterm exam. The mean score on the whole test for these students who got Item 15 correct was 57.6, and the mean score for the entire class was 54.3. The standard deviation on the test was 9.7. In order to calculate the discriminability of Item 15 by the point-biserial method you would enter this information into the formula:

$$\frac{57.6-54.3}{9.7} \cdot \sqrt{\frac{.58}{.42}} = .34 \cdot \sqrt{1.38} = (.34)(1.17) = .40$$

In other words, the correlation between succeeding on item 15 and total test performance is .40.

On short tests there is a problem with using the point-biserial correlation because performance on the item contributes to the total test score. For example, if a test is 6 items long, there is bound to be a positive correlation between getting a particular item correct and the total test score because one sixth of the total score is performance on that item.

In order to compensate for this problem it is sometimes advisable to exclude the item from the total test score. For the six-item test, we might look at the point-biserial correlation between passing Item 1 and the test score derived from Items 2 through 6. In other words, the item we are evaluating (Item 1) is excluded from the total test score.

The point-biserial correlation (r_{pbis}) for an item with total test score is evaluated in very much the same way as the extreme group discriminability index. If this value is ever negative or of low magnitude, the item should be eliminated from the test. The closer the value of the index is to 1.0, the better the item. It should be noted that very easy items, such as those answered correctly 90% or more, usually will not show as good items on the discriminability index. If 90% get an item correct, there is too little variability in performance for a substantial correlation with the total test score.

C.   *Pictures of item characteristics*

A valuable way to learn about items is to draw pictures of their characteristics. This can be accomplished with the *item characteristic curve*. A graph can be prepared for particular items in which the total test score is plotted on the x or horizontal axis and the proportion of examinees passing the items is plotted on the vertical or y axis. The total test score is used as an estimate of the amount of the "trait" possessed by individuals. Because we can never measure traits directly, the total test score is the best approximation we have, Thus the relationship between performance on the item and performance on the test gives some information about how well the item is tapping the information we are interested in.

Drawing the item characteristic curve.   In order to draw the item characteristic curve, you need to define discrete categories of test performance. If the test has been given to large numbers of persons, you can have a category for each test score (65, 66, 67, and so on). However, if the test is given to a smaller group of testees, you might use a smaller number of wide categories (such as 65 to 67). Once you have arrived at these categories, you will need to determine what proportion of the people within each category got each item correct. For example, if you are looking at Item 34, you must determine what proportion of the people with a total test score of 65 got the item correct, what proportion of the people with a total test score of 66 got it correct, and so on.

Once this series of breakdowns has been obtained, you can begin to plot the proportions of correct responses to an item by the total test scores. Examples of what you will get are shown in Figures 6-2 to 6-6.

Figure 6-2 shows the item characteristic curve for a good test item. The gradual positive slope of the line demonstrates that the proportion of people passing the item gradually increases as test scores increase. This means that the item successfully discriminates at all levels of test performance. The curve shown in Figure 6-3 illustrates an item that discriminates very well between people at

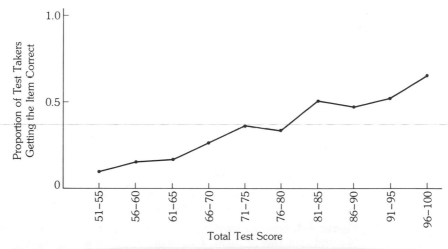

Figure 6-2. Item characteristic curve for a "good" test item. The proportion of test takers getting the item correct increases as a function of total test score.

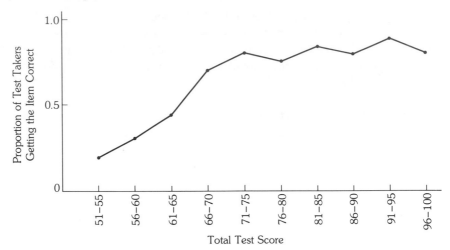

Figure 6-3. Item characteristic curve for a test item that discriminates well at low levels of performance but not at higher levels.

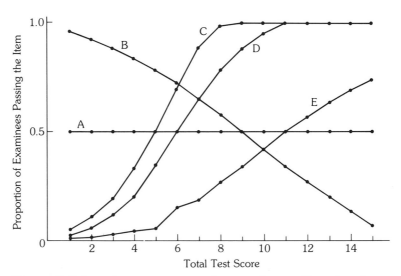

Figure 6-4. Item characteristic curves for several items. (*From* Introduction to Measurement Theory, *by M. J. Allen and W. M. Yen. Copyright © 1979 by Wadsworth, Inc. Reprinted by permission of the publisher, Brooks/Cole Publishing Company, Monterey, California.*)

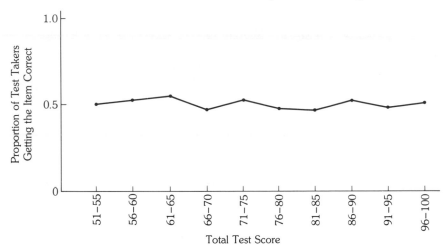

Figure 6-5. An item characteristic curve for a poor item. People with different test scores were equally likely to get the item correct.

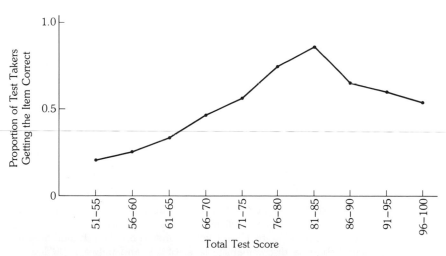

Figure 6-6. Another example of a problem item. Sometimes test takers who "know too much" will rule out the alternative designated as correct.

the lower level of performance. However, all of the people who scored above average on the test got this item correct. Thus it did not provide much discrimination in the higher ranges of performance.

Figure 6-4 shows a variety of item characteristic curves. The items shown in the figure are each sensitive in a particular range. Figures 6-5 and 6-6 show item characteristic curves for poor items. The flat curve in Figure 6-5 indicates that test takers at all levels of ability were equally likely to get the item correct. Figure 6-6 demonstrates a particularly troublesome problem. The item characteristic curve gradually rises, showing that the item is sensitive to most levels of performance. Then it turns down for persons at the highest levels of performance. This suggests that those with the best overall performance on the test did not have the best chances of getting the item correct. This can happen on multiple-choice examinations when one of the alternatives is "none of the above." Students who are exceptionally knowledgeable in the subject area will sometimes be able to rule out all of the choices and choose the "none of the above" alternative. However, one of the alternatives had actually been designated as correct.

Another convenient picture of item characteristics is shown in Figure 6-7. This graph plots the item numbers within the space created by difficulty on one axis and discriminability (point-biserial correlation between item passage and test score) on the other axis. Item 12 has been circled on the graph so that you can

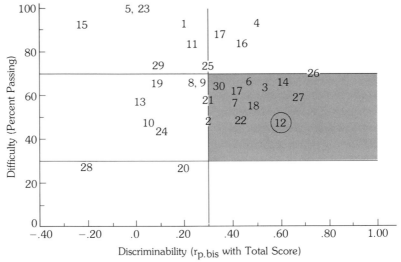

Figure 6-7. Items from a 30-item test are plotted on a graph with discriminability on one axis and difficulty on the other. Each number of the graph represents a test item: 1 is for Item 1 and so on. The shaded area represents items above a discriminability level of .30 and between 30% and 70% in difficulty level. These items would be the best candidates to include in the final version of the test. Item 12 (circled) was passed by 46% of the respondents and was correlated .60 with total test score. Thus it should be retained.

identify it. Of all respondents 46% got this item correct, and its discriminability level is 60. Thus the location of Item 12 on the graph is adjacent to 46 on the difficulty axis and to 60 on the discriminability axis. Earlier in the discussion we noted that "good" items usually fall within the range of .30 and .70 on item difficulty. Thus these boundaries represent the region in which acceptable levels of difficulty and discriminability exist. The shaded region within these boundaries represents the region in which acceptable levels of difficulty and discriminability are achieved. Thus items for the final version of the test should be selected from this area.

Internal criteria. One persistent problem in the practice of item analysis has been our continued dependence on "internal criteria" against which to evaluate items. By internal criteria we mean total test score. The examples we have just given demonstrate how to compare performance on an item with performance on the total test. Similar procedures can be used to compare performance on an item with performance on an "external criterion." For example, if you were building a test to select airplane pilots, you might want to evaluate how well individual items predict success in pilot training or flying performance. The advantages of using external rather than internal criteria against which to validate items were outlined by Guttman (1950) more than 30 years ago. Nevertheless, external criteria are rarely used in practice (Linn, 1980).

D. *Items for criterion-referenced tests*

In Chapter 2 we briefly mentioned the concept of criterion-referenced testing. The traditional use of tests requires that we determine how well someone has done on a test by comparing the person's performance to the performance of others. For example, the meaning of Jeff's 67 on the geography test is determined by his percentile rank in the geography class. Another way of evaluating Jeff's performance is to ask how much he learned in comparison to how much he "should have" learned. Jeff is no longer in competition with everyone else. Instead we have defined what Jeff needs to do in order to be considered knowledgeable about a certain unit. Grades are determined by how much Jeff knows rather than whether or not he knows more than someone else.

A *criterion-referenced test* is one that compares performance to some clearly defined criterion for mastery. This approach is very popular in individualized instruction programs. For each student a set of objectives is defined. These objectives state exactly what the student should be able to do after an edu-cational experience. For example, an objective for a junior high school algebra student might be to be able to solve linear equations with two unknowns. The criterion-referenced test would be used to determine whether this objective had been achieved. After demonstrating this knowledge, the student can move ahead to another objective. Many educators regard criterion-referenced tests as diagnostic instruments. When a student does poorly on some items, the teacher knows that the individualized education program needs more focus in that particular problem area.

There are many problems in the development of criterion-referenced tests. The first step involves clearly specifying the objectives. This is done by writing clear and precise statements about what the learning program is attempting to achieve. These are usually stated in terms of something the student will be able to do. For example, an objective for a unit in high school civics might be to understand the operation of municipal government. Test items that assess the attainment of this objective might ask about taxation powers of local governments, the relation of municipal to state government, and so on.

To evaluate the items in the criterion-referenced test, the test should be given to two groups of students—one group which has been exposed to the learning unit and one which has not. Figure 6-8 shows what the distribution of scores would look like. The frequency polygon looks like a V. The scores on the left side of the V are probably those from students who have not experienced the unit. Scores on the right represent those who have been exposed to the unit. The bottom of the V is called the *antimode*, and it is the least frequent score. This point divides those who have been exposed to the unit from those who have not been exposed. This is usually taken as the cutting point. When people get scores higher than the antimode, we assume that they have met the objective of the test. When they get lower scores, we assume they have not met the objective. In Figure 6-8 the cutting score would be 5.

Criterion-referenced tests have many advantages for newer approaches to education. One growing area in which they have been useful is computer-assisted instruction. For example, a large program created by the American Institutes for Research and the Westinghouse Learning Corporation involved students obtaining much of their education by interacting with a computer terminal. Each student works at his/her own pace on an individualized program

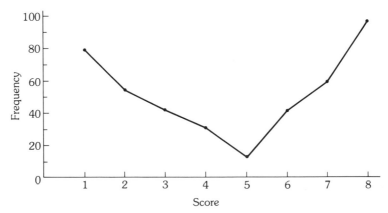

Figure 6-8. Frequency polygon used to evaluate a criterion-referenced test.

of instruction. After exposure to the program, a criterion-referenced test is used to evaluate progress. Students who pass the test can move on to the next unit. Students who do not pass can repeat some of the instruction until they pass. Some people feel this approach to education maximizes individual potential (Flanagan, 1971).

E.   Limitations of item analysis

The growing interest in criterion-referenced tests has posed some new questions about the adequacy of our item analysis procedures. The major problem is that statistical methods for item analysis tell the test constructor which items do a good job of separating students. However, they do not help the students learn. Young children do not care as much about how many items they missed as they do about what they are doing wrong (Davis, 1979). Many times a child will make very specific errors and will continue to make these same mistakes until discovery of why he or she is making the mistake.

For example, an achievement test might ask a fourth-grade student to add .40 and .30. One of the multiple-choice alternatives would be .07, because item analysis had demonstrated that this was a good distractor. The child who selected .07 would not receive a point on the item and also might continue to make similar errors. Although the data are available to give the child feedback on the "bug" in his or her thinking, there is nothing in the testing procedure that initiates this guidance (Linn, 1980). One study involving 1300 fourth, fifth, and sixth graders found that 40% of the children made the same type of errors when given problems of a particular kind (Brown & Burton, 1978). Some researchers in the field of educational measurement now appear to be moving toward testing programs that diagnose in addition to assess (Bloom, 1980; Davis, Jockusch, & McKnight, 1978; Linn, 1980). Tests can have different purposes. In the past we have placed too much emphasis on ranking students and not enough on discovering specific weaknesses or gaps in knowledge (Buros, 1977).

III.   SUMMARY

There is an art and a science to test construction. Writing good items is a complex and demanding task. The first step involves deciding what sort of information you are trying to obtain. True-false items might be used if you are attempting to evaluate absolute judgment. A similar format that is used to evaluate whether or not test takers know "the right information" is the multiple-choice format in which a correct choice must be selected among several alternatives. With these types of formats, the test constructor always must consider the probability that someone will get an answer correct by chance.

Many formats are available for tests that do not have right or wrong answers. The Likert format is popular for attitude scales. Statements are presented and respondents can check the degree to which they agree or disagree with the statements on a five-point scale. A similar format is the category-scaling method in which ratings are obtained on a scale with defined endpoints. The familiar ten-point scale is an example of a category scale. Unfortunately, category scales are subject to some bias when the endpoints are not clearly defined.

Checklists and Q-sorts are among the many item formats used in personality research. These methods require a person to make judgments about whether certain items are descriptive of them or of other people.

Once test items have been created, they can be administered to groups of individuals and the value of the items can be systematically assessed. One method of item analysis requires evaluation of item difficulty. Difficulty is usually assessed by examining the number of persons getting each item correct. In addition to difficulty analysis, test constructors usually examine the correlation between getting any item correct and the total test score. This correlation is used as an index of discriminability.

Another way to learn about the value of items is by drawing a picture of the item characteristic curve. For example, the proportion of people getting an item correct can be plotted as a function of the total test score. Better items are those for which the probability of getting the item correct is highest among those with the highest test scores.

Criterion-referenced tests require a different approach to test construction. With criterion-referenced tests, a person's knowledge is evaluated against what he or she is expected to know rather than against what others know. To evaluate items in criterion-referenced tests, performance for those who would be expected to know the material is compared with performance of others who would not be expected to have mastered the information.

CHAPTER

7

Selection and Personnel Decisions

Learning objectives

When you have completed this chapter, you should be able to do the following:

1. *Discuss the proper methods for selecting a meaningful test.*
2. *Identify the first consideration in determining whether it is worthwhile to administer a test.*
3. *Explain the meaning of base rates in personnel selection.*
4. *Identify three methods that have been developed to estimate the amount of information a test gives beyond what is known by chance.*
5. *Define incremental validity.*
6. *Discuss the significance of utility and decision theory.*
7. *Explain the problem with utility theory equations.*
8. *List several sources that contain valuable information about psychological tests.*

There are many types of psychological tests. In fact the number of tests goes into the thousands. As a student of psychology you will need to learn how to be a good consumer of testing materials.

Table 7-1 presents two sets of items from two "tests." One set is from the Experiential World Inventory. The other set is from the writings of columnist and humorist Art Buchwald. Both sets of items appear to be ridiculous. Yet one set purportedly has a purpose other than to provide humor. Can you tell which test is which?

Just because the promoters of a personality test known as the Experiential World Inventory argue that their measure is valuable you do not have to

TABLE 7-1 Items from two personality scales*

Set 1	Set 2
The sight of blood no longer excites me.	Animals often try to fool me.
	I feel like killing untidy people.
It makes me furious to see an innocent man escape the chair.	I sometimes taste sound.
When I was a child, I was an imaginary playmate.	Someone is making copies of me.
I am bored by thoughts of death.	I sometimes think other people's thoughts.
I become homicidal when people try to reason with me.	I am afraid somebody may cut off my nose.
I don't like it when somebody is rotten.	Old men are indecent.
	I am someone else.
Most of the time I go to sleep without saying goodby.	I would like to drink blood.
Frantic screams make me nervous.	I feel that my ideas may turn into insects.

*From "Objective Personality Tests and Measures," by L. R. Goldberg. Reproduced, with permission, from the *Annual Review of Psychology*, Vol. 25. © 1974 by Annual Reviews, Inc. (Set 1 is from Art Buchwald's column, and set 2 is from the Experiential World Inventory.)

accept their opinion. Instead you must carefully evaluate the information yourself. Do items that ask about drinking blood have more meaning that those asking about being bored by thoughts of death? The answer depends on the evidence the test constructors have to support the meaning of their test. In the case of the Experiential World Inventory there is little reason to believe that scores on this test are more meaningful than the scores on a test created by Art Buchwald, a test he created only for comedy.

This chapter will review methods for selecting a meaningful test. These methods assess whether the test provides useful information.

I. THE TEST MANUAL

Before you use a test, many decisions must be made. Tests are categorized as proprietary and nonproprietary. A proprietary test is one that is the property of the test developer or, in many cases, of a publishing company. A proprietary test is protected by copyright laws, and a user must pay for the privilege of using it. The items of proprietary tests are protected and generally kept restricted. For example, unless you are a professional psychologist, you probably would not have access to the items from widely used tests such as the Minnesota Multiphasic Personality Inventory or the Stanford-Binet intelligence scales. Nonproprietary tests are not protected by copyright in the same way. Most often they are distributed by the test developer or are published in journals. For example, the Internal-External Locus of Control Scale (Rotter, 1966), one of the most widely used measures in personality research, was published in an academic journal. Most users of this scale simply copy the items from the article and pay no royalty to a publisher. However, before you use test items in a written publication, you should check with the publisher. The June/July 1981 *APA Monitor* recently reported that *Boston Magazine* was required to pay psychologist Zick Rubin $5000 for using his love questionnaire without permission (Foltz, 1981).

Testing is a large and profitable business that has not been controlled. In many ways the use of psychological tests is similar to the use of prescription drugs. Although there are no toxic effects of the tests, it is possible that people can be unnecessarily hurt when they are classified improperly by the tests. In order for a new drug to get on the market, it must be tested and meet the standards of the Food and Drug Administration (FDA). There is no equivalent agency that monitors the standards for psychological tests. In place of a federal bureau responsible for overseeing psychological tests, a joint committee of the American Psychological Association, the American Educational Research Association, and the National Council for Measurement in Education created standards and published them in a booklet entitled *Standards for Educational and Psychological Tests*. The short booklet provides a clear set of standards for test developers and users and defines the minimum information necessary for a test manual.

Most commercial test users find proprietary tests best suited for their purposes. If you were to use a proprietary test you would need to be a qualified test administrator who has had appropriate training and experience. To decide whether the test was suited for your purpose you would need to consult the test manual.

The test manual gives all of the basic information needed to administer a test, to score it, and to make sense out of the results. If a test manual is constructed according to the *Standards* defined by the joint committee, it will answer most of the questions you have about the validity, reliability, and norms for the test. Because we covered these topics in earlier chapters, you should now have a good feel for the meaning of norms and the minimum standards for reliability and validity. When evaluating a test, there are a series of questions you should ask, and these are summarized in the checklist in Table 7-2.

For many industrial applications other factors also must be considered. One important criterion is the amount of information the test gives beyond what is known without it. This can be derived from an analysis of base and hit rates.

II.   BASE RATES AND HIT RATES

A test always should provide more information than you would have by chance. Thus tests must be evaluated in terms of how much they contribute beyond what would be known without them. Many times tests are used to place individuals into one of two categories. For example, on the basis of an employment test, a candidate is deemed acceptable or unacceptable. In a medical setting, a test may be used to decide whether a person has a tumor in a certain

TABLE 7-2   Checklist of questions that should be answered in the test manual

Standardization Sample
1. How many subjects were used to establish the reliability, validity, and norms for the test?
2. What were the demographic and personal characteristics of these subjects? Are they similar to those of the group you will give the test to?

Reliability
1. What methods were used to estimate the reliability of the test?
2. Is the reliability high enough for your purposes (usually .90 or above for tests used to make decisions about individuals and .70 or above for research purposes)?

Validity
1. Is there evidence that the test is meaningful for *your purposes*?
2. What specific criteria was the test validated against?

Scoring
1. Are scoring keys available?
2. If the test can be scored by machine, how much does it cost and what sort of report is offered?

Practical Considerations
1. How long does it take to administer the test?
2. Does the test require reading? If so, is it at the right level for the people you will test?
3. How much training is required for the test administrator? How can the training be obtained?

area of the brain. Because tests are not always exactly accurate, the possibility of making an error in assigning someone to a category must be evaluated.

If a test is used to make a dichotomous (two-choice) decision, a cutoff score usually is used. Values above this score might go into the plus category, and values below it might go into the minus category. The plus category might be used to indicate that the person is suitable for the job or that he or she has the tumor. The score marking the point of decision is called the *cutting score*. Establishing a cutting score does not necessarily mean that the decisions will be correct. Sometimes a person will score above the cutting score but will perform as though he or she should not have. For example, suppose that a person scores above the cutting score for an employment test but fails on the job after he or she is selected. This suggests that the test has not done its job. Tests can be evaluated by how well they do in sorting people into the right categories.

By using cutting scores we can divide people into two categories—for example, accept-reject, positive diagnosis-negative diagnosis, and many others. For the purpose of illustration we will use a test that determines which people to hire for a particular job. Those who score above the cutting score might be labeled *acceptable*, and those who score below might be called *unacceptable*. In addition to the scores on the test, it is essential to have some data on how people really do on the job. To do this the employer must define some criterion for deciding whether job performance has been acceptable or unacceptable. Using these two sets of categories, we can construct a chart such as that shown in Table

7-3. There are four cells in this table. Two of the four cells are labeled *hit* because the test has made the correct prediction. *Hits* occur when: 1) the test predicts that the person will be unacceptable and indeed he or she fails, or 2) the test indicates that the person is acceptable and he or she does turn out to be successful. *Misses* occur when the test makes an inaccurate prediction. The *hit rate* is the proportion of cases in which a test accurately predicts success or failure.

TABLE 7-3 Hits and misses for predicting a dichotomous outcome using a cutting score

	Decision on the Basis of Cutting Score	
Performance on the job	*Acceptable*	*Unacceptable*
success	hit	miss
failure	miss	hit

Many times a test does not need to have a good hit rate because the rate of predicting success on the job is high without the test. For example, if we are predicting who will do well in law school, it might be possible to make this prediction on the basis of information other than scores on the Law School Admissions Test (LSAT). For example, college grades might be used. Success on the criterion in this case might be passing the bar examination on the first attempt. The hit rate not using the LSAT would be called the *base rate*. The real value of a test comes from a comparison of the hit rate when the test is used with the base rate without the test. In other words, the hit rate must be better with the test than it would be without it.

For example, suppose the LSAT has a hit rate of 76% for predicting who will pass the bar examination in a certain state. However, 85% of the people taking the test for the first time in that state pass. The LSAT in this case tells us less than the available information. There may be other circumstances in which the hit rate is very low but the base rate is even lower. For example, suppose you need to select people for a position that will involve world class competition. Under the circumstances very few people could be expected to do well—say only 3% would be expected to succeed. If a test could be developed that had a 10% hit rate, it might be considered of value.

Another problem to consider with regard to hit and miss rates is the relative *costs*. Sometimes a miss is very costly. Medical situations provide good examples of costly misses. For instance, consider the costs of concluding on the basis of a test that a tumor is benign (not cancerous) when it is malignant (cancerous). The cost of this sort of miss is that the life of the patient is seriously endangered. In a psychological application, there may be grave consequences of concluding that someone is not suicidal because he or she is below the cutoff score when there is in fact suicide potential. The cost of this sort of miss is that a preventable suicide may occur. These cases are *false negatives*. If the cost of a false negative is high, it may be of value to lower the cutting score. With a lower cutting score, the test will make more errors, but the errors will not be as potentially dangerous.

The other type of miss is the *false positive*. An example of a false-positive situation is one in which someone is selected for a job on the basis of a test. Once on the job the person does poorly and gets fired. Sometimes there are high costs associated with this type of error. For instance, time and money might be invested to train a person who eventually is unable to do the job. In addition, job failure is harmful for the person and might be a blow to self-esteem and self-confidence. If the costs of a false positive are high, it may be of value to raise the cutting score.

Using cutting scores to find hits and misses is an issue in criterion validity (see Chapter 5). Many years ago, Taylor and Russell (1939) demonstrated how to relate validity coefficients to accuracy rates in selection.

A.   *Taylor-Russell tables*

The decision to use a test must depend on what is gained by it. In Chapter 5 we reviewed the concept of criterion validity and showed that tests with significant predictive or concurrent validity coefficients did better than chance in forecasting performance on a criterion. However, knowing that a test is better than chance is not good enough for making choices about whether it will be of value in some application. In the last section we presented the concept of base rates and noted that a worthwhile test must provide more information than would be known from the base rates.

In 1939 Taylor and Russell developed a method for evaluating the validity of a test in relation to the amount that it contributes information beyond the base rates. The method for assessing the value of tests is neatly summarized in a series of tables that have come to be known as the Taylor-Russell tables. To use the tables you must have the following information:

1. *Definition of Success*. For each situation in which the test is to be used, success on the outcome must be defined. This could be that the patient lived, that the person succeeded on the job, or that the student did well in college. Success must be defined clearly by dichotomizing some outcome variable. For example, first-year grade point averages above 2.3 might be defined as success in college and those below might be defined as failures. Or salespersons who achieve average monthly sales over $5000 might be deemed successful, and those who sell less than $5000 might be thought of as unsuccessful.

2. *Determination of Base Rate*. The percentage of persons who would succeed if there were no testing or screening procedure must be determined.

3. *Definition of Selection Ratio*. The selection ratio must be defined. This is the percentage of applicants selected or admitted.

4. *The Validity Coefficient*. Finally, you must have a validity coefficient for the test that usually will be the correlation of the test with criterion.

The Taylor-Russell tables give the likelihood that a person selected on the basis of the test score will be successful. There is a different table for each base rate. Table 7-4 is a Taylor-Russell table for a base rate of .60.

To use the table find the row representing the validity of the test that would be used for selection. Then find the column associated with the proportion of people that can be selected. The number in the body of the table associated with a particular row and a particular column gives you an estimate of the percentage of people that could be expected to succeed when they are selected on the basis of the test.

TABLE 7-4 Taylor-Russell table for base rate of .60*

Validity (ρ_{XY})	Selection ratio										
	.05	.10	.20	.30	.40	.50	.60	.70	.80	.90	.95
.00	.60	.60	.60	.60	.60	.60	.60	.60	.60	.60	.60
.05	.64	.63	.63	.62	.62	.62	.61	.61	.61	.60	.60
.10	.68	.67	.65	.64	.64	.63	.63	.62	.61	.61	.60
.15	.71	.70	.68	.67	.66	.65	.64	.63	.62	.61	.61
.20	.75	.73	.71	.69	.67	.66	.65	.64	.63	.62	.61
.25	.78	.76	.73	.71	.69	.68	.66	.65	.63	.62	.61
.30	.82	.79	.76	.73	.71	.69	.68	.66	.64	.62	.61
.35	.85	.82	.78	.75	.73	.71	.69	.67	.65	.63	.62
.40	.88	.85	.81	.78	.75	.73	.70	.68	.66	.63	.62
.45	.90	.87	.83	.80	.77	.74	.72	.69	.66	.64	.62
.50	.93	.90	.86	.82	.79	.76	.73	.70	.67	.64	.62
.55	.95	.92	.88	.84	.81	.78	.75	.71	.68	.64	.62
.60	.96	.94	.90	.87	.83	.80	.76	.73	.69	.65	.63
.65	.98	.96	.92	.89	.85	.82	.78	.74	.70	.65	.63
.70	.99	.97	.94	.91	.87	.84	.80	.75	.71	.66	.63
.75	.99	.99	.96	.93	.90	.86	.81	.77	.71	.66	.63
.80	1.00	.99	.98	.95	.92	.88	.83	.78	.72	.66	.63
.85	1.00	1.00	.99	.97	.95	.91	.86	.80	.73	.66	.63
.90	1.00	1.00	1.00	.99	.97	.94	.88	.82	.74	.67	.63
.95	1.00	1.00	1.00	1.00	.99	.97	.92	.84	.75	.67	.63
1.00	1.00	1.00	1.00	1.00	1.00	1.00	1.00	.86	.75	.67	.63

To use the table, find the row associated with the validity of the test and the column associated with the proportion of people selected. The numbers in the table show the proportion of cases in which the person selected is expected to succeed.

*From "The Relationship of Validity Coefficients to the Practical Effectiveness of Tests in Selection: Discussion and Tables," by H. C. Taylor and J. T. Russell. *Journal of Applied Psychology*, 1939, 23, 565–578. Copyright 1939 by the American Psychological Association. Reprinted by permission.

For example, suppose that you are put in charge of deciding who will be admitted to a program to train teachers in secondary education. The first thing you must do is decide on a definition of success. After meeting with a committee, you may decide that success will be defined as completing the program and obtaining a satisfactory performance evaluation in student teaching. By studying records, you determine that when no selection procedure was used, 60% of the applicants to the program succeeded on this task. Thus the base rate would be 60% and the Taylor-Russell table for a base rate of .60 would be used. You then consider using the Graduate Record Examination (GRE) to select people for your program because you can only accept 70% of the applicants. A study is done, and it is determined that the correlation between the GRE and success (completing the program and obtaining a satisfactory evaluation in student teaching) is .30. This is the validity of the test for predicting the criterion.

In order to estimate how many people would be expected to succeed if they are selected on the basis of the GRE, we must enter the Taylor-Russell table (Table 7-4) for a base rate of .60. Find the row associated with the .30 validity and move across the table until you are below the column for a selection ratio of .70 (the percentage of applicants you can admit to your program). Using this procedure you should arrive at the number .66, which is the proportion of applicants you would expect to be successful if the selection was on the basis of the GRE. This analysis tells us that 66% of those selected on the basis of GRE scores can be expected to be successful and 60% of those selected at random can be. Should the GRE be required for admittance to your program? To answer this question you must decide whether the increment in 6% associated with the use of the test is worth the extra effort and expense of requiring it.

Looking at Table 7-4 you will see that tests will be more valuable in some situations than in others. For example, the circumstance in which a test is most useful is when the validity of the test is high and the selection ratio is low. This is clear from an inspection of the lower left-hand portion of Table 7-4. Conversely, the situation in which the validity is low and the selection ratio is high (the upper right-hand portion of the table) is one in which the tests will be of little value. When the test has no validity (see the first row of the table), use of the test will be about as good as selecting applicants by chance. Similarly, when nearly everyone is selected (last column) there is little reason to use a test.

Whenever a selection procedure is used, you always should remember that some qualified applicants will be turned away. Use of rational selection procedures should help make the system more fair by decreasing the number of qualified applicants not selected. One way to evaluate the selection procedure is to show the ratio of people selected by the test who then succeed and the ratio of those who would have succeeded but were not selected.

Suppose that you are the personnel manager for a company and that you can choose 30 of 100 applicants for a job. In order to make this decision you have results of a test with a validity of .70. You also know that the base rate for success on the job is .60. Using the Taylor-Russell table for a base rate of .60 you find that 91% of those selected on the basis of the test would be expected to succeed on the job. Because you can select 30 people, this would imply that approximately 27 of them would be expected to succeed and 3 would be expected to fail (91% of 30=27.3).

When you decide to hire 30 of the 100 applicants, you also are deciding not to hire 70 people. It is important to realize that not all of the 70 people would fail if they were selected. In fact many of them will be capable people who have been "misdiagnosed" by the testing procedure. In order to justify your use of the test, it would be your responsibility to explain why your selection procedure is worthwhile, even though it turns down some people who would have succeeded and selects some who fail.

Table 7-5 shows what would happen to all of the 100 applicants. A total of 30 would be accepted, and 70 would be rejected (the selection ratio equals .30). However, because the base rate for success is .60, 60 of the 100 applicants would have succeeded on the job and 40 of them would have failed. The Taylor-Russell table tells us that 91% of those selected on the basis of the test will succeed. This translates into 27 of the 30 selected ($.9 \times 30 = 27.3$), and it also implies that only about 3 of the 30 selected will fail.

Among the 60 people who would have succeeded, only 27 could be selected. This means that 33 people who would have been good choices were rejected. However, among the 40 people who would have failed, an estimated 37 would be in the rejected group. We already know from the Taylor-Russell table that about 91% of those selected by the test would be expected to succeed. Using Table 7-5 we also can calculate the proportion of those rejected on the basis of the test who would be expected to succeed. This comes to $33/70 = .47$. Although the procedure leads to the rejection of many capable applicants, it can be defended as rational because the proportion of those succeeding is much higher among those who are selected by the procedure than among those rejected by the procedure.

TABLE 7-5 What would happen to 100 applicants if 30 people were selected on the basis of a test with a validity of .70 for a job with 60% base success rate?

Performance	Decision		
	Select	Reject	Total
Success	27	33	60
Failure	3	37	40
Total	30	70	

Success ratio given selection$=27/30=.90$ (actually .91 without rounding, see Table 7-4). Success ratio given rejection$=33/70=.47$.

B. Utility theory and decision analysis

The use of Taylor-Russell tables requires that the criterion be a dichotomous variable. However, success usually is measured on a more refined numerical scale. By considering it as only a dichotomous variable we ignore much of the information available to the analyst. For example, instead of considering whether or not someone failed on a job, it seems more reasonable to use a continuum of performance as the criterion. Developments since the publication of the Taylor-Russell tables have attempted to define levels of success rather than considering either success or failure. These formulations are based on utility theory (Brogden, 1946, 1949; Cronbach & Gleser, 1965).

Although the use of decision and utility theory can be of great advantage to the industrial psychologist, the equations used to calculate the value of test information are quite complex. Furthermore, the equations require certain information that is hard to estimate. For example, in order to use the equations, you must know the standard deviation of job performance measured in dollars. To obtain this you must estimate the dollar value associated with different levels of performance on the job. For most jobs this is difficult if not impossible to estimate (Dunnette & Borman, 1979). In summary, the utility methods hold great promise for making rational personnel decisions, yet the difficulty in applying utility formulations has prevented their widespread use.

C. *Incremental validity*

Validity defines the inferences that can be made on the basis of a score or measure (see Chapter 5). Evidence that a test is valid for particular inferences does not necessarily mean that the test is valuable. Even though a test is reliable and valid, the decision to use one must depend upon some additional considerations. For example, does the test give you more information than would be expected if it were not used? What information can the test provide beyond what is already known? This added bit of information gained through using the test is known as *incremental validity*.

The sections on base and hit rates and on Taylor-Russell tables considered problems in incremental validity. In each case methods were presented for evaluating what the test contributed beyond what was known from base rates. The assessment of incremental validity is not necessarily limited to comparisons with base rates. A particularly important aspect of incremental validity is the determination of how much information a test contributes beyond some simpler method for making the same prediction.

Most of the examples given in the preceding sections concerned tests used for selection purposes. However, the same rules and methods apply for tests used for the evaluation of personality or in the practice of clinical psychology.

Recent research on prediction of behavior in particular situations has yielded some simple but startling results. Although it is difficult to predict behavior on the basis of reports by trained clinical psychologists (Meehl, 1954), people are remarkably good at predicting their own behavior (Bem & Allen, 1974; Bem & Funder, 1978; Bandura, 1977). We can learn a lot about whether a person will be able to perform a particular behavior by simply asking.

Frequently, expensive and time-consuming psychological tests are given in order to make predictions about future behavior. Before exerting this effort, it is worthwhile to ask what the tests are adding beyond what would be known if the

■ **FOCUSED DISCUSSION 7-1 How Much Money Can be Saved through Valid Selection?**

A major issue in business and industrial psychology is how to get the most productivity out of employees. Tests are often used in employment settings to select the employees who have the greatest chance of being productive. Some industrial psychologists, however, may have failed to realize just how much economic value can be gained from effective selection procedures. Although Cronbach and Gleser developed methods for evaluating the cost-effectiveness of testing many years ago, their technique was not frequently used because it required the estimation of standard deviation of the dollar value of employee performance. However, newer methods have been developed to estimate this quantity. As a result it is possible to determine how much money is saved by using a valid selection procedure.

One study on the use of these decision models concerned the selection of computer programmers using the Programmer Aptitude Test (PAT). The PAT is a fairly good predictor of job performance in programmers and has a validity coefficient of .76. In a series of analyses it was shown that the use of the PAT, in place of less valid selection procedures, saves considerable money. For example, the U.S. government employs about 17,000 computer programmers. A comparison was made for the dollar savings of using the PAT instead of an alternative procedure with a validity for predicting success on the job of only .20. Twenty percent of the applicants could be selected. The analysis demonstrated that the savings to the government could be $1.2 billion. If this example is expanded to the economy as a whole, the impact of using the PAT for one year would be $10.78 billion. According to this analysis, the gains in productivity associated with using a valid selection procedure are much greater than previously realized (Schmidt, Hunter, McKenzie, & Muldrow, 1979).

Although this analysis is very encouraging, there is at least one problem with the application to programmers. At present, there are more jobs for programmers than there are trained people to fill them. Thus, for the entire economy, the selection ratio cannot be 20%. In fact, nearly 100% of the qualified programmers find work. Gains realized by those who employ the best-qualified programmers are offset by losses to those who employ the less-qualified applicants.

information was obtained in some simpler manner. For example, Holland and Nichols (1964) attempted to find the characteristics that distinguished high school students with high accomplishments from those with less notable credits. They found that a 15-item scale about what activities the students preferred discriminated between the groups as well as a battery of complex personality tests.

Other studies have attempted to determine how a person will be rated by peers on the basis of a variety of tests and self-ratings. The results often demonstrate that simple gross self-ratings are as good at predicting how someone will be rated by peers as are complex personality tests that make inferences about underlying traits (Hase & Goldberg, 1967). Furthermore, self-predictions are no less accurate in forecasting who will go under a hypnotic trance than complex hypnotizability scales (Melei & Hilgard, 1964). Personality tests have been of little value in predicting whether snake phobics will learn to approach a snake after therapy. However, self-predictions have been found to be shockingly accurate (Bandura, 1977).

These examples are not given to convince you that personality tests are meaningless. As you will see in Chapters 15 through 18 personality measures make many valuable and important contributions. However, test users always should ask themselves whether they can gain the same information with a simpler method, with a less expensive method, or with a method that will cause less strain for the subject. Tests should be used when they provide a significant increment in information over what would be obtained with simpler methods. In order to insure that testing is a worthwhile use of time and resources you must carefully select your testing materials.

III.   LOCATING INFORMATION ABOUT PUBLISHED TESTS

When choosing a test for a particular purpose, it is important that you carefully research your options. There are a variety of reference books you should be able to find in the library that provide information about the tests. Each of these books refers you to other journal articles that summarize specific evaluations of the test. In order to get a general overview of the test, seven references are of particular value. These are *Tests in Print II* (Buros, 1974), *The Mental Measurement Yearbook* (Buros, 1978), *Measures for Psychological Assessment* (Chun, Cobb, & French, 1975), *Measuring Human Behavior* (Lake, Miles, & Earle, 1973), *Measures of Social Psychological Attitudes* (Robinson & Shaver, 1973), *A Sourcebook for Mental Health Measures* (Comrey, Backer, & Glaser, 1973), and *Tests and Measurements in Child Development: A Handbook* (Johnson & Bommarito, 1971).

A.   *Tests in Print II*

This exhaustive reference book summarizes information on most of the tests in the English language (Buros, 1974). The book lists the following information: the title of the test, who the test is designed for, when the test was developed (copyright date), the acronym for the test or the set of letters the test is often called by (such as SAT), what subtests are available, whether or not there is a test manual, problems in updating of the test materials, the authors of the test, the publisher of the test, the country in which the test was published, and cross references to the *Mental Measurement Yearbook* and *Personality Tests and Reviews* along with references to relevant journal articles. If you do not know the name of the test, you can locate a test by content area using this source.

B.   *The Mental Measurement Yearbook*

This book is a classic collection of 898 test reviews. It was first begun in

1938 by Oscar K. Buros (1978). After his death in 1978, arrangements were made for the series to be taken over by the University of Nebraska Press. The "MMY," as it is often called, provides comprehensive reviews of testing materials by almost 500 notable psychologists and education specialists. Each review comments on the evidence for the validity and reliability of a test. Often the reviews are quite critical and the reviewer critiques the meaning of the available data. More than 17,000 references for journal articles reviewing the tests are also given. There are now several sourcebooks made up of selected subsections of the MMY. *Vocational Tests and Reviews* (Buros, 1975c) consists of the vocational sections of the seventh MMY and *Tests in Print II*. Similarly, *Personality Tests and Reviews* is made up of the sections on personality tests (Buros, 1975b) and *Intelligence Tests and Reviews* includes the intelligence testing sections (Buros, 1975a).

C. *Measures for Psychological Assessment*

This reference is very similar to *Tests in Print* but includes many measures of mental health published between 1960 and 1970. In contrast to the other reference books, *Measures for Psychological Assessment* (Chunn, Cobb, & French, 1975) contains many references to tests that were never published and to tests that were not determined to be valuable. The references refer the reader to applications in which the test was found to be useful and to others when it was found to be of little value.

D. *Measuring Human Behavior*

The Mental Measurement Yearbook is a large, expensive, and very comprehensive book. *Measuring Human Behavior* (Lake, Miles, & Earle, 1973) attempts to do much of the same thing but is less comprehensive. Reviews and evaluations are provided for more than 80 tests. The reviews are critical and should allow the reader to make a reasonable assessment of the appropriateness of the test for certain applications. In addition, *Measuring Human Behavior* includes 20 reviews of other reference books on psychological measurement.

E. *Measures of Social Psychological Attitudes*

Measures of Social Psychological Attitudes (Robinson & Shaver, 1973) is perhaps the most complete source of information about scales frequently used for research in personality and social psychology. It includes reviews of scales on life satisfaction, self-esteem, locus of control, alienation and anomia, authoritarianism and dogmatism, sociopolitical attitudes, values, general attitudes toward people, religious attitudes, and methodological scales. Each of the numerous reviews describes the variable the scale is designed to measure, gives a description of the scale, and presents evidence for reliability and validity. If the actual items are not presented, a reference is given to help you locate the test. Finally, references to research using the scales are presented.

F. A Sourcebook for Mental Health Measures

Another set of brief test reviews is given in *A Sourcebook for Mental Health Measures* (Comrey, Backer, & Glaser, 1973). This is a very extensive set of abstracts covering about 1100 mental measures. The completion of this book was sponsored by the National Institute of Mental Health to provide a taxonomy of data-collecting devices. This was needed because costly and encyclopedic references such as *The Mental Measurement Yearbook* were not meeting the needs of mental health practitioners. The sourcebook provides brief 300-word abstracts of tests and measures used in all aspects of mental health research and practice. The reviews tend to be less evaluative than those in Buros, but they frequently include some references to published work demonstrating applications.

G. Tests and Measurements in Child Development: A Handbook

Several years ago Johnson and Bommarito (1971) studied all the professional journals in psychology, psychiatry, and education and reviewed professional books and unpublished material in order to find tests measuring aspects of the behavior of children 12 years old and younger. Their search yielded more than 300 instruments that were not published by commercial publishers (nonproprietary). Each of these instruments is summarized in *Tests and Measurements in Child Development: A Handbook*. The summary includes the title of the test, the author, the age level the test is designed for, the type of test (such as behavioral observation, objective, or projective), and information on administration, scoring, special considerations, and sample items. Unfortunately, the Johnson and Bommarito reference does not always provide information on validity, reliability, and norms. This is because such information is not always available for unpublished tests. Nevertheless, this handbook remains one of the best sources of information about tests for children.

IV. SUMMARY

Making a selection among the many published tests has become a technical skill in itself. One of your first considerations should always be whether it is worthwhile to administer this test. How much information does the test give beyond what is known without the test? In personnel selection the base rate is the probability of succeeding without any selection procedure. A variety of methods have been developed to estimate the amount of information a test gives beyond what is known by chance. This depends on the validity of the test, the percentage of people being selected, and the proportion of people expected to succeed if no selection test is used. Taylor-Russell tables can be used for this purpose. When the outcome is defined more precisely than just success or failure, utility and decision theory are sometimes employed. However, the application of the utility theory equations is fairly difficult in most circumstances.

Because there are so many tests available, a wise test consumer will carefully review published information on the test before making a decision. Valuable source books on testing information include *Tests in Print II, The Mental Measurement Yearbook, Measures for Psychological Assessment, Measuring Human Behavior, Measures of Social Psychological Attitudes, A Sourcebook for Mental Health Measures,* and *Tests and Measurements in Child Development: A Handbook*.

8

Test Administration

Learning objectives

When you have completed this chapter, you should be able to do the following:

1. *Know whether the majority of the research evidence shows that White examiners impede the intelligence test performance of Black children.*
2. *Discuss how the relationship between the examiner and the test taker can have an impact on test scores.*
3. *Discuss an expectancy effect and how it might affect a test score.*
4. *Examine the relationship between reinforcing particular responses and test performance.*
5. *Outline some of the advantages of computer-assisted test administration.*
6. *List what characteristics of the state of the subject should be considered when evaluating a test score.*
7. *Know what problems you would need to consider in training your observers if you were in charge of a behavioral-observation study.*

In the last six chapters we discussed many topics related to test construction. Now we are ready to make the transition to using psychological tests. Before moving on to the section on applications, there is one final methodological issue that needs to be covered: the administration of tests.

Test scores are influenced by many factors. However, when we obtain them there is a tendency to think that the observed score is really representative of the true ability or trait we are trying to measure. In Chapter 4 we reviewed the concept of reliability and introduced measurement error. The latter is the difference between the true score and the observed score. Reliability theory is most concerned with random sources of error. In the actual application of tests, many other sources of error must be considered. These include effects of the testing situation, of tester characteristics, and of test-taker characteristics.

I. THE EXAMINER AND THE SUBJECT

A. *The race of the tester*

The effects of race of tester have generated considerable attention because of the concern about bias. Some groups feel that their children should not be tested by anyone except a member of the same race. For example, there has been concern that Black children will receive lower test scores when they are tested by White examiners. Although the effects of racial bias in test administration are discussed very frequently, the exact impact has been studied in relatively few experimental studies. The effects of examiner's race have been reviewed on several occasions by Sattler (1970, 1973a, 1973b, 1973c, 1982). After very careful consideration of the problem and occasional reanalysis of the data, Sattler concluded that there is little evidence that the race of the examiner has much effect on intelligence test scores.

The most common finding in studies of this type is that the race of the examiner has nonsignificant effects on test performance for both Black and White children. These results occurred for both the Stanford-Binet scale and the Peabody Picture Vocabulary Test (Miller & Phillips, 1966; Costello & Dickie, 1970). A similar study with older children (Black sixth graders) also failed to show differences between the children when they were given the Stanford-Binet by a Black examiner and a White one (Caldwell & Knight, 1970).

This same result also has been obtained for group intelligence tests. Scores of Black and White fourth, fifth, and sixth graders were not found to be significantly influenced by having a trained Black or White examiner give the Lorge-Thorndike Group Intelligence Test (Lipsitz, 1969). Although a few studies have shown an effect attributed to the race of the examiner, they are clearly in the minority. In fact, these effects have been found in only 4 of 29 studies (Sattler, 1979a). Sattler & Gwynne (1982) refer to the belief that White examiners impede the test performance of Black children as a myth widely believed but unsupported by scientific studies.

One of the reasons so few studies show effects of the examiner's race on results of IQ tests is that the procedures for properly administering an IQ test are so specific. Anyone giving the test should be doing so according to a very strict procedure. In other words, well-trained Black or White test administrators should be acting in an almost identical fashion. Deviation from this procedure might produce differences in performance associated with the race of the examiner. For example, in the next sections we will show how very subtle (nonverbal) cues can affect test scores. Even though most standardized tests have a very strict administration procedure, there are numerous ways the examiner can communicate a hostile or friendly atmosphere, a hurried or relaxed manner, or an inquisitorial or therapeutic role. These effects may not be a function of race of the examiner per se but may be reflected in strained relationships between members of different ethnic groups.

Sattler (1973c) has shown that there are some situations in which information is affected by the race of the examiner. Thus examiner effects might be expected to be greatest when examiners are given more discretion about the use of the tests. In one study in which a small effect of examiner's race was found, the examiners were paraprofessionals rather than psychologists. In this study White examiners obtained higher scores from White children, while scores for Black or White children were comparable when tested by Black examiners (Abramson, 1969).

B.   The examiner-test taker relationship

Test scores can be affected by the behavior of the examiner and his or her relationship to the test taker. One variable that may affect test scores is rapport. In one study first- through seventh-grade children were given the WISC intelligence test (see Chapter 12) under one of two conditions. Half the children were given the test under enhanced rapport conditions in which the examiner used friendly conversation and verbal reinforcement during the test administration. The other children took the test under a neutral rapport condition. For these children the examiner never initiated conversation or used reinforcement (Feldman & Sullivan, 1971). There was little effect of the examiner's rapport upon the scores of the younger children (just through third grade). However, average IQ scores for the fifth- through ninth-grade students were higher for those who had received the test under the enhanced rapport condition (mean IQ=122) than for the children who had taken the test with a neutral administrator (mean IQ=109). This difference (122−109) is almost a full standard deviation.

Another study compared scores obtained by examiners who made approving comments (such as "good" or "fine") with those obtained by examiners who used disapproving comments ("I thought you could do better than that") or neutral comments. Children who took the test under a disapproving examiner received lower scores than those who had been exposed to a neutral or an approving examiner (Witmer, Bornstein, & Dunham, 1971).

In most testing situations, examiners should not attempt to have a different rapport with different test takers. However, rapport might be influenced by very subtle processes such as the level of performance expected by the examiner.

C.   Expectancy effects

A well-known line of research in psychology has shown that data obtained in experiments sometimes can be affected by what an experimenter expects to find. Robert Rosenthal and his colleagues at Harvard University contributed a large number of experiments on the effects of experimenter expectancy. Because these studies are so well known, many have come to label the effects of experimenter expectancy the "Rosenthal effect." In a typical experiment Rosenthal employs a large number of student experimenters to help collect data on a task such as rating human faces for success or failure. Half the student experimenters are led to believe that the average response will be toward the success side of the scale, and the other half are led to expect that the average response will be on the failure side. The results of these experiments consistently demonstrate that the subjects actually provide data that confirm the experimenter's expectancies. However, the magnitude of the effect is small—about a 1-point difference on a 20-point scale (Rosenthal, 1966).

The experimenter's influence is not limited to human subjects. Other experiments have demonstrated that rats expected to be "maze bright" will learn to run through a maze more quickly than rats expected to be "maze dull." All of the rats are from the same litter, but the experimenter is told to expect a difference (Rosenthal & Fode, 1963).

Several authors have challenged the Rosenthal experiments, claiming that they are based on unsound statistical procedures or faulty design (Barber & Silver, 1968; Ellashoff & Snow, 1971; Thorndike, 1968). Rosenthal acknowledges some problems in his early work and has greatly improved his own skills as a methodologist (Cooper & Rosenthal, 1980). After reviewing many studies, he still maintains that there is an expectancy effect in some situations.

Two aspects of the expectancy effect are important with regard to the use of standardized tests. First, the expectancy effects observed in Rosenthal's experiments were obtained when all the experimenters followed a standardized script. Although gross forms of bias are possible, Rosenthal argues that the expectancy effect results from very subtle uses of nonverbal communication between the experimenter and the subject. The experimenter may not even be aware of his or her role in the process. The second point to consider with regard to the expectancy effect is that it has a very small, subtle effect upon scores. Furthermore, Rosenthal reports that it occurs in some situations but not in others. Determining whether test scores are affected by expectancy requires careful studies for the particular tests being used.

In intelligence testing the expectancy effect can have several different impacts. One type of influence is upon scoring. In a series of experiments, graduate students with some training in intelligence testing were asked to score ambiguous responses from certain intelligence tests. Sometimes they were told that the responses had been given by persons who were "bright," and other times the responses were attributed to "dull" persons. The students tended to give more credit to responses purportedly from bright test takers (Sattler, Hillix, & Neher, 1970; Sattler & Winget, 1970). Other studies have demonstrated that the expectancy effect can occur even if the responses are not ambiguous (Egeland, 1969; Simon, 1969).

A variety of interpersonal process variables have been shown to affect judgment of others (Schneider, Hastorf, & Ellsworth, 1979). These biases may also affect scoring of tests. For example, Donahue and Sattler (1971) demonstrated that students scoring the WAIS intelligence test were more likely to give credit for selected items to examinees they liked or perceived to be warm. Thus examiners must be aware that their relationships with examinees can affect their objectivity for certain types of tests.

Studies in which expectancies have been created for test administrators (giving rather than just scoring tests) have yielded somewhat inconsistent results. Some have shown that there is a significant expectancy effect (Hersh, 1971; Larrabee & Kleinsaser, 1967; Schroeder & Kleinsaser, 1972), while other studies have not demonstrated the expectancy effect (Dangel, 1970; Ekren, 1962; Gillingham, 1970; Saunders & Vitro, 1971).

In reviewing these studies Sattler (1982) noted that the studies showing an expectancy effect tended to have an administrator test only two children (one under a high and one under a low expectancy condition). The studies that did not find an expectancy effect tended to have more subjects tested by each test administrator. The studies using more samples of each tester's behavior should produce more reliable estimates of the expectancy effect (see Chapter 4), and these were the ones where the effect was least often observed. Therefore the studies that failed to show an expectancy effect may be more credible.

Even though the results of studies on expectancy effects are often inconsistent, it is important to pay careful attention to the potentially biasing effect of expectancy. Even Rosenthal's harshest critics do not deny the possible biasing effect of expectancy. Thus it is always important to do as much as you can to eliminate the possibility of experimenter or test administrator bias.

D. *Effects of reinforcing responses*

Because there is such a well-known effect of reinforcement upon behavior, it is very important to administer tests under controlled conditions. Sattler and Theye (1967) reviewed the literature on procedural and situational variables in testing and found that inconsistent use of feedback can damage the reliability and validity of test scores.

Several studies have shown that reward can have an important effect upon test performance. For example, incentives can help improve performance on IQ tests for specific subgroups of children. In one study 6- to 13-year-olds were given tokens (that could be exchanged for money) each time they gave a correct response on the WISC (Wechsler Intelligence Scale for Children) verbal scale. This incentive was effective in improving performance for lower-class White children but not effective for middle-class children or lower-class Blacks (Sweet, 1969).

The incentive need not necessarily be monetary. Many studies have shown that children will work very hard to obtain praise such as "You are doing well" (Eisenberger, 1970, 1972). Several studies have shown that the effects of verbal reinforcement or praise are about as strong as monetary rewards or candy (Cohen, 1970; Quay, 1971; Sattler, 1974; Tiber & Kennedy, 1964). The results of these studies, however, are sometimes complicated. For instance, one study found that girls increased their accuracy on the WISC block design subtest when given any type of reinforcement for a correct response. Boys only increased in accuracy when given chips that could be exchanged for money. However, girls decreased in speed when given reinforcement and boys increased in speed only when given verbal praise (Bergan, McManis, & Melchert, 1971).

There is some evidence that Black children do not respond as well to verbal reinforcers as they do to tangible rewards such as money or candy (Schultz & Sherman, 1976). However, Black psychologist Francis Terrell and his colleagues suggest that this is because the verbal reinforcement often given to the Black children is not culturally relevant. To demonstrate their point they administered the WISC-R intelligence test to lower socioeconomic Black second graders and gave one of four types of feedback for each correct response. One-quarter of the children were given no feedback at all about whether or not they had made a correct response. One group received verbal praise, and another group was given candy. The final group was given culturally relevant verbal praise. For example, after each correct response the Black test administrator remarked "Nice job, Blood" or "Nice job, Little Brother." Using culturally relevant feedback boosted IQ a remarkable 17.6 points, whereas giving the same sort of feedback that was not culturally relevant had very little effect (about 3 points). Tangible rewards boosted performance about 11 points (Terrell, Taylor, & Terrell, 1978). This result is most unusual in light of several previous studies that show only minor effects of reinforcement. Certainly more attention needs to be devoted to the effects of culturally relevant rewards.

Some of the most potent effects of reinforcement have been shown in attitudinal studies. In survey research, the answer given by a respondent is not necessarily right or wrong. Instead, it is an expression of how someone feels about something. Repeated studies have demonstrated that the content of responses in interview studies is affected by the way an interviewer responds (Cannell & Henson, 1974). One of the most interesting demonstrations of this was a study in which respondents in a household survey were asked if they suffered from certain physical symptoms. For half of the subjects, the interviewer gave an approving nod each time a symptom was reported. For the other half, the interviewer remained expressionless. It was shown that the number of symptoms reported significantly increased when approval was given for reporting a symptom. In a similar study two symptoms that no one should report were added to the list. These were "Are your intestines too long?" and "Do the ends of your hair itch?" A greater proportion of people will report that they experience these symptoms if they have been reinforced for reporting other symptoms.

Reinforcement and feedback guide the examinee with regard to which response should be given. Another way to demonstrate the potency of reinforcement involves misguiding the subject. A variety of studies have demonstrated that random reinforcement destroys the accuracy of performance and decreases the motivation to respond (Eisenberger, Kaplan, & Singer, 1974; Koller & Kaplan, 1978). The effects of random feedback have been shown to be rather severe, causing a condition of low motivation for responding, depression, and inability to solve problems. This condition is known as learned helplessness (Abramson, Seligman, & Teasdale, 1978; Seligman, 1975).

Because of the potency of reinforcement on performance, very strict control over the use of feedback by test administrators should be followed. Because different test takers make different responses, it is not possible to insure that advantages due to reinforcement will be the same for all people. As a result, most test manuals and interviewer guides insist that no feedback be given.

It is important to give tests under standardized conditions because situational variables can affect test scores. The *Standards for Educational and Psychological Tests* published by the American Psychological Association and other professional groups emphasize that the directions for the administration of tests should be clearly spelled out in a test manual. These directions should be in sufficient detail to be duplicated in all situations in which the test is given. A good test manual will give the test examiner very detailed and strict instructions that include the exact words to be read to the test takers. Furthermore, it should spell out which questions are to be expected and how they are to be answered.

Inexperienced test administrators often do not fully appreciate the importance of standardization in administration. If you are giving tests or supervising others who are given this responsibility, you must take into consideration that the test may not be reliable or valid if you deviate from the specified instructions. Technical Box 8-1 provides detailed checklists assembled by Traxler (1951) and Clemans (1971) for the administration of group tests. The lists should give you an idea of the amount of detail that must be considered for careful, standardized test administration.

Technical Box 8-1 Sample Checklists for Test Administrators*

In preparation for the Testing Session:

1. For educational tests, match the level of the tests to the level of the students; that is, do not give tests that are too easy or too difficult.

2. See that the tests are on hand well in advance of the date on which they are to be used. Check the quantity of tests immediately upon receipt and, if more are needed, reorder at once. Store in a secure place.

3. Plan *in detail* for the administration of the tests. Choose examiners and proctors with great care. If possible, use examiners who have had previous experience giving the objective type of test. If inexperienced examiners must be used, they should be carefully rehearsed beforehand. *Remember that some very intelligent people are temperamentally unsuited to the exacting routine of adminstering a test.*

One may use relatively inexperienced persons as proctors for tests being given to larger groups, but they should not be placed in charge of the administration of a test.

4. Prepare an examination schedule and see that every person concerned receives a copy. The schedule should give the time and place of each test, indicate just where students to be tested should report and where those who are not taking the test should be, specify what material the examinees will need when taking the test, and give the name of the individual in charge of each examination. It should usually include provision for a make-up test for those who miss the regular testing.

5. Inform students about the examination and its purposes in a manner that will motivate them and encourage their cooperation without creating undue anxiety.

6. Become intimately acquainted with the test materials and the author's recommendations for standardizing administration.

7. Unless security measures prevent it, provide each examiner with a manual, an answer sheet, and a sample copy of the test several days before the examination. Urge the examiners to study the test materials and to take the test, because there is no better way of learning about it. *Most errors in the administration of tests are caused by failure of the examiners to prepare sufficiently beforehand.*

8. Plan procedures for distributing the test materials to the examiners on the day of the examination, except for the review copies mentioned in Point 7.

Before the test

1. Read the directions for administration, examine the test booklet and answer sheet, and rehearse the process of giving the test.

2. Clear up any points of potential confusion by discussion with the general administrator.

During the test

1. Make arrangements so that there will be no interruptions or distractions during the testing period. Persons should not come into or go out of the room unless absolutely necessary. This is especially important for timed tests.

2. Seat the students as specified in the test instructions.

3. When testing is in large groups and proctors are used, see that each proctor understands what is expected of him or her before, during, and at the end of the examination. While the test is in progress, circulate among the proctors keeping them alert to their duties.

4. Make announcements slowly and clearly in a voice that is loud enough to be heard throughout the room. Assume a businesslike and efficient attitude that will command attention, but do not be severe. Remember, some students become nervous when faced with an examination.

5. Supply, or have proctors supply, all students with booklets, pencils, and separate answer sheets, if they are to be used. Announce that the students are not to open their booklets until so instructed.

6. Have the students fill in the blanks on the front of the booklets or answer sheets. Be sure to announce the date, specify how names are to be written and/or coded on the answer sheet, and explain other items that may need clarification. Spend sufficient time on this step to see that the students give all the information

requested correctly. Ages and birth dates are especially important on tests of academic aptitude, because these determine what norms will be used.

7. Hold faithfully to the exact wording of the printed directions unless there is a compelling reason for introducing a variation in them, such as a fire in the building. The preparation of directions for a test is an important aspect of test construction and standardization. The wording of the directions has been carefully thought out by the test author. Do not improvise or introduce shortcuts. If you do, you may influence the test results significantly.

8. Time the examination with extreme care, using an interval timer or a stopwatch. Only in an emergency should a wristwatch be used and only then when it has a second hand and has been checked for accuracy. In many tests accurate timing is the most important single feature of the entire administration procedure. It is advisable to have one of the proctors check your timing to be sure that no error occurs.

9. Move about the room occasionally or have proctors move about to see that all students are working on the right part of the examination, but do not stand gazing over an examinee's shoulder so long that he becomes self-conscious, and do not move nervously from examinee to examinee. Present a reassuring manner—smile occasionally.

10. Do *not* allow necessary disciplinary actions to disrupt the examinees. The sole purpose of discipline in the testing room is to keep everyone working at maximum all the time, with a minimum of disturbance from all sources, *including* the examiner and proctors. Use gestures, facial expressions, and whispers in dealing with examinees during the working period. Make it clear that *no* questions will be answered during working periods except in the event of faulty materials. If anyone speaks aloud or makes semiaudible signs of frustation, smile and put your finger to your lips; if this persists, frown. If a serious disturbance seems imminent, *remove* the disruptive examinee from the room quickly and quietly and make an appointment to clear up the trouble later. Any disciplinary measure that disturbs the group can be just as much of a problem as any disturbance caused by an examinee.

11. Stop the examination immediately when the time is up.

After the test has been given

1. Collect the answer sheets and then the booklets.
2. Have the proctors count and turn in all collected materials promptly.
3. Alphabetize and check the papers against the class list, if required.
4. Follow the procedures that have been established to see that any absent examinees make up the examination. This is a bothersome step, but one that is unavoidable because complete data are essential if the results are to be used successfully in either teaching or guidance.
5. See that the tests are prepared for scoring. Instructions for this step vary and are important, so be certain to follow the directions carefully.

*From William V. Clemans, "Test Administration." In *Educational Measurement* (2nd ed), Robert L. Thorndike (Ed.). Washington, D.C.: American Council on Education, 1971, pp. 197–199.

There are a few occasions requiring deviation from standardized testing procedures. For example, Sattler (1982) acknowledges that special considerations must be given for the blind who cannot read portions of the test, and Kaplan (1979) discusses special considerations for testing the aged. However, many widely used tests have now developed special standardized methods for testing these special populations. In order to assure that tests are given under standardized conditions, some examiners prefer to give instructions through a tape recorder. Others have opted for computer-assisted test administration.

E.   *Computer-assisted test administration*

Computer technology is having an impact on many fields. Testing and test administration are not exceptions. Today most colleges and many grade schools have interactive computer capabilities. Easy access to computer terminals allows the administration of a test through interaction with a computer (Gianetti, Klinger, Johnson, & Williams, 1976).

Interactive testing involves the presentation of test items through a computer terminal and the automatic recording of test responses. The computer also can be programmed to instruct the test taker and to provide some instruction when parts of the testing procedure are not clear. Cronbach (1970) recognized the value of computers as test administrators some time ago. Among the advantages are:

1. excellence of standardization;
2. sequential administration, individually tailored;
3. precision of timing responses;
4. release of human testers for other duties;
5. patience; and
6. control of bias.

Although the potential of computer-assisted testing has been acknowledged for some time, applications of this technology have been relatively few (Gianetti et al., 1976). In the future, however, we can expect to see more computer-assisted test administration—for example, in the application of "tailored" tests. Here the items may be ordered according to level of difficulty. If someone gets several items correct at a certain level of difficulty, the program logic might jump that person ahead to items of greater difficulty. Through this process the program eventually can find an ability level without relying on the subjective biases of the examiner (Recase, 1977).

Computer-assisted test administration does not necessarily depend upon a structured order of test items. Indeed, one advantage of this approach is that the items can be given in any order or in a unique random order for every test taker. The computerized approach does offer many advantages for unique testing situations. For example, if you want to exactly limit the amount of time any one item can be studied, the computer easily can be programmed to flash the items onto the screen for specific durations. Furthermore, the computer-assisted method makes it impossible for test takers to look ahead at other sections of the test or go back to sections that already have been completed (Hoffman & Lundberg, 1976). Comparisons of test scores obtained with computer-assisted or paper-and-pencil administration have not tended to show large differences between the methods (Allen, 1979). Yet the computer method assures standardization and control.

There have been a few serendipitous findings on computer-assisted test administrations. One of the most interesting concerns the use of computers to interview potentially suicidal persons. Many psychologists and psychiatrists believe that people in trouble always must be interviewed by a warm, caring, and empathetic person. These therapists would be appalled if someone experiencing an emotional crisis was interviewed by an electronic computer terminal. However, one study demonstrated that people will divulge more personal information to a machine than they will to a human interviewer. Apparently many people are secretive about their thoughts and feelings and would rather discuss them anonymously.

F. *Subject variables*

A final variable that might be a serious source of error is the state of the subject. It is well known that motivation and anxiety can greatly affect test scores. For example, studies have shown that many college students suffer from a serious debilitating condition known as "test anxiety." Test-anxious students often have difficulty focusing attention on the test items and might be distracted by other thoughts such as "I am not doing well" or "I am running out of time."

Test anxiety is a very important problem in testing and an important area of contemporary research. Therefore, we have devoted an entire chapter to this topic (Chapter 19).

II. BEHAVIORAL ASSESSMENT METHODOLOGY

The increasing use of behavioral observation methodology has been accompanied by many new problems. As we have seen in this chapter, minor variations on standard test administration procedures can have an effect on test scores. However, most of these problems can be overcome by adhering very closely to standard test administration procedures. In behavioral observation studies, the observer has a more active role in recording the data and, as a result, is much more likely to make errors. Some of the problems include reactivity, drift, and expectancies (Kazdin, 1977).

A. *Reactivity*

The reliability of observers in behavioral observation studies is usually assessed in selected sessions in which an experimenter "observes the observers." In other words, someone looks over the observer's shoulder to determine whether he or she is properly recording. Studies have shown that the time when the reliability and accuracy are highest is when someone is checking on the observers. This increase in reliability is called *reactivity* because it is a reaction to being checked. In one study observers rated behavior recorded on a videotape under one of two conditions. First the observers were told that their ratings would be checked against a standard for accuracy. Later the observers were told there was no standard. However, there actually was a standard against which the accuracy of both conditions was checked. The data demonstrated that accuracy dropped by 25% when the observers were led to believe their observations would not be evaluated (Reid, 1970). Indeed, many studies have demonstrated that accuracy and inter-rater agreement decrease when the observers believe their work is not being checked (Kent, Kanowitz, O'Leary, & Cheiken, 1977; Taplin & Reid, 1973).

In order to deal with this problem some experimenters resort to covert operations. For example, the experimenter might randomly check up on the performance of the observers without their knowledge. In general one always should be cautious in interpreting reports on inter-rater reliability. Often the estimate of rater reliability is based on assessment during training. When observers are not observed themselves (such as when they are actually collecting data), their accuracy can be expected to drop.

B. *Drift*

When observers are trained in behavioral observation methods they are given extensive feedback and coaching. After they leave the training sessions it is assumed that they will continue to perform on the job as they did in training. However, studies show that observers have a tendency to "drift" away from the strict rules they followed in training and to adopt their own idiosyncratic definitions of behavior (O'Leary & Kent, 1973; Reid & DeMaster, 1972). The drift may not always be peculiar to the individual observer. Sometimes when many observers work together on the same job they seem to drift away from the original definitions of the behavior, but they do it as a group (O'Leary & Kent, 1973). The occurrence of observer drift suggests that observers should be periodically retrained. Frequent meetings between the observers should be held at which there are discussions about the use of the observation methods. These meetings can eliminate some of the difficulties (Kazdin, 1977).

C. *Expectancies*

The literature on observer expectancies is similar to that on test examiner expectancies. As noted earlier, Rosenthal has accumulated some evidence that expectancies of experimenters can affect the results of behavioral experiments. Some of the Rosenthal experiments show an effect of experimenter expectancies whereas others do not. Similarly, some studies show that test administrator expectancies can affect scores on individual IQ tests whereas other studies do not (Sattler, 1974).

The same sort of inconsistent picture appears for studies on behavioral observation. Some studies have shown that behavioral observers will observe the behavior they expect (Azrin, Holz, Ulrich, & Goldiamond, 1961; Scott, Burton, & Yarro, 1967). On the other hand, some very thorough studies do not demonstrate an expectancy effect (Kent et al., 1974; Redfield & Paul, 1976). Expectancies have been more consistently shown to cause bias in the behavioral observation when observers are given reinforcement for recording a particular behavior (O'Leary, Kent, & Kanowitz, 1975).

The impact of expectancy is very subtle. It probably has some minor biasing effect upon behavioral data. The finding that it occurs significantly in some studies but not others is consistent with the notion that there is a minor but potentially damaging effect of expectancy. In order to avoid this sort of bias, observers should not be informed about what behavior to expect.

D. Statistical control of rating errors

Many efforts to improve the accuracy of raters have produced discouraging results. These attempts to increase rater reliability through extended training have been particularly frustrating for many researchers and applied psychologists because training is expensive and time consuming. Recently a group of psychologists argued that halo or leniency errors can be controlled statistically. This is accomplished through a method known as "partial correlation." Here, the correlation between two variables is found while controlling for the variability in a third variable.

As an example of the method, the group studied 537 supervisory ratings of middle-level managers. Each manager was rated on 15 specific attributes and 1 overall performance rating. Then the variance associated with the overall performance rating was separated from the other ratings. By using this method the variance attributable to the halo effect was reduced and the discriminant validity of the method for rating performance improved (Landy, Vance, Barnes-Farrell, & Steele, 1980).

III. SUMMARY

Standardized test administration procedures are a necessity. Extensive research in social psychology has clearly demonstrated that situational factors can affect scores on mental and behavioral tasks. These effects, however, can be very subtle and may not be observed in all studies. For example, a few studies have shown that the race of the examiner has an impact upon scores for standardized intelligence tests. However, the majority of the studies do not find that the examiner's race has an impact. Similarly, characteristics of the examiner's rapport and expectancies may influence scores on some but not all occasions. Direct reinforcement of specific responses (something that usually should not be done in most testing situations) does have an acknowledged impact.

In order to reduce some of the effects of the examiner there has been an increasing interest in computer-assisted test administration. Computers can administer and score most tests with great precision and with minimum bias. This mode of test administration might be expected to become more common in the near future.

Test scores also are affected by the state of the subject. For example, some students suffer from debilitating test anxiety that seriously interferes with performance.

The use of behavioral observation raises some of the same problems as test administration. In behavioral observation an observer records the responses of others, while in traditional test taking the subject records his or her own behavior. A common problem in behavioral observation is *reactivity*, in which the observer is most accurate only when he or she thinks someone is checking the work. A second problem is *drift,* in which observers gradually come to ignore the procedure they were taught and adopt their own observation method. A third problem is *expectancy* or the tendency for observations to be affected by what the observer expects to observe. The magnitude of these effects is probably small, but the potential bias they introduce is serious enough that precautions should be taken.

APPLICATIONS

9

Introduction to Applied Aspects of Testing

Learning objectives

When you have completed this chapter, you should be able to do the following:

1. *Describe the relationship between psychological tests and the decision-making process.*
2. *Explain why the issue of the uses of test results is at least as important as the issue of test quality.*
3. *Define standard administration.*
4. *Explain the idea of a test battery.*
5. *Distinguish between testing and assessment.*
6. *Identify one of the two most referenced and important intelligence tests.*

Although psychology began as a strictly scientific discipline, as the 1980s dawned there were more positions for appliers of psychological knowledge than there were for strictly scientific pursuits (see Kiesler, 1979). Indeed, many students associate psychology more with its applications in clinical, counseling, educational, and industrial settings than with its scientific base. Furthermore, it seems as though increasingly more students enter psychology with applied interests. Perhaps the interest in applied aspects of psychology reflects a need to find relevance in the educational process. However, because applied psychology depends upon psychology's scientific base, thorough knowledge of scientific principles is essential for a good understanding of any applied branch of psychology, and psychological tests are no exception.

In Chapters 2 through 8 we stressed scientific knowledge and the principles underlying psychological tests. Part 2 on *applications* continues the stress on scientific findings, major principles, and basic concepts. However, consistent with the current interest, Part 2 also provides an in-depth discussion of applied aspects of testing. Our decision to present this material on the application of some of the most highly used tests is based primarily on student interest. However, it also meets the need for an understanding of tests by the increasing numbers of nonpsychologists who make use of tests. Thus the application section provides an overview of many of the most important and highly used psychological tests and also a good introduction for those who may directly or indirectly make use of psychological tests in professional activities.

In the first eight chapters certain key terms and distinctions were introduced and subsequently reviewed to facilitate learning and offer you the opportunity to study the material from a variety of perspectives. In this chapter we will not only introduce some new terms and distinctions, but also review some of the earlier presented concepts. Your success in mastering the application of psychological testing will depend upon your attainment of a firm understanding of several basic ideas and distinctions. Through repetition and presentation of these basic concepts in a variety of contexts, we hope to establish them in your long-term memory.

I. THE ISSUE OF TEST USE

A little knowledge *can be* a dangerous thing, because without a proper perspective there is always the danger of the misuse or improper application of facts. Because psychological tests can be extremely powerful tools, the danger of their misuse is great. Therefore, in learning about the application of tests, one has a responsibility to be cautious and to remain within the boundaries of one's training and experience. Indeed, of all the issues and controversies involving psychological tests, the issue of the uses of tests is perhaps the most critical from an ethical and moral standpoint. For this reason the opening chapter in Part 2 begins with a discussion of the issues involved in using test results.

In our society, especially as it functions today, decisions are constantly made that affect the lives of countless individuals. Most people eventually find themselves grouped, categorized, selected, or rejected (for example, for college or a job). We are not saying this decision process is good or bad; it is simply a reality of contemporary life. By now you are well aware that tests often are used as an aid to this decision process. One important issue facing professional persons and the public alike is whether tests should play a role in the inevitable decision process.

Given that psychological tests are imperfect instruments, what role do you feel tests should play in making decisions? The American Psychological Association, American Educational Research Association, and National Council on Measurement in Education (1974) noted in their *Standards for Educational and Psychological Tests* that some people believe that because tests may be biased or lacking in accuracy, no test should be used until alternative tests are developed. In defense of tests it was argued that the basic issue is not so much one of test quality as an issue of test use. We concur with this argument.

Any test can be misused—regardless of its fairness, lack of bias, and psychometric adequacy. As previously indicated, decisions are going to be made whether or not tests are used. Thus it seems more relevant to ask whether tests can be fairly and appropriately used as an aid in the decision process. The elimination of tests will not solve the problems inherent in the decision-making process. Bias or potential bias would not be eliminated, because people can be just as biased, if not more so, than tests. Thus, in solving the problems of the decision process, we must look beyond tests per se (Reschly, 1981).

Testing continues to flourish despite heavy attacks from both the public and professionals. This seems to indicate that many decision makers consider tests useful. Again, it is not the tests but how they are used that is of central importance. Tests themselves are neither good nor bad, but unless they are properly used, tests can be extremely harmful to individuals as well as to society. Thus the real problem for test users and the public is to insure that tests *are properly used* (for example, see Novick, 1981).

To make proper use of a test, a tester must have complete understanding of the test being used. This involves knowledge of the *standardization sample* and the procedures for administering the test. According to the *Standards for Educational and Psychological Tests,* a test manual must describe the standardization sample and the methods for administering the test. The procedure outlined in the test manual, when followed, is known as a *standard administration* of the test. If the test is not administered according to the procedure specified in the test manual, then it is not appropriate to compare the resulting test data to the standardization sample (which was given a standard administration). Furthermore, the importance of comparing a test result to an appropriate standardization sample should not be minimized. For example, if the standardization sample comprises exclusively middle-class, White Americans, the validity of the test for other populations would be questionable.

In Chapters 4 and 5 you learned about the different types of reliability and validity. In making proper use of tests, however, it is not sufficient to ask "Is this test reliable?" or "Is this test valid?" A test may have an extremely high level of internal consistency, as indicated by high split-half reliability coefficients, and such reliability would provide support for the test. However, a test that is internally consistent is not necessarily reliable over time. Thus, in making appropriate use of a test, one cannot feel comfortable just because the test manual reports that the test is "highly reliable" or "highly valid." One also must know if the test has the type of reliability and the type of validity for one's purposes. If results are needed that are stable across time, for example, you would expect to find evidence of test-retest reliability. Test users therefore must ask, "Does this test have the type of reliability and validity for the purposes for which the test is to be used?" If the answer is "No," then the test should not be used.

To understand a test means to know (1) the characteristics of its standardization sample, (2) the types and quality of its reliability and validity, (3) the reliability and validity of comparable tests, (4) the scoring procedures, (5) the method of administration, (6) the limitations, and (7) the strengths. Information in all these areas should be available in the test manual. One also should know the basic concepts covered in this text.

Even if one understands a test completely, however, it still is vulnerable to misuse unless the tester is trained in its proper use and has had experience with the test, preferably under supervision by an expert. In the absence of the recommended experience, the test user should state the limitations of the results and caution anyone who might use the test score.

State licensing laws and professional ethical codes are designed to protect the public from abuses resulting from test misuse (Danish & Smyer, 1981). Licensing laws attempt to prevent tests from being used by people other than those who are qualified by training and experience. Ethical codes of such organizations as the American Medical Association and American Psychological Association, furthermore, prohibit even highly trained specialists from using procedures beyond their competency. Despite these safeguards, however, the responsibility for proper test use must be shared by all concerned. Teachers, counselors, and others who do not actually administer tests but do make use of test results have a responsibility to understand the appropriate uses and limitations of any test they use. In the absence of such knowledge, test results should be viewed cautiously. For example, if a high-school counselor encounters a result based on a new test, the result should not be used until all the necessary information about the test has been obtained. The counselor should be satisfied that the result can be appropriately applied to the person for whom it is being used.

In addition to precautions on the part of the examiner and anyone else using test scores, the public or consumer of tests also must share in the burden of insuring that tests are properly used and not misused. This means that, as stated earlier, we should become as informed as possible about tests that are used in decisions affecting our lives. One major intent of this text is to provide the consumers of tests as well as the users of tests with sufficient information to become responsible, informed participants in the pervasive field of testing.

II. CONCEPTS AND DISTINCTIONS

In making proper use of tests, you should be familiar with some important concepts, definitions, and distinctions. Below we discuss a test battery, in which results from two or more tests are used together and often in conjunction with other (nontest) sources of data. We also make a distinction between testing and assessment.

A. A test battery

In reading Part 2 of this text you no doubt will quickly conclude that although they are useful in applied settings, even the best available tests leave much to be desired in terms of scientific, or what we will refer to as *psychometric*, adequacy. However, as in medicine, psychological practitioners must make daily decisions on the basis of existing technology. Because of the need for psychological services, practitioners do not have the luxury of waiting until conclusive evidence is published before making application of existing technology. On the other hand, all psychologists are rooted to a scientific perspective. Those who use psychological tests, therefore, usually have a scientific orientation. They are acutely aware of the limitations of the existing technology but often find themselves forced to use the best of what is available.

To deal with their frequently divergent needs for tests that are useful in professional settings and are scientifically sound, psychologists have come up with better ways of using existing tools. One method involves the concept of a test battery. A *test battery* is a collection of tests whose scores are used together in appraising an individual. In employing a test battery the practitioner refuses to accept the validity of a single bit of isolated information. On the contrary, the modern practitioner bases his or her decisions on a variety of data sources. In the test battery a single test score is used in conjunction with other tests and other sources of information, not in isolation. These sources of information may include an interview, direct observations, input from others such as the person's peers or relatives, and records of past performance. In using a test battery in conjunction with other sources of information, the test user integrates a wide variety of findings. This helps to reduce potential errors and avoid pitfalls when only isolated bits of information are relied upon.

B. Testing versus assessment

The terms *testing* and *assessment* often are confused. The goal of "assessment" is to evaluate an individual so that he or she can be described in terms of current functioning and also so that predictions can be made concerning future functioning. Psychological assessment involves the classification of behavior into categories measured against a normative standard (Kaswan, 1981). Tests are used in the assessment process. Thus not all assessment procedures can be called *tests*. In the strictest sense, an assessment procedure is called a test only when its procedures for administration, scoring, and interpretation are standardized; there is a normative sample; and there is evidence in support of its reliability (dependability) and validity (meaning).

A tool useful in the assessment process may or may not qualify as a test.

Indeed, many psychologists have concluded that certain so-called tests would be more appropriately labeled assessment tools because, while they are of use to practitioners in evaluating current and future functioning, they do not meet the requirements of a test. In Part 2 we call many procedures *tests* that others might prefer to call *assessment techniques*. For many of the procedures, especially measures of personality, opinion is divided concerning whether or not the term *test* is appropriate. Thus, where we use the term *test* to describe a particular procedure, your instructor might prefer a term such as *technique* or *assessment tool*.

III.   CRITERIA FOR SELECTION OF TESTS

In view of the large number of available tests, it was no easy matter to decide which to include and which to omit. We thought you might be interested in the major guidelines we used in selecting tests for Part 2 and for deciding how much detail to include about each test.

A.   *Ability tests*

It was not our purpose to discuss *every* test of human ability that has ever been used or even all of those that currently exist. The *Mental Measurement Yearbooks* (for example, Buros, 1972, 1978) and other sources discussed in earlier chapters are designed for this purpose. Our purpose is to help you understand the principles underlying individual and group ability tests so that you will know what to look for in selecting and evaluating them.

In order to include as many tests as possible and also present these in a readable context, our general format is as follows. We briefly describe each test, classify it according to use, provide a general discussion of its psychometric properties, and then attempt to note its major limitations and strengths. For the more important tests we also include some of the major recent research findings. Students requiring more specific or detailed information than provided herein should consult the *Mental Measurement Yearbooks*, the actual test manual, the psychological abstracts, and other sources listed in Chapter 7.

Our primary criterion for selecting a test for discussion demanded that the test illustrate an important concept, a unique property, or an important principle. Whenever more than one test was available to illustrate a specific concept or application, we generally included only the most important for discussion. To evaluate importance we considered how much the test is actually used as revealed in studies of test usage such as those by Lubin, Wallis, and Paine (1971), Sundberg (1961), and Wade and Baker (1977). These have used questionnaire data completed by users of tests to determine the frequency of a test's use in an applied setting.

In evaluating importance, we also consulted the *Mental Measurement Yearbooks* to determine the number of references for any given test. This number of references provided a rough index of the interest the test has generated in the research community. As a final gauge of importance, we surveyed the literature to determine which tests have been discussed by experts in books and reviews exclusively devoted to ability tests, such as Sattler's (1982) text on testing the intelligence of children. We avoided any test in which, in our judgment, the psychometric characteristics were poor. However, any exclusion on our part does not mean a test is psychometrically unsound. Finally, tests of historical value or significance often were included.

It was not hard to ascertain which intelligence tests are most used. Without question the most frequently used ones are the Stanford-Binet intelligence scale and the family of tests known as the Wechsler intelligence scales. Furthermore, more research has been conducted with these two scales than with any other ability test. Buros (1974) listed 215 intelligence tests currently in print. Approximately 93% of the 10,941 references related to these 215 tests pertained to the top 59, with only 857 (or about 7%) of the references on the remaining 156 tests. The Stanford-Binet scale led the list with 1408 references.

However, if the number of references for each member of the family of Wechsler intelligence scales is added together, the total is about 3800. Together the Stanford-Binet intelligence scale and Wechsler intelligence scales account for about half the research done with intelligence tests of any kind and comprise more than half the individual ability tests administered in the United States. Furthermore, principles of all intelligence tests can be easily illustrated in an analysis of the evolution of the Stanford-Binet scale and Wechsler intelligence scales, which we refer to as the "major" intelligence scales. Therefore, in order to achieve the necessary depth for understanding while avoiding the encyclopedic approach, we devote one chapter to the Stanford-Binet scale (Chapter 11) and another to the Wechsler intelligence scales (Chapter 12). These two chapters provide the foundation for understanding all other ability tests, which are discussed in Chapters 13 and 14.

B. Approach to personality tests

Our approach to personality tests concentrates on principles, as does our approach to ability tests. Our discussions of ability as well as personality tests both contain sections in which great detail is presented. We realize that absorbing such detail can be a burden. However, with a detailed knowledge of a relatively few of the most highly used and researched tests, you will acquire a basis for comparing all other tests. What we have tried to do is to present each of the major types and kinds of personality tests with sufficient detail to give you a basis to compare and evaluate new tests or any of the many personality tests not included in our discussion. Unfortunately, there are quite a few such tests, despite our selective orientation. Nevertheless, you will see a clear-cut emphasis on the Minnesota Multiphasic Personality Inventory (MMPI), which is the most frequently referenced structured personality test (and the most referenced of all personality tests), as well as an emphasis on the Rorschach inkblot test, the most frequently referenced projective personality test (Buros, 1972, 1978).

IV. SUMMARY

In this chapter we have provided an introduction to Part 2, the *applications* of psychological tests, and we have discussed the use of test results. Our position, consistent with that of the American Psychological Assocation, is that the major problem today with tests is not their quality or soundness but the way test results are used. Although new and better tests are most welcome, the real challenge is to insure that the available tests are used properly.

One important way of making appropriate use of psychological tests is to use them in a battery. A test battery does not rely on a single bit of information. Rather, data from two or more tests are combined with other sources of information, such as an interview. In the next chapter you will be exposed to the major concepts underlying several types of interviews, including "employment" and "clinical." Because the interview plays such an important role in so many decisions and complements standard tests so well, the importance of interviewing skill as an adjunct to the testing process cannot be overemphasized.

In addition to the issue of test use and the concept of a test battery, Chapter 9 explained our rationale for selecting the tests in Part 2. For the most part, we have included the most highly used and referenced ability and personality tests. You will find an in-depth discussion on a few tests, but these are tests for which thousands of references exist. We have assumed that with a thorough knowledge of a select group of especially important tests and a more general knowledge of a wide variety of other popular tests, you will acquire an ability to evaluate tests. For now, let us proceed to our discussion of interviews.

10

Interview Techniques

Learning objectives

When you have completed this chapter, you should be able to do the following:

1. *Explain the difference between a structured and an unstructured interview.*
2. *Discuss the importance of setting the proper tone for the interview.*
3. *Describe the role of the attitude of the interviewer in the interview process.*
4. *Identify some of the characteristics of effective interviewing.*
5. *List which types of statements tend to keep the interaction flowing or elicit self-exploration in the interviewee.*
6. *Explain the effects of understanding statements on interviewee responses.*
7. *Review the role of the theoretical orientation of the interviewer in the interview process.*
8. *Identify the various sources of error in the interview.*
9. *Explain how interview skills are acquired and developed.*

A young man named John was being considered for a high-level public relations position with his firm in the computer industry. The duties of the position would require him to interact with a wide variety of people, ranging from heads of state and corporation presidents through rank-and-file employees and union officials. In addition, the position would involve making formal policy statements for release to newspapers and television stations throughout the world. He often would have to interact with reporters. Any poorly phrased statement or inappropriate reaction on his part could result in adverse publicity, which could cost his firm millions of dollars. The application process therefore involved an elaborate testing procedure. Included were two lengthy interviews.

The first was with the firm's personnel selection officer; the second was with the firm's clinical psychologist.

Knowing the importance of first impressions (Lyman, Hatlelid, & Macundy, 1981), John was careful to appear neat and well groomed. In his first interview the personnel officer read from a form as she conducted the interview, which went something like this:

> *Officer*: I've read your application form and have gone over your qualifications. Would you now please outline your educational experiences, beginning with high school.
>
> *John*: I graduated from high school in June of 1965 with a major in history and social studies. I began attending college in September of 1965. I graduated in June of 1969 with a major in psychology and minor in business management. I then entered the university's graduate program in business. I obtained my master's degree in business administration.
>
> *Officer*: What is your work history? Begin with your first full-time employment.

John described his work history. The personnel officer then continued a series of questions, which John systematically answered. The questions went something like this:

> How do your education and experience relate to the job for which you are applying?
>
> What educational experiences have you had that might help you function on the job for which you are applying?
>
> What employment experiences have you had that might help you function on the job for which you are applying?
>
> Identify any deficiencies in your educational and work experiences.
>
> What educational and work experiences have you had that might impair your ability to function on the job for which you are applying?

The interview continued in a similar manner. With each question the personnel officer attempted to relate John's educational and work experiences to the particular job duties he was hoping to assume. As her final question the personnel officer asked, "Why do you believe you would make a good candidate for this position?"

John felt good about his interview with the personnel officer. He thought the questions were clear and straightforward, and he was pleased by his answers. The next day he appeared for his interview with the clinical psychologist.

Unlike the personnel officer, the psychologist conducted the interview without the interview questions being in writing. This second interview, which was quite different from the first, went something like this:

Psychologist: John, why don't you tell me a little bit about yourself?

John: Where do you want me to begin?

Psychologist: Oh, it doesn't matter. Just tell me about yourself.

John: I graduated from high school in June of 1965. I majored in history and social studies.

Psychologist: Yes, I see.

John: I then attended college and finally graduate school. My master's degree should help me to assume the duties of the new position.

Psychologist: You feel that your master's degree is a useful asset in your application.

John: Yes, my graduate experiences taught me how to work with others.

Psychologist: With these graduate experiences you learned the art of working with other people.

John: Well, I guess I didn't learn it all in graduate school. I've always managed to get along well with others.

Psychologist: As far as you can tell, you've never had trouble working with people.

John: That's right. As the oldest of three children I've always had responsibility for supervising others. You know what I mean?

Psychologist: Being the oldest you were given extra responsibilities as a child.

John: Not that I resented it. Well, maybe sometimes. It's just that I never had much time for myself.

Psychologist: And having time for yourself is important to you.

John: Yes, of course it is. I guess everybody needs some time alone.

Psychologist: As a person who deals with others all day long you must treasure those few moments you have to yourself.

John: I really do. Whenever I get a chance I like to drive up to the lake all by myself and just think.

Psychologist: These moments are precious to you.

The interview continued like this for about an hour. After it was over, John wasn't sure how well he had done. There didn't seem to be any particular focus or direction to the interview, he believed, as there had been with the personnel officer. It seemed to John as if his second interview touched on everything from his childhood to his personal thoughts. This second interview was quite a contrast to the first.

Think about the two interviews. In what ways were they alike? How did they differ? As you contemplate your answer you will soon realize that there is more than one type of interview and that interviews can differ considerably.

The first interview with the personnel officer was highly structured. The interviewer read from a printed set of questions. The personnel officer's interview was no doubt "standardized." Thus all applicants for the position would be asked the same questions in the same sequence. The second interview, by contrast, was unstructured and therefore unstandardized. The clinical psychologist didn't appear to have any specific or particular questions in mind, and the sequence of questions followed from John's statements. Each applicant no doubt would be asked different questions, depending upon his or her responses.

Can you identify any other differences between the two interviews? The first was narrow or restricted. It focused on two specific areas: John's education and work experiences. The second was broad or unrestricted. It touched on a variety of areas, although the focus of the interview was clearly John himself. The first interview was "directive." The personnel officer directed, guided, and controlled the course of the interview. The second interview was "nondirective." The clinical psychologist let John determine the direction of the interview. When John talked about his master's degree, the psychologist discussed this. When John talked about being the oldest of three children, this became the focus of the psychologist's response. Furthermore, unlike the personnel officer, the psychologist rarely asked questions. Instead, the psychologist tended to comment or reflect upon John's previous statement. Last, but perhaps most important, John's interview with the personnel officer can best be described as an *employment* or *selection interview*. Thus the first interview was designed to elicit information pertaining to John's qualifications and capabilities for particular employment duties. The second interview, on the other hand, can best be described as a *diagnostic interview*. Thus the second interview was designed to elicit information concerning John's emotional functioning. His qualifications were clearly not an issue in the second interview. Rather, in conducting a diagnostic interview, the clinical psychologist was interested in John's feelings, thoughts, attitudes, and the like, which might impede or facilitate John's ability to function competently.

I. THE INTERVIEW AS A TEST

In many respects, an interview is a test. Like any psychological test, an interview is a method for gathering data or information about an individual. This information is then used to describe the individual, make future predictions, or both. Like tests, interviews can be evaluated in terms of standard psychometric qualities such as reliability and validity. Furthermore, there are several types of interview procedures, depending on the type of information that is sought and the goals of the interviewer.

Like any other test the interview involves an interaction between two or more people. Some interviews proceed as do individually administered tests in which the interviewer interacts with a single individual at a time. In other interviews, such as the family interview, a single interviewer interacts with two or more individuals at the same time, just as in any group-administered test. Like any test, an interview has a definite purpose. Unlike a random conversation, an interview generally has a direction and focuses on a particular content area. Even John's interview with the clinical psychologist had direction and focus. Although the interview was nondirective, this did not mean there was *no direction*. The direction of the interview followed John's own statements and previous responses. Although broad, there was a focus—namely, John. Furthermore, just as the person who administers a test must take responsibility for the test administration process, so must the interviewer assume responsibility for the conduct of the interview.

When viewed from a variety of perspectives, an interview is a test: a very important one. Many other tests, such as the Thematic Apperception Test (TAT), for example, cannot be properly used without adequate interview data. The interview, on the other hand, often stands as the only or most important source of data. Good interviewing skills, furthermore, perhaps may be one of the single most important tools for functioning in today's society. Not only is interviewing the chief method for data collection in clinical psychiatry (Mackinnon & Michels, 1971; Stevenson, 1971), but interviewing also is used in all health-related professions including general medicine and nursing. Interviewing also is an essential testing tool in subspecialities such as clinical, industrial, counseling, school, and correctional psychology.

Interviewing also is a tool in social work, vocational and guidance counseling, marriage and family counseling, and so on. Parole boards conduct parole interviews. In addition, interviewing is an essential tool of the researcher. Businesspeople and managers use interviewing to evaluate employees as well as potential clients. Interviewing also is a primary tool of the courtroom attorney. Indeed, interview skills are important in most professions involving people. Contractors or architects must possess sufficient interviewing skills to determine exactly what their customers want them to do. Interviewing also plays a role in everyday life, such as when a parent questions a group of children to find out who is responsible for a broken window. In beginning new relationships on a positive note one also must possess a degree of interviewing skill. Given its broad application, no introductory text on psychological tests could be complete without reference to the interview.

II.   RECIPROCAL NATURE OF INTERVIEWING

Although there are many varied types and purposes of interviews, there are factors common to all interviews. First, all interviews involve mutual or shared interaction (Wiens, 1976). The participants are interdependent upon and influence each other (Heller, 1971, pages 145–148). The transactional or reciprocal nature of the interview process is illustrated in a study by Heller, Davis, and Myers (1966). They found that if one of the participants in the interview increased his or her activity level, the activity level of the other participant also increased. Similarly, a reduction in activity in one of the interview participants was associated with a reduction in the activity of the other. A similar finding was also reported by Matarazzo, Wiens, Matarazzo, and Saslow (1968). Thus the participants in an interview have a profound effect on one another.

In addition to influencing each other's activity, the mood of one of the participants in an interview influences the mood of the other. Heller (1971), for example, reported that when professional actors responded with anger (hostility) to even highly trained experienced interviewers, the interviewers responded in kind. That is, they became angry themselves and directed this back toward the actors. The phenomenon observed by Heller is generally known as *social facilitation* (see Bandura, 1971, page 694). Social facilitation means we tend to act like the models around us. If the interviewer is tense, anxious, defensive, and aloof, the interviewee will tend to respond in kind. Thus, if the interviewer wishes to create conditions of openness, warmth, acceptance, comfort, calmness, and support, he or she must exhibit these qualities.

Social facilitation is one of the most important concepts underlying the interview process. Because the participants in an interview influence each other, obviously the good interviewer must provide a relaxed and safe atmosphere. Through social facilitation, the interviewee then will eventually begin to feel relaxed and safe. However, although participants in an interview influence each other, the good interviewer remains in control and sets the tone of the interview. If the interviewer reacts to the interviewee's tension and anxiety with more tension and anxiety, then a tense situation will rapidly develop. By remaining calm, confident, in control, and self-assured, however, the interviewer will have a calming effect on the interviewee. In our experience even potentially violent prison inmates or disturbed psychotic persons become manageable when the interviewer sets the proper tone. This is consistent with the finding of Schwartz and Hawkins (1965) that modeling influences the behavior even of adult schizophrenic persons.

III.   PRINCIPLES OF EFFECTIVE INTERVIEWING

Setting the tone to facilitate the proper attitudes (for example, relaxation and openness) in the person being interviewed is just one factor in effective interviewing. There are other principles that seem to be common to effective interviewing. Naturally, specific interview techniques and approaches vary depending upon such factors as the type of interview (for example, employment versus diagnostic) and the goals of the interviewer (for example, description versus prediction). Thus there are no hard-and-fast rules that apply to all interview situations. However, there are some principles that aid in the conduct of almost any interview. We present some of these principles because they will help increase your understanding of the factors and processes that underlie the interview. Knowledge of these principles also should help you acquire interview skills of your own.

A. *The proper attitudes*

As Tyler (1969) noted, good interview behavior is actually more a matter of attitude than skill. Experiments in social psychology, for example, have shown that "interpersonal influence" (that is, the degree to which one person can influence another) is related to "interpersonal attraction" (that is, the degree to which there is a shared feeling of understanding, mutual respect, similarity, and the like (Baglan, 1981; Nisbett & Ross, 1980). Attitudes generally related to good interviewing skills include warmth, genuineness, acceptance, understanding, openness, honesty, and fairness. Saccuzzo (1975), for example, studied the initial psychotherapy interviews of first-year clinical psychology graduate students. Patients and therapists both responded to a questionnaire. Their task was to rate the quality of the interview and indicate the topics, concerns, problems, and feelings of the patient as well as the feelings of the therapist.

Although the patients' feelings and concerns were important, the most important factor in the patients' evaluations of the quality of the interview were their perceptions of the interviewer's feelings. The session was given a good evaluation by both interview participants when the patient saw the interviewer as warm, open, concerned, involved, committed, and interested, irrespective of the type or severity of problem or what was talked about. On the other hand, independent of all other factors, when the interviewer was seen as cold, defensive, uninterested, uninvolved, aloof, and bored, the session was rated poorly. To appear effective and establish rapport the interviewer must display the proper attitudes.

B. *Responses to avoid*

In a "stress interview" the interviewer may deliberately induce discomfort or anxiety in the interviewee. As a rule, however, making interviewees feel uncomfortable tends to place them on guard. Guarded or anxious interviewees tend to reveal little information about themselves. However, one of the purposes of the stress interview is to determine how well an individual functions in a stressful, uncomfortable, or demanding situation. Thus the purpose of the interview dictates the type of responses to use or avoid. If the goal is to elicit as much

information as possible, or if one wishes the interview to be considered satisfactory by the interviewee, then certain responses should be avoided. Responses
that should generally be avoided because of their disruptive or limiting effect on
the interview process include *judgmental* or *evaluative statements*, *probing
statements, hostility,* and *false reassurance*.

Judgmental or evaluative statements are particularly apt to inhibit the
interviewee. Being judgmental means evaluating the thoughts, feelings, or actions of another. When we use such terms as good, bad, excellent, terrible,
disgusting, disgraceful, stupid, and the like, we are being evaluative. When we
make an *evaluative statement* we are judging the other person. This tends to put
the person on guard because it communicates that "I don't approve of this
aspect of you." In placing the person on guard we limit his or her ease in
revealing important information. Thus, unless the goal of the interview is to
determine how a person responds to being evaluated or to apply stress by
responding with strong disapproval or displeasure, evaluative or judgmental
statements generally should be avoided in good interview behavior.

Also to be avoided, unless necessary for a specific purpose or type of
interview, are *probing statements*. These demand more information than the
interviewee has been willing to provide voluntarily. The most common way to
phrase a probing statement is to ask a question that begins with "Why?" As
Wiens (1976) noted, asking "Why?" tends to place the person on the defensive.
When we ask "Why?" such as in "Why did you stay out so late?" we are
demanding that the person explain his or her behavior. Such a demand obviously has a judgmental quality. Furthermore, in probing we may induce the
interviewee to reveal something he or she is not yet ready to reveal. If this
happens the interviewee will probably feel anxious and thus not very well
disposed to revealing additional information.

Evaluative and probing statements are just two of the many types of
interviewer responses. To acquire interviewing skill an interviewer must learn all
the various types of responses and when to use or avoid them. Porter (1950), for
example, provides an in-depth analysis of five types of responses, and Gilmore
(1973) reviews several others. The *hostile response* directs anger toward the
interviewee. The *reassuring response* attempts to comfort or support the interviewee, such as "Don't worry, everything will be all right." Porter (1950) argued
that evaluative, probing, and reassuring responses should be avoided. Regarding the latter, the reassuring statement, "false reassurance" almost always
should be avoided. For example, say a friend of yours flunks out of college, loses
his job, and gets kicked out of his home by his parents. You are in fact lying to
this person when you say "Don't worry, no problem, it's okay." This is false
reassurance, and it does nothing to help your friend except perhaps make him
realize that you are not going to assist. The fact of the matter is that what has
happened to your friend is terrible and will require specific action on his part to

prevent even more disastrous developments. Naturally, you should not over-whelm your friend with all the facts at once, but he needs to come to grips with the situation in manageable doses before taking the necessary steps to con-structively solve the problem. The person giving false reassurance usually knows this, and so does the person receiving it.

C. *Effective responses*

Knowing what types of responses to avoid, how does one go about con ducting an effective interview? One major general principle of effective interview-ing is to "keep the interaction flowing." The interview is a two-way process. First one person speaks, then the other, and so on. Furthermore, in general the interviewer uses a minimum amount of effort to keep the interaction flowing. As long as the interviewee's verbalizations are relevant to the purpose of the interview, the interviewer listens with interest by maintaining face-to-face contact.

Except for structured interviews or for a particular purpose, an effective way to initiate the interview process involves the use of an *open-ended* question. This is one that usually cannot be answered specifically, as opposed to a closed-ended question, which can. Examples of open-ended questions include "Tell me a little bit about yourself," "Tell me about what interests you," and "What is it that brings you here to see me?" Examples of closed-ended questions include "Do you like sports?" "Are you married?" and "How old are you?"

A *closed-ended question* brings the interview to a dead halt and thus violates the principle of keeping the interaction flowing. In the example at the beginning of the chapter, even the personnel officer's opening statement was sufficiently open-ended to permit a variety of responses, depending on the characteristics of the interviewee. Where one individual might provide every minute detail of his or her education, for example, a second might simply include major events. In terms of degree, however, the clinical psychologist's opening statement—"Why don't you tell me a little bit about yourself?"—was even more open-ended. Here John could have replied with just about anything.

Open-ended questions give the interviewee wide latitude in choosing the topics that he or she feels are important. As a rule, we can learn a lot more about people when they tell us what they think is important than when we try to guess by asking a series of unrelated closed-ended questions. The open-ended ques-tion requires the interviewee to produce something spontaneously, as opposed to the closed-ended question that generally requires the person to recall some-thing (Wiens, 1976).

Thus you should realize that flexibility is needed in conducting an interview. Except for structured interviews, all interviews cannot be conducted in precisely the same way. In therapeutic or diagnostic interviews the interviewer usually follows only general guidelines in conducting the interview. The goal of such interviews is generally to get to know the person as well as possible. That way we can begin the helping process.

D.   *Responses to keep the interaction flowing*

After asking the open-ended question the interviewer as a rule will let the interviewee respond without being interrupted. That is, the interviewer should remain quiet and listen. When the interview is not structured, once the interviewee's response dies down, the interviewer usually responds in a way that will keep the interaction flowing. A closed-ended question at this point would naturally bring the interview to a halt and should be avoided. Instead, the interviewer should follow the principle of using the minimum effort to keep the interview flowing. Therefore, after the initial response to the open-ended question has been completed, the interviewer could appropriately use a "transitional phrase" such as "Yes," "I see," or "And." These transitional phrases imply that the interviewee should continue talking about the same topic. In John's interview with the clinical psychologist, for example, John stated "I graduated from high school in June of 1965. I majored in history and social studies." The clinical psychologist simply responded with a transition, "Yes, I see." John then continued to elaborate his response.

Sometimes the transitional phrase fails to have the desired effect. When this occurs, it is the interviewer's turn to respond again. The interviewer then should make a response relevant to what has just been communicated. In other words, the interview is thematic: it does not jump from one unrelated topic to another as it might if the interviewer were asking a series of questions. The theme in John's interview with the clinical psychologist involved John. Although the topics did change from John's education to his feelings about being the oldest of three children, John himself remained the central focus. The psychologist accomplished this by making statements that were relevant to what John was saying.

To make a response relevant to what has been communicated the interviewer may use any of the following types of statements: verbatim playback, paraphrasing, restatement, summarizing, clarifying, and understanding. You can view these statements as being on a continuum ranging from a statement that is totally interchangeable with the interviewee's response to a response that adds to or goes beyond it.

In a "verbatim playback" the interviewer simply repeats the interviewee's last response. For example, in his interview with the clinical psychologist John stated that "I majored in history and social studies." The psychologist replied with the transitional phrase "Yes, I see." A verbatim playback, "You majored in history and social studies," would have been equally effective. In either case John most likely would continue to elaborate his previous response. Thus, like the transitional phrase, the verbatim playback generally leads to an elaboration of the interviewee's previous response.

Closely related to the verbatim playback in terms of eliciting elaborations are paraphrasing and restatement responses. "Paraphrasing" and "restatement" responses are both interchangeable with the interviewee's response. A paraphrase tends to be more similar to the interviewee's response than the restatement, but both serve to capture the meaning of the interviewee's response. When John said "My master's degree should help me assume the duties of the new position," the psychologist replied with a restatement, "You feel your master's degree is a useful asset in your application." A paraphrase might have taken the form, "You feel your master's degree will be an important aid in tackling the responsibilities of the new position." In his restatement the psychologist introduced the term *useful asset* to restate John's attitude toward his master's degree. The paraphrase, on the other hand, simply replaced "important aid" for "help" and "tackling the responsibilities" for "assuming the duties." Neither statement, however, added anything to John's.

Summarizing and clarification statements tend to go just beyond the interviewee's response, thus adding to it. In "summarizing" the interviewer pulls together the meaning of several interviewee responses. To John's last statement in the example the psychologist could have replied with a summarizing statement such as, "As a youth you never had much time to yourself because you were responsible for taking care of the two younger children. Today you enjoy those few moments you have to be alone. Whenever you get a chance to be alone you drive to the lake all by yourself and just think." Notice that this summarizing statement involved verbatim playback, paraphrasing, and restating. With these three types of statements the psychologist summarized an entire sequence of responses.

The "clarification" statement, as its name implies, serves to clarify the interviewee's response. When John stated, "Not that I resented it. Well, maybe sometimes. It's just that I never had much time for myself," the psychologist attempted to clarify what John was trying to say. It was not that John resented the extra responsibilities; rather, he simply wanted some time to be alone. Thus the psychologist clarified John's statement by saying "And having time for yourself is important to you."

The clarification statement—like the summarizing, paraphrasing, restatement, and verbatim playback—remains very close to the meaning of the interviewee's response. These responses are relatively interchangeable with the interviewee's own response, or add slightly to it. Each of these responses communicates or facilitates a degree of understanding. At the lowest level the verbatim playback communicates that the interviewer at least heard what the interviewee said. The restatement, paraphrase, and summarizing responses go a bit further and communicate that the interviewer has a good idea of what the interviewee tried to communicate. Even more powerful, however, is the *empathy* or *understanding* response. This communicates that the interviewer understands how the interviewee must feel. When the psychologist stated "These moments are precious to you," he was not simply paraphrasing or restating what John had said. Instead, the psychologist was communicating that he understood how John felt about having time to himself.

Many students have considerable difficulty seeing the value of understanding and other types of statements that stay close to the interviewee's response. Some students consider such statements to be artificial and weak because of their noncommittal quality. However, the rationale for such responses is based on the well-known and well-documented finding that when we communicate to a person that we understand, that person will talk about or explore himself or herself at deeper and deeper levels (Truax & Mitchell, 1971). That is, accurate empathy elicits self-exploration. When the interviewer makes a statement that communicates he or she understands what the interviewee has said, then the interviewee will continue to explore at deeper levels. Consider the following example:

Psychologist: What's been happening today, Bill? (*Open-ended question*)

Bill: My physics teacher yelled at me in front of the whole class.

Psychologist: That's embarrassing. (*Understanding*)

Bill: Not only that, he seems to pick on me all the time.

Psychologist: That must make you angry. (*Understanding*)

Bill: Yeah, I guess so. It seems like he's always finding fault with my work. No matter what I do, he just doesn't like it.

Psychologist: That is really frustrating, Bill. You just can't seem to please him. (*Understanding*)

Bill: The other day we had an exam and I got an F. I checked my answers with Tom, and mine were the same as his. Yet I got an F and Tom got a B.

Psychologist: Hey, that doesn't seem fair. (*Clarification and understanding*)

Bill: You bet it isn't fair. But when I tried to talk to him about it, he refused to listen.

Psychologist: That's scary. (*Understanding*)

Bill: It sure is. If I get one more F, I'll be kicked out of school.

Psychologist: This is really serious. (*Clarification*)

Bill: Yeah. If I get kicked out of school, I couldn't face my parents or friends.

Psychologist: This whole thing has really got you upset. (*Understanding*)

Certainly the psychologist's responses are not the only ones that could have been used. However, you should note how the psychologist, in providing a series of understanding responses, was able to "uncover" the real source of Bill's anguish. The feelings Bill expressed ranged from embarrassment to anger to fear of being kicked out of school and finally to Bill's fear of how his friends and family would view his failure.

Let's consider other possible responses the psychologist could have made to Bill's initial statement, "My physics teacher yelled at me in front of the whole class." The psychologist could have replied: (1) "Why did he do that?" With this probing statement Bill is now forced to defend himself or explain why it happened. He would have to go over the circumstances that preceded the incident, which actually leads away from Bill's real feelings and concerns. (2) "Why did you let him do that to you? That wasn't very smart of you." This evaluative statement also places Bill on the defensive and has the further disadvantage of criticizing him and possibly hurting his feelings. Given this type of reaction from the psychologist, Bill could in no way feel safe in exploring his real feelings. (3) "That man, he's always yelling at somebody. You should report him to his chairperson." With this off-the-cuff advice the psychologist again removes himself from Bill's real concerns. Now the two might spend the rest of their time together weighing the pros and cons of reporting Bill's physics teacher. Still worse, Bill might impulsively follow the advice and get into real trouble if he cannot substantiate his claims. (4) "Don't worry. That physics teacher yells at everyone. It doesn't mean a thing." With this false reassurance Bill no longer is free to express his real concern. The psychologist has already dismissed the whole matter as insignificant.

In short, understanding responses that stay close to the data provided by the interviewee permit the individual to explore the situation out loud and at deeper and deeper levels. In general, interviewing is an uncovering process. Questions, evaluations, reassurances and the like—unless specifically called for as in a structured interview—generally allow only a superficial coverage of the individual. As a rule the problem in interviewing is to obtain verbal information from the interviewee. One good way of accomplishing this goal is by responding with facilitative statements. The facilitative interview provides a positive atmosphere. It begins with an open-ended question followed by understanding statements that capture the meaning and feeling of the interviewee's communication.

E. *Measuring understanding*

Understanding statements can be further understood by an analysis of measures of understanding. Attempts to measure understanding or empathy originated with Carl Rogers' pioneer research into the effects of client-centered therapy (Rogers, 1959, 1961; Walker, Rablen, & Rogers, 1960). It culminated in a 5-point scoring system (Truax & Carkhuff, 1967, pages 46–58). The 5-point system was subsequently revised and presented by Carkhuff and Berenson (1967). Each of the levels in this 5-point system represents a degree or level of empathy. The levels range from a response that bears little or no relationship to the previous statement through a response that captures the precise meaning and feeling of the statement. The highest level of empathy, level five, has relevance primarily for therapeutic interviews. Levels four and three represent various degrees of true empathy or understanding and may be used in all types of unstructured or semistructured (that is, partially structured) interviews. The lowest levels, one and two, have no place in a professional interview and should be avoided. Low level responses, however, occur frequently in everyday conversations. Below we discuss these levels to illustrate how understanding can be measured.

Level one responses.   "Level one responses" bear little or no relationship to the interviewee's response. According to Carkhuff and Berenson (1967) these responses "do not attend to or detract significantly" from the interviewee's responses. A level one conversation might proceed as follows:

Jennifer: Jason, look at my new dress.

Jason: I sure hope it doesn't rain today.

Jennifer: See, it's red with blue stripes.

Jason: If it rains my baseball game might get canceled.

Jennifer: I really love this dress; it's my favorite.

Jason: It's sure going to tick me off if that game gets canceled.

The two might as well be talking to themselves.

Level two responses.   The "level two response" communicates some awareness of the meaning of a statement, but only at a superficial level. The individual making a level two response never quite goes beyond his or her own limited perspective. Level two responses subtract from the communication. For example:

Jennifer: Boy do I feel good, I just got a beautiful new dress.

Jason: I feel bad, it's probably going to rain.

Jennifer: I'll wear this dress to your baseball game.

Jason: If it rains, there won't be a game.

Here the conversation is related, but only tangentially. Neither person is really aware of what is going on in the other. Jason, in particular, is totally insensitive to Jennifer's needs and feelings.

Level three responses.   A "level three response" is one that is interchangeable with the interviewee's statement. According to Carkhuff and Berenson (1967), level three is the minimum level of responding to facilitate the interaction and to be of help to the interviewee. Responses at levels one and two can actually be detrimental to a person in need of help and are clearly non-facilitative. Yet Carkhuff and Berenson's analysis and review of the relevant studies indicate that most Americans respond to each other at levels one and two. Carkhuff and Berenson believe that this low level of responding explains why so many people seem to require professional assistance when dealing with problems. There just are not enough people available who can help others explore their feelings out loud in order to determine how they really feel.

Levels four and five.   Levels four and five not only provide accurate empathy but go beyond the statement given. In "level four" the interviewer adds "noticeably" to the interviewee's response. In "level five" the interviewer adds "significantly" to the response (Carkhuff & Berenson, 1967). We recommend that interviewers learn to respond at levels three and four to maximize self-exploration and the uncovering process in unstructured and semistructured interviews. In our example with Jennifer and Jason, a level four interchange might proceed as follows:

Jennifer: I just got a new dress.

   Jason: You feel glad because you like new clothes.

Jennifer: This one is beautiful; it has red and blue stripes.

   Jason: You really love that new dress, it is a nice addition to your wardrobe.

Active listening.   An impressive array of research has accumulated that documents the power of the understanding response (Bergin, 1971; Patterson, 1974; Truax & Mitchell, 1971). This type of responding, which is sometimes called *active listening*, is the foundation of good interviewing skills for many different types of interviews.

IV.   TYPES OF INTERVIEWS

The previously discussed guides provide a general format for conducting an interview. The specifics would vary, however, depending on the goal, purpose, and theoretical orientation of the interviewer. Maloney and Ward (1976), for example, distinguish among three types of interviews: the evaluation interview, the case history interview, and the mental status examination. Actually, these three types of interviews are not mutually exclusive, but the distinction illustrates the point that the type of information obtained from an interview depends on what the interviewer is looking for. Furthermore, to be more complete, a fourth type of interview also should be included: the employment or selection interview.

A. *Evaluation or assessment interview*

According to Maloney and Ward (1976), the purpose of the "evaluation interview" is to assist in the evaluation of the individual. This type of interview is similar to what Wiens (1976) referred to as the "assessment interview." Maloney and Ward's conception of an evaluation interview provides guides similar to those presented in this chapter for effective interviewing. This similarity is not surprising because both methods are based on the impressive body of literature previously cited that shows accurate understanding leads to self-exploration. Thus Maloney and Ward recommend beginning with an open-ended question with the interviewer "listening, facilitating, and clarifying" during the initial phases of the interview. In addition, Maloney and Ward recommend that the powerful tool of confrontation be included in the process.

The confrontation response is usually most appropriate in therapeutic interviews, but it is a technique that the experienced interviewer should have at his or her disposal. A *confrontation* is a statement that points out a discrepancy or inconsistency. Carkhuff (1969), for example, distinguishes among three types: (1) a discrepancy between what the person is and what he or she wants to become, (2) a discrepancy between what the person says about himself or herself and what he or she does, and (3) a discrepancy between the person's perception of himself or herself and the interviewer's experience.

Carkhuff further notes that there are various degrees of confrontation. In their mildest degree, confrontations may take the form of opening up an issue for consideration, such as "On the one hand you say you want to go out on dates but, on the other hand, you missed five good opportunities to ask someone out." In their more severe or intense degrees, confrontations may take the form, "You had five opportunities to ask a girl for a date! Five! Ever since you've been coming to see me you've been telling me you want a date. You say you want a date, yet you continue to let opportunities pass. Come on, Joe, when are you going to get with it and start living your life the way you know you should."

Carkhuff (1969) classified the confrontation as one of the "action" dimensions of psychotherapy, only to be used after the psychotherapist has spent many sessions developing rapport and mutual understanding. The problem with the confrontation is that it may induce anxiety by bringing conflicts or inconsistencies into a person's awareness when he or she may not be ready to handle them. We therefore strongly recommend that the beginning student leave the confrontation for the more experienced practitioner.

In addition to the confrontation, Maloney and Ward (1976) suggest that direct questions can be used toward the end of the interview to fill in any needed details or gaps in the interviewer's knowledge. This is an excellent suggestion. For unstructured or semistructured interviews we advocate the use of direct questions whenever (1) the data can be obtained in no other way, (2) time is markedly limited and the interviewer is in need of relatively specific information, or (3) the interviewee cannot or will not cooperate with the interviewer. The open-ended, facilitative technique does not work well for nonverbal, intellectually limited, and uncooperative subjects. For these subjects it is exceedingly difficult to get the interview off the ground. Thus direct questioning becomes an absolute necessity. Finally, at the end of an interview direct questions should be used as a clean-up procedure to fill in the missing details.

B.   *Case history interview*

An interview that begins with an open-ended question followed by level three and four responses can yield a wealth of data about an individual. What will be obtained is an in-depth description of those factors most important to the interviewee. However, case history data may or may not be revealed, depending upon its relevance to central issues in the interviewee's life. To obtain a complete "case history," that is, a biographical sketch, specific questioning is often necessary. Case history data may include a chronology of major events in the person's life, a work history, a medical history, and a family history. Family history does not have to be detailed but should include a complete listing of the age and sex of each member in the immediate family. It also is important to note whether any family member including parents, grandparents, uncles, aunts, and siblings have had similar difficulties to those experienced by the interviewee. This is because the occurrence of many conditions runs higher in families than in the general population.

In obtaining the history the interviewer often takes a developmental approach and examines major events in the infancy, early childhood, primary school, secondary school, young adult, mature adult, and older adult years. Maloney and Ward (1976) offer the useful suggestion of beginning with an open-ended question in each major category of case history and completing the details of each category before going on to the next. For example, the interviewer may say "Tell me about your work record." After clarifying the work history, another category such as medical can be explored.

C.   *Mental status examination*

The "mental status examination" is an important tool in psychiatric and neurological examinations. It is a special type of interview used primarily to diagnose psychosis, brain damage, and other major mental health problems. The purpose of the mental status examination is to evaluate a person suspected of neurological or emotional problems in terms of variables known to be related to these problems.

Among the areas covered in the mental status examination are the person's appearance, attitudes, and general behavior. The interviewer also is alert to the emotions emitted by the interviewee. For example, is there one dominant emotion that fluctuates little? Is there an absence of emotion (that is, a flat affect)? Are the emotions appropriate? Do they fluctuate widely? Also evaluated in the mental status examination are the person's thought processes. Intelligence can be evaluated by such factors as speed and accuracy of thinking, richness of thought content, ability to interpret proverbs, memory, and judgment. Especially important in the assessment of schizophrenia, a major form of psychosis involving loss of reality contact, is the quality of the person's thought processes. This can be assessed through an analysis of thought content. For example, is there anything unusual or peculiar about the person's thoughts? Is the person preoccupied with any particular idea? Are the person's ideas realistic?

Other important areas evaluated in the mental status examination include the person's ability to direct and deploy attention. Is the person distracted? Can he or she attend to a task for as long as necessary for successful completion? Sensory factors also are considered. Is the person seeing things that aren't there? What is the accuracy of the person's perceptions?

As a student you must keep in mind that to make proper use of the mental status examination one must have a broad understanding of the major mental disorders and the various forms of brain damage. There is no room for amateurs or self-appointed practitioners when a mental status examination is needed. However, knowledge of those areas covered in the mental status examination can be of use to interviewers interested in knowing the important variables in observing and evaluating another human being.

D. *Employment interview*

The purpose of the "employment interview" is to aid in the selection and promotion decisions in business and industry. It generally has been given its own special place in the psychological literature. A number of important articles and books are exclusively devoted to the employment (selection) interview.

The first extensive review of the employment interview was provided by Wagner (1949), who reviewed a little more than 100 studies devoted to the employment interview. He severely criticized most of the available studies, however, emphasizing that much of the literature consisted of contradicting opinions and how-to-do it formulas. Following Wagner's advice for more and better studies, Webster (1964) presented a series of important experimental investigations into the nature of the employment interview. Two independent reviews of the literature on the employment interview were subsequently published in the mid-1960s (Mayfield, 1964; Ulrich & Trumbo, 1965). Both reviews began where Wagner (1949) had left off. Wright (1969) then reviewed the literature between 1964 and 1969.

Although somewhat dated now, these reviews revealed some extremely valuable information on interviews in general and the employment interview in particular. Interestingly, all of the above reviewers almost unanimously recommended a structured format for the employment interview. A number of studies clearly pointed to the superiority of structured interviews for enabling interviewers to reach agreement concerning their employment decisions based on interviews. Thus, whereas unstructured and semistructured interviews have been dominant in diagnostic and therapeutic settings, the structured interview is emerging as the preferred method for employment purposes. Industrial psychologists thus find the loss of flexibility in structured interviews is more than balanced by the increase in reliability.

One particularly interesting finding in the employment interview literature concerns the powerful impact of early impressions. Webster (1964), for example, reported that early impressions play an especially important role in the final employment decision. It is extremely difficult to overcome the effects of an unfavorable first impression. Similarly, a good first impression can be quite helpful.

Webster and others also have noted that the employment interview often involves a search for negative or unfavorable evidence about a person rather than a search for favorable evidence. In many employment interviews the interviewer will search for negative evidence. If such is found, the person probably will not be hired unless there is a considerable demand for workers and very few individuals to fill open positions. In one study reported by Webster (1964) it was noted that as few as one unfavorable impression was followed by final rejection in 90% of the cases. This rejection rate, however, dropped to 25% when early impressions were favorable. Webster (1964) and others caution employment interviewers against forming an early bias, which might result in rejection of a competent individual.

V.   THEORETICAL ORIENTATION

Another factor to consider in understanding interview procedures is the theoretical orientation of the interviewer. The basic assumptions and theoretical position of the interviewer will affect the type of information sought, the techniques used to get that information, and the subject matter of the decision.

A.   Client-centered approach

The open-ended facilitative approach to interviewing advocated for unstructured and semistructured interviews in this chapter might best be classified as a nondirective or client-centered approach. This approach, as the term client-centered implies, lets the interviewee determine the direction of the interview. It concentrates on allowing the interviewee to closely explore areas of concern. This is why case history data are not always obtained from this type of interview.

B.   Directive approaches

The nondirective client-centered approach can be distinguished from more directive approaches in which the interviewer has a definite idea about the type of information sought and therefore becomes more specific. Case histories or employment interviews, for example, are directive in that the interviewer directs the interview through a specific set of questions.

C. *Behavioral and social learning orientations*

Interviewers with either a behavioral or a social learning theoretical orientation also might be more directive than advocated in this chapter. Certainly behavioral and social learning psychologists could begin as herein suggested for unstructured or semistructured interviews. However, these orientations emphasize the importance of environmental factors in determining behavior. In this orientation the interviewer seeks to ascertain external variables that elicit, maintain, and reinforce problem behavior as well as those environmental factors that suppress positive or adaptive behavior. Maloney and Ward's (1976) suggestion of a series of open-ended and direct closed-ended questions within each content area might be most useful in this type of interviewing and seems to offer many of the advantages of both the client-centered and directive approaches.

D. *Psychoanalytic orientation*

Many of the principles underlying the psychoanalytic method of interviewing have been discussed by Auld (1968). In the psychoanalytic interview the interviewer takes a nonjudgmental attitude, which is labeled as "permissiveness" (Auld, 1968, page 170). Permissiveness means the interviewer accepts, without censure, whatever the interviewee says. To further create the proper atmosphere the interviewer uses "gentleness"—that is, shows no signs of rejection or disapproval. The interviewer also uses "acceptance"—that is, makes the interviewee feel accepted and valued. These principles are clearly analogous to those advocated in this chapter and reflect principles common to many types of interviews.

A psychoanalytic orientation differs from most other approaches in its emphasis on interpretation and analyzing resistance. Unlike the confrontation, which points out discrepancies of which the interviewee has some degree of awareness but is not acting on, the "interpretation" calls to the interviewee's attention unconscious feelings, wishes, fears, and desires. Interpretations are used sparingly and only after long preparation. The interpretation is a powerful tool that can lead to deterioration in the inadequately prepared interviewee. It should be used only by qualified practitioners.

"Resistances" are defined as anything that interferes with the verbal expression of the interviewee (Auld, 1968). Resistances are of particular interest to the psychoanalytic interviewer. Whereas the client-centered interviewer attempts to facilitate communication, the psychoanalytic interviewer is particularly concerned with those factors that prevent the interviewee from expressing himself or herself. It is assumed that resistances are caused by inner suffering or conflict. The interviewer's job is to determine the source of these conflicts and bring them to the awareness of the interviewee.

VI. DEVELOPING INTERVIEWING SKILLS

One controversy in the field of interviewing concerns whether or not interviewing skills can be learned and acquired (Wiens, 1976). General consensus at this time is that interviewing skills can be acquired. To acquire such skills you should familiarize yourself with research and theory on the interview. By understanding the principles and underlying variables in the interview, you will have taken the first step toward acquisition of interviewing skills.

A second factor in acquiring interviewing skills is supervised practice. It is still true that experience is the best teacher. No amount of book learning can compare to having one's taped interview analyzed by an experienced interviewer.

A third factor in the acquisition of interviewing skills has to do with the principles under which any skill is acquired. As a student you must begin with a conscious effort to apply the principles learned from books and supervisors. For example, you must continually make an effort to apply the principles involved in keeping the interaction flowing. In addition, you must continually ask yourself questions such as "What does this person mean? Am I communicating that I understand? Is the person exploring at deeper levels? What is being communicated nonverbally?"

In the initial phase of learning any new skill, it almost seems like you must attend to a hundred things at once—an impossible task. However, if you make a persistent effort, gradually you will begin to respond appropriately by habit. Thus experienced interviewers automatically attend to the person's appearance, nonverbal communications, emotional tone, and so on. They do so not because they were endowed with special abilities, but because they trained themselves to do so. With practice a behavior can be completed automatically and with little effort. This is true for many of the skills of successful interview behavior.

VII. SOURCES OF ERROR IN THE INTERVIEW

In making appropriate use of the interview you must develop an awareness of the various sources of error or potential bias in interview data. In acquiring a knowledge of these sources of error you can try to compensate for their negative effects. Furthermore, in acquiring this knowledge you will develop a better awareness of the limitations inherent in judging human beings on the basis of the interview.

A. *Sources of error in the meaning and accuracy of interview data*

Many sources of interview error can be attributed to the extreme difficulty we have in making accurate, logical observations and judgments. Suppose, for example, in his first day of teaching a fifth-grade class a schoolteacher observes that one child follows all the rules and directions but a second child just cannot seem to stay out of trouble. If that teacher is not careful, he might develop a bias in his judgments toward both these children. He might see the first child as good, even if she breaks the rules for several weeks in a row. On the other hand, he might see the second child as bad, even if she follows the rules for the rest of the school term. Similarly, a child may turn in a composition replete with grammatical and spelling errors. This child may have just had a bad day. However, even if his or her next paper is relatively free of errors, the teacher will have a tendency to look for them and to view the child as weak in grammar. Furthermore, the teacher may see the child as weak in other areas just on the basis of his early impression of the child's grammatical skills.

Thorndike (1920) labeled this tendency to judge specific traits on the basis of a general impression the "halo effect." Thorndike became aware of the halo effect when he noticed that ratings of behavioral tendencies (that is, traits) based on interview data tended to correlate more highly than could be reasonably expected.

Thus there appears to be a human tendency to generalize in our judgments on the basis of a single, limited experience. In the interview, halo effects occur when the interviewer forms a favorable or unfavorable early impression. The early impression then biases the remainder of the judgment process. Thus, with an early favorable impression or positive halo, the interviewer will have difficulty seeing the negatives. Similarly, with an early unfavorable impression, or negative halo, the interviewer will have difficulty seeing the positives. In short, halo effects impair objectivity and must be consciously avoided by the effective interviewer.

Similar to the halo effect is the tendency to judge on the basis of one outstanding characteristic. Hollingworth (1922) first called this error tendency "general standoutishness." One prominent characteristic can bias the interviewer's judgments and prevent an objective evaluation. In an early paper Burtt (1926), for example, noted the tendency of interviewers to make unwarranted inferences from personal appearance. A well-groomed, attractive individual might be rated higher in intelligence than a poorly groomed, unattractive individual, even though the latter individual is more intelligent than the former. Again, one characteristic prevents an objective evaluation.

Sources of error such as the halo effect and the tendency to judge on the basis of one outstanding characteristic reduce the validity of interview data. Recall that validity tells us about the meaning of test scores. Errors that reduce the objectivity of the interviewer produce inaccurate judgments, thus biasing the meaning or validity of the evaluation. These error tendencies perhaps explain why the predictive validity of interview data vary so widely. Wagner (1949), for example, reported studies that attempted to correlate judgments from interview data with such factors as grades, intelligence, and performance on standardized tests. The correlations ranged from .09 to .94 with a median of .19. Studies reviewed by Ulrich and Trumbo (1965) revealed a similar range of predictive validity coefficients, with correlations as low as $-.05$ and as high as .72 when ratings based on interview data were correlated with a variety of indices such as job performance. Carlson, Thayer, Mayfield, and Peterson (1971) reported similar findings.

Clearly the validity of interview data always must be questioned. Yet the interview can provide a wealth of unique data. The safest approach is to consider interview data as tentative: a hypothesis or set of hypotheses to be confirmed by other sources of data. Interview data may be of dubious value without the support of more standardized procedures. Results from standardized tests, on the other hand, are often meaningless if not placed in the context of case history or other interview data. The clear and simple conclusion is that the two go together, each complementing the other. Both are essential in the process of evaluating human beings.

B.   *Sources of error in the stability of interview data*

Recall that reliability refers to the stability, dependability, or consistency of test results. For interview data the critical questions in terms of reliability have centered around interinterviewer agreement (agreement between two or more interviewers). As with the validity studies, reliability coefficients for interinterviewer agreement vary widely. Wagner (1949), for example, found a range of reliability coefficients from .23 to .97 (median .57) for ratings of traits (enduring behavioral tendencies). The range of coefficients for ratings of overall ability was even wider (−.20 to .85; median .53). Ulrich and Trumbo's (1965) more recent review reported similar findings. Webster (1964) argued that one reason for fluctuations in interview reliability is that different interviewers look for different things. Where one might focus on strengths, for example, another might focus on weaknesses. The two disagree because their judgments are based on different aspects of the individual. Furthermore, as Webster also noted, the theoretical orientation of the interviewer influences the type of information sought and therefore the basis for decisions.

In considering the reliability of interviews you should realize that agreement among interviewers varies for different types of interviews. The research suggests that a highly structured interview, in which specific questions are asked in a specific order, can produce highly stable results. For example, if we ask a person his or her name, date of birth, parents' names, and addresses of all residences within a particular time span and then ask the same questions a year later, results should be nearly identical. Reliability would only be limited by the memory and honesty of the interviewee and the clerical capabilities of the interviewer. Although this is an extreme example, it should be clear that highly structured interviews that ask a set of specific questions in a specific order should produce fairly dependable results. The problem is that such structure can limit what can be obtained from the interview, thus defeating the purpose of interviews designed to provide a broad range of data.

Unstructured or semistructured interviews frequently provide data that cannot to be obtained from other sources. However, the dependability of such results will clearly be limited. The same question may not be asked twice, or it may be asked in a different way. Thus interviewers readily acknowledge the limited reliability of interview data. In exchange, however, the interview offers the possibility of obtaining data that cannot be obtained from other sources (Wiens, 1976). However, where reliability is the most important goal, a standardized interview is indicated.

VIII.   RESEARCH APPROACHES TO THE STUDY OF INTERVIEWING

The interview has been studied from a wide variety of perspectives. Our purpose in this section will be to provide you with a few of the major approaches that have been taken in research attempts to understand the interview process.

A. *Nonverbal communication*

Interviewees communicate through both verbal and nonverbal means. "Nonverbal methods of communication" include such factors as facial expressions, body posture, body movements, and tone quality of the voice. All these factors have been studied and clearly play a role in the interview process. Consider the case where a friend of yours has just received some bad news. You ask, "Are you all right?" She hangs her head low and in a quiet voice says, "Yeah, I'm okay." Actually, her nonverbal behavior indicates she is *not* all right. Indeed, when there is a discrepancy between the verbal and nonverbal behavior, the odds are that the nonverbal behavior is the more accurate reflection of a person's feelings. People lie, distort, and color their communications much less often in their nonverbal than in their verbal communication.

Excellent analyses of nonverbal behavior in the interview situation have been conducted by Ekman and Friesen (1968) and Mahl (1968). Ekman and Friesen (1968) discussed the assumptions underlying studies of nonverbal behavior. Among these assumptions are nonverbal behavior (1) communicates emotions, (2) provides qualities as to how the verbal discourse should be interpreted, and (3) is less affected than verbal behavior by attempts to censor communication. One of the findings reported by Ekman and Friesen (1968) is that experts (Dittmann, 1962) as well as naive judges (Ekman, 1965a, 1965b) can reliably judge emotion (that is, affect) from nonverbal behavior. The implication is that it is possible to reliably evaluate nonverbal communication. Another interesting finding reported by Ekman and Friesen (1968) has to do with the activity of the person's feet. In a case study these authors found evidence that suggested the movement of the interviewee's feet can reflect anger, annoyance, and irritation. Even more revealing are the movements of the hands, which may reflect how the person feels about himself or herself (Ekman & Friesen, 1968). Such findings tend to support Freud's (1905) statement that "If his lips are silent, he chatters with his finger-tips; betrayal oozes out of him at every pore."

One of the best-known analysts of nonverbal interview behavior is G. F. Mahl (1968). His general approach is to have an experienced investigator observe an interview through a one-way mirror without hearing the voices. The investigator then attempts to infer the meaning of gestures. Mahl's (1968) results again indicate that nonverbal behavior alone can reveal considerable information about an individual. Mahl's data suggests, for example, that moderate amounts of scratching and rubbing the nose may be related to aggression turned against the self (that is, depression), whereas playing with one's wedding ring may suggest marital conflict (Mahl, 1968).

One of the most interesting new developments in the field of nonverbal communication was the introduction of the Profile of Nonverbal Sensitivity (PONS) test (Rosenthal, Hall, DiMatteo, Rogers, & Archer, 1980). The PONS test provides quantitative indices of a person's abilities to accurately decode nonverbal cues given by another person who is shown in a film. The test provides scores for accuracy in reading facial expressions, body movements, posture, and voice tone. Extensive validity studies support the use of the PONS test for evaluating and training professionals who are involved in therapeutic interviews. For example, among six samples of counselors, psychotherapists, or advanced students in these fields, supervisor ratings of therapeutic skill correlated with nonverbal sensitivity as measured by the PONS test. In other studies it has been shown that the physicians' accuracy in the body movement and posture portion of the PONS test was significantly correlated with favorable ratings of the doctors by their patients (DiMatteo, 1979).

B. Quantitative aspects of interview behavior

Other major areas of focus in interview research include the analysis of silence (Matarazzo et al., 1968); the analysis of acoustical properties of speech such as pitch, frequencies, intensities, and timbre (Matarazzo & Wiens, 1972); and the timing of verbal interactions (Wiens, Matarazzo, & Saslow, 1965). All these factors have been found to be related to the communication process. Findings have been so encouraging that some investigators have proposed models in which computers could be programmed to analyze the meaning of interview data based quantitative characteristics such as length of silences, pitch, tone quality, and analysis of body movements (Jaffe, 1968).

IX. SUMMARY

In a structured interview the interviewer asks a specific set of questions. In the structured standardized interview these questions are printed. The interviewer reads the questions in a specific order or sequence. In the unstructured interview there are no specific questions or guidelines for the interviewer to follow. Thus each unstructured interview is unique. Unstructured interviews provide considerable flexibility, but at the expense of stability of interview data.

An interview is an interactive process. The participants (interviewer and interviewee) influence each other. Good interviewers set the tone of the interview by maintaining a warm, open, confident atmosphere.

Good interviewing is a matter of attitude. A study by Saccuzzo (1975) showed that interviewees give positive evaluations to interviewers when the interviewer is seen as warm, genuine, accepting, understanding, open, committed, and involved. Poor evaluations were given when attitudes and feelings opposite to these were exhibited by the interviewer. Good interview behavior involves developing the proper attitudes and displaying them during the interview.

Good interviewing also involves avoidance of statements that are judgmental, probing, evaluative, or hostile. An interview should begin with an open-ended question—that is, one that cannot be answered yes or no or with a short, specific response. The process of interviewing then involves the facilitation of the flow of communication. Closed-ended questions, which can be answered with a "Yes" or "No" or a specific response, usually bring the interview to a halt and typically should be reserved for instances where less directive procedures fail to produce the desired information.

Transitional phrases such as "I see" help keep the interview flowing. Statements that communicate understanding or are interchangeable with the interviewee's responses tend to elicit self-exploration at deeper and deeper levels. These responses include verbatim playback, paraphrasing, restatement, summarizing, clarification statements, and understanding statements.

Efforts to assess the quality of understanding statements have led to a 5-point scale system developed by Truax, Carkhuff, and co-workers. A large body of knowledge has shown that understanding statements are extremely powerful in helping the interviewee uncover and explore underlying feelings.

There are various types of interviews including the evaluation or assessment interview, the case history interview, the mental status examination, and the employment interview. The interviewer's theoretical orientation may determine what he or she looks for in the interview as well as the conduct of the interview. Client-centered interviewers, to a large degree, permit the interviewee to determine the direction of the interview. Behavioral and social learning interviewers, on the other hand, are more directive. Psychoanalytic interviewers focus on resistance and interpretation.

There are two primary sources of error in the interview: those pertaining to validity or meaning of interview data and those pertaining to the dependability or reliability of interview data. The tendency to draw general conclusions about an individual based on the limited data of a first impression limits the meaning and accuracy of interview data. Such tendencies have been labeled the "halo effect" and "standoutishness." Furthermore, predictive validity coefficients for interview data vary widely. Reliability of interview data has been measured primarily in terms of agreement among interviewers on variables such as intelligence, overall ability, and traits. The more structured the interview, the more interviewers agree. Thus, like predictive validity coefficients, reliability coefficients for interview data vary widely.

Interviewing skills are developed by acquiring knowledge about good interview behavior and principles, supervised practice, and a conscious effort to form the right habits. However, the interview is highly fallible. Interview data can best be seen as the complement of other sources of data.

11

Tests of Mental Ability:
The Binet Scale

Learning objectives

When you have completed this chapter, you should be able to do the following:

1. *Explain how Binet defined intelligence.*
2. *Identify Binet's two guiding principles of test construction.*
3. *Describe the concept of age differentiation.*
4. *Explain some of the implications of Binet's use of the concept of general mental ability.*
5. *Describe the concept of mental age (MA).*
6. *Describe the intelligence quotient (IQ) concept.*
7. *Identify some improvements in the 1937 revision of the Stanford-Binet intelligence scale.*
8. *Describe the psychometric properties of the 1937 Stanford-Binet intelligence scale.*
9. *Define deviation IQ.*
10. *Identify the major improvement in the 1972 revised norms for the Stanford-Binet intelligence scale.*

What is the best way of maximizing the educational experiences for each unique member of the society? There is no getting away from the fact that human beings differ. Some are tall, and some are short. Some prefer sugar with their coffee, and others like it black. Some work well with their hands but abhor math. Others may be geniuses at math but clumsy and inept when working with their hands. How can we provide for the unique needs of each individual in a way that maximizes his or her interests and abilities when we must, at the same time, provide for the needs of the group as a whole?

Is it fair to take a child with little ability and no interest in math and force this child to compete with others with ability and interest in math? The child with little ability will suffer considerable failure in this situation and perhaps begin to think poorly of himself or herself as a result. Suppose, on the other hand, the child with low ability in math is removed from a regular class and placed with other children, all of whom are labeled "slow learners." Would the experience of being removed from a regular class not be even more damaging to the child's feelings of self-worth and competence? Taking the other side for a moment, how fair is it to children with exceptional abilities in math to receive less than an adequate educational challenge because others with less ability slow down the pace of instruction?

Suppose we did remove certain children from regular classrooms in order to provide special instruction to children with special needs. The rest of the class then might have a greater opportunity to learn at a faster pace. However, how are we to distinguish the child of limited ability from the child of adequate ability who is not performing because of attitude, motivation, personality, or cultural factors (see, for example, Fox 1981)? Whom can we trust to make the final decision concerning who is limited and who is not? It would be tragic if a child of average or better abilities were placed in a special program that failed to adequately stimulate the child. It is well known that in addition to low intelligence, many other factors can account for poor school performance (Scarr, 1981). If a child is placed in a "slow learners" class because of shyness, fear of authority, family problems, emotional upset, cultural differences, or someone's personal bias, then this child may fail to develop maximally, and society as well as the child suffers. Indeed, any decision to isolate children of normal abilities from those with limited abilities has social, economic, political, legal, and moral significance.

The problems we have been discussing are not new. A decision made by the French minister of public instruction around the turn of the century has strongly influenced educational practices to this day. The French minister made a decision that some of you might criticize today: to create a procedure for identifying intellectually limited individuals so that they could be removed from the regular classroom and given special educational experiences. It was this decision that provided the force behind the development of modern intelligence tests and all the heated controversy presently associated with them (Hebb, 1981).

In 1904 the French minister appointed a commission to implement his decision. The commission was given a definite assignment: to recommend a procedure for identifying the so-called subnormal (intellectually limited) child. One of the members of this commission was Alfred Binet, who had demonstrated his qualifications for the job by his earlier research on human abilities (Binet, 1890a,b). The task of the commission was indeed formidable. No one doubted that human beings were capable of incredible accomplishments, which were obviously a reflection of intelligence. Nor was there much doubt that differences existed between individuals in their level of intelligence. But how was one to define intelligence?

Binet had few guideposts. A study by Wissler (1901) indicated that simple functions such as reaction time, sensory acuity, and the like failed to discriminate well among individuals of high and low scholastic ability. Therefore, Binet looked for complex, rather than simple, processes in his struggle to understand human intelligence. However, there were few available definitions of intelligence and certainly no consensus concerning the nature of human intelligence. Binet's first problem became that of deciding what he wanted to measure—that is, to define intelligence.

I. IN SEARCH OF A DEFINITION OF INTELLIGENCE

Binet was sailing in uncharted waters. It is one thing to take an established method or tool and find a way to improve upon it. Once the basic idea of the airplane had become established and a workable model had been developed, it was not long before countless small refinements produced a product that could not even be imagined in the 19th century. The difficult task lies in developing the basic idea and a workable model in the first place. Such was the task facing Binet and the commission appointed by the French minister of public instruction. In meeting the challenge he faced, Binet finally decided on a definition of intelligence.

In his definition Binet departed from what was perhaps the dominant view of his day. Psychologists in the university and laboratory settings tended to view intelligence in terms of a collection of separate and distinct processes. Memory, for example, was viewed as separate and distinct from concentration. Memory and concentration, in turn, were both viewed as separate from reasoning. If intelligence consisted of separate and distinct abilities, one approach to its measurement would be that of determining the complete set of abilities and then developing a way to measure each one.

Suppose that intelligence comprises separate, distinct abilities and that each of these could be identified. There would still be the problem of determining how the various abilities interacted to produce a final product: intelligent behavior. In solving a problem you don't use only memory or reasoning or concentration. You use all these abilities and perhaps others. Together these abilities interact to produce a final product: the solution. What is more important, reasoning or memory? Such questions pose another problem in defining intelligence in terms of separate abilities. How does one determine the contribution of each ability to the final evaluation? Individuals with the best memories, for example, may not be the most intelligent. Certain abilities seem to contribute more to the final evaluation than others. Finally a point is reached at which a better memory no longer enhances intelligent behavior.

To deal with the problems of a definition of intelligence in terms of an undetermined number of separate and distinct processes of unknown relative contribution, Binet decided to concentrate on developing a general, overall measure of intelligence. Binet did not necessarily disagree with the concept of separate and distinct abilities. However, the problem of isolating the complete set of hypothetical abilities and developing a measure for each was far greater than the problem of measuring a general or pervasive factor that plays a role in all intelligent behavior. Thus Binet restricted his task to that of measuring "general mental ability," which was not seen as a single unified process. If Binet could find a way of measuring at least some of the factors related to the total or final product of the interaction among a set of separate processes, general mental ability, then at least he would have a basis for meeting his goal of finding a way to distinguish the limited child from the brighter one.

Binet eventually defined intelligence in terms of one's capacity to (1) find and maintain a definite direction or purpose, (2) adjust strategy if necessary to achieve that purpose, and (3) evaluate or criticize the strategy so that necessary adjustments could be made. He believed intelligence was "the tendency to take and maintain a definite direction; the capacity to make adaptations for the purpose of attaining a desired end; and the power of auto-criticism" (Terman, 1916, page 45).

II. BINET'S PRINCIPLES OF TEST CONSTRUCTION

In choosing a definition, Binet took the necessary first step in developing a measure of intelligence. However, he was still faced with the problem of deciding exactly what he wanted to measure. Binet believed that intelligence, as he defined it, expressed itself through the judgmental, attentional, and reasoning facilities of the individual (Binet & Simon, 1905). He therefore decided to concentrate on finding tasks related to these three facilities.

In developing tasks to measure judgment, attention, and reasoning, Binet used trial and error as well as experimentation and hypothesis-testing procedures. However, he was guided by two major concepts that to this day provide the underlying principle to the Binet scale and all of its many revisions and offshoots. These principles, which perhaps represent Binet's most profound contribution to the study of human intelligence, remained unchallenged in mental testing until recently (Garcia, 1981). They provided the core foundation for many subsequent generations of human ability tests.

A. *Principle 1: Age differentiation*

Principle 1, *age differentiation*, refers to the simple fact that older children have greater capabilities than younger. For example, whereas most 9-year-olds can tell that a 50-cent coin is worth more than a quarter, a quarter is worth more than a dime, and so on, most 5-year-olds cannot. Binet searched for tasks that could be completed by between 66.67% to 75% of the children of a particular age group and also be completed by a smaller proportion of younger children but a larger proportion of older ones. Thus Binet eventually assembled a set of tasks that could be completed by an increasingly higher proportion of children with increasing age.

With these tasks he was able to estimate the mental ability of a child in terms of his or her completion of tasks designed for the average child of a particular age, regardless of the child's actual or chronological age. A particular 5-year-old child, for example, might be able to successfully complete tasks that the average 8-year-old could complete. On the other hand, another 5-year-old might not be capable of completing even those tasks that the average 3-year-old could complete. Thus, with the principle of age differentiation it became possible to determine the equivalent age capabilities of a child independently of chronological age. This equivalent age capability was eventually called "mental age." If a 6-year-old completed tasks for the average 9-year-old, then the 6-year-old had demonstrated that he or she had capabilities equivalent to the average 9-year-old. With capabilities equivalent to the 9-year-old, the 6-year-old had a mental age of 9.

B.   Principle 2: The concept of general mental ability

In addition to the principle of age differentiation, Binet was guided in his selection of tasks by his decision to measure only the total product of the various separate and distinct elements of intelligence, "general mental ability." With the concept of general mental ability Binet freed himself from the burden of identifying each element or independent aspect of intelligence. He also was freed from ascertaining the relative contribution of each element to the whole. Binet's decision to measure general mental ability was based on practical considerations. The search for tasks now could be restricted to anything related to the total or final product of intelligence. The value of any particular task then could be judged in terms of its correlation with the combined result (total score) of all other tasks. Tasks with low correlations could be eliminated and tasks with high correlations retained.

To better understand the effect of Binet's decision to evaluate general intelligence, consider this analogy. Water is composed of two elements, hydrogen and oxygen. Each molecule of water is composed of two atoms of hydrogen and one atom of oxygen. The total product of two hydrogen atoms and one oxygen atom is water. In attempting to measure water, one could take the position that you must first identify the elements of which water is composed and then measure them. On the other hand, you also could argue that what you really should do is measure the properties of water itself, not the properties of hydrogen or oxygen. Both arguments are valid.

Binet's decision to measure the total product, general mental ability, is only one possible solution to the problem of measuring human intelligence. In support of Binet, other investigators have held the view of a general intelligence factor in human beings (Vernon, 1950; Jensen, 1970), which Spearman (1927) referred to as *g*. Spearman's *g* is the general factor that enters into all aspects of intelligence. One basic implication of the concept of general intelligence is that one has good judgment, good concentration, good reasoning, good attention, and the like—not because of isolated, specific capabilities in each of these areas—but because of some underlying unity: general intelligence. While Binet may not have endorsed the concept of general intelligence, his decision to measure the total product certainly opened the possibility of measuring general intelligence in human beings.

III. THE EARLY BINET SCALES

Using the principles of age differentiation and general mental ability, Binet and another appointee of the French minister of public instruction, T. Simon, collaborated to develop the first version of what was eventually to be called the *Stanford-Binet Intelligence Scale*. The first version was called the *1905 Binet-Simon Scale*. The original Binet scale was limited compared to present-day applications of intelligence tests. Its purpose was restricted to identifying mentally defective children in the Paris school system.

A. *Nature of the 1905 Binet-Simon scale*

The 1905 Binet-Simon scale was an individual intelligence test consisting of 30 items presented in an increasing order of difficulty. Item 4, for example, tested the subject's ability to recognize food (for example, to discriminate between chocolate and wood). Item 14 required subjects to define familiar objects such as a fork. The most difficult item, 30, required subjects to define and distinguish between paired abstract terms (for example, sad and bored). Binet proposed that Item 9, which required subjects to name designated objects in a picture, was the approximate limit of the average 3-year-old. Therefore, average 3-year-olds were not expected to complete Item 10, which required subjects to compare the length of two lines and designate the longer. Any 3-year-old demonstrating this ability could be considered brighter than the average 3-year-old. A 3-year-old who could successfully complete Item 14, which required the subject to define familiar objects, would be performing at the upper limit of the average 5-year-old.

In Binet's time three levels of intellectual deficiency were designated by terms no longer in use today because of the derogatory connotations these terms have acquired for the general public. *Idiot* was used to describe the most severe form of intellectual impairment, *imbecile* to designate moderate levels of impairment, and *moron* for the mildest level of impairment. Binet believed that the ability to follow simple directions and imitate simple gestures (Item 6 on the 1905 scale) was the upper limit of adult idiots. The ability to identify parts of the body or simple objects (Item 8) would rule out severe intellectual impairment in an adult. The upper limit for adult imbeciles was Item 16, which required the subject to state the differences between two common objects such as wood and glass. Item 23 consisted of a series of increasing weights. The examiner would place the weights in ascending order, remove one, and then scramble them. The subject's task was to identify the missing weight. This was believed to be approximately the upper limit of adult morons. Successful completion of Item 24, giving rhymes to selected words, and/or Item 25, providing the correct word to an incomplete sentence, therefore would contraindicate mild levels of retardation in an adult.

The collection of 30 tasks of increasing difficulty in the Binet-Simon scale provided the first major measure of human intelligence. It therefore was a scientific breakthrough. Binet had solved two major problems of test construction. He determined exactly what he wanted to measure, and he developed items for this purpose. He fell short, however, in several other areas of measurement. The 1905 Binet-Simon scale lacked an adequate measuring unit to express results, adequate normative data, and evidence in support of its validity. The classifications Binet used (idiot, imbecile, and moron) can hardly be considered adequate for expressing results and, as Binet himself was aware, little had been done to document the scale's validity. Furthermore, norms for the 1905 scale were based on only 50 children who had been considered normal based on an average school performance.

B. The 1908 scale

Binet was interested in producing a sound scientific instrument rather than in defending his position at the expense of progress. He therefore made a major effort to deal with the limitations of the 1905 scale in his second major revision. This second revision appeared in 1908, just three years after the initial scale had been introduced. In the 1908 scale Binet and Simon retained the principle of age differentiation. Indeed, the 1908 scale was an *age scale*, which means items were grouped according to age level rather than simply in order of increasing difficulty as they had been in the 1905 scale.

In the 1908 scale the standardization sample was increased more than fourfold. This new sample consisted of 203 Paris schoolchildren. Grouped by age, the criterion for inclusion of an item at any particular age level was that it must have been successfully passed by two-thirds to three-fourths of a representative group of children at that age. Table 11-1 provides a sample of some of the items included at each age level.

The 1908 Binet scale was a clear improvement over the 1905 scale. However, Binet had done little to meet one persistent criticism: the verbal/language emphasis of the scale. The scale provides many tasks in a variety of areas. As an individual test, it requires from 30 to 85 minutes of professional time to administer to a single person. Yet for all this time and effort, the scale produces only one score, which is almost exclusively related to verbal, language, and reading ability. Binet's rationale for providing only one score of course was based on the notion of general mental ability, for which a single score is appropriate as well as logically consistent. Unfortunately, however, Binet made little effort to diversify the range of abilities tapped. As a result the scale has remained heavily weighted on language, reading, and verbal skills at the expense of other factors such as the integration of visual and motor functioning (for example, eye-hand coordination).

TABLE 11-1 Sample items from the 1908 scale

Age Level Three (Five Items)
1. Point to various parts of face.
2. Repeat two digits forward.

Age Level Four (Four Items)
1. Name familiar objects.
2. Repeat three digits forward.

Age Level Five (Five Items)
1. Copy a square.
2. Repeat a sentence containing ten syllables.

Age Level Six (Seven Items)
1. State age.
2. Repeat a sentence containing 16 syllables.

Age Level Seven (Eight Items)
1. Copy a diamond.
2. Repeat five digits forward.

Age Level Eight (Six Items)
1. Recall two items from a passage.
2. State the differences of two objects.

Age Level Nine (Six Items)
1. Recall six items from a passage.
2. Recite days of week.

Age Level Ten (Five Items)
1. Given three common words, construct a sentence.
2. Recite months of the year in order.

Age Level 11 (Five Items)
1. Define abstract words (for example, justice).
2. Determine what is wrong with absurd statements.

Age Level 12 (Five Items)
1. Repeat seven digits forward.
2. Provide the meaning of pictures.

Age Level 13 (Three Items)
1. State the differences between pairs of abstract terms.

C. *Mental age*

Perhaps the major improvement in the 1908 scale was the introduction of the concept of mental age. Here Binet attempted to solve the problem of expressing the results in adequate units. A subject's mental age was based on his or her performance compared to the average performance of individuals in a specific chronological age group. In simple terms, if a 6-year-old can perform the tasks that can be done by two-thirds to three-fourths of the representative group of 8-year-old children, then this child has a mental age of 8. A 10-year-old who can do no more than pass items that two-thirds to three-fourths of the representative group of 5-year-olds can pass is said to have a mental age of 5.

Calculations of mental age scores became possible because of the shift to an age scale in the 1908 revision. In deriving a child's mental age score, the first step is to determine what is known as the *basal age*. As it is used in modern revisions of the Binet scale, basal age refers to the highest age level at which an individual passes every group of tasks (that is, test) at a particular age level. As indicated in Table 11-1, the 1908 scale had five items at the 3-year level, four at the 4-year level, five at the 5-year level, and so on. In terms of basal age, if a child misses one or more tasks at ages 6 and 5 but passes all tasks at age 4, then his or her basal score is 4 years of age.

In administering the Binet scale, the first goal is to establish the basal age. Thus all tasks need not be given to all subjects. For example, when testing a 7-year-old with average school performance, the examiner probably would begin the test administration at the tasks of the 7-year level. If the child passes each group of tasks at this level, tasks below the 7-year level need not be administered. If this 7-year-old child successfully passes all the tests at the 8-year level, however, then this becomes the basal age unless the child then passes each group of tasks at a still higher year level. However, if the 7-year-old misses even one group of tasks at the 7-year level, then all tasks at the 6-year-old level must be administered and so on, until all tests at a particular age level are passed. Hence a 7-year-old child may have a basal age score of 6, 5, 4, or even lower, depending on the highest year level at which every group of tasks is passed.

Once the basal age is determined testing continues until the subject misses evey group of tasks at a given year level. The year level at which all tests are failed is called the *ceiling*. For those tests passed at age levels between the basal and the ceiling, the subject receives a designated amount of credit in terms of mental age. In the 1908 revision subjects were given 1-year credit of mental age for each five tasks successfully passed beyond the basal. This method had the drawback of not allowing credit for a fraction of a year. Table 11-2 shows how mental age might have been calculated from the 1908 scale. The table illustrates the inequities resulting from failure to allow fractional credit.

IV.   THE 1916 SCALE: TERMAN'S STANFORD-BINET INTELLIGENCE SCALE

Binet and Simon again revised their intelligence scale in 1911, but this third version contained only minor improvements. A few new tasks were added to the 59 in the 1908 scale. Seven tasks heavily related to scholastic achievement were removed in an effort to enhance validity as a measure of intelligence rather than simply scholastic skills. In addition, the age range was increased to include adults.

By the time of the 1911 Binet-Simon revision, the potential utility of the Binet scale had gained recognition in developed countries throughout Europe and in the United States. In the United States, for example, Goddard published a translation of the 1905 Binet-Simon scale in 1908, and he published a version of the 1908 scale in 1911 (Herrnstein, 1981). Other Americans subsequently published a variety of versions of the Binet scale. These included Yerkes's 1915

TABLE 11-2 Mental age from the 1908 scale

Child 1
Chronological age: 6 years 6 months
Basal age: 4 years
Number of tasks passed beyond basal: 14
Number of years credit beyond basal: 2 (5 passes=1 year)
Mental age: 4+2=6

Child 2
Chronological age: 6 years 6 months
Basal age: 4 years
Number of tasks passed beyond basal: 10
Number of years credit beyond basal: 2
Mental age: 4+2=6

Child 3
Chronological age: 6 years 6 months
Basal age: 5
Number of tasks passed beyond basal: 4
Number of years credit beyond basal: 0
Mental age: 5

and 1923 versions, Herring's 1922 version, and Kuhlmann's 1912, 1922, and 1930 versions. However, it was the 1916 Stanford-Binet version, developed under the direction of L. M. Terman, that flourished and became, for quite some time, the dominant intelligence scale in the world.

A. Development of the 1916 Stanford-Binet intelligence scale

In developing the 1916 Stanford-Binet version Terman relied heavily on Binet's earlier work. The principles of age differentiation, general mental ability, and the age scale were retained. The basal, ceiling, and mental age concepts also were retained. The 1916 revision included 59 items from the previous Binet-Simon scales, four tasks from existing American tests, and many originally constructed tasks (Terman, 1916). Thus the scale was once again lengthened, this time to 90 items.

The 1916 scale contained other improvements as well. The age range was increased to include children from 3 through 14 years as well as average and superior adults. Many of the items from the earlier Binet scales were modified, and their locations were altered in line with results from more recent experimentation. An alternate item was added to each age level. This alternate item could be used when one of the original items at a particular age level could not be appropriately administered or was somehow invalidated because of an administration error.

Terman's 1916 revision also increased the size of the standardization sample. Originally Terman and his colleagues had studied the records of 2300 subjects consisting of 1700 normal children, 200 defective and superior children, and 400 adults (Terman, 1916). However, in order to achieve homogeneous groups at each age level, the total sample below the 14-year age level was reduced to 1000 children. Each child in this group, however, was within two months of his or her birthday.

Unfortunately, the entire standardization sample of the 1916 revision consisted exclusively of native-born White children from California. Thus, although the standardization sample had been markedly increased, it was far from representative. In fact, given that geographic location may affect test performance (Lewandowski & Saccuzzo, 1976; Saccuzzo & Lewandowski, 1976), this sample cannot even be considered representative of White native-born Americans. Nevertheless, the increased sample size was a step in the right direction and was clearly an improvement over the meager 50 and 203 individuals of the 1905 and 1908 Binet-Simon versions.

B. *The intelligence quotient (IQ) concept*

The 1916 scale provided the first significant application of the *intelligence quotient* (IQ) concept (Herrnstein, 1981). The IQ concept that, as Herrnstein (1981) noted, had been recommended by Stern (1912), used a subject's mental age in conjunction with his or her chronological age to obtain a ratio score. This ratio score presumably reflected the subject's rate of mental development. Table 11-3 illustrates how the IQ was determined.

TABLE 11-3 The intelligence quotient concept

Child 1
Chronological age (CA): 6 years
Mental age (MA)*: 6 years
$$IQ = \frac{MA}{CA} \times 100 = \frac{6}{6} \times 100 = 100$$

Child 2
Chronological age (CA): 6 years
Mental age (MA): 3 years
$$IQ = \frac{MA}{CA} \times 100 = \frac{3}{6} \times 100 = 50$$

Child 3
CA=6; MA=12; IQ=200

Adult 1
CA=50; MA=16
$$IQ = \frac{16}{16} \times 100 = 100$$
16←(the maximum CA)

*As determined by the basal age plus the number of tasks completed on the Binet scale beyond the basal.

In calculating IQ, the first step is to determine the subject's chronological age. To obtain this we need only know his or her birthday. Second, the subject's mental age is determined by his or her score on the scale, which is determined by adding the appropriate amount of mental age credit to the basal. Finally, to obtain the IQ, the chronological age (CA) is divided into the mental age (MA) and multiplied by 100 to eliminate fractions.

$$IQ = \frac{MA}{CA} \times 100$$

As you can see in Table 11-3, when the MA is less than the CA, the IQ will be below 100. In this case the subject was said to have slower than average mental development. When the converse occurred—that is, when the MA exceeded the CA—the subject was said to have faster than average mental development.

The IQ score altered the nature of the measuring unit that was used in expressing the results. However, as will be seen, the method may have actually been a step backward, and the MA/CA method of calculating IQ scores was ultimately abandoned. The 1916 scale had a maximum possible mental age of 19.5 years. That is, if every group of items was passed, a mental age score of 19.5 would result. Given this limitation in the magnitude of mental age, anyone older than 19.5 would have an IQ of less than 100, even if all items were passed. Therefore, a maximum limit on the chronological age had to be set. Because it was believed at the time of the 1916 revision that mental age ceased to improve after 16 years of age, 16 was used as the maximum chronological age.

V.   THE 1937 SCALE

The 1937 revision remains as the heart of the Binet scale. Although the 1937 scale was subsequently revised in 1960 and restandardized in 1972, all items in the current version came from the 1937 scale. With few exceptions the current psychometric adequacy of the Stanford-Binet intelligence scale can be judged only by data obtained on the 1937 revision.

A.   *General improvements in the 1937 scale*

The 1937 scale extended the age range down to the 2-year-old level. The mental age range also was increased because new tasks were added. This increased the maximum possible mental age to 22 years 10 months. Scoring standards and instructions were improved to reduce ambiguities, enhance standardization of administration, and increase interscorer reliability. Furthermore, a number of performance items, which required the subject to do something like copy designs, were added in an effort to deal with criticisms concerning the scale's emphasis on verbal skills.

The standardization sample also was markedly improved. Whereas the 1916 norms were restricted to Californians, the new subjects for the 1937

Stanford-Binet standardization sample came from 11 states spread across a variety of regions in the United States. Furthermore, subjects were selected according to father's occupation. In addition to improvements in its representativeness, the standardization sample was substantially increased. Unfortunately, the standardization sample included only Whites as well as an excess of urban versus rural subjects (Terman & Merrill, 1937). Nevertheless, this improved sample represented a most desirable trend. The 3184 individuals included in the 1937 standardization sample represented more than a threefold increase from the 1916 scale and was more than 63 times larger than the original sample of the 1905 scale.

Perhaps the most important improvement in the 1937 version was the inclusion of an "alternate equivalent form." Forms L and M were designed to be equivalent in terms of both difficulty and content. Furthermore, with two equivalent forms, psychometric properties of the scale could be readily examined.

B. *Psychometric properties of the 1937 scale*

Subjects in the 1937 standardization sample were tested on both forms within a period of from one day to one week after the initial testing. Results were extremely impressive with a correlation of above .91 for unselected cases (Terman & Merrill, 1937). As McNemar (1942) noted, however, reliability coefficients were higher for older subjects. Thus results for younger individuals were not as stable as those for older ones. Reliability figures also varied as a function of IQ level, with higher reliabilities in the lower IQ ranges (that is, less than 70) and poorer reliability coefficients at the higher IQ ranges.

Lowest reliabilities occurred in the younger age groups at the higher IQ ranges. These findings were explainable, at least in part, by the fact that the nature of the items changed in terms of becoming more and more verbally weighted as one proceeded from younger to older age ranges. Bayley (1955), furthermore, suggested that environmental influences during the early years might result in the development of abilities not demonstrated on the earlier tests. In other words, learning during the early developmental years may influence test scores in later years, a hypothesis that was subsequently substantiated (Kagan & Freeman, 1963). In any case, IQ scores in younger children are far from stable.

Despite variations in the reliability for different IQ and age ranges, the reliability of the 1937 scale was quite impressive. Indeed, the Binet scale remains one of the most reliable psychological tests of any kind. However, along with differing reliabilities, each age group in the standardization sample produced its own unique standard deviation of IQ scores. This differential variability in IQ scores as a function of age created the single most important problem in the 1937 scale. More specifically, despite the great care that was taken in selecting the standardization sample, different age groups showed significant differences in the standard deviation of IQ scores. As reported by Terman and Merrill (1937), standard deviation of the IQ at age 6 was approximately 12.5. The standard deviations at ages $2\frac{1}{2}$ and 12, on the other hand, were 20.6 and 20.0, respectively. Because of these discrepancies in the standard deviations at different age levels, IQs at one age level were not equivalent to IQs at another. This concept is elaborated in Focused Example 11-1.

■ **FOCUSED EXAMPLE 11-1**

Recall our discussion of standard deviations and percentiles in Chapter 3. A score that is two standard deviations above the mean is approximately at the 98th percentile. Therefore, if the mean IQ is 100, a 6-year-old, where the standard deviation is 12.5, would need an IQ of 125 to be two standard deviations above the mean. Being two standard deviations above the mean, this child would be at about the 98th percentile. However, at 12 years of age, where the standard deviation is 20, the same child would now need an IQ of 140 to be two standard deviations above the mean and in the 98th percentile. Thus a child at age 6 who obtained an IQ of 125 would be two standard deviations above the mean and in the 98th percentile. If this same child obtained an IQ of 125 at age 12, he or she would only be 1.25 standard deviations above the mean (remember, the standard deviation at age 12 is 20) and thus only at about the 89th percentile. Thus, in the 1937 scale, an IQ at one age range was not comparable to an IQ at another age range in terms of percentiles.

Tied to the reliability of the Binet scale is its standard error of measurement. As discussed in Chapter 4, measurement error refers to differences between the subject's true score and the score obtained by a measuring device. To determine how much the Binet IQ is affected by short-term errors of measurement, Forms L and M were administered a few days apart. Despite an impressive correlation exceeding .90 (Terman & Merrill, 1937), a relatively large difference occurred in the average IQs for the two testings, especially at the higher IQ ranges. For example, the average difference in IQ equaled 5.9 for IQs of 130, 5.1 for IQs of 100, but only 2.5 for IQs of 70. As might be predicted from reliability data, measurement error was far greater at the younger age levels. Thus the true score for a 5-year-old who obtained an IQ of 130 would be expected to show considerable fluctuation (McNemar, 1942).

Despite problems with reliability, the validity of the 1937 scale was strongly supported. Clearly the scale had content validity. Examination of its content reveals that the subject engages in everything from simple manipulation of objects to complex abstract reasoning. The 1937 Stanford-Binet scale also had well-documented predictive validity. In one sense, however, the scale's high level of predictive validity is rather a mixed blessing. Thus the high correlations between the 1937 scale and school success (Terman & Merrill, 1953; Watson, 1951) suggest the scale is largely a measure of scholastic aptitude, academic achievement, verbal ability, and reading skills. However, the evidence in support of the scale is not limited to predictive validity. "Biserial correlational analysis" revealed a sizable correlation between each item and the total test score (Terman

& Merrill, 1937). That is, each item contributed substantially to the total test score, just as the concept of general mental ability demanded. Because more items were passed with increasing age, the concept of age differentiation and thus the construct validity of the scale also was supported. Finally, factor analytic studies supported the validity of the scale (Sattler, 1982).

VI. THE 1960 STANFORD-BINET REVISION

Twenty-three years after the 1937 revision, the test originated by Binet in 1905 was again revised into its present-day format. The 1960 revision, still widely used today, consists entirely of items from Forms L and M of the 1937 scale. Terman and Merrill (1960) argued that the purpose of having an alternate form had been served. Reliabilities and standard error of measurement had been determined, and the scale more than met rigorous psychometric standards. However, by 1960 many of the items had become outdated, and experience revealed a number of scoring and test administration ambiguities.

The idea of the 1960 revision was to create a single instrument by selecting the best from the two forms of the 1937 scale. Tasks that showed an increase in the percentage passing with an increase in age—the major criterion and guiding principle for all versions of the Binet scale—were given the highest priority. Also given priority were tasks that correlated highly with scores as a whole—the second major guiding principle behind the Binet scale. In addition, instructions for scoring and test administration were improved, and IQ tables were extended from age 16 to 18 (Terman & Merrill, 1960).

A. *Administering the Stanford-Binet intelligence scale*

Table 11-4 illustrates the mechanics of the modern Binet scale. Each year level contains a number of tests, including an alternative test. Each test, in turn, contains one or more tasks. To successfully pass a test, a subject must pass a certain number of tasks. To pass Test 1 in the example, the subject must pass at least one of two tasks. To pass Test 2, the subject must pass at least two of three tasks.

Recall the central importance of the basal age score in administering the Binet scale. The basal score in the modern Stanford-Binet is the highest year level at which the subject successfully passes all tests. The problem for the examiner is to determine which year level to begin the testing with in order to maximize the chances of locating the subject's basal age as quickly as possible. To determine the most appropriate year level in which to begin the testing requires considerable examiner skill. If the examiner begins at too low a year level, then the items will be too easy for the subject. Theoretically, the examiner can begin the testing at any year level.

To use an extreme example, the examiner can begin the testing at year Level II for an 8-year-old child of average intelligence. Clearly year Level II is far too low to begin testing an 8-year-old of average intelligence. The child will no doubt pass all the tests at every year level through at least VI or VII and perhaps year Level VIII. Assuming the child passes all tests at every year level through VIII and then misses at least one test at year Level IX, his or her basal score would be 8 years of age. The results for all year levels prior to Level VIII would not be included in the computation of the child's mental age or IQ.

In addition to being a waste of time, beginning too low may fatigue the child so that he or she is too tired to concentrate when the more difficult tasks are presented at the later year levels. Furthermore, beginning too low may lower the validity of the test results if the child becomes bored or establishes an inappropriate set by incorrectly concluding that all items are too easy. On the other hand, if the examiner begins at too high a year level, the child may become discouraged, lose motivation, and give up easily on all difficult items. Clearly the Binet scale must be administered by a well-trained, competent, and sensitive examiner. Establishing a working relationship with the subject (that is, rapport) is one of the most important factors in a valid Binet administration.

TABLE 11-4 Mechanics of Binet scale record form for year Level II

Year II

_____ Test 1 (subject must pass one task to pass)
Task a
Task b

_____ Test 2 (subject must pass two tasks to pass)
Task a
Task b
Task c

•

•

_____ Test 6 (contains only one task)
Task a

_____ Alternative Test (subject must pass five tasks to pass)
Task a
Task b

•

•

Task f

In further understanding the Binet scale, recall that testing continues until the ceiling, in which the individual misses every test at a given age level. The 1960 revision ranged in age from Levels II through XIV and then had levels for Average Adult (AA) as well as three levels of Superior Adult (SA). Ages for Levels II through V were broken down into half-year intervals (for example, II, II–6 months, III, III–6 months, and so on). Each interval from II through XIV contains six tests. The adult levels contain between six and eight tests. In addition each year level includes a supplementary or alternative test. The subject receives a certain amount of mental age credit for each test beyond the basal. Between age Levels V through AA, for example, two months of credit are given for each test passed. Table 11-5 illustrates the method of determining mental age. As with the 1937 version, the maximum mental age is 22 years 10 months.

B. The deviation IQ concept

One persistent problem in measuring human intelligence has been that of finding an adequate unit for expressing results. In 1908 the concept of mental age was introduced, only to be extended by the intelligence quotient (IQ) concept in the 1916 revision. The IQ was retained in the 1937 revision; however, as noted earlier, standard deviations of IQs obtained by the formula IQ=MA/CA×100 were not always the same at all age levels in the standardization sample. As a result of this variability in standard deviations at the various age levels, an IQ at one age level was not comparable (that is, did not have the same meaning) to an identical IQ obtained at a different age level (see Focused Example 11-1).

TABLE 11-5 Sample test summaries

Child 1, chronological age: 5 years 6 months

Year level	Number of tests passed	Mental age credit
IV	6	Basal age (all tests passed)
V	5	10 months (2 months per test)
VI	1	2 months (2 months per test)
VII	0	Ceiling

Mental age=4 years+10 months+2 months=5 years

$IQ=\frac{5}{5.5}\times100=90.9=91$

Child 2, chronological age: 7 years 0 months

Year level	Number of tests passed	Mental age credit
VII	6	Does not apply
VIII	6	Basal
IX	2	4 months (2 months per test)
X	3	6 months (2 months per test)
XI	4	8 months (2 months per test)
XII	1	2 months (2 months per test)
XIII	2	4 months (2 months per test)
XIV	0	Ceiling

Mental age=8 years+4 months+6 months+8 months+2 months+4 months=10 years

$IQ=\frac{10}{7}\times100=142.9=143$

In addition to a lack of comparability at different age levels, the IQ concept is limited in that an individual's MA gradually ceases to increase as maturity is reached. As a result the IQ concept is limited to the point where increases in chronological age no longer produce equivalent increases in the mental age. This point begins at about 16 years of age, depending on the type of item. Furthermore, the IQ concept does not take into account possible declines in MA that may occur during aging. In an effort to deal with the limitations of the intelligence quotient (IQ), the 1960 Binet scale revision incorporated Wechsler's (1939) "deviation IQ" methodology.

The deviation IQ, as it is used in the Stanford-Binet scale, is simply a standard score with a mean of 100 and a standard deviation of 16. With the mean set at 100, the deviation IQ was ascertained by evaluating the standard deviation of mental age for a representative sample at each age level. New IQ tables were then constructed that corrected for differences in variability at the various age levels. In correcting for these differences in variability, the 1960 IQ tables now produced IQs that were comparable from one age level to another (Terman & Merrill, 1960). The deviation IQ method eliminated one of the major problems of the intelligence quotient concept. With the deviation IQ, scores finally could be directly compared across age groups. Thus scores could be interpreted in terms of standard deviations and percentiles with the assurance that IQ scores for every age group corresponded to the same percentile.

C. Recent evidence on the psychometric qualities of the 1960 scale

The 1960 revision did not include a new normative sample or restandardization. The investigators argued that psychometric data accumulated on the 1937 scale could be transformed to the 1960 scale (Terman & Merrill, 1960). We might describe the scale's psychometric qualities by the term *inherited validity*. In fact, the little work that has been reported does tend to confirm the assumption that psychometric characteristics of the 1937 scale have been inherited by the 1960 scale (Brittain, 1968; Share et al., 1964). However, the assumption of inherited psychometric properties has not gone uncriticized (Fraser, 1965). Berger (1970), in particular, charged the deviation IQs of the 1960 revision were based on data obtained with the 1937 scales. As Berger correctly noted, the 1960 ratio IQs may not have the same properties (distribution statistics) as those observed in the 1937 scale. Thus the IQs and MAs of the 1960 revision may be limited in accuracy.

D. The 1972 revised norms

As in the past, criticisms of the Binet scale have been met by positive action rather than by defensive arguments. By 1972 a new standardization group consisting of a representative sample of 2100 children (about 100 at each Stanford-Binet age level) had been obtained for use with the 1960 revision (Thorndike, 1973). Unlike all previous norms, the 1972 norms included non-

Whites. The mean deviation IQ remained at 100 and the standard deviation at 16. Interestingly, IQs derived from the 1972 norms tended to be lower for a given subject than those obtained with the 1960 norms.

VII. EVALUATION OF THE BINET SCALES

The measure of intelligence first developed under the guidance of Binet is indeed a living test. Between 1905 and 1972 numerous efforts have been made to improve and update the scale and maintain its validity. However, certain points should be noted. First, the tasks are old. Some of the items on the present form are no more than modifications of tasks from the earliest versions, and no new tasks have been introduced since 1937. Second, the scale continues to be heavily weighted in the verbal areas and, more than anything else, seems to be related to scholastic achievement in general and reading comprehension in particular. Because it is an age scale, items are listed according to age with no regard to content. Therefore, the scale produces only a single score. Attempts to describe subjects in terms of specific abilities such as memory or reasoning are dubious at best. Sattler (1982), for example, presented a comprehensive summary of Binet scale interpretative procedures. Yet he concluded that the validity, reliability, and utility of most Binet scale interpretation procedures are unknown and that some are downright hazardous. However, Chase and Sattler (1980) offer some suggestions for reducing the hazards.

Proponents of the Binet scale, however, argue that the weight of evidence continues to support its psychometric adequacy. Indeed, the Binet scale is probably the most powerful psychological test in existence for predicting scholastic achievement. Proponents further argue that although it produces only one score, the Binet scale provides an extremely useful context for observing behavior. The Binet scale examiner can obtain a wealth of data by observing a person solving problems and performing tasks of varying difficulty. Factors such as reaction to frustration or success can be readily observed. The examiner also can observe such factors as the person's approach to problem solving (for example, trial and error versus a systematic approach). Thus the Binet scale provides the examiner with an opportunity to observe behavior in a standard setting and thus offers a wealth of information in addition to a score that can be compared against relatively recent and representative normative data.

VIII. SUMMARY

Rather than being a collection of separate and distinct processes (such as reasoning, memory, and concentration), Binet's definition of intelligence involved the concept of general mental ability. Binet eventually defined intelligence in terms of the capacity (1) to find and maintain a definite direction or purpose, (2) to make adaptations—that is, strategy adjustment if necessary to achieve that purpose, and (3) for self-criticism so that necessary adjustment in strategy can be made.

Binet's two major principles of test construction were age differentiation and general mental ability. Differentiation refers to the fact that with increasing age, children develop increasing capabilities. Thus older children have greater capabilities than younger ones.

With his use of the concept of general mental ability, Binet freed himself from the burden of identifying each and every element or independent aspect of intelligence. He also was freed from ascertaining the relative contribution of each element to the whole. In his decision to use the concept of general mental ability Binet restricted his search for measures of intelligence to anything related to the whole or final product of intelligence rather than to hypothetical individual processes underlying intelligence.

Mental age is a unit of measure for expressing results of intelligence tests. The concept was introduced in the second revision of the Binet scale in 1908. A subject's mental age is based on his or her performance compared to the average performance of individuals in a specific chronological age group. For example, if a 6-year-old child can perform tasks that can be done by the average 8-year-old, then the 6-year-old child is said to have a mental age of 8.

The intelligence quotient (IQ), like mental age, is a unit of measure for expressing results of intelligence tests. Introduced in the Terman 1916 Stanford-Binet revision of the Binet scale, the intelligence quotient (IQ) is a ratio score. Specifically, the IQ is the ratio of a subject's mental age (as determined by his or her performance on the intelligence scale) and chronological age. This ratio is then multiplied by 100 to eliminate fractions:

$$\text{Intelligence quotient} = \frac{\text{Mental age (MA)}}{\text{Chronological age (CA)}} \times 100$$

or

$$IQ = \frac{MA}{CA} \times 100$$

For example, if a 6-year-old child obtains a mental age of 12, his or her intelligence quotient would be determined as follows:

$$IQ = \frac{12 \text{ (MA)}}{6 \text{ (CA)}} \times 100 = 200$$

The 1937 scale made a number of general improvements over the 1916 one. The age range was extended, scoring standards and instructions were improved, and a number of performance items were added. These performance items, which required subjects to do something such as copy designs rather than say something, reduced the verbal emphasis of the Binet scale. In addition, an alternative equivalent form was added and the size and representativeness of the standardization sample were improved.

In general the 1937 scale proved to be a highly reliable instrument. However, reliability fluctuated for different age and IQ ranges. Reliability was poor for younger children at the upper IQ levels. Reliability was far better for older age groups and for low (for example, 70) and average (for example, 96–106) IQ ranges. The 1937 scale proved to be valid from a number of perspectives. In addition to content validity, construct validity, and validity support from factor analytic studies, the 1937 scale demonstrated considerable predictive validity. As a predictor of scholastic achievement, the 1937 scale has few competitors.

The deviation IQ, as it is used in the Stanford-Binet scale, is a standard score with a mean of 100 and a standard deviation of 16.

The 1972 revised norms for the Stanford-Binet intelligence scale included non-Whites for the first time in the long history of the scale.

12

The Wechsler Intelligence Scales

Learning objectives

When you have completed this chapter, you should be able to do the following:

1. *Identify the major motivation for the development of the Wechsler scales.*
2. *Briefly describe the point and performance scale concepts.*
3. *List the verbal and performance subtests of the WAIS-R and briefly describe the function purportedly measured by each subtest.*
4. *Explain the declining age standard on the WAIS-R.*
5. *Tell how IQ scores are determined on the WAIS-R.*
6. *Describe the reliability of the WAIS and WAIS-R.*
7. *Describe the validity of the WAIS and WAIS-R.*
8. *Identify some of the major advantages and disadvantages of the WAIS and WAIS-R.*
9. *Briefly describe the WISC, WISC-R, and WPPSI.*

Susan's family had just moved from a small rural town to a large metropolis on the East Coast. At the age of 9 she was still shy around strangers and lacked confidence. Her attempt to adjust to a new school was a disaster. Because she started in the middle of the school term, all the other children seemed way ahead of her. She felt hopelessly behind. To make matters worse she had an unusually strong fear of failure. Rather than make an error, she would remain silent even if she knew an answer. With all her negative experiences in the new school, she began to develop a poor attitude toward school tasks and avoided them. Eventually she was referred to the school psychologist for testing. To Susan this referral was the school's way of punishing her for not doing her homework.

Fearful, upset, and angry, she made up her mind not to cooperate with the psychologist.

When the time finally came for her appointment, Susan began to cry. The principal was called in to accompany her to the psychologist's office. All the psychologist's attempts to comfort Susan did little to reduce her fear and anxiety. Finally the psychologist decided to begin the testing. He started with a relatively simple task that requested Susan to repeat digits. The psychologist stated "I'm going to say some numbers. Listen, because when I'm through I want you to say them as I do." He began the first set of digits and stated in a soft, clear voice "Six, three, one." Susan did not even respond. She had been staring blankly at the walls and did not listen to what the psychologist had said. The psychologist attracted her attention and said "Now say what I say: four, two, seven." This time Susan heard, but again she remained mute.

Now think for a moment. How many different factors were involved in the psychologist's ostensibly simple request to repeat three digits forward? To comply with this request Susan would have had to direct her attention to the words of the psychologist, possess adequate hearing, and understand the instructions. She would also have to cooperate, make an effort, and be capable of repeating what was in her mind. Certainly her familiarity with numerals—that is, her previous learning and experience—could influence her performance. If the children in her new school had more exposure to numerals than she, then they would have an advantage over her in this regard. Furthermore, her lack of confidence, negative attitude toward school, fear of failure, and shyness all played a role in her performance. A more confident, less fearful child with positive attitudes toward school would have a clear advantage over Susan. Thus, in addition to memory, many nonintellective factors (for example, attitude, experience, and emotional functioning) play an extremely important role in a person's ability to perform a task even as "simple" as repeating three digits forward.

Both Binet and Terman were aware of the influence of nonintellective factors on results from intelligence tests. However, David Wechsler is perhaps one of the most influential advocates of the role of nonintellective factors in these tests. In the fourth edition of his book *The Measurement and Appraisal of Adult Intelligence*, Wechsler (1958, pp. vii–viii) stated "Factors other than intellectual ability, for example, those of drive and incentive, are involved in intelligent behavior."

In the highly influential fifth revision of Wechsler's (1958) book, Matarazzo (1972, p. 132) added to Wechsler's statement on the role of nonintellective factors in IQ tests: "Although the IQ is the best single measure of intelligence, it is neither the only nor a complete measure of it. It [IQ] is a function of other factors besides sheer intellectual ability." Wechsler (1981) subsequently reasserted the importance of nonintellective factors but warned that "no amount of drive will develop a dullard into a mathematician."

I. THE WECHSLER INTELLIGENCE SCALES

The role of nonintellective factors is apparent in the intelligence scales bearing the name of Wechsler. Just two years after the Binet scale's monumental 1937 revision, its supremacy as a measure of human intelligence was challenged by Wechsler's contribution to human intelligence testing, the Wechsler-Bellevue Intelligence Scale. With so many different and varied abilities associated with intelligence, many of which were affected or influenced by a unique set of nonintellective factors, Wechsler objected to the single score offered by the Binet scale. In constructing his own intelligence test, Wechsler deviated considerably from many of the central concepts in the Binet scale.

Wechsler (1939) capitalized on the inappropriateness of the Binet scale as a measure of the intelligence of adults. The Binet scale items were selected for use with children, not adults. Thus, Wechsler concluded that the Binet items lacked validity when answered by adults. As a result, examiner-subject rapport was often impaired in a Binet scale testing with adults. Wechsler (1939) further noted that the Binet scale's emphasis on speed, with timed tasks scattered throughout the scale, tended to unduly handicap older adults. Furthermore, mental age norms were clearly not applicable to adults. In addition, Wechsler criticized the Binet scale because it did not consider possible deterioration in intellectual performance with increasing age.

A. *Advances in intelligence testing: Point and performance scale concepts*

Many of the differences between the Wechsler and Binet scales are quite profound. Two of the most critical differences are (1) Wechsler's use of the point scale concept rather than an age scale and (2) Wechsler's inclusion of a performance scale.

The point scale concept.   Recall that since its 1908 revision the Binet scale grouped items by age level. Each age level included a group of tasks that could be passed by two-thirds to three-fourths of the individuals at that age level. In the age scale format, the arrangement of items has nothing to do with their content. At a particular year level there might be one task related to memory, a second related to reasoning, and a third related to skill in using numerical data. Another year level might also include a task related to memory but then include other tasks related to concentration or language skills. Thus various types of content are scattered throughout the scale. Furthermore, subjects do not receive a specific amount of points or credit for each task completed. For example, if a Binet scale subject was required to pass three out of four tasks in order to receive credit for a particular test, then passing only two tasks would produce no credit at all for that test.

In a *point scale* credits or points are assigned to each item. All items of a particular content can then be grouped together. Within each content area, items can be presented in order of increasing difficulty. By arranging items according to content and assigning a specific number of points to each item, Wechsler was able to construct an intelligence test that yielded not only a total overall score as in the Binet, but also gave additional scores for each content area. Thus, with the point scale concept Wechsler was able to devise a test that permitted an analysis of the individual's ability in a variety of content areas (for example, judgment, vocabulary, and range of general knowledge).

The performance scale concept.   The Binet scale has been persistently and consistently criticized for its emphasis on language/verbal skills. In dealing with this problem, Wechsler included an entire scale that provided a measure of nonverbal intelligence: a *performance scale*.

In addition to its advantage as a measure of adult intelligence and its ability to yield separate scores for various functions rather than a single score, Wechsler's approach thus had a third major advantage over the Binet scale. The performance scale consists of tasks that require a subject to do something (for example, copy symbols or point to a missing detail) rather than to simply answer questions.

Although the Binet scale contains some performance tasks, these tend to be concentrated at the early age levels. Furthermore, the results of a subject's response to a performance task on the Binet scale are extremely difficult to separate from the results of verbal tasks. Thus, it is not possible on the Binet scale to determine the precise extent to which a subject's response to a performance task increased or decreased the total score. The Wechsler scale, however, included two separate scales. The verbal scale provided a measure of verbal intelligence, and the performance scale provided a measure of nonverbal intelligence.

The concept of a performance scale was far from new. Prior to the development of the Wechsler scale several performance tests were available as a supplement or alternative to the verbally weighted Binet scale (such as the Leiter International Performance Scale, which is discussed in the next chapter). However, Wechsler's new scale offered the possibility of a direct comparison of an individual's verbal and nonverbal intelligence. Thus, both verbal and performance scales were standardized on the same sample, and results for both scales were expressed in comparable units.

The purpose of a performance scale is to overcome (to the extent possible) language, cultural, and educational factors in measuring intelligence. Furthermore, if verbal tasks provide a useful context in which to observe behavior, then tasks requiring the subject to do something can offer an even richer and more varied context in which to observe a subject's approach to problem solving. Indeed, performance tasks tend to require a longer interval of sustained effort, concentration, and attention than most verbal tasks. Therefore, despite their relative insensitivity to language, educational, and cultural factors, performance tasks are generally more vulnerable to emotional disorders (Rapaport et al., 1968). With a performance and a verbal scale, Wechsler went a long way toward resolving one of the major problems in the Binet scale.

B. *The Wechsler-Bellevue intelligence scale*

Despite his conceptual improvements, Wechsler's first effort to measure adult intelligence, the Wechsler-Bellevue scale (Wechsler, 1939), was poorly standardized. Its normative sample consisted of a nonrepresentative sample of 1081 Whites from the eastern section of the United States (primarily New York residents). By 1955, however, Wechsler had revised the Wechsler-Bellevue scale into its modern form, the Wechsler Adult Intelligence Scale (WAIS), which was revised in 1981 (Wechsler, 1981).

C. *Standardization of the Wechsler adult intelligence scales*

The WAIS, which was no more than an extension and technical improvement of the Wechsler-Bellevue scale, was designed for individuals 16 years of age and older. The standardization sample of 1700 adults was distributed over seven age levels, contained an equal number of males and females, and was representative of the U.S. population according to the 1950 census in terms of geographic location, urban versus rural area, race (White versus non-White), occupational level, and education. For each age level two institutionalized mentally retarded individuals, one man and one woman, were included in the sample. Supplementary norms were also developed for the elderly; these norms were based on 475 individuals over 59 years old. The most recent revision of the WAIS, the WAIS-R, is based on the 1970 census and a representative sample of 1880 individuals distributed over nine age groups who were tested between 1976 and 1980.

II. SCALES AND SUBTESTS OF THE WAIS-R

Like Binet, Wechsler defined intelligence in terms of the capacity to act purposefully and to adapt to the environment. Intelligence is, he stated, "the aggregate or global capacity of the individual to act purposefully, to think rationally and to deal effectively with his environment" (Wechsler, 1958, p. 7). Wechsler believed that intelligence comprised specific elements that could be individually defined and measured. However, these elements were seen as interrelated—that is, not entirely independent. This is why he used the term *global* or *aggregate*. Wechsler's definition implies that intelligence comprises a number of specific interrelated functions or elements and that general intelligence is the result of the interplay of these elements. Theoretically, by measuring each of the elements, general intelligence could be measured by summing up the individual's capacity on each element. Thus, Wechsler made an effort to measure separate abilities, which Binet had avoided in his decision to adopt the concept of general mental ability. In creating the WAIS and WAIS-R, Wechsler identified 11 elements or functions, 6 related to verbal intelligence and 5 to nonverbal intelligence. Table 12-1 lists each of these 11 subtests and the basic function they purportedly measure (Rapaport et al., 1968; Sattler, 1982; Wechsler, 1958; Zimmerman, Woo-Sam, & Glasser, 1973).

TABLE 12-1 WAIS-R subtests

Verbal scales	**Major function measured**
Information	Range of knowledge
Comprehension	Judgment
Arithmetic	Concentration
Similarities	Abstract thinking
Digit span	Immediate memory, anxiety
Vocabulary	Vocabulary level
Performance scales	**Major function measured**
Digit symbol	Visual-motor functioning
Picture completion	Alertness to details
Picture arrangement	Planning ability
Block design	Nonverbal reasoning
Object assembly	Analysis of part-whole relationships

A.   The verbal subtests

The six verbal subtests are (1) information, (2) comprehension, (3) arithmetic, (4) similarities, (5) digit span, and (6) vocabulary. Each of these is briefly discussed below.

The information subtest.   College students typically find the information subtest a relatively easy task. As in all Wechsler subtests, items are presented in order of increasing difficulty. Item 6 asks something like "Name four famous U.S. presidents." Like all Wechsler subtests, the information subtest involves both intellective and nonintellective components. These components include the ability to comprehend instructions, follow directions, and provide a response. Although purportedly a measure of the subject's range of knowledge, factors such as curiosity and interest in the acquisition of knowledge tend to influence test scores. Figure 12-1 illustrates how a score on the information subtest can be parceled into components.

The comprehension subtest.   Like the information subtest, the comprehension subtest is given without any specific preparatory instructions. The examiner simply reads each question and waits for the response. The comprehension subtest has three types of questions. The first places the subject in a situation and asks what should be done in that situation. For example, a person might be asked something like "What should you do if you find an

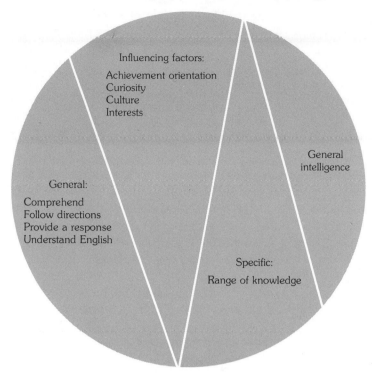

Figure 12-1. Information Subtest: Intellective and Nonintellective Components. (*Based on factor analytic and logical analyses of intellective and nonintellective components in the information subtest.*)

injured person lying in the street?" The second type of question asks the subject to provide a logical explanation for some rule or phenomenon such as "Why do we bury the dead?" The third type of question asks the subject to define proverbs such as "A stitch in time saves nine." Previous learning and scholastic aptitude play a far smaller role in the comprehension subtest than in the information subtest; generally, the comprehension subtest measures common sense. In addition, emotional difficulties frequently reveal themselves on this subtest and lower the person's score. For example, a psychopathic individual might respond to the question concerning what to do if you find an injured person as follows: "Tell somebody I didn't do it." A phobic neurotic might respond "Make sure I don't get any blood on myself." A schizophrenic might say "Run." In each case the person's emotional disturbance interferes with his or her judgment, resulting in an inappropriate response.

The arithmetic subtest.   The only instructions for administering the arithmetic subtest of the WAIS are "Now let us try these." If the examiner stated "Now we are going to do some math problems," many people might become anxious because of mental blocks or fear of arithmetic. Actually the arithmetic subtest contains 14 relatively simple problems. The ninth most difficult item is as easy as this: "A man with $17.50 spends $7. How much does he have left?" Obviously you need not be a mathematician to figure this one out. However, you must be able to retain the figures in memory while manipulating them. In a few cases, such as in retarded or educationally deprived subjects, arithmetic skills sometimes play a significant role. Generally, however, concentration, motivation, and memory are the major factors underlying performance. Figure 12-2 illustrates some of the intellective and nonintellective components for the arithmetic subtest as revealed by factor analytic and logical analyses.

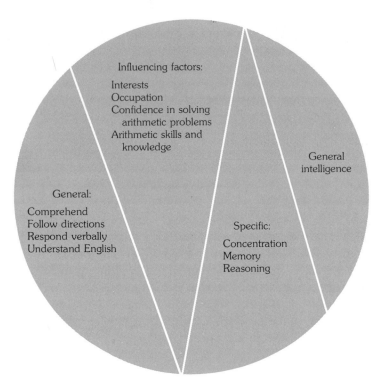

Figure 12-2.   Arithmetic Subtest: Intellective and Nonintellective Components.

The similarities subtest.   The similarities subtest consists of 14 paired items of increasing difficulty. The subject's task is to identify the similarity between the items in each pair. The subject may be asked, for example, "In what way are a horse and a cow alike?" Many of the early, easier items are so well known that responses simply reflect previously learned associations (Zimmerman et al., 1973). However, the more difficult items definitely require the subject to think at an abstract level. This subtest measures the subject's ability to see the similarity between apparently dissimilar objects or things.

The character of a person's thought processes can also be seen in many cases. For example, schizophrenic persons tend to give concepts that have meaning only to them—that is, idiosyncratic concepts. An idiosyncratic response to the hypothetical horse and cow item might be "Both are places to hide." Such a response has meaning only to the schizophrenic person, who may further explain "My favorite hiding place is on my uncle's farm." Brain injured and mentally retarded individuals tend to have difficulty thinking abstractly. The character of their thought processes is concrete. A concrete response is highly specific, such as "A cow and a horse both have four legs."

The digit span subtest.   The digit span subtest requires the subject to repeat digits, read at the rate of one per second, forward and backward. In terms of intellective factors, the digit span subtest measures short-term auditory memory. As with other Wechsler subtests, however, nonintellective factors (for example, attention) often influence the results. For example, a large body of literature has shown that anxiety in the test situation impairs performance on the digit span subtest (Boor & Schill, 1968; Edwards, 1966; Hodges & Spielberger, 1969).

The vocabulary subtest.   The ability to define words is not only one of the best single measures of intelligence, but it is also the most stable and least deteriorating aspect of intelligence (Rapaport et al., 1968). Vocabulary tests are included on nearly every individual test involving verbal intelligence. The relative stability of the vocabulary scale is one of its most important features. If an individual has shown deterioration (that is, lowered performance compared to a higher level at some earlier time) because of emotional factors or brain damage, vocabulary would be one of the last subtests to be affected. For example, the poor concentration of schizophrenic persons lowers performance on arithmetic or digit span long before vocabulary is negatively affected. Whereas mild concentration difficulties lower optimal performance on arithmetic and digit span, such difficulties do not affect vocabulary until they become quite severe. Because the vocabulary subtest provides an estimate of general verbal intelligence that is relatively stable and independent of deterioration, it can be used to evaluate base line intelligence (that is, what a person's intellectual capacity probably was prior to an emotional illness, brain injury, or trauma).

B.   Raw scores, scaled scores, and the verbal IQ

The six verbal subtests constitute the verbal scale of the WAIS-R. Each subtest produces a raw score—that is, a total number of points. Information, for example, contains 29 items scored 1 or 0. The highest possible raw score on information is 29. The maximum possible raw score on vocabulary, on the other hand, is 70. Clearly a raw score of 29 on information is not comparable to a raw score of 29 on vocabulary.

To deal with the lack of comparability of raw scores of the individual subtests, the raw scores for each subtest are converted to a standard or *scaled score* with a mean of 10 and a standard deviation of 3. On the WAIS-R a raw score for any given subtest yields the same scaled score regardless of age because norms for WAIS and WAIS-R scaled scores were based on a reference sample of 500 cases ranging between 20 and 34 years of age selected from the standardization sample. For a given subject the scaled score on one subtest can be directly compared to any other. For example, a scaled score of 10 is at the 50th percentile for all subtests. Thus a person's relative strength on any subtest can be directly compared to his or her strength on any other. This feature of the WAIS-R opens the possibility of pattern analysis, in which a person's pattern of weaknesses and strengths can be related to particular problems. Figure 12-3 illustrates a possible WAIS-R pattern.

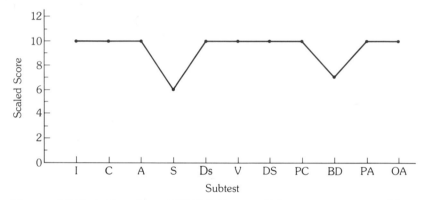

Figure 12-3. A Hypothetical WAIS-R Pattern. Subtests are represented by initials (for example, I=information, Ds=digit span, and DS=digit symbol).

In Figure 12-3 the subject obtained an average scaled score on every subtest except similarities and block design. In pattern analysis an effort would be made to determine what type of problem would lower performance on these subtests. It is assumed that the person's other (average) subtest scores indicate that he or she is capable of average performance in all areas. The relatively low scores on similarities and block design are assumed to reflect deterioration. Because these scores are both related to abstract thinking (verbal and nonverbal, respectively), the question becomes "What type of problem would cause deterioration in abstract thinking?" In answering this question the tester may gain insights into the nature of the person's problem.

To obtain the verbal IQ the scaled scores on each of the six verbal subtests are summed. This sum is then compared to the standardization sample of the person's age group. You should note that the same scaled score sum produces different IQs depending on age. For example, a sum of 60 yields a verbal IQ of 97 in the 25–34 age group, but this same sum yields a verbal IQ of 109 in the 70–74 age group for the WAIS-R. The reason older subjects require a lower scaled score sum to produce the same or even higher IQ as middle-aged subjects is discussed in Focused Example 12-1. Tables are provided in the manual so that, given the person's age and summed scaled scores, the IQ can be looked up. The verbal IQ for each age level is a deviation IQ with a mean of 100 and a standard deviation of 15.

■ **FOCUSED EXAMPLE 12.1 THE DECLINING AGE STANDARD**

One of the important debates within psychology has centered around the question "Does intelligence decrease in the later years of life?" Analysis of the WAIS standardization had indicated that scores rise until the late 20s or 30s and then decline until about age 60. After age 60 there seemed to be a relatively sharp decline in intelligence (Doppelt & Wallace, 1955). However, the WAIS was standardized cross-sectionally. This means a different sample of subjects was tested at each age level. In contrast to the cross-sectional method is the longitudinal method. In the longitudinal method the same subjects are tested at various points in time. Obviously the longitudinal method provides far greater control over important variables than the cross-sectional one.

When the same individuals are tested several times over a long period (longitudinal method), there is control over educational opportunities (more colleges are available today than were available 40 years ago), cultural experiences, technological advances (for example, the availability of television), and a host of other factors. Furthermore, a longitudinal study precludes the possibility of inadvertently having unusually bright (or limited) individuals at one particular age group, which would bias the results. However, a longitudinal study requires many years to complete. In standardizing the WAIS, Wechsler could not afford to take the same group of adults and test them at various points in their lives over a 50-year span. However, recent evidence from longitudinal studies has indicated that intelligence actually does not decline anywhere near as dramatically as indicated by an analysis of Wechsler's cross-sectional normative sample. In fact, the evidence indicates that except in certain abnormal conditions and just prior to death, intelligence remains fairly stable throughout the life span (Matarazzo, 1972).

The reason for the dramatic differences between a verbal IQ for a scaled score sum of 60 in the 25–34 age group (IQ=97) and the verbal IQ for a sum of 60 in the 70–74 age group (IQ=109) is that WAIS and WAIS-R norms are based on cross-sectional data. The decline in intelligence in the later years of life indicated by the cross-sectional data is reflected in the IQ conversions for a particular age group. The average sum of the verbal subtest scaled scores in the WAIS cross-sectional standardization sample, for example, was about 48 in the 70–74 age range. The average sum in the 25–34 age range, however, was 61. Therefore, in order to obtain a verbal IQ of 100, someone in the 70–74 age range would need a sum of scaled scores of 48, whereas someone in the 25–34 age range would need a sum of 61. This phenomenon is known as the declining age standard.

The purpose of the declining age standard was to avoid penalizing aging adults. If intelligence did in fact decline with age, and all subjects were compared to the performance of adults at their peak as in the Binet scale, then younger subjects would obtain consistently higher IQ scores than older subjects. A subject who showed no more decline in intelligence above and beyond the normal aging process would still manifest substantial reductions in the IQ score. Unless corrected for, the end result would be that few elderly would obtain even average scores and most would fall in the below average or retarded ranges. However, inasmuch as the longitudinal data show that intelligence does not decline significantly throughout the life span, the declining age standard actually has the reverse of its intended effect when subjects tested 20 or 30 years ago are retested and evaluated in terms of cross-sectional norms. An adult tested at 34 years of age in 1955 would actually gain 5–10 IQ points if tested in 1982. As Matarazzo (1972) noted, the age norms of the WAIS score require periodic updating, which is one reason the WAIS was revised in 1981.

C. *The performance subtests*

The five performance subtests of the WAIS and WAIS-R are digit symbol, picture completion, block design, picture arrangement, and object assembly. Each of these is discussed below.

The digit symbol subtest. The digit symbol subtest requires the subject to copy symbols. In the upper part of the standard WAIS form for recording responses are the numbers 1 through 9. Under each number is a symbol (see Figure 12-4). After completing a short practice sample, the subject is given 90 seconds to copy as many symbols as possible. The subtest measures such factors as ability to learn an unfamiliar task, visual-motor dexterity, degree of persistence, and speed of performance (Zimmerman et al., 1973). Naturally the subject must have adequate visual acuity and appropriate motor capabilities to successfully complete this subtest.

The picture completion subtest. In the picture completion subtest the subject is shown a picture in which some important detail is missing, such as a horse without a tail. The subject is asked to tell (Wechsler, 1955) which part is missing; however, credit can be obtained simply by pointing to the missing part. As in all five WAIS and WAIS-R performance subtests, picture completion is timed: the subject is given 20 seconds to locate the missing detail. As simple as this task would seem from a test administration standpoint, the importance of an experienced examiner becomes clear in a close examination. If the subject points, the examiner must ascertain that the right detail has been identified. In addition, the experienced examiner will not immediately go to the next item if 20 seconds have elapsed but the subject has not yet responded. If the subject appears to be contemplating a response, the examiner will generally permit a response, even though no credit can be obtained beyond the time limit. An experienced examiner knows that it is unwise to force a subject to struggle over a picture when it is clear that he or she has no idea of the answer. Discretion is

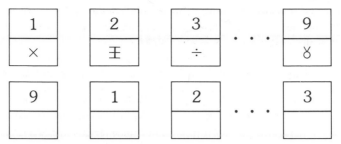

Figure 12-4. Digit Symbol: An Illustrative Example. The top row contains divided boxes with a number in the upper half and a mark underneath. The bottom row contains divided boxes with numbers on top but no marks. The subject's task is to supply the appropriate mark in the lower half of the bottom row.

necessary in giving this, as well as other, WAIS and WAIS-R performance subtests.

The block design subtest.   Block design tasks have long been included in nonverbal measures of intelligence (Arthur, 1930; Kohs, 1923). Materials for the block design subtest include nine blocks. Some sides are all red, some sides are all white, and some sides are red on one-half and white on the other. The materials also include a booklet with pictures of the blocks arranged according to a specific design or configuration. The subject is asked to arrange the blocks into the designs that appear in increasing difficulty. The block design subtest requires the subject to reason, analyze spatial relationships, and integrate visual and motor functions. The input information (that is, pictures of designs) is visual, but the response (output) is motor. The subtest provides an excellent measure of nonverbal concept formation or abstract thinking (Rapaport et al., 1968).

The picture arrangement subtest.   The picture arrangement subtest also requires the subject to notice relevant details. In addition, however, the subject must be able to plan adequately and notice cause-and-effect relationships (Zimmerman et al., 1973). The subtest consists of ten items, each of which contains a series of related pictures such as those found in most comic strips. The pictures are placed in a mixed-up order, and the subject is asked to put them in the right order so that they tell a story. Because the individual must find the logical sequence of events, the subtest taps nonverbal reasoning ability. Because some of the items involve social or interpersonal content, it has been suggested that the subtest also taps the ability to accurately interpret social situations (Sattler, 1982; Zimmerman et al., 1973).

The object assembly subtest.   Object assembly consists of four puzzles (four cut-up objects) that the subject is asked to put together as quickly as possible. The subtest measures the ability of the subject to see part/whole relationships and involves "visual analysis and its coordination with simple assembly skills" (Zimmerman et al., 1973).

D. Performance IQs

As with the verbal subtests, the raw scores for each of the five performance subtests are converted to scaled scores based on the 500 cases in the 20–34 age group of the standardization sample. The mean and standard deviation are the same as for the verbal subtests, 10 and 3 respectively. The performance IQ is determined by summing the scaled scores on the five performance subtests and comparing this score to the appropriate age group. The performance IQ, like the verbal IQ, is a deviation IQ with a mean of 100 and a standard deviation of 15.

E. Full-scale IQs

The full-scale IQ follows the same principles of the verbal and performance IQs. It is obtained by summing the scaled scores of the six verbal subtests with the five performance subtests and comparing the subject to his or her appropriate age group. Again, a deviation IQ with a mean of 100 and a standard deviation of 15 is obtained.

III.   INTERPRETIVE FEATURES OF THE WAIS AND WAIS-R

The WAIS and WAIS-R provide a rich source of data that often furnish cues of significance in the diagnosis or evaluation of emotionally disordered states. Of particular significance in evaluating disordered states is the comparison of verbal and performance IQs and analysis of the pattern of subtest scores (Guertin, Ladd, Frank, Rabin, & Hiester, 1966, 1971).

A. Verbal-performance IQ comparisons

In providing a measure of nonverbal intelligence in conjunction with a verbal IQ, the WAIS and WAIS-R provide an extremely useful opportunity not offered by the Binet scale. First, the inclusion of the performance IQ aids in the interpretation of the verbal IQ (Sattler, 1982). Assume, for example, that a subject obtains a verbal IQ (VIQ) in the retarded ranges (such as VIQ=70). If the performance IQ is also approximately 70, then results with the verbal IQ have been confirmed and we have a good indication that the individual is, in fact, intellectually retarded. Suppose, however, that the performance IQ exceeded 100. Then we have a case where the individual is at least average in his or her nonverbal skills but two standard deviations below the mean in the verbal area. Even though the full-scale IQ might still fall within the retarded ranges, it is quite unlikely that such a person is mentally retarded. Instead, language, cultural, or educational factors might account for the differences in the two IQs.

Discrepancies between the verbal and performance IQs may also result from emotional problems or brain damage (Wechsler, 1958). For example, the left hemisphere of the brain is primarily responsible for the verbal/language functions in most people. If a person obtains a low verbal IQ and a high performance IQ, then this may suggest left-hemisphere impairment. Similarly, a high verbal IQ relative to the performance IQ may suggest right-hemisphere impairment. Indeed, the overwhelming weight of the literature examined in a review of the WAIS by Guertin et al. (1966, 1971) indicated that a discrepancy between the verbal and performance IQs is an indicator of brain damage when the pattern involves a low verbal and a high performance IQ.

B. Pattern analysis

The 11 separate subtest scores of the WAIS and WAIS-R offer an opportunity for pattern analysis. In pattern analysis relatively large differences between subtest scaled scores are evaluated. Wechsler (1958) believed that certain patterns of WAIS scores might be related to certain types of emotional problems. He reasoned that different types of emotional problems might have a differential effect on the subtests. Hysterics, for example, use denial and repression—that is, put things out of awareness as a defense mechanism. Therefore they should show lapses in their long-term store of knowledge, which might reflect itself in a relatively low score on the information subtest. Schizophrenia involves poor concentration and impaired judgment, which might be reflected in relatively low scores on arithmetic and comprehension. Wechsler (1958) provided a host of patterns tentatively proposed to have diagnostic significance.

Following Wechsler's (1958) proposed patterns a large number of investigators empirically studied the potential validity of pattern analysis (Guertin et al., 1966, 1971; Guertin, Rabin, Frank, & Ladd, 1962). Results were inconclusive and contradictory. Indeed, Frank (1970) surveyed the literature relevant to the diagnostic and personality implications of the WAIS. He concluded that the available research was so poorly controlled that the best thing to do would be to forget the work that had been done and start all over again from scratch.

Following Frank's criticisms of the literature and all but dismissal of the potential of pattern analysis, Lewandowski and Saccuzzo (1975, 1976) and Saccuzzo and Lewandowski (1976) listed a number of methodological considerations that must be followed in order to fairly answer the questions concerning the validity of pattern analysis. These authors argued that although the validity may be dubious, the question has yet to be satisfactorily resolved. They further suggested that the question concerning validity might be resolved if appropriate methodological rigor is used in the design of relevant studies. The purpose of Lewandowski and Saccuzzo (1975) and Saccuzzo and Lewandowski (1976) was to illustrate how their methodological considerations might be applied in validating a specific Wechsler intelligence scale pattern for a particular disordered state. These authors failed to confirm many of Wechsler's (1958) hypotheses concerning the meaning of certain subtest patterns, which had been based on his examination of the standardization sample. However, they found that a definite, reliable pattern of subtest scores could be associated with individuals who had been incarcerated for delinquency. This work was subsequently cross-validated and confirmed by Wickham (1978).

Although the issue of the validity of pattern analysis has yet to be resolved, clinical practitioners continue to interpret Wechsler subtest patterns. The hypothetical cases below illustrate what WAIS-R scores might mean to a clinician.

C.   *Hypothetical case studies*

Consider the following example of a 16-year-old high school junior who obtained a "D" average despite a previously stable "B" average. Standard achievement tests found his reading and arithmetic grades appropriate. Scaled scores were as shown in Table 12-2 (remember, the mean is 10 and standard deviation is 3).

TABLE 12-2 Scaled scores

Verbal scales	*Performance scales*
Information: 11	Digit symbol: 4
Comprehension: 9	Picture completion: 10
Arithmetic: 7	Block design: 5
Similarities: 11	Picture arrangement: 11
Digit span: 5	Object assembly: 6
Vocabulary: 11	
Scaled score sum: 54	Scaled score sum: 36
Verbal IQ: 104*	Performance IQ: 83*
Sum of scaled scores for verbal and performance scales: 90	
Full-scale IQ: 93*	

*According to tables provided in the WAIS-R manual.

The previously stable "B" average indicates that this individual is probably of at least average intelligence. The rapid decline in his grades, however, suggests some dramatic change or shift in functioning. His scaled score of 11 on vocabulary is above the mean. Because vocabulary is a relatively stable measure of IQ, the scaled score of 11 also indicates this individual's IQ of 93 is likely to be an underestimate of his intelligence. Assuming that this individual's typical scaled score performance would be about 11, as reflected in his scaled score on vocabulary and confirmed by his scaled scores on information and similarities, we find evidence for deterioration in his judgment (comprehension), concentration (arithmetic), and immediate memory (digit span) in the verbal areas. We also find it in his visual motor speed and integration (digit symbol), nonverbal reasoning (block design), and ability to see part-whole relationships (object assembly) in the performance areas.

When we consider all the areas of impairment, as indicated by relatively low-scaled scores, we must hypothesize the possibility of some type of brain injury or tumor, because these will impair performance on all of the subtests in which the subject has shown evidence of deterioration. With the possibility of a brain tumor, a medical examination and additional tests are both necessary.

In the absence of evidence to the contrary, the clinician would strongly suspect that the subject's shift in grades may be due to brain injury or tumor. However, the clinician would consider other possibilities as well. Environmental or situational factors could lead to impairment on the various WAIS-R subtests. For example, the subject may have become involved with drugs, so this possibility must be examined. Furthermore, the pathology of schizophrenia may cause similar decrements in performance. Therefore, signs of peculiar behavior or other symptoms of schizophrenia should be ruled out by interview and perhaps a projective test (see Chapter 17). Also ruling out situational, environmental, or schizophrenic factors, the examiner might interview to determine whether the subject has suffered a recent blow to the head. If these possibilities prove to be negative, the subject should be immediately referred for a neurological examination by an appropriate medical specialist.

In considering this illustration, as well as the one below, it is important not to lose your perspective. Remember that the validity of pattern analysis is still questionable. Saccuzzo and Lewandowski (1976) found a pattern for acting-out behavior that was later substantiated by Wickham (1978). However, the evidence in support of the validity of most patterns, for reasons that will be discussed more fully in the pages ahead, is still questionable. Our illustrations are designed to give you a flavor of the approach that is taken by many practicing psychologists, who cannot wait for the final piece of evidence before using the tools available to them. They must make decisions, and they do the best they can within the limits of the available research and their experience.

As you no doubt have observed, the above analysis resulted in several speculations, and the clinician exercised the usual caution in interpreting and using the results. For our next example, we present a pattern very much like the one that Saccuzzo and Lewandowski (1976) and Wickham (1978) found in acting-out delinquents. The figures are based on the WAIS rather than the WAIS-R.

In this example, we have the scaled scores of a 16-year-old female with chronic school problems. She was identified as a slow learner in the earlier grades, and she reads far below her grade level. Her scores were as shown in Table 12-3.

The subject is nearly 1 standard deviation above the mean in her performance IQ, and all of her subtests in the performance area are at or greater than the mean. Clearly she is not lacking intellectual potential. Thus, her verbal IQ of 89 is very likely an underestimate of her intellectual capacity. Furthermore, she obtains an above average score on similarities, a noneducationally related measure of abstract thinking skills. Her major areas of weakness are in the

TABLE 12-3 Scaled scores for a slow learner

Verbal scales	Performance scales
Information: 3	Digit symbol: 12
Comprehension: 7	Picture completion: 11
Arithmetic: 4	Block design: 13
Similarities: 11	Picture arrangement: 10
Digit span: 10	Object assembly: 12
Vocabulary: 8	
Scaled score sum: 43	Scaled score sum: 58
Verbal IQ: 89	Performance IQ: 112

Sum of scaled scores for verbal and performance scales: 101
Full-scale IQ: 99

subtests related to academic achievement, information and arithmetic. In addition, she shows some impairment in her judgment. Her verbal IQ thus appears to be lowered due to her lack of motivation for academic achievement and poor judgment. Her pattern of subtest scores is one typically found in poor readers and delinquents.

IV. PSYCHOMETRIC PROPERTIES OF THE WAIS AND WAIS-R

The WAIS and WAIS-R do well, both in reliability and validity. Below is a summary of these qualities.

A. *Reliability*

Reliability coefficients for the WAIS have been impressive and attest to the internal and temporal reliability of the verbal, performance, and full-scale IQs. Using the split-half method for all subtests except for digit span[1] and digit symbol[2], Wechsler (1955) reported reliability coefficients for the 18–19, 24–34, and 45–54 age groups of the standardization sample. Coefficients were .97 for the full-scale IQ of all three groups, .96 for the verbal IQ in all three groups, and .93 or greater for the performance IQ in all three groups. Figures for the WAIS-R are comparable (Wechsler, 1981).

Reports of test-retest WAIS reliabilities, although not as impressive, have ranged from .98 for full-scale IQs of psychiatric patients (Coons & Peacock, 1959) to .78 for retarded subjects (Silverstein, 1968). In a study involving a 13-year test-retest interval with normals, Kangas and Bradway (1971) reported a coefficient of .73 for the full-scale IQ. Results with verbal and performance IQs generally tend to run just a bit lower than those for the full-scale IQ. However, Kangas and Bradway (1971) reported a reliability of only .57 for the performance IQ after a 13-year interval. There are not sufficient data available to evaluate the WAIS-R, but figures reported by Wechsler (1981) are encouraging.

[1] For digit span, digits forward was compared to digits backward.
[2] For digit symbol, a parallel form was used to estimate reliability.

The Wechsler (1981) WAIS-R manual reports an overall standard error of measurement of 2.53 for the full scale IQ, 2.74 for the verbal IQ, and 4.14 for the performance IQ. The figures for the WAIS were about the same.

Test-retest reliability coefficients for the 11 subtests have tended to vary widely. For data presented by Wechsler (1955), information, vocabulary, and digit symbol produced coefficients in the .90s. Similarities, picture completion, and block design produced coefficients in the .80s. The lowest coefficients were produced by picture arrangement and object assembly, where the coefficients were in the .60s. The figures for the WAIS-R are only slightly better. These relatively low coefficients indicate the potential hazards of pattern analysis. If the individual subtests are not stable, then clearly patterns would also lack stability, limiting the potential validity of pattern interpretation.

Perhaps you can now understand why the validity of pattern analysis is questionable and difficult to document. The dependability of pattern analysis depends on subtest intercorrelation as well as the separate reliabilities of the subtests. As the subtest intercorrelations increase and the reliabilities of individual subtests decrease, pattern analysis becomes increasingly dubious (Saccuzzo, Braff, Shine, & Lewandowski, 1981).

B. Validity

Evidence for the validity of the WAIS comes from a variety of sources. Wechsler (1958) argued that the WAIS has content validity in that the functions tapped by the subtests fit the definition of intelligence. Furthermore, similar tasks have been used in other IQ measures and are of proven clinical utility.

Construct validity has been shown by the intercorrelations of the subtests as well as of the verbal and performance IQs. These correlations suggest that the WAIS measures a general intelligence factor. Factor analytic data have also tended to produce factor structures consistent with the notion of a general factor, measuring general intelligence (for example, Spearman's g, which was discussed in Chapter 1), and more specific factors measuring verbal, perceptual, and memory abilities (Cohen, 1957).

Wechsler (1958) further reported that when used in guidance and counseling, mean IQ differences are found among various educational (such as high school versus college) and occupational (for example, engineers versus blue-collar workers) groups in the expected directions. The WAIS has also been correlated with a wide range of tests with coefficients running as high as .897 for the Binet and full-scale IQ (Giannell & Freeburne, 1963) through .68 for the full-scale IQ and progressive matrices (see Chapter 14) and .44 for the performance IQ and progressive matrices (McLeod & Rubin, 1962). In general, correlations with other tests run between .4 and .8.

The WAIS-R used about 80% of the WAIS items (Wechsler, 1981). Wechsler argued that the validity of the WAIS-R is probably comparable to the

WAIS. However, he calls for additional research for a more precise evaluation of the recently developed WAIS-R.

V.   EVALUATION OF THE WAIS AND WAIS-R

The WAIS and WAIS-R offer a number of advantages over the Binet scale. As point scales they permit a reporting of results in terms of functions. Furthermore, the WAIS and WAIS-R use scaled scores that allow a direct comparison of each subtest. The WAIS and WAIS-R offer both a verbal and a performance IQ, permit a pattern analysis, and (like the Binet scale) have impressive psychometric properties. However, individual subtests of the WAIS and WAIS-R are not highly reliable, and the validity of pattern analysis therefore is questionable. Furthermore, being based on the 1950 census, the WAIS is outdated. The new revision of the WAIS, however, deals with many of these problems.

The most common, and perhaps the most serious, criticism of the WAIS is its weakness in measuring extreme IQs. The lowest IQ possible is 41. One can obtain a verbal IQ of 41 if all items are missed except one, which asks the subject to name the colors of the American flag. When all items are missed, the IQ score cannot be determined. Thus, the WAIS cannot measure the lower levels of mental retardation and tends to overestimate IQs at these levels. However, the WAIS has a relatively low ceiling at the upper levels, and it tends to underestimate IQs at the upper levels. Furthermore, although the WAIS clearly measures something more than verbal and language skills, like the Binet it may be measuring only a limited subset of those factors that express intelligent behavior. Finally, validity coefficients sometimes leave much to be desired. The WAIS-R has done little to deal with these problems.

VI.   DOWNWARD EXTENSIONS OF THE WAIS-R: THE WISC, WISC-R, AND WPPSI

Most of the basic ideas of the WAIS and WAIS-R apply to its downward extension, the WISC, which was first published in 1949 and revised in 1974. The WISC measures intelligence from ages 5 through 15 years 11 months (the revised WISC, WISC-R, taps ages 6 through 16 years 11 months 30 days). The basic ideas of the WAIS and WAIS-R also apply to the Wechsler Preschool and Primary Scale of Intelligence (WPPSI). The WPPSI measures intelligence in children from 4 to $6\frac{1}{2}$ years old. These extensions of the WAIS have been thoroughly discussed by Sattler (1982) in a comprehensive textbook devoted to testing intelligence in children. Basic ideas that apply to all Wechsler scales (WAIS, WAIS-R, WISC, WISC-R, and WPPSI) and that have already been discussed in the section on the WAIS and WAIS-R will not be duplicated here, nor will the details previously provided on the WAIS and WAIS-R. If you understand the WAIS and WAIS-R, then you should have little difficulty with the

WISC, WISC-R, and WPPSI. Therefore, only the major distinguishing features of these Wechsler scales will be presented.

A. *The WISC*

The Wechsler Intelligence Scale for Children (WISC) originated from Form II of the Wechsler-Bellevue scale. Its purpose was to provide a point scale measure of intelligence for children between the ages of 5 and 15 years 11 months. Whereas the WAIS contains 11 subtests, all of which are used in the calculation of IQ scores, the WISC contains 12 subtests, two of which are supplementary. Within the WISC verbal scale are information, comprehension, arithmetic, similarities, and vocabulary. Digit span is a supplementary subtest. These subtests parallel the corresponding WAIS and WAIS-R subtests in content and functions measured. Items are arranged in order of difficulty and are grouped by content.

One of the major differences between the WAIS-R and WISC has to do with termination of a subtest administration. In general the WISC terminates a subtest administration after a fewer number of consecutive errors than does the WAIS-R. This is to prevent younger or duller subjects from experiencing too many failures and to reduce administration time, which usually takes about an hour.

The verbal scales of the WISC.   The information subtest of the WISC contains items such as "Who was the first President of the United States?" Some items, however, are more difficult, such as "Who was the first person who sailed around the world?" Like its counterpart on the WAIS and WAIS-R, the WISC comprehension subtest puts the subject in a situation or asks a question requiring common sense in order to measure judgment. A WISC comprehension item might ask "What should you do if you were the first person to see a house on fire?" As in the WAIS-R, the early items of the arithmetic subtest are fairly simple. Later items, however, can be difficult even for adults, such as "27 is three-fourths of what number?" As in the WAIS-R, the similarities subtest contains items that require the subject to state the similarity between two objects or things, such as brick and wood. The vocabulary and digit span subtests are identical in format to their counterparts on the WAIS-R.

The performance scales of the WISC.   As in the verbal subtests, the performance subtests of the WISC parallel those of the WAIS-R. Indeed, the formats for picture completion, picture arrangement, block design, object assembly, and coding (called digit symbol on the WAIS) are nearly identical. The major difference between the WAIS-R and WISC on the performance scale is the content, which is geared toward children on the WISC. The only WISC subtest not included on the WAIS-R is mazes, a supplementary subtest that asks the subject to use a pencil to find his or her way through a maze. This subtest measures planning ability and perhaps general intelligence.

Standardization of the WISC.   The WISC standardization sample consisted of White male and female children. These 2200 children were selected to be representative of the 1940 census. The sample was biased, however, in that it contained an overabundance of middle- and upper-socioeconomic individuals. Nevertheless, the sample was impressive. It contained 100 boys and 100 girls at each age from 5 through 15 years. These children were selected from four geographic locations in the United States representing both rural and urban sections of the country. Finally, the normative sample for the WISC was distributed according to parental occupation (Wechsler, 1949). Although impressive, this sample is clearly not representative of minority groups and individuals in the lower socioeconomic strata.

Raw scores and scaled scores.   To score the WISC, scaled scores are calculated from raw scores on the basis of norms at each age level. This procedure differs from that for the WAIS-R where scaled scores are obtained from a representative sample at only one age level. However, as for the WAIS-R, the mean scaled score is set at 10 and the standard deviation at 3. Scaled scores are summed for verbal, performance, and full-scale IQs. These totals are then compared against a single table of standard scores with a mean of 100 and a standard deviation of 15 for each of the three IQs—verbal, performance, and full scale.

Interpretation: Hypothetical case studies.   Interpretation of the WISC also parallels that for the WAIS and WAIS-R. Consider the following example. A male, 7-year-old, White, English-speaking child who is having school problems obtains the scaled scores shown in Table 12-4.

TABLE 12-4 Scaled scores for a boy having school problems

Verbal scales	Performance scales
Information: 4	Picture completion: 5
Comprehension: 5	Picture arrangement: 2
Arithmetic: 3	Block design: 6
Similarities: 0	Object assembly: 6
Vocabulary: 1	Coding: 4
Scaled score sum: 13	Scaled score sum: 23
Verbal IQ: 53	Performance IQ: 62
Sum of scaled scores for verbal and performance scales: 36	
Full-scale IQ: 54	

This child showed deficiencies in all areas measured by the WISC. In no case did he obtain a scaled score that was as high as even 1 standard deviation below the mean. This child is consistently impaired in all areas, and so his full-scale IQ of 54, more than 2 standard deviations below the mean, is clearly indicative of mental retardation. Thus, the WISC is consistent with mental retardation. However, additional data (for example, a medical examination and a history of social functioning) would be necessary if the diagnosis of mental retardation is to be made (Malgady, Barcher, Davis, & Towner, 1980).

Consider another example of a 9-year-old, White, female, English-speaking child who is having school difficulties (see Table 12-5).

TABLE 12-5 Scaled scores for a girl having school problems

Verbal scales	Performance scales
Information: 10	Picture completion: 11
Comprehension: 1	Picture arrangement: 3
Arithmetic: 2	Block design: 9
Similarities: 5	Object assembly: 1
Vocabulary: 8	Coding: 10
Scaled score sum: 26	Scaled score sum: 34
Verbal IQ: 70	Performance IQ: 78
Sum of scaled scores for verbal and performance scales: 60	
Full-scale IQ: 71	

Although this child has a verbal and a full-scale IQ that are both 2 standard deviations below the mean and thus in the defective ranges according to the WISC manual, analysis of her profile pattern indicates average or better performance in three areas: information, picture completion, and coding. Her average or better capabilities in these areas would make a diagnosis of mental retardation highly suspect and premature. However, the wide variability in subtests, known as *subtest scatter*, indicates her performance is below what she might have accomplished at some previous time. This lowered performance from previous levels suggests deterioration. Her major areas of weakness in the verbal areas are in her judgment (comprehension subtest), concentration (arithmetic subtest), and abstract thinking (similarities subtest). Her adequate scores on coding and block design, however, indicate no apparent brain damage or visual motor difficulties. The most likely hypothesis in this case is that emotional difficulties are responsible for this child's school problems.

Reliability of the WISC.   Reliability coefficients for the WISC were obtained as they were for the WAIS and WAIS-R subtests. Split-half reliabilities were obtained for three age groups: $7\frac{1}{2}$, $10\frac{1}{2}$, and $13\frac{1}{2}$. Each of these age groups contained 200 cases. Reliabilities for full-scale, verbal, and performance IQs ranged from a high of .96 for the verbal IQ in the two oldest age groups to a low of .86 for the performance IQs in the youngest age group. Coefficients for full-scale IQs ran in the low .90s. Standard errors of measurement were comparable to those of the Binet scale and ran between 3.0 and 5.6.

Reliability coefficients for individual subtests are much less impressive, with most in the .60s, .70s, and .80s. As with the Binet scales, reliability coefficients were poorer for the younger groups. Test-retest coefficients tend to run in the high .70s for all three IQs (Gehman & Matyas, 1956).

WISC validity.   The only claims to validity provided in the WISC test manual (Wechsler, 1949) are the intercorrelations of the verbal, performance, full-scale IQs and each of the 12 subtests. Presumably, high intercorrelations would support the validity of the WISC as a measure of general intelligence. Unfortunately, some of the coefficients presented in the manual are disappointingly low. With the exception of the intercorrelations of verbal, performance, and full-scale IQs, few coefficients exceeded .45 and many correlations in the .20s and .30s were obtained. Despite these relatively poor intercorrelations among the subtests, investigations have shown that the WISC does correlate well with academic criteria (Littell, 1960) as well as with other tests such as the Stanford-Binet, where 47 studies have found correlation coefficients ranging from .30 to .94 (Sattler, 1974).

B.   The revised WISC (WISC-R)

In 1974 the WISC was revised. This revision is referred to as the Wechsler Intelligence Scale for Children—Revised (WISC-R). The scale is quite similar to the WISC. Although the order of subtest administration was modified, 72% of the WISC items were retained. The WISC-R was extended one year to include individuals 16 years 11 months and 30 days. Therefore it provides some overlap with the WAIS-R, which begins at 16, where the WISC had ended. A textbook devoted entirely to WISC-R interpretation is available (Kaufman, 1979).

The major improvement in the WISC-R is that the standardization included non-Whites as well as Whites and that the sample was selected according to the 1970 U.S. census. Reliability coefficients were obtained as they had been for the WISC, WAIS, and WAIS-R, with results comparable to those for the WISC except that slightly better coefficients were obtained for some of the individual subtests as was the case when the WAIS was revised. A test-retest reliability study of 303 children from the standardization sample was also reported in the test manual. Results were impressive, with coefficients in the .90s for the three IQ scores and coefficients in the .60s, .70s, and .80s for the individual subtests. Although a bit higher than those for the WISC, intercorrelations of WISC-R subtests are relatively low, with many coefficients in the .20s or lower but several in the .60s.

The correlation between the WISC-R and other Wechsler scales is rather good. Because the WISC-R overlaps with both the WAIS for 16-year-olds and the downward extension of the WISC (the WPPSI for 6-year-olds), the WISC-R could be correlated with both the WAIS and WPPSI. All coefficients were in the .80s and .90s. The manual also reported correlations with the WISC-R and

Stanford-Binet scale, with the majority of coefficients in the .60s and .70s. Research indicates the WISC R compares quite favorably with the WISC (Davis, 1978; Munford & Munoz, 1980).

C. *The Wechsler Preschool and Primary Scale of Intelligence (WPPSI)*

Prior to revising the WISC, Wechsler (1967) published a scale for use with children 4 to 6½ years of age. This scale parallels the WAIS, WAIS-R, WISC, and WISC-R in format, in method of determining reliabilities, and in subtests. Only three unique subtests were included: (1) animal house, a timed test requiring the child to place a colored cylinder in an appropriate hole in front of an animal, (2) geometric design, a perceptual motor task, and (3) sentences, a supplementary subtest of immediate recall. Reliability coefficients are comparable to those obtained with the other Wechsler scales. Validity studies, however, have found a rather wide range of correlation coefficients (.33 to .92) when the WPPSI is correlated with the Binet scale (Sattler, 1974). WPPSI correlations with other tests have produced a similar range of coefficients (Sattler, 1982).

VII. SUMMARY

Motivation for the development of the Wechsler scales began with the search for a more appropriate measure of adult intelligence than provided by the Binet scale. The first product of this effort was the Wechsler-Bellevue scale.

In a point scale a specific number of credits or points is assigned to each item. As a result, all items of a particular content can be grouped together. A performance scale measures nonlanguage intelligence, as opposed to a verbal scale, which measures language/verbal intelligence. In a performance scale the subject is required to do something rather than to answer questions.

The six verbal subtests of the WAIS and WAIS-R and the functions they purportedly measure are as follows:

1. Information: range of knowledge
2. Comprehension: judgment
3. Arithmetic: concentration
4. Similarities: abstract thinking
5. Digit span: immediate memory, anxiety
6. Vocabulary: vocabulary level

The five performance subtests of the WAIS and WAIS-R and the functions they purportedly measure are as follows:

1. Digit symbol: visual-motor functioning
2. Picture completion: alertness to details
3. Picture arrangement: planning ability

4. Block design: nonverbal reasoning
5. Object assembly: analysis of part-whole relationships

The WAIS and WAIS-R use a declining age standard. This means that elderly subjects must obtain fewer correct responses in order to achieve the same IQs as young adults. The declining age standard resulted from the cross-sectional nature of the WAIS standardization sample. This sample, which involved testing different subjects of differing ages at about the same time, suggested that intelligence declined with age. However, longitudinal studies, which test the same subjects at varying intervals across the life span, have indicated intelligence remains relatively stable across the life span. The implication is that the WAIS norms must be periodically revised, as they were in 1981 with the WAIS-R.

Three IQ scores can be obtained from the WAIS and WAIS-R: verbal IQ, performance IQ, and full-scale IQ. The verbal and performance IQs are obtained by converting the raw score of each subtest to a standard score of 10 with a standard deviation of 3. The scaled scores are then summed separately for the verbal and performance IQs. Each of the IQs can be determined from a table, which converts the summed scaled scores into a standard score with a mean of 100 and a standard deviation of 15. To obtain the full-scale IQ the scaled scores for the verbal and performance IQs are summed. This sum is again compared to a table of norms, which converts it to a standard score (mean=100; SD=15).

The reliability coefficients of the WAIS and WAIS-R are excellent for verbal, performance, and full-scale IQs, both in terms of temporal stability and internal consistency. Reliabilities for the individual subtests, however, vary widely.

Evidence for the validity of the WAIS comes from a variety of sources. The WAIS tends to be predictive of achievement and correlates well with other tests purporting to measure intelligence. Factor analytic studies also support the validity of the WAIS. Wechsler believes that the data in support of the WAIS also support the validity of the WAIS-R.

Among the major advantages of the WAIS are that it (1) is appropriate for adults, (2) uses deviation IQs, (3) has strong evidence of reliability and validity, (4) uses a point scale, (5) includes a performance scale, and (6) offers the possibility of pattern analysis. The WAIS-R has the same advantages.

Major disadvantages of the WAIS are that (1) it has poor reliability for the individual subtests, (2) it is a poor measure of extreme (high and low) levels of intelligence, and (3) many of its items, as well as its norms, are outdated. The WAIS-R takes care of the last problem but not the first two.

The WISC is a downward extension of the WAIS-R for measuring children's intelligence. First published in 1949, the WISC was revised in 1974. The revision is called the Wechsler Intelligence Scale for Children—Revised (WISC-R).

The WPPSI is a downward extension of the WISC and WISC-R for measuring intelligence in very young children (4 to $6\frac{1}{2}$ years). It was published in 1967.

13

Other Individual Tests of Ability

Learning objectives

When you have completed this chapter, you should be able to do the following:

1. *Identify the advantages and disadvantages of the alternative individual ability tests compared to the Binet and Wechsler scales.*
2. *List six differences among the alternative individual ability tests.*
3. *Discuss the strengths and weaknesses of the Bayley Scales of Infant Development compared to other measures of infant intelligence.*
4. *Identify some of the purposes of the Columbia Mental Maturity Scale.*
5. *Explain the major theory behind tests of learning disability.*
6. *Explain the main idea behind testing for brain damage.*
7. *List three possible reasons for errors on the Bender Visual Motor Gestalt Test.*
8. *Describe the general reaction among reviewers to the Torrance Tests of Creative Thinking.*
9. *Identify a major problem with the Wide Range Achievement Test.*

For assessing general intelligence in relatively normal individuals, the Binet and Wechsler scales are exceptionally good instruments. However, consider individuals with sensory, physical, or language handicaps. The standardization samples of the two major scales do not include handicapped individuals. For example, how can we fairly evaluate the Binet performance of someone who has been blind for life? What about individuals who are unable to speak? Clearly, there are numerous instances where a score based on the major scales would be either impossible to obtain or seriously biased against the individual.

Thus, a number of individual tests have been created to meet special problems or measure specific abilities.

I.   GENERAL FEATURES OF ALTERNATIVE INDIVIDUAL ABILITY TESTS

Before beginning our discussion of specific tests, some general comments are in order. As you will see, there is quite an array of individual ability tests. However, most were designed primarily to provide an alternative to the Binet and Wechsler scales. It is instructive to compare the general features of the alternative individual tests to the Binet and Wechsler scales.

A.   *Alternative individual ability tests compared with the Binet and Wechsler scales*

Recalling the information in Chapters 11 and 12 on the Binet and Wechsler scales, you may find it instructive to consider individual ability tests, particularly individual intelligence tests, as they compare with these two important scales. Although most individual intelligence tests other than the Binet and Wechsler scales are newer and less well established than the two major scales, these factors alone do not explain why no other individual intelligence test is used as much as these two major scales (see Lubin et al., 1971). Despite limitations of the Binet and Wechsler scales, none of the alternatives are clearly superior from a psychometric standpoint. Some of the alternative individual intelligence tests are weaker in terms of the representativeness and/or quality of the standardization sample. Some are less stable, and still others are limited in terms of documented validity. Some have inadequacies in the test manual, in terms of either unclear or poorly standardized administration instructions, and others provide insufficient information concerning psychometric adequacy, appropriate uses, and limitations. Some of the alternatives compare poorly on all counts. Except for their advantages for specific purposes, perhaps none of the alternatives can be considered better than the two major scales when all relevant factors are considered.

Although usually weaker in terms of psychometric properties, many of the alternatives to the major scales are not as reliant on a verbal response as are the Binet and Wechsler verbal scales. Many require the subject only to point or to make any response indicating yes or no and thus are not as dependent on complex integration of visual and motor functioning as are the Wechsler performance subtests. Like the Wechsler scales, most of the alternatives contain a performance scale or subscale. Indeed, it was the dearth of performance tasks in the Binet scale that helped to stimulate the development of many alternative individual tests of ability.

In providing a performance component (many alternatives are exclusively performance scales), alternatives to the Binet scale, and even to the Wechsler in some cases, have particular relevance for special populations. In many respects, the alternatives to the major intelligence scales were developed to fill in gaps in the applicability of the major scales. Some were designed for special populations such as individuals with sensory limitations (for example, the deaf) and/or physical limitations (for example, the paralyzed or partially paralyzed). Others were designed to evaluate those with language limitations such as the culturally deprived, certain brain-damaged individuals, and foreign-born or non-English-speaking individuals. Still others were designed to assess learning difficulties.

Because they were designed for special populations or special purposes, the existence of alternatives is justifiable. However, their specificity often limits the range of functions or capabilities that can be measured. Thus, the greater specificity of some alternatives may be considered a weakness as well as a strength. Although the alternatives may be much more suitable for special populations than are the major scales, an IQ score based on one of the alternatives, with rare exceptions, cannot be used interchangeably with a score from one of the major scales. The alternatives are most appropriate when used for their own unique purposes. In addition, the alternatives are often useful as a supplement for results obtained with one of the major scales, for screening purposes, for follow-up or reevaluations, and/or when insufficient time is available to administer one of the major scales.

Because they are designed for special populations, some alternatives can be administered totally without verbal instructions (for example, through pantomime or chalkboard instructions). A few of the alternatives can be administered and scored without a single word being spoken. Furthermore, most are less related to reading ability than is the Binet scale, and a few are almost totally independent of reading ability. As a consequence the scores from many alternatives contain less variability due to scholastic achievement than either the Binet or even the Wechsler scales, in which some subtests are influenced by attitude toward scholastic achievement.

B. Alternatives compared with each other

To construct and publish a useful test, it is necessary to develop a better (for example, a more psychometrically sound) method than is currently available. In the absence of this requirement one may develop a test to measure some factor not being tapped by any existing measure or may provide a test for a particular group for which existing procedures have proved to be inadequate. If there are no specific advantages in a new test, most examiners would probably stay with the more established test. This is true even if they are given a choice between a more established test in which they have experience and an equally sound new test for the same purpose. Therefore, most alternatives tend to differ from each other in some important way. Alternatives to the major scales that do no more than attempt to measure abilities in the same way, only better, have met with little success.

In comparing individual intelligence tests other than the Binet and Wechsler scales, we find that some are restricted to very young children, others are for older children and adolescents, and still others are for both children and adults. Thus, one difference among the alternatives to the major scales is the age range. A second important difference concerns what is measured. Some of the alternatives attempt to measure language or vocabulary skills through nonverbal techniques, some purport to measure nonverbal or nonlanguage intelligence, and others are most strongly related to perceptual-motor skills. Alternatives also differ in the type of score that results. Some produce only a single score as in the Binet scale. Others, however, produce several scores, as in the Wechsler scale. Another difference among the alternatives can be found in the type of response required of subjects. As previously indicated, whereas some present the items in a multiple-choice format, requiring that the subject choose or point to a correct alternative, others simply require the subject to indicate yes or no by whatever means possible.

There are still other important differences among the alternative individual tests of human ability. Some require simple motor skills, while others demand more complex motor behavior. A few, like the Wechsler scale, sample a wide range of abilities; others are quite narrow in the range of abilities sampled. Still another difference concerns the target population (for example, the deaf, blind, physically handicapped, learning disabled, language impaired, and foreign-born). Furthermore, some provide timed tasks while others do not. Some claim to have significance for personality and clinical diagnosis; others are exclusively related to an ability.

Another difference exists in the amount of examiner skill and experience necessary for administration. Whereas some require as much skill and experience as do the Binet or Wechsler scales, others require only minimal examiner skill and could probably be administered by a trained paraprofessional under the supervision of an experienced professional. To facilitate memory and to avoid confusing the various tests in this chapter, you are advised to compare and contrast the various procedures to the Binet and Wechsler scales and to each other in terms of the major properties of tests. Table 13-1 summarizes the major distinguishing features among the alternatives.

II. SPECIFIC ALTERNATIVE INDIVIDUAL ABILITY TESTS

The earliest individual ability tests were typically designed for specific purposes or populations. One of the first, the Seguin Form Board Test (Seguin, 1866), actually preceded the Binet. Seguin's test was of the performance variety and produced only a single score. It consisted of a simple form board in which objects of various shapes were placed in a board containing appropriately shaped holes (such as squares or circles). The Seguin Form Board Test was used primarily to evelute mentally retarded adults and emphasized speed of performance. A version of the Seguin Form Board Test is still available. Quite a bit

TABLE 13-1 Summary of differences among individual ability tests other than the Binet and Wechsler scales

Difference	Definition or example
Age range	Different tests are designed for specific age groups
What is measured	Verbal intelligence, nonverbal intelligence, and so on
Type of score	Single score versus multiple scores
Type of skill required	Simple motor, complex motor, and so on
Range of abilities sampled	Single specific ability versus a wide range of abilities
Target population	Deaf, blind, learning disabled, and so on
Timing	Some are timed, others are not
Personality versus ability	Some claim to have relevance for personality and clinical diagnosis as well as ability
Examiner skill and experience	Some require far less examiner skill and experience to administer and interpret than others

after the development of the Seguin test, the Healy-Fernald Test (1911) was developed as an exclusively nonverbal test for adolescent delinquents. Although it produced only a single score, the Healy-Fernald test provided several types of tasks, rather than just one as in the Seguin Form Board task, and there was less emphasis on speed. Shortly after publication of the Healy-Fernald test, Knox (1914) developed a battery of performance tests for non-English-speaking adult immigrants to the United States. The test was one of the first that could be administered without language. Speed was not emphasized. In sum, early individual ability tests other than the Binet scale were for specific populations, produced a single score, had nonverbal performance scales, and gradually decreased the emphasis on speed from the earliest to the more recent tests. These early procedures demonstrated the feasibility of constructing nonverbal performance individual tests that could provide an alternative to the verbally dependent Binet scale, could be administered without verbal instructions, and could be used with children as well as adults.

A. Infant and preschool scales

An important category of alternative individual tests of ability attempts to measure intelligence in infants and young children. Five such tests are discussed below.

Brazelton Neonatal Assessment Scale (BNAS). The BNAS (Brazelton, 1973) is purportedly an individual intelligence test for newborn infants between 3 days and 4 weeks of age. Despite its relatively recent development, the Brazelton scale is rapidly becoming one of the most popular infant intelligence assessment tools. In addition to its practical uses, it is finding its way into medical as well as psychological research (Reynell, 1975). One major reason for the popularity of the Brazelton scale is that it provides an assessment at an earlier age than any other infant intelligence test. Its closest competitors begin where it leaves off: at 4 weeks of age. Thus, the Brazelton scale filled a gap in infant intelligence testing that existed for many years—assessing intellectual functioning during the first 28 days of life.

Developed by a Harvard pediatrician, the Brazelton scale produces 47 scores, 27 behavioral items, and 20 elicited responses (Buros, 1978). These scores are obtained in a variety of areas including neurological, social, and behavioral aspects of a newborn infant's functioning. Factors such as reflexes, responses to stress, startle reactions, cuddliness, motor maturity, ability to habituate to sensory stimuli, and hand-mouth coordination are all assessed. Reviews of the Brazelton scale have been favorable. Sostek (1978) stated that the Brazelton has "the greatest breadth of the available neonatal examinations" (p. 208), and an earlier review described it as "rigorous" (Wolkind, 1974).

Despite its breadth and rigor, the Brazelton scale is limited because of a lack of normative data. Although examiners and researchers can state that one infant scored higher than another in a particular area, there is no standard sample against which to compare test results. In addition, more research is needed concerning the meaning and implication of scores. The scale purportedly aids in assessing the infant's role in the mother-infant social relationship, and, presumably, high scores are associated with high levels of intelligence. Like most infant intelligence measures, however, the Brazelton scale has poorly documented predictive and construct validity. Furthermore, despite relatively good interrater reliability for trained examiners with coefficients ranging from .85 to .90 (Sostek, 1978), test-retest reliability (that is, reliability over time) leaves much to be desired. As for all measures of intelligence prior to age 8, when development is rapid and uneven, test-retest reliability coefficients for the Brazelton scale are typically poor and unstable.

In conclusion, the Brazelton scale appears to hold promise in assessing abilities of infants through the first 28 days of life. As a measure of the neurological, motor, and social functioning of humans during the first few weeks of life, the Brazelton scale has been well received and is popular among researchers and applied practitioners alike. However, there is a real need for normative data and predictive validity studies. Until these are provided, interpretive conclusions should be stated tentatively and with caution.

Gesell Developmental Schedules (GDS).   The Gesell Developmental Schedules—also known as the Gesell Maturity Scale, the Gesell Norms of Development, and the Yale Tests of Child Development (see Buros, 1974)—are one of the oldest and most established infant intelligence measures. First published in 1925 (Gesell, 1925), the Gesell scale has been subjected to extensive research and refinement. One of the leading infant intelligence measures from the 1930s through the 1960s, the Gesell scale continues to be used by those interested in assessing infant intelligence. However, the 1970s saw a substantial decline in research activity, and the Gesell scale was not included in the most recent *Mental Measurement Yearbook* (Buros, 1978) because insufficient research had been conducted to warrant its inclusion.

One reason for the popularity of the Gesell scale is that its current use is based on normative data from a carefully conducted longitudinal study of early human development (see Gesell et al., 1940). The idea behind procedures that are based on developmental data is that human development unfolds in stages or in sequences over time. Gesell and colleagues obtained normative data concerning these various stages in the maturational process. With data on when specific developmental milestones manifest themselves (for example, when the infant first rolls from back to stomach unassisted, when words are first uttered, or when the child learns to walk); it becomes possible to compare the rate of development of any infant or young child to established norms. If the individual shows behavior or responses associated with a more mature level of development than typically found for his or her chronological age, then it can be assumed that the person is ahead in development compared with others of the same age. Increased development, in turn, can be related to high intelligence.

In the Gesell scale an individual's *developmental quotient* (DQ) is determined according to a test score, which is evaluated by assessing the presence or absence of behavior associated with maturation. The DQ score concept parallels the mental age (MA) concept. Thus, the Gesell produces an intelligence quotient (IQ) score similar to that of the Binet scale. The formula for IQ in the Gesell scale is as follows:

$$IQ = \frac{\text{Developmental Quotient}}{\text{Chronological Age}} \times 100$$

or more simply

$$IQ = \frac{DQ}{CA} \times 100$$

Normative data for the Gesell scale were obtained from a sample of 107 American-born male and female (49 boys, 58 girls) Caucasian infants whose parents were of northern European descent and who were judged to be normal. Any student who has studied the present text to this point will readily and immediately recognize the lack of representativeness of this sample. However, these infants were carefully studied. Beginning at 4 weeks of age, they were examined at two-week intervals until the 8th week of life. From the 8th through 56th weeks they were examined at four-week intervals (12th, 16th, 20th, and so on). The sample was examined again at 1½ and 2 years of age and also at yearly intervals between ages 2 and 6. Major assessment areas included motor, adaptive, language, and social behavior.

Gesell and colleagues (see, for example, Gesell & Amatruda, 1947) believed the Gesell scale could be used for a wide variety of purposes in addition to the estimation of intelligence from patterns and rates of development. They also believed the scale could be used for assessing normal, subnormal, and superior infants and young children. The scale was also seen as having value in the assessment of developmental deviations, neurological impairment, personality organization, and emotional or temperamental characteristics (Gesell & Amatruda, 1941).

Early reviews of the Gesell scale were mixed, ranging from those that were highly laudatory to those that criticized it on various grounds. Favorable reviews commented on its broad scope in assessing development, intelligence, and medical problems in infants and young children (Firestone, 1942; Wilson, 1942). However, critics noted its restricted standardization sample and scattering of information in that at least three different books had to be consulted to find information that should have been summarized in a single test manual or book (Doll, 1942; Koch, 1942).

Despite years of extensive use, the Gesell scale still has a number of problems. The most recent review provided by the *Mental Measurement Yearbooks* criticized the Gesell scale for the same problems identified by reviewers in the 1940s (Werner, 1965). The original standardization sample, obviously nonrepresentative, continues to be used. In addition to being limited, restricted, and small by today's standards, the original Gesell scale standardization sample is also outdated, especially in view of the many changes that have taken place since the 1940s (for example, changes in child-rearing practices, advances in nutrition and pediatric care, technological advances, and exposure to television).

In addition to limitations in its standardization sample, the Gesell scale has limited documentation in terms of reliability and validity. Despite what would seem like unlimited opportunity for a reliability assessment, documentation of the Gesell scale's reliability rests primarily on a study showing correlations ranging in the low to high .90s between DQs obtained by examiners and observers, all of whom were trained by the same person (see Knobloch & Pasamanick, 1960). Prior to this study, reliability data on the Gesell scale was essentially nonexistent (Werner, 1965). Validity studies, furthermore, have not been encouraging.

Although some studies have reported an excellent correlation (such as .87 based on 195 cases) between the Gesell scale and the Stanford-Binet scale for 3-year-olds (Knobloch & Pasamanick, 1960), results with infants have been rather discouraging. In one of the few available validity studies, Gardener and Swiger (1958) found a high negative correlation ($-.64$) between DQ and CA in 128 young infants. Furthermore, the available research suggests the Gesell scale has little, if any, predictive validity for normal (Escalona & Moriarty, 1961) as well as abnormal (Share, Webb, & Koch, 1961) infants.

In conclusion, Gesell's concept of empirically determining developmental sequence norms in evaluating infants and young children is logical and promising. When first constructed, the Gesell scale was nothing short of a breakthrough in infant ability testing. The use of a nonrepresentative sample in its initial development, furthermore, was not at all unusual. However, since its early construction, little has been done to improve the Gesell scale according to today's more rigorous standards. The declining interest in the Gesell scale therefore comes as no surprise. Although the Gesell scale is of value to the highly trained and experienced examiner, the available empirical data indicate that it is not highly accurate for predictive purposes.

Bayley Scales of Infant Development (BSID).   As with many infant tests, the underlying idea of the Bayley Scales of Infant Development is the same as that underlying the pioneer in infant testing, the Gesell scale. Like the Gesell, the Bayley bases its assessments on normative maturational developmental data. Published only four years before the Brazelton scale, the Bayley scale was the product of 40 years of study (Bayley, 1969). Designed for infants between 2 and 30 months of age, the Bayley scale produces two main scores (mental and motor) and 30 ratings of behavior. To assess mental functions, the Bayley scale uses measures such as the infant's response to a bell, the ability to follow an object with the eyes, and, in older infants, the ability to follow oral instructions. The heart of the Bayley scale is the motor scale because a major underlying assumption is that later mental functions are dependent on motor development (Bayley, 1969).

Unlike the Gesell and Brazelton scales, the standardization of the Bayley scale is excellent. With a normative sample of 1262 infants between 2 and 30 months—divided into subgroups by sex, race, socioeconomic status, rural versus urban area, and geographic region according to the 1960 census, the Bayley scale is the best standardized test of infant ability available to date.

Like the Stanford-Binet scale, raw scores on the Bayley scale are converted to standard scores with a mean of 100 and a standard deviation of 16. Given the care and effort that Bayley put into its development, the positive reviews of the Bayley scale (for example, by Damarin, 1978a) come as no surprise. In addition to its exemplary standardization, median split-half reliability coefficients run around .88 for the mental scale and .84 for the motor scale, with ranges from the low .80s to low .90s for the mental scales and ranges from the high .60s to low .90s for the motor scales (Bayley, 1969).

Research interest in the Bayley scale continues to grow, as evidenced by the increase in the number of references found in a recent *Mental Measurement Yearbook* (Buros, 1978). Nevertheless, the Bayley scale is relatively new and more validity studies are needed. In terms of construct validity, Bayley (1969) reported that the performance scale increases with increasing chronological age. She also reported correlations clustering in the high .40s and high .50s for the mental scale and Stanford-Binet IQs for preschoolers at three age levels: 24, 27, and 30 months. Although modest, these correlation coefficients are respectable in view of the typical instability found at these early age levels. However, more validity data are needed and so, like other tests of infant ability, the Bayley scale offers an excellent opportunity for researchers interested in uncovering the nature of ability during the earliest stages of life. The work that has been done has been quite encouraging (for example, Beck, 1979).

In conclusion, despite present limitations in the available research (especially concerning the meaning of test scores), the superior standardization of the Bayley scale and encouraging results—where adequate data are available—suggest an important role for the Bayley scale in the field of infant ability testing during the remainder of the 20th century. Given its solid standardization, its sampling of both motor and mental abilities, the care taken by its author in its construction, and the interest shown to date, the Bayley scale is an exceptionally promising one.

Cattell Infant Intelligence Scale (CIIS).   Another noteworthy infant ability test is the Cattell Infant Intelligence Scale (CIIS), which is also based on normative developmental data. Designed as a downward extension of the Stanford-Binet scale for infants and preschoolers between 2 and 30 months of age, the Cattell scale purports to measure intelligence in infants and young children (P. Cattell, 1940). Patterned after the Binet in an age scale format, the Cattell scale contains five test items for each month of age between 2 and 12 months and five items for each two-month interval between 12 and 36 months of age. The items are similar to those of other infant tests such as the Gesell scale. Tasks for infants include attending to a voice or following objects with the eyes. Tasks for young children involve form board-type procedures and the manipulation of common objects. The ability to follow oral instructions becomes an increasingly important factor with increasing age.

The Cattell Infant Intelligence Scale parallels the Binet scale administration and scoring procedures; and if a young child passes an item at the 30-month level, the examiner is instructed to immediately begin at Level III of the Stanford-Binet scale. However, scores are expressed in terms of mental age (MA) and intelligence quotient (IQ) rather than in terms of deviation IQs as in the modern Stanford-Binet scale.

For examiners who require a Gesell-type developmental infant test with a standardization that is more adequate than the Gesell scale, the Cattell Infant Intelligence Scale stands with the Bayley scale (BSID) as one of the most important available options (Damarin, 1978b). In fact, in his review of the Cattell scale, Damarin found little difference between the types of tasks in the Bayley scale and those in the Cattell scale. However, the Cattell scale is obviously the older scale; it was copyrighted nearly three decades before the Bayley scale. Unfortunately, being an older, more established instrument is no advantage for the Cattell Infant Intelligence Scale. On the contrary, normative data for the

Cattell scale compare unfavorably to that of the Bayley scale in several respects. In addition to being outdated when compared to the standardization sample of the Bayley scale and more than four times smaller, the Cattell scale sample is based primarily on children of parents from the lower and middle classes and, therefore, is not representative of the general population.

Because its normative data are considerably weaker than those of the Bayley scale, it seems appropriate to ask whether the Cattell Infant Intelligence Scale has any advantages over its more recent competitor, the Bayley scale. In answering this question, we find that evidence in support of the reliability and validity of the two instruments is similar. If time is limited, the Cattell scale may be preferable because it only takes about half as long to administer. However, it produces only a single score rather than the two scores and 30 observations of the Bayley scale. Thus, its shorter administration time is balanced by more restricted results. Furthermore, as a downward extension of the Stanford-Binet scale, the Cattell scale seems to be in need of updating in that the former no longer uses the intelligence quotient for calculating scores. Thus, IQ scores from the Cattell scale may not be comparable to deviation IQs on the Binet scale.

In conclusion, we tend to disagree with Damarin's assessment that it may be premature for examiners to shift from the Cattell scale to the Bayley scale. Except for experienced examiners, who can use the Cattell scale as a standard procedure with which to compare infants and young children against their own internal norms based on years of experience, as a more modern procedure the Bayley scale appears to offer some important advantages. Thus, for new and less experienced test users, the Bayley scale deserves careful consideration.

McCarthy Scales of Children's Abilities (MSCA).   Thus far our discussion has included individual ability tests appropriate for newborns, infants, and young children. The McCarthy Scales of Children's Abilities (MSCA) complements these ability tests for the young. A product of the early 1970s, the McCarthy scale measures ability in children between 2.5 and 8.5 years of age. It picks up just about where the Bayley scale leaves off. Overall, the McCarthy scale is a carefully constructed individual test of human ability. In fact, were it not for its relatively meager validity data, the McCarthy scale might well have reached the status of the Wechsler scale (WPPSI), which overlaps with the McCarthy scale's age range. Indeed, the McCarthy scale seems to offer some advantages over the WPPSI and even the Binet scale for the 2.5 to 8.5 age range. Unfortunately, because of McCarthy's death (she died before the test was even published), the task of strengthening the McCarthy scale rests on the shoulders of interested researchers.

On the positive side, the McCarthy scale produces a pattern of scores as well as a variety of composite scores. Its battery of 18 tests samples a wide variety of functions long held to be related to human intelligence. Of the 18 scales, 15 are combined into a composite score known as the *general cognitive index*

(GCI). The general cognitive index is a standard score with a mean of 100 and a standard deviation of 16. Presumably, the index reflects how well the child has integrated prior learning experiences and adapted them to the demands of the scales. It is not unreasonable to assume that McCarthy believed that the general cognitive index reflected intelligence and that her definition of intelligence must have included something like the ability to integrate past learning and adapt it to the solution of new problems. Sattler (1978), for example, argued that the definition of McCarthy's general cognitive index is similar to definitions of the intelligence quotient (IQ) and most likely was meant as a substitute for the IQ concept.

The 15 tests constituting the general cognitive index are divided into three scales: verbal (five tests), perceptual-performance (seven tests), and quantitative (three tests). Two additional scales can be derived by combining the three tests not included in the general cognitive index with two from the perceptual-performance scale to produce a motor scale. Combining all four memory-related tests from the general cognitive index produces a memory scale. In all, the McCarthy scale contains six overlapping scales including the general cognitive index.

The psychometric properties of the McCarthy scale are relatively good. Although the six scales were grouped by McCarthy on the basis of her experience and knowledge, with the aim of obtaining a set of scales with diagnostic potential (that is, the scales were grouped by nonempirical methods), factor analytic studies have tended to produce strong support for her groupings. A factor analysis of the standardization data by Kaufman (1975a), for example, resulted in four factors roughly corresponding to the general cognitive index, verbal, memory, and motor scales.

Thus, the empirical data support the potential of pattern analysis for diagnostic purposes. The standardization sample, furthermore, conforms to present-day standards of rigor. The 1032 children in this sample were stratified according to race, geographic region, father's occupation, and urban-rural residence according to the 1970 U.S. census. The sexes were evenly distributed, and at least 100 children were included in each of the age groupings, which consisted of 10 separate groupings for each half-year interval from $2\frac{1}{2}$ through $8\frac{1}{2}$.

Raw scores for each of the 18 tests are weighted by a factor of .5, 1, or 2, and then summed in the appropriate combinations to yield composite raw scores for each of the six scales except the general cognitive index. The composite raw score for the index is obtained from the composite scores on the verbal, perceptual-performance, and quantitative scales. These raw scores are then converted into standard scores with a mean of 50 and a standard deviation of 10 (Silverstein, 1978). Norms are available for each of the ten age groups. Thus, subjects can be compared to members of their own age group.

Reliability coefficients for the McCarthy scale are excellent. These coefficients were determined by the split-half method unless this procedure was inappropriate when the test-retest procedure was used.

Reliability coefficients of the ten age groups for the general cognitive index tend to run in the low .90s. Coefficients for the other five scales range from the high .70s to high .80s. Temporal stability (that is, test-retest) coefficients are also good, with coefficients in the .90s for the general cognitive index and with median coefficients in the mid-.90s for the other five scales. Thus, the six scales of the McCarthy scale hold their own when compared to the three Wechsler IQs (VIQ, PIQ, and FSIQ).

Validity data are also encouraging. Although concurrent validity data are limited, correlations with the Stanford-Binet scale and the WPPSI are quite good. The general cognitive index correlates .81 with the Binet IQ and .71 with the WPPSI full-scale IQ. Additional validity coefficients based on small samples are provided in the manual and by Hunt (1978).

The McCarthy scale is psychometrically sound. Its six scores permit pattern analysis and possible diagnostic interpretation. As with any relatively new test, however, more data are needed in support of the scale's validity (Ammons & Ammons, 1974). Especially lacking are construct validity studies to aid and support interpretations. Until such data can be produced, McCarthy scale results should be interpreted with caution. Nevertheless, the McCarthy scale appears to have considerable potential, and the many favorable reviews of this relatively new individual test of ability are encouraging (Hunt, 1978; Sattler, 1978; Silverstein, 1978). If researchers are successful in providing additional documentation of validity, the McCarthy scale may provide stiff competition for even the most established individual ability tests for the 2.5-to-8.5 age range.

B. General individual ability tests for handicapped and special populations

In addition to tests for infants and young children, a number of alternatives are specifically designed to provide a more valid measure of intellectual functioning than the Binet and Wechsler scales for cases in which the major scales may be biased or inappropriate. As you will see, each of these general individual ability tests for handicapped and special populations contains unique strengths and limitations.

Columbia Mental Maturity Scale (CMMS).   A variety of sensory and physical limitations often make a valid administration of the Binet, Wechsler, or even many of the major alternative scales (such as the McCarthy scale) quite impossible. Therefore, for children suffering from physical limitations (for example, cerebral palsy), speech impairments, language limitations, or hearing loss, an instrument is needed that does not create bias against them. One such instrument is the Columbia Mental Maturity Scale (CMMS), which evaluates ability in normal and variously handicapped children from 3 through 12 years of age. The test often provides a more suitable measure of intelligence than do the more established scales when it is used for individuals with special needs.

The Columbia scale was revised in the early 1970s (Burgemeister, Blum, & Lorge, 1972). One of its distinguishing characteristics is that it requires neither a verbal response nor fine motor skills. Purported to be a measure of general reasoning ability, the Columbia scale requires the subject to discriminate similarities and differences by indicating which drawing does not belong on a 6-by-9-inch card containing from three to five drawings, depending on the level of difficulty. The task, then, is a multiple-choice one in nature.

The 1972 edition of the Columbia scale contains 92 different cards grouped into eight overlapping levels, or scales, according to chronological age. Testing begins at a scale commensurate with the child's age. Included among the advantages of the Columbia scale are its relative independence of reading skills, ease of administration and scoring, and the clarity of its test manual (Egeland, 1978). Subjects are not timed, so pressure is minimal.

One problem with earlier versions of the Columbia scale was its poor standardization sample. However, the 1972 standardization sample is quite impressive. It consists of 2600 children divided into 13 levels from 3 years 6 months through 9 years 11 months. Each level contains 200 children, and the sample is stratified according to the U.S. population in terms of the major important variables including sex, race, geographic region, and parent's occupation. Clearly, the minimum acceptance standards for a standardization sample increased substantially during the 1970s; ability tests that do not meet these standards understandably tend to be overlooked. Unlike their predecessors, modern constructors of new tests must provide strong standardization data. With its restandardization, the Columbia scale is again a highly competitive ability test.

Raw scores from the Columbia scale can be converted to a standard score with a mean of 100 and a standard deviation of 16, which is known as the age deviation score (ADS). The age deviation score can be expressed in terms of percentiles. Raw scores, furthermore, can also be converted to mental age equivalents. As is typically found in the better or more recent tests, the child is compared to his or her own age group (that is, the 200 children at his or her age group in the standardization sample).

The Columbia scale manual contains data on both split-half and test-retest reliability for various age groupings in the standardization sample. The scale is internally as well as temporarily consistent for short intervals. Coefficients range between .85 and .90 for both split-half and test-retest reliabilities.

Although we have seen great strides in terms of minimum acceptable normative and reliability requirements in individual tests of ability, typical validity requirements appear to be weaker. The Columbia scale, like so many other individual ability tests, could benefit greatly from additional validity documentation. The available validity data reported in the manual and elsewhere have been encouraging. However, sufficient data do not exist for a complete evaluation. The highest correlate of the 1972 edition is the 1959 edition of the Columbia scale. Thus, the newer scale overlaps considerably with the older scale, with a correlation of about .84 according to the manual. The Columbia scale's correlation with the Stanford-Binet scale, as reported in the manual, is .67. Correlations with group ability tests are similar.

The Columbia scale has one important difficulty of which all of its users should be aware. The scale is highly vulnerable to random error. A young child can obtain a score of 82 simply on chance alone, and a score in the average ranges can be obtained with just a few lucky guesses (Kaufman, 1978). Theoretically, if 100 apes were administered the lower levels of the Columbia scale, an alarming number might obtain scores in the average ranges for human beings.

In conclusion, the Columbia scale is a well-standardized, reliable instrument useful in assessing ability for a variety of sensory, physical, and language handicapped individuals. Because of its multiple-choice nature, however, and consequent vulnerability to chance variance, results should be used with caution. When used with subjects for whom the major scales would be appropriate, the Columbia scale might best be seen as a screening device. The importance and value of the Columbia scale can be found in its relevance to a variety of special populations. Even for these populations, however, the Columbia scale might be more safely employed if used in conjunction with those Wechsler subtests that can be given, depending on the disability of the child involved. If the child can point, for example, Wechsler's picture completion can be given in conjunction with the Columbia scale as an additional check on the accuracy of the results. If the child is physically handicapped but can speak, then some of the Wechsler verbal subtests can be used with the Columbia scale to support results.

Peabody Picture Vocabulary Test (PPVT).   Similar to the Columbia scale in several respects is the Peabody Picture Vocabulary Test (PPVT) developed by Dunn (1959, 1965). Although its age range of 2½-to-18 years is considerably wider than that for the Columbia scale, both are multiple-choice tests that require a subject only to indicate yes or no in some manner. Primarily for the physically or language handicapped, the Peabody test cannot be used with the deaf because the subject must be able to hear the instructions. The Peabody test purports to measure hearing or receptive vocabulary, presumably a nonverbal estimate of verbal intelligence. Although untimed, the Peabody test can be administered in 15 minutes or less, and it requires no reading ability. Test stimuli consist of 150 plates, each containing four numbered pictures. The subject's task is to indicate which of the four pictures is best related to a word read by the examiner. Items are arranged in increasing order of difficulty, and administration entails determination of a basal and ceiling performance as in the Stanford-Binet scale. The number of incorrect responses is subtracted from the ceiling to produce a total score. This total score can then be converted to a deviation IQ (M=100 and SD=15), percentile rank, and/or mental age.

Although they constitute a relatively large group, the more than 4000 children included in the Peabody standardization sample were all White children from the Nashville, Tennessee, area. Furthermore, except for subjects under age 9, Peabody test norms were obtained through the use of large-scale group administration. Thus, the validity comparing an individual administration to this sample is subject to question.

Despite problems in the way its standardization sample was obtained, the Peabody test has generated considerable research and practical interest, perhaps because it includes two parallel forms and provides a measure of verbal ability without requiring a verbal response. Alternate form reliabilities reported in the manual, furthermore, are generally reasonable. These reliabilities range from .67 for younger children through .84 for the upper age ranges. Other studies, however, have reported an alternate form reliability ranging from .37 to .97, with a median of .77 (Sattler, 1974). Criterion validity studies have produced varied and inconsistent results. Such inconsistencies, however, are quite common in validity studies of many individual ability tests. Correlations with the Binet scale range all the way from .22 to .92, with similar findings for the WISC and a variety of other types of ability tests.

In conclusion, the Peabody test has a number of positive attributes and some negative ones. On the positive side are its ease of administration and utility for certain handicapped groups. On the negative side, its standardization method, in conjunction with the problems inherent in the multiple-choice format, indicate that the Peabody test cannot be used in place of the major ability scales (that is, the Binet and Wechsler scales) except for specific cases where the major scales may not be appropriate. In one study, for example, subjects were selected from the Nashville area and thus were similar to those in the standardization sample in terms of geographic location. The researchers attempted to determine the efficiency of the Peabody test in estimating WISC IQs in a low-functioning delinquent population. The Peabody test was found to be weak in this regard in that for WISC full-scale IQs from 60 through 80, the Peabody score was almost always 70 (Condit, Lewandowski, & Saccuzzo, 1976).

Thus, the Peabody test overestimated the IQs of subjects with WISC IQs less than 70 and underestimated WISC IQs less than 80 so that regardless of the WISC IQ the Peabody IQ remained about 70. Perhaps this result can be explained by the Peabody test's large standard error of measurement, which ranges between 6 and about 8.6. In any case, current interest in the Peabody test should be accompanied by additional research. As a caution, it should be noted that Peabody test administration does not require a highly trained examiner. This may appear to be an advantage to some, but to us this means that Peabody test results should be interpreted with extra care whenever the qualifications of the examiner are unknown.

Leiter International Performance Scale (LIPS).   Whereas the Columbia and Peabody tests measure verbal aspects of intelligence, the Leiter

International Performance Scale (LIPS) is strictly a performance scale whose intent is to provide a nonverbal alternative to the Stanford Binet scale for the age range of 2 to 18 years. First developed in the 1930s and last revised in 1948, the Leiter scale has experienced a recent decrease in interest among researchers, although the scale finds rather frequent use in clinical settings. The Leiter scale purports to provide a nonverbal measure of general intelligence through sampling a wide variety of functions from memory through nonverbal reasoning. It can be administered without the use of language, and it requires no verbal response from subjects.

Presumably it can be applied to a rather large range of handicapped individuals, particularly the deaf and language disabled. Like the Peabody test, the Columbia scale, and most recent tests for the handicapped, the Leiter scale is untimed. Patterned after the Binet scale, the 54 tests of the Leiter scale are arranged in an age scale format at yearly intervals from 2 through 18. Despite its many positive features and utility for subjects who cannot or will not provide a verbal response, the Leiter scale has some noteworthy problems. It was published during a time when it was common to construct a test and to leave the job of psychometric documentation to users and general researchers. The Leiter manual failed to include information routinely found in modern test manuals. However, the Leiter scale's validity documentation is extremely good with a range of criterion validity coefficients from .52 to .92 (median .83).

We agree with Sattler (1974) that the Leiter scale merits consideration as an aid to clinical diagnosis in handicapped children. As with other tests discussed in this chapter, however, we must encourage the test user to exercise caution in interpreting Leiter test results because more research is needed into the meaning of test scores. It is hoped that interested researchers will see the need for additional investigations into the properties of the Leiter scale. In addition, a careful standardization of the Leiter scale would be most welcome.

C.   *Broad-range individual ability tests: Child through adult*

Whereas the tests discussed in the previous sections tend to apply to a specific population or age group, broad-range individual ability tests can usually be applied to individuals of all ages. In addition, these tests are designed to estimate intelligence in both normal and a wide variety of special populations.

Porteus Maze Test (PMT).   Another popular but poorly standardized nonverbal performance measure of intelligence is the Porteus Maze Test (PMT), which has been one of the more important individual ability tests since it was first published about the time of World War I. As its name implies, the Porteus Maze Test consists of maze problems. Like the Leiter scale, the Porteus test can be administered without verbal instruction and thus can be used for a variety of special and handicapped populations. In favor of the Porteus test is a large body of empirical findings reported in various editions of the *Mental Measurement Yearbook*. These findings add construct validity to the test.

However, the Porteus test has no manual. Furthermore, its standardization sample is quite old (Doctor, 1972). Despite its problems the Porteus test, like so many other tests discussed in this chapter, meets an important need in providing a measure of ability for a variety of handicapped groups for whom the Binet and Wechsler scales are inappropriate. However, as with many similar tests, a restandardization would greatly improve the quality of the Porteus test, whose usefulness is evident by the fact that it has survived for so many years.

Other broad-range tests.   The widespread use and interest in tests such as the Peabody, Leiter, and Porteus are clearly an indication of the need for strictly nonverbal and/or performance measures of intelligence, especially for the handicapped. Therefore it is unfortunate that so many of the available instruments are in need of restandardization and/or additional reliability or validity documentation. Clearly more work is needed to improve the status of ability tests for handicapped individuals. Newer procedures—such as the Columbia scale, the Quick Test (Ammons & Ammons, 1962), the Pictorial Test of Intelligence (French, 1964), and the Slosson Intelligence Test (Slosson, 1963)—may offer some hope, but these also have limitations.

Much can be said for the Quick Test, except that the standardization sample is not representative of the general population. The Slosson test also is useful as a quick measure of intelligence, but it is heavily dependent on language skills. The Pictorial Test of Intelligence is almost as sound as the Columbia scale and can be used for similar purposes. In general the Columbia scale and the Pictorial Test of Intelligence are perhaps the most strongly supported general ability measures for a broad range of handicaps. Each of the tests for the handicapped, however, has its own unique advantages and disadvantages. All should be interpreted with caution and should be subjected to additional research investigation.

III.   INDIVIDUAL TESTS OF ABILITY FOR SPECIFIC PURPOSES

The tests discussed below are the best examples, according to our criteria, of individual ability tests for a variety of specific abilities such as learning ability and memory. Our discussion is far from complete, but it does focus on important or instructive instruments. The students interested in encyclopedic coverage should consult the *Mental Measurement Yearbook*.

A.   *Learning disabilities: Illinois Test of Psycholinguistic Abilities (ITPA)*

One of the newest and fastest growing areas in education and psychology involves the study of specific learning disabilities. One major idea behind the notion of learning disabilities is that a child may be average in intelligence but fail in school because of a specific deficit or disability that prevents learning. Of the mushrooming tests designed to assess learning disabilities, none is more illustrative of the theory of learning disabilities and has generated more interest than the controversial Illinois Test of Psycholinguistic Abilities (ITPA).

Based on modern concepts of human information processing, the ITPA assumes that failure to respond correctly to a stimulus can result not only from a defective *output* (that is, *response*) system but also from a defective *input* and/or *information processing system*. Consistent with information processing theory (for example, see Haber, 1969), the Illinois test assumes that a human response to an outside stimulus can be viewed in terms of discrete stages or processes. Stage 1, the input stage, involves the reception of incoming environmental information by the senses. Thus, the information must first be received by the senses before it can be analyzed. During Stage 2 of processing, input information is analyzed or processed. Finally, having processed the information, the individual must make a response, the final stage of processing.

Assuming that a learning disability can occur at any of these three levels of processing, the Illinois test further theorizes that the child may be impaired in one or more specific sensory modalities. Input information may be visual, auditory, or tactile. The Illinois test provides three subtests that measure the individual's ability to receive input information in terms of visual, auditory, or tactile input independently of processing and output factors. Three additional subtests are available that provide independent measures of processing in each of these three sense modalities, and other subtests provide independent measures of motor and verbal output.

By providing relatively independent measures for each of these areas, the Illinois test purports to have value in isolating the specific site of a learning disability. For example, a child may produce age appropriate scores for all three input and all three processing subtests but may have an unusually low score on motor (but not verbal) output. This result would indicate that, although the child is able to receive and process information as well as others do, he or she has trouble in expression through the motor areas. The child's problem can thus be localized to motor output, and the treatment can be focused on enhancing motor skills. However, if the problem involves auditory processing, then this area becomes the focus.

Designed for use with children 2 through 10, the Illinois test has found widespread use and interest among educators, psychologists, learning disability specialists, and researchers. This popularity, however, cannot be attributed to its psychometric qualities. Not only is the Illinois test one of the most difficult individual ability tests to administer, but the manual presents no reliability or validity data. Although normative data are provided, the exact nature of the normative sample is difficult to ascertain from the manual—a problem that has been severely criticized (Lumsden, 1978). In fact, the Illinois test has been criticized on a variety of grounds, including inadequate validity, excessively low reliabilities for individual subtests, and failure to provide normalized standard scores. The reviews of both Lumsden (1978) and Wiederholt (1978) conclude that the test should not be used in the assessment of learning disabilities.

The field of learning disability assessment is relatively new and so are tests in this area. As a result, new tests of learning disabilities are in the same stage as early intelligence instruments. However, when judged by modern standards for individual ability tests, especially those which purportedly measure intelligence, even the most established and highly used test of learning disabilities (the Illinois test) compares unfavorably in a variety of respects. Nevertheless, the information processing approach underlying the Illinois test appears most promising and deserves a second look.

In considering learning disability tests, a number of conclusions seem warranted. First, test constructors should attempt to respond to the same criticisms that led to changes in the Binet and Wechsler scales. Second, much more empirical and theoretical research is needed. Finally, users of learning disabilities tests in general and the Illinois test in particular should take great pains to understand the weaknesses of these procedures and to not overinterpret results.

B. Brain damage

Four individually administered procedures with relevance in assessing brain damage are briefly described below. These procedures attempt to measure abilities usually affected by brain damage. Low scores thus are indicative of possible brain damage. The four procedures range all the way from one that takes about 8 hours to administer to one whose average administration time is about five minutes.

The Reitan Battery.   There are many methods of assessing brain damage. One approach, though far from the only one and perhaps not even the best, is through psychological tests. One advantage of such tests is that they are not physically harmful. Some medical procedures, such as those involving injections of fluids into the spinal cord, can be quite dangerous and painful. But psychological tests tend to be less precise and specific than medical assessment tools. One of the best-known experts in assessing brain damage (that is, organicity) through psychological tests is R. M. Reitan (for example, see Reitan, 1962, 1968, 1976). He gathered and refined a wide variety of psychological tests of organicity to create the 8-hour Reitan Battery. Refer to Reitan's publications for a discussion of his comprehensive battery. Also available is a relatively recent text devoted exclusively to assessment of brain damage through psychological tests (Lezak, 1976). Research with the Reitan Battery supports its usefulness in assessing brain damage (Williams, Heaton, & Lehman, 1980).

Benton Visual Retention Test (BVRT).   Brain damage tests are based on the concept of *psychological deficit*. According to this concept, a poor performance on a specific task is related to or caused by some underlying deficit. By knowing the underlying function or ability measured by a specific psychological test, the test examiner can relate a poor performance on that test to this underlying function. This is the idea behind the Benton Visual Retention Test (BVRT), which assumes that visual memory ability is easily impaired by brain damage. Thus, a deficit on a visual memory task would be consistent with possible brain damage.

Designed for individuals aged 8 and over, the Benton test consists of geometric designs that are briefly presented and then removed. The subject is asked to reproduce the designs from memory. The responses are scored according to criteria in the manual. The subject loses points for mistakes and omissions and gains points for correct or partially correct responses. Norms are then available to evaluate scores. As the number of errors increase, the subject begins approaching the organic (brain damaged) range.

Bender Visual Motor Gestalt Test (BVMGT).   Also used in the assessment of brain damage and similar to the Benton test is the Bender Visual Motor Gestalt Test (BVMGT). The Bender test has a variety of uses and is among the most popular individual tests (Lubin et al., 1971). It consists of nine geometric figures (such as a circle and a diamond) that the subject is simply asked to copy. A number of specific errors have been identified for each design, and the Bender test is scored according to the number of errors. Developmental norms are available that describe the number of errors associated with children aged 5 through 8 (see Koppitz, 1964). By the age of 8, any child of normal intelligence can copy the figures with only one or two errors. Therefore, anyone over 8 who cannot copy the figures may be suffering from some type of deficit.

Research with the Bender test (see Koppitz, 1964) has shown that errors can occur for individuals whose mental age is less than 8 (for example, because of low intelligence), individuals with organicity, and individuals with emotional problems. Errors associated with organicity have been identified, and a variety of scoring systems for organicity are available.

Memory-for-Designs Test (MFD).   Another simple drawing test involving perceptual-motor coordination is the Memory-for-Designs Test (MFD). Requiring only a ten-minute administration, the Memory-for-Designs Test can be used for individuals 8.5 to 60 years of age. Empirical data have tended to support its use as an indicator of brain injury (Graham & Kendall, 1946; Graham & Kendall, 1960; Kendall & Graham, 1948). As with the Benton test, the subject attempts to draw a briefly presented design from memory. Drawings are scored from 0 to 3 depending on how they compare with representative sample drawings from normal controls and persons with varying degrees of brain injury. A raw score total based on all 15 drawings can then be corrected for age and intelligence by reference to a table. This corrected score can then be evaluated against a relatively large (825) normative sample.

Reported split-half reliability indices are quite good (.92), and test-retest indices range from .81 to .90 (Graham & Kendall, 1946; Graham & Kendall, 1960). Like so many psychological tests, additional validity documentation of the Memory-for-Designs Test is needed. The studies that are available, however, have been quite supportive (Garrett, Price, & Deabler, 1957; Howard & Shoemaker, 1954; Hunt, 1952).

Evaluation of perceptual-motor drawing tests of organicity. Like all psychological tests of brain damage when used in isolation, the Benton, Bender, and Memory-for-Designs tests have been criticized because of their limitations in validity documentation. However, all three can be used as screening devices. An excessive number of errors on any of these procedures provides a signal for the examiner that more in-depth testing or a medical evaluation may be necessary.

C.   *Creativity: Torrance Tests of Creative Thinking (TTCT)*

The 1960s and 1970s saw a growing interest in the assessment of a previously overlooked ability: creativity. Recently there has been an explosion of new creativity tests. Like learning disability tests, most creativity tests are still in the early stages of development. One of the better, more established, and more popular of these creativity tests is known as the Torrance Tests of Creative Thinking (TTCT).

Like many other creativity tests, the Torrance tests measure a variety of areas or aspects of creative thinking (for example, fluency, flexibility, originality, and elaboration). Scores on the TTCT can be obtained in each of these areas. However, like individual ability tests for the handicapped and tests of learning disability, the TTCT does not quite meet the standards of the Binet and Wechsler scales in terms of standardization, reliability, and validity. Reliability studies have varied widely (for example, .35 to .73 for a three-year period), and validity studies have tended to be varied as well as inconclusive (Hattie, 1980). Reviewers typically suggest that more work is needed (Baird, 1972; Thorndike, 1972). Unlike some creativity tests, the TTCT was conservatively presented as a research tool, but little has been done to prevent the test from being used in applied settings.

In sum, the Torrance tests are typical of creativity tests. Applied practitioners demand such a tool for their work, and, although inconsistent, available data reflect its merit and fine potential. As with so many other tests, however, more work is needed. Results from the new creativity tests must be viewed as tentative and with caution.

D.   *Individual achievement tests: The Wide Range Achievement Test (WRAT)*

We have already discussed the popular distinction between intelligence and achievement. As you know, tests of intelligence presumably measure potential capability, whereas achievement tests presumably measure what the person has actually acquired or done with that potential. Although scores from "intelligence tests" and "achievement tests" often overlap widely, discrepancies sometimes are found between purported measures of intelligence and measures of achievement. Such discrepancies may occur if a person of average potential has not made full use of that potential. Such a person would tend to score higher on a general ability test than on a specific achievement test, especially if the general ability test minimizes the effects of learning and the achievement test is highly specific. Similarly, a person may score average on a general intelligence test but—because of a high level of interest, motivation, or special training—score above average on achievement. Thus, despite the overlap between intelligence and ability tests, comparisons of achievement and intelligence test data can sometimes be extremely revealing.

Most of the achievement tests are group tests, and these are discussed in the next chapter. Perhaps the most popular and widely used individual achievement test is the Wide Range Achievement Test (WRAT). The Wide Range Achievement Test permits an estimate of grade level functioning in reading, spelling, and arithmetic. It can be used for ages 5 and over and has two levels for each of the three achievement areas.

Revised in 1976, the Wide Range Achievement Test is easy to administer. It also is highly popular. However, although it is useful as a general measure of how an individual has developed his or her abilities in spelling, arithmetic, and reading, test users must again be cautioned. Experience has shown that norms for the Wide Range Achievement Test are not entirely representative. For example, average readers in the 11th grade (50th percentile) will score about two years behind when compared with individuals for the test's norms. Such individuals might be inappropriately labeled "reading disabled."

The norm problem with the Wide Range Achievement Test underscores our repeated warning for caution in the use of test results. All test users should learn as much as they can about the tests they use. Statements from the test publishers or distributors of tests, and even statements in the test manuals always must be carefully examined.

IV.   SUMMARY

The number of individual ability tests is almost overwhelming. Most of these tests are for highly specific purposes, and their strength lies in their specificity. Table 13-1 summarized some of the major differences among the various alternative individual tests of ability. Of the infant and preschool scales there is much to be said for the Bayley Scales of Infant Development. The McCarthy Scales of Children's Abilities appear to be promising tests for measuring intelligence in young children, but more work is needed. Overall, general ability tests for handicapped and special populations should be used cautiously. Among the tests of ability for the handicapped, the Columbia Mental Maturity Scale is one of the most promising.

Learning disability tests are based on information processing theory. These tests are relatively new so that their results should also be viewed with caution. These tests, like creativity tests, have a long way to go if they hope to reach the standards of the Binet and Wechsler scales. A number of useful drawing tests such as the Bender, the Benton, and the Memory-for-Designs are all excellent economical screening devices for organicity. These tests attempt to measure an ability related to brain functioning. From a deficit, brain damage is inferred. The Bender Visual Motor Gestalt Test, in addition to being a screening device for brain damage, can also be related to intellectual and emotional functioning. Finally, although achievement and intelligence tests often overlap, sometimes a comparison between the two can be useful. One of the major individual achievement tests is the Wide Range Achievement Test. This test, however, may sometimes lead to incorrect conclusions because of problems with its norms.

CHAPTER

14

Group Ability Tests: Intelligence, Achievement, and Aptitude

Learning objectives

When you have completed this chapter, you should be able to do the following:

1. Compare group and individual ability tests.
2. Identify the major characteristics of group tests.
3. List four general rules for using results from group ability tests.
4. Evaluate the adequacy of the available group ability tests for use in kindergarten through 12th grade.
5. Identify and evaluate two major group ability tests for college entrance.
6. Identify and evaluate two major group ability tests for graduate school entrance.
7. Identify some of the advantages of the Goodenough-Harris Drawing Test.
8. Identify some popular group ability tests used in business and industry.

In Chapters 11, 12, and 13 we considered the individual ability tests. In the present chapter we cover group tests of ability.

I. COMPARISON OF GROUP AND INDIVIDUAL ABILITY TESTS

The Binet and Wechsler scales are the most extensively used and respected of the individual ability tests. Individual tests, you will recall, require a single examiner for a single subject. The examiner provides the instructions according to a standardized procedure stated in the test manual. The subject responds, and the examiner records the response verbatim. The examiner then evaluates and scores the subject's response, and this scoring process usually involves considerable skill. In contrast, group tests can be administered to more than one person at the same time by a single examiner. The examiner may read the instructions and impose time limits. But subjects record their own responses, which usually are choices between two or more alternatives. Scoring is typically objective and requires no skill on the part of the examiner, who simply adds the number of correct responses and in some cases subtracts a certain percentage for incorrect responses. Individual and group tests are alike in that both involve a comparison of a subject's test score to a standard sample, and scores from both types of tests can typically be converted into standard scores and percentiles.

In addition to differences in whether a single individual or a group of individuals is tested at once, who records the response (examiner or subject), and objectivity of scoring, there is still another important difference between group and individual tests. In most individual tests the examiner takes responsibility for eliciting a maximum performance. If a problem exists that might inhibit a maximum performance—for example, if a subject is frightened, nervous, uncooperative, or unmotivated—the examiner takes responsibility for neutralizing this problem in order to elicit the best possible performance from the subject. In an individual test the examiner may encourage guessing—for example, by saying in a warm, friendly, supportive tone "Sure you know that, just guess." Indeed, one major assumption of those using results from most individual tests is that the test score represents the upper limits of a person's capabilities; if this isn't the case, the examiner must state so in a written report or memo to guard against misuse of the results.

Those using the results of group tests, however, must assume the subject is already cooperative and motivated. Subjects are not praised for responding as they are on individual tests, and there are no safeguards to prevent a person from receiving a low score for reasons other than low ability, such as lack of motivation, lack of cooperation, or emotional upset. As a result of this lack of safeguards low scores on group tests are often difficult to interpret. With high scores, especially very high scores, it is logical to assume that the subject was motivated and has mental abilities commensurate with the obtained score. Low scores, however, may have been due to low mental ability, lack of interest, inadequate motivation, clerical errors in recording responses, or a host of other factors.

A. *Advantages of individual tests*

A major advantage of individual over group tests is that individual tests can provide a wealth of information about a subject above and beyond the test score. Individual tests allow examiners to observe behavior in a standard situation. Because the instructions and methods of administration are always as identical as possible, the situation in which subjects take an individual test is typically the same. Therefore differences observed in behavior and attitudes are most likely a reflection of differences in the individuals taking the test. One person may respond quickly and enthusiastically when correct but become hesitant or withdrawn following failure. Another person may react to failure by trying harder and may actually do better in the face of frustration and failure.

After examiners have gained experience with an individual test and know how to use it properly, they have the opportunity to observe different reactions from individuals placed in the same situation. Experienced examiners eventually develop internal norms. They have an idea of how most subjects react to a certain task or situation and can easily identify unusual reactions. The opportunity to observe behavior in a standard situation can be invaluable to an examiner trying to understand the unique attributes of a person and in adequately interpreting the meaning of a test score.

By providing the opportunity to observe behavior under standardized conditions, individual tests add a whole new dimension to the information that can be obtained from an interview. Some subjects won't talk and some can't talk for a variety of reasons. How is the examiner to gain an understanding of such individuals? Information provided by friends or relatives cannot be relied on because friends and relatives are rarely objective and usually they are not trained in observing human behavior. Simply observing the person in a natural setting may provide some useful information, but then the examiner has nothing to compare these observations with. Thus, in allowing observations of behavior under standard conditions, individual tests provide an invaluable opportunity for the examiner to obtain information beyond the information that can be obtained in an interview.

B.   *Advantages of group tests*

Group tests also have unique advantages. Group tests are cost-efficient in that they minimize the amount of professional time necessary for administration and scoring, involve less expensive materials, and usually require less skill in and training of examiners than do individual tests. Scoring for group tests is more objective and hence typically more reliable than the subjective scoring of many individual tests. Group tests can be used with large numbers of individuals, and, when combined with data from other sources, group test results can often yield information as useful and meaningful as that obtained from individual tests.

Whereas individual tests find their greatest application in the assessment and diagnosis of psychological or medical problems in the clinical situation, the application of group tests is far broader. Group tests are used in the schools at every level from kindergarten through college and graduate school. They are also extensively used by the military, in industry, and for a variety of research problems. Group test results can be used for screening and selection purposes; to assess mental, vocational, or special abilities; to assess mastery of a particular discipline or subject area; and to assess interests and aptitudes for specific occupations or job duties.

If the benefits of individual observation and unique interpretation of test scores are minimal for the examiner's purpose or if many individuals must be tested in a limited time with limited personnel, then group tests, administered with care and interpreted with an understanding of their properties, strengths, and limitations, can be extremely valuable tools.

II. GENERAL FEATURES OF GROUP TESTS

A. *Characteristics of group tests*

Generally speaking, group tests can be characterized as paper-pencil or booklet-pencil tests in that the only materials required are a printed booklet of test items, a scoring key, an answer sheet, and a pencil. Most group tests are of the multiple-choice variety, where the subject must select one alternative from as many as eight possible responses. Some group tests also require a free response, such as completing a sentence or design.

There are, by far, more group than individual tests, and, like individual tests, group tests vary among themselves in a variety of respects. One major difference is whether the test is primarily verbal, thus requiring reading or language skills, is primarily nonverbal, or combines verbal and nonverbal tasks. Some group tests group items by type (for example, all verbal analogy problems are in the same section, with items arranged in order of increasing difficulty). A test of this kind is ideally suited for producing a variety of scores such as those obtained from the Wechsler tests. Other group tests present different tasks arranged in no particular or systematic order. A test of this kind typically produces a single score related to general ability. Group test scores can be converted to a variety of units. Most produce percentiles or some type of standard score, but a few produce ratio or deviation IQs.

B. *Selecting group tests*

In selecting a group test one should remember that there are a sufficient number of psychometrically adequate group tests for almost any purpose. Therefore, the test user need never settle for any tests but those whose psychometric soundness has been well documented. This is especially the case for ability tests used in the schools.

In view of the ready availability of psychometrically sound instruments we do not discuss here poorly standardized or marginally reliable tests. However, as with our discussion of individual tests, our treatment of group tests is not comprehensive. Therefore, tests not included in our discussion are not necessarily psychometrically unsound instruments. Our criteria for selection of tests for this discussion parallel our criteria for selection of individual tests. We were especially influenced by the *Mental Measurements Yearbooks* in this regard. We gave highest priority to established, highly used tests that continue to generate interest among researchers and practitioners. If several tests are similar in design, construction, and purpose, we generally include only the one or two most highly referenced in the *Mental Measurements Yearbooks*. However, we also include tests that illustrate concepts or meet specific needs. Finally, we include a few recent tests as well as tests of historical value.

C. *Using group tests*

Overall, tests included in our discussion are as reliable and well standardized as the best individual tests. However, as for some individual tests, validity data for some group tests are weak, meager, contradictory, or all three. Therefore, all users of group tests must be careful in interpreting and making use of test scores. These tests should not be seen as a simple solution to the decision-making process. Rather, their main value arises when they are used in conjunction with other data.

Test use is an especially important issue where group tests are concerned because results from these procedures are probably used by more people than results from individual tests. Therefore, for the thousands of teachers, educators, school administrators, personnel staff members in industry, counselors, and others who routinely have access to results from group tests, we have a few suggestions.

Use results with caution.   Never consider scores in isolation or as absolutes. Try to include the test score as only one bit of data, to be tentatively accepted unless not confirmed by other data. Be especially careful in using these tests for prediction, except for predicting relatively limited factors over a brief time. Avoid overinterpreting test scores or attributing to test scores more value than is warranted by their limitations.

Be especially suspicious of low scores.   Users of group tests must of necessity assume the subjects understand the purpose of testing and want to do well and are equally rested and free of emotional problems. Many group tests also require reading ability as well as an interest in solving test problems. When any of these assumptions and requirements are not met, an artificially low score can result.

Consider wide discrepancies a warning signal.   When an individual exhibits wide discrepancies either between two or more test scores or between a test score and behavior or other sources of data, all may not be well with the individual (assuming the discrepancy is not the result of a clerical error). The discrepancy may reflect emotional problems or severe stress. For example, a child with high test scores may obtain poor grades because of emotional upset. Or a child with good grades may obtain a poor test score because of a crisis, such as a death in the family.

When in doubt, refer.   With low scores, wide discrepancies, or whenever there is sufficient reason to doubt the validity or fairness of a test result, the safest course is to refer the subject for individual testing by a competent professional person. If given the reasons for the referral, a professional trained in individual test use can generally ascertain the cause of the problem and provide the unique interpretation called for in such cases. In this area, it is well to know one's limitations. It is often dangerous as well as reckless to take on a responsibility appropriate for a trained specialist.

III. GROUP TESTS IN THE SCHOOLS: KINDERGARTEN THROUGH 12TH GRADE

Our discussion of specific group ability tests begins with three of the soundest and most popular tests used in the public school system. These are the Kuhlmann-Anderson Test, the Cognitive Abilities Test, and the Henmon-Nelson Test.

A. *Kuhlmann-Anderson Test, seventh edition*

The Kuhlmann-Anderson Test (KAT) is a group intelligence test with eight separate levels for all grades, kindergarten through 12th grade. Each of the eight levels of the KAT contains several tests, with a variety of items for each test. As with most multilevel batteries, which cover multiple levels or age (grade) ranges, KAT items are primarily nonverbal at lower levels, requiring minimal reading and language ability. However, whereas most multilevel batteries become increasingly verbal with increasing age or grade level, the KAT remains primarily nonverbal throughout. Thus, the KAT is not only suited to young children but can also be useful for those who might be handicapped in following verbal procedures.

One of the oldest, most carefully constructed, and most thoroughly established of the group tests for school children, the KAT was refined and improved through several revisions made between 1927 and 1967. A reflection of the quality of the KAT is the fact that many of its items can be found on a variety of other group tests.

Results of the most recent (seventh) edition of the KAT can be expressed in verbal, quantitative, and total scores. At some levels, total scores can be expressed as a deviation IQ. Scores at other levels can be expressed as *percentile bands*. A percentile band is like a confidence interval. It provides the range of percentiles that are likely to represent a subject's true score. It is created by forming an interval that is one standard error of measurement above and below the obtained score and converting the resulting values to percentiles.

The overwhelming majority of reviews have praised the KAT for its construction, standardization, and other excellent psychometric qualities. Normative data have been continually improved and are based on more than 10,000 representative subjects. Reliability coefficients are quite good, with split-half coefficients running in the low .90s and test-retest coefficients ranging from the low .80s to low .90s. Validity is well documented. The KAT correlates highly with a variety of ability tests and in particular has an impressive correlation with the Stanford-Binet. In one study with an earlier edition, the KAT was found to correlate almost perfectly with the Stanford-Binet when measurement errors were taken into account (Dearborn & Rothney, 1941).

In sum, the KAT is an extremely sound, sophisticated group test. Its nonverbal items make it particularly useful for special purposes. However, its impressive validity and reliability also make it one of the group ability tests of choice for all grade levels.

B. *Cognitive Abilities Test*

A revision of the popular Lorge-Thorndike Intelligence Test, the Cognitive Abilities Test (CAT) is another sound group instrument for evaluating ability in children in kindergarten through 12th grade. The CAT has two levels. The primary level produces only a single score; the upper level (grades 3 through 12) produces verbal, nonverbal, and quantitative scores. Normative data are not as extensive or as carefully stratified in the CAT as in the KAT. However, reliability and validity coefficients for the two tests are comparable. Like the KAT, the CAT is a sound, well-constructed group ability test.

C. *Henmon-Nelson Test*

A third well-standardized, highly used, and carefully constructed test for all grade levels is the Henmon-Nelson Test (H-NT) of mental abilities. Whereas the KAT contains eight levels and the CAT two, the H-NT is broken down into four levels by grade (kindergarten through 2, 3 through 6, 6 through 9, 9 through 12). Although it produces only a single score believed to reflect general intelligence, two sets of norms are available. One set is based on raw score distributions by age, the other on raw score distributions by grade. Raw scores can be converted into deviation IQs as well as percentiles. The availability of only a single score has been a continued source of controversy (see Lefever, 1959). However, a single score is consistent with the purpose of the test, which is to obtain a relatively quick measure of general intelligence (it takes approximately 30 minutes to complete the 90 items).

As with the KAT, normative data for the H-NT are based on a large sample. Current normative data are representative of the U.S. population according to the 1970 census. In fact, the standardization of the H-NT is one of the best found in any test. Subjects were selected from 250 schools on the basis of clustering and randomizing procedures to ensure representativeness.

As in the other tests for school-age individuals, most of the reliability coefficients, both split-half and test-retest, reported in the manual run in the .90s. Furthermore, the H-NT correlates well with a variety of intelligence tests (median .76, range .50 to .84), as well as with achievement test scores (median .79, range .64 to .85). Correlations with grades, though not as high, are quite impressive, with a median coefficient of .60.

In sum, the H-NT is an exceptionally well-standardized group test for all grade levels. It produces a single score related to intelligence, achievement, and grades. Administration time is brief, and its psychometric adequacy is well documented.

D. *Summary*

The KAT, CAT, and H-NT are all sound, viable instruments. The KAT is especially useful if nonverbal items are needed. The CAT might be used when data concerning differential ability in verbal, quantitative, and nonverbal areas are needed. Finally, for a quick, highly predictive instrument, the H-NT is extremely valuable. The three tests can be used in conjunction, for follow-up or for reevaluation purposes, to avoid repetition of test material or to check the stability or validity or both of a score obtained with just one of the three. Other tests are available, but these three tests are clearly among the best and most widely used group tests for school children in kindergarten through the 12th grade.

IV. COLLEGE ENTRANCE TESTS

Two of the most popular college entrance tests are the College Board Scholastic Aptitude Test and the Cooperative School and College Ability Tests. These are discussed below.

A. *College Board Scholastic Aptitude Test (SAT)*

Tests in Print II (Buros, 1974) lists more references for the College Board Scholastic Aptitude Test (SAT) than for any ability test other than the Stanford-Binet and Wechsler tests. Thus, the SAT leads all other group tests in relevant published research and exceeds all individual ability tests in this regard except for the Binet and Wechsler tests. Many of you have taken the SAT or a similar college entrance test and are perhaps interested in finding out more about it. Indeed, the SAT or a related test has probably played at least some role in deciding your future (see, for example, Hargadon, 1981).

In use since 1926, the SAT is administered on specific dates at centers established by the publisher (Buros, 1974). Rather than being an intelligence test, the SAT purports to predict the potential for higher education of high school seniors at the upper ability levels, thus the term *aptitude* in its name.

The SAT produces two scores, a verbal (SAT-V) and a mathematical (SAT-M) score. The SAT-V is composed of carefully selected and analyzed items involving sentence completion, identification of opposites, use of analogies, and paragraph comprehension. The SAT-M covers arithmetic, algebra, and geometry. The SAT-V and SAT-M are administered in two timed sections. Seventy-five minutes are allowed for each section. The two sections correlate in the high .60s, with a definite increasing relationship between the two over the last three decades (see, for example, Wallace, 1972). Presumably, this increasing correlation reflects a decreasing emphasis on specific knowledge (DuBois, 1972b); however, the math section tends to be "wordy" (Wallace, 1972), and so the relationship may be in part due to a verbal influence in the math section.

The SAT is one of the most stable tests of any kind. The five-option, multiple-choice tasks are scored by a formula that adjusts for guessing. Test-retest, internal consistency, and alternative-form reliability coefficients consistently range from the high .80s to low .90s.

In addition to documenting stability, researchers have put much work into validity documentation. Validity data have not been as spectacular as reliability data, although results are quite good. Predictive validity coefficients for freshman grades do, however, vary widely depending on one's major. Lowest coefficients are in the teens and highest coefficients are in the low to mid .60s. Median and modal coefficients, which run from the low to high .30s, are only modest. However, as many have noted, when combined with the high school record, the SAT can be extremely useful in predicting freshman college grades. DuBois (1972b), for example, notes that "typical validities are .39 for SAT-V, .33 for SAT-M, .55 for the high school record, with a multiple correlation of the order of .62" (p. 344).

The psychometric soundness of the SAT is based on years of experience, statistical analyses of the results from tens of thousands of administrations, and careful item selection. Although present norms are based on a relatively old sample consisting of over 10,000 students who took the test in 1941, the psychometric adequacy of the SAT is perhaps better documented than that for any other ability test. Separate norms as a function of various demographic variables (sex, race) are not available, but evidence shows the test is equally valid for all groups (see Wallace, 1972).

There is little basis on which to criticize the SAT and much to be said for its soundness as a predictor of grades during the early years of college when it is used in conjunction with other sources of data like the high school record. The psychometric adequacy of the SAT may be the highest possible for any such test, and the SAT is likely to play a role in college entrance decisions for some time to come, despite attacks from the public and a decline in average SAT scores (see Zajonc & Bargh, 1980).

The major weakness of the SAT as well as of other major college entrance tests lies in its relatively poor predictive power in discriminating the grades of students who score in the middle ranges (total scores between 900 and 1200). It is not uncommon for a student at the mean on the SAT to have a higher college grade point average than a student who scores a standard deviation above the mean on both sections, perhaps because factors such as motivation, determination, personality, emotional stability, and home and social life also influence freshman grades. In other words, test scores and high school performance records aren't the only determinants of college success.

B. *Cooperative School and College Ability Tests*

The second most referenced test at the college level in *Tests in Print II* (Buros, 1974) is the Cooperative School and College Ability Tests (SCAT), developed in 1955. In addition to the college level, the SCAT covers three precollege levels beginning at the fourth grade. The SCAT purports to measure school-learned abilities as well as one's potential to undertake additional schooling.

Although the SCAT is well designed and constructed, Butcher (1972) questions the representativeness of the SCAT standardization sample. Psychometric documentation of the SCAT, furthermore, is neither as strong nor as extensive as that for the SAT. Another problem is that little empirical data are provided in support of the major assumption that previous success in acquiring school-learned abilities can predict future success in acquiring such abilities. Even if this assumption were accurate, and it probably is, grades, which also reflect school-learned abilities, should provide about as much information as the SCAT, especially at the college level. In view of these considerations, we concur with Butcher (1972) that additional evidence on the SCAT would be highly desirable. Also, despite its reasonably good correlation with the SAT, we see little advantage of the SCAT over the SAT for prediction of college success. Nevertheless, the research interest shown in the SCAT seems to indicate a potential future for this test, especially as more is learned about its properties.

V. GRADUATE SCHOOL ENTRANCE TESTS

If you plan to go to graduate school, then you very likely will be required to take a graduate school entrance test. The two most popular of these are the Graduate Record Examination Aptitude Test and the Miller Analogies Test.

A. *The Graduate Record Examination Aptitude Test*

The Graduate Record Examination Aptitude Test, better known as the GRE, is one of the most commonly used tests for graduate school entrance. Almost any student who wishes to pursue graduate work in psychology, as well as in many other disciplines, is likely to be confronted with the GRE. Offered throughout the year at designated examination centers, which are located mostly at universities and colleges, the GRE purports to be a measure of general scholastic ability. It is most frequently used in conjunction with grade point average, letters of recommendation, and other academic factors in the highly competitive graduate school selection process. The GRE contains a general section that produces verbal, quantitative, and reasoning scores. In addition to this general test, which is used for all college majors, the GRE contains an advanced section that measures achievement in at least 20 majors, such as psychology, history, and chemistry.

In some respects the GRE parallels the SAT. With a mean of 500 and a standard deviation of 100, as in the original standardization sample of the SAT V, the verbal section covers reasoning, identification of opposites, use of analogies, and paragraph comprehension. The quantitative section covers arithmetic reasoning, algebra, and geometry as in the SAT-M. However, the normative sample for the GRE is only about one-fifth the size of the SAT sample (about 2000 college seniors tested at 11 colleges in 1952). The psychometric adequacy of the GRE is also less spectacular than that of the SAT, both in the reported coefficients of validity and reliability and in extensiveness of documentation. Nevertheless, the GRE is a relatively sound instrument.

The stability of the GRE based on Kuder-Richardson and odd-even reliability is adequate, with coefficients only slightly lower than those of the SAT. However, the predictive validity of the GRE is not highly convincing. Independent studies of the GRE vary from those that find moderate correlations between the GRE and grade point average to those that find no or even a negative relationship between the two. Although it can be said that high GRE scorers tend to complete graduate school more often than low scorers for certain programs, general predictive studies have proved somewhat discouraging.

Those who aspire to go to graduate school might be asking at this point "With its limitations, why is it that the GRE has such a critical effect on my chances for going to graduate school and on my future career?" Indeed, many graduate school hopefuls have asked this question. One answer is that many schools have developed their own local norms and psychometric documentation and are able to use the GRE, either independently or in conjunction with other sources of data, to predict success in their programs. Furthermore, many graduate selection committees use the GRE broadly, as in requiring a minimum cutoff score to apply. The basic problem is that there are more qualified applicants for graduate school than there are available resources to train them and job markets to absorb them. Therefore, the difficult job of selection must have some basis.

Graduate schools also frequently complain that grades are no longer good predictors of scholastic ability because of *grade inflation*—the phenomenon of rising average college grades despite declines in average SAT scores. Thus, many people claim that a "B" today is equivalent to a "C" 15 or 20 years ago, and that an "A" today is equivalent to a "B." Another complaint is that the Freedom of Information Act grants students the right to examine their files, including letters of recommendation. The argument is that professors and other sources of student recommendations cannot be open or candid, knowing the student may some day read the letter. Thus, as the validity of grades and letters of recommendation becomes more questionable, greater reliance is being put on test scores. Fair or not, this is the reality. However, students with relatively poor GRE scores need not feel devastated and can take heart in the knowledge that their score is not necessarily predictive of success in graduate school.

One trend in graduate selection in psychology has been the consideration of nontraditional factors such as research experience and publications. Saccuzzo and Schulte (1978), for example, surveyed American Psychological Association approved and nonapproved clinical and nonclinical psychology programs and found that the most important consideration beyond grades and GRE scores was research experience and professional publications. Although apparently rare according to their results, research publications can do more to enhance a new application or previously rejected application for graduate study than can retaking the GRE, taking additional courses to improve grades, or even obtaining a master's degree. Regarding a master's degree, Saccuzzo and Schulte found that the possession of such a degree made no difference in the selection considerations of most psychology programs. In addition, possession of a master's degree decreased chances for admission in twice as many programs as those in which it increased chances. The message is clear. Students who believe themselves to be more capable than their undergraduate grades and GRE scores indicate simply must demonstrate this capability through research endeavors.

Another issue to consider is whether to study for the GRE. In addition to study books and guides, many courses are offered to those hoping to increase their chances of success (see Anastasi, 1981). Some of these courses are offered through recognized universities, but there are no restrictions on who can offer them or on how much students are charged. Students can pay over $300 for such courses. Unfortunately, no published data support such courses or study guides. Certainly you should attempt to prepare as much as possible for this important exam; however, be advised that many of those who offer study programs have not yet bothered to document their value. We would at the least want to know the track record of any course requiring a large sum of money in advance.

B. Miller Analogies Test

A second major graduate school entrance test is the Miller Analogies Test (MAT). Like the GRE, the MAT is designed to measure scholastic aptitudes for graduate-level studies. However, unlike the GRE, the MAT is a strictly verbal test. It requires the student to discern in 50 minutes logical relationships for 100 varied analogy problems ranging in difficulty up to the most difficult items found in any test. Knowledge of specific content and a wide vocabulary are extremely useful in this endeavor. However, the most important factor appears to be the ability to see relationships as well as a knowledge of the various ways analogies can be formed (by sound, number, similarities, differences, and so forth). The MAT is used in a variety of specializations and fields, and special norms are available for various fields.

Odd-even reliability data for the MAT are quite adequate, with reported coefficients in the manual in the high .80s. Unfortunately, as with the GRE, predictive validity support for the MAT is lacking. Despite a substantial correlation with the GRE (coefficients run in the low .80s), validity coefficients reported in the manual for grades vary considerably from sample to sample and are only modest (median in the high .30s). Generally, the psychometric adequacy of the MAT is reasonable when it is compared with ability tests in general, but the GRE and grade point average remain as its primary correlates. Furthermore the MAT is not predictive of research ability, creativity, and other factors important to graduate school and professional performance. However, as an aid in discriminating among graduate applications and adults at the highest level of verbal ability, the MAT is an excellent device.

VI. NONVERBAL GROUP ABILITY TESTS

As we noted in our discussion of individual tests that do not require the use of language, nonverbal tests are needed for evaluating individuals who are either handicapped or limited in the verbal/language realm. As with their individual test counterparts, nonverbal group tests may be performance tests, which require the subject to do something (draw, solve maze problems), or they may be paper-pencil tests, which provide printed nonverbal relationship items and instruct the subject to select the best of two or more multiple-choice responses. Like the nonverbal individual tests, some nonverbal group tests can be administered without the use of language.

A. *Progressive Matrices*

The Progressive Matrices (PM) test is one of the best known and most popular of the nonverbal group tests. Only the SAT, Wechsler, and Binet tests are referenced more in Buros (1974). The PM may be group or individually administered and covers an age range from 5 through elderly adults. Instructions are simple, and if necessary the PM can be administered by demonstration without the use of language. The PM consists exclusively of one of the most commonly found type of stimuli in nonverbal tests of any kind, matrices. The 60 matrices of the PM are graded in difficulty. Each contains a logical pattern or design with a missing part. The subject's task is to select the appropriate design from up to eight alternative choices. There is no time limit, and the test purports to measure general intelligence, or Spearman's g factor (Spearman, 1927).

The PM, a product of England, was designed to assess military recruits independently of educational factors. The lack of U.S. norms for the PM is a constant source of criticism. Futhermore, the test manual has several problems. It contains only minimal reliability data and no validity data. In spite of these limitations, the PM and PM-like tests have flourished. The versatility of matrices in ability testing can be seen in their wide application for such groups as young children, the culturally deprived, and the language-handicapped. Analysis of available reliability studies shows a rather respectable range of coefficients from the high .70s to low .90s (see Bortner, 1965). Early studies also revealed a fairly large correlation between the PM and the Stanford-Binet (r=.60) (Keir, 1949), Wechsler performance IQ (r=.70), and Wechsler verbal IQ (r=.58) (Hall, 1957).

In spite of the absence of U.S. norms and problems with its test manual, the PM is a widely used test that is supported by a large body of empirical findings. Although it uses only a single nonverbal task, the incomplete matrix, the PM is especially valuable because, to a large degree, it eliminates the verbal/language and educational components found in so many other tests whose chief goal is to measure ability independently of these factors. Perhaps some day the PM or something similar will be standardized on a sample of Americans. Such work is needed, long overdue, and has considerable potential for interested investigators.

B. *Goodenough-Harris Drawing Test*

A remarkable nonverbal intelligence test that can be either group or individually administered is the Goodenough-Harris Drawing Test (G-HDT). The G-HDT is one of the simplest, quickest, easiest to administer, and least expensive of all ability tests. A pencil and white unlined paper are the only needed materials. The subject is instructed to draw a picture of a whole man and to do the best job possible. The G-HDT was standardized by determining those characteristics of human figure drawings that differentiated subjects in various age groups. More than 70 scorable items were discerned. Subjects get credit for each item included in their drawings. As a rule, each detail is given one point. For example, if only a head is included with no facial features, then the subject receives only one point. Points are added for additional details such as facial features and clothing.

The G-HDT was originally standardized in 1926 and was restandardized in 1963. Scoring of the G-HDT follows the principle of age differentiation—older children tend to get more points because of the greater accuracy and detail of their drawings. Thus, mental ages can be determined by comparing scores with those of the normative sample. Raw scores can be converted to standard scores with a mean of 100 and a standard deviation of 15. Split-half, test-retest, and interscorer reliability coefficients are good, with ranges in the high .60s to low .90s for both old and revised forms (J. A. Dunn, 1972). Scores begin leveling off at about age 14 or 15 (Anastasi, 1972b), so the use of the G-HDT is restricted primarily to children. Correlations with the Stanford-Binet have ranged from .36 to .74 (J. A. Dunn, 1972).

Because of their ease of administration and short administration time, the G-HDT and other human-figure drawing tests are extensively used in a battery of tests (Lubin, Wallis, & Paine, 1971). Relatively recent, representative norms and good validity documentation allow the examiner to obtain a quick rough estimate of a child's intelligence. Interest in the G-HDT runs high, with the number of references listed in Buros (1974) fewer only than those for the PM, the SAT, and the Wechsler and Binet tests. However, the G-HDT is most appropriately used in conjunction with other sources of information in a battery of tests; results based on G-HDT data alone could be quite misleading.

C. *IPAT Culture Fair Intelligence Test*

All cultures tend to reinforce certain skills and activities at the expense of others. One purpose of nonverbal and performance tests is to remove factors related to cultural influences so that pure intelligence, independent of learning, culture, and the like, can be measured. Experience and empirical research have shown that such a test has yet to be developed (see Olmedo, 1981). Indeed, many doubt whether such an accomplishment is even within the realm of possibility (Tannenbaum, 1968).

The IPAT Culture Fair Intelligence Test was designed to eliminate language influences in an ability test and to provide an estimate of intelligence that is relatively free of cultural influence. Although it is no more successful in this regard than any other such attempt, the popularity of the Culture Fair Intelligence Test reflects the strong desire among users for a test that reduces cultural factors as much as possible.

Constructed in the 1940s under the direction of R. B. Cattell, the Culture Fair Intelligence Test is a paper-pencil procedure that covers three levels (ages 4 to 8 and mentally defective adults; ages 8 to 12 and randomly selected adults; and high school age and superior adults). Two parallel forms are available. Standardization varies according to age level. Kuder-Richardson reliabilities run only in the .70s with substantially lower test-retest coefficients. The test has been correlated with a wide variety of other tests with mixed results. Correlations with the Wechsler and Binet tests are quite good, with a range of .56 to .85 (Tannenbaum, 1968). Also in support of the Culture Fair Intelligence Test is the finding that normative data from Western European countries, the United States, and Australia are comparable. Thus, if one wishes to estimate intelligence in a Western European or Australian individual, the Culture Fair Intelligence Test is probably the instrument of choice.

VII. **GROUP TESTS FOR SPECIFIC PURPOSES**

There are an almost uncountable number of group tests for an endless variety of purposes. In addition to group tests used to assess intelligence, academic aptitude, and factors relevant for personnel and occupation selection, there is an endless variety of tests for specific populations. The Black Intelligence Test of Cultural Homogeneity (BITCH), for example, is designed to be a culture fair intelligence test for Blacks. The Barranquilla Rapid Survey Intelligence test (BRSI) purports to measure intelligence in Spanish-speaking persons. Inasmuch as intelligence tests for specific groups are new and poorly documented, we mention them here only to make you aware of the richness and variety of available tests.

A. *Tests for use in industry: The Wonderlic Personnel Test (WPT)*

Business and industry make extensive use of tests, especially as an aid in making decisions concerning employment, placement, and promotion. One widely used such test is the Wonderlic Personnel Test (WPT). Based on a popular instrument, the Otis Self-Administering Tests of Mental Ability, the WPT is a quick (12-minute) test of mental ability in adults. Normative data are available on over 50,000 adults 20 to 65 years old. Five forms, whose intercorrelations range from .82 to .94, are available. Odd-even reliability coefficients are also excellent, with a range between .88 and .94 reported in the manual. The main drawback of the WPT is its meager validity documentation. However, the WPT is a quick, stable, paper-pencil, intelligence test with extensive norms. It is widely used for employee-related decisions in industry but has its greatest value when local validity data are available. In the absence of local data, test scores must be interpreted with some caution.

B. *Tests for assessing occupational aptitude*

The number and variety of group ability tests for measuring aptitude for various occupations are staggering. The General Aptitude Test Battery (GATB), for example, is a nonreading ability test that purportedly measures aptitude for a variety of occupations.

In measuring potential ability (aptitude) for specific vocations, a number of fine tests are available. The Differential Aptitude Test (DAT) is especially useful in assessing clerical competence, such as clerical speed and accuracy and grammar. The Bennett Mechanical Comprehension Test and the Revised Minnesota Paper Form Board Tests are two popular measures of mechanical ability. The Accounting Orientation Test has shown some promise in measuring accounting skills. To assess business skills and readiness for graduate study in business, there is the Admission Test for Graduate Study in Business. There are also special ability tests for advanced study in dentistry (for example, the Dental Admission Testing Program), law (for example, the Law School Admission Test), and medicine (for example, the Medical College Admission Test).

VIII. SUMMARY

Group ability tests are available for just about any purpose, and there appears to be no end to the construction of this type of test. Relative ease in scoring and administration gives group ability tests a major advantage over individual tests, and, in many cases, the results from group tests are as stable and valid as those from individual tests. However, low scores, wide discrepancies between two group test results, or wide discrepancies between a group test result and some other indicator such as grades should be a reason for exercising caution in interpreting results. When in doubt, users of group ability tests should refer the problem to a competent professional who can administer an individual ability test.

The public school system makes perhaps the most extensive use of group ability tests. Indeed, many sound tests exist for all levels from kindergarten through 12th grade. College and graduate school entrance tests also account for a large proportion of the group ability tests used in the United States.

In addition to their use in the educational system, a considerable number of group ability tests play an important role in personnel decisions. A number of ability tests have been developed for personnel selection in business and industry. Other group ability tests can be used by the vocational counselor to assess ability for certain occupations. Still other group ability tests measure aptitude for advanced or professional training. In viewing group ability tests, one gets the impression that there is almost no limit to the scope and applicability of psychological tests.

15

Structured Personality Tests

Learning objectives

When you have completed this chapter, you should be able to do the following:

1. *Identify the major characteristics of a structured personality test.*
2. *Identify the underlying assumption of the first structured personality test (the Woodworth Personal Data Sheet).*
3. *Identify the assumptions of early structured personality tests based on the logical-content strategy.*
4. *Briefly discuss the strategy used in construction of the MMPI.*
5. *Describe the K and F scales on the MMPI.*
6. *Identify major psychometric weaknesses of the MMPI.*
7. *Explain how factor analysis is used in structured personality test construction.*
8. *Briefly describe the Cattell 16PF.*
9. *Briefly describe the EPPS and explain the meaning of an ipsative score.*

In his junior year at college, Mike went to the university counseling center to find out more about himself. To aid him in his quest for self-understanding, a psychologist suggested that he respond to a long list of items known as the California Psychological Inventory (CPI). The CPI is a structured personality test (procedure) that provides a list of statements and asks the subject to respond "true" or "false" to each. The statements were something like these: "I like to read mystery stories." "I am usually alert to my environment." "I would rather follow others than be the leader." "I like to solve difficult problems." "My father is a good man." It took Mike about an hour to respond to the 480 items of the CPI.

A week later he returned for an interpretation of his test scores. The psychologist told Mike that the test indicated he was highly effective in dealing with other individuals; his response pattern was similar to that produced by individuals who make effective leaders. The CPI also indicated that Mike was able to control his desires and impulses and express them effectively and appropriately.

How did the psychologist decide that Mike's responses to certain items reflected specific traits and characteristics (such as leadership ability and control of impulses)? How accurate were the psychologist's interpretations? Did the interpretations really reflect Mike's characteristics? How stable are the results? Can we expect that after ten years the CPI will still indicate that Mike has leadership qualities? We explore these and other questions in this chapter on the structured personality tests.

Tests came into existence in an effort to solve problems facing modern societies. Tests of mental ability were created to distinguish those with subnormal mental abilities from those with normal abilities in order to enhance the education of both groups. However, there is far more to being human than having normal or subnormal mental capabilities. It is not enough to know that a person is high or low in such factors as speed of calculation, memory, range of knowledge, and abstract thinking. To make full use of information about a person's mental abilities, it is also important to know how that person uses these abilities. All the mental abilities in the world are useless in a totally withdrawn individual who sits in the corner of a room all day. But even a relatively small number of mental abilities can go far in a high-energy individual who is organized, persistent, determined, and highly motivated, and who relates well to others. These nonintellective aspects of human behavior are typically distinguished from mental abilities and are referred to as personality characteristics.

Even prior to the development of the first Binet scale, Binet had hypothesized that a person's pattern of intellectual functioning might reveal information about personality factors (Binet & Henri, 1895, 1896). Subsequent investigators agreed with Binet's hypothesis (Hart & Spearman, 1912; Terman, 1916; Thorndike, 1921; E. Webb, 1915), and the hypothesis continues to find support to this day (Eysenck, 1967; G. H. Frank, 1970, 1976; Wechsler, 1943, 1958, 1981). However, specific tests of human personality were not developed until World War I created a need to separate people on the basis of emotional functioning. Thus, the impetus for the development of measures of functioning above and beyond mental abilities came from a need to separate groups on the basis of emotional well-being.

Like the early developers of tests of mental ability, early developers of personality tests were traveling in uncharted territory. Imagine yourself faced with the task of measuring some aspect of human behavior. How would you begin? You could observe and record a person's behavior. This approach, however, would not have helped early investigators because their problem was to find a way of identifying emotionally unstable military recruits. The volume of applicants for military service in the United States during World War I was so great that it became impossible to successfully use the one available method of the time, the interview. A measure of emotional functioning was needed to evaluate large numbers of people and to screen out those unfit for military service. To meet this need, psychologists employed the *self-report question-naire*. Self-report questionnaires provide a list of statements and require subjects to respond in some way to each, such as marking "true" or "false" to indicate whether the statement applies to them.

The general procedure in which the subject is asked to respond to a written statement is known as the *structured*, or *objective, method* of personality assessment, as distinguished from the projective method (to be discussed in Chapter 17). As their name implies, structured measures of personality are characterized by structure and lack of ambiguity. A clear and definite stimulus is provided, and the requirements of the subject are evident and specific. An example of a structured personality test item is "Respond yes or no to the statement 'I am happy.'" In contrast, a projective test item may provide a picture of an inkblot and ask "What might this be?" In a projective personality test the stimulus is ambiguous and the subject has no guidelines as to what type of response is required.

I. STRATEGIES OF STRUCTURED PERSONALITY TEST CONSTRUCTION

Many approaches to or strategies of test construction have been tried during the evolution of structured personality tests.

A. *Overview of the strategies*

Like measures of mental ability, efforts to measure nonintellective, personality factors evolved through a number of phases. New features were added as problems with the old approaches became evident. In the realm of structured personality testing, a number of approaches or strategies have been tried. There is some disagreement concerning how these strategies should be classified, what they should be called, and even how many distinctly different strategies exist (Gynther & Gynther, 1976). At the broadest level, the strategies are empirical or nonempirical (deductive). Each of these two major strategies can be further divided into two major substrategies. Empirical strategies may use either the method of criterion groups or the method of factor analysis. Deductive strategies may be of either the logical-content variety or the theoretical variety. These four strategies are discussed more or less in the order in which they came to prominence in the field of structured personality testing. Table 15-1 provides a summary of the strategies.

The deductive strategies use reason and deductive logic to determine the

TABLE 15-1 Summary of strategies for structured personality test construction

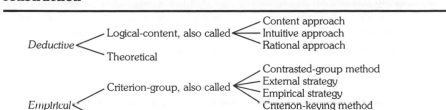

meaning of a test response, and empirical strategies use statistical or experimental methods or both. For the deductive strategies, in the logical-content method, items are selected on the basis of simple face validity; in the theoretical approach, test construction is guided by a particular psychological theory. For the empirical strategies, in the criterion-group approach, items are selected to distinguish a group of individuals with certain characteristics, known as the criterion group, from a control group; the factor analytic approach uses the statistical technique of factor analysis to determine the meaning of test items.

B. Deductive strategies

The two deductive strategies are the logical-content and theoretical approaches.

Logical-content strategy. The logical-content strategy, as its name implies, uses reason and deductive logic in the development of personality measures. This strategy has also been referred to as the content approach (Maloney & Ward, 1976), the intuitive approach (Goldberg, 1974), and the rational approach (J. S. Wiggins, 1973). In the most general use of this strategy, the test designer tries to logically deduce the type of content that should measure the characteristic to be assessed. For example, if you want to measure eating behavior, it makes sense to include statements such as "I frequently eat between meals." Statements that have no direct logical relevance to eating behavior, such as "I enjoy solving complex puzzles," would not be included in tests employing the logical-content strategy. The principal distinguishing characteristic of the logical-content strategy is that it assumes that the test item describes the subject's personality and behavior. If a person marks "true" to the statement "I am outgoing," then it is assumed that he or she is outgoing. Initial efforts to measure personality used the logical-content approach as the primary strategy.

Theoretical strategy. The theoretical strategy, as its name implies, begins with a theory concerning the nature of the particular characteristic to be measured. As in the logical-content approach, an attempt is then made to deduce items. In the theoretical approach, however, items must be consistent with the theory. If the theory hypothesizes that personality can be broken down into six major areas, an effort is made to develop items that tap each of these six areas. In addition to being guided by theoretical concerns, rather than simply selecting any item that seems to measure a particular characteristic, theoretical strategies also demand that every item in a scale be related to the characteristic that is being measured. Thus, the theoretical approach attempts to create a homogeneous scale and, to this end, may employ statistical procedures such as item analysis.

C. Empirical strategies

Empirical strategies make no assumptions about the meaning of a test response or the nature of personality. These strategies retain the self-report features of the deductive strategies in that subjects are asked to respond to items that are descriptive of their own views, opinions, and feelings. However, empirical strategies attempt to use experimental research to empirically determine the meaning of a test response or the major dimensions of personality or both.

Criterion-group strategy. The criterion-group strategy, sometimes known as the contrasted-group method (Goldberg, 1972b), the external strategy (Goldberg, 1974), or even the empirical strategy (Maloney & Ward, 1976), begins with a known or criterion group. The criterion group is one that possesses a certain characteristic, such as a group of individuals known to be aggressive or a group known to be schizophrenic. Test constructors select and administer a group of items to all individuals in this criterion group as well as to a control group from the normal population. They then attempt to locate items that distinguish the criterion and control groups. This procedure always involves the use of an *external criterion*—a group known to possess certain characteristics—and involves contrasting the criterion and control groups. Thus, the terms *contrasted-group* or *external-criterion* strategy are frequently used interchangeably with the term *criterion-group strategy*.

Hypothetically, suppose that a group of aggressive individuals mark "true" to items such as "I am not aggressive," "I like to attend concerts," and "I would rather read than write" significantly more than do individuals in a normal control comparison group. These items can then be included on an aggression scale. When new subjects endorse a large proportion of items on the aggression scale, we may then hypothesize that they are aggressive because they endorsed the same items that distinguished aggressive individuals from control individuals. The content of the items is of little consequence. What is important is that aggressive individuals marked "true" to these items, and this endorsement discriminated the aggressive individuals from the control group. As J. S. Wiggins (1973, p. 394) notes, depressed individuals respond "false" significantly more than normals to the statement "I sometimes tease animals." There is no logical or rational reason for this response. It is important to remember that the actual content or face validity of an item in the criterion-group strategy is of little importance. Instead, the approach attempts to determine which items discriminate the criterion and control groups.

Once distinguishing items have been determined for one sample of subjects representing the criterion group, the next step is to cross-validate the scale by checking its discriminating power for an independent criterion sample—individuals also known to possess the characteristics to be measured   against a new control group. If the scale significantly distinguishes the two groups, then it is said to have been cross-validated. Once a scale has been developed, data from the normal controls can be used to obtain standard scores. It can then be determined how far above or below the mean of the normal group each new subject scores in standardized units. Thus, a subject's score on each scale can be converted to percentiles (see Chapter 2).

After a scale has been constructed and cross-validated, a third step in the criterion approach is typically employed. In this step, additional research is conducted in order to empirically ascertain what it means when subjects endorse a large number of items on a particular scale (for example, Svanum & Dallas, 1981). An independent group that scores two standard deviations above the mean on an aggression scale, for example, may be intensely studied to determine how they describe themselves, how others describe them, characteristics of their family background, and so on. Hence, when a person scores two standard deviations above the mean on a particular scale, it is known that the items endorsed by this individual were those that distinguished a criterion group from a control group and that high scores on this scale tend to be obtained by individuals who possess certain characteristics as indicated by empirical research.

Factor analytic strategy.   The factor analytic strategy uses the statistical procedure of factor analysis to empirically derive the basic dimensions of personality. As you will recall from Chapter 3, factor analysis is a technique for boiling down or reducing data to a small number of descriptive units or dimensions. A test, for example, may have two scales that correlate highly, such as hostility and aggression. The correlation between the two means that they overlap in what they measure—that is, they share common variance. Both, for example, may be related to characteristics of a paranoid personality, a personality problem characterized in part by aggression and hostility. The same test may also have two other scales, suspicion and defensiveness, factors also associated with the paranoid personality. These two scales may correlate not only with each other but also with the hostility and aggression scales. Thus, all four scales may overlap, or share common variance. If it can be shown that a substantial proportion of the variability in all four scales is related to some common factor, then a factor analyst would argue that the test actually has only one scale, which is related to the paranoid personality.

Factor analysts begin with an empirical data base consisting of the intercorrelation of a large number of items or tests. They then factor analyze these intercorrelations, typically in such a manner as to find the minimum number of areas of common variance to account for as much of the variability in the data as possible. They then attempt to label these factors by ascertaining what all the items related to a particular factor have in common.

II.   CRITERIA USED IN SELECTING TESTS FOR DISCUSSION

There are far too many structured personality tests to adequately discuss them all even in a book devoted exclusively to the subject let alone in a single chapter. (We prefer the term *tests* for general purposes, although for specific procedures other terms like *inventories*, *techniques*, *scales*, and *assessment procedures* are often preferred.) However, all available structured personality tests can be classified according to whether they use one or some combination of the four strategies discussed above: logical-content, theoretical, criterion-group, and factor analytic. We selected the tests included in the discussion that follows because they illustrate each of the major strategies and because of their (1) widespread use as indicated by surveys of psychological test usage in the United States (Lubin, Wallis, & Paine, 1971; Sundberg, 1961); (2) interest to the research community as determined by the number of references listed in the personality sections of the *Mental Measurements Yearbooks*; and (3) historical value as determined by the introduction of new concepts in structured personality testing. In selecting these criteria, we were guided by those used by Gynther and Gynther (1976) in their excellent overview of structured personality tests.

III.   THE LOGICAL-CONTENT STRATEGY

We begin our discussion with the first personality test ever developed, the Woodworth Personal Data Sheet. We then present two examples of early logical-content tests. The Mooney Problem Checklist is a relatively recent example of the logical-content approach.

A.   *Woodworth Personal Data Sheet*

The first personality inventory ever, the Woodworth Personal Data Sheet, was developed during World War I and published in its final form after the war (Woodworth, 1920). Its purpose was to identify military recruits likely to break down in combat. Prior to the Woodworth, military recruits were screened in psychiatric interviews. However, because of a shortage of psychiatrists, adequate interviewing of all applicants became impossible. This need for alternative screening methods was the impetus for the development of tests of personality.

The final form of the Woodworth contained 116 questions to which the individual responded "yes" or "no." The items were selected from lists of symptoms known to be related to emotional disorders and from the questions asked by psychiatrists in the conduct of their screening interviews. In effect, the scale was a paper-pencil psychiatric interview. The Woodworth consisted of questions similar to these: "Do you drink a fifth of whiskey a day?" "Do you wet the bed at night?" "Do you frequently daydream?" "Do you usually feel in good health?" "Do you usually sleep soundly at night?" The Woodworth yielded a single score, which provided a single global measure of functioning. Only those recruits reporting many symptoms were subsequently given an interview. In this way, the military was able to concentrate its efforts on the most likely candidates for rejection from service on the basis of emotional problems.

Although its items were selected through the logical-content approach, the Woodworth had two additional features. First, items that were endorsed by 25% or more of a normal sample in the scored direction were excluded from the test. This technique tended to reduce the number of false positives—that is, the number of subjects who would mark a number of items in the scored direction when, in fact, they were not risks and would most likely be cleared in an actual interview. Second, only those symptoms that occurred twice as often in a previously diagnosed neurotic group than in normals were included in the first version of the test.

The success of the Woodworth in solving the problem of mass screening provided a stimulus for the development of a host of structured tests (inventories) aimed at measuring personality characteristics. These tests borrowed items from each other, particularly the Woodworth, and used a variety of methods for clustering and scoring items. However, all were alike in that they assumed face validity of a test response.

B. Early multidimensional logical-content scales

Two of the better known early tests developed by using the logical-content strategy were the Bell Adjustment Inventory, which is still in clinical use (Lubin et al., 1971), and the Bernreuter Personality Inventory. The Bell Adjustment Inventory attempts to evaluate the subject's adjustment in a variety of areas such as home life, social life, and emotional functioning. The Bernreuter Personality Inventory could be used for subjects as young as 13 or 14 years old and included items related to six personality traits such as introversion, confidence, and sociability. The Bell and the Bernreuter were both first published in the 1930s, and both represented at least some advance over the Woodworth in that they produced more than one score. These multidimensional procedures were the forerunners of many modern tests, which yield a variety of scores rather than a single overall index.

C. Mooney Problem Checklist

Few modern tests rely on the logical-content method of test construction. Perhaps the most recent important example is the Mooney Problem Checklist, which was published in 1950. The Mooney contains a list of problems that reoccurred in clinical case history data and in the written statements of problems submitted by approximately 4000 high school students. It is like the Woodworth in that in clinical practice subjects who check an excessive number of items are considered to have difficulties. The major interpretive procedure is to assume face validity of a test response. Thus, if a subject puts a check by an item related to finances, it is assumed that the person is having financial difficulties.

D. Criticisms of the logical-content approach

Psychologists involved in the development of the Woodworth and the plethora of subsequent tests probably thought they had discovered a miracle. These tests proved extremely useful as screening devices and methods of obtaining information about a person without the necessity of an extensive interview. Before long, however, the weaknesses of the logical-content strategy became evident.

In assuming face validity of test items, the logical-content strategy also assumes that the subject takes a normal approach to the test, complies with the instructions, reads each item, and answers as honestly as possible. Even assuming the validity of these assumptions, subjects may not be capable of objectively evaluating their own behavior in the area covered by the test item (for example, "I never drink too much alcohol"). Even if subjects are capable of accurate self-evaluation, they still may not interpret the test item in the same way as the test constructor or test user, which is also an implicit assumption of the logical-content strategy.

A. Ellis (1946) argued that none of the above assumptions is necessarily true, and assuming that they are is certain to produce errors. Indeed, structured personality tests based on the logic of face validity were so sharply criticized (Landis, 1936; Landis, Zubin, & Katz, 1935; McNemar & Landis, 1935) that the entire structured approach to personality was all but discarded until it was finally rescued by the introduction of a new conceptualization in personality testing, the empirical criterion-group strategy (Dahlstrom, 1969a).

IV.   THE CRITERION-GROUP STRATEGY

Just when the development of an adequate structured personality test seemed nothing more than a pipe dream, the Minnesota Multiphasic Personality Inventory (MMPI) introduced a number of innovations in the construction of structured personality tests. The main idea—assume nothing about the meaning of a subject's response to a test item—though not entirely new, was the only possible way of meeting objections from critics of structured personality tests based on face validity. Since the logical-content approach had been beaten to death because of its many assumptions, developers of the MMPI argued that the meaning of a test response could be determined only through empirical research.

A.   *Minnesota Multiphasic Personality Inventory*

The MMPI is a 566-item true-false self-report questionnaire. Statements are typically of the self-reference type, such as "I like good food" and "I never have trouble falling to sleep." The subject is asked to mark "true" or "false" for each statement as it applies to himself or herself. The heart of the test consists of three major validity scales (the "cannot say" scale, which measures the number of items not responded to, is not included here as a major validity scale) and ten clinical scales. The validity scales provide information concerning the person's approach to testing, such as whether an attempt was made to fake bad by endorsing more items of pathological content than could be justified by any person's actual problems or whether an attempt was made to fake good by avoiding pathological items. The ten clinical scales were originally designed to identify psychological disorders, such as neurosis and schizophrenia. Today, the clinician uses the pattern of scores, codebooks that provide extensive research summaries on the meaning of test scores, and clinical judgment to assess the meaning of the clinical scales. As we discuss in greater detail later in the chapter, each of the three validity and ten clinical scales contains between 15 and 78 items. Subjects obtain a raw score on each scale based on the number of items marked in the scored direction. Raw scores are then converted to standardized scores, which are called *T*-scores, with a mean of 50 and a standard deviation of 10.

Forms.   The MMPI comes in a variety of forms. The Group Form lists the items in a reusable paper booklet, and the subject records the answers on a standard answer sheet. This form can be scored by hand or by machine. Form R is a hard-cover, spiral-bound booklet. A box form lists each item on a card and asks the subject to sort each card into "true," "false," and "cannot say" piles. There is also a standard tape recording of the MMPI items, which subjects can listen to. Some forms contain fewer than the full 566 items because only 399 items are actually used in the three major validity and ten clinical scales. The remaining items are for special scales and research purposes. Graham (1977) describes in detail the various MMPI forms and ordering information.

Purpose.   As with the Woodworth, the purpose of the MMPI is to assist in distinguishing normal from abnormal groups. Specifically, it was designed to aid in the diagnosis or assessment of the major psychiatric or psychological disorders, and, for the most part, it continues to be used for this purpose. According to the test manual (Hathaway & McKinley, 1967), the test can be used with persons 16 years of age or older who have had at least six years of schooling. However, care must be taken to make sure the individual can read at the sixth-grade level and has an IQ within normal limits. (See Focused Example 15-1.)

■ **FOCUSED EXAMPLE 15-1   READING THE MMPI**

In one interesting case that we had the opportunity to observe, a 16-year-old female was being detained by the juvenile court. Her mother reported her to the police, stating she could not be controlled. A few hours before her preliminary hearing, the judge requested psychological testing to aid in the assessment process. A psychology intern, who was inexperienced with the MMPI, was the only professional staff member available, and he tried to carry out the judge's orders himself by administering a quick MMPI. The intern warned the girl of the validity scales, stating that he could tell if she tried to fake. When she was presented with the test booklet, the girl groaned, stating "This test is too hard." The intern assured her not to worry, that there were no right or wrong answers. "Oh, I hope I pass," the girl said, "I'm not good at tests."

She finished moments before the time of her court hearing, after taking more than two hours rather than the usual hour required to complete the MMPI. The intern immediately scored it and found that she had marked nearly half of the 64 items in the scored direction on the F scale, one of the validity scales containing highly pathological content. Since the average for the general population on this scale is four items in the scored direction, with an average of eight items in the scored direction for delinquents, the girl's endorsement of 30 items clearly indicated she had not taken a normal approach to testing and suggested to the intern that she had faked by deliberately endorsing pathological items in order to appear disordered.

In court the judge asked the intern what the results showed. "I can't tell," said the intern, "because she tried to fake." "Did you fake?" asked the judge. "No sir," said the girl, "I swear I didn't." The judge told her to go back and take the test again.

Irate, the intern again warned the girl not to fake. "Oh, I hope I pass," she moaned. "Just answer truthfully and you'll pass," said the intern. She completed the test, and the intern immediately scored it. Results were almost identical to those for the previous testing. The intern rushed into the testing room and scolded the girl for faking again. "I knew I'd flunk that test," she said, "it was too hard for me." Finally it dawned on the intern to question whether she could read the test. A reading test revealed that she could read only at the fourth-grade level. Most of the items were therefore incomprehensible to her. The embarrassed intern was forced to go back into court and explain what had happened. No doubt he never again made the mistake of administering the MMPI when the subject's reading level was in doubt.

Development of the scales.   Beginning with a pool of 1000 items selected from a wide variety of sources, including case histories, psychological reports, textbooks, and existing tests, the authors of the test, S. R. Hathaway, a psychologist, and J. C. McKinley, a physician, finally selected 504 items that were judged to be relatively independent of each other. The scales were then determined empirically by presenting the items to criterion and control groups in order to find those items that distinguished the criterion groups from the controls.

The criterion groups used in the development of the MMPI consisted of psychiatric inpatients at the University of Minnesota Hospital. These psychiatric patients were divided into eight groups according to their psychiatric diagnoses. The original pool of psychiatric patients stood at 800, but this number was substantially reduced in order to find homogeneous groupings with sufficient agreement on diagnoses. The final eight criterion groups each consisted of about 50 patients: hypochondriacs, individuals preoccupied with the body and fears of illness; depressed patients; hysterics, primarily individuals who showed a physical problem with no physical cause, such as hysterical blindness; psychopathic deviates — delinquent, criminal, or antisocial individuals; paranoids, individuals who showed symptoms including poor reality testing (for example, delusions in which they falsely believed that people were plotting against them); psychasthenics, individuals with a neurotic disorder characterized by excessive doubts and unreasonable fears; schizophrenics, individuals with a psychotic disorder involving dramatic symptoms such as hallucinations (seeing things that aren't there) and thinking problems such as illogical reasoning; and hypomanics, individuals with a disorder characterized by hyperactivity and irritability.

Those in the criterion groups were then compared to about 700 controls consisting primarily of relatives and visitors of the patients in the University of Minnesota Hospital. The use of this control group has been among the greatest sources of criticism for the MMPI. Clearly there is little basis for calling the relatives of patients in a large city university hospital representative of the general population, although the control group was augmented by other subjects such as a group of recent high school graduates. Difficulties with its control group partially explain the failure of the MMPI to reliably identify disordered states.

Despite the weakness of the control group, the MMPI did provide a reference sample against which the criterion groups could be compared. After an item analysis was conducted, items that separated the criterion from control groups were included on one or more of the eight scales. To cross-validate the scales, independent samples of the criterion and control groups were administered the items. To qualify as cross-validated, a scale had to distinguish the criterion group from the control at the .05 level of significance.

In addition to the eight scales described above, two others were added: the masculinity-femininity (MF) scale, which contained items differentially endorsed by males and females, and the social-introversion (Si) scale, which was developed by Drake (1946) to identify outgoing individuals. These latter two scales plus the eight scales described above constitute the ten clinical scales of the MMPI.

Because the logical-content approach had been criticized for its many assumptions, Hathaway and McKinley developed validity scales to measure test-taking attitude and to assess whether the subject took a normal, honest approach to the test. The L, or lie, scale was rationally designed to detect individuals attempting to present themselves in an overly favorable way.

The K scale served the same purpose, but it was empirically constructed. In deriving the K scale, Hathaway and McKinley compared the MMPI scores of nondisturbed individuals showing normal patterns with the MMPI scores of individuals who were known to be disturbed but who produced normal MMPI patterns in that they showed no scales that deviated significantly from the mean. The K scale thus attempts to locate those items that distinguished normal from abnormal groups when both groups marked the test in such a way as to produce a normal pattern. It was assumed that pathological groups would produce normal patterns because of defensiveness, a tendency to hide or deny psychological problems, and that this defensiveness could be determined by comparing these individuals to nondisturbed normals.

The F scale, designed to detect individuals who attempt to fake bad, consists of those items endorsed by less than 10% of the control group. Of the 64 items on the F scale, most of which contain pathological content such as "Odd odors come to me at times," the average number of items endorsed in the scored direction is four. Clearly, anyone marking a lot of these items is taking an unusual approach to the test. Thus, high F scores bring the validity of the whole profile into question.

Finally, although it is referred to as a validity scale, the "cannot say" scale consists simply of the items to which the subject failed to respond either "true" or "false." If as few as 10% of the items are omitted, the entire profile becomes invalid. As a result, many present-day clinicians discourage the subject from omitting items because providing the option produces little useful information and can easily lead to a completely invalid profile.

Initial interpretations.   For all the scales, the control group provided the reference for which standard scores (T-scores) were determined. With a mean of 50 and standard deviation of 10 for each scale, scores on each scale could be directly compared, and each scale could be interpreted as a percentile. Subjects with T-scores of 50 were thus at the mean of the control sample; T-scores of 70, two standard deviations above the mean, were considered significantly elevated.

The original approach taken in MMPI interpretation was simple and straightforward. Because the scales significantly discriminated the criterion from control groups and withstood the test of cross validation, most users assumed that individuals with characteristics similar to those of a criterion group would produce significant elevation on the appropriate scale. Schizophrenics, for example, would show significant elevation on the schizophrenia scale, hysterics would show elevation on the hysteria scale, and so on. Unfortunately, this turned out to be a false assumption. Experience with the MMPI rapidly revealed that few subjects showed elevation on only a single scale. When elevation did occur, it was found in two, three, four, or even in all the scales. Thus, there was a problem: What did the test mean when someone showed elevation on the hysteria, psychopathic deviate, schizophrenia, and hypomania scales? There is no such thing as a hysterical psychopathic hypomanic schizophrenic.

The failure of the MMPI to identify psychological disorders by producing simple, neat elevations on a single scale led to the use of pattern, or configural, analysis, which the test authors (Hathaway & McKinley, 1943) had originally suggested. This change led to an avalanche of studies and proposals for identifying clinical groups on the basis of patterns of MMPI scores (Meehl & Dahlstrom, 1960; Henrichs, 1964; Taulbee & Sisson, 1957). However, early investigations (Garfield & Sineps, 1959; Loy, 1959) as well as more recent investigations (Fowler & Coyle, 1969; Meikle & Gerritse, 1970) revealed the futility of this approach. Either the rules were so complex that only an extremely small portion of the profiles met the criteria, as for the Gilberstadt and Duker (1965) rules, or the rules led to diagnoses that were no more accurate than those made by untrained nonprofessionals (Meehl, 1954, 1956, 1957; Meehl & Rosen, 1955).

Meehl's extension of the empirical approach.   Even before the weight of evidence began documenting the failure of the MMPI to reliably identify individuals in the various diagnostic categories, regardless of whether one scale or a pattern of scale elevation was used in the evaluation, the MMPI and the criterion-group approach to personality assessment were rescued by Paul Meehl. Pointing to the possible advantages of analyzing the two highest scales showing elevation, known as the two-point code, Meehl (1951) began to emphasize the importance of conducting research on individuals who showed specific two-point codes and other configural patterns in order to empirically determine the meaning of MMPI elevations. Thus, having failed to work as anticipated, the MMPI was salvaged by finding homogeneous profile patterns and determining the characteristics of individuals showing these patterns. In other words, new criterion groups could be established consisting of individuals grouped on the basis of similarities in their MMPI profiles. In this approach the characteristics of a criterion group consisting of subjects who showed elevation on two scales (for example, the psychopathic deviate and hypomania scales) could be empirically determined. The difference in approach meant that MMPI configural patterns, rather than psychiatric diagnosis, became the criterion for the selection of homogeneous criterion groups.

Because the original idea of the contrasted-group method was abandoned in favor of finding criterion groups based on MMPI patterns and then studying these groups, we use the term criterion-group strategy rather than contrasted-group strategy to describe the MMPI and related tests. The more recent approach does not attempt to distinguish the criterion group from a control group. Instead, the characteristics of the criterion groups are evaluated through empirical means such as peer ratings, physician ratings, and demographic characteristics. The upshot has been an eruption of studies describing the characteristics of individuals showing certain MMPI patterns. Manuals such as the MMPI handbook (Dahlstrom, Welsh, & Dahlstrom, 1972, 1975) and other MMPI books (for example, Marks, Seeman, & Haller, 1974) summarize these studies.

In conjunction with his proposed extension of the empirical approach to personality assessment, Meehl and others (Hathaway, 1947; Welsh, 1948) began to advocate a change in the names of the scales. Since elevation of the schizophrenia scale did not necessarily mean the person was schizophrenic, the use of such a name was awkward as well as confusing. They therefore suggested that the scales be called by number rather than name. Table 15-2 lists the scales by their number. Only clinical scales were given numbers; validity scales retained their original names.

TABLE 15-2 MMPI scales

Symbol currently in use	Old Name	Number of items in scale*	Common interpretation of elevation
Validity scales			
L	Lie Scale	15	Naive attempt to fake good
K	K Scale	30	Defensiveness
F	F Scale	64	Attempt to fake bad
Clinical scales			
1	Hypochondriasis	33	Physical complaints
2	Depression	60	Depression
3	Hysteria	60	Immaturity
4	Psychopathic deviate	50	Authority conflict
5	Masculinity-femininity	60	Masculine or feminine interests
6	Paranoia	40	Suspicion, hostility
7	Psychasthenia	48	Anxiety
8	Schizophrenia	78	Alienation, withdrawal
9	Hypomania	46	Elated mood, high energy
0	Social introversion	70	Introversion, shyness

*Because of item overlap, the total number of items here is 654.

Note: The validity scales (L, K, and F) determine the individual's approach to testing (normal or honest, fake bad, fake good). Of the ten clinical scales, two were developed rationally (5 and 0). The remaining eight scales were developed through the criterion-group method. Numerous interpretive hypotheses can be associated with each MMPI scale. However, the meaning of any MMPI scale depends on the characteristics of the subject (age, race, sex, socioeconomic status, education, IQ, and so forth).

With the use of numbers, MMPI patterns could now be given a numerical code. For each of the two most commonly used coding systems (Hathaway, 1947; Welsh, 1948), the clinical scales are listed in rank order from highest *T*-score to lowest. A symbol is then used to indicate the level of elevation. In Welsh's (1948) system, for example, *T*-scores of 90 (four standard deviations above the mean) and greater are designated by *; *T*-scores between 80 and 89 are designated by "; *T*-scores between 70 and 79, by '; *T*-scores between 60 and 69, by −; and so on for each ten-point interval down to # placed to the right of *T*-scores below 29. For example, the code 13* 2" 7' 46890− means that Scales 1 and 3 have *T*-scores above 90, Scale 2 above 80, Scale 7 above 70, and the remaining scales between 60 and 69. This pattern would be referred to as a one-three two-point pattern or, more simply, a 13 code, based on the two highest scales.

Psychometric properties.   Dahlstrom and Welsh (1960, pp. 472–474) evaluated the *reliability* of the MMPI. The results they report are not overly encouraging. For intervals of less than one year, test-retest reliability coefficients range from the low .50s to the low .90s (median .80s) for psychiatric patients. For test-retest intervals of four years or more, however, a considerable drop occurs, with a range of .13 to .54 (median .30) for high school students and a range of .16 to .73 (median .40) for college students. Proponents of the MMPI have argued that high reliability is not to be expected from the MMPI because it measures psychiatric conditions that change with treatment. Indeed, Scale 2 in particular, the depression scale, has been shown to change following successful treatment with psychotherapy (Bergin, 1971). Nevertheless, long-term reliability figures are better for psychiatric groups than for nonpsychiatric groups. Given the relative absence of psychological disorders in nonpsychiatric groups, stability figures for the MMPI are disappointingly poor. Like test-retest coefficients, split-half reliability coefficients, which range all the way from .05 to .96 (median .70s), have done little to provide firm support for the reliability of the MMPI.

Another factor to consider in evaluating the psychometric adequacy of the MMPI is the *composition of the scales*. Because of the way in which scales were originally constructed, many items are on more than one scale and some items are on as many as six. Scale 8, which has more items than any other scale (78 items), contains only 16 unique items (Dahlstrom et al., 1972, p. 232).

Perhaps as a result of item overlap, *intercorrelations among the clinical scales* are extremely high. For example, Scales 7 and 8 correlate between .64 and .87 depending on the sample studied (Dahlstrom & Welsh, 1960). This high incorrelation among the scales has led to a number of factor analytic studies (Dahlstrom & Welsh, 1960; Dahlstrom et al., 1972, 1975; Welsh, 1956; Block, 1965), which consistently show that only two factors account for most of the variance of the ten MMPI scales. These factors have been variously labeled throughout the literature. Because of the high intercorrelations among the scales and results from factor analytic studies, the validity of pattern analysis is questionable.

Still another psychometric problem with the MMPI is the *imbalance in the way items are keyed*. Many individuals approach structured tests with a *response style*, or bias, which is a tendency to mark an item in a certain way irrespective of content. One of these tendencies is *acquiescence*, the tendency to agree or to endorse an item as true. Given the possibility of response tendencies, one would expect an equal number of items in the keyed direction for the categories "true" and "false." Not so; all the items on the L scale and 29 of the 30 items on the K scale are keyed false. Scales 7, 8, and 9 are keyed on a 3:1 true-false ratio.

Major works devoted to the MMPI (Dahlstrom & Welsh, 1960; Dahlstrom et al., 1972; Hathaway & McKinley, 1967) strongly emphasize the importance of taking into account the *demographic characteristics of the subjects* in interpreting profiles. This advice is indeed warranted in that most of the studies have shown that age (Gynther & Shimkunas, 1966; J. T. Webb, 1970), sex (Aaronson, 1958; J. T. Webb, 1970), race (Gynther, 1972; Gynther, Fowler, & Erdberg, 1971; Strauss, Gynther, & Wallhermfechtel, 1974), place of residence (Erdberg, 1969), and other demographic factors such as intelligence, education, and socioeconomic status (Gynther & Shimkunas, 1965; S. E. Nelson, 1952; Thumin, 1969) are all related to the MMPI scales. This overwhelming evidence supporting the covariation between demographic factors and the meaning of MMPI scores clearly shows that two exact MMPI profile patterns can have quite different meanings depending on the demographic characteristics of each subject.

The major source of *validity* for the MMPI comes from the multitude of research studies that describe the characteristics of particular profile patterns. Volume II of the revised MMPI handbook (Dahlstrom et al., 1975), for example, cites approximately 6000 studies with the number of new studies increasing every year (for example, Bennett & Schubert, 1981; Conley, 1981). This body of research provides ample evidence of the construct validity of the MMPI. Indeed, it is primarily the existence of this huge body of data that has allowed the MMPI to survive despite its poor showing when subjected to rigorous psychometric analysis.

A number of studies, for example, have related MMPI response patterns to alcoholism. In fact, some evidence indicates that the MMPI might be useful in the early detection of individuals who later become alcoholics (Hoffman, Loper, & Kammeier, 1974; Kammeier, Hoffman, & Loper, 1973; Loper, Kammeier, & Hoffman, 1973). The MMPI was administered to a group of men while they were still in college. The original MMPI response patterns of those individuals who later became alcoholic were compared to those of a control group who did not become alcoholic. Results showed that the subjects who eventually became alcoholic had significantly higher scores on one validity scale (F) and two clinical scales (4 and 9). Thus, these scales may be related to characteristics that contribute or lead to alcoholism in males. Interestingly, the original MMPI response pattern of those in the alcoholic group was the same as their retest pattern after they had become alcoholic.

Current status.   Rodgers (1972) calls the MMPI a "psychometric nightmare." Indeed, the inadequacies of the MMPI in the representativeness and size of its normative sample, in the item overlap among the scales, in the imbalance in true-false keying, in the high intercorrelation among the scales, in the relatively poor reliability, and in the lack of generalizability across demographic variables justify such a characterization. However, because of the wide body of empirical results concerning the meaning of the MMPI scores, the test continues to thrive. The test is obviously of practical value to the clinician. Despite its drawbacks and the development of a multitude of new tests based on other strategies, the MMPI continues to be used more than any other test in the field of structured personality measures (Lubin et al., 1971). Even though the test seemed to fail miserably in its original purpose, clinical practitioners prefer to use it to evaluate psychological disorders, in part because so many MMPI studies have been summarized and are readily available to assist in making use of the scores. The widespread and persistent use of the MMPI is also due to the fact that results from the MMPI are typically viewed as hypotheses to be verified or ruled out by other sources of data (Graham, 1977). Thus, the MMPI has evolved as one of the critical elements in a battery of tests typically consisting of an interview, intelligence measure, projective test (see Chapter 17), and the MMPI. The MMPI also has clinical utility in that, with experience, a clinician can develop an idea of what a schizophrenic or neurotic MMPI pattern looks like in a particular population (of hospitalized inpatients, for example). In short, despite its weaknesses, the MMPI continues to be used more than any other structured personality test, most likely because it leads all other structured tests in the amount of research devoted to its validation. We therefore believe the emphasis on the MMPI in this chapter is justified, and, despite keen competition, it will take some time before the MMPI is replaced as the primary structured personality assessment tool.

B.   *California Psychological Inventory*

The CPI (Gough, 1957, 1969) is second only to the MMPI in popularity as a structured personality test constructed primarily by the criterion-group strategy. For 11 of the 18 CPI scales, criterion groups (for example, males versus females; homosexual males versus heterosexual males) were contrasted to produce measures of personality that were categorized into four classes: Class 1, interpersonal effectiveness; Class 2, intrapersonal controls; Class 3, academic orientation; and Class 4, attitudes toward life (Gough, 1968).

More than a third of the 480 items are almost identical to items in the MMPI, and many others are quite similar to MMPI items (Megargee, 1972). However, the test does more than share items with the MMPI. Like the MMPI, the CPI shows considerable intercorrelation among its scales. Factor analytic studies have shown that two factors associated with internal controls (Class 2 scales) and interpersonal effectiveness (Class 1 scales) account for a large part of the variance (Megargee, 1972). Also as in the MMPI, true-false scale keying is often extremely unbalanced. Furthermore, reliability coefficients are not much more impressive than those reported for the MMPI (Megargee, 1972). Short-term test-retest coefficients range from .49 to .90 depending on the sample; long-term coefficients range from .38 to .77 (Megargee, 1972). In addition, the method used to establish some criterion groups has been questioned. For example, for some of the scales subjects were placed in criterion groups on the basis of ratings by friends.

The advantage of the CPI is that it can be used with normal subjects. The MMPI is generally not appropriate with normal subjects, and the meaning of nonelevated profiles is not well established. Therefore, if the intent is to assess normal individuals for interpersonal effectiveness and internal controls, the CPI is a good candidate for the measure. Goldberg (1972b) goes so far as to say that the CPI is probably as useful or more useful than any comparable existing instrument. Furthermore, as with the MMPI, a considerable body of literature has focused on the CPI. Each new piece of literature extends the utility of the test and adds to its construct validity. Therefore, the future of the CPI as a measure of normal personalities has some potential despite its limitations as noted by critics such as R. L. Thorndike (1959) and Walsh (1972).

V. THE FACTOR ANALYTIC STRATEGY

Structured personality tests, as they exist today, share one common set of assumptions. These assumptions, simply stated, are that humans possess characteristics or traits that exhibit themselves across situations (are stable); vary from individual to individual; and can be measured. Nowhere are these assumptions better illustrated than in the factor analytic strategy of test construction.

As you will recall, factor analysis is a statistical procedure for reducing the redundancy in a set of intercorrelated scores. For example, one major technique of factor analysis, the principal-components method (Hotelling, 1933), finds the minimum number of common factors to account for an interrelated set of scores. As noted in the previous section, two factors can account for most of the variance in both the CPI and MMPI, which suggests that these tests are actually measuring only two unique components and that all scales are related to these two components.

The advantages of factor analysis are quite evident. However, prior to the advent of the high-speed computer, even simple factor analyses required several weeks and even several months of tedious arithmetic operations on a hand calculator. Therefore, the development of the factor analytic strategy awaited the technological refinement of computers. One individual, R. B. Cattell, has distinguished himself in using the factor analytic strategy of structured personality assessment; his work is the focus of this section.

A. Guilford's pioneer efforts

One usual strategy in validating a new test is to correlate the scores on the new test with the scores on other tests purporting to measure the same entity. J. P. Guilford's approach was related to this procedure; however, instead of individually comparing one test to a series of other tests, Guilford and his associates determined the interrelationship (intercorrelation) of a wide variety of tests and then factor analyzed the findings in an effort to find the major underlying dimensions common to all personality tests. If results from existing personality tests could be reduced to only a few factors, then items correlating highly with these factors could be used in a new test that would capture the major dimensions of personality.

The result of the initial attempt to apply this strategy was a series of inventories, which Guilford and his associates published in the 1940s (the STDCR, Guilford, 1940; the GAMIN, Guilford & Martin, 1943; the Temperament Survey, Guilford & Zimmerman, 1949). These procedures were ultimately collapsed into a single scale, the Guilford-Zimmerman Temperament Survey (Guilford & Zimmerman, 1956).

The Guilford-Zimmerman Temperament Survey reduces personality to ten dimensions, each of which is measured by 30 different items (Guilford, 1959). The ten dimensions are general activity, restraint, ascendance (leadership), sociability, emotional stability, objectivity, friendliness, thoughtfulness, personal relations, and masculinity. The test presents a list of statements, most of which are self-statements as in the MMPI, and the subject's task is to indicate "yes" or "no" for each statement. Three validity, or verification, keys are included to detect falsification and to evaluate the validity of the profile, as in the MMPI. Standard scores were obtained from college group reference samples, and split-half reliabilities are good, ranging from .75 to .85. However, this first major factor analytic structured personality test failed to catch on, perhaps because it was overshadowed by the MMPI and also because of the arbitrary, subjective way of naming factors. The Guilford-Zimmerman Temperament Survey is now primarily of only historical interest.

B.   *Cattell's contribution*

Rather than attempt to uncover the major dimensions of personality by intercorrelating personality tests, R. B. Cattell began with all the adjectives applicable to human beings in order to empirically determine and measure the essence of personality. Beginning with a monumental catalog of all the adjectives (trait names) applying to humans in an unabridged dictionary, Allport and Odbert (1936) reduced their list to 4504 "real" traits. Adding to the list traits found in the psychological and psychiatric literature, Cattell then reduced the list to 171 terms that he believed accounted for the meaning of all items on the original list. College students then rated their friends on these 171 terms, and the results were intercorrelated and factor analyzed. The 171 terms were reduced to 36 dimensions, which were called *surface traits* (R. B. Cattell, 1957). Subsequent investigation through factor analysis finally produced 16 distinct factors that accounted for all the variables. Thus, Cattell had reduced personality to 16 basic dimensions, which he called *source traits*.

The product of Cattell's marathon task was the Sixteen Personality Factor Questionnaire, better known as the 16PF (R. B. Cattell, 1949), which was subsequently revised based on continued factor analysis (Cattell, Eber, & Tat-suoka, 1970). Consistent with the factor analytic strategy, items that correlated highly with each of the 16 major factors, or source traits, were included, and those with relatively low correlations were excluded.

Great care was taken in the standardization of the 16PF. Separate norms were provided for males alone, females alone, and males and females combined for each of three groups: U.S. adults, college students, and high school seniors. Thus, nine sets of norms are available. To further deal with the covariation of structured personality test data and demographic variables that plagues the MMPI, the 16PF provides age corrections for scales that significantly change with age. Six forms of the test are available, two parallel forms for each of three levels of vocabulary proficiency, ranging from newspaper-literate adults through the educationally disadvantaged. For the educationally disadvantaged, a tape-recorded (oral) form is also available. Norms for the various forms are based on more than 15,000 subjects, representative of geographic area, population densi-ty, age, family income, and race according to figures provided by the U.S. census.

Unlike the MMPI and CPI, the 16PF contains no item overlap, and keying is balanced among the various alternative responses. Short-term test-retest correla-tion coefficients for the 16 source traits are impressive, with a range of .65 to .93 and a median coefficient of .83. Long-term test-retest coefficients, however, which range from .21 to .64, are not so impressive. Also a bit disappointing are the correlations between the various forms, which range from a low of .16 to a high of .79, with median coefficients in the .50s and .60s depending on which forms are correlated. For whatever reason, it may be that measures of human personality are limited in long-term stability. If it cannot be shown that per-sonality tests can produce good long-term stability coefficients, then the whole trait approach is open to question, and those who advocate the situation as the determinant of human personality would be supported. Despite the method used for deriving factors, the 16 source traits of the 16PF do intercorrelate, with some correlations as high as .75 (Cattell et al., 1970). To deal with this overlap, the 16 factors themselves were factor analyzed, which resulted in four second-order factors. Scores can be obtained for these second-order factors. Analysis of the psychometric properties of the 16PF thus reflects the effort Cattell and his colleagues have made in attempting to provide a psychometrically sound in-strument.

Other important features of the test are its provision of a parallel inventory for ages 12 to 18, the Jr. Sr. High School Personality Questionnaire, and still another parallel extension for use with children 8 to 12, the Children's Per-sonality Questionnaire. Cross-cultural studies have been conducted in Western Europe, Eastern Europe, the Middle East, Australia, and Canada (Gynther & Gynther, 1976). Furthermore, various research investigations have supported the validity of Cattell's personality test (Cattell et al., 1970). To extend the test to assessment of clinical populations, items related to psychological disorders have been factor analyzed (Cattell & Bolton, 1969; Delhees & Cattell, 1971a), resulting in 12 new factors in addition to the 16 needed to measure normal personalities. These new factors were then used in the construction of a clinical instrument, the Clinical Analysis Questionnaire (CAQ) (Delhees & Cattell, 1971b).

Cattell and his colleagues are to be commended for their innovative and persistent efforts to provide a psychometrically sound, objective test of personality. Although the 16PF is not so well established as the MMPI because it is newer and was originally designed to measure normal rather than abnormal personality, if any existing test is to replace the MMPI, one good candidate would be the family of tests originating from, and including, the 16PF.

VI. THE THEORETICAL STRATEGY

Despite the outstanding efforts of Cattell in using the factor analytic strategy to determine the major dimensions of personality and to eliminate many of the psychometric problems of tests devised by using the logical-content and criterion-group strategies, the factor analytic strategy is also not without criticism. One major criticism of factor analytic approaches is the subjective nature of the process of naming factors. To understand this problem, it is necessary to understand that each score on any given set of tests or variables can be broken down into three components: common variance, unique variance, and error variance. *Common variance* is the amount of variance a particular variable holds in common with other variables. Common variance results from overlap between what two or more variables are measuring. *Unique variance* is highly specific and refers to factors uniquely measured by the variable. In other words, unique variance refers to some factor measured only by the variable in question. *Error variance* is variance attributable to error. Factor analytic procedures generally identify sources of common variance at the expense of unique variance. Thus, important factors may be overlooked when the data are categorized solely on the basis of blind groupings by computers. Furthermore, all the computer can do is identify the groupings. The factor analyst must determine what factors these groupings measure, and there are no definite criteria or rules for naming factors. If five items such as daring, outgoing, determined, excitable, and fearless load high on a factor, what should this factor be called? In factor analysis, your name for this factor has about as much validity as anybody else's.

To avoid the potential disagreement and biases stemming from factor analytic approaches, structured personality tests guided in their construction by theory have been proposed. In this approach, items are selected to measure the variables or constructs specified by a major theory of personality. After items have been selected and grouped into scales, a construct-validity approach is taken. Presumably, predictions are made concerning the nature of the scale, and, if the predictions hold up, the scale is supported.

A. *Edwards Personal Preference Schedule*

One of the most well-known examples of a structured personality test developed by using the theoretical strategy is the Edwards Personal Preference Schedule (EPPS) (A. L. Edwards, 1954, 1959). (Again, we use the term *test* in the general sense. According to Edwards, the EPPS is not a test in the strict sense because there are no right or wrong answers.) The EPPS is used extensively in counseling centers (Lubin et al., 1971) and has been researched more than any other personality inventory except for the MMPI (Gynther & Gynther, 1976, p. 247). In addition to illustrating the theoretical strategy, the EPPS illustrates some interesting concepts in personality test construction, such as the concept of ipsative scores, which we discuss later.

The theoretical basis for the EPPS is the need system proposed by Murray (1938), which has probably been the most influential theory in personality test construction to date. Among the human needs proposed by Murray are the need to accomplish (achievement), the need to conform (deference), and the need for attention (exhibition). In developing the EPPS, Edwards selected 15 needs from Murray's list and constructed items with content validity for each of these needs.

Having selected items based on theory, Edwards was able to avoid the blind, subjective, and atheoretical approaches of other strategies. However, he was still faced with the perpetual problems of response styles and biases, problems the MMPI had dealt with by including special scales to detect faking or unusual test-taking approaches. Edwards was especially concerned with faking and *social desirability*, the tendency to say good things about yourself or to mark items that you believe will be approved by the examiner, irrespective of accuracy.

To deal with these sources of bias, Edwards attempted to rate each of his items on social desirability. He then formed pairs of items that were comparable in social desirability and required subjects to select the one item in the pair that was more characteristic of their likes or feelings. Subjects cannot simply provide the socially desirable or expected response because each item in the pair is presumably equal on social desirability. There is also not much point in faking— that is, selecting the less characteristic item. In addition, there is no problem of balancing scored items, such as is presented by the true-false imbalance of the MMPI.

As a further check on the validity of EPPS results, Edwards included a consistency scale, consisting of 15 pairs of statements repeated in identical form. In other words, of the 210 pairs of statements, only 195 are different. The 15 pairs occurring twice are presented more or less randomly throughout the test. With this format, the number of times a subject makes the identical choice can be converted to a percentile based on normative data. The EPPS also permits an analysis of within-subject consistency, which consists of the correlation of odd and even scores in the 15 scales.

Norms for the EPPS were based on over 1500 college men and women and approximately 9000 adults from the general population selected from urban and rural areas in 48 states. Separate normative data are available for each of these two groups as well as for high school students. For a given raw score on each of the 15 scales, a percentile can be immediately obtained from the pro-file sheet.

To better understand the EPPS, you should bear in mind that in construct-ing it, Edwards listed items for each of the scales and then paired them with items from the other 14 scales. When subjects make a choice, they are selecting between one of two needs. In other words, in each choice a subject is selecting one need at the expense of another. With this procedure, it becomes possible to express the selection of items on one scale relative to the selection of items on another in order to produce an *ipsative score*. Ipsative scores present results in relative terms rather than as absolute totals. The implication is that two individ-uals with identical relative, or ipsative, scores may differ markedly in the absolute strength of a particular need. Ipsative scores compare the individual against himself or herself and produce data that reflect the relative strength of each need for that person; each person thus provides his or her own frame of reference (see Mullins, Weeks, & Wilbourn, 1978).

Although only short-term (one-week) test-retest reliability figures are pre-sented in the manual, the coefficients, which range from .74 to .88, are quite respectable. Split-half reliabilities, which range from .60 to .87 as reported in the manual, although not as impressive, are satisfactory. Furthermore, intercorrela-tions among the scales are lower than for either the MMPI or 16PF, ranging between $-.34$ and .46.

The EPPS indeed has a number of interesting features. Its forced-choice method, which requires subjects to select one of two items rather than to respond "true" or "false" ("yes" or "no") to a single item, is an interesting solution to the problem of faking and other sources of bias. Because each subject provides his or her own frame of reference, the relative strength of needs, as well as the internal consistency for each individual subject, can be determined. Item content follows established theoretical lines. The 15 identical pairs aid in the evaluation of the validity of the profile. Norms are based on large samples and are available for adults from the general population as well as for high school and college students. Ipsative scores based on these norms can be converted to percentiles. Reliability data are adequate for the short term, and the 15 scales of the EPPS have lower intercorrelations than do the scales of the major tests developed by using factor analytic and criterion-group strategies. Last, but not least, the test is among the most researched of the personality inventories and is used extensively in applied settings.

Despite its impressive features and extensive use and the widespread interest it has engendered, the EPPS has not been well received by reviewers. Radcliffe (1965), Stricker (1965), and Heilbrun (1972) have all been critical. Part of the problem is that studies have shown that, like other structured personality tests, the EPPS can be faked in spite of its forced-choice procedure (Dicken, 1959). Other data raise questions concerning the test's ability to adequately control social-desirability effects (Feldman & Corah, 1960; N. Wiggins, 1966). The appropriateness of converting ipsative scores, which are relative, to normative percentiles is also questionable. Gynther and Gynther (1976) believe the major problem with the EPPS is the rather meager data in support of its validity. Although a number of studies have attempted to discriminate among a variety of groups (for example, smokers vs. nonsmokers) with the EPPS, the EPPS has a "paucity" of nontest correlates (Gynther & Gynther, 1976), and little is being done to correct the problem.

Since the first attempts at test construction, the major spirit has been one of gradual improvements following criticism and the identification of problems. The EPPS seems to have originated in this spirit, and it is unfortunate that efforts are not being made to improve it. Many more validity studies are needed (Stricker, 1965), and a new revision is long overdue (Heilbrun, 1972).

B. *Personality Research Form*

A result of a recent attempt to use the theoretical strategy in constructing a structured personality test is the Personality Research Form (PRF) (Jackson, 1967). Like the EPPS, the PRF was based on Murray's (1938) theory of needs. However, unlike Edwards, the constructors of the PRF developed specific definitions of each need. In this way, items for each scale could be as independent as possible, an important consideration in creating homogeneous scales. To further increase homogeneity of scales, over 100 items were tentatively written for each scale and were administered to over 1000 college students. Biserial correlational analysis then located items that correlated highest with the proposed scale while at the same time showing relatively low correlations with other scales, particularly social desirability. In other words, strict definitional standards and statistical procedures were used in conjunction with the theoretical approach. This use of a combination of procedures is the latest trend in personality test construction.

To aid in the assessment of validity, a scale analogous to the F scale of the MMPI was constructed. Like the MMPI F scale, the PRF infrequency scale consists of items with low endorsement rates for a standard sample. Thus, high rates of endorsement on this scale throw doubt on the validity of the results. A social-desirability scale similar to the K scale of the MMPI is also included. Two sets of parallel forms (four forms in all) as well as a form based on the best items from other forms were developed.

Items are presented in a true-false format but are balanced in true-false keying. Unlike the scales of the MMPI, the PRF scales have no item overlap. Furthermore, scales are relatively independent, with most intercorrelation coefficients at ±.30 (Gynther & Gynther, 1976).

Internal-consistency coefficients reported in the manual (Jackson, 1967) are extremely good, with a range of .80 to .94 (median .92). Factor analytic studies (Jackson, 1970) have supported the validity of the PRF. Furthermore, many studies have supported the test's construct validity (Edwards & Abbott, 1973; Trott & Morf, 1972) as well as predictive validity (Kusyszyn, 1968).

Because it is a relatively new instrument, it is difficult to assess the future of the PRF. Clearly it possesses sound psychometric properties, which perhaps accounts for its preponderance of favorable reviews (Anastasi, 1972a; E.L. Kelly, 1972; J. S. Wiggins, 1973). In any case, by combining theory with rigorous statistical procedures, the PRF appears to have established a new trend in the construction of structured personality tests.

VII.   SUMMARY

Structured personality tests are self-report procedures that provide statements to which the subject either must respond "true" or "false" ("yes" or "no") or must choose the most characteristic of two or more alternatives. These tests are highly structured and provide a definite, unambiguous stimulus for the subject. Scoring is straightforward and usually involves the summing of the number of items marked in a scored direction.

The original pressure to develop personality tests came from the demands created by World War I for a screening instrument to identify emotionally unstable recruits who might break down under the pressures of combat. The initial structured personality instrument, the Woodworth Personal Data Sheet, was based on a logical-content strategy in which items were interpreted in terms of face validity.

Not long after their appearance, tests based on the logical-content strategy fell into disrepute. The problem with these tests was the numerous assumptions underlying them. Included in these assumptions were that the subject complies with the instructions and provides an honest response; that the subject understands the items and is an accurate observer capable of evaluating his or her own behavior and responding in a nondefensive manner; and that the subject, test constructor, and test interpreter all define the questions in the same way. A review by A. Ellis (1946) seriously questioned each of these assumptions.

The first major advance in structured personality assessment came with the MMPI, which employed a strategy involving criterion groups. In this criterion-group strategy, groups possessing known characteristics were contrasted with a control population. Items that distinguished the criterion group were included in a scale that was then cross-validated on an independent sample of criterion and control subjects. The MMPI revitalized structured personality tests. It made no assumptions about the meaning of a subject's response to a test item but rather attempted to empirically discern its meaning. In the criterion-group strategy, the content of the item is irrelevant. If a subject marks "true" to the statement "I hear loud voices when I'm alone," it is not assumed that he or she hears loud voices when alone.

In addition to its advantages over logical-content tests in avoiding assumptions, the MMPI had the added feature of validity scales. The two most important MMPI validity scales are the K scale, which measures social desirability, and the F scale, which consists of 64 infrequently endorsed items to pick out subjects taking an unusual or unconventional approach to testing. Theoretically, excessively high scores on the validity scales can be used to identify biased results, thus avoiding the problems of faking and social desirability inherent in the logical-content approach.

Despite its extensive use and the widespread interest in it by researchers, the MMPI has been described as a psychometric nightmare. Among its problems are an inadequate normative sample, both in size and representativeness; extreme item overlap among the scales; an imbalance in true-false keying; high intercorrelation among the scales; poor long-term reliability coefficients; and lack of generalizability across demographic variables.

The factor analytic strategy of test construction has been used in an effort to overcome some of the problems inherent in the criterion strategy. Factor analytic strategies attempt to find areas of common variance in order to locate the minimum number of variables or factors that account for a set of intercorrelated data. R. B. Cattell has been the most important representative of this approach.

Employing the factor analytic approach to find the common variance of all trait-descriptive terms in the dictionary, Cattell reduced an original item pool of over 4000 items to 16 and created the 16PF. Great care was taken to provide adequate norms. Nine separate normative samples based on demographic variables, plus an age-correction scale, are available. Also available are three sets of parallel forms for individuals of varying levels of vocabulary proficiency.

The EPPS has found its primary use in counseling centers. It employs a forced-choice strategy that requires subjects to choose the more applicable of two statements. Ipsative scores, which use the subject as his or her own frame of reference, express results in terms of the relative strength of a need.

16

Tests for Choosing Careers

Learning objectives

When you have completed this chapter, you should be able to do the following:

1. Describe the use of the criterion-keying method in the development of the SVIB.
2. List some of the criticisms of the SVIB.
3. Describe how the SCII improved on the SVIB.
4. Describe how the KOIS differs from the SVIB and SCII.
5. Outline some of the controversial issues in interest measurement.
6. Compare the approaches to career placement taken by Osipow, Super, and Roe.
7. State why it is important to study the characteristics of work environments.
8. Discuss several ways in which work environment can affect behavior.
9. List several methods of job analysis.
10. Describe the template-matching method of assessment.

At age 35, Harry found himself faced with a dilemma. He had studied hard for many years to become a dentist, but what he had known for many years was becoming obvious—he really did not like dentistry. Although Harry had chosen dentistry as an occupation, he had not given detailed consideration to what the practice of dentistry was like before making a commitment to the field.

Harry could trace his interest in becoming a dentist to an experience he had during his childhood. As a young boy he liked to play golf, and, while on the course one day, Harry met a dentist who explained that the practice of dentistry was lucrative and that it still allowed practitioners enough time to play golf and engage in other activities. Harry was a good student and the encounter with the golfer-dentist made him think that dentistry would afford him the ideal lifestyle. Harry liked his science classes when he entered college, and he continued to be an outstanding student. After four years in a state university, he was accepted by a good dental school.

In dental school Harry began to question his career choice for the first time. Two things became apparent by the end of his third year. First, he did not really enjoy doing dental work. He found himself uneasy when his patients fussed in the chair, and he disliked subjecting people to the discomfort associated with the dental procedures. Second, Harry discovered that he was not interested in the same things as were other people in the field of dentistry.

After completing dental school, Harry did a brief tour of duty in the Air Force as a dentist. When he left the service, he decided he wanted to get away from dentistry for a while and enrolled in art school. However, despite his dislike for dentistry, he returned to practice because of the large personal and financial investment he had already made in the profession. Dentistry paid well, and it was difficult to give it up; retraining in a field of more interest to him would be difficult and costly. During the ten years following dental school, Harry quit and reentered dental practice on three separate occasions. Throughout the entire experience, he remained unhappy with his choice of a profession.

Although Harry is a fictitious name, this story is true, and it recounts the lives of many people in many careers who feel they have made the wrong choice. Some of the misery talented people like Harry have experienced could have been avoided with proper career counseling and guidance. In this chapter we examine the contribution of psychological tests to the selection of and preparation for a career.

The term *career* denotes adventure to many people. As a noun, it means swift course and as a verb it means to go swiftly or wildly. The Latin root is *carrus*, chariot. Thus the term for today's rat race of the work world has its roots in the exciting chariot races of the Romans (Super & Hall, 1978). And careers can indeed be exciting and the essence of life if they are properly selected. They can also lead to misery and unhappiness if they are not carefully chosen, as we saw in the example of Harry. Psychological tests can be helpful in the selection of the right career. The first step in the identification of an appropriate career path is the evaluation of interests.

I.   MEASURING INTERESTS

If you want to enter a career that will be satisfactory to you, it is important to identify your interests. Some people need little help in finding work that interests them. However, others can benefit from the guidance given by a psychological test. In the more than 60 years since the introduction of interest inventories, millions of people have been exposed to feedback about their own interests in order to help them make wise career choices.

The first interest inventory was introduced in 1921 and was called the Carnegie Interest Inventory. By the time the *Mental Measurements Yearbook* was published for the first time in 1939, it found 15 different interest measures to discuss (Datta, 1975). The two most widely used interest tests were introduced relatively early. The Strong Vocational Interest Blank was first released in 1927, and the Kuder Preference Survey made its first appearance in 1939. Today there are more than 80 interest inventories in use (Diamond, 1979). However, the Strong (now called the Strong-Campbell Interest Inventory) remains the most widely used test in research and practice.

A. *The Strong Vocational Interest Blank*

Shortly after World War I, psychologist E. K. Strong, Jr., and some of his colleagues began to carefully examine the activities that were liked and disliked by members of different professions. During the course of their study, they came to realize that people in different professional groups had different patterns of interests. To some extent, you might expect this to occur because people tend to choose lines of work that are of interest to them. Carpenters might be expected to be interested in woodworking, and painting might be of more interest to an artist than to a salesperson. However, Strong and his colleagues also found that people in the same line of work also had similar hobbies, liked the same types of entertainment, and read the same types of books and magazines.

With this research as a base, Strong set out to develop a test that would match the interests of a subject to the interests and values of a criterion group of people who were happy in the careers they had chosen. This procedure is called *criterion keying*, or the *criterion-group approach* (see Chapter 15 for a discussion of this approach). The test that was created with this method was called the Strong Vocational Interest Blank (SVIB).

In the early studies, groups of individuals from many professions and occupations responded to approximately 400 items dealing with likes and dislikes related to these occupations and to leisure activities. The Strong procedure then determined whether the interests of new subjects were similar to those of the criterion groups.

In the revised 1966 version of the SVIB the 399 items were related to 54 occupations for men. A separate form was available for 32 different occupations for women. Items in the SVIB were weighted according to how frequently an interest occurred in a particular occupational group as opposed to how frequently it occurred in the general population. Raw scores were converted to standard scores with a mean of 50 and standard deviation of 10. Each criterion group used in the construction of the SVIB contained about 300 persons, which made for a healthy normative sample. Numerous reliability studies produced impressive results, with odd-even and short-term test-retest figures generally running between the low .80s and low .90s. Long-term (20-year) test-retest coefficients ran in the respectable .60s. Validity data indicated that the SVIB was good for predicting job satisfaction (for example, Strong & Campbell, 1966).

One of the most interesting findings to emerge from the hundreds of published studies using the SVIB is that patterns of interest remain relatively stable over a long period of time. Strong made a practice of asking a group of Stanford University students who took the test in the 1930s to take the test again as they grew older. These studies showed that interests remain relatively stable over a period as long as 22 years. Of course, most people did modify their interests slightly over this period, and a few people made complete turnabouts. Nevertheless, the great majority remained steady.

Studies with the SVIB also showed that interest patterns are fairly well established by age 17. For example, Stanford students who were premedical majors and eventually became physicians scored high on the physician scale of the SVIB. When recontacted throughout life, they tended to remain high on that scale (Tyler & Walsh, 1979). Other studies showed some instability of interests during adolescence with the patterns becoming stable by the time of the senior year in high school (Campbell & Hansen, 1981).

Despite the widespread acceptance and use of the SVIB, disenchantment with the test began to mount in the late 1960s and early 1970s. Critics cited a sex bias in the scales because different tests were used for men and women. Others complained about the lack of theory associated with the test.

B. The Strong-Campbell Interest Inventory

In 1974, psychologist D. P. Campbell published a new version of the SVIB, which he called the Strong-Campbell Interest Inventory (SCII). The SCII was Campbell's (1974) response to the shortcomings of the SVIB. Items from both the men's and women's forms of the SVIB were merged into a single form, which included scales devoid of sex bias. For example, the scales for waiter and waitress were merged. Items that referred to gender (for example, salesman) were appropriately modified.

The SVIB had also been attacked because it lacked a theoretical orientation. In the development of the SVIB, Strong had focused on the match between the interests of a subject and those of people who enjoyed working in various fields. However, he shied away from providing a theoretical explanation for why certain types of individuals liked working in some fields and disliked employment in others. In the SCII, Campbell incorporated Holland's (1975) theory of vocational choice. After many years of study, Holland postulated that interests are an expression of personality and that people can be classified into one or more of six categories according to their interests. These categories are listed in Table 16-1. One detailed study using all 437 occupation titles from the Bureau of the Census demonstrated that Holland's system is better able to describe work activities, general training requirements, and occupational rewards than is a variety of competing vocational classification systems (Gottfredson, 1980). Holland's work came to the attention of Campbell because the six personality factors in Holland's theory were quite similar to the patterns of interest that emerged from many years of research with the SVIB. In addition, the factors

TABLE 16-1 Holland's six personality factors

Factor	Interest pattern
Realistic	Enjoys technical material and outdoor activities.
Investigative	Is interested in science and the process of investigation.
Artistic	Enjoys self-expression and being dramatic.
Social	Is interested in helping others and in activities involving other people.
Enterprising	Is interested in power and political strength.
Conventional	Likes to be well organized and has clerical interests.

Adapted from Holland (1975).

postulated by Holland could be used for either men or women. Thus, Holland's theory and his six personality factors became incorporated into the SCII (Tyler & Walsh, 1979).

The SCII in its current form is divided into seven parts, which are summarized in Table 16-2. The test, which still retains the core of the SVIB, now has 325 items, to which a person responds "like," "dislike," or "indifferent."

TABLE 16-2 Summary of the seven parts of the Strong-Campbell Interest Inventory

Section	Name	Number of Items	Examples of Items
1	Occupations	131	Actor/actress, criminal lawyer, freelance writer, office clerk, X-ray technician
2	School subjects	36	Algebra, art, economics, literature, zoology
3	Activities	51	Cooking, taping a sprained ankle, watching an open-heart operation
4	Amusements	39	Fishing, boxing, listening to religious music, skiing, attending lectures
5	Types of people	24	Military officers, ballet dancers, very old people
6	Preference between two activities	30	Being an airline pilot or being an airline ticket agent, taking a chance or playing safe, reading a book or watching television
7	Your characteristics	14	Wins friends easily, can prepare successful advertisements, has patience when teaching others

Adapted from Campbell & Hansen (1981).

Various agencies provide automated scoring services for the SCII, and most of them summarize several different scores for each profile. The first score is a summary of general themes, which are based on Holland's six personality types (Table 16-1). For example, the profile might provide information about the general types of activities the person enjoys, the kinds of people the person might work well with, and the most suitable general occupational environment.

The second score summary given in a report is for the administrative indexes. These are of less personal importance to the test taker but are needed in order to be sure that errors were not made in the administration, scoring, or processing of the test.

The third set of scores provides a summary of the person's basic interests. For example, they suggest whether the person was high, low, or about average in preference for science, mechanical activities, and athletics. This information is reported in standardized T-scores (see Chapter 2). (Remember that T-scores have a mean of 50 and a standard deviation of 10. Thus a T-score of 60 would be 1 standard deviation above the mean or would be in approximately the 84th percentile.)

The final set of summary scores given in the SCII profile is for the occupational scales. These scales occupy most of the space on the SCII profile. The profile shows the person's score for each of 124 occupations, which are broken into six general occupational themes. The scoring for the occupational scales differs from the scoring for the general theme and basic interest scales because the occupational scale compares the test taker's score with the scores of people working in the various professions. The general theme and basic interest scales compare the test taker's score with those of people in general. If you took the SCII, for each scale you would be assigned a score indicating the degree of similarity—very dissimilar, dissimilar, average, similar, or very similar—between your interests and the interests of people who are happy in their chosen occupations. Many of the occupations are divided so that different criterion groups are provided for males and females. For example, if your score was in the very similar category for the occupation social worker (for female), this finding would suggest that your interests were very similar to those of women who had been employed as social workers and had enjoyed the profession.

Several systems provide computerized reports for SCII profiles. Focused Example 16-1 shows the interpretive report for a 28-year-old female research psychologist named Jean A. As you can see, the report provides plentiful information about her interests as well as information about the meaning of the SCII.

C. The 1981 SCII revision

A new version of the SCII was released in Spring, 1981. Although the testing materials (that is, test booklets and answer sheets) did not change, the SCII profile was expanded to include 162 occupational scales, 99 of which have been developed since 1977. In the new revision, every occupational criterion group is represented by a national sample. In addition, special precautions were taken to rule out potential difficulties in interpretation. For example, one of the criticisms of the SCII has been that members of the criterion groups may have been older than those who would be just entering the work force. In the revised SCII, younger and older members of each criterion group were compared to determine whether interests and values of the recent entrants to the work force differed from those of workers who had been on the job for many years. The new SCII also includes male and female norms for nearly every occupation. There are now only four male and four female occupations for which there are

■ FOCUSED EXAMPLE 16-1 PORTIONS OF A COMPUTERIZED SCII INTERPRETIVE REPORT FOR JEAN A.

```
        ***********************************************
        ****      GENERAL OCCUPATIONAL THEMES     ****
        ****                                      ****
        ***********************************************
```

PSYCHOLOGICAL RESEARCH HAS INDICATED THAT INTERESTS CAN BE GROUPED INTO SIX CATEGORIES, EACH OF WHICH CAN BE DESCRIBED BY A GENERAL THEME. IMMEDIATELY BELOW ARE YOUR SCORES—LISTED FROM HIGH TO LOW—ON THESE SIX GENERAL THEMES. A GRAPH OF YOUR RESULTS ALSO HAS BEEN PROVIDED. THE SIX THEME NAMES ARE SHOWN AT THE RIGHT OF THE GRAPH, WITH THEIR ABBREVIATIONS LISTED IN THE SCALE COLUMN. AVERAGE SCORES ON THESE SCALES RANGE BETWEEN 43 AND 57. SCORES BELOW 43 ARE GENERALLY CONSIDERED LOW AND INDICATE THAT YOU PROBABLY SHARE FEW OF THE CHARACTERISTICS OF THAT THEME. SCORES ABOVE 57 GENERALLY ARE CONSIDERED HIGH AND SUGGEST THAT MANY OF THE CHARACTERISTICS OF THAT THEME PROBABLY FIT YOU.

```
                YOUR      3      4      5      6      7
SCALE           SCORE  ...0.....0.....0.....0.....0.....0.....

I-THEME          58     *****************************          (INVESTIGATIVE)
A-THEME          51     ************************              (ARTISTIC)
S-THEME          45     *********************                 (SOCIAL)
E-THEME          42     *******************                   (ENTERPRISING)
C-THEME          37     ****************                      (CONVENTIONAL)
R-THEME          36     ***************                       (REALISTIC)
```

ALL OF THE INTERESTS AND CHARACTERISTICS FOR ONE THEME, HOWEVER, MAY NOT FIT EXACTLY ANY ONE PERSON. MOST PEOPLE SCORE HIGH ON TWO OR EVEN THREE THEMES, THUS DISPLAYING CHARACTERISTICS OF MORE THAN ONE CATEGORY. SOME PEOPLE SCORE LOW ON ALL THEMES, INDICATING THAT DEFINITE PATTERNS OF INTERESTS, AS MEASURED BY THESE THEMES, HAVE NOT DEVELOPED YET. THIS IS PARTICULARLY TRUE FOR YOUNG PEOPLE. GENERALLY, THE HIGHER YOUR SCORE, THE MORE CHARACTERISTICS YOU SHARE WITH THAT PARTICULAR THEME. MEN AND WOMEN SCORE SOMEWHAT DIFFERENTLY ON THE SAME THEME, AND THIS HAS BEEN TAKEN INTO ACCOUNT BY COMPARING YOUR SCORES WITH THE AVERAGES FOR YOUR SEX.

```
        ***********************************************
        ****         OCCUPATIONAL SCALES          ****
        ****                                      ****
        ***********************************************
```

THE NEXT GROUP OF RESULTS ARE OCCUPATIONAL SCALES. THEY INDICATE HOW SIMILAR YOUR INTERESTS ARE TO THE INTERESTS OF EMPLOYED PEOPLE IN VARIOUS OCCUPATIONS. THE AVERAGE WORKER SCORES ABOUT 50 ON THE SCALE WHICH IS BASED ON HER OR HIS OCCUPATION, AND ABOUT TWO-THIRDS OF THESE WORKERS

HAVE SCORES OF 45 AND HIGHER ON THEIR OCCUPATION SCALE. IN THE GENERAL POPULATION, THE AVERAGE RANGE OF SCORES FOR ADULTS IS BETWEEN 26 AND 44. SCORES BELOW 26 INDICATE LITTLE SIMILARITY OF INTEREST WITH PEOPLE IN THAT OCCUPATION. YOUR SCORES ARE LISTED TO THE LEFT OF EACH OCCUPATIONAL SCALE, AND ARE RANKED FROM HIGH TO LOW WITHIN EACH OF THE GROUPS OF VERY SIMILAR, SIMILAR, AVERAGE RANGE, DISSIMILAR, AND VERY DISSIMILAR INTERESTS.

RESEARCH HAS INDICATED THAT PEOPLE WHO ENTER AN OCCUPATION WHERE THEY HAVE SIMILAR SCORES TEND TO REMAIN IN THAT OCCUPATION AND ARE MORE SATISIFIED THAN IF THEY ENTER AN OCCUPATION WHERE THEY HAVE DISSIMILAR SCORES. FURTHERMORE, THESE SCORES MAY INDICATE INTEREST IN AN OCCUPATION THAT YOU MAY NOT HAVE CONSIDERED BEFORE AND CAN HELP YOU THINK ABOUT VARIOUS OTHER CAREERS. THE FOLLOWING SCORES INDICATE HOW YOUR INTERESTS MATCH THOSE OF FEMALES IN VARIOUS OCCUPATIONS.

VERY SIMILAR 55+	SIMILAR 54–45	AVERAGE RANGE 44–26	DISSIMILAR 25–16	VERY DISSIMILAR 15–
58 PHYSICIAN	52 OPTOMETRIST	43 DENTAL HYGIENIST	25 SOCIAL WORKER	15 EXEC HOUSEKEEPER
	50 PSYCHOLOGIST	42 VETERINARIAN	23 BUYER	13 LANGUAGE TEACHER
	49 COLLEGE PROF.	42 DENTIST	23 GUIDANCE COUNS.	13 ELEM. TEACHER
	49 PHYS. THERAPIST	41 MATHEMATICIAN	23 RECREATION LEAD.	12 SOC. SCI TEACHER
	48 MEDICAL TECH.	41 ENGINEER	22 DENTAL ASSISTANT	10 SECRETARY
	46 DIETITIAN	40 ARTIST	21 CREDIT MANAGER	8 DEPT STORE SALES
	46 PHARMACIST	40 SPEECH PATHOL.	21 BANKER	8 HOME ECON. TCHR.
		39 ACCOUNTANT	21 LIFE INS. AGENT	5 CHRISTIAN ED DIR
		38 MATH-SCI. TEACH.	21 ENGLISH TEACHER	3 ART TEACHER
		38 LANGUAGE INTERPR.	20 INSTRUM ASSEMBL.	1 BUSINESS ED TCHR
		37 LAWYER	19 INT. DECORATOR	
		37 MUSICIAN	17 LIC. PRAC. NURSE	
		37 ADVERTISING EXEC.		
		37 CHEMIST		
		35 COMPUTER PROGR.		
		35 ENTERTAINER		
		34 PHYS ED. TEACHER		
		34 X-RAY TECHNICIAN		
		33 REPORTER		
		32 LIBRARIAN		
		31 OCCUP. THERAPIST		
		31 PHYSICIST		
		30 YWCA STAFF		
		29 REGISTERED NURSE		
		28 BEAUTICIAN		
		27 FLIGHT ATTENDANT		
		27 ARMY OFFICER		

* * * * * * * * * * * * * * * * * * * *

BELOW ARE YOUR HIGHEST OCCUPATIONAL SCALE SCORES. YOU SHOULD PAY PARTICULAR ATTENTION TO THOSE OCCUPATIONS WHERE YOUR SCORES INDICATED THAT YOU HAD THE MOST SIMILAR INTERESTS. YOU WILL HAVE THE BEST CHANCE OF FINDING SATISFACTION IF YOU DECIDE ON AN OCCUPATION WHERE YOUR INTERESTS ARE SIMILAR WITH YOUR CO-WORKERS AND LESS CHANCE IF YOUR INTERESTS ARE DISSIMILAR. IF YOU RECORDED THE SAME LIKES AND DISLIKES AS THE WORKERS, YOUR SCORE WILL BE HIGH FOR THAT OCCUPATION. IF YOUR LIKE AND DISLIKE RESPONSES WERE DIFFERENT FROM THOSE OF PEOPLE IN THE OCCUPATION, YOUR SCORE WILL BE LOW AND YOU WOULD NOT LIKELY BE SATISFIED IN THAT KIND OF WORK.

AS BEFORE, PAGE REFERENCES ARE GIVEN FOR THE OCCUPATIONAL OUTLOOK HANDBOOK (OOH), WHICH PRESENTS ADDITIONAL INFORMATION ON EMPLOYMENT OPPORTUNITIES AND RELEVANT WORK SITUATIONS. REFERENCES ALSO ARE LISTED FOR THE DICTIONARY OF OCCUPATIONAL TITLES (DOT) FOURTH EDITION-1975. THE DOT GIVES DETAILED JOB DESCRIPTIONS OF THE DUTIES AND FUNCTIONS OF EACH OCCUPATION AND CAN BE FOUND IN YOUR LOCAL LIBRARY OR PURCHASED FROM THE U.S. GOVERNMENT PRINTING OFFICE FOR $12.00. THE FIRST DOT REFERENCE IS FOR PAGE NUMBER AND THE SECOND DOT REFERENCE IS FOR THE DOT CODE FOR THAT PARTICULAR OCCUPATION.

YOUR HIGHEST SCORES APPEARED ON THE FOLLOWING SCALES AND INDICATE THE GREATEST DEGREE OF SIMILARITY BETWEEN YOUR ANSWERS AND THOSE OF FEMALES IN THESE OCCUPATIONS-

58 PHYSICIAN------- PHYSICIANS DIAGNOSE, TREAT, AND ATTEMPT TO PREVENT PHYSICAL ILLNESSES. EIGHT YEARS OF COLLEGE TRAINING, A ONE-YEAR RESIDENCY, AND A PASSING SCORE ON A STATE BOARD EXAMINATION ARE NECESSARY BEFORE AN INDIVIDUAL IS LICENSED TO PRACTICE MEDICINE. PERSONS INTERESTED IN THIS FIELD MUST BE WILLING TO STUDY A GREAT DEAL THROUGHOUT THEIR CAREERS TO KEEP UP WITH THE LATEST MEDICAL ADVANCES. HIGH MORAL STANDARDS, EMOTIONAL STABILITY, A PLEASANT PERSONALITY, AND AN ABILITY TO MAKE DECISIONS IN EMERGENCIES ARE ALSO IMPORTANT. DIFFERENT SPECIALTIES ARE OBSTETRICS, GYNECOLOGY, AND SURGERY. THE EMPLOYMENT OUTLOOK FOR THIS FIELD IS EXPECTED TO BE VERY GOOD THROUGH THE MID-1980S.

OOH 463-466
DOT 53-54
DOT 070.010-.101

52 OPTOMETRIST------- OPTOMETRISTS EXAMINE EYES AND PRESCRIBE CORRECTIVE LENSES AND TREATMENT. SIX YEARS OF COLLEGE TRAINING AND A PASSING SCORE ON A STATE BOARD EXAMINATION ARE REQUIRED TO BE GRANTED A LICENSE. PERSONS INTERESTED IN THIS CAREER SHOULD HAVE BUSINESS APTITUDE, SELF-DISCIPLINE, AND AN ABILITY TO DEAL TACTFULLY WITH PATIENTS. RELATED OCCUPATIONS ARE OPHTHALMOLOGIST AND OPTICIAN. EMPLOYMENT FOR THIS OCCUPATION IS EXPECTED TO GROW ABOUT AS FAST AS THE AVERAGE FOR ALL OCCUPATIONS.

OOH 459-461
DOT 63
DOT 079.101

50 PSYCHOLOGIST------- PSYCHOLOGISTS STUDY THE NORMAL AND ABNORMAL BEHAVIOR OF INDIVIDUALS AND GROUPS TO UNDERSTAND AND EXPLAIN THEIR ACTIONS. PSYCHOLOGISTS TEACH, COUNSEL, OR DO EXPERIMENTAL RESEARCH. A MASTERS DEGREE IS THE MINIMAL REQUIREMENT FOR ENTRANCE INTO THIS FIELD, AND A PH.D. IS BECOMING INCREASINGLY IMPORTANT. PERSONS CONSIDERING THIS FIELD MUST BE EMOTIONALLY STABLE, MATURE, SENSIBLE, PATIENT, AND ABLE TO DEAL EFFECTIVELY WITH

OOH 528-531
DOT 48-49
DOT 045.061-.107

PEOPLE. RELATED OCCUPATIONS ARE PSYCHIATRIST AND PSYCHOMETRIST. EMPLOYMENT IS EXPECTED TO GROW FASTER THAN FOR MOST OCCUPATIONS.

* *

THE U.S. GOVERNMENT PRINTING OFFICE PROVIDES SUBSECTIONS OF THE OOH IN PAMPHLET FORM IF THE BOOK ITSELF IS NOT READILY AVAILABLE TO YOU. THE BULLETIN NUMBER AND COST FOR EACH REPRINT THAT WOULD BE HELPFUL FOR YOU ARE LISTED BELOW. THESE PAMPHLETS CAN BE ORDERED FROM THE U.S. GOVERNMENT PRINTING OFFICE (MINIMUM ORDER IS $1.00).

BULLETIN
NO.   COST   TITLE
1955-27 $.50   HEALTH PRACTITIONERS
1955-30 $.50   LAWYER, CITY MGR. + SOCIAL SCIENCE OCCUPATIONS
1955-12 $.50   EDUCATION AND RELATED OCCUPATIONS

USING YOUR HIGH OCCUPATIONAL SCALE SCORES AS GUIDES, YOU SHOULD SEEK ADDITIONAL INFORMATION ABOUT THOSE AREAS WHERE YOUR INTERESTS ARE FOCUSED. ASK YOUR LIBRARIAN FOR FURTHER INFORMATION ON JOBS IN THESE AREAS, TALK TO PEOPLE IN THESE FIELDS, READ BOOKS AND PERIODICALS THAT ARE RELEVANT, AND SO FORTH.

TO LEARN MORE ABOUT THE LIFE AND WORK OF PEOPLE IN OCCUPATIONS WHERE YOU HAVE HIGH SCORES, THE FOLLOWING BOOKS ARE SUGGESTED FOR FURTHER INFORMATION—

—LONE WOMAN. BY DOROTHY CLARK WILSON. LITTLE, BROWN, AND CO., 1970.
—YOUR FUTURE IN OPTOMETRY. BY JAMES R. GREGG. RICHARDS ROSEN PRESS, 1971.
—CAREERS IN PSYCHOLOGY. AMERICAN PSYCHOLOGICAL ASSOCIATION, ED., 1975.

* *

not norms for the opposite sex (Campbell & Hansen, 1981). In summary, the 1981 revision takes a sound psychological test and eliminates some of its few remaining problems.

D.   The Kuder Occupational Interest Survey

Although the SCII is probably the most widely used interest inventory today, many other interest inventories compete for large shares of the market. The Kuder Occupational Interest Survey (KOIS) ranks second in popularity. The KOIS is one of several interest scales that grew out of the original Kuder Preference Survey published in 1939. Throughout the years, the Kuder has always been an alternative to the SVIB-SCII and has always advertised its unique features.

The KOIS presents the test taker with 100 triads (sets of three) of alternative activities. For each triad, the test taker selects the most preferred and the least preferred alternatives. Scoring of the KOIS scales gives the same information yielded by the earlier Kuder Preference Surveys—data on ten general occupational interests (for example, outdoor interests versus social service interests). However, in its newer form (Kuder, 1975) the KOIS examines the similarity between a test taker's interests and the interests of people employed in different occupations in a manner very similar to that of the SCII. One of the distinguishing features of the KOIS is that it has a separate set of scales for college majors. Thus in addition to suggesting which occupational group might be best suited to a test taker's interests, the KOIS may also provide direction with regard to selection of a major.

In 1979 five new scales were added to the KOIS. These were the first in a series of new scales that emphasize nontraditional occupations for men and women. By September 1980, a total of 13 new scales had been added with additional ones planned. Examples of new scales are architect (female norms), journalist (female norms), and film/television producer/director (male norms) (Kuder, 1979).

Although each test taker is evaluated with regard to the norms for many occupational and college major groups, the KOIS provides a summary of an individual's highest scores by signaling them with an asterisk. Table 16-3 shows one of these summaries. The scores are rank ordered in the table. Those toward the top are for the vocations in which this test taker showed the highest interest. The higher the score, the greater the similarity between the test taker and people who are actually engaged in that line of work or who are enrolled in that college major. A score above .45 is typically obtained by about 80% of the people in the actual vocation or college major. Most students will have some scores above, and they may want to pay particular attention to them. For example, the scores in Table 16-3 suggest that the woman has interests that resemble those of women working in technical jobs and in computer programming.

Recent studies show that the psychometric properties of the KOIS are very

TABLE 16-3 Summary report for Kuder Occupational Interest Survey

Report of Scores   Kuder Occupational Interest Survey   Form DD

NAME STUDENT ONE   FEMALE   99991   DATE 01/20/81

OCCUPATIONAL SCALES	NORMS M	NORMS F	OCCUPATIONAL SCALES (CONTINUED)	NORMS M	NORMS F	COLLEGE MAJOR SCALES	NORMS M	NORMS F
>COMPUTR PROGRAMR		.60*	ENG.HEAT/AIR CON	.43		>BIOLOGICAL SCI		.64*
>DENTIST		.57*	METEOROLOGIST	.43		>PSYCHOLOGY		.64*
SOC WORKR,SCHOOL		.57*	>SOC WORKER,GROUP		.42	HEALTH PROFES		.59*
>ARCHITECT		.56*	AUTO SALESPERSON	.42		>MATHEMATICS		.59*
>PHYSICIAN		.56*	>COUNSELOR,HI SCH	.42				
>FILM/TV PROD/DIR		.55*	ENGINEER, ELEC	.42		>ART AND ART EDUC	.58*	
>PHYS THERAPIST		.54*	ENG.MINING/METAL	.42		>BIOLOGICAL SCI	.58*	
ENGINEER		.53	TRAVEL AGENT	.42		>FOREIGN LANGUAGE		.57
>ACCT,CERT PUBLIC		.52	>VETERINARIAN	.42		>FOREIGN LANGUAGE	.57*	
>COMPUTR PROGRAMR	.52*		>X-RAY TECHNICIAN	.42		>MUSIC & MUSIC ED	.57*	
>FILM/TV PROD/DIR	.52*		STENOGRAPHER		.41	>PSYCHOLOGY	.57*	
PSYCHIATRIST	.52*		ENGINEER, CIVIL	.41		DRAMA		.56
>PSYCH, CLINICAL	.52*		RADIO STATON MGR	.41		>HISTORY		.56
STATISTICIAN	.52*		DENTAL ASSISTANT		.40			
>AUDIOL/SP PATHOL		.51	ENGINEER, INDUS	.40		>POLITICAL SCI		.56
PSYCHOLOGIST		.51	>FLORIST	.40		PREMED/PHAR/DENT	.56*	
>PSYCH, CLINICAL		.51	>LIBRARIAN	.40		>SOCIOLOGY	.56*	
>AUDIOL/SP PATHOL	.51*		PLANT NURSRY WKR	.40		>ART AND ART EDUC		.55
OPTOMETRIST	.51*		>FLORIST		.39	PHYSICAL SCIENCE	.55*	
>ARCHITECT	.50*		BUYER	.39		>ENGLISH		.54
PEDIATRICIAN	.50*		CLOTHIER, RETAIL	.39		SOCIAL SCI, GENL		.54
PHOTOGRAPHER	.50*		>JOURNALIST	.39		HOME ECON EDUC		.54
>PHYS THERAPIST	.50*		>MATH TCHR,HI SCH	.39				
PODIATRIST	.50*		PERSONNEL MANAGR	.39		>MUSIC & MUSIC ED		.54
PSYCH,INDUSTRIAL	.50*		TV REPAIRER	.39		>PHYSICAL EDUC		.54
ELEM SCHL TCHR	.49*		>COUNSELOR,HI SCH		.38	AIR FORCE CADET	.54*	
>NURSE	.49*		SECRETARY		.38	ARCHITECTURE	.53*	
PSYCHOLOGY PROF	.49*		FORESTER	.38		>MATHEMATICS	.53*	
>SOC WORKER,PSYCH	.49*		>LIBRARIAN		.37	>SOCIOLOGY		.52
OCCUPA THERAPIST		.48	>MATH TCHR,HI SCH		.37	>ELEMENTARY EDUC	.52*	
>SOC WORKER,PSYCH		.48	RELIGIOUS ED DIR		.37	>ELEMENTARY EDUC		.51
>DENTIST	.48*		MINISTER	.37				
MATHEMATICIAN	.48*		REAL ESTATE AGT	.37		NURSING		.51
PSYCH,COUNSELING	.48*		SCHOOL SUPT	.37		>ENGLISH		.49
DIETITIAN, ADMIN		.47	BEAUTICIAN		.36	>HISTORY		.49
CHEMIST	.47*		PRIMARY SCH TCHR		.35	LAW-GRAD SCHOOL		.49
>LAWYER	.47*		PRINTER	.35		MILITARY CADET		.49
>JOURNALIST		.46	HOME DEMONST AGT		.34	>POLITICAL SCI		.48
>SCIENCE TCHR, HS		.46	>VETERINARIAN		.34	ENGINEERING,CHEM		.47
>SOCIAL CASEWORKR		.46	>INSURANCE AGENT	.34		ENGINEERING,ELEC		.47
>INTERIOR DECORAT	.46*		YMCA SECRETARY	.34				
OSTEOPATH	.46*		>BANKER	.33		>PHYSICAL EDUC	.47*	
PHARMACIST	.46*		>BOOKKEEPER	.33		BUS ED & COMMERC		.46
>SCIENCE TCHR, HS	.46*		BANK CLERK		.32	ECONOMICS		.46
>SOCIAL CASEWORKR	.46*		>BOOKKEEPER		.31	ENGINEERING,MECH		.46
>INTERIOR DECORAT		.45	BLDG CONTRACTOR	.31		ENGINEERNG,CIVIL		.44
>LAWYER		.45	COUNTY AGRI AGT	.31		BUS ACCT AND FIN		.43
NUTRITIONIST		.45	PLUMBING CONTRAC	.31		BUS & MARKETING		.43
>BANKER		.44	POSTAL CLERK	.31		BUS MANAGEMENT		.43
DIETITIAN,SCHOOL		.44	DEPT STORE SALES		.30			
HOME EC TCHR COL		.44	OFFICE CLERK		.30	FORESTRY		.43
>INSURANCE AGENT		.44	SUPERVSR,INDUSTR	.30		ANIMAL HUSBANDRY		.42
SOC WORKER,MEDIC		.44	ELECTRICIAN	.29		AGRICULTURE		.39
>X-RAY TECHNICIAN		.44	WELDER	.29		TCHG CATH SISTER		.38
>ACCT,CERT PUBLIC	.44		BRICKLAYER	.28				
>BOOKSTOR MANAGER	.44		PAINTER, HOUSE	.28		V 52		
ENGINEER, MECH	.44		POLICE OFFICER	.28				
PHARMACEUT SALES	.44		AUTO MECHANIC	.27				
>PHYSICIAN	.44		FARMER	.27				
>SOC WORKER,GROUP	.44		TRUCK DRIVER	.27				
>BOOKSTOR MANAGER		.43	MACHINIST	.25				
DEAN OF WOMEN		.43	PLUMBER	.24				
>NURSE		.43	CARPENTER	.22				

M	.42	S	.49
MHI	.30	F	.42
W	.45	D	.53
WBI	.34	MO	.40

SRA   Your scores are reported to you in rank order, on all scales. They show to what extent the choices you marked were like those typical of satisfied people in the occupations and college majors listed. Your top scores are followed by an asterisk (•). (For additional information and for an alphabetical list of scales, see the other side of this report.) > INDICATES TWIN SCALES, WITH SCORES IN M AND F COLUMNS.

("Report of Scores" from Kuder Occupational Interest Survey, Form DD. c 1979, 1970, 1968, 1965 Science Research Associates, Inc. Reprinted by permission.)

good. Short-term reliabilities tend to be high (between .80 and .95), and increasing evidence indicates that scores remain stable as long as 19 years (Zytowski, 1976). One study on the predictive validity of the KOIS showed that half of a group of adults who had been given an early version of the KOIS while they were high school students were working in fields that the high school KOIS suggested they enter. Predictive validity for the college major scales was even better. There was closer correspondence between interests and the occupation a person was working in for those who had completed college. A college degree provides more freedom than does a high school diploma in finding work that is personally desirable (Zytowski, 1976).

Other studies on the KOIS reveal that high school students report greater confidence in their knowledge of themselves when they are given KOIS results than when they are not. But knowing the results of the KOIS did not make the high school students more confident or more satisfied with their career plans, except when the students expressed a special interest in learning about the test results (Zytowski, 1977). Even though the KOIS has been less thoroughly studied than the SVIB-SCII, a growing amount of evidence indicates that it may be quite useful for guidance decisions for high school and college students.

E.   The Minnesota Vocational Interest Inventory

One of the criticisms of the SCII and the KOIS has been that they emphasize professions that require college and professional training. Although an increasing number of Americans eventually obtain a college degree, most workers still do not graduate from college. The Minnesota Vocational Interest Inventory (MVII) is designed for men who are not oriented toward college and emphasizes skilled and semiskilled trades (Clark, 1961; Clark & Campbell, 1965). The MVII is modeled after the SVIB scales and has nine basic interest areas including mechanical interests, electronics, and food service, as well as 21 specific occupational scales including those for plumber, carpenter, and truck driver. The MVII has been used extensively by the military and by guidance programs for non-college-bound individuals.

F.   The Career Assessment Inventory

A more modern interest inventory for nonprofessionally oriented adults than the MVII is the Career Assessment Inventory (CAI). Developed by Charles B. Johansson, the CAI is written at the sixth-grade reading level and is designed for the 80% of Americans who have fewer than four years of postsecondary education. The CAI provides information similar to that yielded by the SCII. Each test taker is evaluated on six occupational theme scales: realistic, investigative, artistic, social, enterprising, and conventional. The second portion of the CAI report describes basic interests. Each test taker is evaluated in 22 specific areas, including carpentry, business, and food service. The third section of the report is a series of occupational scales. As with the SCII and other interest inventories, scores for the 89 occupational scales on the CAI were obtained by using a criterion-keying method. The interests of the test takers are matched to the interests of truck drivers, secretaries, waitresses, and so forth.

Validity and reliability studies reported in the test manual suggest that the

CAI has desirable psychometric properties. Scores tend to be quite stable, and people who find employment in occupations for which they have expressed strong interest tend to remain at their jobs and find more satisfaction with work than do those who have low scores for those occupations. The test developer also took special pains to be certain that the CAI was culturally fair and that sex bias was avoided. In many ways, the CAI has become the working person's SCII (Johansson, 1976; Johansson & Johansson, 1978).

G.   *General issues in the measurement of interests*

Despite the common and enthusiastic use of interest inventories, several problems have repeatedly surfaced, including faking, sex bias, and mismatches between abilities and interests.

Faking.   Interest inventories are usually used to give individuals guidance with regard to career choice. However, in some situations interest inventories are used to make placement decisions. For example, the U.S. Navy considers vocational interest scores in assigning men and women to advanced training. In such employment and personnel situations, test takers may be motivated to give the response they think the employer will regard favorably. Simulation studies have demonstrated that students who are asked to fill out a personality test as though they were applying for a job differ in their responses from those who are told to answer the questions as though the results would be used for guidance (Rushmore, 1956). Some studies in real-life situations have produced similar results. High school students taking a personality test for guidance purposes tended to score as less responsible and less stable than they did when they took the same test later for summer employment placement (Gordon & Stapleton, 1956).

Even though some studies do show a tendency toward faking when the results are to be used for employment decisions, there is also evidence to the contrary (McCormick & Ilgen, 1980). In one study done by the U.S. Navy, applicants took the SVIB twice, once as an applicant for a Navy scholarship program and again on another occasion—either in high school or in college one year after they had applied for the scholarship. The results of the study demonstrated that the SVIB scores were virtually the same under both circumstances. In other words, motivation to fake SVIB responses in order to get a scholarship did not have a significant impact on test scores (Abrahams, Neumann, & Gilthens, 1971). Several other studies have also failed to find substantial faking on interest inventories.

Although faking is widely discussed as a problem in interest inventory administration, recent evidence shows that the effects of faking are minor. Recent changes in testing policies have also reduced the disguised use of personality and interest tests. Nevertheless, in some circumstances you may wish to take the motivation of the test takers into consideration.

Sex bias.   The use and development of interest inventories have not been acceptable to all members of society. In particular, advocates of women's rights justifiably pointed out that the early interest inventories contributed to the discrimination against women (Birk, 1974; Diamond, 1979; Peoples, 1975). The Association for Evaluation in Guidance appointed a Commission on Sex Bias in Measurement, which concluded that interest inventories contributed to the policy of guiding young men and women into sex-typed careers. The interest inventories were much more likely to direct women into work roles that are traditional for women, such as nursing, clerical service, and elementary school teaching. The SVIB, which was the major interest inventory at the time of the Commission report, has separate forms for men and for women. Careers on the women's form, it was noted, tended to be lower in status and to command lower salaries (Harmon, Cole, Wysong, & Zytowski, 1973).

In response to these criticisms, the SCII began using the same forms for both men and women. However, in the 1977 SCII manual, D. P. Campbell (1977) noted that Strong (who is no longer alive) may have felt that using the same norming tables for both men and women would have harmed the validity of the test. A unisex interest inventory, according to Strong, ignores the social and statistical reality that men and women have different interests. In other words, knowing the sex of the test taker tells us a lot about his or her interests. Nevertheless, the new SCII has made major efforts to reduce sex bias.

We must emphasize that the new SCII has reduced but not eliminated sex bias. Although the basic interest and general theme portions of the SCII compare a respondent's responses to those from a combined male/female reference group, the occupational scales are normed separately for men and women. Further, the interpretive comments that are provided by most scoring services are geared toward the test taker's sex group (Minton & Schneider, 1980). We anticipate that the value of using the same or different norms for men and women will be a matter of continuing controversy and debate. The current versions of both the SCII and the KOIS reflect the growing concern about sex bias.

Aptitudes and interests.   Extensive research on interest inventories (Campbell & Hansen, 1981) reinforces an important but often overlooked point: interest inventories measure interests; they do not measure the chances that people will be successful in jobs that they find interesting. The norm groups for the Strong inventories consist of people who are successful enough in various fields to remain working in them for defined periods of time. However, degree of success is not defined. If you obtain a high score for a particular occupation, you have interests that are similar to the people working in that field. Self-rated satisfaction with chosen careers does appear to be higher for those whose interests match those of others working in the field. But repeated studies have emphasized that your chances of succeeding in that job depend on aptitudes and abilities.

II. MEASURING PERSONAL CHARACTERISTICS FOR JOB PLACEMENT

Interests are just one of the many factors that must be considered in career planning and placement. Career choices depend on matches between people and jobs. Employers want to find the right person for the job, and job hunters continually seek that one job that is just right for their personal skills and interests. Thus, psychologists and vocational guidance specialists look at job placement from many different perspectives. Some focus on the person and his or her characteristics, others attend to the work environment, while still others concentrate on unique combinations of persons and situations. To begin, let's look at some of the theories and measurement methods that focus on the person.

A. *Trait factor approach: Osipow's vocational dimensions*

Samuel Osipow has been a leading figure in the field of counseling psychology for many years. Osipow's (1973) approach to career guidance is to give extensive tests covering personality, abilities, interests, and personal values in order to learn as much about a person's traits as possible. This approach involves the administration of an extensive battery of tests, including many of the ones we have covered in the last several chapters (Purdue pegboard, Seashore Measure of Musical Talents, SCII, KOIS). Results from this large battery of tests were factor analyzed (see Chapter 3) to find common factors of traits that characterize different occupational groups. People requiring guidance are given the battery of tests in order to learn about their traits. Then the counselor matches their traits to the traits that characterize the different occupations.

Osipow's approach has been used extensively in research and practice and has undoubtedly helped many people find their own occupational niches. However, the approach has also come under fire for overemphasizing the person and paying too little attention to the work environment. Further, some critics suggest that Osipow's system focuses too much on a single point in time and does not attend sufficiently to the process by which someone reaches a career decision (Tyler & Walsh, 1979).

B. *The Career Maturity Inventory: Super's developmental theory*

Many theories of career choice draw on stage theories from life-span developmental psychology, which is the study of personal development throughout the life cycle. Noted counseling psychologist Donald Super proposes that individuals go through five developmental stages that are relevant to their career choices and aspirations (Super, 1953). Table 16-4 summarizes the stages. Super believes that people enter careers in order to express themselves. Activities in the world of work are expressions of the worker's self-concept. The developmental stages define the vocational behavior that is expected of an individual during given portions of the life cycle. The correspondence between vocational behavior and the expected behavior for that age period is called *vocational maturity*.

TABLE 16-4 Stages in Super's developmental vocational maturity model

Stage	Age Range
Crystalization	14–18
Specification	18–21
Implementation	21–24
Stabilization	25–35
Consolidation	35 on

Several tests measure vocational maturity. The best known and most widely used of these is the Vocational Maturity Inventory (VMI), which later became the Career Maturity Inventory (CMI) (Crites, 1973). This test provides scores for vocational maturity, attitude, self-knowledge or vocational competence, choosing a job, problem solving, occupational information, and looking ahead. Most of the psychometric data on the CMI are impressive. In particular, the vocational competence portion is well constructed, and data obtained with it seem to demonstrate the expected properties. For example, high school students do show an expected year-to-year increase in scores on the vocational competence scale. This is the result that would be expected as the students become more vocationally mature (Crites, 1974). Unfortunately, some problems with the CMI still remain. For example, it appears that 12th graders score as less vocationally mature than do 11th graders, which is inconsistent with the notion that students should become more vocationally mature with age (Crites, 1973).

C. The California Occupational Preference Survey: Roe's career-choice theory

Anne Roe, who is another major theorist in counseling psychology, believes that career choice is the result of the type of relationship a person has had with his or her family during childhood. After extensive research on the personalities of scientists who had entered different fields of study, Roe came to the conclusion that some people are interested primarily in other people, while other people are not. Children reared in a warm and accepting environment, according to Roe, become people-oriented adults, while those exposed to a cold and aloof environment at home become more interested in things than in other people (Roe & Klos, 1969; Roe & Siegelman, 1964).

Roe's theory identifies person or nonperson orientation as the major factor in career choice. Those who are people oriented seek careers in which they will have contact with others. They may find careers in service areas, the arts, or entertainment. Individuals who are not person oriented may prefer occupations that minimize interpersonal relationships, such as those in science or technology or those involving outdoor activities. In an elaboration of the theory, Roe and Klos (1969) classified occupational roles according to two independent continua. The first had orientation to purposeful communication at one extreme and orientation to resource utilization at the other. The second had orientation to interpersonal relations at one extreme and orientation to natural phenomena at the other. Table 16-5 summarizes the vocations that might fall within the space created by these two continua. Placement in a particular job within a field depends on the ability and training of the individual.

TABLE 16-5 Examples of career fields for individuals rated on Roe's continua

	High on orientation to purposeful communication	High on orientation to resource utilization
High on orientation to interpersonal relations	Arts and entertainment; uses tastes	Business contacts; uses persuasive techniques
High on orientation to natural phenomena	Science; uses "laws"	Technology; uses mechanics

Adapted from Roe and Klos (1969).

To measure the characteristics described in Roe's theory, R. R. Knapp and his associates developed the California Occupational Preference Survey (COPS). This test requires respondents to indicate on a four-point scale the degree to which they like or dislike 168 different occupational activities. The COPS gives scores in six different fields: aesthetic, business, linguistic, scientific, service, and technical. Scores are also given for professional versus skilled orientation as well as for outdoor versus clerical orientation. (The COPS has been expanded to become the California Preference System Inventory, which includes nine occupational clusters; Knapp & Knapp, 1976.) Reliabilities for the COPS have been reported to be in the .90s. Normative data have been reported for 512 high school males and 589 high school females. However, few validity studies are available at this point, and we must wait to learn more about the meaning of COPS scores.

D. Are there stable personality traits?

Imagine that you have the responsibility for hiring employees for a large business and that you want to do everything you can to convince your supervisors that you have done a good job. To do so, you want to make certain decisions about the personalities of the people you interview, and you need to communicate this information to the people who will supervise the employees. For example, you might ask whether they have the traits of kindness, honesty, trustworthiness, reliability, and dedication. We often believe knowledge of such personality traits provides us with a convenient way of organizing information about others, for describing how they have behaved in the past, and for making predictions about how they will act in the future (Kelly, 1967; Jones & Nisbett, 1971).

Much of the study of personality has been devoted to creating categories of traits, developing methods for measuring them, and finding out how groups of traits cluster together. Indeed, the very concept of personality assumes that the characteristics of a person are stable over time. If Richard is a hard-working person, we expect him to be hard working in many different situations. Although we commonly use trait names in this way to describe other people, the evidence that personality characteristics are stable is a little shaky. For example, Mischel (1968, 1979) has shown that personality traits are simply not good predictors of how people will behave in particular situations. In a well-argued attack on trait theorists, Mischel (1968) demonstrated that knowing how someone scores on measures of psychological traits rarely gives better than chance insight into how the person will act in any situation. Thus, trait theorists were forced to retreat and rethink their assumptions.

Another problem for traditional trait theories is raised by research on a relatively new approach to personality and social psychology known as *attribution theory*. Originally, attribution theory considered only how people make judgments about others. However, there has been an enormous expansion of interest in attribution. Research in this area now covers all aspects of how people attempt to understand the causes of events in their lives.

The ideas behind attribution theory were first presented by Heider (1944, 1958) but were not made popular until the late 1960s. Recent attribution theorists suggest that events in a person's environment can be caused by one of three sources: persons, entities (things or some aspect of the environment), and times (situations) (H. H. Kelly, 1967). To determine which of these (or which combination) has caused the event, an observer uses three criteria: distinctiveness, consensus, and consistency. For example, if we are looking for an explanation of why John is unhappy with his job today, we need to ask whether it has to do with something that happened on the job this particular day (distinctiveness), whether others in the same situation also dislike the job (consensus), or whether John is unhappy on all workdays (consistency).

Attribution theory is thus less concerned with predicting behavior in particular situations than it is with studying how individuals make judgments about the causes of behavior. Some researchers have suggested that the selection of an explanation for behavior depends on the role played by the person offering the judgment. When we are observers and are making judgments about other people, we tend to use dispositional, or trait, explanations. However, we do not use trait explanations for our own behavior. When we are the *actors* in a situation, we see our own behavior in terms of the situation. In other words, we describe others in terms of traits, but we explain our own behavior in terms of situations. Why is there a difference between the attributions of actors and observers? Jones and Nisbett (1971) suggest that we know more about ourselves than we know about others. By searching our memory, we can remember behaving in many different situations. However, when we make judgments about others, we do not have as much information about how situations caused them to act differently.

To summarize, Mischel and the attribution theorists feel that psychologists have devoted too much attention to personality traits and not enough attention to situations. Thus, they recommend attention to the effect of situations on behavior.

III.   MEASURING CHARACTERISTICS OF THE WORK SETTING

To study the influence of situations, we need methods to describe and measure them. These methods are described in this section.

A.   *The social-ecology approach*

Ecology is the branch of biology that studies the relationship between living organisms and their environments. Organisms must adapt to the physical environment in order to survive. Similarly, environments can have an impact on the social lives of their inhabitants. Thus psychologists have recently come to recognize the importance of studying people within natural environments and of analyzing the impact physical environments have on social behavior (Wicker, 1979). As well-known environmental psychologist Daniel Stokols proclaims, "At a time when environmentalists and economists are proclaiming that 'small is beautiful,' the research literature on human behavior in relation to its environmental settings continues to expand at a staggering rate" (1978, p. 253). This field of study is called *environmental psychology*. A similar area is *ecological psychology*, which focuses on events that occur in a behavioral setting. We will refer to these topics of study together as *social ecology*. One of the most important areas in social ecology is the study of behavioral settings.

Each day, you participate in a variety of behavioral settings. For example, your psychological testing class is a behavioral setting. The program for this setting might include a lecturer who comes to deliver a prepared talk to a group of students. The lecturer might arrive two to three minutes late and enter a room in which students are enjoying conversation with one another. However, after the arrival of the lecturer, the room grows quiet, and as the presentation begins attention is focused on the speaker. Physical arrangements in the room facilitate this social interaction. For example, the chairs face the front of the room, and there is a blackboard available for the lecturer's use. Barker has made the study of behavioral settings his life work. For many years, he and his colleagues described the publicly available behavioral settings in two small towns: Oskaloosa, Kansas, and Leyburn, England. Each of these towns included many behavioral settings such as card games, court sessions, and special businesses. Barker's work involved documenting each setting by describing how long interactions lasted, who participated, the sexes of the people in the setting, and so on (Barker & Schoggen, 1973; Barker, 1979; Schoggen, 1979; Wicker, 1979).

The study of behavioral settings reveals a great deal about the social rules of the environment. For example, in both the small towns (Oskaloosa and Leyburn) women spent less time in public behavioral settings than did men. The studies also confirmed what many feminists have been saying all along—that women are limited to certain settings. For example, women in both towns were observed most often in such behavioral settings as churches and schools. They were also often found in settings that favored social talking and less often in business and governmental settings.

Behavioral settings are truly self-regulating ecologies. When a component of the system is missing, the activities in the program are changed to correct the imbalance. For example, if there are no chairs in your psychological testing class, students will probably go out looking for them in order to bring the situation into balance. If someone in the class makes too much noise, social forces will come into operation to eliminate the disruption (Wicker, 1979). Thus, in order to avoid social condemnation, you must act according to the rules for that behavioral setting. A catcall during psychology class might bring you strange and rejecting looks because it is out of place. Yet in the behavioral setting of a rock concert, it is perfectly appropriate. Social adjustment requires that you know the rules of many social behavioral settings and that you follow them.

The study of behavioral settings also involves examining the relationship between work satisfaction and the requirements of the job. Wicker and Kirmeyer (1976) used this approach in a study of coping behavior among rangers in Yosemite National Park. During the summer the workload for the rangers varies greatly because the number of people entering the behavioral setting differs. When the workload increases, the rangers feel more challenged and needed on the job and also use more strategies to cope with their jobs. By the end of the summer, when the workload is the heaviest, the challenge of heavy crowds is no longer associated with job satisfaction. Instead, the rangers were less able to cope, and they felt physically and emotionally drained. In order to understand the relationship between work setting and satisfaction, many aspects of the ecology must be considered. These include the workload, coping strategies, and the duration of work overload. It also requires making a precise description of the work environment.

B.   *Classifying environments*

How do different environments affect your behavior? Are you able to work better when the sun is out? Or do you get more tired and irritable on hot days? Most of social psychology is based on the premise that behavior is influenced by situations. Some of the early work in the field of environmental psychology involved building classification systems for various situations. You might think of this as similar to the work done by many early personality psychologists who built elaborate systems to classify personality types (for example, aggressive, masculine). The environmental psychologists built elaborate systems to classify the characteristics of environments that had been shown to affect individual or group behavior.

Table 16-6 shows a classification system created by Moos (1973). It includes six characteristics of environments and gives some examples. For example, many studies demonstrate that characteristics of the people in your environment affect your behavior. The likelihood that a high school girl will begin to smoke, for example, can be greatly influenced by the number of other girls who already smoke or who approve of smoking. Over the years, Moos and his collegues have developed many different measures to evaluate characteristics of environments. A summary of some of these scales is shown in Table 16-7.

TABLE 16-6 Six characteristics of environments

Characteristics	Examples
Ecological dimensions	Architectural design, geographic location, weather conditions
Behavioral settings	Office, home, store
Organizational structure	Percentage of women in the student body, number of people per household, average age of group
Characteristics of inhabitants	Proportion of students who date, drink, or vote
Psychosocial and organizational climate	Work pressure, encouragement of participation, orientation toward helping with personal problems
Functional or reinforcing properties	Is aggression reinforced on the football field; is it reinforced at home?

Adapted from Moos (1973).

Moos's work on measuring the characteristics of environments is important for the field of vocational psychology because it demonstrates how personal characteristics of the work environment affect job choice and worker satisfaction. For example, workers are more satisfied with work environments that promote quality interactions between workers and supervisors than they are with environments in which these relationships are kept more distant. The quality of the relationship between workers and supervisors also enhances productivity (Moos, 1976d). Some evidence also indicates that workers in supportive work environments are less likely to develop disabilities caused by stress on the job (Moos, 1976d) than are workers in nonsupportive environments. A pleasant work environment is also good for business. For example, bank customers who perceive bank employees as being friendly and supportive are less likely to withdraw their money in order to switch banks than are customers who dislike the social environment of the bank (Moos, 1976d).

TABLE 16-7 Summary of scales used to evaluate different environments

Type of Environment	Scale	Reference
Treatment environments	Ward Atmosphere Scale	Moos (1976e)
	Community Oriented Programs Environment Scale	Moos (1976a)
Institutional environments	Correctional Institutions Environment Scale	Moos (1976b)
Educational institutions	University Residence Environment Scale	Moos and Gerst (1976)
	Classroom Environment Scale	Moos and Truckett (1976)
Community environments	Work Environment Scale	Moos and Insel (1976)
	Group Environment Scale	Moos and Humphrey (1976)
	Family Environment Scale	Moos (1976c)

In sum, behavioral settings and social environments are coming to be recognized as important factors in job and personal satisfaction. The study of work environments is a relatively new area that we expect to blossom in the coming decade.

C. Job analysis

In addition to knowing how to classify work environments, the industrial psychologist also needs to be able to describe and measure characteristics of the job. Employers often want to describe activities of their workplace to determine what type of personnel is needed or why some employees are unhappy working in the setting. There are many available methods for doing so. Zedeck and Blood (1974) summarize the five basic methods: checklists, critical incidents, observations, interviews, and questionnaires.

Checklists are used by job analysts to describe the activities and working conditions that are usually associated with a job title. An example of a checklist for a research assistant in behavioral research is shown in Table 16-8. The first column of the checklist shows the activities associated with the job title, and the other columns list the frequency of occurrence of these activities. The task for the job analyst is simply to record how frequently each activity occurs for persons in this job classification.

TABLE 16-8 Job checklist for research assistant

Activity	Frequency of occurrence				
	Per hour	Per day	Per week	Per month	Per year
Photocopying		1			
Typing			2		
Attending meetings				1	
Meeting with subjects			3		
Ordering supplies				1	
Writing reports					1

The assistant would be expected to photocopy materials once per day, type twice per week, meet with subjects three times per week, and so on.

Checklists have been criticized because they do not provide an integrated picture of the job situation and they do not provide information about specific behaviors. In contrast to Moos's environment scales, checklists are less predictive of whether someone will like a particular job environment.

Critical incidents are observable behaviors that differentiate successful from unsuccessful employees. The critical-incident method was developed by Flanagan (1954). By acquiring specific descriptions of the behaviors of successful employees and their unsuccessful counterparts, one can learn something about the differences between the two groups. An example of a critical incident that might describe a successful employee is "Always arrives at meetings on time." A critical incident describing an unsuccessful employee might be "Leaves work area disorganized."

Observation is another method for learning about the nature of the job. As we discussed in Chapter 8, information gathered through observation methods can sometimes be biased because people change their behavior when they know they are being watched. In order to avoid this problem, the participant-observation method is sometimes used. A participant observer is someone who participates in the job and functions as though he or she were one of the workers.

Interviews can also be used to find out about the job. The difficulty with interviews is that some workers may give information to an interviewer that is different from the information they would give to another employee because they are uncomfortable or because they fear that what they say may be held against them. Another problem is that an interviewer who is unfamiliar with the job may not ask the right questions. Some methods that may help you get more information out of an interview are discussed in Chapter 10.

Questionnaires are commonly used to find out about job situations, but we do not recommend using them unless special precautions are taken. Many employers favor questionnaires because they are inexpensive. However, the employer may never know whether the respondent understood the questions and the type of information gained is limited to the specific questions. A more serious problem is that there is a selective return rate in questionnaire studies. Employees who feel very favorable or very unfavorable toward the company may be more likely to complete the questionnaire and to return it.

IV. MEASURING THE PERSON-SITUATION INTERACTION

Two different perspectives have been presented in this chapter. First we reviewed research and methods from counseling psychology that emphasized the importance of characteristics or traits of persons in their career satisfaction. Then we shifted gears and began discussing the characteristics of work situations and how they may affect people.

To a growing number of psychologists, whether traits or situations are more important in determining behavior is "a pseudo question" (Endler, 1973). It is meaningless to ask whether trait or situation is more important in explaining behavior when it is clear that behavior is always a joint function of characteristics of the person and characteristics of the situation. This position is a compromise between trait and situational approaches to personality assessment. It acknowledges the importance of personality characteristics as well as the role of situations (Endler & Hunt, 1968; Endler, 1973; Endler & Magnusson, 1976; Magnusson & Endler, 1977). The interactionists support their position by reporting the proportion of variance in behavior that is explained by person, by situation, and by the interaction between person and situation. You might think of this explanation by thinking of a pie divided to represent all the different influences on human behavior. Figure 16-1 shows the pie. One slice represents the proportion of the variation attributable to personality traits. Another slice represents the proportion of the variation caused by situational influences. A third slice is for the interaction between situational influences and dispositional, or trait, influences. This interaction is caused by unique combinations of traits and situations. For example, an interaction might describe how Harry reacts to being a dentist. This cause is different from the characteristics of Harry (in all situations) or the effects of performing the role of a dentist. Careful studies applying a statistical method known as analysis of variance have separated the proportion of variance attributable to each of these factors. As shown in Figure 16-1, the interaction accounts for a larger portion of the variance in behavior than does either the person or the situation (Magnusson & Endler, 1977).

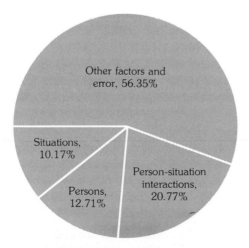

Figure 16-1. Factors influencing behavior. A pie is divided according to the proportion of variation in behavior accounted for by trait, situation, and the interaction between trait and situation. The interaction is first among the three sources of influence. However, unexplained, or error variance is much larger than any other factor. (*Adapted from data in Bowers, 1973.*)

Although it is revealing that unique combinations of persons and situations explain more of the variation than does either influence by itself, the interaction position still explains only some of the people some of the time (Bem & Allen, 1974). As Figure 16-1 shows, the largest slice of the pie represents *error variance*, the proportion of the total not explained by the three sources of influence. After reviewing many studies on the influences of person and situation, Sarason, Smith, and Diener (1975) concluded that none of the three sources account for an impressive share of the variation when compared with the amount of variation left unexplained. Although the interaction is a slightly better predictor than either the trait or the situation, it is only slightly better. Thus, the need was still present for measurement methods that could be used to predict more of the people more of the time. Bem and Funder (1978) proposed one such method.

By 1978, many psychologists were convinced that the interaction between person and the situation accounts for most of the variance in behavior (Bem & Allen, 1974; Endler & Magnusson, 1976; Magnusson & Endler, 1977). However, finding exact person-situation interactions was difficult. One important study by Bem and Allen (1974) demonstrated that some individuals may be consistent with regard to some personality characteristics yet inconsistent with regard to others. This is a radical departure from traditional trait approaches to personality, which assume that all traits characterize all people to some degree and do so consistently. Instead, Bem and Allen proposed that some traits characterize some people, and other traits characterize other people. Some people may not be characterized by any traits at all. Bem and Allen demonstrated this proposal by asking college students to rate whether their behavior would be consistent or inconsistent in different situations. These ratings were made for different traits, such as friendliness and conscientiousness. They found that students who identified themselves as consistently friendly did indeed appear to be friendly in a variety of situations. In contrast, those who rated themselves as inconsistently friendly were found to be friendly in some situations but unfriendly in others. Thus, friendliness does not characterize all people. Some people are consistent on this characteristic, while others are not. Yet the same people who are inconsistent on friendliness may be consistent on another trait such as conscientiousness. An even more exciting aspect of this finding is that the students could predict their own consistencies and inconsistencies very well; fancy testing devices were not needed!

This insight called for new measurement methods that would lead to accurate predictions of behavior. Bem and Funder (1978) introduced a descriptive system that could be used to take advantage of our ability to predict our own behavior in particular situations. They call their approach the Template-Matching Technique. The system attempts to match personality to a specific template of behavior. For example, consider how to answer the question "Should Tom become an insurance salesperson?" Assuming you know nothing about Tom, perhaps the best way to guide him would be to describe how several hypothetical people might react to working in this job. You might say, for example, that people who are shy may have difficulty approaching new customers or that people with families may not like insurance sales because of the irregular work hours. Now Tom can predict his own reaction to the job by matching his characteristics with the set of templates you have provided for him.

Along the same lines, Bem and Funder propose that "situations be characterized as sets of template-behavior pairs, each template being a personality description of an idealized type of person expected to behave in a specified way in that setting" (1978, p. 486). The probability that a particular person will behave in a particular way in a situation is a function of the match between his or her characteristics and a template. For example, if Tom's personality characteristics matched the template for those who hated being insurance salespersons, he might be best advised to avoid that career.

The difficulty with a technology of person-situation interactions is that there are so many potential combinations of persons and situations. Bem and Funder were able to demonstrate that they could predict behavior very well in three particular situations; yet the number of potential person-situation combinations staggers the mind (Cronbach, 1975a).

The template-matching model is interesting because it represents convergence of thought among psychologists with quite different training and backgrounds. Bem and Funder, the originators of the template-matching idea, were trained in the area of personality and social psychology. However, the person-situation interaction resembles what educational psychologists call the aptitude-treatment interaction (Cronbach, 1975a). Further, the template-matching idea is quite similar to a popular theory of career choice that Holland (1973) proposes. Holland suggests that there are six clusters of personality and interest traits; these are the same six clusters represented as the six general themes on the SCII (see Table 16-1). Holland contends that there are six vocational environments corresponding to these traits and that people will be happiest if they are able to match their personal characteristics to the characteristics of the work environment (Holland, 1975; Holland & Gottfredson, 1976). For example, an investigative individual will be most content if he or she can work in an investigative field such as science.

In general, career satisfaction depends on an appropriate match between person and job. The developing technology for finding job-person matches holds great promise for the field of career counseling and guidance testing.

V.   MEASURING ATTITUDES

Throughout this chapter we have talked about such phenomena as satisfaction and preference. These constructs are attitudes. An attitude is defined as a "positive or negative affective reaction toward a denotable abstract or concrete object or proposition" (Bruvold, 1970, p. 11). Attitude measurement is complex, and thorough discussion would require a book in itself. We cited a few of the basic principles of attitude-scale construction in Chapter 6. Following is a brief overview of some popular methods for measuring attitudes. If you would like more details on attitude measurement, we suggest A. L. Edwards (1957), Torgerson (1958), and Nunnally (1978).

A. *Attitude scales*

Attitude scales are mechanisms to assign numbers to attitudes according to a well-defined set of rules. There are many types and formats for attitude scales, but the most common are the Likert format and the Thurstone format.

Likert format.   The Likert format for attitude scales presents subjects with a group of statements and asks the extent to which they agree or disagree. For example, you might be given a group of statements such as "The more noise at a party, the more fun it is." or "Most married men would cheat on their wives if given the opportunity." For each of these items you would be asked to express the extent to which you agree or disagree on a five-point scale: strongly agree, agree, neither agree nor disagree, disagree, strongly disagree. Each of these alternatives is assigned a number (for example, 1 for strongly agree through 5 for strongly disagree), and your score on the scale is the sum of your responses to all the items in the scale. These scores can then be interpreted in relation to norms that are established by giving the same items to many people who represent well-defined groups.

In constructing a Likert scale the researcher must be sure that the scale is *unidimensional*—in that it represents only a single attitude. The two example items above do not represent the same attitudinal dimension and would not be included in the same scale. Scale constructors usually need to employ complex statistical methods, such as factor analysis, to determine whether their scales are indeed unidimensional.

Thurstone format.   Construction of a Thurstone scale is more complex than the construction of a Likert scale. This method was developed by psychologist L. L. Thurstone; it adopts methods used by experimental psychologists who study psychophysics. The first stage in the development of a Thurstone scale requires assembling a large number of statements about a particular attitude. For example, one of Thurstone's best-known studies considers attitudes toward the church. Each statement is printed on an individual card, and a group of judges sorts them into 11 piles representing differing degrees of the attitude. For example, the first pile might be used for statements that express the highest appreciation for the values of the church; the successive piles might be used for statements indicating increasing degrees of disfavor toward the church; and the final pile might be used for statements indicating strongest negativism toward the church. The purpose of this exercise is to establish scale values for each item. The scale values thus reflect the judgment of the group that originally rated the items. During this process, many ambiguous or irrelevant items are thrown out so the scale becomes refined. The final scale includes only a subset of the original statements and is composed of items with equally spaced scale value. Once the scale values are established, we can learn about the attitudes of other people by summing the scale values of items they are willing to endorse.

B. *Interviews and surveys*

Survey research is used to find out information about some population when such information cannot be obtained more cheaply in some other way. We would probably not do a survey to find out how many people live in the United States because the Bureau of the Census provides this information every decade. However, when we need some unavailable information yet do not have the resources to question every single person, we use survey methods to help us estimate how a large group would respond on the basis of interviews of a smaller sample drawn from it.

One example of the use of survey methods is the determination of how many people watch specific television programs. You have probably never been contacted by a television pollster, yet your television viewing habits are estimated each week. The Neilsen Company, which is the major television viewership assessment organization, places electronic devices on the television sets of a limited number of American families. The devices record which stations are watched at all hours of the day and night. On the basis of a very small sample of households (about 1200 nationwide), Neilsen can make a fairly accurate estimate of the number of persons watching particular programs.

The major principle in survey research is that the sample be random, thus assuring that all different types of people are represented. When the samples are not random, results become inaccurate. In a famous case, a magazine called the *Literary Digest* attempted to forecast the outcome of the 1936 presidential contest between Franklin D. Roosevelt and Alfred M. Landon. The magazine drew its sample from lists of automobile registration and from telephone books. In 1936, auto owners and those with phones tended to be wealthy and Republican. The poll showed that Landon would win by a landslide. However, the results of the election were just the opposite; Roosevelt won by one of the greatest margins in history. Thus, survey results will be of little value if the sample is not random. Election polls using as few as 2000 respondents to represent all the voters in the nation have repeatedly been shown to be accurate when the small samples are drawn randomly.

VI. SUMMARY

In the beginning of this chapter we presented the true case of Harry, a dentist who felt he had made the wrong career choice. Harry's problem might have been avoided through proper interest testing and career counseling. Several methods for assessing vocational interests are available. The best known of these is the SVIB, an empirically keyed test that matched the interests of male and female test takers with those of people who were satisfied with their career choices. Although it was among the most widely used tests in the history of psychology, the SVIB was harshly criticized for its sexist orientation and for its atheoretical orientation. A new version, the SCII, responds to these criticisms by including male and female keys in the same form and by embracing Holland's theory of occupational themes.

The KOIS is the next most frequently used interest test. In contrast to earlier versions, the present KOIS provides occupational scores similar to those given by the SVIB. A unique feature of the KOIS is that it provides scores for college majors. Other occupational interest measures are also available, including the MVII and the CAI, which are designed for use with non-college-oriented individuals.

Several prominent counseling psychologists have proposed that career placement be guided by personality traits. Osipow used multivariate statistics to identify clusters of interests and abilities that characterized those in different occupations. Super and Crites favored a developmental perspective, suggesting that career satisfaction is related to vocational maturity. Roe believed that different approaches to child-rearing produced some individuals who were people oriented and others who were thing oriented. People-oriented individuals find their way into people-oriented careers, and those who are not oriented toward people gain more satisfaction from work that involves less contact with people.

In 1968, Mischel demonstrated that personality measures may not always be accurate in predicting behavior in particular situations. At about the same time, many attribution theorists began demonstrating that people explain the behavior of others by using personality traits. However, when asked about their own behavior, they tend to attribute cause to the situation. These developments gave rise to the development of measures to assess characteristics of social environments and work settings.

Out of these new developments grew a new perspective on personality. This was the interactional perspective, which emphasized that all behavior is the product of both personal characteristics and the situation in which the behavior occurs. The interactional perspective gave rise to new assessment techniques such as the Template-Matching technique, which attempts to predict behavior by finding the optimal match between characteristics of persons and aspects of the situation.

To assess such phenomena as job satisfaction, applied psychologists often have to measure attitudes in addition to more enduring personality characteristics. Attitude scales are mechanisms to assign numbers to attitudes according to well-defined rules. Two popular methods for attitude-scale construction are the Likert method and the Thurstone method. Survey research is a method of obtaining attitudinal and other information about a large number of people on the basis of responses obtained from a small sample. To obtain reliable information, surveys must use random sampling methods, and the questions must be carefully worded.

17

Projective Personality Tests

Learning objectives

When you have completed the material in this chapter, you should be able to do the following:

1. *Define the projective hypothesis.*
2. *Identify five individuals who played a dominant role in the development of the Rorschach.*
3. *Describe the Rorschach stimuli.*
4. *Briefly describe Rorschach administration and scoring.*
5. *List the pros and cons of the Rorschach.*
6. *Describe the Holtzman.*
7. *Describe the TAT stimuli.*
8. *Briefly describe TAT administration.*
9. *Identify the factors that should be considered in evaluating the TAT.*
10. *List some of the major similarities and differences between the Rorschach and the TAT.*

A few years ago the wife of an army sergeant sued for divorce after 14 years of marriage. The wife claimed that her husband was "mentally unstable and deranged." She accused him of beating her, often for no apparent reason. The sergeant went to a psychologist to "prove" his sanity. In addition to an interview, an ability test (the Wechsler Adult Intelligence Scale), and an objective personality test (the Minnesota Multiphasic Personality Inventory), the psychologist administered the Rorschach inkblot test. The Rorschach is one of the best known and most widely used of the projective personality tests. According to the psychologist's evaluation, the Rorschach indicated that the sergeant was free of unusual or bizarre thought processes. The psychologist concluded that, based on the Rorschach and other test results, the sergeant was mentally stable, contrary to his wife's claims.

The matter went to court; the psychologist was called to the witness stand. The cross-examination by the wife's attorney proceeded as follows:

ATTORNEY: Based on the Rorschach and other tests, you concluded that this man is mentally stable.

PSYCHOLOGIST: I did.

ATTORNEY: What is the Rorschach?

PSYCHOLOGIST: The Rorschach is a projective psychological test that contains ten cards with inkblots on them. Five of the inkblots are black and gray; two are black, gray, and red. The remaining three are composed of a variety of pastel colors of various shades.

ATTORNEY: How do you administer a Rorschach?

PSYCHOLOGIST: The subject—that is, the person taking the test—is shown each of the cards, one at a time. The subject is required to state what the inkblot might be.

ATTORNEY: You mean to say that you can tell whether a person is sane or insane by the way he or she interprets 10 black, gray, and variously colored inkblots?

PSYCHOLOGIST: That is correct.

ATTORNEY: Your honor, this is ridiculous. For 14 years a man beats his wife for no apparent reason, but the psychologist says he's normal because he passed an inkblot test.

Put yourself in the wife's position. How do you think she felt when the psychologist said her husband was not unstable because of the way he interpreted inkblots? How would you feel if a psychologist told you that your father or mother would have to be hospitalized in a psychiatric facility because of the way he or she responded to ten variously colored inkblots? If this procedure irritates you or if you object on the grounds that the Rorschach is scientifically unsound, you are not alone. Without much difficulty you could find plenty of support for your position. Indeed, in an analysis of the scientific status of the Rorschach, Schwartz and Lazar (1979) conclude that projective personalty tests in general and the Rorschach in particular "are not scientific, in the ordinary sense of the term" (p. 10). Furthermore, many, such as Snyder, Shenkel, and Lowery (1977), question the objectivity of interpretations from projective tests.

Projective tests, such as the Rorschach, are among the most controversial and misunderstood of the psychological tests. The Rorschach has been vigorously attacked on a variety of scientific and statistical grounds (Eysenck, 1959; Jensen, 1965; Knutson, 1972). Yet, in Lubin, Wallis, and Paine's (1971) survey of psychological test usage in the United States, the Rorschach was reported to be in use in 91% of the 251 clinical settings surveyed. Why is there such widespread use and acceptance of projective tests like the Rorschach in spite of severe attacks from prominent researchers and psychometricians? To answer this question, we need to take a look at the rationale for and nature of projective tests.

I. THE PROJECTIVE HYPOTHESIS

The primary rationale underlying projective tests is the *projective hypothesis*. Numerous definitions have been advanced for the projective hypothesis, with credit for the most complete analysis commonly given to L. K. Frank (1939). Simply stated, the projective hypothesis proposes that when people attempt to understand an ambiguous or vague stimulus their interpretation of that stimulus reflects their needs, feelings, experiences, prior conditioning, thought processes, and so forth. When a frightened little boy looks into a dark room and sees a huge shadow that he interprets as a monster, he is projecting his fear onto the shadow. The shadow itself is neutral. It is neither good nor bad, fearsome nor pretty. What the child really sees is a reflection of the inner workings of his mind.

The concept of projection is not new. Exner (1976) notes, for example, that Leonardo da Vinci used ambiguous figures to evaluate young art students. Leonardo presented potential students with an ambiguous figure and presumably evaluated imagination according to the quality of the artistic form the students created from it. The concept of projection is also reflected in Shakespeare's "Nothing is either good or bad, but thinking makes it so."

Thus, two or more individuals may interpret any ambiguous or unclear situation in different, or even opposite, ways. Suppose your instructor returns an exam with 60% marked at the top. You may look at the number and react positively, remarking "Yea, I passed." Another student with precisely the same mark at the top, however, may react with immediate disappointment and anger, stating "What's wrong with that teacher; I studied hard for that exam." Now suppose your instructor announces "This was a difficult exam; the highest score in the class was 60%, which is an A." The point here is that the number 60% has no specific meaning. Yet, both you and another student reacted to it as if it did. Projective tests are sufficiently ambiguous or vague that numerous interpretations are possible to the same stimulus. Because numerous interpretations are possible, your particular interpretation can be seen as a reflection of your needs, thought processes, characteristics, and so on.

Although what the subject finally sees in a stimulus is assumed to be a reflection of personal qualities or characteristics, some responses may be more revealing than others. If, for example, you say that a round figure is a ball, you provide a relatively straightforward interpretation of the stimulus. The stimulus itself is low on ambiguity; it is round and shaped like a ball. In viewing this stimulus a high percentage of people would probably see, although not necessarily report, a ball. Even this simple response, however, can reveal a lot about you. Your response indicates that you are able to perceive the world as others do, are accurate in your perception of the external environment, and are willing to provide a conventional response. Suppose, however, you said that this same stimulus looked like a square peg in a round hole. Assuming the stimulus is actually round and contains no lines or shapes resembling a square peg, your perception of the stimulus does not conform to its actual property (roundness). Thus, your perception may not be accurate. Your response may also indicate that you are unwilling to provide the obvious, conventional response. Or your response may indicate that you perhaps feel out of place, like a square peg in a round hole.

In understanding projective tests, you should realize from the start that absolute, definite conclusions should never be drawn from any single response to an ambiguous stimulus. The examiner may only hypothesize what a test response means. Even the same response to the same stimulus may have several possible meanings depending on the characteristics of the people who make the response. Many factors can influence your response to a stimulus on a projective test. Your response, for example, may reflect a recent experience or an early experience of which you are unaware (Lindzey, 1952). It may reflect something you have witnessed (a bloody murder) or imagine (flunking out of college) rather than something you have actually experienced (Lindzey, 1952). It may reflect your day-to-day problems, such as an argument with your boyfriend or girlfriend. With all these possible factors influencing a response, it is little wonder that the validity of projective tests is difficult to document. Interpretation of projective tests requires highly trained, experienced practitioners. Even a highly trained expert, however, can easily draw the wrong conclusions, and often even the most experienced experts disagree among themselves. As in the example at the beginning of the chapter, the experts claim that they can use projective tests to draw valid conclusions. Researchers, however, remain unconvinced.

II.   THE RORSCHACH INKBLOT TEST

As an example of a psychological test based on the projective hypothesis, the Rorschach has few peers. For many years the Rorschach was without question the dominant personality test discussed in the *Mental Measurements Yearbooks* in both research citations and clinical use. Indeed, no general discussion of psychological tests is complete without reference to the Rorschach, whereas the omission of dozens of other tests would hardly be noticed.

A. *Historical antecedents*

Like most concepts, the notion of employing inkblots to study human functioning did not simply pop out of thin air. More than 25 years before the birth of Herman Rorschach, originator of the test that bears his name, Kerner (1857) noted that individuals frequently report idiosyncratic or unique personal meaning when viewing inkblot stimuli. The wide variety of possible responses to inkblots makes them valuable in studying a particular individual. Indeed, the idea of using inkblots to assess personality functioning was proposed by Binet (Binet & Henri, 1896) when Rorschach was only 10 years old. Several investigators then supported Binet's position concerning the potential value of inkblots in investigating human personality (Dearborn, 1897; Kirkpatrick, 1900), and their support led to the publication of the first set of standardized inkblots by Whipple (1910). Rorschach, however, receives credit for finding an original and important use for inkblots: identifying psychological disorders. Rorschach's investigation of inkblots began around 1911 and culminated in 1921 with the publication of his famous book *Psychodiagnostik*. A year later, he suddenly and unexpectedly died of a serious illness at the early age of 37.

Like many unconventional ideas, Rorschach's work was initially viewed with suspicion and even disdain. The sole psychiatric journal of Rorschach's homeland, Switzerland, did not even review *Psychodiagnostik* (Allison, Blatt, & Zimet, 1968). In fact, there were only a few foreign reviews of the book, and these tended to be critical. When David Levy first brought Rorschach's test to the United States from Europe, he found a cold, unenthusiastic response. American psychologists judged the test to be scientifically unsound, and psychiatrists found little use for it. Nevertheless, the use of the test gradually increased, and eventually it became quite popular.

Five individuals have played dominant roles in the use and investigation of the Rorschach. One of these, Samuel J. Beck, was a student of Levy's. Beck was especially interested in studying certain patterns, or as he called them "configurational tendencies," in Rorschach responses (S. J. Beck, 1933). Beck, who died in June 1980, eventually wrote several books on the Rorschach and influenced several generations of Rorschach practitioners (S. J. Beck, 1944, 1945, 1952). A second dominant person was Marguerite Hertz. Hertz, like Beck, stimulated considerable research on the Rorschach during the initial years when the test first established its foothold in the United States (Hertz, 1937, 1938). Bruno Klopfer, who emigrated to the United States from Germany, also published several key Rorschach books and articles and played an important role in the early development of the Rorschach (Klopfer & Kelley, 1942; Klopfer & Davidson, 1944). Zygmunt Piotrowski (1947, 1964) and David Rapaport (Rapaport, Gill, & Schafer, 1945, 1946) came somewhat later than Beck, Hertz, and Klopfer. As with the three who preceded them, however, both Piotrowski's and Rapaport's influences continue to be felt to this day. As Exner (1976, p. 75) notes, the development of the Rorschach can be attributed primarily to the efforts of these five individuals. Like most scholars, however, the five often disagreed. Their disagreements are the source of many of the current problems with the Rorschach. Each expert developed a unique system of administration, scoring, and interpretation. They all also found disciples willing to accept their biases and to use their systems.

B. *Stimuli, administration, and interpretation*

Rorschach constructed each stimulus card by dropping ink on a piece of paper and folding it. The result was a unique, bilaterally symmetrical form against a white background. After apparently experimenting with thousands of such blots, Rorschach selected ten. Five were black and gray, two contained black, gray, and red, and three contained pastel colors of various shades. An example of a Rorschach card is shown in Figure 17-1.

The Rorschach is an individual test. In the administration procedure each of the ten cards is presented to the subject with minimum structure. After some preliminary remarks concerning the purpose of testing, the examiner hands the first card to the subject and asks something like "What might this be?" No restriction is placed on the type of response permitted, and no clues are given concerning what is expected. If the subject asks for guidance or clarification, the examiner gives little information. If, for example, the subject asks "Do I use the whole thing or just part of it?" the examiner replies "As you like it" or "Whatever you choose." Anxious subjects or individuals who are made uncomfortable by unstructured situations frequently ask questions, attempting to find out as much as possible before committing themselves. The examiner, however, may not give any cues that might reveal the nature of the response that is expected. Furthermore, in view of the finding that the examiner may inadvertently reveal information or reinforce certain types of responses through facial expressions and other forms of nonverbal communication (E. Lord, 1950),

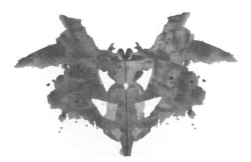

Figure 17-1. An example of a card from the Rorschach. (*From "Rorschach Inkblot Test," by H. Rorschach. In Psychodiagnostik. Copyright © 1942 by Verlag Hans Huber. Reprinted by permission.*)

Exner (1974) advocates an administration procedure in which the examiner sits next to the subject rather than face to face.

Notice that the examiner is nonspecific and, to a large degree, vague. This lack of clear structure or direction with regard to demands and expectations is a primary feature of all projective tests. The idea is to provide as much flexibility as possible so that the subject's response is a reflection of the subject. If the examiner inadvertently provides too many guidelines, then the response may simply reflect the subject's tendency to perform as expected or to provide a socially desirable response, as discussed in Chapter 15. Therefore, an improper administration that provides too much structure invalidates the results. Interpretations from such administrations are dubious.

Each card is administered twice. During the free-association phase of the test the examiner presents the cards one at a time and asks "What might this be?" If the subject gives only one response to the first card, the examiner may say "Some people see more than one thing here." The examiner usually makes this remark only once. If the subject rejects the card—that is, states that he or she sees nothing—the examiner may reply "Most people do see something here, just take your time." The examiner records every word and even every sound made by the subject verbatim. In addition, the examiner records how long it takes a subject to respond to a card (reaction time) and the position of the card when the response is made (upside down, sideways).

The purpose of the second phase of Rorschach administration, the inquiry, is to allow the examiner to score the subject's responses. Responses are scored according to at least five dimensions including location (where the perception was seen), determinant (what determined the response), form quality (to what extent the response matched the stimulus properties of the inkblot), content (what the perception was), and frequency of occurrence (to what extent the response was popular or original; popular responses occur once in every three protocols on the average). A complete discussion of these special scoring categories is beyond the scope of the present text. For further information on scoring and interpretation, you are referred to Exner's (1974) Rorschach textbook and to Exner and Weiner (1981).

In scoring for location the examiner must determine where the subject's perception is located on the inkblot. To facilitate determining this location, a small picture of each card, known as the location chart, is provided. If necessary, on rare occasions, an examiner may give a subject a pencil and ask the subject to outline the perception on the location chart. In scoring for location the examiner notes whether the subject used the whole blot (W), a common detail (D), or an unusual detail (Dd). Location may be scored for other factors as well, such as for the *confabulatory response* (DW). In the confabulatory response the subject overgeneralizes from a part to the whole. We discuss this response in detail later on.

A summary of a subject's location choices can be extremely valuable. The examiner may, for example, determine the number and percentage of W, D, and Dd responses. This type of information, in which scoring categories are summarized as a frequency or percentage, is known as the *quantitative*, structural, or statistical aspect of the Rorschach as opposed to the *qualitative* aspects, which pertain to the content and sequence of responses. Normal subjects typically produce a certain balance of W, D, and Dd responses. When a subject's pattern deviates from the typical balance, the examiner begins to suspect problems. However, no one has been able to demonstrate that a particular deviation is linked to a specific problem. A substantial deviation from what is typical or average may suggest a number of possibilities. Such deviation alerts the examiner to the possibility that the protocol may be invalid. Or the subject may be original or unconventional and thus fail to respond according to the typical pattern. Or the subject may have a perceptual problem such as occurs with certain types of brain damage or with severe emotional problems. Interestingly, the relative proportion of W, D, and Dd location choices varies with maturational development. Ames, Metraux, and Walker (1971), for example, note that W responses occur most frequently in the 3- to 4-year-old group. As the child grows older, the frequency of W responses gradually decreases until young adulthood. Thus, adult protocols with a preponderance of W responses may suggest immaturity.

Like other quantitative aspects of the Rorschach, location patterns and frequencies have been studied in a large number of experimental investigations. These investigations provide information concerning the meaning of various response patterns and thus contribute to the construct validity of the Rorschach. Unfortunately, many of the results of the studies conflict with the opinions of experts. Furthermore, many studies supporting the validity of the Rorschach have not been successfully replicated. The ability to form W responses, for example, has been linked to intelligence. Presumably, the W response requires an ability to organize the entire inkblot into a single, meaningful percept, and this organization process requires intelligence. However, because W responses are related to intelligence only for specific cards, there is a low correlation (about .40) between the number of W responses and IQ (Abrams, 1955; Holzberg & Belmont, 1952; Lotsoff, 1953; McCandless, 1949; Wishner, 1948).

Having ascertained the location of a response, the examiner must determine what it was about the inkblot that led the subject to see that particular percept. This factor is known as the determinant. One or more of at least four properties of an inkblot may determine or lead to a response: its form or shape, movement, its color, and its shading. If the subject uses only the form of the blot to determine a response, then the response is scored F and is called a pure form response. Responses are scored for form when the subject justifies or elaborates a response by statements such as "It looks like one," "It is shaped like one,"

"Here are the head, legs, feet, ears, and wings." In all these examples the response is determined exclusively on the basis of shape. In addition to form, a perception may be based on movement, color, shading, or some combination of these factors. These other determinants, furthermore, can be subdivided. Movement may be human (M), such as two people hugging; animal (FM), such as two elephants playing; or inanimate (m), such as sparks flying.

As with location, the presence (or absence) of each determinant as well as the relative proportion of the various determinants can be related to a number of hypotheses and empirical findings. Consider the movement response. Most Rorschach experts agree that whether and how a subject uses movement can be most revealing. The meaning of movement, however, is unclear because of disagreements among experts and contradictory or unclear experimental findings. Many experts believe the movement response is related to motor activity and impulses. Numerous movement responses, for example, may suggest high motor activity or strong impulses. The ratio of M to FM responses, furthermore, has been linked by some experts to a person's control and expression of internal impulses. In addition, like many other quantitative aspects of the Rorschach, the movement category varies with development. Ames et al. (1971), for example, found more FM than M responses from children than from adults. Thus, a high proportion of FM responses in an adult may indicate immaturity or a primitive capacity to deal with impulses. As you think about these inferences, however, you should keep in mind that most are no more than hypotheses. An examiner who blindly accepts one interpretation of a particular quantitative aspect can be making a big mistake. Certainly one who blindly accepts a particular interpretation of a Rorschach pattern is ignoring the available literature. Focused Example 17-1 illustrates the value of using highly trained experts to interpret Rorschach patterns.

Finding the determinant is the most difficult aspect of Rorschach administration. Because of the difficulties of conducting an adequate inquiry and the present lack of standardized administration procedures, wide variations exist today among examiners in the conduct of the inquiry. It has been known for years that examiner differences influence the subject's response (Gibby, Miller, & Walker, 1953). As a result of this problem, much of the Rorschach literature is confounded by differences in administration and scoring alone. This is one of the reasons why good experimental investigations of the Rorschach are rare.

Scoring content, however, is a relatively simple matter. Most authorities list a number of content categories such as human (H), animal (A), and nature (N). An inquiry is generally not necessary to determine content.

Similarly, most experts generally agree on the so-called populars, those responses that are frequently given for each card. Furthermore, Exner's (1974) comprehensive system, which includes as populars only those responses that occur once in three protocols on the average, provides a standardized method for scoring populars.

■ **FOCUSED EXAMPLE 17.1   EXPERT INTERPRETATION OF THE RORSCHACH**

Rorschach experts resolutely maintain that, if properly used, the Rorschach can be an invaluable tool. Scientists remain unconvinced. In our judgment, the key issue revolves around test use. As we have stated, Rorschach interpretations should be viewed only as tentative hypotheses. Those hypotheses that can be confirmed by other sources of data can be seen as having more validity than those that cannot be confirmed. When the Rorschach is rigidly or blindly interpreted, the scientist's disdain becomes justified. When the Rorschach is interpreted cautiously and in conjunction with other sources of data, however, a highly trained expert may astound even the most critical scientist.

One of us had a predoctoral internship at a Veterans Administration Hospital in which Marguerite Hertz, one of the five original Rorschach experts, was a consultant. Every second Thursday of the month Hertz would interpret an actual Rorschach protocol presented by one of the interns or staff members. Her interpretations were so detailed and exact that we, as scientists inexperienced with the Rorschach, doubted the validity of her interpretations. When other interns or the staff psychologists agreed with everything Hertz said, we became even more skeptical. We thought they were just awed by Hertz's reputation and were afraid to challenge this spirited woman.

When our turn came to present a Rorschach, we used the protocol of a patient we had seen in psychotherapy for several months. We knew this patient very well. We fully expected Hertz to make errors in her interpretation. We were determined to point these out to the group, thus exposing the group's error in accepting Hertz's previous interpretations. We were shocked, however, when Hertz was able to describe this patient after reading only the first four or five responses and examining the quantitative summary of the various scoring categories and ratios. Within 25 minutes Hertz not only told us what we already knew but began to tell us things we hadn't seen but which were obviously true once pointed out. This experience was most unsettling. Having started with a strong bias against the Rorschach, we could not dismiss what Hertz had done without concluding that there must be some value in it.

Later we found that Hertz's secret was her experience. She had given or studied so many Rorschachs that she had an intuitive feeling for the meaning of a particular pattern. After having seen the Rorschach patterns of dozens if not hundreds of disturbed individuals, she could easily identify a problem. Indeed, her knowledge and experience were so broad that she could even distinguish among specific types of disturbances based on the Rorschach.

We still feel the scientific status of the Rorschach leaves much to be desired. However, our experiences with the Rorschach, which include direct observation of interpretations from prominent experts, have led us to reconsider its value. If experts can make accurate interpretations, then it may be premature to reject the Rorschach without further experimental investigations. However, until the experts can specify the exact processes underlying correct interpretations from the Rorschach, the criticism from scientists will continue.

Scoring form quality, the extent to which the percept matches the stimulus properties of the inkblot, is difficult. Some experts argue that if the examiner can also see the percept, then the response has adequate form quality. If the examiner cannot see it, then the response has poor form quality and is scored F−. Obviously such a subjective system is grossly inadequate because scoring for form quality may then depend on the intelligence, imagination, skill, and even psychological state of the examiner. Exner's (1974) comprehensive system, which uses the usual frequency of the occurrence of various responses in evaluating form quality, is more objective and thus more scientifically acceptable than the method based on the examiner's ability to see the percept.

Table 17-1 summarizes our discussion of Rorschach scoring. Our discussion has obviously been incomplete, but perhaps you now have an idea of how a projective test can be scored to yield quantitative data. These quantitative data, in turn, are important because they permit the accumulation of norms for particular groups. If subjects deviate from the typical or expected performance, then the examiner must determine the reason underlying the deviation. This process often leads to valuable information about the individual (Exner, Gillespie, Viglione, & Coleman, 1982; Wiener-Levy & Exner, 1981).

Rorschach scoring is obviously difficult and complex. The purpose of the above discussion is to familiarize you with some of the many possibilities and to provide an introduction to Rorschach scoring for students planning an applied specialty. Use of the Rorschach requires advanced graduate training. You should not attempt to score or use a Rorschach without formal and didactic graduate instruction and supervised experience. Without this detailed training you might make serious errors because the procedure is so complex.

In addition to the quantitative aspects, Rorschach protocols may be evaluated for nonquantitative, or qualitative, features. These features include the specific content as well as an analysis of the sequence of responses. One important aspect of a qualitative interpretation is an evaluation of content that is reported frequently by emotionally disturbed, retarded, or brain damaged individuals but infrequently by the normal population. Such responses can be used to discriminate normal from disordered conditions. Confabulatory (DW) responses illustrate the value of qualitative interpretations. In the DW response, the subject overgeneralizes from a part to a whole: "It looked like my mother because of the eyes. My mother has large piercing eyes just like these." Here the subject sees a detail—"large piercing eyes"—and overgeneralizes so that the entire inkblot looks like his or her mother. Although one such response has no clear or specific meaning, when a subject makes a number of confabulatory responses, a disordered state becomes increasingly likely. These responses are infrequently given by the normal population yet are often given by brain damaged, mentally retarded, or emotionally disturbed individuals. Naturally, the examiner must evaluate interviews, the case history, the presenting problem, and results from other tests before accepting the validity of a qualitative analysis

TABLE 17-1 Summary of Rorschach scoring

I. LOCATION

Definition: Where on the blot was the percept seen (located)?

Types: *
1. Whole (W). The whole inkblot was used.
2. Common detail (D). A common or well-defined part of the inkblot was used.
3. Unusual detail (Dd). An unusual or poorly defined part of the inkblot was used.

II. DETERMINANT

Definition: What feature of the inkblot determined the response?

Typoo: *
1. Form (F). The shape or outline of the blot determined the response ("because the inkblot looked like one").
2. Movement (M, FM, m). Movement was seen ("two animals *walking* up a hill").
3. Color (C). Color played a role in determining the response ("a brown bear," "pink clouds").
4. Shading (T). Texture or shading features played a role in determining the response ("a furry bear because of the shading").

III. FORM QUALITY

Definition: To what extent did the percept match the stimulus properties of the inkblot?

Types: *
1. F+ or +. Percept matched stimulus properties of the inkblot in an exceptionally good way.
2. F. Percept matched stimulus properties of the inkblot.
3. F− or −. Percept matched the stimulus properties of the inkblot poorly.

IV. CONTENT

Definition: What was the percept?

Types: *
1. Human (H).
2. Animal (A).
3. Nature (N).

V. POPULAR-ORIGINAL

Definition: How frequently is the percept seen in normative samples? (Popular responses are seen in about one out of every three protocols.)

---

*This list is incomplete and does not cover the entire range of possibilities. The information given is designed to illustrate quantitative scoring of a projective test.

of a Rorschach protocol. A problem arises when the examiner or a researcher tries to use a single Rorschach feature to predict or define a specific disordered state (see Focused Example 17-2).

To the extent that confabulatory responses can be scored and summarized, they become increasingly like quantitative data. On a continuum of quantitative responses to qualitative responses, confabulatory responses are somewhere in the middle. A more strictly qualitative interpretation can be found in our earlier example in which the response "square peg in a round hole" was interpreted to mean that the individual felt out of place. Obviously, the closer an interpretation is to the qualitative end of the continuum, the more subjective and less reliable the interpretation. If the criteria for scoring responses such as the confabulatory can be made more stringent and less subjective, these responses may eventually reach the status of quantitative data. What can be done with quantifying Rorschach data is limited only by the creativity of researchers and the ability to find reliable ways of translating various types of content into quantitative data.

■ FOCUSED EXAMPLE 17-2 THE DANGER OF BASING RORSCHACH INTERPRETATIONS ON INSUFFICIENT EVIDENCE

We had the opportunity to become involved in a case in which an individual claimed that the negligence of a large company in sealing pipes together caused a leak of gas that resulted in brain damage. This individual consulted an attorney who sent her to a psychologist. The psychologist administered a Rorschach. Based on his findings, the psychologist concluded the person was brain damaged and thus had a legitimate case. The company called us and asked whether the Rorschach could be used to diagnose or identify brain damage. We replied that certain Rorschach patterns may be consistent with brain damage but that you couldn't prove a person was brain damaged simply on the basis of Rorschach results.

Laywers for the company brought in the psychologist's report and a copy of the Rorschach protocol. The person suspected of brain damage provided only six responses, far fewer than the 22 to 32 responses typically found for the ten Rorschach cards. The protocol was as follows:

	Free Association	Inquiry	Scoring
Card 1	A bat	Here are the wings, there is the head	W F A P

Discussion:
The W indicates the whole inkblot was used in the percept. The F indicates that only the form or shape (not color, movement, or shading) determined the response. The A stands for animal content. The P indicates this response is a popular (that is, one that is commonly given).

Card 2	I don't know	No, I still don't	Rejection

Discussion:
When the subject fails to provide a response, this is known as a rejection. Some examiners present the card again in the inquiry and ask "Now do you see anything?" A rejection could indicate a number of things. The typical or classical interpretation of a rejection is guardedness or defensiveness.

Card 3	I don't know (Q) No, I don't see anything	I said I don't know	Rejection

Discussion:
The (Q) indicates the examiner questioned the subject further, thus attempting to elicit a response. Notice the defensive quality in the subject's response during the inquiry.

Card 4	A gorilla	All of it; big feet, head, body	W F A
Card 5	A moth	Whole thing; wings, feelers, head	W F A P
Card 6	I don't know	No, nothing	Rejection
Card 7	A bird without a head	Wings, but no head (Q) All of it	W F– A

Discussion:

The F− indicates a poor correspondence between the response, bird, and the stimulus properties of the inkblot. Bird is an unusual response to this inkblot.

Card 8	Animals, maybe rats trying to steal something	Just two animals on the sides	D F A P

Discussion:

The two animals were formed from two common details (D). It was scored P since this response is a popular (that is, frequently occurring).

Card 9	I don't know	No, it doesn't look like anything to me	Rejection
Card 10	Nothing, wait, looks like a bug here	Just a bug, legs, pinchers, head	D F Insect

The psychologist who conducted this Rorschach administration stretched the interpretation, in our judgment, when he claimed this person was brain damaged. The argument presented was that a small number of responses, a preponderence of W responses, a lack of determinants other than form, and misperception (the poor form quality response to card 7) were all consistent with brain damage. Because the protocol contained qualities commonly found in the protocols of brain damaged individuals, the psychologist argued that he had found evidence for brain damage.

We looked at this Rorschach protocol and concluded that its information alone could in no way be considered sufficient evidence for brain damage. First, a small number of responses, in itself, cannot be attributed to any single factor. A small number of responses can be found in retarded, depressed, and extremely defensive individuals as well as in those who are brain damaged. Second, the small number of responses led to an imbalance in the proportion of W to D responses. Data on the typical ratio of W to D responses are based on protocols with 20 to 30 responses. With only six responses, all bets are off. You can't say anything about the balance with so few responses. And, in any case, there is no clear evidence that brain damaged persons give a preponderance of W responses. Third, the one F− response proves nothing. A single F− response does not necessarily indicate anything in particular let alone brain damage or disturbed perceptions. On the contrary, the subject gave three popular responses, indicating she was capable of accurate perceptions. How else could she see things that are so commonly seen by others? Fourth, lack of determinants other than form can have several possible interpretations. The significance of the exclusive use of form in this protocol is dubious, however, in view of the small number of responses. A protocol with 30 responses, all determined exclusively by form, would have quite a different meaning. Notice how the total number of responses can influence or alter the meaning of Rorschach data. The Rorschach places no limit on the number of possible responses.

We suggested that other tests be used to evaluate brain damage in this individual. Taking a conservative approach, we did not deny that this person was brain damaged. We simply stated that the Rorschach in no way documented the presence of brain damage. The person in question, however, dropped her suit after our analysis was communicated to her attorney and her psychologist.

C. *Psychometric properties*

Evaluating the Rorschach on classical psychometric properties (standardization, norms, reliability, validity) has proved exceptionally difficult, and this attempt to document or refute the adequacy of the Rorschach has produced one of the greatest divisions of opinion within the entire field of psychology. Time and again scientific psychologists have evaluated the available empirical data and concluded that the Rorschach is inadequate when judged by traditional standards. Despite these negative evaluations the Rorschach has flourished in clinical settings (Lubin et al., 1971; Sundberg, 1961).

In evaluating the Rorschach you should keep in mind that there is no universally accepted method of administration. Some examiners provide lengthy introductions and explanations; others provide almost none. Most of the experts state that the length, content, and flavor of administrative instructions should depend on the subject. Yet, empirical evidence indicates that the method of providing instructions and the content of the instructions influence a subject's response to the Rorschach (Goetcheus, 1967). Given the lack of standardized instructions, comparisons of the protocols of two different examiners are tenuous at best. There is no scientifically legitimate excuse for this lack of standardization, which contributes to the inherent difficulties in validating the Rorschach. Suppose, for example, it is hypothesized that the total number of responses to a Rorschach is related to level of defensiveness. Even if an adequate criterion measure of defensiveness could be found, if examiner instructions influence the number of responses, one examiner might obtain an average of 32 responses, whereas a second might obtain 22, independently of defensiveness. If protocols from both examiners are averaged in a group, any direct relationship between number of responses and defensiveness can easily be masked or distorted. Until a universally accepted method of Rorschach administration is used, researchers must standardize the Rorschach administration procedures themselves or risk confounding their results.

In addition to nonuniform administration, Rorschach scoring procedures are also not standardized. One system scores for human movement whenever a human is seen, while another has elaborate and stringent rules for scoring human movement. The former system obviously finds much more human movement than does the latter, even when the same test protocols are evaluated. Without standardized scoring it is extremely difficult to determine the frequency, consistency, and meaning of a particular Rorschach response. One result of unstandardized Rorschach administration and scoring procedures is that reliability investigations have produced varied and inconsistent results, and, even when reliability is shown, validity is questionable.

Researchers, however, must also share in the responsibility for the contradictory and inconclusive findings that permeate the Rorschach literature. Many research investigations of psychological tests such as the Rorschach have failed to control important variables including race, sex, age, socioeconomic status, and intelligence. If a particular variable such as race influences test results, as the research indicates (see Lewandowski & Saccuzzo, 1976), then studies that fail to control race may lead to false conclusions.

Whether the problem is lack of standardization, poorly controlled experiments, or both, there is little agreement regarding the scientific status of the Rorschach (Aronow, Reznikoff, & Rauchway, 1979). As Buros (1970) notes, "This vast amount of writing and research has produced astonishingly little, if any, agreement among psychologists regarding the specific validities of the Rorschach" (p. xxvi). In brief, the meaning of the thousands of published Rorschach studies is still debatable. For every supportive study there appears to be a negative or damaging one.

A number of studies have used the test-retest method to evaluate the reliability of the Rorschach over time. As with the objective personality tests, long-term test-retest reliability cannot be documented. Considering both long- and short-term test-retest correlation coefficients, early studies found a range of coefficients from as low as .38 to as high as .86 (Ford, 1946; Fosberg, 1941). More recent studies have produced similar findings (Exner, 1976, pp. 5-6). To complicate matters, average test-retest correlations vary across populations such as children versus adults (Ford, 1946; Eichler, 1951). Furthermore, wide ranges (.16 to .96) are found when specific scoring categories (for example, color or movement) rather than average correlations are used (Holzberg & Wexler, 1950). Split-half reliabilities have been equally discouraging.

Alternative forms for the Rorschach have also failed to produce meaningful results (Eichler, 1951; Harrower & Steiner, 1945). To our knowledge there have been no recent attempts to develop an alternative form. The problem involves developing another set of ten cards equivalent to the originals yet dissimilar enough to be called different. The subjective element in such a task is incredible.

Despite the consistently poor showing of the Rorschach during decades of research, many Rorschach experts and some researchers have rejected the negative studies on the grounds that they are poorly controlled, naive, or biased (Blatt, 1975; Holt, 1970; Lewandowski & Saccuzzo, 1976). Proponents of the Rorschach also claim that long- or even short-term test-retest coefficients are of little relevance in assessing the Rorschach if its use is restricted to evaluating current rather than future functioning. In addition, Rorschach proponents argue that despite its poor psychometric properties, the Rorschach can be valuable in obtaining specific information about a single individual (Aronow et al., 1979). Rorschach practitioners maintain, finally, that Rorschach results are not used blindly but are interpreted in conjunction with other information. When other sources of data are employed, errors can be reduced and predictive accuracy can be increased. Table 17-2 summarizes some of the pros and cons of the Rorschach.

Obviously the final word on the Rorschach has yet to be spoken. Far more

TABLE 17-2 Summary of arguments for and against the Rorschach

Against	In favor
1. Lacks a universally accepted standard of administration, scoring, and interpretation.	1. Lack of standardized procedures is a historical accident that can be corrected.
2. Evaluations of data are subjective.	2. Test interpretation is an art not a science; all test interpretation involves a subjective component.
3. Results are unstable over time.	3. Measures current functioning; results need not be stable over time; low or variable test-retest reliability coefficients should not be considered damaging.
4. Is unscientific.	4. Has a large empirical base.
5. Is inadequate by all traditional standards.	5. Available evidence is biased and poorly controlled and has therefore failed to provide a fair evaluation.

research is needed, but unless practitioners can agree on a standard method of administration and scoring the researcher's hands will be tied. Fortunately for the Rorschach, the first steps toward an adequate evaluation have already been taken. In a heroic effort, Exner (1974) distilled the best elements of the various Rorschach systems and proposed a comprehensive system. Exner's comprehensive system provides standard administration procedures that were developed and refined on the basis of empirical analysis. Likewise, scoring has been designed to increase interscorer reliability. Normative frequency tables based on empirical investigations are available to aid in evaluating quantitative factors. Although additional work is still needed, Exner and his colleagues are improving the psychometric qualities of the Rorschach. Interpretive suggestions are based on experimental investigations rather than on theoretical dogma or personal bias. If Exner's goal of providing a standard administration and scoring system can be realized, the 21st century may find the Rorschach elevated to a position unimaginable 20 years ago. In any event, both opponents as well as proponents still have a long way to go before the psychological community will be able to achieve a consensus on this most controversial test (Howes, 1981).

III. AN ALTERNATIVE INKBLOT TEST: THE HOLTZMAN

Among the prime problems of the Rorschach, from a psychometric viewpoint, are its variable number of responses from one subject to another, lack of standard procedures, and lack of an alternative form. To meet these difficulties while maintaining the advantages of the inkblot methodology, the Holtzman Inkblot Test was created (Holtzman, Thorpe, Swartz, & Herron, 1961). In the Holtzman the subject is permitted to give only one response per card. Administration and scoring procedures are standardized and carefully described. An alternative form is available that correlates well with the original test stimuli.

Interscorer as well as split-half reliabilities are comparable to those found for objective personality tests (Gamble, 1972).

Both forms, A and B, of the Holtzman contain 45 cards. Each response may be scored according to 22 dimensions. Many of these dimensions are similar to those found in the Rorschach and include location, determinant, and content. Responses may also be scored for such factors as anxiety and hostility. For each scoring category or variable, norms are presented for several samples ranging from 5-year-olds through adults. Given the psychometric advantages of the Holtzman, it is interesting that the test hasn't even begun to challenge the Rorschach's popularity.

Gamble (1972) reviewed the literature on the Holtzman and concluded that there were insufficient data to adequately compare the Holtzman to the Rorschach. The main difficulty with the Holtzman appears to be its validity (Gamble, 1972; Zubin, 1972). The few available validity studies are hardly impressive. As Zubin (1972) notes, those studies that show a positive relationship between the Holtzman and various criterion measures are based on qualitative rather than quantitative features. Thus, the available supportive evidence is highly subjective and depends on examiner skill rather than formal interpretive standards. In short, the Holtzman cannot, at this time, be considered any more useful than the Rorschach, despite its superior psychometric features. Nevertheless, the Holtzman is a relatively young test compared with the Rorschach, and it is still too early to form a judgment concerning its clinical utility relative to the Rorschach.

IV. THE THEMATIC APPERCEPTION TEST

The Thematic Apperception Test (TAT) is a product of U.S. psychology that is comparable to the Rorschach in many ways including its importance and its psychometric problems. It was first introduced in 1935 by Christina Morgan and Henry Murray of Harvard University. As with the Rorschach, use of the TAT grew rapidly after its introduction. Also as with the Rorschach, serious questions have been and continue to be raised concerning its psychometric adequacy. Unlike the Rorschach, however, the TAT has been relatively well received by the scientific community. The TAT also differs from the Rorschach in that it is based on Murray's (1938) theory of needs, whereas the Rorschach is basically atheoretical. The TAT and the Rorschach differ in other respects. The TAT authors were conservative in their evaluation of the TAT and scientific in their outlook. The TAT was not oversold as the Rorschach had been, and no extravagant claims were made. Unlike the Rorschach, the TAT was not billed as a diagnostic instrument—that is, a test of disordered emotional states. Instead, the TAT was presented as a measurement instrument for evaluating human personality characteristics.

The TAT has also distinguished itself from the Rorschach in that its nonclinical research uses are just as important as its clinical uses. Indeed, the TAT is one of the most important techniques used in personality research (for example, Atkinson, 1981; McClelland, Atkinson, Clark, & Lowell, 1953; McClelland & Atkinson, 1948; Turner, 1970). As stated, the TAT is based on Murray's (1938) theory, which distinguishes 28 human needs, including the needs for sex, affiliation, and dominance. Many of these needs have been extensively studied in personality research by using the TAT. Murray's need for achievement—"the desire or tendency to do things as rapidly and/or as well as possible" (Murray, 1938, p. 164)—alone has generated countless studies involving the TAT. A review of the relevant literature by Birney (1968) cites well over 100 studies on this one need, most of them by McClelland (1951a, 1951b, 1958, for example). The TAT measure of the achievement need has been related to factors such as parental perceptions, parental expectations, and parental attitudes toward their children. Need achievement is also related to the standards you as a student set for yourself (for example, academic standards). Studies such as those on the achievement motive have increased the construct validity as well as the scientific respectability of the TAT.

A. *Stimuli, administration, and interpretation*

The TAT is more structured and less ambiguous than is the Rorschach. TAT stimuli consist of pictures depicting a variety of scenes. There are 29 pictures and one blank card, for a total of 30 test stimuli. Specific cards are designed for males, others for females. Some of the cards are appropriate for older subjects; others are for young subjects. A few of the cards are appropriate for all subjects. Card 1, for example, can be given to any subject. It shows a boy, neatly dressed and groomed, sitting at a table upon which is a violin. In his description of Card 1, Murray stated that the boy is "contemplating" the violin. According to experts such as Bellak (1975), Card 1 of the TAT tends to reveal a person's relationship toward parental figures.

Other TAT cards tend to elicit other kinds of information. Card 4 is a picture of a woman "clutching the shoulders of a man whose face and body are averted as if he were trying to pull away from her" (Bellak, 1975, p. 51). This card elicits information concerning male/female relationships. Bellak (1975) and others (Rapaport et al., 1945, 1946) provide a description of the TAT cards along with the information each card tends to elicit. This knowledge is essential in TAT interpretation. Figure 17-2 shows Card 12F, which sometimes elicits conflicting emotions about the self. Other feelings may also be elicited.

Standardization of administration and especially scoring procedures are about as poor, if not worse, for the TAT as for the Rorschach. Most examiners typically state something like "I am going to show you some pictures. I want you to tell me a story about each picture. Tell me what led up to the story, what is happening, what the characters are thinking and feeling, and what the outcome will be." In the original design of the test, 20 cards were to be administered to

Figure 17-2. Card 12F from the Thematic Apperception Test. This card often gives the subject a chance to express her attitudes toward a mother or daughter figure. Sometimes attitudes toward marriage and aging also emerge. (*From "Thematic Apperception Test." Reprinted by permission of Harvard University Press,* © *1943, 1971. All rights reserved.*)

each subject, 10 cards in each of two separate one-hour sessions. In actual practice, however, only 10 or 12 cards are typically used (Bellak, 1975, p. 47). As with the Rorschach and almost all other individually administered tests, the examiner records the subject's responses verbatim. The examiner also records the reaction time—the time interval between the initial presentation of a card and the subject's first response. By recording reaction time, the examiner can determine whether the subject has difficulty with any particular card. Because each card is designed to elicit its own themes, needs, and conflicts, an abnormally long reaction time may indicate a specific problem. If, for example, the reaction time substantially increases for all cards involving heterosexual relationships, then the examiner may hypothesize that the subject is experiencing difficulty in this area.

There are by far more interpretive and scoring systems for the TAT than for the Rorschach. In his excellent review of the TAT literature through 1962, Murstein (1963) states "There would seem to be as many thematic scoring systems as there were hairs in the beard of Rasputin" (p. 23). Murstein summarizes most of the major methods of interpretation for the TAT, grouping them into quantitative and nonquantitative methods. Unlike the quantitative aspects of the Rorschach, which are considered to be extremely important by most examiners, quantitative methods of TAT interpretation are rather unpopular. Most TAT examiners find the available scoring systems overly elaborate, complex, and time consuming. They therefore tend to use only nonquantitative methods of interpretation.

Almost all methods of TAT interpretation take into account the hero, needs, press, themes, and outcomes. The hero is the character in each picture with whom the subject seems to identify. In most cases the story revolves around one easily recognizable character. If a number of characters seem to be important, the character most like the storyteller is selected as the hero. Of particular importance are the motives and needs of the hero. Most systems, including Murray's original, consider the intensity, duration, and frequency of each need to be indicators of the importance and relevance of that need. In TAT interpretation, press refers to the environmental forces that interfere with or facilitate satisfaction of the various needs. Again, factors such as frequency, intensity, and duration are used to judge the relative importance of these forces. The frequency of various themes (for example, depression) and outcomes (for example, failures) is also a prime indicator of their importance.

To understand the potential value of the TAT in evaluating personality characteristics, you should realize that quite different responses to the same card are elicited from different individuals. For example, for Card 1, in which a boy is contemplating a violin, one subject may say: "This boy's mother has just reminded him to practice the violin. The boy hates the violin and is wondering what he can do to make his practice session less boring. As he daydreams, his mother scolds him so he picks up the violin and plays, resenting every minute." Another subject may respond: "The boy has just come home from school and is getting ready to practice the violin. He hopes to become a great violin player someday but realizes he's just an average, ordinary person. He picks up the violin and plays, dreaming about success." A third story may go as follows: "It's violin practice again and the boy is fed up. Do this, do that, his parents are always trying to live his life. This time he fixes them, he picks up the violin, smashes it, and goes out to play baseball."

Think about these three different stories. Because the stimulus was the same in each case, differences in the stories must in some way reflect differences in the storytellers. The primary issue, however, is exactly what is revealed in these stories. Many years ago Lindzey (1952) analyzed a number of assumptions underlying the TAT. Table 17-3 lists these major assumptions. Although there were problems with many of the studies cited by Lindzey, positive evidence was found in support of these assumptions. By understanding these assumptions, you can get an idea of the complexity of TAT interpretation.

Although Lindzey's analysis was conducted some time ago, many TAT practitioners are guided by the assumptions listed in Table 17-3. The primary assumption—in completing an incomplete or unstructured situation, the individual may reveal his or her own strivings, dispositions, and conflicts—provides a rationale and support for projective tests in general. Most of the other nine

TABLE 17-3 Lindzey's assumptions for TAT interpretation

Primary assumption:
In completing an incomplete or unstructured situation, the individual may reveal his or her own characteristics (strivings, dispositions, conflicts).

Other assumptions:
1. The storyteller ordinarily identifies with one person in the drama. The characteristics (wishes, strivings, conflicts) of this imaginary person may reflect those of the storyteller.
2. The storyteller's characteristics may be represented indirectly or symbolically.
3. All stones are not of equal importance.
4. Themes directly related to stimulus material are less likely to be significant than those unrelated to stimulus material.
5. Recurrent themes (those that show up in three or four different stories) are particularly likely to mirror the characteristics of the storyteller.
6. The stories may reflect momentary characteristics of the storyteller (those aroused by temporary environmental factors) as well as enduring characteristics.
7. Stories may reflect events from the past that the storyteller has only observed or witnessed. However, the selection of these stories suggests that the events may still be a reflection of the storyteller's own characteristics.
8. Group membership or sociocultural factors may also be reflected in the stories.
9. Dispositions and conflicts that are inferred from the storyteller's creations may be unconscious and thus may not always be reflected directly in overt behavior or consciousness.

Adapted from Lindzey (1952).

assumptions, however, pertain specifically to the TAT. As these assumptions indicate, although a story is a reflection of the storyteller, a multitude of factors may influence the story. Therefore, all TAT experts agree that conducting a complete interview and taking a case history must accompany any attempt to interpret the TAT. No matter how careful and thorough such an interview, however, final conclusions and interpretations are still based on many factors including the skill and experience of the examiner.

B. Psychometric properties

Many experts consider the TAT, like the Rorschach, to be psychometrically unsound. With the unstandardized procedures for administration, scoring, and interpretation it is easy to understand why psychometric evaluations have produced inconsistent, unclear, and conflicting findings. For example, division of opinion is so wide that, whereas one expert finds impressive evidence of intrinsic validity (Harrison, 1965), others have found TAT validity to be almost nil (Varble, 1971). Not only is the interpretation of the TAT subjective, but analysis of the TAT literature is also a matter of subjective interpretation. In other words, as with the Rorschach, two experts can look at the same research data yet draw different or even opposite conclusions. It should be no surprise, then, that for almost every positive empirical finding there is a countering negative empirical finding.

An analysis of existing results does reveal that when specific variables are studied, such as the achievement need, respectably high reliability figures are found (Exner, 1976; Murstein, 1963). Test-retest reliabilities appear to fluctuate, however, and to diminish as the interval between the two testing sessions increases. Tomkins (1947), for example, found that a test-retest correlation coefficient of .80, obtained after a two-month interval, diminished to .50 after a ten-month interval for an independent sample. However, Atkinson (1981) has recently argued that the validity of the TAT does not depend on test-retest reliability. Split-half reliabilities have been consistently poor. It should be noted, however, that, like Rorschach proponents, many TAT proponents do not consider the split-half method appropriate because each card is designed to produce its own theme and content. Agreement among interpreters, however, varies considerably, with correlations ranging from the low .30s to the .90s, with the greatest agreement among similarly trained examiners (Harrison, 1940; Harrison & Rotter, 1945; Mayman & Kutner, 1947).

Validity studies have produced even less clear findings. Most experts agree that the TAT has content validity for evaluating human personality. However, criterion validity has been difficult to document. In an early but often cited study, Harrison (1940) found that his own inferences based on TAT stories correlated .78 with hospital records for specific variables. And he reported that he was 75% correct in diagnosing patients into major categories, such as psychotic versus neurotic, using TAT data. In a more recent study by Little and Shneidman (1959), however, 12 specialists for each of four tests (TAT, Make-a-Picture Story, Rorschach, MMPI) were asked to match the judgments of a group of criterion judges who had conducted extensive interviews with each of the subjects. Not only was there little agreement between the test judges and criterion judges, but of the four tests the TAT faired poorest, having both the lowest reliability and the poorest predictive validity. However, as indicated earlier, the validity of TAT does not seem to require test-retest reliability (Atkinson, 1981), and the TAT does have considerable construct validity in view of the number of research studies involving it.

As we review the psychometric properties of the TAT we find that, like the Rorschach, the TAT has a number of significant problems. In spite of these problems, however, the TAT continues to find widespread application in clinical as well as research settings. As with the Rorschach, the most pressing need appears to be that of establishing standardized administration and scoring procedures. Until such standardization is achieved, the TAT will continue to fare poorly according to traditional psychometric standards.

V.   ALTERNATIVE APPERCEPTION PROCEDURES

An alternative thematic apperception test (Ritzler, Sharkey, & Chudy, 1980) has been constructed by selecting pictures from the *Family of Man* photo-essay collection (Museum of Modern Art, 1955). According to the authors of this long overdue attempt to update the TAT methodology, the new procedure can be quantitatively scored. It provides a balance of positive and negative stories and a variety of action and energy levels for the main character. In comparison, the TAT elicits predominantly negative and low-energy stories (Ritzler et al., 1980). Preliminary results with this new procedure, known as the Southern Mississippi TAT (or SM-TAT), have been encouraging. These results indicate that the SM-TAT preserves many of the advantages of the TAT while, at the same time, providing a more rigorous and modern methodology than that offered by the TAT. Naturally, further research is needed, but the authors of this new attempt to modernize the TAT are to be applauded.

The versatility and usefulness of the TAT approach are illustrated not only by attempts such as that of Ritzler et al. (1980) to update the test but also by the availability of special forms of the TAT for children and other special forms for the elderly. The Children's Apperception Test (CAT) was created to meet the special needs of children age 3 through 10 (Bellak, 1975). The CAT stimuli contain animal rather than human figures as in the original TAT. The Gerontological Apperception Test uses stimuli in which one or more elderly individuals are involved in a scene with a theme relevant to the concerns of the elderly like loneliness and family conflicts (Wolk & Wolk, 1971). The Senior Apperception Technique is an alternative to the Gerontological Apperception Test and is parallel in content (Bellak, 1975; Bellak & Bellak, 1973).

VI. SUMMARY

According to the projective hypothesis, interpretations of an ambiguous or vague stimulus reflect the subject's own needs, feelings, experiences, prior conditioning, thought processes, and so forth.

The Rorschach is the preeminent projective test. Five individuals played a dominant role in the development of the Rorschach: Beck, Hertz, Klopfer, Piotrowski, and Rapaport. Rorschach stimuli consist of ten black, gray, red, and various pastel inkblots. These stimuli were formed by dropping ink on a piece of paper and folding the paper.

Rorschach administration involves two phases. During the free-association phase the examiner presents each card with a minimum of structure. During the second phase, the inquiry, the examiner presents each card again to obtain sufficient information for scoring purposes. The five major Rorschach scoring categories are location (where), determinant (why), content (what), popular-original (frequency of occurrence), and form quality (correspondence of percept to stimulus properties of the inkblot).

The Rorschach is highly controversial. On the negative side the Rorschach has been attacked for its lack of standardized methods for administration, scoring, and interpretation. It has been criticized because interpretations are subjective and results are unstable over time. The weight of scientific evidence has been unfavorable. On the positive side, efforts are being made to establish standardized procedures. In the hands of an expert the Rorschach can reveal a wealth of information about a single individual and unfavorable scientific evidence is disputable.

The Holtzman is a recently developed alternative to the Rorschach. The Holtzman overcomes much of the scientific criticism of the Rorschach, but the value and importance of this relatively new procedure have not yet been determined.

The TAT is another projective test; it enjoys wide research as well as clinical use. The TAT stimuli consist of 29 pictures depicting a variety of scenes and one blank card. Card 1, for example, consists of a scene in which a boy, neatly dressed and groomed, is sitting at a table upon which is a violin. The boy is contemplating the violin. Specific cards are suited for adults, children, males, and females.

In administering the TAT, the examiner requests the subject to make up a story. The story should include the events that led up to the scene, what the characters are thinking and feeling, and the outcome.

Like the Rorschach, the TAT has strong supporters but has also been attacked on a variety of scientific grounds. Although not psychometrically sound by traditional standards, the TAT is in widespread use. Like the Rorschach, it is capable of providing a wealth of information about a single individual.

Some of the similarities between the TAT and Rorschach are as follows: They are both individual projective tests for measuring human functioning and personality characteristics. Both are poorly standardized for administration, scoring, and interpretation. Both have poor test-retest reliability, especially for long intervals. Reliability coefficients for both tests vary widely. Both are highly criticized yet both are extensively used and enthusiastically adopted by practitioners. Both provide a rich source of information about a single individual, and both are supported by a wide body of empirical findings.

Some of the differences between the TAT and Rorschach are as follows: The Rorschach stimuli are inkblots; the TAT stimuli depict various scenes. Thus, TAT stimuli are more meaningful than Rorschach stimuli. The TAT is based on Murray's (1938) theory of needs; the Rorschach is atheoretical. Formal scoring and quantitative features are important in the Rorschach but are of little significance in the TAT. The TAT finds extensive use in research as well as in clinical settings; the Rorschach is primarily a clinical tool. TAT interpretation is guided by a variety of assumptions, which were listed and explored by Lindzey (1952). Rorschach interpretation still depends on the opinion of experts and on research surveys such as those contained in Exner's (1974) Rorschach textbook.

18

Alternatives to Traditional Psychological Tests

Learning objectives

When you have completed the material in this chapter, you should be able to do the following:

1. *Identify the differences between behavioral and traditional assessment procedures.*
2. *Identify the difference between the beliefs underlying traditional tests and the beliefs underlying behavioral tests.*
3. *Briefly describe behavioral assessment based on operant conditioning.*
4. *Identify the main difference between behavioral self-report techniques and traditional self-report techniques.*
5. *List four types of behavioral self-report techniques.*
6. *Briefly describe the functional, or behavior-analytic, approach to behavioral assessment.*
7. *Explain how cognitive-behavioral assessment differs from other types of behavioral assessment.*
8. *List four types of cognitive-behavioral assessment.*
9. *Describe a cognitive functional analysis.*
10. *Briefly describe community and psychophysical assessment.*

A middle-aged high school teacher once contacted us regarding her 7-year-old son. At the age of 4 the boy had suffered from an illness in which he was unable to eat solid food for 25 days because it made him gag. If he managed to swallow, he became extremely nauseous. Ever since he recovered from the illness, he had been reluctant to eat all but a few select foods. His usual menu consisted of cold cereal for breakfast, a peanut butter sandwich for lunch, and plain spaghetti for dinner. He refused to eat meat or vegetables of any kind. His parents tried everything, but nothing worked. The mother was concerned that the boy was not developing properly. She had taken him to a pediatrician who told her that unless something could be done to get the boy to eat he would have to be hospitalized. The physician suggested psychiatric intervention and gave the boy one month to improve.

After explaining the presenting problem, the mother asked us whether we could administer a test that might help explain why the child wasn't eating. A school psychologist had suggested to her that psychological tests might be useful in facilitating the treatment process. If we could understand why the boy wasn't eating, perhaps this information would aid in the treatment. In the course of our interview we discovered that the boy had been in psychiatric treatment when he was 5. The treatment had lasted about one year with little improvement. Partly because of this previous failure and partly because of her desperation, the mother insisted we do some testing. As we thought about the various tests we might use, we could see little value in using any of the traditional tests for this presenting problem.

We did administer the Wechsler Intelligence Scale for Children and found the boy had above-average intelligence (full-scale IQ=115). In achievement, as measured by the Wide Range Achievement Test, the boy was functioning about a half grade level above his present grade placement in both reading and arithmetic. Thus, intellectual and achievement factors could not account for the problem; the ability tests yielded little information in this case. Personality tests were more revealing than the ability tests but, unfortunately, were not very useful. We administered the Children's Apperception Test, and our interpretation confirmed our suspicion that the boy's eating problem originated with the trauma he had suffered when he was unable to eat solid foods. In simple terms, the boy had a deep-seated fear of eating.

Knowing why the boy wasn't eating certainly wasn't much help. One of the weaknesses of the traditional tests we had used in this case is that they provide little information concerning possible treatment approaches. When we explained the situation to the mother she pleaded, "Isn't there any other type of test you can give him? Isn't there a test that might also indicate what type of treatment would be most effective?" Thanks to advances within psychology, we were able to answer "yes."

We told the mother that a whole new approach to testing had been developed by psychologists in the specialty based on learning principles known as behavior modification, or behavior therapy. Collectively, these new and nontraditional testing techniques are known as *behavioral assessment*. "Please try these new procedures," she said. "I don't care if they are new and perhaps untested," she continued, "if they might help, by all means use them."

Would you be willing to try a new, nontraditional testing procedure? If so, you are not alone. Traditional psychological tests may be extremely valuable in the hands of highly trained experts, but they still fall short on several grounds. The traditional tests that we have discussed thus far offer little information concerning treatment approaches. As a rule, these traditional procedures also provide little information concerning how a person might behave in a particular situation. Even if these traditional procedures do explain the reason behind a particular symptom, this information is often of little value to the overall treatment process. Thus, in addition to limitations in reliability, validity, norms, and the like, traditional psychological tests have been criticized on a number of other grounds. These numerous weaknesses with traditional tests perhaps explain both the decline in the status of traditional tests and the sudden explosion of new alternative tests.

I. THE STATUS OF TRADITIONAL PSYCHOLOGICAL TESTS AND AN OVERVIEW OF THE ALTERNATIVES

In 1953, Shaffer conducted a survey asking clinical psychological practitioners to rank order their primary responsibilities. The practitioners ranked psychological testing first among all their duties. Only 14 years later, Holt (1967) wrote "Diagnostic testing today is in a funk" (p. 44). A number of authors explored the reasons for this dramatic decline in the role and status of psychological testing (Lewandowski & Saccuzzo, 1976; Saccuzzo, 1976). In addition to the unreliability and poorly documented validity of traditional procedures, many psychologists rejected traditional tests because of their lack of grounding in the psychological sciences and their poor relationship to treatment.

The psychologists' aversion of traditional testing procedures was paralleled by attacks from the public. As noted by Rapaport, Gill, and Schafer (1968), books written for the general public strongly attacked psychological tests during the interval between Shaffer's (1953) survey and Holt's (1967) assessment of the status of testing. In summarizing the general spirit of these attacks, Rapaport et al. (1968) provided this statement: "Although their instruments are unscientific and invalid, psychologists are reading our minds, invading our privacy, imposing a yoke of conformity on employees, and stifling originality in school children, driven by morbid sexual curiosity and the cynical pursuit of money" (p. 32). These accusations led to an inquiry by the Senate Subcommittee on Constitutional Rights and the House Subcommittee on Invasion of Privacy (Dahlstrom, 1969b). Although neither of these subcommittees succeeded in documenting deliberate and widespread misuse of tests (Brayfield, 1965), public attacks against testing continued. There was, for example, a call for a moratorium on all tests until improved procedures were developed (APA, 1974).

In response to these criticisms, psychologists began to develop testing techniques based on the psychological sciences, on principles and concepts developed in psychological laboratories. Grounded in psychological findings and theories, these tests, although new, provide genuine alternatives to traditional testing procedures.

These alternatives to traditional testing procedures fall into three main categories. The first, and by far the largest, category is generally referred to as behavioral assessment, which can be broken down into a number of sub-categories including procedures based on operant conditioning, self-report techniques, Kanfer and Saslow's behavior-analytic, or functional, approach, cognitive techniques, and psychophysiological techniques. The second category consists of the community testing procedures. The third category consists of newly emerging psychophysical and signal detection procedures. We discuss each of these procedures in the sections that follow.

II. BEHAVIORAL ASSESSMENT PROCEDURES

Traditional testing procedures are based on a medical model. According to this model, the overt manifestations of a disordered psychological condition (for example, overeating or undereating) are only symptoms or surface expressions of an underlying cause. In other words, disordered behavior is caused by some other characteristic or by an early experience of the person. In the example at the beginning of this chapter, the boy's avoidance of food was, in a sense, originally caused by the trauma of an illness in which solid food made him nauseous. Treatment in this model is based on the idea that, unless the cause of a symptom is removed, a new symptom may develop. Thus, one major function of traditional psychological tests is to ascertain the hypothetical underlying causes of disordered behaviors.

In behavioral assessment, by contrast, the symptom of a disordered condition is considered the real problem. If the person eats too much, then the problem is simply overeating and not some hypothetical underlying cause. The overeating may, in fact, have been caused by some early experience, just as the 7-year-old boy in our example avoided eating because of his previous illness. However, in behavioral assessment, the eating behavior becomes the direct target of treatment. Therefore, the testing procedure evaluates eating behavior.

You shouldn't think that behavioral assessment denies, ignores, or negates the causes of psychological disorders. On the contrary, certain techniques of behavior assessment include an evaluation of the factors that precede, coexist with, and follow (maintain) disordered behavior. These may be environmental factors (for example, working conditions, home situation), thought processes (for example, internal dialogue), or both. Thus, behavioral assessment often includes an evaluation of the internal or external factors that lead to and maintain disordered behavior as well as an evaluation of the behavior itself.

Behavioral assessment is more direct than traditional psychological tests. All the major reviewers of the distinction between traditional and behavioral assessment agree that behavioral assessment is characterized by fewer inferential assumptions and remains closer to observables (Goldfried, 1976; Goldfried &

Kent, 1972; Mischel, 1968; J. S. Wiggins, 1973). Through behavioral assessment it might be found, for example, that just prior to eating the 7 year old boy in our example says to himself "I don't want to eat; it will make me sick." Subsequently, the boy refuses to eat. As he leaves the dinner table his mother might say "That's O.K., honey, you don't have to eat." The boy's self-statement "I don't want to eat" precedes the disordered behavior. His avoidance of food is the core of the disorder. His mother's comment, plus the boy's relief that he doesn't have to eat, reinforces or maintains the disorder. In behavior assessment, preceding and subsequent factors may be analyzed, but the focus is usually on behavior. The treatment process thus involves an attempt to alter the disordered behavior (for example, increasing the frequency of eating behavior). Treatment may also involve modification of the internal dialogue before and after the boy eats and modification of the mother's behavior so that she no longer reinforces avoidance of food and instead reinforces eating.

In traditional procedures, the boy's failure to eat would be viewed only as a symptom. Testing would be aimed at determining the cause of this symptom (the early trauma of the illness he had when he was 4), and treatment would be directed at the cause rather than at the behavior itself. Presumably, by giving the boy insight into the causes of his behavior, a psychologist could get the boy to understand why he wasn't eating. When he achieved this understanding, he would no longer need to avoid eating.

It is beyond the scope of this text to debate the pros and cons of the behavioral and medical models. Our goal is to help you understand the differences between the two. Suffice it to say that behavioral testing procedures have added a whole new dimension to the field of psychological testing.

A. Procedures based on operant conditioning

In operant conditioning, we observe the various responses or behaviors of an individual. Once a response has occurred, we can then do something to that response to alter the probability of its recurrence. We may present something positive following the response to increase the rate of recurrence, or we may present something negative or aversive to reduce the rate of recurrence. In behavioral assessment based on operant conditioning, our first task is to identify the critical response or responses involved in the disorder. We can then evaluate these critical responses for frequency, intensity, or duration. This evaluation establishes the base line (usual rate of occurrence) for the particular behavior. According to a system developed by Kanfer and Saslow (1969), if the behaviors occur too frequently, they are called behavioral excesses. If they occur too infrequently, they are called behavioral deficits. Obviously, when there is a behavioral excess, treatment is aimed at reducing the frequency, intensity, or duration of the behavior in question. When there is a behavioral deficit, treatment is aimed at increasing the frequency, intensity, or duration of the behavior. Table 18-1 outlines the steps in behavioral assessment based on operant conditioning.

TABLE 18-1 Steps in a behavioral assessment

Step 1. Identify critical behaviors.
Step 2. Determine whether critical behaviors are excesses or deficits.
Step 3. Evaluate critical behaviors for frequency, duration, or intensity (that is, obtain a base line).
Step 4. If excesses, attempt to decrease frequency, duration, or intensity of behaviors; if deficits, attempt to increase behaviors.

After attempting to increase or decrease the behavior (treatment intervention), psychologists observe the effect of the intervention on the behavior in question relative to the base line. If, for example, the goal was to decrease the behavior, then there should be a decrease relative to the base line. Should the critical behavior remain at or above base-line levels, then intervention has failed.

In the example at the beginning of this chapter with the 7-year-old boy, we decided to use behavioral assessment based on operant conditioning. In this case, the critical behavior was obvious, frequency of eating. Furthermore, the critical behavior was a deficit—that is, the boy wasn't eating enough. To evaluate the critical behavior, Step 3, we asked the boy's mother to record the amount and kind of food that the boy ate each day. Using standard calorie references, we converted the amount of food the boy ate into calories. The base line looked something like the graph in Figure 18-1. The boy was eating an average of about 800 calories a day, with a range between 600 and 1000 calories on any given day. This number of calories is too few to prevent a small, gradual weight loss.

Because the behavior was a deficit, the goal was to increase his frequency of eating. For our intervention, we used a reward system based on points. The plan was that the boy be given points for everything he ate. The more he ate, the more points he could get. Following each meal his mother recorded the number of points that he received as well as the cumulative total. She posted this record

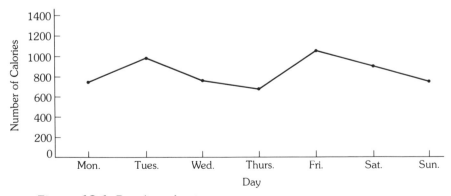

Figure 18-1. Base line of eating.

on a bulletin board in the boy's room so he could observe his own progress. She also posted a chart that we had worked out with her and the boy. The chart listed toys and other rewards that he could trade for points. For example, he could exchange 10 points for a package of baseball cards any time he wanted. He could also save his points for bigger prizes. For 350 points he could get a miniature pinball machine he had been wanting, and so on. In the treatment procedure his mother recorded exactly what he ate each day just as she did during the pretreatment assessment, in which the base line was obtained. This record was then converted into calories, and each week we made a graph of his day-to-day calorie intake.

The intervention proved highly effective. Within one week he had earned about 200 points and was well on the way to securing a pinball machine. The graph for this first week of treatment is shown in Figure 18-2. As the graph indicates, the boy doubled his average intake of calories to about 1600 (range 1400 to 1800 calories) during the first week of treatment. Thus, his intake of calories was far above base line following the intervention. Assessment continued throughout the treatment and also provided feedback concerning the effects of the treatment. In the second week, the boy's consumption of calories fell below the dramatic increases of the first week, but it never fell below base line levels. In six weeks the boy gained about eight pounds. He had earned just about every toy he had ever wanted. At this point his mother became concerned that he might gain too much weight or that she might go broke paying for rewards. After consultation with us, she terminated the point system. Following termination there was a substantial drop in his eating behavior for three or four days, but then it increased to about normal levels for his age.

Apparently the boy's parents had developed a different attitude about his eating behavior. So did the boy. Everybody concerned now knew the boy could

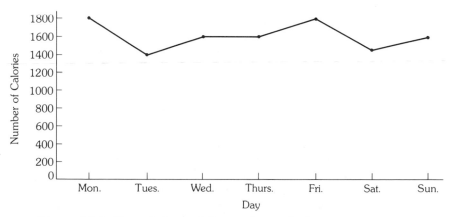

Figure 18-2. Eating behavior following first week of intervention.

eat without negative consequences. Thus, the parents refused to permit the boy to get away without eating, and the boy no longer had an excuse not to eat. Although the therapy never attempted to get at an original or hypothetical underlying cause of the behavior, the boy was in every sense cured. He wasn't hospitalized, and his eating behavior was adequate six months following treatment. His mother complained that he was still a finicky eater but that his weight was within normal limits.

The operant approach is the core of all behavioral assessment procedures. It can be used in solving a variety of problems including stopping smoking, spending more time studying, and losing weight. In each case you first calculate a base line. Then you implement an intervention. Finally, you observe the effects of your intervention on the base line. If you feel you don't study enough, you can try the approach yourself. To assess your study behavior, record the number of minutes you study each day for one week. This is your base line. Then decide on a reward you can give yourself. Every day record how long you study. Give yourself the reward whenever you study longer than 75% of the average for your base line. See whether this procedure doesn't increase the time you spend studying.

B. *Self-report techniques*

In our example the frequency of the 7-year-old boy's disordered eating behavior was recorded by his mother because the assessment process required that someone observe the boy. Not all problems, however, can be so easily and readily observed (Mitchell, 1979). Furthermore, when a parent or relative of the subject does the observing and recording, the practitioner must depend on the skill, accuracy, and honesty of the well-meaning but untrained relative. Thus, in the ideal situation, the practitioner, or a trained assistant, takes the responsibility for observing the individual to be assessed. The practitioner directly observes and records specific problem behaviors in a variety of situations and notes the factors that precede and maintain these behaviors. Naturally, like any observer, the practitioner must make himself or herself as inconspicuous (unobtrusive) as possible so as not to interfere with or influence the subject. Unfortunately, it is difficult, time consuming, and often unrealistic for a trained professional to follow a subject around recording behaviors, and in most cases it is difficult for the observer to avoid influencing the subject. Indeed, it has long been known that even the presence of an observer may alter the behavior of an individual (Polansky, Freeman, Horowitz, Irwin, Papanis, Rapaport, & Whaley, 1949).

One attempt to deal with the problems inherent in obtaining observational data is the self-report technique. The typical self-report is a list of statements about particular situations. The subject's task may be either to respond "true" or "false" to each statement or to circle a number (1 to 5, 1 to 7, for example) to indicate the importance or relevance of the statement. Table 18-2 gives examples of the types of statements used. Self-report techniques assume that the person's responses reflect individual differences and are measures of some other observable phenomenon (Tasto, 1977). If, for example, one person circles 5 for fear of snakes and another person circles 1, we would assume that direct observation of these two individuals when they are actually confronted with snakes would reveal different, measurable responses. The person who circled 5 might scream and run, for example. The person who circled 1 might simply ignore the snake. Thus, a person's response is assumed to be related to a behavior that can actually be observed. In place of direct observation, the practitioner accepts the face validity of the subject's responses.

TABLE 18-2   Examples of behavioral self-reports

Circle 1 if the item elicits no fear
   2 if the item elicits some fear
   3 if the item elicits a little fear
   4 if the item elicits a lot of fear
   5 if the item elicits extreme fear

Worms	1	2	3	4	5
Bats	1	2	3	4	5
Psychological tests	1	2	3	4	5
Dogs	1	2	3	4	5
Snakes	1	2	3	4	5
Highways	1	2	3	4	5
Men	1	2	3	4	5

Circle true or false as the item applies to you.

I like to talk when in a group.	True	False
I relate easily to the opposite sex.	True	False
I like to walk in dark places.	True	False
I like to give speeches to large groups.	True	False
I feel most comfortable with strangers.	True	False
I feel most comfortable with family.	True	False
I feel most comfortable with friends.	True	False
I like to be the leader in a group.	True	False
I would rather follow than lead in a group.	True	False

Behavioral assessment has concentrated on phenomena such as fear, and this concentration illustrates the major distinction between behavioral self-report procedures and traditional self-report procedures. Behavioral self-report procedures focus on situations that lead to particular response patterns. Traditional procedures focus on relatively enduring internal characteristics of the individual (personality traits) that lead to particular response patterns. In the behavioral approach, situations are seen as the primary determinant of behavior. In the traditional approach, characteristics that the person brings to a situation are seen as the primary determinant of behavior. Thus, in the behavioral approach, a person is not simply fearful and therefore fearful no matter what the situation; a person is fearful only in certain circumstances or situations.

The Fear Survey Schedule. The Fear Survey Schedule (FSS) is the oldest and most researched of the behavioral self-report procedures. It has been in clinical and experimental use since the 1950s. Since the FSS was first introduced into the literature by Akutagawa (1956) as a 50-item test, it has undergone a variety of changes, and versions now have from 50 to 122 items (Lawlis, 1971) with ratings of fear on either five- or seven-point scales. Items are typically related to situations that involve fear and avoidance behaviors, such as fear of open places, fear of snakes, fear of dead animals. Subjects rate each item according to the degree to which they experience that particular fear. Items for the FSS have been derived both from clinical observation of actual cases (Wolpe & Lang, 1964) and from experimental investigations in laboratory settings (Geer, 1965). The FSS attempts to identify those situations that elicit fear and thus avoidance. Once these situations are identified, treatment can be aimed at helping the person to deal with these situations, thus reducing fear.

Social avoidance and depression. Since the introduction of the FSS, behavioral practitioners have developed numerous other self-report techniques to measure a variety of problems. Watson and Friend (1969) attempted to measure anxiety in social situations with their 28-item true-false Social Avoidance Distress (SAD) scale and 30-item Fear of Negative Evaluation (FNE) scale. Lubin (1965) published a Depression Adjective Check List (DACL) to assist in the behavioral treatment of depression. In Lubin's depression scale, subjects indicate whether each of 32 adjectives "applies to me" or "does not apply to me." Eight forms are available.

Assertiveness. Many individuals have difficulty speaking up for themselves, and often, when they finally do speak up, they wind up being aggressive. Suppose, for example, someone cuts in front of you in a long line to see a popular movie. Assertiveness experts might suggest that you calmly and firmly inform this person of the location of the end of the line. If you encounter resistance, you calmly explain that everyone has been waiting in line and that the only polite and appropriate thing for the intruder to do is to go to the end of the line. Many people, however, have difficulty acting appropriately in this type of situation. They may stew inside or may go to the other extreme and display aggression, such as striking the intruder or throwing a temper tantrum.

A number of behavioral practitioners have constructed measures of assertiveness. Table 18-3 illustrates the type of item found in a behavioral assessment self-report questionnaire for assertiveness, such as the Assertive Behavior Survey Schedule (ABSS) (see Cautela & Upper, 1976). If you were taking the ABSS, you would indicate the responses you would make in specific situations in which assertiveness is indicated. You would also be asked to speculate on the consequences of assertiveness for you. Thus, the ABSS can help determine

TABLE 18-3 Sample questions from a behavioral assertiveness questionnaire

I. Suppose you were in the following situations. How would you respond? Indicate by circling number 1, 2, or 3.
  A. You have ordered filet mignon for you and your date at an expensive restaurant. You wanted yours cooked rare. The waiter brings it well done. What would you do?
    1. Tell the waiter to bring you another, cooked the way you wanted it.
    2. Complain to the waiter, but eat what he had brought for you anyway.
    3. Say nothing.
  B. You are at a bank. You've been waiting in line for nearly ten minutes. Finally, you reach the head of the line. A man with a large brief case comes from the outside and steps right in front of you. What would you do?
    1. Tell him to go to the end of the line.
    2. Tell him there is a long line, but let him go in front of you anyway.
    3. Say nothing.
II. In those situations in which you say nothing, what are you afraid of? (Check the best answer.)
  A. Being yelled at (   )
  B. Being beat up (   )
  C. Being embarrassed (   )
  D. Being rejected (   )
  E. Violating a personal or religious belief (   )
  F. Expending excessive energy (   )

Adapted from Cautela and Upper (1976, pp. 97–98).

whether you can be assertive if necessary, situations in which you might have difficulty being assertive, and your personal attitude toward assertiveness.

The availability of many other assertiveness questionnaires illustrates the importance this topic has in behavioral assessment. Another approach, for example, was developed by Rathus (1973). The Rathus Assertiveness Schedule (RAS) consists of 30 items, which subjects rate on a six-point scale depending on the extent to which the item applies to them. McFall and Lillesand (1971) developed still another assertiveness procedure, the 35-item Conflict Resolution Inventory (CRI). The CRI describes a series of unreasonable requests and asks whether the subject would refuse the request. For example, a fellow classmate who missed the last lecture asks you to recopy your notes, neatly of course, and bring them to his house that night so that he can study for the exam scheduled for the next day. Would you comply? What would you say to this person? How would you feel about your response?

Self-report battery.   Cautela and Upper (1976) have proposed the use of a self-report battery incorporating many of the commonly used self-report techniques, such as a variety of behavioral self-rating checklists and the FSS. The battery contains three types of scales. Primary scales request general information such as historical data. These scales assess general needs. Secondary scales are designed to yield information about the need for specific techniques such as relaxation or assertiveness training. The tertiary scales are highly specific.

These scales are designed to yield information about specific problems such as alcohol and drug abuse, overeating, and inappropriate sexual behavior.

Evaluation of self-report procedures.   Obviously, any practitioner with a problem to assess can simply devise and publish a self-report device. Indeed, there appears to be no shortage of such practitioners. Unfortunately, little psychometric data, if any, are ever presented to aid in an evaluation of these devices. The little information that is presented usually is based on poorly controlled correlational studies.

The lack of psychometric data on behavioral self-report measures may be the result of the relative newness of these procedures. This lack, however, may also reflect a feeling of many behavioral practitioners that their techniques are fundamentally different from traditional procedures and therefore need not be judged by the same criteria. Nevertheless, in their use of self-report techniques, behavioral psychologists appear to be repeating history and reinventing the wheel. In introducing their self-report battery, for example, Cautela and Upper (1976) do not hesitate to admit that the prototypes of current self-report techniques are tests such as the Woodworth Personal Data Sheet, which was discussed in Chapter 15. Early paper-and-pencil structured personality tests, which were finally abandoned in the 1930s, are indeed difficult to distinguish from many present-day self-report procedures. Both implicitly assume a test response can be interpreted on the basis of face validity. Thus, all the problems of interpretation in terms of face validity (subject capacity and willingness to be truthful, response biases, poor reliability, poor validity, lack of norms) generally apply to current behavioral self-report techniques.

Unfortunately, only one of the currently available self-report techniques, the FSS, has been subjected to anything close to an adequate psychometric analysis, and the results are not at all encouraging. In fact, the FSS may be worse than the Rorschach in meeting traditional psychometric standards. Tasto (1977) lists at least seven different forms of the FSS, with little agreement as to which one is best. No standardized administration procedure exists, and there is little agreement as to how the FSS should be scored or interpreted. The generalizability of the FSS is questionable because most of the studies with the procedure have used only college students as subjects. Reliability studies have shown that the FSS is internally consistent, with split-half reliability coefficients exceeding .9 (Geer, 1965; Hersen, 1971). However, test-retest reliability studies have produced varied and inconsistent results (Suinn, 1969a; Braun & Reynolds, 1969). Almost no norms are available. Efforts to provide evidence of the validity of the FSS by correlating it with traditional measures of anxiety, such as the Taylor Manifest Anxiety Scale, have produced correlations as high as .80 (Lang & Lazovik, 1963) and as low as .39 (Geer, 1965).

Clearly, behavioral practitioners have a long way to go before behavioral self-report procedures can be offered as anything more than idiosyncratic clinical tools. Unfortunately, many behavioral practitioners may be unaware of the fact that self report procedures possess many of the problems of the early objective personality tests (for example, the Woodworth), which have long since been abandoned. However, self-report techniques are only one type of behavioral assessment. Other, more scientifically sound procedures are also beginning to blossom.

C. *Kanfer and Saslow's functional approach*

In our discussion of behavioral assessment procedures based on operant conditioning, we mentioned Kanfer and Saslow's (1969) concept of behavioral deficits and excesses. At this point we would like to discuss this approach in detail, as the approach goes beyond principles of operant conditioning. Indeed, Kanfer and Saslow are among the most important pioneers in the field of behavioral assessment.

Kanfer and Saslow's method of behavioral assessment provides an alternative to the traditional diagnostic labeling of the medical model (neurotic, psychotic, and so forth). These authors propose what they called a *functional (behavior-analytic) approach* to assessment. Rather than labeling people schizophrenic or neurotic, this approach focuses on behavioral excesses and deficits. As previously indicated, a behavioral excess is any behavior or class of behaviors described as problematic by an individual because of excesses in its frequency, intensity, duration, or because of its inappropriateness. The functional approach adheres to the underlying assumptions of the learning approach to the study of disordered behavior. This approach assumes that normal and disordered behavior both develop according to the same laws and differ only in extremes. Taking a shower, for example, is a normal behavior. What about taking two showers a day? Clearly the laws governing acquisition of the behaviors involved in taking one shower are the same as those for taking two showers. What about eight showers a day? Consider three hour-long showers a day, or showers taken just after company comes for an unexpected visit. The behavior is deviant only because of its excessive frequency, intensity, duration, or its inappropriateness. Similarly, most of us blow off steam by yelling every now and then. However, if you yell every 30 seconds at an extreme intensity, and you keep on yelling for up to half an hour, especially when you go to the public library, then your yelling is clearly extreme and maladaptive.

Behavioral deficits are classes of behaviors described as problematic because they fail to occur with sufficient frequency, adequate intensity, in appropriate form, or under socially expected conditions (Kanfer & Saslow, 1969). Lack of assertiveness, for example, may be viewed as a behavioral deficit. Again, the behavior, or lack of it, is not by itself a disorder. If, for example, a gang of boys drive their motorcycles into the parking spot you were prepared to pull into, then it may not be too wise to say "That's my spot; there's another around the block." Finding another parking spot yourself is probably far more adaptive behavior. However, if people are always taking things from you and you never speak up and you view your disinclination to speak up as a problem, then you may have a behavioral deficit.

Besides isolating behavioral excesses and deficits, a functional analysis also involves other procedures, including clarifying the problem and making suggestions for treatment. In the traditional approaches, knowing a person has a particular disorder or conflict does little in the way of suggesting treatment strategies. However, when behavioral excesses are identified, efforts can be made to reduce the intensity, frequency, and so forth, of these behaviors. When behavioral deficits are identified, efforts can be made to provide new behaviors or increase the frequency of existing behaviors.

D.   *Cognitive-behavioral assessment procedures*

Whereas behavioral assessment based on operant conditioning, self-reports, and Kanfer and Saslow's functional analysis are relatively established, cognitive-behavioral assessment is a new and exciting development. The more established techniques of behavioral assessment, in general, concentrate on overt behavior and the situations that lead to particular behavioral patterns. Cognitive-behavioral assessment, however, evaluates the thinking patterns and processes that lead to behavior, including beliefs, expectations, and statements that the person makes to himself or herself (self-statements). As with other areas of behavioral assessment, treatment interventions and the testing processes are linked.

In a discussion and review of cognitive-behavioral assessment, Kendall and Korgeski (1979) discuss several different types of cognitive-behavioral assessment: thought sampling, assessing imagery, assessing beliefs, and assessing self-statements. We will briefly discuss each of these procedures. In the thought-sampling approach, there is an effort to obtain a random sample of a person's thoughts. Klinger (1978), for example, provides the individual with a portable beeper, which goes off at varying intervals. When it does, the individual records his or her thoughts at the moment using a Thought Sampling Questionnaire (TSQ). The TSQ allows the individual to rate inner experience on a variety of variables including vividness and controllability. Klinger, Barta, and Mahoney (1976) have shown that people spend more time thinking about their current concerns than about other subjects. Therefore, the TSQ presumably provides a measure of the person's most important and pressing current concerns (Kendall & Korgeski, 1979, p. 4).

The ability to visualize or imagine is essential in many techniques of behavior therapy. Therefore, a number of procedures have been developed to assess how well an individual can visualize. Hiscock (1978) examines these various procedures. Unfortunately, Hiscock's review reveals a very poor correlation among the various measures of imagery. Thus, far more work is needed in this area if the behavioral tests of imagery are to achieve respectable levels of validity.

According to the social-learning viewpoint, human behavior is often determined by beliefs and expectations rather than by what may be true in reality. If, for example, your instructor announces that there is to be an exam the third week of classes, you will no doubt do most of your studying for it the day or two before if you are like most students. Suppose, however, you miss the class just before the announced exam. Further suppose that a "friend" of yours plays a trick on you. He telephones and tells you the exam has been canceled. If you believe him and therefore expect that there will be no exam, will you study as hard as you would have before (if at all)? It's unlikely. The exam will still be given (reality), but your behavior is different because you believe the exam has been canceled. In view of the importance of beliefs and expectations in determining behavior, a number of behavioral tests have been developed to measure them. R. A. Jones (1968), for example, developed a 100-item Irrational Beliefs Test (IBT) to measure irrational beliefs (for example, the belief that you must always succeed to be worthwhile). Initial results with the IBT have been promising. Researchers, for example, have reported a significant positive relationship between the IBT and traditional measures of anxiety (Goldfried & Sobocinski, 1975) and of depression (R. E. Nelson, 1977). Thus, initial findings have tended to support the criterion validity of the IBT.

What people say to themselves also influences behavior. If you tell yourself that you can't learn statistics, then you are likely to avoid statistics. Furthermore, when confronted with a difficult statistics problem, you are likely to give up easily. If you tell yourself you like statistics, however, you probably look forward to studying statistics. When you confront a difficult statistics problem, you are likely to take your time and systematically figure out the answer. Self-statements have been shown to be influential in behaviors as diverse as assertiveness (Schwartz & Gottman, 1976) and coping behavior in cardiac patients (Kendall, Williams, Pechacek, Graham, Shisslak, & Herzoff, 1979). Interestingly, positive and negative self-statements don't function in the same way. Apparently, negative self-statements do far more harm than positive self-statements do good. Thus, treatment generally involves identifying, then eliminating, negative self-statements rather than increasing positive self-statements. Try to become aware of your own self-statements for a moment. What do you say to yourself as you go about your daily activities? The odds are, if you are making a lot of negative self-statements, you are hindering your personal efficiency and ability to cope.

One of the most important examples of the cognitive-behavioral assessment approach is Meichenbaum's (1976) technique called *cognitive functional analysis*. The premise underlying a cognitive functional analysis is that what a person says to himself or herself plays a critical role in behavior. The cognitive functional analyst is thus interested in internal dialogue such as self-appraisals and expectations. Again, what do you say to yourself about yourself as you go about your daily activities? Do you constantly criticize or belittle yourself? Or do you always reassure yourself of your capabilities? Research clearly indicates these self-statements influence your behavior and even your feelings (Meichenbaum, 1976).

Meichenbaum's cognitive functional analysis is an extension of previously discussed behavioral assessment procedures. Like other forms of behavioral assessment, cognitive functional analysis is concerned with ascertaining the environmental factors that precede behavior (environmental antecedents) as well as the environmental factors that maintain behavior (environmental consequences). In addition, however, a cognitive functional analysis attempts to ascertain the internal or cognitive antecedents and consequences for the behavioral sequence (the internal dialogue). What does the person say to himself or herself prior to, during, and following behavior? What is said prior to the behavior may influence what is done. What is said during the behavior may influence the manner in which the behavior manifests itself. What is said following the behavior may influence its probability of recurrence (Meichenbaum & Turk, 1976).

If thoughts influence behavior, then modifying thoughts can lead to modifications in behavior. That is, to the extent that thoughts play a role in eliciting or maintaining a behavioral sequence, modification of the thoughts underlying the sequence should lead to behavioral changes. If, for example, the thought "I must have a cigarette" is consistently associated with the behavioral sequence involved in smoking, then changing that thought to "My lungs are clean, I feel healthy, and I have no desire to smoke" should modify the person's pattern of smoking behavior.

Paralleling Meichenbaum's technique of cognitive functional analysis are procedures and devices that allow a person to test himself or herself. These procedures are typically known as self-monitoring devices. Because behavioral practitioners value the role and responsibility of the individual in the therapeutic process, they have developed a wide variety of these devices. In the simplest case, an individual is required to record the frequency of a particular behavior— that is, to monitor it so that the individual becomes aware of the behavior. To monitor your smoking behavior, simply count the number of cigarettes you smoke each day. To monitor your weight, weigh yourself each morning and record the number of pounds.

Some self-monitoring procedures are quite sophisticated (Mahoney, 1974). For example, a mechanical counter marketed to the general public can be attached to the jaw in order to count the number of bites a person takes when eating. The idea is to take fewer bites each day, even if it's only one fewer than the day before. Presumably, this procedure will ultimately result in a lower intake of food and eventually weight loss. Related to mechanical counters are timing devices that permit an assessment of how long a person engages in an activity. In one method, the subject is required to plug in a clock every time he or she studies, thus recording total study time. The goal is to increase this length of time, either by increasing the length of individual study sessions or by increasing the total study time within a specific period. These self-monitoring assessment tools are limited only by the imagination of the practitioner. Azrin and Powell (1968), for instance, developed an electronic device attached to a cigarette case. The device counts the number of times the case is opened. Treatment is aimed at opening the case a fewer number of times each day. Naturally, it would be easy to cheat with these devices, but to think of this possibility is to miss the point of these procedures. These devices help people help themselves by increasing awareness through feedback. You test yourself. If you cheat, you cheat yourself.

E. *Psychophysiological assessment procedures*

Traditional psychological tests consist primarily of questionnaires or puzzle and game tasks. The new behavioral assessment procedures, however, have led to the development of technical hardware for use in the assessment process. such as Klinger's (1978) beeper to sample thoughts and Azrin and Powell's (1968) electronic device to measure the number of times a cigarette case is opened. Of particular relevance are the recent developments in the relatively new area of psychophysiological assessment (see Lang, 1971). Seen as a variant of behavioral assessment by some and as an independent category by others, psychophysiological methods of assessment utilize such indicators as heart rate, blood pressure, galvanic skin response (GSR), and skin temperature to assess psychological problems. In essence, psychophysiological assessment procedures attempt to quantify physiological responses. This quantification is then translated into psychological factors (Kallman & Feuerstein, 1977). Thus, physiological data are used in drawing inferences concerning the psychological state of the individual. L. Epstein (1976), for example, maintains that such quantification not only is possible but can also be reliably accomplished.

The feasibility of psychophysiological assessment received support in an early study conducted by Ax (1953). Ax demonstrated that the fear response was related to specific physiological changes such as increases in blood pressure and skin conductance levels. He found that he could distinguish fear and anger based on physiological data. Ax's early work had interesting implications. For instance, it suggested the possibility of assessing abnormally chronic and intense anger or fear through strictly physiological methods. This type of assessment would be a quantum leap from traditional procedures, which depend on a voluntary response from the subject. In addition, as with other methods of behavioral assessment, psychophysiological assessment has direct implications for treatment.

Despite Ax's early work, the impetus for the development of psychophysiological assessment didn't come until Kamiya's (1968) remarkable discoveries. Prior to Kamiya's pioneer research in biofeedback, it had been generally believed that the human nervous system could be easily divided into two parts: the voluntary, which is under conscious control, and the involuntary, which is automatic (subconscious) and not under conscious control. Kamiya showed that, if a person is given information (feedback) regarding the so-called involuntary functions, that person can learn to exert a large degree of conscious control over these processes. He showed, for example, that a person could learn to control brain-wave patterns. His work suggested the possibility of conscious control of other processes such as heart rate, blood pressure, and skin conductance. Thus, if a psychological problem, such as chronic anger, can be reduced to physiological events and if these physiological events can be quantified, then biofeedback can be used to alter these physiological processes in a positive way. Research in this regard is promising (L. Epstein, 1976; Lang, 1971) but still in only the exploratory stages.

The polygraph and related devices that measure blood pressure, heart rate, and galvanic skin response (GSR) have been the primary tools of the psychophysiological assessment specialist. However, imaginative researchers continue to add to this hardware. For example, psychophysiologists have been particularly interested in measuring sexual response and sexual arousal in males and females. Measures of sexual arousal make use of the fact that sexual arousal is directly related to the flow of blood into the penis in males and into the vagina in females (Masters & Johnson, 1966). Using this knowledge, researchers have developed measures of sexual arousal in both males and females. In males, for example, penile erection can be measured by the penile transducer (Zuckerman, 1971). This device encircles the penis. As erection occurs, an electrical signal is generated, and this signal can then be recorded. The procedure can be used to determine the type of stimuli (pictures, fantasies, males, females, and so forth) that lead to arousal in males as well as the strength of the male sexual response. The penile transducer and related devices are much more objective than are traditional tools. Again, however, this type of assessment is still in the exploratory stages and thus far from perfected.

Psychophysiological hardware seems to hold considerable promise for raising the scientific respectability of psychological testing. A number of problems still remain, however, and considerably more research and development are needed. One of the most serious problems in psychophysiological assessment concerns artifacts. For instance, movement by the person many result in recording a physiological response that did not occur. In many cases, furthermore, direct measurement is difficult if not impossible. In measuring brain-wave patterns, for example, electrodes are placed on the head, whereas the electrical current measured actually comes from the brain. Thus, the skull distorts the electrical impulse measured by the recording device. There are other problems as well. Among these problems is the long-known effect of initial values (Wilder, 1950). According to the concept of initial values, the strength of a response is influenced by the absolute prestimulus strength. Is an increase in heart rate from

60 to 85 beats per minute or an increase from 110 to 125 beats per minute the stronger response? Obviously, one must take initial values into account in evaluating the strength, intensity, and significance of a physiological response. In spite of these problems, psychophysiological procedures appear to hold great promise for the future of psychological testing.

III. OTHER ALTERNATIVES TO TRADITIONAL PSYCHOLOGICAL TESTS

Of the alternatives to traditional psychological tests, behavioral assessment is by far the most important and most extensively developed. However, just as psychology itself has grown and expanded, so too have testing techniques. One of the newer specialties is the emerging field of community psychology (Iscoe & Spielberger, 1970). As its name implies, community psychology is interested in the community as a whole rather than in a particular individual or group of individuals. Because traditional psychological tests focus on the individual, community psychologists have had to develop new procedures relevant to communities.

In addition to community testing procedures, psychologists are working on the development of still other new approaches. Among the best examples of these other new approaches are procedures based on psychophysical and signal detection methodology. Psychophysics is the branch of psychology interested in determining the relationship between a physical stimulus (light, for example) and the human response to that stimulus. Although the field of psychophysics is far from new, efforts to use psychophysical principles as an alternative to traditional psychological tests are still in their infancy.

A. *Community testing procedures*

Community testing procedures are related to behavioral assessment in that the focus is on situations rather than on the individual. However, whereas behavioral testing procedures measure the effect of certain situations on the individual, community testing procedures analyze the characteristics of specific situations. Both community and behavioral assessment, however, are more concerned with the effects of situations on individuals than are the traditional procedures. In community procedures, the situations under study are those that occur in communities (effects of slums, overcrowding, large shopping centers, for example).

J. G. Kelly (1969), for example, believes that behavior can be judged only in relation to the context in which it occurs. He therefore attempts to assess such factors as the individual in relation to the physical environment, the individual in relation to the social environment, and one aspect of the social environment in relation to another. In their book on community psychology, Bindman and Spiegel (1969) discuss several methods of community testing that are already in existence. One of these is Klein's (1969) procedure. Klein's approach involves an evaluation of four aspects of the community: the physical characteristics, the self-image, the major groups and the interrelationships among these groups, and the major forces and the interplay among them. These community approaches have opened up a whole new area of psychological testing.

B. *Psychophysical and signal detection procedures*

Still another new alternative to traditional procedures uses methods based on psychophysical data and signal detection analysis. In these procedures, a signal is presented, and the subject is required to report whether he or she saw it. Many variations in presenting a signal are possible. The examiner can vary the strength of the signal, use more than one signal and require the subject to guess which one has been presented, or follow the signal with noise or another signal to determine the effects of one signal on another.

Saccuzzo and colleagues (Saccuzzo, 1977b, 1981; Saccuzzo & Braff, 1981; Saccuzzo, Kerr, Marcus, & Brown, 1979; Saccuzzo & Miller, 1977; Saccuzzo & Schubert, 1981) suggest that psychological disorders may be evaluated, and perhaps detected in their early stages, by psychophysical methods. In a series of studies beginning with Saccuzzo, Hirt, and Spencer (1974), Saccuzzo has provided considerable evidence that the severe psychological disorder schizophrenia may be related to the speed with which information is transferred throughout the nervous system. If schizophrenia does in fact develop because of slow processing by the individual, then it would seem sensible to use a direct measure of processing speed to assess schizophrenia rather than indirect procedures such as the Rorschach.

Indeed, information processing speed can be assessed by flashing two stimuli in brief succession in a tachistoscope. If a stimulus, such as the letter T, is presented and then terminated, the information is first registered by the nervous system. After the information is registered by the nervous system, it enters a brief perceptual memory system, which Neisser (1967) calls iconic storage. The person does not become consciously aware of the stimulus until it is transferred to the higher brain centers, where it is compared with previous learning. The rate of this transfer of information is the speed of information processing (Saccuzzo et al., 1974).

If a stimulus is presented, terminated, then followed by a second, noninformational stimulus, such as a random pattern, the second and first stimulus may integrate in the visual system. Only this unidentifiable composite will then be transferred to the higher brain centers. Obviously, if this occurs, the individual is not able to identify the originally presented T. However, if the T is transferred to the higher centers before the noninformational stimulus is presented, the person is able to identify the letter. By finding the minimum interval between presentation of the letter and presentation of the noninformational stimulus at which the noninformational stimulus no longer interferes with processing of the letter, it becomes possible to estimate how long it took the letter to reach the higher centers (Saccuzzo & Miller, 1977). Thus, speed of information processing can be determined by finding this minimum interval.

Saccuzzo and colleagues have shown that schizophrenic persons can be distinguished from normal persons and others (for example, neurotic persons) on the basis of information processing speed. In brief, normal persons require a much shorter interval to avoid the effects of the noninformational stimulus. For example, Saccuzzo et al. (1974) showed that normal persons and hospitalized nonschizophrenic persons reached maximum performance with only a 150-millisecond interval between presentation of the letter and presentation of a second, noninformational stimulus. Schizophrenic persons, however, required an interval of 300 milliseconds to reach maximum performance. This finding suggests that schizophrenic persons process information more slowly than normal persons do and that schizophrenic persons can be distinguished from normal persons on the basis of the length of the interval between the two stimuli required for maximum performance. This approach, which is only in its infancy, offers a variety of advantages over other procedures: scoring can be simplified, administration can be easily standardized, and the effects of the examiner can be minimized.

IV. SUMMARY

Behavioral procedures differ from traditional tests in that they are more direct, have fewer inferential assumptions, and remain closer to observables. Traditional tests are based on the medical model, which views the overt manifestations of psychological disorders merely as symptoms of some underlying cause. This underlying cause is the target of the traditional procedures. Behavioral tests are based on the belief that the overt manifestations of psychological disorders are more than mere symptoms. Although these overt manifestations may be caused by some other factor, they, rather than a hypothetical cause, are the targets of behavioral tests.

In behavioral assessment based on operant conditioning, the first task is to identify the critical response or responses involved in a disorder. These critical responses are then evaluated for frequency, intensity, or duration. Resulting data provide the base line for the particular behaviors. Once a base line is obtained, an intervention is introduced. The effect of this intervention on the base line is then observed.

Self-report techniques of behavioral assessment focus on situations that lead to particular response patterns; traditional procedures focus on determining internal characteristics of the individual that lead to particular response patterns. Furthermore, more than traditional procedures, the behavioral procedures purport to be related to observable phenomena. Four types of behavioral self-report techniques are the FSS, the ABSS, the DACL, and the self-report battery.

Kanfer and Saslow (1969) developed the functional, or behavior-analytic, approach to behavioral assessment. Rather than labeling people as schizophrenic or neurotic, this approach focuses on behavioral deficits and behavioral excesses. A behavioral excess is any behavior described as problematic because of excesses in its frequency, intensity, duration, or because of its inappropriateness; a behavioral deficit is the opposite (occurs too infrequently, for example).

Behavioral assessment based on operant conditioning, self-reports, and functional analyses concentrate on overt behaviors and the situations that lead to particular behavioral patterns. Cognitive-behavioral assessment, by contrast, evaluates thinking patterns and thinking processes that lead to behavior, including beliefs and expectations. Kendall and Korgeski (1979) discuss several approaches to cognitive-behavioral assessment, including thought sampling, assessing imagery, assessing beliefs, and assessing self-statements.

One of the most important examples of the cognitive-behavioral assessment approach is Meichenbaum's (1976) technique, cognitive functional analysis. The premise underlying a cognitive functional analysis is that what a person says to himself or herself plays a critical role in determining behavior. A cognitive functional analysis ascertains environmental factors that precede behavior as well as environmental factors that maintain behavior. In addition, a cognitive functional analysis attempts to ascertain the internal or cognitive antecedents and consequences for a behavioral sequence.

Of the alternatives to traditional psychological tests, behavioral assessment is by far the most important and most extensively developed. However, at least two other types of alternative testing procedures can be identified. Community testing procedures assess community characteristics and the relationships between a person and the community. A second alternative to behavioral assessment is the new psychophysical and signal detection approaches.

CHAPTER

19

Measures of Test Anxiety

Learning objectives

When you have completed the material in this chapter, you should be able to do the following:

1. *List the three major types of situations that cause stress.*
2. *Define anxiety and describe how it is usually expressed.*
3. *Describe the difference between state anxiety and trait anxiety.*
4. *Describe the type of anxiety the Taylor Manifest Anxiety Scale was designed to measure.*
5. *Name the first test designed to measure test anxiety.*
6. *Discuss some of the different theoretical orientations that underlie the different test-anxiety measures.*
7. *Discuss the different components of test anxiety.*
8. *Describe the type of test anxiety that helps rather than hurts performance.*
9. *Explain the high correlations among most test anxiety scales.*
10. *Describe treatments that can be used to reduce test anxiety.*

It is the day of your final exam. You have studied hard, and you have every reason to expect an "A." As you enter the classroom you have a stiff feeling in the back of your neck. Sweat moistens the pencil as you get it out. Finally the long, complicated instructions are over, the materials are distributed, it is time to work. Yet despite all your preparation the test does not go the way you would prefer. Instead of concentrating on the task of test taking, you worry about not doing well or you think about running out of time. When it is all over, you feel cheated. You knew the material well, but your grade on the exam does not reflect your knowledge.

If this story describes a situation you have experienced, you have company. Although there are no good figures, this experience is a typical one for hundreds of thousands of students and other test takers each year. Test anxiety is thus a common problem among college students and a major factor diminishing the validity of tests.

Test anxiety is also an important and active area in psychological research. There are a good many theories (Wine, 1980) about the relationship of anxiety to performance, and these theories have led to the development of a variety of specific test-anxiety scales and measures (see Sarason, 1980). In this chapter we review the general concepts of anxiety and stress, and then we review in some detail the theory and measurement of test anxiety.

I. STRESS AND ANXIETY

Stress is a response to situations that involve demands, constraints, or opportunities (Sarason & Sarason, 1980). During our lifetimes all of us will experience some psychological stress. The extent to which it bothers us at different times in our lives, however, will be different for each of us. For some people stress is a debilitating problem, interfering with virtually every aspect of their lives. For others, stress causes problems in particular situations. For still others, stress helps them accomplish important goals. The study of psychological stress has gained an increasingly central position within psychological and biomedical sciences. It has become clear that psychological stress can interfere with performance on mental and academic tests (Sarason, 1975), and it is increasingly apparent that stress is a major factor in the disease process. Some medical investigators now believe that stress is involved in 50% to 80% of all illnesses.

Psychological stress has three components: frustration, conflict, and pressure. Frustration occurs when the attainment of a goal is blocked. It may take different forms, but the principle remains the same. If after being a premed student for four years you are rejected by all major medical schools, for example, frustration is likely to result. Or if you want to get into a disco and are refused entrance, you may also become frustrated. In each case something or someone has blocked the attainment of a goal. Conflict is a type of stress that occurs when a choice must be made between two or more important goals. For example, you must decide between going to law school and going to graduate school in psychology. The final type of stress is pressure to speed up activities. External pressure occurs when your professor assigns a lot of extra reading right before the midterm exam; internal pressure occurs when no such reading is assigned but you take it upon yourself because it fits your style and aspirations (Coleman, 1973).

Exposure to stressful situations can cause an observable reaction known as anxiety. *Anxiety* is an unpleasant emotional state marked by worry, apprehension, and tension. When you are anxious, your autonomic nervous system becomes activated: your heart beats fast; your pulse rate goes up; your hands tend to sweat. The amount of anxiety you experience depends, in part, on the intensity of the stress-producing stimulus as you perceive it. It results from your evaluation of the situation (Spielberger, 1972): How potentially harmful is the situation for you? How threatening? How dangerous?

II.   GENERAL MEASURES OF ANXIETY

A.   *The State-Trait Anxiety Inventory*

Actually, there are two types of anxiety. Anxiety as described in the preceding paragraph is *state anxiety*, an emotional reaction that varies from one situation to another. *Trait anxiety* is a personality characteristic, reflecting the noticeable differences among the frequencies and intensities of people's emotional reactions to stress; it is a characteristic of the person and not of the situation confronted. Interest in these two types of anxiety led Charles D. Spielberger to develop the state-trait anxiety theory, which in turn led to the development of the State-Trait Anxiety Inventory (STAI). The STAI provides two separate scores: one for state anxiety (A-State) and another for trait anxiety (A-Trait). The STAI A-Trait scale consists of 20 items; subjects indicate how they generally feel about each item on a four-point scale. A similar set of items is used to evaluate A-State.

There is good evidence for the validity and the reliability of the STAI. For example, test-retest reliabilities are .73 to .86 for the trait scale. The state scale, which is supposed to be inconsistent over time, indeed has low test-retest reliability (.16 to .54). As we noted in Chapter 5, validity defines the range of inferences that can be made on the basis of a score or a measure. Validity studies have shown that the STAI can be used to make several important and useful generalizations. For example, concurrent validity studies have shown that the STAI trait scale correlates well with other measures of trait anxiety. Spielberger, Gorsuch, and Lushene (1970) report a variety of studies in which the STAI trait scale was correlated with the Taylor Manifest Anxiety Scale (see below). It was also associated with another trait-anxiety scale known as the IPAT Anxiety Scale (Cattell & Scheier, 1961) for the same groups of college students and psychiatric patients. The correlations with the Taylor and the IPAT ranged from .75 to .85, which are quite impressive and suggest that these three scales are, for the most part, measuring much of the same psychological dimension. Other scales attempting to measure trait anxiety do not do so well. One example is the Affect Adjective Checklist developed by Zuckerman (1960). It correlated only moderately with other tests designed to measure trait anxiety. In this case the concurrent validity correlations ranged from .41 to .57 (Spielberger et al., 1970). This information tells us that the STAI seems to measure the same thing as other

scales that purport to assess trait anxiety and that some other scales do not seem
to do so well.

In order for us to give a test a positive recommendation we must go beyond
the observation that it correlates well with other tests that supposedly measure
the same thing. At least two other conditions must be met. First, we must show
that the test measures something that the other tests do not. This is discriminant
evidence for construct validity (see Chapter 5). If a new test just does what the
old tests could already do, there is no need to develop a new test. Second, the
test must be shown to have meaning beyond what is known through its relations
to other tests. Just because a test correlates with other tests does not mean that it
is valid for the inferences we want to make. It is possible that the other tests are
themselves meaningless.

A good example of a validity study for the STAI is reported by Spielberger,
Auerbach, Wadsworth, Dun, and Taulbee (1975). This study took advantage of
the natural anxiety associated with anticipation of surgery. Patients who were
scheduled to undergo surgery were given the STAI before and after the medical
procedure. Patients who had undergone major surgery showed less state anxiety
after they had been told they were recovering well than they did before the
operation. This finding demonstrates that state anxiety fluctuates with the
situation—just as the test constructors say it will. Trait anxiety was not affected
by the situation; it remained the same before and after surgery. People high in
trait anxiety simply continued to respond in an anxious way, even in situations
that evoked little or no anxiety among people low in trait anxiety. Each component of the STAI thus appears to measure what it is supposed to measure. And
the two components are clearly assessing different aspects of anxiety.

B. The Taylor Manifest Anxiety Scale

The Taylor Manifest Anxiety Scale grew out of a different tradition within
psychology. Janet Taylor was a student (and later wife and widow) of the famous
learning psychologist Kenneth Spence. Originally, Taylor was interested in the
conditioning of the eyelid response. In eyelid-conditioning experiments, puffs of
air are administered to the eyelids in order to cause a blinking response. Over a
series of trials, subjects learn to anticipate the puff, and the blink comes to
precede rather than follow the air puff. The observation that stimulated the
development of the Taylor Manifest Anxiety Scale was that some individuals
learned to anticipate the air puff more rapidly than others.

According to Spence's learning theory, performance of a response is partially a function of motivation. In this case, the motivation is anxiety. Thus Taylor
needed to measure anxiety. She began by selecting items from the MMPI (see
Chapter 15) that described anxiety states. A partial list of these items and the
answers that indicate high anxiety are presented in Table 19-1. Taylor reasoned
that her list of items about these rather private events tapped an inferred drive
state (Taylor, 1953). When she divided subjects into groups high and low on

manifest anxiety, she found that the rate of anticipatory eye blinking was greater for the high anxiety subjects than for the low anxiety subjects. This experiment demonstrates both the validity of the scale for learning experiments and the plausibility of Taylor's hypothesis about eyelid conditioning and anxiety (Taylor, 1951).

In recent years, the Taylor scale has been found to be of less value because anxiety research has often required more specific measures. Anxiety is no longer regarded as a global trait; rather, there has been a growing tendency to consider specific types of anxiety and to use specific measures. One type of anxiety that has attracted an enormous amount of research attention is test anxiety.

TABLE 19-1   Ten items from the Taylor Manifest Anxiety Scale

---

I have very few headaches. (False)
I cannot keep my mind on one thing. (True)
I frequently notice my hand shakes when I try to do something. (True)
I practically never blush. (False)
I have nightmares every few nights. (True)
I sweat very easily even on cool days. (True)
I have a great deal of stomach trouble. (True)
I am usually calm and not easily upset. (False)
I am happy most of the time. (False)
I have been afraid of things or people that I know could not hurt me. (True)

From "A Personality Scale of Manifest Anxiety," by J. Taylor. In *Journal of Abnormal and Social Psychology*, 1953, *48*, 286. Copyright 1953 by the American Psychological Association. Reprinted by permission.

III. MEASURES OF TEST ANXIETY

Few topics in contemporary psychology are as well studied as test anxiety. Test anxiety affects large numbers of students at most levels of the educational system. Most of the readers of this book have experienced some form of test anxiety. For some of you this may have been a debilitating form of test anxiety that interfered with your performance on an exam.

We discuss research on text anxiety in more detail than research on other topics for three reasons: This is a topic that is relevant to many college students. Test-anxiety research is relevant to many major psychological theories. And test anxiety is a factor that may interfere with performance on all sorts of tests.

Test anxiety has been the object of a lot of theoretical research within psychology for more than 30 years. Much of this research was stimulated by a theory of test anxiety proposed by George Mandler and Seymour Sarason (1952). These theorists described test anxiety as a drive, or motivational state, that could become manifest in two different types of responding—task relevant and task irrelevant. Task-relevant responses are directed toward accomplishing the task at hand. They direct the energy associated with the test situation toward the goal of achieving a good grade. These responses may actually reduce anxiety. The major difficulty for students with test-anxiety problems is with task-irrelevant responses. In a test-taking situation, these students begin responding in a way that interferes with their performance on the test. Usually, they begin thinking in self-oriented ways; they entertain thoughts such as "I am going to fail." Because they entertain these thoughts at the expense of devoting attention to the items on the test, the result is often a disappointing performance.

Although Mandler and Sarason were from the same theoretical persuasion as Taylor, they concluded that the Taylor Manifest Anxiety Scale was too general as a measure of test anxiety. They decided instead to develop a specific measure of test anxiety and called their product the Test Anxiety Questionnaire. Over the years, people have discovered some inadequacies with this questionnaire and have transformed it into other measures such as the Test Anxiety Scale (Sarason, 1958), the Liebert-Morris Emotionality and Worry Scales (Liebert & Morris, 1967), and the Test Anxiety Inventory (Spielberger, Anton, & Bedell, 1976). Others have used different sources of items to construct tests such as the Achievement Anxiety Test (Alpert & Haber, 1960) and the Suinn Test Anxiety Behavior Scale (Suinn, 1969b). In the following sections we review each of these test-anxiety measures.

A. *The Test Anxiety Questionnaire*

The Test Anxiety Questionnaire (TAQ) is the granddaddy of all test-anxiety measures. It was the outgrowth of the Mandler and Sarason (1952) test-anxiety theory. The theory distinguishes between two different drives, or motivational states, that operate in test-taking situations. One is the *learned task drive*, which is the motivation to emit responses relevant to the task at hand. The other is the *learned anxiety drive*. The learned anxiety drive has two components: task-relevant responses and task-irrelevant responses, which were described above. Mandler and Sarason developed a 37-item questionnaire (the TAQ) that assesses a person's predisposition to think or act in a way that interferes with the completion of a task. In other words, they attempted to build a measure to assess the task-irrelevant responses in the learned-anxiety-drive portion of their theory. Some of the items from the TAQ are presented in Table 19-2. You might check the items to see whether they describe the way you feel during testing situations. Responses to the TAQ items are obtained on a 15-centimeter graphic scale. On the scale the end points and the midpoint are identified. For example, a student is asked whether he or she avoids intelligence tests more or less than other students avoid them. The endpoints of the scale are "more often than other students" and "less often than other students." The midpoint is simply labeled "midpoint."

The reliability of the TAQ is very good. Early studies using a group of 100 Yale students demonstrated that the split-half reliability was .99, and a coefficient of .82 was obtained in a test-retest study over a six-week period. Some validity evidence showed that students who were high in test anxiety actually did more

TABLE 19-2 Some of the questions used in the Test Anxiety Questionnaire

4. If you know that you are going to take a group intelligence test, how do you feel *beforehand*?

I...I...I

Feel very confident   Midpoint   Feel very unconfident

9. *While* taking a group intelligence test to what extent do you perspire?

I...I...I

Perspire not at all   Midpoint   Perspire a lot

17. Before taking an individual intelligence test, to what extent are you (or would you be) aware of an "uneasy feeling"?

I...I...I

Am not aware of it at all   Midpoint   Am very much aware of it

24. In comparison to other students, how often do you (would you) think of ways of avoiding an individual intelligence test?

I...I...I

More often than other students   Midpoint   Less often than other students

26. When you are taking a course examination, to what extent do you feel that your emotional reactions interfere with or lower your performance?

I...I...I

Do not interfere with it at all   Midpoint   Interfere a great deal

From "A Study of Anxiety and Learning," by G. Mandler and S. B. Sarason. In *Journal of Abnormal and Social Psychology*, 1952, 47, 166–173. Copyright 1952 by the American Psychological Association. Reprinted by permission.

poorly on intellectual tasks than did students who were low in test anxiety (Mandler & Sarason, 1952).

B. The Test Anxiety Scale

One of the early criticisms of the TAQ was that it dealt with state anxiety rather than trait anxiety. The first revision of the TAQ began to consider individual or personality differences in test anxiety. In 1958 Irwin Sarason, the brother of Seymour Sarason (the original codeveloper of test-anxiety theory), rewrote the TAQ items in a true-false format to create the 21-item Test Anxiety Scale (TAS). Irwin Sarason agreed with the earlier theory that test anxiety produced interfering responses during test-taking situations, but he also recognized personality differences between people who were high or low in test anxiety. He believed that less test-anxious people respond to test-taking situations by increasing their effort and attention toward the problem they are working on. Highly test-anxious persons react to the threatening situation by making self-oriented and personalized responses, often criticizing themselves rather than working on the test problems.

As you can see, the focus on the test-anxiety problem shifts from the situation in the TAQ to the person in the TAS. Although the TAS and the TAQ are quite similar and are indeed highly correlated, one measure assesses anxiety associated with situations while the other determines which persons are highly test anxious.

Since the introduction of the TAS, Sarason has accumulated convincing evidence that it does make a meaningful distinction between more and less test-anxious individuals. For example, there is a difference in the way they respond to instructions. In some experiments, the experimenter intentionally gives instructions that are stress producing—for example, by telling the students that they are expected to finish in a limited time or by telling them that the test they are taking correlates well with measures of intelligence. For subjects who score low on the TAS, these instructions may actually help. Usually less test-anxious students score better under stress-producing conditions. The opposite seems to be true for the more test-anxious group. These individuals tend to do better when the instructions are neutral or reassuring rather than stress producing (Paul & Eriksen, 1964; Sarason, 1958, 1959, 1961, 1975). These studies are valuable for at least two reasons. First, they show that the TAS does make meaningful distinctions between people. Second, they suggest that differences in school performance may be associated with personality characteristics other than intelligence.

Furthermore, the research gives specific hints about the nature of test anxiety. Only the more test anxious say negative things to themselves instead of thinking about the problems on the test. This interference with thought has been found to be most severe for test-anxious people while they are working on difficult tasks (Sarason & Palola, 1960).

Some studies demonstrate that students who score high and low on the TAS also use information in different ways. Those with low scores on the TAS tend to increase their efforts when they are told they have not done well. In other words, if they do not do well, they may try to do better. But, given the same feedback, test-anxious persons plunge into themselves instead of plunging themselves into the task (Sarason, 1975; Mandler & Sarason, 1952; Marlett & Watson, 1968).

The differences between more and less test-anxious individuals can also be detected in the way they respond to neutral feedback. After they have been given neutral feedback, students who score high on the TAS tend to respond as though they had just been given bad news, and they do not have much faith in their future success. Those who score low on the TAS tend to be optimistic about their future performance after they have been given neutral feedback (Meunier & Rule, 1967).

Some studies have even shown that when test-anxious individuals are placed in situations in which they will be evaluated (like describing themselves orally for a half hour), they attend most to negative references to themselves. They may not expect others to evaluate them well, and they actively search their environment for information to prove to themselves that this is true. For example, if someone leaves the room during a test, a test-anxious subject may interpret the behavior as an indication that he or she is not working fast enough (Sarason, 1975).

Research using the TAS is among the most extensive in the test-anxiety literature, and it confirms the validity of the TAS as a personality measure. The research shows that poor performance on tests may result from a combination of two factors: being a test-anxious person and being in a situation that arouses anxiety. When they come to an anxiety-arousing testing situation, highly test-anxious individuals may not be able to focus on the task at hand, which in this case is performing well on the test. Instead, they may have to contend with many interfering thoughts such as "My mind's a blank" or "I really feel stupid." Those of you who have had this experience know how distressing it can be. When you should be concentrating on calculating the statistics problem or picking the correct multiple-choice alternative, you begin instead to think that you are running out of time or that you are going to fail.

You may also experience some physiological changes: your heart rate may speed up, your mouth may get dry, you may begin to sweat, you may get an upset stomach or a stiff neck. Recognizing these physical side effects of test taking, some researchers have proposed that these emotional responses be measured separately.

C.   The Liebert-Morris Emotionality and Worry Scales

Liebert and Morris (1967) propose that test anxiety has two distinct and different components—emotionality and worry. Emotionality is the physical response to test-taking situations. Liebert and Morris view emotionality as awareness of autonomic arousal. In testing situations, you experience emotionality when your heart speeds up or your neck gets stiff. They regard worry as the mental preoccupation with failing and with the personal consequences of doing poorly.

Liebert and Morris began their investigation of test anxiety by doing a factor analysis on the TAQ. Factor analysis is a technique that can be used to reduce a large number of items to a smaller and more manageable set (see Chapter 3). One of the advantages of factor analysis is that it can identify the number of dimensions that are being measured by a collection of items. The test-anxiety measures we have discussed (the TAQ and the TAS) both assume that high or low scores imply only that the subject is high or low on a single construct known as test anxiety. After performing their factor analytic studies, Liebert and Morris concluded that it was not correct to think of test anxiety as a single dimension. Their studies revealed that there were two independent factors in test anxiety: emotionality and worry.

Table 19-3 shows the items that resulted from Liebert and Morris's factor analysis. Items 1-5 were associated with the emotionality factor. As you can see, all these items are statements about physiological arousal or about being upset. Items 6-10 were associated with the worry factor. These items are the typical self-oriented responses that characterize test-anxious individuals. These two components make up the two separate subscales of the Liebert-Morris Emotionality and Worry Scales.

TABLE 19-3 The Liebert-Morris Scales

Directions: Read each of the following statements carefully. To the left of each item indicate how you feel right now in relation to the upcoming ability test you will be taking. Use the following alphabetical scale:

a. The statement does *not* describe my feeling, condition, etc.
b. The feeling, condition, etc., is *barely* noticeable.
c. The feeling, condition, etc., is *moderately* intense.
d. The feeling, condition, etc., is *strong*.
e. The feeling, condition, etc., is *very strong*.

	Factor	
1.	Emot.	I am so nervous that I cannot remember facts which I really know.
2.	Emot.	I feel my heart beating faster.
3.	Emot.	I am so tense that my stomach is upset.
4.	Emot.	I have an uneasy, upset feeling.
5.	Emot.	I feel very panicky about taking the test.
6.	Worry	I do not feel very confident about my performance on the test.
7.	Worry	I feel I may not be as well prepared for the test as I could be.
8.	Worry	I am worrying a great deal about the test.
9.	Worry	I find myself thinking of how much brighter the other students are than I am.
10.	Worry	I am thinking of the consequences of doing poorly on the test.

Reprinted with permission of authors and publisher from: Liebert, R. M., & Morris, L. W. Cognitive and emotional components of test anxiety: A distinction and some initial data. *Psychological Reports*, 1967, *20*, 975–978.

Liebert and Morris felt that worry was related to one's own confidence in performing well on a test. More formally, they postulated that worry was inversely correlated with the expectation of success. If you expect to do well, you should obtain a low score on the worry scale. If you expect to do poorly, relative to others, you should obtain a high score. Liebert and Morris regarded emotionality as a transient state. Emotionality should be greatest when you are most uncertain and apprehensive about taking a test, and it should decline as your uncertainty lessens.

To provide evidence for their ideas, Liebert and Morris divided 54 college students into three groups, which differed in their expectations for performing well on an upcoming class exam. One-third of the students had a high expectation of success, a third had a low expectation of success, and the final group had a medium expectation of success. In support of the theory, lower expectations for success were related to higher scores on the worry measure, and scores on the emotionality items were unrelated to expectation of success (Liebert & Morris, 1967).

Additional evidence for the validity of the Liebert-Morris Scales was provided by an experiment by Spiegler, Morris, and Liebert (1968). In these studies the Liebert-Morris Scales were given to college students on three separate occasions: five days before an exam, immediately before the exam, and immediately after. Emotionality, which is the component of the measure that is supposed to vary depending on the situation, increased as the test date approached, peaked immediately before the exam, and fell sharply after the exam was over. Worry remained relatively constant across the three testing periods. This research therefore confirmed the claim that test anxiety involves two separate processes.

Morris and Liebert (1970) attempted to relate their measure of test anxiety to pulse rate, expectation of success on an exam, and test grades. They found that those who worried more also expected to do more poorly on an exam and indeed had poorer grades. According to their theory, pulse rate should have been closely associated with emotionality scores. However, they found pulse rate equally related to emotionality and to worry. The situation became confused even further when Doctor and Altman (1969) reported that college sophomores showed substantial decreases in worry after a test. Remember, emotionality rather than worry is supposed to change from one situation to the next. Doctor and Altman suggested that worry may be divided into two components. One component is true worry, which is the traitlike component Liebert and Morris intended to measure. The other part of worry is related to the perceived unpleasantness of the testing situation. When the test is over, this type of worry goes away. Within this framework, it is possible to explain why worry may decrease after an exam.

However, the problems with the Liebert-Morris Scales did not end here. Therapy studies began appearing in the literature that depended on the Liebert-Morris Scales to measure emotionality and worry separately. For example, Finger and Galassi (1977) did a study in which two different treatments were used for students who had problems with test anxiety. One treatment was expected to affect emotionality, while the other treatment was designed to affect worry. Contrary to what had been expected, treatments that affected emotionality also affected worry. In other words, it appeared that emotionality and worry functioned as a single process in test anxiety and that the Liebert-Morris Scales were not making a meaningful distinction between two types of test anxiety. Richardson, O'Neil, Whitmore, and Judd (1977) did a separate factor analysis on the Liebert-Morris Scales. Contrary to Liebert and Morris, Richardson and his colleagues did not find support for the hypothesis that emotionality and worry are two different factors.

D.   The Test Anxiety Inventory

In the midst of this controversy, Spielberger et al. (1976) created a separate test-anxiety scale to measure the emotionality and worry components of test anxiety. Spielberger's contribution drew from the same set of items as the other test-anxiety scales; he called this one the Test Anxiety Inventory (TAI). (Focused Example 19-1 illustrates some of the overlap in items on the various test-anxiety measures.) As we mentioned earlier in the chapter, Spielberger developed a theory that separates anxiety into two parts: trait anxiety and state anxiety. After many years of research on state-trait anxiety theory, Spielberger decided to amend the theory to deal with complex learning.

■ FOCUSED EXAMPLE 19-1 COMMON ITEMS ON TEST-ANXIETY INVENTORIES

Although there are many test-anxiety measures, most of them have drawn their items from the TAQ (Mandler & Sarason, 1952). The items have been rewritten and have been put into different formats, but they are essentially the same despite the fact that the different scales are used in research that supports quite different theories. Following are some of the similar items from the different scales.

TAQ	TAS	Liebert-Morris Scales	TAI
If you know that you are going to take a group intelligence test, how do you feel beforehand? (very confident to very unconfident)	If I knew I was going to take an intelligence test, I would feel confident and relaxed beforehand.	I do not feel very confident about my performance on the test.	I feel confident and relaxed while taking tests.
Before taking an individual intelligence test, to what extent are you (or would you be) aware of an "uneasy feeling"? (not at all to very much)	I have an uneasy, upset feeling before taking a final examination.	I have an uneasy, upset feeling.	While taking final examinations, I have an uneasy, upset feeling.
When you are taking a course examination, to what extent do you feel that your emotional reactions interfere with or lower your performance? (do not interfere with it at all to interfere a great deal)	When taking a test, my emotional feelings do not interfere with my performance.	I am so nervous I cannot remember facts which I really know.	(not included)
(not included)	I sometimes feel my heart beating faster during important exams.	I feel my heart beating faster.	I feel my heart beating very fast during important tests.

Some of the validation studies for these test-anxiety scales demonstrate that a new scale correlates well with established measures. As you can see here, it is not surprising that the TAQ, the TAS, the Liebert-Morris Scales, and the TAI are highly intercorrelated. After all, they ask nearly the same questions!

The state-trait anxiety theory, just like the Liebert and Morris view of test anxiety, includes an emotionality and worry component. In the state-trait theory, worry is considered analogous to trait anxiety, and emotionality is considered analogous to state anxiety. Worry is a personality trait—different people worry different amounts about tests. The manner in which arousal is expressed in particular situations is emotionality. Spielberger's theory differs from traditional test-anxiety theories in emphasizing the role of emotionality in test anxiety.

Traditional test-anxiety theory considers worry to be the most important problem that interferes with performance on tests. The state-trait theory focuses on emotionality as the factor that lowers performance more. Differences between people who are high or low on worry are important because those high on worry experience more emotionality in testing situations than do those who score low on worry.

The state-trait theory may become clear if we consider an example. Suppose that you are high on worry and your friend is low on worry. According to traditional test-anxiety theories it is your worry that causes you to perform poorly on examinations, probably because you become preoccupied with thoughts about yourself during the examinations. For example, you may think to yourself: "Oh, no, some people just handed in their tests. I must be going too slow. What if I flunk?" Your friend, who is low on worry, would not be distracted by these thoughts. She would be able to focus attention on the task of completing the exam. The state-trait theory has a similar interpretation for these problems, but it has a different theoretical explanation. This theory emphasizes the role of emotionality in the process. If you are high in trait anxiety, you have a tendency to become more aroused when you are under stress than does your friend who is low in trait anxiety: your heart beats faster, your blood pressure goes higher, and you have more responses that are irrelevant to the task at hand. Your friend does not get as excited when under pressure and does not have these physiological responses.

Spielberger's 20-item TAI has not been used in enough studies for us to assess its value. However, in preliminary reports, Spielberger et al. (1975) offer convincing psychometric evidence for the value of the test. Reliabilities for male subjects are reported to be .87 and .90 for the emotionality and the worry components respectively. For female subjects they are .90 and .91 (alpha coefficients). Also, there is a significant negative correlation between the TAI and grade point average for both males ($-.31$) and females ($-.18$). This finding suggests a small but significant tendency for those students with higher scores on the TAI (or those students who are more anxious) to get poorer grades in school.

E.   The Achievement Anxiety Test

If you experience test anxiety, you may find that some aspects of the experience are not so bad for you. In fact some aspects of the experience may even be good for you. One approach to the measurement of test anxiety that takes these aspects into account and that is different from some of the others we have already talked about was presented many years ago by Alpert and Haber (1960).

Their Achievement Anxiety Test (AAT) is a 19-item scale that gives scores for two different components of anxiety: facilitating anxiety and debilitating anxiety. Debilitating anxiety is similar to the anxiety that all the other scales attempt to measure. The debilitating-anxiety scale measures the extent to which anxiety interferes with performance on tests. The novel component of the AAT is facilitating anxiety, a state that can motivate performance. This type of anxiety gets you worried enough to study hard. If you are not anxious at all, you may not be motivated enough to gear up for the exam. Thus facilitating anxiety is helpful, and debilitating anxiety is harmful.

The AAT has some rather impressive evidence for reliability and validity. Test-retest reliabilities over a ten-week period were reported to be .83 for the AAT facilitating scale and .87 for the debilitating component. If the two components are really measuring opposing functions of anxiety, they should be negatively correlated with each other. Evidence suggests that indeed they are negatively correlated ($-.37$). The debilitating scale of the AAT was designed to measure a process similar to that measured by the TAS, and the correlation between these two measures is .64. The AAT facilitating scale was designed to measure a type of anxiety that is opposite to that measured by traditional test-anxiety scales, and the correlation between this scale and the TAS is significantly negative ($-.40$).

There is other good evidence for the validity of the AAT. For example the facilitating scale correlates positively with grade point average (.37), while the debilitating scale correlates negatively with college grades ($-.35$) (Alpert & Haber, 1960). One study at a large West Coast university demonstrated that the AAT scales predict grade point average nearly as well as does the Scholastic Aptitude Test (McCordick, Kaplan, Smith, & Finn, 1981). Because of these advantages, the AAT has been a favorite in many research studies on test anxiety (Desiderato & Koskinen, 1969; Ihli & Garlington, 1969; McCordick et al., 1981; Meichenbaum, 1972).

F.   The Suinn Test Anxiety Behavior Scale

By now you are probably thinking that there is a test-anxiety scale for almost any situation. Before we leave this area, we must mention a final one. This scale was developed for a particular orientation to the study of test anxiety—the behavioral approach. Most of the test-anxiety scales we have already discussed consider thoughts or cognitions about test anxiety—for example, worrying about a test. In contrast, the Suinn Test Anxiety Behavior Scale (STABS) was designed to assess how much anxiety different behavioral situations can be expected to produce. The scale consists of 50 behavioral situations. A subject must indicate on a five-point scale the amount of anxiety the situation would produce. Particularly tough situations might be ones the subject later learns to be less sensitive to through psychotherapy. In fact items for systematic desensitization can be taken directly from subjects' responses to the STABS items (Suinn, 1969).

When it was evaluated over a four-week period, the test-retest reliability of the STABS was .74, and it remained about the same (.78) in a six-week retest evaluation. Validity evidence shows that the STABS correlates .60 with the TAS and −.24 to −.28 with errors in classroom examinations and final grades in classes (Suinn, 1969). The STABS has been used in some experiments that attempt to determine the effects of behavioral treatments for test anxiety (Aponte & Aponte, 1971; Kaplan, McCordick, & Twitchell, 1979). In general it has been favorably reviewed, and it is one of the few measures that differs substantially from the other test-anxiety scales. In particular, the STABS has great potential for use among behaviorally oriented psychologists.

IV.   TREATMENTS FOR TEST ANXIETY

Throughout this chapter we have repeatedly stressed that test anxiety can be a debilitating problem for many college students. If you have problems with test anxiety, you may gain some comfort from knowing that clinical psychologists have sharpened their skills for dealing with test anxiety in recent years. The most successful approaches have been those that use some form of behavior modification. The most popular treatments are systematic desensitization (Wolpe, 1969) and cognitive behavior modification. In systematic desensitization a student systematically learns to relax and then experiences the thought of successively more threatening situations. Cognitive behavior modification (Meichenbaum, 1972; Kaplan et al., 1979) combines systematic desensitization with training in which a student learns to say positive things to himself or herself. For example, the student may learn to relax muscles in order to combat emotional responses during a test and then may also learn to make self-statements such as "I am not going to let this get to me" or "Just relax; I'm in control; concentrate on the exam."

The success of these approaches depends to some extent on the measures used to evaluate them. For example, systematic desensitization is quite effective when it is evaluated by changes in the TAQ, the TAS, or the AAT. However, systematic desensitization and most other therapies are less effective if the measure used is an increase in grade point average. When combined with training in study skills, however, systematic desensitization again appears to be effective even when the measure is grade point average (Allen, 1972; Anton, 1976; Smith, 1977; Spielberger et al., 1976).

Thus, test-anxious college students may need help not only in reducing their test anxiety but also in improving their study skills. Additional benefits appear when a self-talk component is added to the study skills–desensitization treatment package. Thus, clinical psychologists now are beginning to feel that they have the technology to help college students cope with the debilitating effects of test anxiety. Furthermore, these new approaches appear to effect improvements in classroom performance in addition to positive changes in

---

■ FOCUSED EXAMPLE 19-2 TEST ANXIETY AND THE FUNNY TEST

Perhaps the most unusual treatment for test anxiety was reported by Smith and several of his colleagues (Smith, Ascough, Ettinger, & Nelson, 1971). These psychologists were aware that some students in their classes had difficulties with test anxiety. They were also aware of several theories that suggest that a good laugh may help alleviate anger and anxiety. Smith and his colleagues used the TAS to determine which of their students were low and which were high in test anxiety. Then half the students in each group were given a funny version of their midterm. The other half were given a serious version.

In the funny version, one-third of the items were intended to be humorous. For example, one of the items about abnormal behavior read:

> Claiming to be a slot machine, Julius has been standing against a wall in a Las Vegas casino for six years making bell-like sounds and occasionally complaining that he is being tilted. Which other member of Julius's family is most likely to exhibit bizarre behavior? Alternatives: (a) his mother; (b) his sister; (c) his identical twin; (d) it is impossible to make a probability statement.

The results demonstrated that the humorous items did help relieve some of the test anxiety. On the serious version of the test, the highly anxious students did not do as well as those who did not experience much test anxiety. However, on the test with some funny items, the differences between high and low test-anxious students disappeared.

---

scores on anxiety inventories (McCordick et al., 1981; Meichenbaum, 1977; Meichenbaum & Butler, 1980). (Focused Example 19-2 describes a different approach to treating test anxiety.)

V. SUMMARY

Test anxiety is a fact of life for many students. In this chapter we reviewed some of the existing research on the theory and measurement of test anxiety. Research on test anxiety was an outgrowth of general theories of learning. Early studies by Taylor identified anxiety as a motivational state that could be measured with a short scale. Using the scale she was able to relate anxiety to a general theory that had previously depended primarily on evidence from animal studies. Later developments divided anxiety into state and trait components.

Eventually specific test-anxiety theories were proposed, and test anxiety became an area of study in itself. As test-anxiety theory developed, many scales were devised to measure test-anxiety problems. Different theories emphasized that test anxiety is a general motivational state, is a personality trait, or is related both to situations and to the characteristics of the test taker. In other words, there are many different theories of test anxiety and many different ways of measuring it. Recent developments in psychotherapy hold great promise for the successful treatment of test anxiety.

We believe that test anxiety will continue to be an active area for research for three reasons: Test anxiety is related to many general theoretical issues in psychology. Test anxiety is a real problem for many college students. And findings from studies of test anxiety may help us gain an understanding of anxiety in general.

PART

3

ISSUES

20

Test Bias

Learning objectives

When you have completed the material in this chapter, you should be able to do the following:

1. *Discuss some of the current controversies surrounding the use of intelligence tests.*
2. *Give some of the arguments for and against the belief that the content of standardized tests is biased in favor of White, middle-class children.*
3. *Explain how criterion validity studies, which review the slopes and intercepts of regression lines, are used in the study of test bias.*
4. *Discuss some of the problems with popular tests such as the Chitling Test and the BITCH.*
5. *List the components of the SOMPA and some of the advantages and disadvantages of this system.*
6. *Describe how different social, political, and ethical viewpoints are represented by different definitions of test fairness.*
7. *Discuss some of the opportunities for developing improved predictors for minority-group members.*
8. *Describe some of the problems with the criteria commonly used to evaluate standardized tests.*
9. *Describe how differences in test scores can be used to justify efforts to change the social environment.*
10. *Using the information from this chapter and from other sources, write an essay for or against the use of standardized tests for minority children.*

Psychological testing is not a field without controversy. Since the early 1970s serious and emotional debates have flourished about the meaning of tests for the placement and classification of individuals. This chapter reviews the issue of test bias, which is at the heart of the controversy. The issue of test bias is so controversial that it has inspired some court evaluations of the meaning of tests for minority-group members.

Although test bias is the unmistakable issue of the day, we should not give the impression that it is the first controversy about mental testing. Controversy has surrounded mental testing since test reports began in 1905, and the issues have been debated on and off since the 1920s (Cronbach, 1975b; Haney, 1981).

I. WHY IS THE ISSUE CONTROVERSIAL?

A basic tenet of U.S. society is that all persons are created equal. This cornerstone of political and social thought is clearly defended in the Constitution. Yet all individuals are not treated equally, and the history of social action is replete with attempts to remedy this situation. Psychological tests are among the many practices that counteract the idea that all people are the same. Tests are designed to measure differences between people, and often the differences tests measure are in desirable personal characteristics such as intelligence and aptitude. Test scores that demonstrate differences between people may suggest to some that people are not created with the same basic abilities.

The most aggravating problem is that certain ethnic groups, on the average, score differently on some psychological tests. The most controversial case concerns intelligence tests. On the average, Black Americans score 15 points lower than White Americans on standardized IQ tests. (See Chapter 11 for the meaning of IQ scores.) This difference is equal to about one standard deviation. Nobody disagrees that the two distributions greatly overlap and that there are some Blacks who score as high as the highest Whites. There are also some Whites who score as low as the lowest Blacks. Yet only about 15% to 20% of the Black population score above the average White score, and only about 15% to 20% of the White population score below the average Black score. Figure 20-1 shows the overlap between these two populations.

This is not a debatable issue. If you were to administer the Stanford-Binet or the Wechsler (see Chapter 12) to large random samples of Black and White Americans, you would most likely get the same results. The dispute has not been over whether these differences exist but over where the responsibility for the differences lies. Many have argued that the differences are due to environmental factors (Kamin, 1974; Rosenthal & Jacobson, 1968), while others have suggested that the differences are biological (Jensen, 1969, 1972; Munsinger, 1975). We will not discuss the environmental versus the biological debate because this is a technical issue that is independent of the problems with tests.

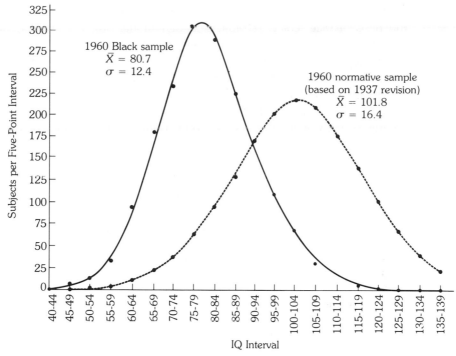

Figure 20-1. IQ distributions for Black and for White Americans. Although the distributions overlap, the means are different. Only about 15% to 20% of the Black population score above the White mean. The IQs were measured using the Stanford-Binet. (*From "A Normative Sample of Intelligence and Achievement of Negro Elementary School Children in the Southeast United States," by W. A. Kennedy, V. Van de Riet, and J. C. White, Jr. In* Monographs of the Society for Research in Child Development, *1963, 28* [No. 90], *68. Reprinted by permission.*)

II.   TEST FAIRNESS AND THE LAW

The U.S. government has attempted to establish clear standards for the use of psychological tests. Regulation of tests comes in many forms, including executive orders, laws created by legislative bodies, and actions by the courts. The most important legal development was the passage of the 1964 Civil Rights Act. Title VII of this act created the Equal Employment Opportunity Commission (EEOC). The EEOC in 1970 published guidelines for employee-selection procedures. In 1978, it released a new document entitled *Uniform Guidelines on Employee Selection Procedures.* These are the major guidelines for the use of psychological tests in education and in industry.

The 1978 guidelines are stricter, more condensed, and less ambiguous about the allowable uses of psychological test scores than were the 1970 guidelines. The original Act clearly prohibited discrimination in employment on the basis of race, color, religion, sex, or national origin. However, the 1978 guidelines made clear that any screening procedure, including the use of psychological tests, may be viewed as having adverse impact if it systematically rejects substantially higher proportions of minority than nonminority applicants. When any selection procedure does so, the employer must demonstrate that the procedure has validity for the inferences the employer wants to make. These criteria for the validity of a selection procedure are similar to those discussed in Chapter 5. However, the guidelines are specific about the acceptable criteria for the use of a test; we review these criteria in detail in Chapter 21. The guidelines have been adopted by a variety of federal agencies including the Civil Service Commission, the Department of Justice, the Department of Labor, and the Department of the Treasury. The Office of Federal Contract Compliance has the direct power to cancel government contracts held by employers who do not comply with these guidelines. In the next few years it is almost certain that these guidelines will provide the basis for law suits filed by both minority and non-minority job applicants who feel they have been mistreated in their employment pursuits.

III.   THE TRADITIONAL DEFENSE OF TESTING

In this chapter we focus on a central issue: are standardized tests as valid for Blacks and other minority groups as they are for Whites? All the types of validity we discussed in Chapter 5 come into play when the issue of test bias is considered (Cole, 1981). Some psychologists argue that the tests are differentially valid for Black and White persons. Because the issue of differential validity is so controversial and so emotionally arousing, it has forced psychologists to think carefully about many issues in test validation. Differences between ethnic groups on test performance do not necessarily indicate that the test is biased. The question is whether the test has different meanings for different groups. In psychometrics, validity defines the meaning of a test.

A.   *Content validity*

Several years ago *Newsweek* magazine published an article on cultural fairness in testing. The article listed several items from the general information portion of the Stanford-Binet that might be problematical for persons with disadvantaged backgrounds. Test constructors and users were accused of being biased because some children have never had the opportunity to learn about some of the items, and other items may be answered differently (but still correctly) by members of different ethnic groups.

Many researchers also argue that scores on intelligence tests are affected by language skills that are inculcated as part of a White, middle-class upbringing but are foreign to inner-city children (Kagan, Moss, & Siegel, 1963; Lesser, Fifer, &

Clark, 1965; Mercer, 1971; Pettigrew, 1964; Scarr-Salapatek, 1971; Woodring, 1966). As a result of being unfamiliar with the language, some children have no chance of doing well on standardized IQ tests. For example, an American child is not likely to know what a shilling is, but a British child probably does. Similarly, the American child would not be expected to know where one puts the petrol. We assume that only a British child would understand this term. Some psychologists argue that asking an inner-city child about opera is just as unfair as asking an American child about petrol. In both cases the term is not familiar to the child (Hardy, Welcher, Mellits, & Kagan, 1976).

Flaugher (1978) considered the accusations about the bias in psychological tests and concluded that many of them are based on misunderstandings. Many people feel that a fair test is one that asks questions they can answer. By contrast, a biased test is one that does not reveal all the test taker's strengths. Flaugher argued that the purpose of aptitude and achievement tests is to determine whether a person knows certain bits of information that are drawn from large potential pools of items. The test developers are indifferent to the opportunities people have to learn the information on the tests. The meaning they eventually assign to the tests comes from correlations of the test scores with other variables.

Some psychologists have argued that the linguistic bias in standardized tests does not cause the observed differences (Clarizio, 1979a). For example, Quay (1971) administered the Stanford-Binet to 100 children in an inner-city Head Start program. Half of the children in this sample were given a version of the test that used a Black dialect, while the others were given the standard version. The results demonstrated that the advantage produced by having the test in a Black dialect translates into less than a one-point increase in test scores. This finding is consistent with other research findings demonstrating that Black children can comprehend standard English about as well as they can comprehend nonstandard Black dialect (Clarizio, 1979a; Copple & Succi, 1974). This finding does not hold for White children, who seem to be functional only in the standard dialect.

Systematic studies have failed to demonstrate that biased items in well-known standardized tests are the culprits responsible for the differences between ethnic groups (Flaugher, 1978). One approach has been to find people who have expertise in judging the unfairness of particular items. Once these unfair items have been eliminated, the test should be less biased. Unexpectedly, the many attempts to purify tests using this approach have not yielded positive results. In one study 16% of the items in an elementary reading test were eliminated after experts reviewed them and labeled them as potentially biased toward the majority group. However, when the new version of the test, which had the bad items "purged," was used, the differences between the majority and the minority school populations were no smaller than they had been when the original form of the test was used (Bianchini, 1976).

Another approach to the same problem is to find classes of items that are most likely to be missed by members of a particular minority group. If a test is biased against that group, there should be significant differences between the minority and nonminority groups on certain categories of items. These studies are particularly important because if they identify certain types of items that discriminate between groups, these types of items can be avoided on future tests. Again, the results have not been encouraging; studies have not been able to clearly identify categories of items that discriminate between groups (Flaugher, 1974). The studies do show that groups differ on certain items, but it has not been clear whether these are real or chance differences. When groups are compared on large numbers of items, some differences will occur for chance reasons.

A final approach to this problem is to find items that systematically show differences between ethnic groups. Then these items are thrown out, and the test is rescored. In one study, 27 items from the SAT were eliminated because they were the specific items on which ethnic groups differed. Then the test was rescored for everyone. Although it seems as though this procedure should have eliminated the differences between groups, it actually had only slight effects because the items that differentiated the two groups tended to be the easiest items in the set. When these items were eliminated, the test was harder for everyone (Flaugher & Schrader, 1978).

In summary, studies have not supported the popular belief that items have different meanings for different groups. However, we must continue to scrutinize the content of tests. On some occasions careful reviews of tests have turned up questionable items. Many tests are carelessly constructed, and every effort should be taken to purge items that have the potential for being biased.

B. *Criterion validity*

Each night on the evening news the weatherperson forecasts the conditions for the next day. We come to depend on these forecasts if they have a history of being accurate. In evaluating the weather report, we are making a subjective assessment of validity. In a similar way we evaluate tests by asking whether they forecast future performance accurately. Standardized tests such as the SAT have been evaluated and found to be satisfactory in predicting performance during the first year of college. These tests clearly do not give us all the information we would need for perfect prediction. Yet they do give us enough information that we should pay attention to them.

College administrators who use the test scores are faced with difficult problems. On the average, minority applicants have lower test scores than nonminority applicants. At the same time most universities and colleges are attempting to increase their minority enrollments. Because minority applicants are considered as a separate category, it is appropriate to ask whether the tests have differential predictive power for the two groups of applicants.

As we mentioned in Chapter 5, the criterion validity of a test is assessed by the coefficient of correlation between the test and some criterion. The higher the correlation, the more confident we are about making predictions. If college grades are the criterion (the variable we are trying to forecast), the validity of a test such as the SAT would be represented by the correlation between the SAT and first year college grades. If students who score well on the SAT do well in college and students who score poorly on the SAT get lower grades, the test might be considered valid for aiding in the decision of admitting college students.

In Chapter 3 we reviewed the interpretation of regression plots as they relate to the validity of psychological tests. Plots like the one in Figure 20-2 were shown, and we explained how to obtain a predicted criterion score from a test score. This was done by finding the test score on the horizontal axis of the graph and drawing a line directly upward until you hit the regression line. Then the line was drawn directly over to the left until it came to rest on the vertical axis. This gave you the predicted criterion score. The only difference between Figure 20-2 and Figure 3-8 is that we have added an ellipse around the regression line. This ellipse is called an *isodensity curve*. It is used to encircle a specified portion of the cases that constitute a particular group.

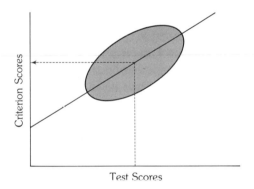

Test Scores

Figure 20-2. A sample regression plot. The slope of the line shows the relationship between a test and a criterion. The steeper the slope of the line, the better the prediction of the criterion score.

Figure 20-3 shows a regression line that represents each of two groups equally well. Group A appears to be performing less well than Group B on both the test (predictor) and the criterion scores. You can demonstrate this for yourself by selecting some points from the test scores for Group A and finding the expected scores on the criterion. Now by repeating this exercise for a few points in Group B, you will find that Group A is expected to do more poorly on the criterion because it did more poorly on the test. However, for both Group A and Group B the relationship between the test score and performance on the criterion is the same. Thus, there is little evidence for test bias in Figure 20-3.

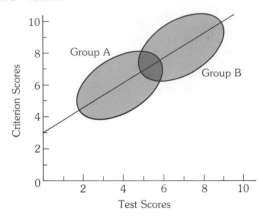

Figure 20-3. A single regression slope can predict performance equally well for two groups. However, the means for the two groups differ.

Figure 20-4 represents a different situation. Here there is a separate regression line for each group. The slopes of the two lines are the same, and that is why the two lines are parallel. However, the *intercepts*, or points at which the regression lines cross the vertical axis, differ. If you pick a particular test score, you get one expected criterion score if you use regression line A and another expected criterion score if you use regression line B. For a test score of 8 the expected criterion score from regression line A is 6, while the expected criterion score from regression line B is 10. The dotted line in Figure 20-4 is based on a combination of regression lines A and B. Now try finding the predicted score for a test score of 8 from this combined (dotted) regression line. You should get 8. Thus, the combined regression line actually overpredicts performance on the criterion for Group A and underpredicts performance for Group B. According to this example the use of a single regression line produces discrimination in favor of Group A and against Group B.

Several psychologists were surprised to find that this situation seems to fit the use of the SAT (Cleary, 1968; Kallingal, 1971; Pfeifer & Sedlacek, 1971; Temp, 1971). Each of these studies showed that the relationship between college performance and SAT scores was best described by two separate regression equations. Using a combined regression equation, which is commonly the case in practice, overpredicts how well minority students will do in college and tends to underpredict the performance of majority-group students. In other words, it appears that the SAT used with a single regression line yields biased predictions and the bias is in favor of minority groups and against majority-group students.

Notice that the lines in Figure 20-4 are parallel, indicating that the slope of the lines is about the same for each group. Equal slopes translate into equal predictive validity. Most standardized aptitude and achievement tests do confirm

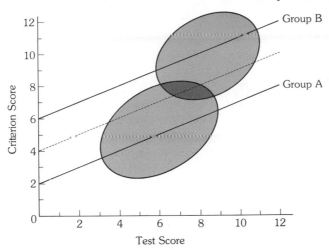

Figure 20-4. Regression lines with equal slopes but different intercepts.

the relationships shown in the figure. Thus, there is little evidence that tests such as the SAT predict college performance differently for different groups. Whether separate or combined regression lines are used depends on different definitions of bias. (We return to this issue later in the chapter. As we will see, the interpretation of tests for assessing different groups can be strongly influenced by personal and moral convictions.) It is worth noting that the situation shown in Figure 20-4 is independent of differences in mean scores. The differences in mean scores in the figure are equal to the differences between the two regression lines.

A third situation outlined by Cleary and her colleagues (Cleary, Humphreys, Kendrick, & Wesman, 1975) is shown in Figure 20-5. In this figure there are two regression lines, but the lines are no longer parallel. In this situation the coefficient for one group is different from the coefficient for the other group. In the situation presented in Figure 20-4, we found that each group was best represented by its own regression line. In this case, using a common regression line causes error in predicting scores for each group. However, the situation depicted in Figure 20-4 is not hopeless, and indeed some psychologists feel that this situation is useful because it may help increase the accuracy of predictions (Cleary, 1968). However, Figure 20-5 demonstrates a more hopeless situation. In this case the test is differentially valid for the two groups, meaning that the test will have an entirely different meaning for each group. Although empirical studies have rarely turned up such a case, there are some known examples of differential slopes (Mercer, 1979). An extensive discussion of differential validity is presented by Bartlett and O'Leary (1969). Focused Example 20-1 illustrates the application of both content and criterion validity.

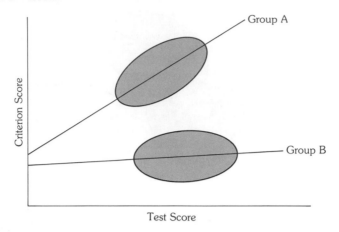

Figure 20-5. Regression lines with different slopes suggest that a test has different meanings for different groups. This is the most clear-cut example of test bias.

IV.   OTHER APPROACHES TO TESTING MINORITY-GROUP MEMBERS

To many American psychologists the defense of psychological tests has not been totally satisfactory. Although some consider the defense of the tests to be strong enough, others emphasize that we must try to find selection procedures that will end all discriminatory practices and protect the interests of minority-group members. Those who do not think that the tests are fair suggest one of two alternatives: outlaw the use of psychological tests for minority students (Williams, 1974) or develop psychological assessment strategies that suit minority children. Advocates of the first alternative have launched a legal battle to establish restrictions on the use of tests. This battle is discussed in detail in Chapter 21. In this section we review various approaches to the second alternative. In particular, we look at three different assessment approaches, the Chitling Test, the Black Intelligence Test of Cultural Homogeneity, and the System of Multicultural Pluralistic Assessment. Each of these approaches is different, yet they are all based on one common assumption: minority children have not had the opportunity to learn how to answer items on tests that reflect traditional, White, middle-class values.

A.   *Ignorance versus stupidity*

In a California trial about the use of testing in public schools, *Larry P. v. Wilson Riles,* the judge made an abrasive but insightful comment. Both sides in the case agreed that minority children perform more poorly on the standardized tests. The major issue debated by the witnesses was the meaning of the scores. One side argued that the scores reflect the underlying trait of intelligence. In other words, they allegedly measure how smart a child is. Witnesses for the other

■ FOCUSED EXAMPLE 20-1 SCORING THE WISC FOR INNER-CITY CHILDREN

The WISC requires that a test administrator follow a rigid protocol in allowing credit for certain types of responses. Over the years many people have questioned whether these scoring procedures should be so stringent. In particular they have suggested that some children may be giving an appropriate response for the subculture they are familiar with even though that response may not be given credit. A large study conducted in the inner portion of Baltimore (the Johns Hopkins Child Development Study) favors this conclusion (Hardy et al., 1976).

As part of the Johns Hopkins study, 200 children from the inner city of Baltimore were given selected questions from the WISC. For this study, however, the standard WISC scoring instructions were abandoned, and an attempt was made to understand the reasoning behind the children's answers. For example, the WISC question "What would you do if you were sent to buy a loaf of bread, and the grocer said he did not have any more?" was given. The WISC scoring instructions state that the correct answer is "Go to another store." Among the 200 children in the study, 61 gave an incorrect response. However, when the examiners probed the children about their responses, they discovered that many of the children had given replies that were reasonable considering their circumstances. For instance, the rigid WISC scoring procedures do not allow credit for the response "Go home." Yet many of the inner-city children explained that there were no other stores near their homes and that they were not allowed to go away from home without permission. Others reported that they used family credit to shop and would need to go home to get money if they needed to go to another store. In each of these cases, the researchers suggested that the children had given correct and reasonable responses to the question given their own circumstances (Hardy et al., 1976).

Other psychologists emphasize the need for strict scoring procedures if the use of intelligence tests is to be reliable. Standardization implies that all children take the test with the same set of rules. Beyond this objection, the methodology of the Johns Hopkins study has been called into question. Sattler (1979b) carefully reviewed the study and found a variety of methodological problems. In particular, there was no control group of children who were not from the inner city. Thus, it is not possible to determine whether children in general would have benefited from a more liberal interpretation of the criteria for a correct answer. There is abundant evidence that permitting a tester to exercise judgment about the reasonableness of a response results in higher scores for children from many different walks of life. Under most circumstances this procedure does not result in greater validity for the test (Sattler, 1974).

Another of Sattler's objections is that the study may have had serious rater bias. It is quite likely that the psychologists who tested the inner-city children knew that the study was on test bias and that their interpretations of a reasonable response were influenced by a subjective predisposition.

Ultimately a test is evaluated by its criterion validity. How well does it do its job in predicting performance on some criterion of interest? Many psychologists argue that any scoring procedure is all right if it enhances the relationship between a test and a criterion. In the Johns Hopkins study, no information was offered about the benefits of a liberal scoring system for the criterion validity of the test (Hardy et al., 1976). Thus, different scoring procedures may make the scores of inner-city children higher, but it remains to be determined whether the revised procedures would make the tests more meaningful (Sattler, 1979b). Most studies on criterion validity suggest that IQ tests are not differentially meaningful for different groups of children (Hall, Huppertz, & Levi, 1977; Hartlage & Steele, 1977; Henderson, Fay, Lindemann, & Clarkson, 1973; Lamp & Traxler, 1973; Lunemann, 1974; Palmer, 1970).

side suggested that the tests measure only whether the child has learned the appropriate responses needed to perform well on the test. This position claims that the tests do not measure how smart the child is but only whether the child has been exposed to the information on the test. After hearing the testimony for the different points of view, the judge mumbled that the issue was really one of ignorance versus stupidity. Although this comment appears abrasive and racist, it is quite insightful. There are two potential explanations for why some children do more poorly on standardized tests than other children. One explanation is that they are less intelligent. Put bluntly this would be the stupidity explanation. The other explanation is that some children do more poorly because they are ignorant. In other words, they simply have not learned the right responses for a particular test. If ignorance is the explanation, differences in IQ scores are less to be concerned about because they can be changed. The stupidity explanation is more damning because it implies that the lower test scores obtained by Black students are a product of some deficit that cannot be easily changed.

The term *ignorance* implies that differences can easily be abolished. Just as some minority children are ignorant about how to answer items that might predict success in the White, middle-class culture, White, middle-class children could be labeled ignorant about how to succeed in the world of a ghetto child. This proposition is illustrated by the Chitling Test.

B. *The Chitling Test*

Many years ago animal psychologists talked about higher and lower animals. The higher animals were considered to be intelligent because they could do some of the same things humans can do, and the lower animals were considered to be unintelligent because they could not perform like humans. However, in 1969, a famous article by Hodos and Campbell changed the thinking of many students of animal behavior. Hodos and Campbell argued that all animals are equally intelligent for the environments in which they live. We cannot compare the intelligence of a rat with that of a cat because a rat is adapted to a rat's environment and a cat is adapted to a cat's environment. Both animals are best suited to survive in the environment they occupy.

The same insight seems not to have permeated the world of human affairs. Because of poverty and discrimination, minority and nonminority children grow up in different environments. To be successful in each of these environments requires different skills and knowledge. A psychological test may consider survival in only one of these environments, and this is usually the White, middle-class environment. Thus, using one of these tests for impoverished children is analogous to testing a cat on a task designed to determine how well a rat is adapted to a rat's environment.

The Chitling Test was developed by Black sociologist Adrian Dove to demonstrate that there is a body of information about which the White middle class is ignorant. Dove named his effort the Dove Counterbalance General Intelligence Test, but it has become known as just the Chitling Test ("Taking the Chitling Test," 1968). A major aim in developing the Chitling Test was to show that Blacks and Whites are just not talking the same language.

Some of the items from the Chitling Test are shown in Table 20-1. Try to answer the questions and tally up your scores. Most of you may not do too well because you have not been exposed to Black culture. Minority-group members who have grown up in a ghetto should clearly outperform you. On this test, a White, middle-class student would probably score as culturally deprived.

TABLE 20-1 Selected items from the Dove Counterbalance General Intelligence Test (the Chitling Test)

1. A "handkerchief head" is: (a) a cool cat, (b) a porter, (c) an Uncle Tom, (d) a hoddi, (e) a preacher.
2. Which word is most out of place here? (a) splib, (b) blood, (c) gray, (d) spook, (e) Black.
3. A "gas head" is a person who has a: (a) fast-moving car, (b) stable of "lace," (c) "process," (d) habit of stealing cars, (e) long jail record for arson.
4. "Bo Diddley" is a: (a) game for children, (b) down-home cheap wine, (c) down-home singer, (d) new dance, (e) Moejoe call.
5. If a pimp is uptight with a woman who gets state aid, what does he mean when he talks about "Mother's Day"? (a) second Sunday in May, (b) third Sunday in June, (c) first of every month, (d) none of these, (e) first and fifteenth of every month.
6. If a man is called a "blood," then he is a: (a) fighter, (b) Mexican-American, (c) Negro, (d) hungry hemophile, (e) Redman or Indian.
7. What are the "Dixie Hummingbirds"? (a) part of the KKK, (b) a swamp disease, (c) a modern gospel group, (d) a Mississippi Negro paramilitary group, (e) deacons.
8. T'Bone Walker got famous for playing what? (a) trombone, (b) piano, (c) "T-flute," (d) guitar, (e) "hambone."

The correct answers are: (1) c, (2) c, (3) c, (4) c, (5) e, (6) c, (7) c, and (8) d. *(From "Taking the Chitling Test," by A. Dove. In* Newsweek, *1968, 72, 51–52. Copyright 1968 by Newsweek, Inc. All Rights Reserved. Reprinted by permission.)*

However, we must caution you about the meaning of the test. At present, no more than face validity has been established. No body of evidence demonstrates that the test successfully predicts performance on any important criterion. If we want to predict which students will do well in college, the Chitling Test will be of no benefit. In fact, standardized tests predict performance for both minority and nonminority students, and the Chitling Test predicts performance for neither group. It may well be that the Chitling Test will turn out to be a valid test for inferring how streetwise someone is. Yet we must await validity evidence before we can make any generalizations. Dove described his efforts to develop an intelligence test as "half serious." But we have seen that the test does identify an area of content on which the races differ and Blacks outperform Whites.

C. *The Black Intelligence Test of Cultural Homogeneity*

Some psychologists regard most achievement and intelligence tests as instruments of racism. Most racist actions are felt to be illogical and emotional. However, the use of intelligence tests is seen as a subtle and thus more danger-ous racist move because the tests are supported by scientific validity studies (Garcia, 1981). Robert Williams, a well-known Black psychologist, has labeled this phenomenon *scientific racism* (1974). Williams views IQ and standardized achievement tests as "nothing but updated versions of the old signs down South that read 'For Whites Only'" (1974, p. 34).

Of particular interest to Williams and his colleagues is the assessment of the ability to survive in the Black community. Indeed they feel that assessment of survival potential with a Survival Quotient (SQ) is more important than assess-ment of IQ, which only indicates the likelihood of succeeding in the White community. As a beginning, Williams developed the Black Intelligence Test of Cultural Homogeneity (BITCH), which asks respondents to define 100 vocabu-lary words relevant to Afro-American culture. The words came from the *Afro-American Slang Dictionary* and from Williams's personal experience interacting with Black Americans. Black persons obtain higher scores than their White counterparts on the BITCH. When Williams administered the BITCH to 100 16-to 18-year-olds from each group, the average score for Black subjects was 87.07 (out of 100). The mean score for the Whites was significantly lower (51.07). Williams argues that traditional IQ and achievement tests are nothing more than culture-specific tests that assess how much White children know about White culture. The BITCH is also a culture-specific test, but one on which the Black subjects outperform the Whites.

Although the BITCH does tell us a lot about the cultural loading in intelli-gence and achievement tests, it has received mixed reviews. The reliability data reported by Williams show that the BITCH is quite reliable for Black test takers (standard error less than 3 points on the 100-point scale) and acceptably reliable for White test takers (standard error about 6). (Conventional tests have similar reliabilities for both groups; Oakland & Feigenbaum, 1979.) However, little convincing validity data on the BITCH are available. Although the test manual does report some studies, the samples are small and not representative of any clearly defined population (Cronbach, 1978). The difficulty is that we cannot determine whether the BITCH does predict how well a person will survive on the streets, how well he or she will do in school, in life, or in anything else. To support the conclusion that the BITCH is an intelligence test, we must have some evidence. The test does assess word association, but it seems to give no information on reasoning abilities.

Further studies are needed to determine whether the BITCH does what it is supposed to do. One of the rationales for the test is that it will identify children who have been unfairly assigned to classes for the Educable Mentally Retarded (EMR) on the basis of IQ scores. In one study, Long and Anthony (1974) attempted to determine how many Black EMR children would be reclassified if they were retested with the BITCH. Among a small and limited sample of 30 Black EMR high school students from Gainesville, Florida, all the students who performed poorly on the WISC also performed below the first percentile on the BITCH. Using the BITCH served to reclassify none of the students. However, this was just one small and nonrepresentative study. In its present state, the BITCH can be a valuable tool for measuring White familiarity with the Black community. When White teachers or administrators are sent to schools that have predominantly Black enrollments, the BITCH may be used to determine how much they know about the culture. Furthermore, the BITCH may be used to assess the extent to which a Black person is in touch with his or her own community. As Cronbach (1978) notes, people with good abstract reasoning skills may function poorly if they are unfamiliar with the community in which they live. Similarly, people with poor reasoning skills may get along just fine if they are familiar with the community.

D. The System of Multicultural Pluralistic Assessment

No assessment technique covered in this book challenges our traditional beliefs about testing as much as the System of Multicultural Pluralistic Assessment (SOMPA) (Mercer, 1979). This system, developed by sociologist Jane Mercer, has already been adopted by several states. Before we discuss the SOMPA and the evaluations of it, it is instructive to review Mercer's beliefs about the social and political implications of testing.

Mercer feels that our beliefs about what is fair and what knowledge exists are related to the social structure. She agrees with sociologist K. Mannheim (1936) that members of the politically dominant group provide the interpretation of events within a society and they do so from their own perspective. The traditional psychometric literature on IQ tests provides a scientific rationale for the dominant group to keep minority-group members in their place by demonstrating that the minority-group members do not have the language and knowledge skills to perform well in a White cultural setting. The feedback given to the minority groups is not that they are ignorant about the rules for success in another culture (just as the dominant group would be in a minority culture) but that they are stupid and unlikely to succeed. Mercer emphasizes that we must take into consideration that some individuals are working from a different knowledge base.

It is not possible to give a complete description of the SOMPA here. The system is complex, and many technical issues have been raised about its validity and its applicability (Brown, 1979a, 1979b; Clarizio, 1979a, 1979b; Goodman, 1977, 1979; Mercer, 1979; Oakland, 1979).

One important philosophical assumption underlies the development of the SOMPA. This assumption is that all cultural groups have the same average potential. Any differences between cultural groups are assumed to be caused by differences in access to cultural experiences. Those who do not perform well on the tests are not well informed about the criteria for success that are usually set forth by the dominant group. However, within groups that have had the same cultural experiences, not all individuals are expected to be the same; and assessment of these differences is a better measure of ability than is assessment of differences between cultural groups.

Mercer has been concerned about the consequences of labeling a child as mentally retarded (Mercer, 1972). She has convincingly argued that many children are incorrectly identified as retarded and that they suffer severely as a result of this inaccurate branding. In particular, she is distressed that classes for EMR students have disproportionate numbers of minority children. Mercer maintains that some minority students score low on the traditional tests because they are ignorant about the ways of the dominant culture and are not in any way mentally retarded. Another reason for misclassification is medical problems. Thus a fair system of evaluation must include medical assessment. It must also include the assessment of children relative to other children who have had similar life experiences. The basic point of divergence between the SOMPA and earlier approaches to assessment is the SOMPA attempt to integrate three different approaches to assessment: medical, social, and pluralistic.

One of the most consistent findings in the field of public health is that members of low-income groups have more health problems than do those who are economically better off. The *medical* component of the SOMPA system asks "Is the child an intact organism?" (Mercer, 1979, p. 92). The rationale for this portion is that medical problems can interfere with a child's performance on mental measures and in school.

The *social-system* component attempts to determine whether a child is functioning at a level that would be expected by social norms. For example, does the child do what is expected by family members, peer groups, or the community? Mercer feels that test users and developers typically adopt only a social-system orientation. For example, if a test predicts who will do well in school, it is forecasting behavior that is expected by the dominant social system. However, Mercer emphasizes that the social-system approach is a narrow one because only the dominant group in society defines the criteria for success (Reschly, 1981).

The *pluralistic* component of the SOMPA recognizes that different subcultures are associated with different life experiences. Only within these subgroups do individuals have common experiences. Thus, tests should assess individuals against others in the same subculture. It is important to recognize the distinction between the criteria for defining deviance in the pluralistic model and in the social-system model. The social-system model uses the norms of society as the criteria, while the pluralistic model uses the norms within a particular group.

The SOMPA attempts to assess children relative to each of these models. The medical portion of the SOMPA package includes physical measures such as visual tests, tests of hearing, and tests of motor functioning. The social-system portion is similar to most assessment procedures. The entire WISC-R is given and evaluated according to the regular criteria. Finally, the pluralistic portion also uses WISC-R scores but evaluates them against those for groups that have similar social and cultural backgrounds. In other words, the WISC-R scores are adjusted for socioeconomic background. These adjusted scores are known as *estimated learning potentials* (ELPs).

The major dispute between Mercer and her many critics is over the validity of the SOMPA. Mercer (1979) points out that a test itself is not valid or invalid but the inferences that are made on the basis of the test scores are. She insists the ELPs cannot be validated in the same way as are other test scores. (Validating a test by predicting who will do well in school is appropriate only for the social-system model.) Mercer argues that the criteria for evaluating the ELP must be different. She states that the appropriate validity criterion for ELPs should be the percentage of variance in WISC-R scores that is accounted for by sociocultural variables. Many SOMPA critics (Brown, 1979a; Clarizio, 1979b; Goodman, 1979; Oakland, 1979), however, feel that a test should always be validated by demonstrating that it predicts performance. The correlation between ELPs and school achievement is around .40, while the correlation between the WISC-R and school achievement is around .60 (Oakland, 1979). Thus, ELPs are a poorer predictor than WISC-R scores of school success. Mercer refutes these critics by arguing that the test is not designed to identify which children will do well in school. Its purpose is to determine which children are mentally retarded. This can be done only by comparing children with others who have had the same life experiences.

Accepting Mercer's argument may produce a quota system for EMR classes. Using ELPs should make the proportions of ethnic groups in EMR classes more representative than they now are. Because several states have adopted the SOMPA, we may soon be able to determine the ultimate effect of the system. There is no question that it will identify many fewer minority children as EMR students. This may please some taxpayers because the costs of educating EMR students are higher than average. Only time will tell whether children no longer considered EMR students will benefit. Mercer's (1972) research suggests that a big part of the battle is just getting more children labeled as normal. Her critics retaliate by suggesting that the effects of labeling are weak and inconsequential. They argue that no matter what these children are called they will need some special help in school.

V. SUGGESTIONS FOR SOLUTIONS

This chapter has been about problems associated with the finding of ethnic differences in test scores. We have hit you with many different arguments from many different perspectives. In the following pages we offer some solutions. However, we must warn you that the different solutions depend on different social and political beliefs about the definition of bias.

A. *Ethical concerns and the definition of test bias*

It is difficult to define the term *test bias*. Different authors have different views (Cole, 1981; Darlington, 1978; Flaugher, 1978; Hunter & Schmidt, 1976). These different definitions represent commitments to underlying ethical viewpoints about the way various groups ought to be treated. Hunter and Schmidt (1976) identify three ethical positions that set the tone for much of the debate: unqualified individualism, the use of quotas, and qualified individualism. All these positions are concerned with the use of tests to select people either for jobs or for training programs (including college).

Supporters of *unqualified individualism* would use tests to select the most qualified individuals they could find. In this case users of tests would be indifferent to the race or sex of applicants. The goal would be to predict those who would be expected to perform best on the job or in school. According to this viewpoint, a test is fair if it finds the best candidates for the job or for admission to school. If race or sex were a valid predictor of performance over and above the information in the test, the unqualified individualist would see nothing wrong with considering this information in the selection process.

A quite different ethical approach to selection is to use *quotas*. Quota systems explicitly recognize race and sex differences. If the population of a state is 20% Black, then supporters of a quota system might argue that 20% of the new medical students in the state-supported medical school should also be Black. Selection procedures are regarded as biased if the actual percentage of applicants admitted is different from the percentage in the population; each group should have a fair share of the representation (Gordon & Terrell, 1981). This fair-share selection process gives less emphasis than the testing process to how well people in the different groups are expected to do once they are selected (Darlington, 1971; Hunter & Schmidt, 1976; R. L. Thorndike, 1971).

The final moral position considered by Hunter and Schmidt might be viewed as a compromise between unqualified individualism and a quota system. *Qualified individualism*, like unqualified individualism, embraces the notion that the best qualified persons should be the ones selected. But unqualified individualists also take information about race, sex, and religion into consideration if it helps predict performance on the criterion. Not to do so results in underprediction of performance for one group and overprediction of performance for another group. Qualified individualists, however, recognize that, although failing to include group characteristics (race, sex, and religion) may lead to differential accuracy in prediction, this differential prediction may counteract known effects of discrimination. It may, for example, lead to underprediction of the performance of the majority group and overprediction of the performance of the minority group. The qualified individualist may choose not to include information about personal characteristics in selection because ignoring this information may serve the interest of minority-group members.

Each of these ethical positions can be related to a particular statistical definition of test bias, and we now turn to these definitions. Table 20-2 shows several different models of test bias based on different definitions of fairness. All these models are based on regression lines as we discussed above. The models discussed in Table 20-2 are relevant to tests that are used for selection purposes, including job-placement tests and tests used to select students for college or for advanced-degree programs.

The straight regression approach described in Table 20-2 (see also Cleary, 1968) represents the unqualified-individualism position. The result of this approach is that a large number of majority-group members may be selected. In other words, this approach maintains that an employer or a school should be absolutely color and gender blind. The reason for considering ethnicity or sex is to improve prediction of future performance. This approach has been favored by business because it assures the highest rate of productivity among the employees who are selected by the procedure.

At the other extreme is the quota system. To achieve fair-share representation, separate selection procedures are developed. One procedure, for example, is used to select the best available Black applicants, and another procedure is used to select the best available non-Black applicants. If a community has 42% Black residents, the first procedure would be used to select 42% of the employees, and the other procedure would be used to select the other 58%.

The difficulty with the quota system is that it may lead to greater rates of failure among some groups. Suppose, for example, that a test had been devised to select telephone operators and that the test did indeed predict who would succeed on the job. However, the test selected 70% women and only 30% men. The quota system would encourage the use of separate cutoff scores so that the proportion of men selected would approach 50%. But, because the women scored higher on the average, they would perform better on the job, resulting in a higher rate of failure among the men. Thus, although quota systems often aid in increasing the selection of underrepresented groups, they also make it likely that the underrepresented groups will experience failure.

Table 20-2 shows two other models (Cole, 1973; Darlington, 1971; R. L. Thorndike, 1971). These models represent compromises between the quota and the unqualified-individualism points of view. In each of these cases there is an attempt to select the most qualified persons yet there is some adjustment for being from a minority group. When persons from two different groups have the

TABLE 20-2 Different models of test fairness

Model	Reference	Use of regression	Rationale	Effect on minority selection	Effect on average criterion performance
Regression	Cleary (1968)	Separate regression lines are used for different groups. Those with the highest predicted criterion scores are selected.	This is fair because those with the highest estimated level of success are selected.	Few minority-group members selected.	High.
Constant Ratio	R. L. Thorndike (1971)	Points equal to about half of the average difference between the groups are added to the test scores of the group with the lower score. Then a single regression line is used, and those with the highest predicted scores are selected.	This is fair because it better reflects the potential of the lower-scoring group.	Some increase in the number of minority-group members selected.	Somewhat lower.
Cole/ Darlington	Cole (1973), Darlington (1971, 1978)	Separate regression equations are used for each group, and points are added to scores of those from the lower group to assure that those with the same criterion score have the same predictor score.	This is fair because it selects more potentially successful persons from the lower group.	Larger increase in the number of minority-group members selected.	Lower.
Quota	Dunnette and Borman (1979)	The proportion of persons to be selected from each group is predetermined. Separate regression equations are used to select those persons from each group who are expected to perform highest on the criterion.	This is fair because members of different subgroups are selected based on their proportions in the community.	Best representation of minority groups.	About the same as for the Cole/ Darlington model.

Based on Dunnette and Borman (1979).

same test score, these procedures give a slight edge to the person from the lower group and put the person from the higher group at a slight disadvantage. Although these approaches have been attacked for being based on faulty logic (Hunter & Schmidt, 1976, 1978), plausible defenses have been offered. The effect of these procedures is to increase the number of persons selected from underrepresented groups. However, these procedures also reduce the average performance score on the criterion.

We cannot tell you which of these approaches is right and which is wrong. That decision depends on your own values and judgment about what is fair.

B. *Improving the use of selection devices*

We have contended that the observed differences between minority and nonminority groups on standardized tests are a problem. Sometimes a problem stimulates us to think differently; in the words of famous entrepreneur Henry Kaiser: "A problem is an opportunity in work clothes." Another reason for the differences in test scores may be that different strategies for solving problems characterize different subcultures. Knowing how groups differ in their approaches to problem solving can be of benefit for two reasons. First, it can help us learn important things about the relationship between socialization and problem-solving approaches. This information can guide the development of pluralistic education programs (Castaneda & Ramirez, 1974). Second, knowing more about the ways different groups approach problems can lead to the development of improved predictors of success for minority groups (Goldman, 1973).

Along these lines, Goldman (1973) has proposed the differential process theory, which maintains that for many tasks different strategies may lead to an effective solution. According to this theory, strategies—the ways people go about solving problems (Frederiksen, 1969)—mediate between abilities and performance.

An example of differential process at work is that Black college students (on the average) tend to score higher on the verbal subtest of the SAT than they do on the quantitative subtest. White students (on the average) score about the same on both subtests. As the result of socialization experiences, it is possible that Black students structure the task of getting through school differently—they develop their verbal skills rather than their quantitative abilities. This result may also reflect differences in the opportunity to learn proper quantitative skills because of unequal educational opportunity. In any case, Black students tend to choose college majors that emphasize their verbal abilities. It may thus be appropriate to build specific tests that predict how well these students will do in the majors they choose. These tests could deemphasize quantitative skills if they are shown to be unrelated to success for these particular majors. In other words, the test would be validated for the specific majors chosen by Black students.

C. *Developing different criteria*

Criterion validity is the correlation between the test and the criterion. But what are the criteria against which the tests used to assess the potential of children in the public schools are evaluated? Most of these tests are simply valid predictors of how well children will do on other standardized tests. In other words, most standardized tests are evaluated against other standardized tests. The difficulty is that the criterion may be the test dressed in different clothes. For example, an intelligence test may be evaluated to determine how well it predicts performance on a standardized achievement test. This test is measuring not native ability but achievement. Differences in scores on this test between minority and nonminority groups are therefore due to opportunity to learn rather than ability to learn.

If we do not accept standardized tests as a criterion against which tests can be evaluated, how can we determine the meaning of the tests? There is considerable debate about whether classroom grades should be allowed as the criterion. Supporters of the use of classroom grades claim that these grades are the only independent measure of how well the child is doing. It is no surprise, they maintain, that there is a correlation between IQ tests and scores on standardized achievement tests because both measure a similar domain of content. However, they do argue that IQ tests do not predict classroom grades for minority children and, therefore, are not valid for minority youngsters. The support for this position comes from a single study by Goldman and Hartig (1976). In this study, scores on the WISC were found to be unrelated to teacher ratings of classroom performance for minority children. For the nonminority children, there was a significant relationship between IQ and teacher ratings. If the criterion becomes classroom grades rather than another standardized test, the IQ test appears valid for nonminority but not for minority children.

Supporters of the use of the tests do not want classroom grades to be the criterion for three reasons. First, teacher-assigned grades are unstandardized and are open to subjective bias (Sattler, 1979a). For example, teachers have been known to reward effort more than ability (Weiner & Kukla, 1970). Second, there are few available studies in which grades have been used as the criterion. Third, the one frequently cited study (Goldman & Hartig, 1976) is open to other explanations. In this study, the teachers rated the classroom performance of nearly all the minority children as poor. These low ratings resulted in little variance on the criterion measure. As we learned in Chapter 3, any variable for which there is no variability cannot correlate well with other variables.

The problem with criterion measures becomes even more apparent for measures used with adults. We know, for example, that the Medical College Admission Test (MCAT) predicts success in medical school. Yet, as Focused Example 20-2 demonstrates, it does not predict who will be a successful doctor. Similarly, the Law School Admission Test (LSAT) predicts performance in law school. Yet there is little evidence that it predicts who will be a good attorney. The professional school admission tests may be weeding out candidates who would not do so well on the narrowly defined criterion of medical school or law school grades. In doing so, they may be eliminating people who are potentially better doctors and lawyers than those who are admitted. Imagine, for example, that a White and a Chicano doctor are trained equally well in the science of medical care and that both are practicing in a public hospital in a Chicano neighborhood. The Chicano doctor will more likely be effective because that

■ **FOCUSED EXAMPLE 20-2 EVALUATING THE MEDICAL COLLEGE ADMISSION TEST**

The ultimate goal in medical practice is the successful diagnosis and treatment of patients. Thus, selection of medical students should proceed with this objective in mind. However, the MCAT is designed to predict only how well students will do in medical school. Studies do show that the MCAT is an adequate predictor of medical school grades. But how meaningful are medical school grades?

The importance of medical school grades has been a matter of some debate. For example, one study that considered measures of physician success in practice found that grades were unassociated with measures of real-life performance (Loughmiller, Ellison, Taylor, & Price, 1970). In another study of 217 physicians who were practicing in Utah, 76 measures of doctor performance were taken. Among over 1000 correlations between grades and performance on these measures, 97% were nearly 0. On the basis of these results, the criteria for admission to medical school were seriously questioned (Taylor, Price, Richards, & Jacobsen, 1965). Although tests may predict medical school grades, it is unclear whether grades or the tests give us much information about who will be a successful doctor.

doctor understands the culture and the language of the patients and thus is better at understanding specific complaints and symptoms. The White doctor may do a poorer job at diagnosing the problems. The MCAT would have done its job poorly by focusing on the short-term criterion of medical school grades. Further work is needed to develop measures that are good predictors of the long-range goal of clinical success (Goldman & Hewitt, 1976).

D. *Changing the social environment*

It is not hard to determine that majority and minority children grow up in different social environments. You can learn this by reading any sociology textbook or by getting in your car and driving to the nearest inner-city ghetto. Given this disparity in environment, it is not surprising that tests favor the majority. Many critics of tests seem to hold the tests responsible for inequality of opportunity (Flaugher, 1978). One view of test scores is that they are an accurate reflection of the effects of social and economic inequality (Green, 1978).

To understand this argument we must consider the purpose of testing. In educational settings, tests such as the SAT or the GRE or even IQ tests are usually considered to be tests of aptitude—they measure some trait that is inborn and unlikely to change if the person is put in a different environment. But most experts now agree that the tests are measuring not aptitude but achievement. The scores can be changed with proper nurturing. Verbal and numerical abilities are acquired through experience. Thus, low test scores should not be viewed as insurmountable problems; they can be improved.

Much of what has been said in this chapter is consistent with the view that tests do point up differences between minority and nonminority students. Furthermore, systematic attempts to show that this problem is the fault of the tests have not been convincing. Many minority students do well on the tests, and the tests accurately predict that these students will do well on the criterion. A Black student and a White student who each achieve a score of 1100 on the SAT are predicted to do equally well in college, and studies show that indeed they do perform at about the same level.

Blaming the tests for observed differences between groups may be a convenient way to avoid a much larger problem. No one has suggested that the tuberculin test is unfair because it demonstrates that poor people have the disease more often than wealthy people do. Public health officials have correctly concluded that some people live in environments that predispose them to the disease. Getting rid of scales that identify underweight children will not cure malnutrition (Flaugher, 1978). Although measuring intelligence may not be the same as testing for tuberculosis or measuring weight (Mercer, 1979), the analogy may be worth considering.

If unequal access to adequate education and to stimulating experiences results in differences in test scores, it would be more useful to change the social environment than to continuously bicker about the tests. The tests may only be the bearers of bad news. By documenting how severe the problem is, the tests may be telling us that overcoming this problem will be expensive, will be difficult, and may take many years. Blaming the tests for a problem that they did not cause seems to be shortsighted and nonproductive (Green, 1978).

VI.   SUMMARY

In this chapter we have examined two sides of the issue of test bias. A summary of some of the arguments for and against the use of tests is given in Table 20-3. As the table shows, there are strong differences of opinion about the value of intelligence and aptitude tests for minority-group members. As a result of the challenge to traditional tests, new approaches such as the Chitling Test, the BITCH, and the SOMPA have been developed. Among these, the SOMPA is clearly the most sophisticated. All of these new approaches rest on the assumption that social groups do not differ in their average potential. These approaches have been challenged because they do not have the same sort of validity evidence as is available for the traditional tests.

Part of the debate about test bias results from different moral views about what is fair. Some have argued that a testing and selection program is fair if it selects the best-suited people, regardless of their social group. This approach may lead to overrepresentation of one group. Another moral position supports selection procedures that select members from different racial and ethnic groups

TABLE 20-3 For and against the use of tests

Against	For
The Stanford-Binet was standardized on only 1000 children and 400 adults. None of these people were Black (Guthrie, 1976).	Although the tests were not standardized on minority-group members, they have now been used to test millions of children of all races. The tests appear to have the same validity for minority students as they do for majority students. Therefore neglecting to include minorities in the original validation studies was not relevant (Sattler, 1979a).
The use of intelligence tests can have a damaging social impact. For example, differences in IQ between different ethnic groups were used to limit immigration of certain groups into the United States during the early years of the 20th century (Kamin, 1974).	Examination of the Congressional record covering the debates about the 1924 Immigration Act failed to uncover discussion of intelligence-test data or claims that the mean IQ of Americans would decline if the immigration of certain groups was allowed (DuBois, 1972a).
If a teacher just thinks some children have higher IQs, the actual test scores of those children will improve (Rosenthal & Jacobson, 1968).	Studies documenting the effects of self-fulfilling prophecies and teacher expectations overinterpreted their original data, contained some results that are statistically impossible, and cannot be depended on (Snow, 1969; Elashoff & Snow, 1971; R. L. Thorndike, 1968).
Minority children can only be damaged by the continued use of psychological tests.	Psychological tests can be used to identify the most capable members of each group. Without the tests people will be selected on the basis of personal judgment, which might be more racist than the tests (Cronbach, 1975b).
The validity of IQ tests was documented using other standardized tests as the criterion rather than measures of classroom performance (Mercer, 1979).	The objective tests are better validity criteria than classroom performance, which is more subjective. Teachers may grade on the basis of effort rather than ability (Sattler, 1979a).
Most test administrators are White; the scores of Black children would improve if they were tested by Black examiners (Forrester & Klaus, 1964; Pasamanick & Knobloch, 1955).	Some studies do indeed show that race of the examiner is an important factor. However, most studies do not. Among 28 different studies on the effects of the examiner's race, 24 fail to show that race of the examiner has a significant impact on scores (Sattler, 1979a).

according to their proportions in the general population. A third moral position is a compromise between the preceding two.

Although test bias is sure to remain an area of considerable controversy, there are some positive potential solutions. For example, tests might be evaluated against outcome criteria that have relevance for minority-group members.

A current raging controversy is over the nature of differences in test performance. One group believes the differences are genetic or biological in origin
(Jensen, 1969, 1972), while another group believes the differences result from
differences in the social environment (Kamin, 1974; Olmedo, 1981). The social-
environment explanation seems to be the more popular. If we accept this view,
differences in test performance might suggest to us that we need to escalate our
efforts to wipe out inequality. If we endorse the genetic position, we are acknowl-
edging that little can be done to equalize performance among different groups.

21

Testing and the Law

Learning objectives

When you have completed the material in this chapter, you should be able to do the following:

1. Describe the bases on which the federal government can regulate the use of psychological tests.
2. Describe the EEOC guidelines and their importance.
3. Describe how the New York Truth in Testing Law affects the use of psychological tests.
4. Discuss the impact of PL 94-142.
5. Discuss the importance of Hobson v. Hansen.
6. Describe the issue in Diana v. State Board of Education and how it differs from the major issue in Larry P. v. Wilson Riles.
7. Compare and contrast the decisions in Larry P. v. Wilson Riles and Parents in Action on Special Education v. Hannon.
8. Discuss the importance of Regents of the University of California v. Bakke.
9. Describe how the courts are involved in the use of personnel tests.
10. Discuss your own views on the role of the courts in the regulation of psychological tests.

In 1969 the California Department of Education began requiring the use of standardized IQ tests to diagnose retardation. Students scoring below 85 on the WISC or the Stanford-Binet were sent to special classes for the Educable Mentally Retarded (EMR). Larry P. was one of the approximately 6000 Black children who were assigned to EMR classes on the basis of the tests. However, a few years later, Larry P. and five of his Black schoolmates were retested by Black psychologists, who reported higher IQ scores. On the basis of these new and higher test scores, Larry and the others were placed back in the regular school track.

Larry P.'s battle was not as simple as being retested to gain an equitable placement. Instead, a class-action law suit was filed on behalf of the six Black children (representing the class of all similar students); this case challenged the right of the state to use IQ tests for classroom placement, arguing that the tests were racially discriminatory and therefore violated both the California constitution and the 14th Amendment to the United States Constitution, which guarantees equal protection of the laws.

It took until 1977 for the case to be heard in the U.S. District Court. After hearing and reviewing more than 11,000 pages of testimony by psychologists and interested parties, Judge Robert Peckham released a 131-page opinion in October 1979 forbidding the placement of Black children in EMR classes on the basis of standardized test scores. Thus, the ultimate decision about the use of psychological tests was not made by trained psychologists, by professional educators, or by interested citizens. Rather, it was made by the courts.

The same year the decision in Larry P.'s case was released, the state of New York passed a truth in testing law, and a similar bill was introduced on the floor of the U.S. House of Representatives. In addition, a Florida judge ruled that Black students who did not receive all their education in integrated schools could not be denied a high school credential on the basis of a minimum competence test. By the end of the 1970s the use of psychological tests had become a major legal issue. These courtroom and legislative battles over the appropriate use of psychological tests set the stage for the many current conflicts over testing.

In this chapter we review some of the major legal issues concerning the use of psychological tests. We begin by covering some of the basic laws regulating the use of tests, and then we report on how the courts have interpreted some of these laws. Focused Example 21-1 discusses the meaning of the word "law."

I. LAWS GOVERNING THE USE OF TESTS

A. *Federal authorities*

Many people commonly believe that the federal government has unlimited authority to regulate almost any activity. Actually, the circumstances under which the federal government can regulate are limited. Until fairly recently, the most commonly used authority for regulation was interstate commerce.

Interstate commerce.   The Constitution gives most of the power to the states. Each state has its own constitution, which generally defines the relationship between the state and its citizens. It is up to the states to make policies for the recognition of other administrative units, such as cities and

■ FOCUSED EXAMPLE 21·1   WHAT IS A LAW?

As common as it is for each of us to refer to laws, many people are confused about what exactly constitutes the law. Most people think of law only as statutes. *Statutes* are the rules written by legislative bodies at any level of government. Before proposed statutes become law, they are called *bills* or *propositions*.

In addition to statutes, *constitutions* have the force of law. In the United States there is a federal Constitution, and each state has its own constitution. In law suits (or litigation) it is frequently argued that a policy violates a constitutional rule or principle. The U.S. Constitution is considered the supreme law of the land because any federal, state, or local law is invalid if it is judged to conflict with the Constitution. State or local laws that are inconsistent with a state constitution can also be declared invalid.

Statutes and constitutions are typically worded in general terms. Frequently, they give authority to a specific agency to write *regulations*. For all intents and purposes, these regulations are also laws. For example, the Civil Rights Act of 1964 (a statute) created the Equal Employment Opportunity Commission (EEOC), which wrote guidelines for fair employment practices; these guidelines are regulations. Although these regulations were not created by any elected officials, they are laws that must be adhered to.

The final form of law is *judicial opinion*. Statutes, constitutions, and regulations must be applied to the specific facts. Thus courts of law are frequently called on to interpret the law in view of a given factual situation. In doing so, the courts offer opinions that consider specific cases against the background of statutes, constitutions, and regulations. Once a court offers an opinion on a specific case, the opinion becomes law. For example, in the case of *Larry P. v. Wilson Riles*, a judge rendered the opinion that IQ tests could not be used to place Black children in EMR classes. This opinion is the law in California unless a higher court reverses the U.S. District Court opinion (Wing, 1976).

counties, that exist within the states. The Constitution does not directly recognize cities, counties, or school districts. The only restriction on the states' authority to pass laws is that no state can pass or enforce a law that is inconsistent with the Constitution.

The federal government is charged with regulating interstate commerce because each state has only that authority necessary to attend to its own affairs. Interstate commerce is business activity involving two or more states. For example, a test that is developed by a New Jersey company and shipped (over state lines) to be administered for profit in Kansas clearly involves interstate commerce. Some legal authorities now believe that interstate commerce involves almost all activities. Thus, the federal government can regulate many activities under the umbrella of interstate commerce.

The regulation of interstate commerce is clear and direct. Federal agencies such as the Federal Trade Commission create specific policies for the regulation of specific products and activities. Congress also devotes much of its energy to the creation of laws that regulate specific business activities. These extensive and well-documented policies represent direct regulation. The other form of governmental regulation is indirect. This is the power to regulate through the control of spending.

Control of spending.   The U.S. government is a big spender. So big, in fact, that virtually all major American business institutions depend to some extent on federal revenues. This spending gives the federal government considerable leverage. It can withhold money whenever federal authorities consider it just to do so. In effect, the government has the right to say "do it our way or we will not pay."

This policy is straightforward for cases in which the government is a customer and needs to regulate the product it is purchasing. For example, when the federal government is paying for the development of a test, it has the right to withhold payment unless the work is done according to governmental standards. However, this power is frequently exercised in an indirect manner. For example, the government has standards for equality in employment, and it has the authority to ask that institutions conform to this standard. The government can say in effect "conform to our employment guidelines or we will not pay you to develop a test."

Most school districts are happy to receive federal funds to implement certain programs. However, they may not be enthusiastic about implementing other policies. For example, a district may have a school lunch program for under-privileged children, and it may enthusiastically support this program. The government may then ask the district to build ramps for handicapped children however, and the district may not be inclined to follow through. There is no criminal penalty for deciding not to build the ramps. However, the government has the authority to withhold the funds for the desired program (lunches) unless there is compliance with the second order (ramps).

Virtually all public and most major private institutions can be regulated in this way because of their dependence on federal contracts and grants. And institutions in the private sector that do not depend as heavily on federal funds can be regulated through interstate commerce. Government regulation is thus difficult to escape.

Guidelines of the Equal Employment Opportunity Commission.   One of the major ways in which the government exercises its power to regulate testing is through interpretations of the 14th Amendment to the Constitution. The 14th Amendment guarantees all citizens due process and equal protection. However, specifying the conditions under which due process and equal protection are afforded has taken a long time. Gradually, the way in which these principles are implemented has been carefully refined. The clearest statement from the federal government has been with regard to employee testing and personnel procedures.

During the presidency of Lyndon Johnson, Congress enacted the Civil Rights Act of 1964, one of the most important pieces of legislation of the century. Title VII of the act and its subsequent amendments created an Equal Employment Opportunity Commission (EEOC). In 1970 the commission released a set of guidelines that defined fair employee-selection procedures. In 1978, the guidelines were revised and simplified, were published as the *Uniform Guidelines on Employee Selection Procedures*, and were jointly adopted by the EEOC, the Civil Service Commission, and the Departments of Justice, Labor, and the Treasury. These guidelines thus affect most public employment and can also be imposed in institutions that receive governmental funds (Novick, 1981).

The intent of the guidelines is to prohibit discrimination. The document makes it clear that an employer cannot discriminate on the basis of race, color, sex, national origin, or religion. The guidelines are particularly concerned with selection procedures that might have *adverse impact*. Adverse impact is interpreted according to the four-fifths rule, which is one of the most controversial components of the guidelines. The four-fifths rule is stated as follows:

> A selection rate of any race, sex, or ethnic group which is less than four-fifths ($\frac{4}{5}$) (or 80%) of the rate for the group with the highest rate will generally be regarded by the federal enforcement agencies as evidence of adverse impact, while a greater than four-fifths rate will generally not be regarded by federal enforcement agencies as evidence of adverse impact.

This means that a selection procedure may be suspected of having adverse impact if it gives any homogeneous group of employees four-fifths or more of the jobs. For example, if an employer hires 90% of the White male applicants and only 20% of the Black male applicants, the selection procedure violates the four-fifths rule. The employer then has to demonstrate that extenuating circumstances make the standards unreasonable. One of the most interesting problems with the four-fifths rule has been that efforts to recruit minorities reduce the percentage from that group that is hired. By recruiting members of many minority groups, an employer can hire a smaller percentage of those recruited. Active recruiting may result in selection of a smaller percentage of minority-group members. Thus, the rule, which was designed to protect minority-group members, may discourage the aggressive recruiting of these groups. The EEOC acknowledges these problems and has developed exceptions for particular circumstances. The authorization of these exceptions for specific individual cases is left up to the EEOC and, in many cases, will be left to the courts (McCormick & Ilgen, 1980).

The guidelines are explicit and include many careful definitions of terms such as *validity*. Whenever a psychological test or other selection device is employed and its use results in adverse impact (or the overselection in one group), extensive evidence for the validity of the selection procedure must be presented. Much of the text of the EEOC guidelines is devoted to a discussion of the minimum requirements for the validity of a selection procedure. In essence, the guidelines parallel the discussion presented in Chapter 5. Technical Box 21-1 gives the EEOC requirements for criterion validity.

Technical Box 21-1. EEOC Guidelines for Criterion Validity

Technical standards for criterion-related validity studies—(1) *Technical feasibility.* Users choosing to validate a selection procedure by a criterion-related validity strategy should determine whether it is technically feasible (as defined in section 16) to conduct such a study in the particular employment context. The determination of the number of persons necessary to permit the conduct of a meaningful criterion-related study should be made by the user on the basis of all relevant information concerning the selection procedure, the potential sample, and the employment situation. Where appropriate, jobs with substantially the same major work behaviors may be grouped together for validity studies, in order to obtain an adequate sample. These guidelines do not require a user to hire or promote persons for the purpose of making it possible to conduct a criterion-related study.

(2) *Analysis of the job.* There should be a review of job information to determine measures of work behavior(s) or performance that are relevant to the job or group of jobs in question. These measures or criteria are relevant to the extent that they represent critical or important job duties, work behaviors, or work outcomes as developed from the review of job information. The possibility of bias should be considered both in selection of the criterion measures and their application. In view of the possibility of bias in subjective evaluations, supervisory rating techniques and instructions to raters should be carefully developed. All criterion measures and the methods for gathering data need to be examined for freedom from factors which would unfairly alter scores of members of any group. The relevance of criteria and their freedom from bias are of particular concern when there are significant differences in measures of job performance for different groups.

(3) *Criterion measures.* Proper safeguards should be taken to insure that scores on selection procedures do not enter into any judgments of employee adequacy that are to be used as criterion measures. Whatever criteria are used should represent important or critical work behavior(s) or work outcomes. Certain criteria may be used without a full job analysis if the user can show the importance of the criteria to the particular employment context. These criteria include but are not limited to production rate, error rate, tardiness, absenteeism, and length of service. A standardized rating of overall work performance may be used where a study of the job shows that it is an appropriate criterion. Where performance in training is used as a criterion, success in training should be properly measured and the relevance of the training should be shown either through a comparison of the content of the training program with the critical or important work behavior(s) of the job(s) or through a demonstration of the relationship between measures of performance in training and measures of job performance. Measures of relative success in training include but are not limited to instructor evaluations, performance samples, or tests. Criterion measures consisting of paper-and-pencil tests will be closely reviewed for job relevance.

(4) *Representativeness of the sample.* Whether the study is predictive or con-current, the sample subjects should insofar as feasible be representative of the candidates normally available in the relevant labor market for the job or group of jobs in question, and should insofar as feasible include the races, sexes, and ethnic groups normally available in the relevant job market. In determining the repre-sentativeness of the sample in a concurrent validity study, the user should take into account the extent to which the specific knowledges or skills which are the primary focus of the test are those which employees learn on the job.

Where samples are combined or compared, attention should be given to see that such samples are comparable in terms of the actual job they perform, the length of time on the job where time on the job is likely to affect performance, and other relevant factors likely to affect validity differences; or that these factors are included in the design of the study and their effects identified.

(5) *Statistical relationships.* The degree of relationship between selection proce-dure scores and criterion measures should be examined and computed, using professionally acceptable statistical procedures. Generally, a selection procedure is considered related to the criterion, for the purposes of these guidelines, when the relationship between performance on the procedure and performance on the crite-rion measure is statistically significant at the .05 level of significance, which means that it is sufficiently high as to have a probability of no more than one (1) in twenty (20) to have occurred by chance. Absence of a statistically significant relationship between a selection procedure and job performance should not necessarily discour-age other investigations of the validity of that selection procedure.

(6) *Operational use of selection procedures.* Users should evaluate each selec-tion procedure to assure that it is appropriate for operational use, including estab-lishment of cutoff scores or rank ordering. Generally, if other factors remain the same, the greater the magnitude of the relationship (e.g., correlation coefficient) between performance on a selection procedure and one or more criteria of per-formance on the job and the greater the importance and number of aspects of job performance covered by the criteria, the more likely it is that the procedure will be appropriate for use. Reliance upon a selection procedure which is significantly related to a criterion measure but which is based upon a study involving a large number of subjects and has a low correlation coefficient will be subject to close review if it has a large adverse impact. Sole reliance upon a single selection instru-ment which is related to only one of many job duties or aspects of job performance will also be subject to close review. The appropriateness of a selection procedure is best evaluated in each particular situation and there are no minimum correlation coefficients applicable to all employment situations. In determining whether a selec-tion procedure is appropriate for operational use the following considerations should also be taken into account: the degree of adverse impact of the procedure, the availability of other selection procedures of greater or substantially equal validity.

(7) *Overstatement of validity findings.* Users should avoid reliance upon techniques which tend to overestimate validity findings as a result of capitalization on chance unless an appropriate safeguard is taken. Reliance upon a few selection procedures or criteria of successful job performance when many selection proce-dures or criteria of performance have been studied, or the use of optimal statistical

weights for selection procedures computed in one sample, are techniques which tend to inflate validity estimates as a result of chance. Use of a large sample is one safeguard; cross validation is another.

(8) *Fairness*. This section generally calls for studies of unfairness where technically feasible. The concept of fairness or unfairness of selection procedures is a developing concept. In addition, fairness studies generally require substantial numbers of employees in the job or group of jobs being studied. For these reasons, the Federal enforcement agencies recognize that the obligation to conduct studies of fairness imposed by the guidelines generally will be upon users or groups of users with a large number of persons in a job class, or test developers; and that small users utilizing their own selection procedures will generally not be obligated to conduct such studies because it will be technically infeasible for them to do so.

(a) *Unfairness defined*. When members of one race, sex, or ethnic group characteristically obtain lower scores on a selection procedure than members of another group and the differences in scores are not reflected in differences in a measure of job performance, use of the selection procedure may unfairly deny opportunities to members of the group that obtains the lower scores.

(b) *Investigation of fairness*. Where a selection procedure results in an adverse impact on a race, sex, or ethnic group identified in accordance with the classifications set forth in section 4 above and that group is a significant factor in the relevant labor market, the user generally should investigate the possible existence of unfairness for that group if it is technically feasible to do so. The greater the severity of the adverse impact on a group, the greater the need to investigate the possible existence of unfairness. Where the weight of evidence from other studies shows that the selection procedure predicts fairly for the group in question and for the same or similar jobs, such evidence may be relied on in connection with the selection procedure at issue.

(c) *General considerations in fairness investigations*. Users conducting a study of fairness should review the A.P.A. Standards regarding investigation of possible bias in testing. An investigation of fairness of a selection procedure depends on both evidence of validity and the manner in which the selection procedure is to be used in a particular employment context. Fairness of a selection procedure cannot necessarily be specified in advance without investigating these factors. Investigation of fairness of a selection procedure in samples where the range of scores on selection procedures or criterion measures is severely restricted for any subgroup sample (as compared to other subgroup samples) may produce misleading evidence of unfairness. That factor should accordingly be taken into account in conducting such studies and before reliance is placed on the results.

(d) *When unfairness is shown*. If unfairness is demonstrated through a showing that members of a particular group perform better or poorer on the job than their scores on the selection procedure would indicate through comparison with how members of other groups perform, the user may either revise or replace the selection instrument in accordance with these guidelines, or may continue to use the selection instrument operationally with appropriate revisions in its use to assure compatibility between the probability of successful job performance and the probability of being selected.

(e) *Technical feasibility of fairness studies*. In addition to the general conditions needed for technical feasibility for the conduct of a criterion-related study an investigation of fairness requires the following:

(i) An adequate sample of persons in each group available for the study to achieve findings of statistical significance. Guidelines do not require a user to hire or promote persons on the basis of group classifications for the purpose of making it possible to conduct a study of fairness; but the user has the obligation otherwise to comply with these guidelines.

(ii) The samples for each group should be comparable in terms of the actual job they perform, length of time on the job where time on the job is likely to affect performance, and other relevant factors likely to affect validity differences; or such factors should be included in the design of the study and their effects identified.

(f) *Continued use of selection procedures when fairness studies not feasible.* If a study of fairness should otherwise be performed, but is not technically feasible, a selection procedure may be used which has otherwise met the validity standards of these guidelines, unless the technical infeasibility resulted from discriminatory employment practices which are demonstrated by facts other than past failure to conform with requirements for validation of selection procedures. However, when it becomes technically feasible for the user to perform a study of fairness and such a study is otherwise called for, the user should conduct the study of fairness.

From "EEOC Guidelines." Equal Employment Opportunity Commission, 1978.

Although the validity requirements are specifically applicable to psychological tests, they also apply to other selection devices such as employment forms and interviews. (See Focused Example 21-2 for an example.) In addition, they apply to other job requirements including educational and work-experience requirements. In summary, the EEOC guidelines provide clear, unambiguous regulations for the use of any assessment device in the selection of employees.

As you might expect, many employers were furious about the EEOC guidelines. They saw them as additional governmental interference with their conduct of business and as a means of inhibiting them from hiring the best person for a job. Although it is easy to sympathize with their concern about excessive bureaucratic red tape, historical evidence supports the implementation of the guidelines. The basic rationale for the EEOC guidelines was provided by the equal protection clause in the 14th Amendment to the Constitution. The 14th Amendment was ratified in the post-Civil War era, but the equal protection clause was not a major basis for public policy for nearly 100 years—until the court battles over school desegregation and the activities of the Civil Rights Movement led to the passage of the 1964 Civil Rights Act. Even after the passage of this important law, employers still did not follow fair employment practices. The specific EEOC guidelines were therefore necessary in order for the intent of the law to be realized. Without the specific guidelines, more than 100 years passed without employers recognizing the legal requirement of equal protection.

■ FOCUSED EXAMPLE 21-2   CONTENT VALIDITY AND SEXUAL HARASSMENT DURING A PARAMEDIC EXAM

The EEOC guidelines make it clear that questions asked on employment tests and during employment interviews must be relevant to performance on the job. However, not all agencies are in full compliance with this regulation, particularly with regard to job interviews. This noncompliance was a source of irritation to Sandra Buchanan when she appeared before the Los Angeles City Fire Department for an interview for a paramedic job. During the interview she was asked as much about her sex life as she was about her four years of paramedic training and experience. For example, she was asked: "Have you ever had semipublic sex?" "Have you had sex on the beach?" "Have you had sex in a parked car?" "Have you ever exposed yourself indecently?" "Have you molested any children?" "Do you have any homosexual contacts?"

Ms. Buchanan was so disturbed by these questions that she filed a complaint with the Civil Service Commission. In the ensuing investigation, the fire department was asked to show how the questions about sex related to the paramedic job. Its response was that the questions create stress and therefore give the department a chance to observe how a person handles himself or herself in stressful situations. The department also argued that it needed to delve deeply into the backgrounds of applicants because paramedics are entrusted with important responsibilities. One member of the fire department argued that the question on indecent exposure was necessary because "they have a dormitory situation that is quite different from other jobs; the nature of this job makes some of the questions job related that would not be related in other jobs."

The commission decided that the department had to reinterview Ms. Buchanan. It was instructed to review the questions and eliminate those that were not job related. It appeared that the commission agreed with Ms. Buchanan's attorney, who argued, "It is time that the city of Los Angeles stop asking 'How's your sex life?' and get back to the business of finding the most qualified person for the job of Los Angeles paramedic" (quoted from *Los Angeles Times*, June 29, 1979).

It is worth noting that the guidelines are used only for cases in which adverse impact is suspected. When adverse impact is not suspected, organizations are under little pressure to use valid selection procedures (McCormick & Ilgen, 1980). As Guion (1976) observes, "organizations have the right even to be fairly stupid in their employment practices as long as they are stupid fairly" (p. 811).

B. Specific laws

Other regulatory schemes attempt to control the use of tests. Two examples are the New York Truth in Testing Law of 1979 and the Education for All Handicapped Children Act of 1975.

Truth in testing laws.   The New York Truth in Testing Law is one of the most controversial measures ever to hit the testing field. The New York law was motivated by an extensive investigation of the Educational Testing Service (ETS) by the New York Public Interest Research Group (NYPIRG). Other testing companies are affected by the law, but the New York law was written with ETS specifically in mind.

ETS was created by the College Entrance Examination Board, the American Council on Education, and the Carnegie Foundation in 1948. Its original and best-known mission was to create and administer aptitude tests such as the SAT. By 1979, ETS was responsible for over 300 testing programs including the Graduate Management Admission Test (GMAT), the Graduate Record Examination (GRE), the Multi-State Bar Exam, and the Law School Admission Test (LSAT). The assets of the company exceeded $25 million, and its gross yearly income exceeded $80 million.

NYPIRG seemed upset by the wealth and success of ETS, yet what bothered NYPIRG more was the power ETS has. Each year several million persons take tests designed and administered by ETS, and the results of these tests have pronounced impacts on their lives (Brill, 1973; Kiersh, 1979; Levy, 1979). Many educational programs take the scores seriously. Students scoring poorly on the LSAT, for example, may be denied entrance to law school, and this rejection may eventually affect many important aspects of their lives. Higher scores may have resulted in a higher income, more occupational status, and greater self-esteem for them.

On investigation, NYPIRG became dissatisfied with the available information on test validity, the calculation of test scores, and the financial accounting of ETS. The Truth in Testing Law responds to these objections by requiring testing companies to (1) disclose all studies on the validity of a test, (2) provide a complete disclosure to students about what scores mean and how they were calculated, and (3), on request by a student, provide a copy of the test questions, the correct answers, and the student's answers.

The first two portions are essentially noncontroversial. The test developers argue that they do disclose all pertinent information on validity, and they do release many public documents highlighting the strengths and weaknesses of their tests. We have written to ETS many times and have never been refused any report. Furthermore, ETS strongly encourages institutions using their tests to perform local validity studies. Any of these studies can be published in scholarly journals (which are found in most college libraries) with no interference from ETS. However, NYPIRG provided some evidence that ETS and other testing companies have files of secret data that they do not make public because these data may reflect poorly on the product. The second aspect of the law was included because ETS sometimes reports index scores to schools without telling students how the index was calculated and the exact index value being reported.

The controversial third portion of the law may turn out to seriously decrease the value of testing programs. Requiring that the test questions be returned to students means that the same questions cannot be used in future versions of the test. Several problems are expected to result from this policy. First, it decreases the validity of the test. With the items constantly changing, the test essentially becomes a new test each time the items change. As a result, it is impossible to accumulate a record of construct validity.

Second, it is difficult to equate scores across years. For example, a graduate school must often consider students who took the GRE in different years. If the test itself is different each year, it is difficult to compare the scores of students who took the test at different times. Although the bill eventually adopted in New York did allow testing companies to keep some of the items secret for equating purposes, this practice falls short of being a satisfactory solution. Equating can be accomplished, but it may be difficult without increasing the chances of error.

Third, the most debated problem associated with the disclosure of test items is that it will greatly increase the costs to ETS and other testing companies. ETS will probably not absorb these inflated costs but will pass them on to the consumer. Just how high the cost of taking a test will go is a matter of conjecture. Experts within the testing industry warn that the costs could be more than twice what they were before the law was passed. NYPIRG doubts that the costs of writing new items will have any substantial impact on the cost of taking the test. Only 5% of the student fees for taking a test go to question development, while 22% to 27% go to company profit. Backers of the law feel there should be only minimal increases in fees and that ETS, as a nonprofit and tax-exempt institution, should take the cost of writing new items out of its substantial profits.

One immediate impact of the New York Truth in Testing Law was that it stimulated other similar proposals. The most important of these was the Educational Testing Act of 1979, which was offered to the U.S. House of Representatives in July 1979. The Educational Testing Act, which was proposed by Representatives Ted Weiss, Shirley Chisholm, and George Miller, was essentially the same as the New York Truth in Testing Law; the major provisions of the bills were almost identical. In effect, the Educational Testing Act of 1979 attempted to make the New York law a federal law. However, the federal bill was not enacted into law.

There is no question that the truth in testing bills were introduced by sincere and well-intentioned legislators. However, the laws are disturbing for two reasons. First, they politicize a process that has in the past been primarily academic. The issues in the debate were not presented in a scholarly fashion. Instead, they were presented (on both sides) in an adversarial manner. The debate thus got out of the hands of psychologists who have the training to interpret some of the complex technical issues. For example, in his testimony before a subcommittee of the House Education and Labor Committee, Representative Weiss made many references to the bias in the tests. His major argument was that there are mean differences between different ethnic groups in test scores. As we discussed in Chapter 20, mean difference is not generally considered evidence for test bias among psychologists, and psychologists came to this conclusion after many years of careful debate and study.

ETS does make booklets available to the public that present information on the scoring system, the validity, the reliability, and the standard error of measurement for each of their tests. Persons with no background in testing probably will not comprehend all this information. Each of you, after completing your testing course, will have little difficulty interpreting the manuals, but, as you know, it has taken you a long term of hard study to get to this point. The authors of the bills fail to recognize that the proper use of tests and test results is a technical problem that requires technical training in advanced courses such as psychological testing. After all, we do not expect people to be able to practice medicine without the technical training given in medical school.

Second, we must consider the ultimate impact of the truth in testing legislation. One side argues that the new laws will make for a fairer and more honest testing industry. The other argues that students will now have to pay a higher price for a poorer product. If the requirement of test-item disclosure results in lower validity of the tests (which it most likely will), there will be greater error in selecting students than now exists. In other words, selection for admissions may become more random.

The Education for All Handicapped Children Act of 1975.   In 1975 Congress passed a law that is having a major impact on the use of psychological tests. PL 94-142 (the 142nd Public Law passed by the 94th Congress) guarantees a publicly financed education to all handicapped children. The law is detailed with regard to its major requirement—that an individually tailored educational plan be developed for each handicapped child. The additional requirement that the educational characteristics of each handicapped child be assessed necessitates the use of tests. In particular, children may be identified for placement in programs funded through PL 94-142 by the use of psychological tests. For example, tests may be used to identify children for EMR classes, which receive funding under the law.

However, the law clearly specifies that the tests must be reliable, valid, and nondiscriminatory with regard to the non-English speaking, the poor, members of minority groups, and the bilingual. A debate has erupted about which tests meet these criteria. Jane Mercer, the creator of the SOMPA (see Chapter 20), argues that her test meets the requirements of the law, while the WISC and Stanford-Binet do not. In fact, she suggests that the SOMPA system is the only test that conforms to the law (Mercer, 1979). Her critics interpret the law as requiring traditional tests such as the Stanford-Binet and WISC and assert that the SOMPA cannot be used under the law (Clarizio, 1979a; Sattler, 1979a). A court test may be required to determine which tests can be used.

II. SOME MAJOR LAWSUITS

Legislation is not the only way to change policy. There are other options for those who have particular conflicts. One option that is being used with increasing frequency is litigation, or the law suit. Law suits are usually considered to be the last resort for resolving personal conflicts. For example, if you feel you have been wronged and you have been unable to persuade those who have offended you through other legal means, you may file a law suit. In doing so, you trust the court system to make a fair judgment about your case.

There have already been many law suits concerning the use of psychological tests, and we expect the number to dramatically increase in the years to come. Some of the most important of these law suits are discussed in this chapter. It is important to realize that each of these cases was complex and involved considerably more evidence than we can cite here.

A. Early desegregation cases

The 14th Amendment requires that all citizens be granted the equal protection of the laws. At the end of the 19th century, it was being argued that segregated schools did not offer such protection. In the famous 1896 case of *Plessy v. Ferguson,*[1] the Supreme Court ruled that schools could remain segregated but that the quality of the schools must be equal. This was the much-acclaimed separate-but-equal ruling.

Perhaps the most influential ruling in the history of American public school education came in the case of *Brown v. Board of Education*[2] in 1954. In the *Brown* case, the Supreme Court overturned the *Plessy v. Ferguson* decision and ruled that the schools must provide nonsegregated facilities for Black and White students. In its opinion the court raised several issues that would eventually affect the use of psychological tests.

The most important pronouncement of *Brown* was that segregation was a denial of equal protection. In coming to its decision, the court made extensive use of testimony by psychologists. This testimony suggested that Black children could be made to feel inferior if the school system kept the two races separate.

The story of the *Brown* case is well known, but what is less often discussed is the ugly history that followed. Many school districts did not want to desegregate, and the battle over busing and other mechanisms for desegregation continues today in many areas. Many of the current arguments against desegregation are based on fear of children leaving their own neighborhoods or on the stress on children who must endure long bus rides. The early resistance to the *Brown* decision was more clearly linked to the racist belief of Black inferiority.

[1]163 U.S. 537 (1896).
[2]347 U.S. 483 (1954), 349 U.S. 294 (1955).

B.   *Stell v. Savannah-Chatham County Board of Education*[3]

The most significant racist court case occurred when legal action was taken to desegregate the school system of Savannah, Georgia, on behalf of a group of Black children. The conflict began when attorneys for two White children intervened. They argued that they were not opposed to desegregating on the basis of race but that Black children did not have the ability to be in the same classrooms as Whites. Testimony from psychologists indicated that the median IQ score for Black children was 81 while that for White children was 101. Because there was such a large difference in this trait (which was assumed to be genetic), the attorneys argued that it could be to the mutual disadvantage of both groups to congregate them in the same schools. Doing so might create even greater feelings of inferiority among Black children and might create frustration that would eventually result in antisocial behavior.

The court essentially agreed with this testimony and ruled that the district should not desegregate. The judge's opinion reflected his view of what was in the best interest of all of the children. Later, this decision was reversed by Judge Griffin Bell of the U.S. Court of Appeal for the Fifth Circuit. In doing so, the court used the precedent set forth by *Brown* as the reason for requiring the Savannah district to desegregate. It is important to note that the validity of the test scores, which were the primary evidence, was never discussed (Bersoff, 1979, 1981).

C.   *Hobson v. Hansen*[4]

Stell was just one of many cases that attempted to resist the order set forth in the famous *Brown* desegregation case. Like *Stell*, many of these cases introduced test scores as evidence that Black children were genetically incapable of learning or being educated in the same classrooms as White children. The courts routinely accepted this evidence. Given the current controversy over the use of psychological tests, it is remarkable that several years passed before the validity of the test scores became an issue.

The first major case to examine the validity of psychological tests was *Hobson v. Hansen*. The *Hobson* case is relevant to many of the current law suits. Unlike the early desegregation cases, it did not deal with sending Black and White children to different schools. Instead, it concerned the placement of children once they arrived at a school. Although the courts had been consistent in requiring schools to desegregate, they tended to take a hands off approach with regard to placement of students in tracks once they arrived at their desegregated schools.

The *Hobson* case contested the use of group standardized ability tests to

---

[3]220 F. Supp. 667, 668 (S.D. Ga. 1963), rev'd 333 F.2d 55 (5th Cir. 1964) cert. denied, 379 U.S. 933 (1964).
[4]269 F. Supp. 401 (D. D.C. 1967).

place students in different learning tracks. Julius W. Hobson was the father of two Black children placed in a basic track by the District of Columbia School District. Carl F. Hansen was the superintendent for the district. Within the district, children were placed in honors, regular, general, and basic tracks on the basis of group ability tests. The honors track was designed to prepare children for college, while the basic track focused on skills and preparation for blue-collar jobs. Placement in the basic track makes it essentially impossible to prepare for a high income/high prestige profession.

The rub in *Hobson* was that racial groups were not equally represented among those assigned to the basic track. In effect, the tracking system served to racially segregate groups by placing Black children in the basic track and White children in the other tracks. Psychological tests were the primary mechanism used to justify this separation.

The *Hobson* case was decided in 1967 by Judge Skelly Wright of the federal district court of Washington, D.C. Just two years before the decision, the Supreme Court had ruled that a group is not denied equal protection by "mere classification" (Bersoff, 1979). Nevertheless, Judge Wright ruled against the use of the tracking system when based on group ability tests. After extensive expert testimony on the validity of the tests for minority children, the judge concluded that the tests discriminated against them. An interesting aspect of the opinion was that it claimed that grouping would be permissible if it were based on innate ability. The judge asserted that ability test scores were influenced by cultural experiences, and the dominant cultural group had an unfair advantage on the tests and thereby gained admission to the tracks that provided the best preparation for high income/high prestige jobs.

D. *Diana v. State Board of Education*[5]

The decision in *Hobson v. Hansen* opened the door for a thorough examination of the use of standardized tests for the placement of students in EMR tracks. The case of *Diana* has particular implications for the use of standardized tests for bilingual children. Diana was one of nine Mexican-American elementary school children who had been placed in EMR classes on the basis of the WISC or Stanford-Binet. These nine children represented a class of bilingual children. They brought a class action suit against the California State Board of Education, contending that the use of standardized IQ tests for placement in EMR classes denied equal protection because the tests were standardized only for Whites and had been administered by a non-Spanish-speaking psychometrist. Although only 18% of the children in Diana's school district had Spanish surnames, this group made up nearly one-third of the enrollment in EMR classes.

When originally tested in English, Diana achieved an IQ score of only 30. However, when retested in Spanish and English, her IQ bounced to 79, which

[5]C.A. No. C-70 37 RFP (N.D. Cal., filed Feb. 3, 1970).

was high enough to keep her out of the EMR classes in her school district. Seven of the other eight plaintiffs also achieved high enough scores on retesting in Spanish to be taken out of the EMR classes.

When faced with this evidence, the California State Board of Education decided not to take the case to court. Instead, they adopted special provisions for the testing of Mexican-American and Chinese-American children. These provisions included the following: (1) If English was not the primary language, the children would be tested in their primary language. (2) Questions based on certain vocabulary and information that the children could not be expected to know would be eliminated. (3) The Mexican-American and Chinese-American children who had been assigned to EMR classes would be reevaluated with tests that used their primary language and nonverbal items. (4) New tests would be developed by the state that reflected Mexican-American culture and that were normed for Mexican-American children (Bersoff, 1979). Later studies confirmed that bilingual children do score higher when tested in their primary language (Bergan & Parra, 1979).

The combination of the judgment in *Hobson* and the change in policy brought about by *Diana* forced many to seriously question the use of IQ tests for the assignment of children to EMR classes. However, these decisions were quite specific to the circumstances in the particular cases. *Hobson* dealt with group tests but did not discuss individual tests. However, individual tests are used more often than group tests to make final decisions for EMR placement. The ruling in *Diana* was limited strictly to bilingual children. These two cases were thus not relevant to Black children placed in EMR classes on the basis of individual IQ tests. This specific area was left for the most important court battle of them all—*Larry P. v. Wilson Riles.*

E.   Larry P. v. Wilson Riles[6]

In October 1979, Judge Robert Peckham of the Federal District Court for the Northern District of California handed down an opinion that declared that "the use of IQ tests which had a disproportionate effect on Black children violated the Rehabilitation Act, the Education for All Handicapped Children Act, Title VI, and the 14th Amendment when used to place children in EMR classes." Attorneys for Larry P., one of six Black elementary school students who were assigned to EMR classes on the basis of IQ test results, had argued that the use of standardized IQ tests to place Black children in EMR classes violated both the California constitution and the equal protection clause of the 14th Amendment (Opton, 1979) as well as those laws mentioned above.

The court first ruled in the case of *Larry P.* in 1972. It found that the school district incorrectly labeled Larry as EMR and violated his right to equal educational opportunity. As a result, a preliminary injunction was issued that prohib-

[6]343 F. Supp. 1306 (N.D. Cal. 1972), aff'd 502 F.2d 963 (9th Cir. 1979).

ited that particular school district from using IQ tests for EMR placement decisions. Later, the California Department of Education called for a temporary moratorium on IQ testing until another court opinion on the validity of the tests could be obtained (Opton, 1977). The *Larry P.* case came before the same court that had issued the preliminary injunction in order to obtain a ruling on test validity for Black children.

During the trial, both sides geared up for a particularly intense battle. Wilson Riles was the Black superintendent of public instruction in California; he had instituted many significant reforms that benefited minority children. Thus, it was particularly awkward to have a nationally recognized spokesperson for progressive programs named as the defendant in an allegedly racist scheme.

In defense of the use of tests, Riles and the state called many nationally recognized experts on IQ tests including Lloyd Humphreys, Jerome Sattler, Robert Thorndike, Nadine Lambert, and Robert Gordon. These witnesses presented rather extensive evidence that IQ tests, particularly the Stanford-Binet and the WISC (which were used to test Larry and the others), were not biased against Blacks. Although the tests had not originally been normed for Black populations, studies had demonstrated that they were equally valid for use with Black and White children. (Many of the arguments supporting the use of tests for all races are summarized in Chapter 20.) If the tests were not biased, then why did Larry and the others receive higher scores when they were retested by Black psychologists? The defense argued that the Black psychologists did not follow standard testing procedures and that IQ test scores are not changed when standardized procedures are followed.

Statements from special-education teachers were also presented. The teachers argued that the children involved in the case could not cope with the standard curriculum and that they required the special tutoring available in the EMR classes. The children had not been learning in regular classes, and the schools investigated cases in which there was doubt about the placement. For all these children, the assignment to EMR classes was deemed appropriate (Sattler, 1979a).

The Larry P. side of the case also had its share of distinguished experts, including George Albee, Leon Kamin, and Jane Mercer. The arguments for Larry were varied. His lawyers argued that all humans are born with equal capacity and that any test that assigns disproportionate numbers of children from one race to an EMR category is racist and discriminatory. The witnesses testified that dominant social groups had historically used devices such as IQ tests to discriminate against less powerful social groups and that the school district had intentionally discriminated against Black children by using unvalidated IQ tests. Specifically, the tests were used to keep Blacks in dead-end classes for the mentally retarded, in which they would not get the training they needed to move up in the social strata. Furthermore, the plaintiffs suggested that labeling someone as EMR has devastating social consequences. Children who are labeled as

EMR lose confidence and self-esteem (Mercer, 1973), and eventually the label becomes a self-fulfilling prophecy (Rosenthal & Jacobson, 1968). In other words, labeling a child as mentally retarded may cause the child to behave as though mentally retarded.

The judge was clearly persuaded more by the plaintiffs than by the defense. He declared that the tests "are racially and culturally biased, have a discrimina-tory impact on Black children, and have not been validated for the purpose of [consigning] Black children into educationally dead-end, isolated, and stigmatiz-ing classes." Furthermore, the judge stated that the Department of Education had "desired to perpetuate the segregation of minorities in inferior, dead-end, and stigmatizing classes for the retarded."

The effect of the ruling, which is now being appealed, was a permanent discontinuance of IQ testing to place Black children in EMR classes. The decision immediately affected all Black California school children who had been labeled as EMR. More than 6000 of these children must be reassessed in some other manner.

There are strong differences of opinion about the meaning of the *Larry P.* decision. Harold Dent, one of the Black psychologists who had retested Larry P. and the other children, hailed the decision as a victory for Black children:

> For more than 60 years psychologists have used tests primarily to justify the majority's desire to "track" minorities into inferior education and dead-end jobs. The message of *Larry P.* is that psychologists must involve themselves in the task mandated in the last sentence of the court's opinion: "this will clear the way for more constructive educational reform" [quoted in Opton, 1979].

Others did not share the belief that the *Larry P.* decision was a social victory. Nadine Lambert, who was an expert witness for the state, felt it was a terrible decision. On learning of it, she remarked, "I think the people who will be most hurt by it are the Black children" (quoted in Opton, 1979). Banning the use of IQ tests opens the door to completely subjective judgments, which may be even more racist than the test results. Opponents of the *Larry P.* decision cite many instances in which gifted Black children were assumed to be average by their teachers but were recognized as highly intelligent because of IQ test scores.

F. *Parents in Action on Special Education v. Hannon*[7]

Just as the case of *Larry P.* was making headlines in California, a similar case came to trial in Illinois. The case was a class-action law suit filed on behalf of two Black children (representing the class of all similar children) who had been placed in special classes for the educable mentally handicapped (EMH) on the basis of IQ test scores. Attorneys for the two student plaintiffs argued that the children were inappropriately placed in EMH classes because of racial bias in

[7]USDC NI11; J. Grady pub. 7/7/80.

the IQ tests. They suggested that the use of IQ tests for Black children violates the equal protection clause of the Constitution and many federal statutes.

In their presentation to the court, the plaintiffs relied heavily on the recent *Larry P.* decision, which held that the WISC, the WISC-R, and the Stanford-Binet IQ tests are biased and inappropriate for the testing of minority children. However, Judge John Grady of the U.S. District Court came to exactly the opposite conclusion of Judge Peckham, who had presided over the *Larry P.* case. Judge Grady found evidence for racial bias in the three major IQ tests to be unconvincing. In his opinion, he noted that the items objected to were only a fraction of the items on the entire test. For example, witnesses for the plaintiffs never mentioned whole subtests on the WISC and WISC-R, such as arithmetic, digit span, block design, mazes, coding, and object assembly. The judge noted that these subtests were not biased in favor of either Black or White children because most youngsters of both groups would have never confronted problems of this type before. The items for which there were legitimate objections were too few to have an impact on test scores.

Thus, less than one year after the historic *Larry P.* case, another court concluded "Evidence of racial bias in standardized IQ tests is not sufficient to render their use as part of classification procedures to place Black children in 'educable mentally handicapped' classes violative of statutes prohibiting discrimination in federally funded programs." It now seems likely that this whole issue may require a hearing by the Supreme Court. Focused Example 21-3 presents conflicting statements from the two judges in these cases.

■ FOCUSED EXAMPLE 21-3 DIFFERENT OPINIONS FROM DIFFERENT JUDGES

We often think that two judges looking at the same evidence will come to the same conclusion. However, many times judges differ sharply in their opinions. When confronted with different opinions from Judges Peckham (*Larry P. v. Wilson Riles*) and Grady (*Parents in Action on Special Education v. Hannon*), Sattler (1980) juxtaposed quotes from the two judges on selected issues in the cases. Below are some of the statements demonstrating that the judges viewed the issues differently.

Judge Robert Peckham	Judge John Grady

What are the functions of special classes for the educable mentally retarded or educable mentally handicapped?

". . . EMR classes are designed to separate out children who are *incapable* of learning in the regular classes. . . . Further, the curriculum was not and is not designed to help students learn

"The EMH curriculum is designed for the child who cannot benefit from the regular curriculum. It is designed for children who learn slowly, who have short attention spans, slow reaction

the skills necessary to return to the regular instructional program. . . . Finally, consistent with the first two aspects of EMR classes, the classes are conceived of as 'dead-end classes.' Children are placed there, generally at about eight to ten years of age, because they are thought to be incapable of learning the skills inculcated by the regular curriculum. They are provided with instruction that deemphasizes academic skills in favor of adjustment, and naturally they will tend to fall farther and farther behind the children in the regular classes."

time, and difficulty retaining material in both the short term and the long term. The curriculum also recognizes the difficulty an EMH child has in seeing similarities and differences, in learning by implication, in generalizing and in thinking abstractly. The curriculum thus involves much repetition and concrete teaching. Subjects are taught for short periods of time, in recognition of the children's short attention spans."

How much emphasis is given to the IQ in placing children in mentally retarded or educable mentally handicapped classes?

"The available data suggest very strongly that, even if in some districts the IQ scores were not always determinative, they were pervasive in the placement process. . . . Retardation is defined in terms of the IQ tests, and a low score in effect establishes a *prima facie* case of retardation."

"The IQ score is not the sole determinant of whether a child is placed in an EMH class. First, the score itself is evaluated by the psychologist who administers the test. The child's responses are recorded verbatim, and the significance of his numerical score is a matter involving judgment and interpretation. . . . The examiner who knows the milieu of the child can correct for cultural bias by asking the questions in a sensitive and intelligent way. . . . Finally, the IQ test and the psychologist's evaluation of the child in the light of that test is only one component of several which form the basis for an EMH referral."

Was the issue of test validity important in the trial?

". . . If defendants could somehow have demonstrated that the intelligence tests had been 'validated' for the purpose of EMR placement of black children, those tests could have been utilized despite their disproportionate impact. . . . However, defendants did not make these showings."

"We do not address the broader questions of whether these IQ tests are generally valid as measures of intelligence, whether individual items are appropriate for that purpose, or whether the tests could be improved. Those questions are not involved in this case."

To what extent do socio-economic factors account for the findings that black children score lower than white children on intelligence tests?

". . . It is clear that socio-economic status by itself cannot explain fully the undisputed disparities in IQ test scores and in EMR placements. . . . The insufficiency of the above explanation leads us to question the cultural bias of IQ tests. The first important inferential evidence is that the tests were never designed to eliminate cultural biases against black children; it was assumed in effect that black children were less 'intelligent' than whites."

"It is uncontradicted that most of the children in the EMH classes do in fact come from the poverty pockets of the city. This tends to suggest that what is involved is not simply race but something associated with poverty. It is also significant that many black children who take the tests score at levels high enough to preclude EMH placement. Plaintiffs have not explained why the alleged cultural bias of the tests did not result in EMH-level scores for these children. Plaintiffs' theory of cultural bias simply ignores the fact that Black children perform differently from each other on the tests. It also fails to explain the fact that some black children perform better than most whites. Nationally, 15 to 20 percent of the blacks who take the tests score above the white mean of 100."

To what extent does black children's use of non-standard English affect their performance on intelligence tests?

"At the outset, it is undeniable that to the extent black children speak other than standard English, they will be handicapped in at least the verbal component of the tests. . . . Dr. [Asa] Hilliard and other witnesses pointed out that black children are more likely to be exposed to non-standard English, and that exposure will be reflected in IQ scores."

"The evidence does not establish how the use of non-standard English would interfere with performance on the Wechsler and Stanford-Binet tests. . . . Dr. [Robert J.] Williams testified that a black child might say, 'John go to town' instead of 'John is going to town,' or 'John book' instead of 'John's book.' . . . What is unclear is how the use of such non-standard English would handicap a child either in understanding the test items or in responding to them. . . . Moreover, responding to a test item in non-standard English should not affect a child's score on the item, since the examiners are specifically instructed by the test manuals to disregard the form of the answer so long as the substance is correct. . . . But there are no vocabulary items on the IQ tests, so far as I can tell, which are peculiar to white culture."

To what extent do differences between black culture and white culture affect black children's performance on intelligence tests?

"To the extent that a 'black culture' —admittedly a vague term   exists and translates the phenomenon of intelligence into skills and knowledge untested by the standardized intelligence tests, those tests cannot measure the capabilities of black children. . . . On the basis of their different cultural background, which results particularly in lower scores on IQ tests, black children are subjected to discrimination analogous to that borne by many San Francisco Chinese, who, because of their cultural background, could not communicate effectively in English. Certainly many Chinese Americans would succeed in those schools even without remedial English. Nevertheless, the failure to provide English-language teaching foreclosed substantial numbers of students from any meaningful educational opportunity. This same result occurs from the use of IQ tests and a biased placement process."

"Dr. Williams did not explain how he relates the other characteristics of black culture to performance on the tests. It is not clear, for instance, how the extended family as opposed to the nuclear family would pertain to performance on the tests. Like Dr. [Leon] Kamin's description of the racist attitudes of Goddard, Yerkes and Terman, Dr. Williams's description of black culture has not been connected to the specific issue in this case. . . . Dr. Kamin's argument that the black child does not obtain the same 'information,' and Dr. [George] Albee's argument that the black child does not share in the dominant white culture, seem inapplicable to most items on all three of the tests in question. As already noted, many of the categories of test items have no precise counterpart in the experience of any children, of whatever race. Others have almost precise counterparts in the everyday experience of American children of all races. Any number of test items could be cited to illustrate this point."

Generally, to what extent are intelligence tests racially biased?

"The answer, as should be clear from the earlier discussion of the history and biases of IQ tests, is that validation has been assumed, not established, for blacks. The tests were developed and standardized in the United States on white, essentially middle-class groups. . . ."

"All but a few of the items on their face appear racially neutral. . . . I conclude that the possibility of the few biased items on these tests causing an EMH placement that would not otherwise occur is practically nonexistent."

Does the use of intelligence tests violate some provisions of Public Law 94-142 (Education for all Handicapped)?

". . . Defendants have failed to take the steps necessary to assure the tests' validity. They have committed a serious error that Title VII regulations warn against in the employment situation: 'Under no circumstances will the general reputation of a test, its author,

"The requirement that 'materials and procedures' used for assessment be non-discriminatory, and that no single procedure be the sole criterion for assessment, seems to me to contemplate that the process as a whole be non-discriminatory. It does not require

or its publisher, or casual reports of test utility be accepted in lieu of evidence of validity.' Whether or not the tests in fact do what they are supposed to do, the law is that defendants must come forward and show that they have been validated for each minority group with which they are used. This minimal burden has not been met for diagnosing the kind of mental retardation justifying EMR placement."

that any single procedure, standing alone, be affirmatively shown to be free of bias. The very requirement of multiple procedures implies recognition that one procedure, standing alone, could well result in bias and that a system of cross-checking is necessary."

From "Different Opinions for Different Judges: Judges Peckham (*Larry P. v. Wilson Riles*) and Grady (*Parents in Action for Special Education v. Hannon*)," by J. Sattler. In *American Psychological Association Monitor*, 1980, *11* (11) 7-8. Copyright 1980 by the American Psychological Association. Reprinted by permission.

G. *Debra P. v. Turlington*[8]

Some people feel that a test is biased if it contains questions that particular test takers cannot answer. One 1979 lawsuit in Florida involved ten Black students who had failed in their first attempt to pass Florida's minimum competence test, the State Student Assessment Test. Debra P. was one of the students, and the case took her name. In Hillsborough County, where the suit was filed, about 19% of the students in the public school system were Black. However, Black students constituted 64% of those who failed the test.

Minimum competence tests similar to the one used in Florida have been adopted by more than 30 states, and 19 states require the exam for graduation. If they meet other requirements, students who do not pass the exam are given a certificate of completion that acknowledges that they attended high school but does not carry the same status as a high school diploma. Examples of items from a minimum competence test are shown in Table 21-1.

The Florida suit charged that the test should not be used for minority students when most of their education occurred before the schools were desegregated. Thus the dispute was over whether the same test should be used for students who may have had unequal opportunities to learn in school. Attorneys for the students argued that their clients had been in inferior schools and had been the subjects of continued discrimination. Thus they should not be held to the standards for majority students, who had better opportunities.

Ralph D. Turlington was the commissioner of education and one of the defendants in the case. He argued that basic minimum standards must be applied in order to certify that students have enough information to survive in situations that require high school level sophistication. These standards, it was argued, must be absolute. Either students know the basic information or they do

[8]474 F. Supp. 244 (M.D. Fla. 1979).

TABLE 21-1 Examples of items from a minimum competence test

Use the following table to answer question 1:

12 inches=1 foot	1,760 yards=1 mile
3 feet=1 yard	5,280 feet=1 mile

1. Sara needs to wrap string around 8 boxes. Each box needs a piece of string 72 inches long. How many yards of string does she need?
    A. 8 yards   B. 16 yards   C. 48 yards   D. 576 yards

2. The Florida sales tax on cars is 4%. The sticker price on a car including extras, title, transportation, and dealer preparation is $3,200. What is the total cost of the car including sales tax?
    A. $3,204   B. $3,212   C. $3,314   D. $3,328

3. The graph below shows the changes in the cost of coffee during a one-year period. According to this graph, how much did the cost of a pound of coffee change from April 1 to July 1?
    A. $.50   B. $1.00   C. $1.50   D. $2.50

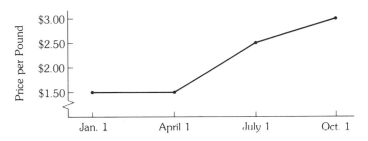

Chocolate Chip Cookies

1 cup brown sugar	2 eggs	1 tsp. salt
1 cup white sugar	1 tsp. baking soda	1 tsp. vanilla
1 cup shortening	2¼ cups flour	1 pkg. chocolate chips

Preheat oven to 350 degrees. In a medium-sized mixing bowl, combine sugar and shortening. Add vanilla and eggs. In another bowl sift together flour, salt, and baking soda. Add sifted ingredients to sugar and shortening mixture. Add chocolate chips. Mix all ingredients together and drop by teaspoon on a cookie sheet. Bake at 350 degrees for 10 minutes.

4. From the above recipe, what should be sifted with baking soda? A. vanilla and eggs B. sugar and shortening   C. flour and salt   D. chocolate chips and salt

Answers to sample questions:
1. B   2. D   3. B   4. C
    From *State Student Assessment Test. Part II: Answers to Your Questions.* Reprinted with permission of the State of Florida, Department of Education.

not. According to the commissioner, "To demand that a 12th-grade student with a 3rd-grade reading level be given a diploma is silly."

The Florida case illustrates the kind of law suit we might expect in the future. It pits two sides with reasonable arguments against each other. One side argues that minority children have worked hard in school under great disadvantage and cannot be expected to have learned the things majority children know. In recognition of their work they deserve a diploma. The other side argues that there should be an absolute standard for basic information (Seligmann, Coppola, Howard, & Lee, 1979).

The court essentially sided with the commissioner. The judge did not challenge the validity of the test. However, he did suspend the use of the test for four years, after which all the students who had any part of their education in segregated schools would have graduated. Then, according to the opinion, the test could be used. In a review of the case Lerner (1981) argued that the minimum competence tests should continue to be used. As an attorney, Lerner finds little legal justification for court involvement in the testing programs.

H.   *Regents of the University of California v. Bakke*

Alan Bakke was an engineer in his 30s who decided to apply to the University of California, Davis, medical school in the early 1970s. Although Bakke had a high grade point average and good MCAT scores, he was denied admission. Bakke decided to investigate the matter. He discovered that his test scores were higher than those of minority students who had gained admission to the medical school under a special affirmative action program. Bakke eventually sued the university on the grounds that he had been discriminated against because he was not a minority-group member. The suit ended in the Supreme Court and is considered to be one of the most important cases of the century.

Although many arguments were presented in the *Bakke* case, one of the major ones concerned the use of test scores. Under the affirmative action program, the cutoff value for MCAT scores was higher for nonminority than for minority students. In defense of the special admissions program it was argued that the tests were not meaningful (valid) for minority students. However, evidence was also presented that the tests were equally meaningful for both groups.

The Supreme Court ruling was not specific with regard to the use of tests. The court ruled that the university had to admit Bakke and that it had denied him due process in the original consideration of the case. It also implied that the use of different cutoff scores was not appropriate. However, the court did acknowledge that race could be taken into consideration in selection decisions. This acknowledgment was interpreted by the EEOC as meaning that affirmative action programs based on numerical quotas could continue (Norton, 1978).

After the Bakke decision, the high court seemed unwilling to hear further reverse-discrimination cases. For example, a week after Bakke, the court refused to hear a challenge to a strong affirmative action plan that created reverse discrimination (*EEOC v. A.T.&T.*).

I.   *Personnel cases*

Most of the cases we have discussed involved educational tests. Several other important law suits have dealt with the use of tests in employment settings. Through a series of Supreme Court decisions, specific restrictions have been placed on the use of tests for the selection of employees. The most important of

■ **FOCUSED EXAMPLE 21.4   COACHING AND THE BIAS IN APTITUDE TESTS**

One of the criticisms of standardized achievement tests is that coaching may improve performance. So widespread is the belief that coaching is helpful that SAT, LSAT, and GRE preparatory schools have become a big business. If coaching does improve performance for these tests, then they are not really aptitude tests but achievement tests. Those who believe that coaching works have accused the Educational Testing Service of being biased and fraudulent because their tests do not measure pure aptitude.

One of the major problems with studies on coaching is that few of them include a proper control group. Thus, when students improve after their coaching classes, it is not clear whether it was due to the coaching, their commitment to improve performance (evidenced by signing up for coaching), or some other personality characteristic associated with enrolling in a coaching course. The few studies with proper control groups show a very small but significant gain in performance as a function of obtaining coaching. But is the small gain worth the effort? (Anastasi, 1981)

Systematic reviews of the entire coaching literature suggest that the more time spent in preparation for the test, the greater the increase in score. However, the relationship is nonlinear. Small increases in preparation time result in some improvement in test performance; but as preparation time increases, lesser returns in performance are realized. According to Messick and Jungeblut (1981, p. 191), who completed the review, "The student contact time required to achieve average score increases much greater than 20 to 30 points (on a 200 to 800 point scale) for both the SAT-V and the SAT-M rapidly approaches that of full time schooling."

these cases are *Griggs v. Duke Power Company*,[9] *Albemarle Paper Company v. Moody*,[10] and *Washington v. Davis*.[11] The effect of these decisions has been to force employers to define the relationship between test scores and job performance and to define the measure of job performance. However, none of the decisions denies that tests are valuable tools in the personnel field and that the use of tests can continue.

The courts have also been asked to decide on issues of test administration. For example, an employee of the Detroit Edison Company was not promoted because of a low test score. In his defense, his union suggested that the low score might have been an error and requested a copy of the test to check the scoring. Detroit Edison did not want to release the test because it feared that the union would distribute the items to other employees. By a vote of five to four, the Supreme Court ruled on the side of Detroit Edison (*Detroit Edison Co. v.*

[9]401 U.S. 424(a) (1971).
[10]442 U.S. 405 (1975).
[11]96 U.S. 2040(c) (1976).

N.L.R.B. [12]). It is interesting that in a major decision such as this, a single vote can make a difference in policy (Cronbach, 1980).

J.   A critical look at law suits

As surely as the sun will rise tomorrow, there will be more court battles over the use of psychological tests. The problems that we as psychologists are unable to resolve ourselves will eventually be turned over to someone else for a binding opinion. This procedure may not be in the best interest of the field of psychology or of the people whom we serve.

It is difficult to be an uncritical admirer of the courts. As Lerner (1979) notes, inconsistencies in court decisions are commonplace. Even worse, judges who make important decisions about the use of tests often have little background in psychology or testing. On completing this course, you should be better able to evaluate most of the evidence than some of those who ultimately make the decisions in courtrooms. Often judges obtain their entire education about testing during the course of a trial.

In the near future we must grapple with many tough issues. For example, many current social problems seem related to the differential distribution of resources among the races in American society. Changing the income distribution seems to be one of the only ways in which effective social change can occur. To accomplish this redistribution, we must get minority children in appropriate educational tracks, into professional schools, and into high income positions. The courts have ruled that psychological tests are blocking this progress.

Psychologists themselves are not of one mind regarding the use of psychological tests. However, as we noted in Chapter 20, current research tends not to confirm the widely held belief that the tests are systematically biased. The field of psychometrics, after long and careful consideration of the problems, has come to a conclusion opposite that of the courts, which have given the issue a briefer evaluation. In the end however, the courts have the power, and their judgment is the law.

III.   SUMMARY

With increasing frequency, tests are coming under legal regulation. One of the major sets of regulations has been provided by the EEOC. This commission, which was created by the Civil Rights Act of 1964, has issued strict guidelines for the use of tests. The guidelines clearly spell out the minimum criteria for validity and reliability of psychological measures.

Tests have also come to be regulated by statute. Recently, the state of New York passed a truth in testing law that places many requirements on commercial testing companies. One of the controversial components of this law is that it requires testing companies to disclose the actual test items to test takers. In the

[12]99 S. Ct. 1123 (1979).

past, test items have been protected by copyright. Thus, test items will have to be constantly rewritten, and this procedure may have a damaging effect on the reliability and the validity of the tests. Following the passage of the New York law, a bill with the same goals was introduced on the federal level. This was the Educational Testing Act of 1979, which was not passed into law. A few years earlier, Congress passed PL 94-142, which outlined standards for the assessment of potential among handicapped children.

Many law suits have had an effect on the use of tests. In *Stell v. Savannah-Chatham County Board of Education*, the court ruled that differences between Blacks and Whites in IQ scores could not be used as a justification for keeping the schools segregated. In *Hobson v. Hansen* group tests were found to be inappropriate for the assignment of Black children to EMR classes. The concern over IQ tests was extended in *Diana v. State Board of Education*. This case, which was settled out of court, established that IQ tests could not be used with bilingual children, and it stimulated the development of new methods of assessment for these children. The impact of each of these decisions was magnified in *Larry P. v. Wilson Riles*, in which tests were banned as a means of assigning Black children to EMR classes. In 1980, a court apparently reversed this decision in the case of *Parents in Action on Special Education v. Hannon*. In *Debra P. v. Turlington*, a court ruled that a minimum competence test could be used only when the students had received their entire education in integrated schools.

The regulation of testing through statute (laws passed by legislators), regulation (rules created by agencies), and litigation (law suits) has only recently become common. In the future we can expect more interactions between testing and the law.

22

The Future of Psychological Testing

Learning objectives

When you have completed the material in this chapter, you should be able to do the following:

1. *Explain why the question of whether humans possess stable traits is an issue in the testing field.*
2. *Explain the issue of actuarial versus clinical prediction.*
3. *Identify human rights as they pertain to testing.*
4. *Explain the problem of labeling.*
5. *Explain the issue of divided loyalties.*
6. *Identify some important responsibilities of test users and test constructors.*
7. *Identify three important current trends in the testing field.*
8. *Describe the future prospects of testing.*

No one can predict the future with certainty. However, by examining current trends in conjunction with pressures and forces that are currently shaping the testing field, we can deepen our understanding of testing and venture a few educated guesses about the future. The future of testing will depend ultimately on numerous complex, interacting forces. Identifying each force individually tends to oversimplify reality. Therefore, you should recognize that the forces identified separately here do not operate in isolation but rather interact with each other in highly complicated ways.

I. PRESSURES SHAPING THE FIELD OF TESTING

The pressures currently shaping the testing field include professional issues, moral issues, ethical issues, and social issues.

A. *Professional issues*

Three major professional issues play an especially important role in the current status and the future of psychological testing: theoretical concerns, the adequacy of tests, and actuarial versus clinical prediction.

Theoretical concerns.   One of the most important considerations underlying tests is the dependability (reliability) of test results. Reliability places an upper limit on validity. According to the *Standards for Educational and Psychological Tests* of the American Psychological Association, the American Educational Research Association, and the National Council on Measurement in Education (APA, 1974), a test that is totally unreliable (unstable) has no meaning. There may be exceptions to this rule (Atkinson, 1981), but current practice generally demands that tests possess some form of stability. As a corollary, whatever is being measured must itself have stability. When we say a test has reliability, we are implying that test results are attributable to a systematic source of variance, which is stable itself. In other words, the test is presumed to measure a stable entity. There are various types of reliability, depending on the different purposes of the tests. Each test must possess the type of reliability that is appropriate for the uses to which it is put (APA, 1974).

Most existing tests measure what we assume is a stable entity—either the individual as he or she presently functions or some temporally stable characteristic of the individual. In measuring current functioning, we may say something like "the person is emotionally unstable" or "the person is out of contact with reality," or we may provide a diagnostic label such as "schizophrenic" or "neurotic." In describing current functioning, we imply that the person functions this way in a fairly stable, though perhaps short-term, manner, independently of the situation or environment. In other words, we assume we can describe the person in absolute terms, as if in a vacuum, independently of external factors. Similarly, and even more strikingly, when we purport to measure a temporally stable characteristic of an individual, we are assuming that we are measuring an enduring quality that will manifest itself over time regardless of immediate or long-term external (situational, environmental, and so forth) factors. Again, we assume that what we are measuring exists in absolute terms—that is, in a vacuum or independently of external factors.

Whether we are measuring current functioning or a temporally stable characteristic, the assumption is always that the systematic source of variance measured by the test is due entirely to the person as opposed to some factor external to the person. When we purport to measure a stable characteristic of an individual and find less than perfect temporal reliability, we assume that the imperfections are due to test-related inadequacies, such as measurement error, or to minor fluctuating subject variables, such as fatigue. Thus, we assume that the characteristic or variable being measured is stable, that it exists, and that our ability to measure it is limited only by the adequacy of the test instrument. Therefore, the more accurate a test, the more stable the results should be.

In simple terms, in using tests we assume that people possess stable characteristics (for example, intelligence) and stable response tendencies (for example, traits) that hold up across situations and exist independently of the environment. This assumption may be most unfortunate in view of results of empirical investigations. Even the best tests have yet to achieve such temporal stability that differences over time can readily be attributed solely to measurement error or fluctuating subject variables. Even more striking, as we established in Chapters 15 through 17, no personality test has a high degree of long-term stability. In the realm of personality in particular, little empirical data have supported the view that humans possess traits that are stable over the long term and across situations (Mischel, 1968). Hence, one of the main assumptions underlying tests, that humans possess stable characteristics and response tendencies independently of external factors, may not be entirely correct.

This theoretical issue is relevant to psychology as a whole and to personality psychology in particular. Early formulations of human personality tended to view it as consisting of enduring and stable traits (behavioral dispositions). Freud and many of his followers, for example, believed that early experiences, memories, traumas, and anxieties often resulted in behavioral dispositions that persisted throughout life. Views such as Freud's, however, were challenged by those who saw human personality as changing rather than as fixed and stationary as well as by those who saw that situations and external factors also influence behavior.

Almost every test discussed in this text is based on the assumption that human characteristics can be measured independently of the context in which these characteristics occur (the environment), a theory that is not only disputable but that has failed to find significant support. Psychological tests can be no better than the science of psychology underlying them. As the science clarifies basic theoretical issues, changes in testing are to be expected in order that the tests conform to the available knowledge. In the meantime, it must be acknowledged that perhaps the single most important theoretical assumption of tests, that human characteristics are stable and can be measured independently of the environment, is debatable.

Human behavior may be the result of long-term stable behavioral tendencies (traits), the external or internal environments that precede, coexist with, and follow behavior, or some other factor such as the interaction between traits and environments. Either our tests have a long way to go before they will be able to measure the precise determinants of human behavior or, for predictive purposes, current conceptualizations and underlying assumptions of tests are not precise enough.

Based on our review of the psychometric qualities and limits of mental-ability and personality tests, we conclude that humans must continually change. One explanation for the far from perfect reliability of tests in general and the relatively poor long-term reliability of personality tests in particular is that as the individual adapts and adjusts to an ever-changing environment, the individual changes.

Most definitions of intelligence, for example, include the ability to adapt or change according to circumstances.

A theory consistent with the available data would postulate that all normal humans possess ability to adapt to changing circumstances. This ability is itself a combination of factors that can and do change. We can refer to these combined factors as the individual's index of adjustment, which we believe is correlated with scores on major ability tests in use today. An individual with a high index of adjustment can adapt more readily and perhaps find more effective solutions to environmental pressures than can those with a low index. However, reacting to the environment may not only change behavioral tendencies but also influence the index of adjustment. Repeated failures or consistent success, for example, may increase rigidity, which in turn can lower the index of adjustment. However, an extremely demanding environment, such as one that forces the individual to call on latent reserves, may increase the index. In this theory, ability and personality are ever changing and are measurable only within the context in which they occur.

The point here is that all psychological tests are based on implicit theories of human functioning. Unfortunately, the validity of these theories and their underlying assumptions are far from proven. Furthermore, there is no consensus concerning a definition of human intelligence as well as no consensus concerning the essence of human personality, whether it be normal or abnormal. A revolution in psychological theory, therefore, could revolutionize psychological tests. In any case, today's tests are no better than the theories and assumptions that underlie them.

The adequacy of tests.   A second professional issue in testing concerns the adequacy of existing tests. This entire text has been aimed at providing you with the knowledge needed to evaluate tests. To this end, the text is filled with statements concerning standardization, norms, scoring, interpretation, test design, reliability, and validity. Thus far, however, our discussion has been in relative terms; we have identified tests that are superior to other tests according to traditionally accepted psychometric standards. We have not established absolute, external criteria against which to evaluate tests. But many psychologists as well as nonpsychologists have questioned whether even the best existing tests possess sufficiently sound psychometric qualities to warrant their use.

As we noted in Chapter 9, the real issue in testing is how tests are used. In support of this position, APA (1974) argues that decisions are going to be made whether or not tests are used in the decision-making process. As convincing as this argument is, it is also true that it may be better to have no test at all than one that leads to an incorrect conclusion more often than it leads to a correct one. There may be, and no doubt are, situations in which all concerned would be better off without test results than they would be with them.

We are not advocating that all tests be eliminated until better ones are developed, but we do believe that the issue of the adequacy of tests should be viewed from all possible perspectives. Some tests, such as many individual and group ability tests, are generally adequate in reliability. However, just about any test could benefit from greater validity documentation. Clearly, the quality or adequacy of existing tests viewed in absolute rather than relative terms is a factor that must be considered when evaluating current and future trends in testing.

Actuarial versus clinical prediction. A third professional issue, which is related to the issue of the adequacy of tests, concerns the accuracy of predictions made by test users. Throughout this book we have argued that tests provide a standard setting in which behavior can be observed and that practitioners can use this situation in conjunction with experience and local norms to gain a greater degree of accuracy in their observations and decisions than would otherwise be possible. Certainly users of psychological tests must feel this way or they simply would not waste their time with tests. However, can tests truly help in the assessment process, or are practitioners fooling themselves, repeating their errors and teaching their errors to students? Indeed, test users rarely, if ever, receive feedback on the accuracy of their predictions and decisions based on tests.

Again, we do not know the answer, but the issue must be seen from all sides. The early work of Meehl (Meehl, 1954; Meehl & Rosen, 1955) and others (Little & Shneidman, 1959) drew attention to the limits of test data even in the hands of trained practitioners. In more recent analyses, Sawyer (1966) and Sines (1970) reviewed a number of studies that compared an actuarial approach, in which test results were analyzed by a set of rules, against a clinical approach, in which trained professionals analyzed test results. These reviews indicated that the set of rules was more accurate than the interpretations of trained professional practitioners, even when the practitioners knew the rules. This research confirmed Meehl's (1954) earlier finding that trained practitioners could not improve on predictions based on statistical formulas. Other studies and analyses, however, indicate that the trained practitioner is a better predictor than actuarial formulas, especially when using data from a variety of sources including a test battery, interview, and case history (for example, Goldberg, 1970; Holt, 1970; Wiggins & Kohen, 1971). In either case, we again find professional disagreement at the most basic levels.

B. *Moral issues*

Professional issues alone will not determine the future of testing. The field is also presently being shaped by moral issues—human rights, labeling, and invasion of privacy. These moral issues are an extremely important influence in the testing field.

Human rights.   Several different kinds of human rights are relevant to psychological testing. Among these rights is the right not to be tested (APA, 1974). Individuals who do not want to subject themselves to testing should not, and ethically cannot, be forced to do so. APA (1974) also states that test takers have the right to know test scores and interpretations as well as the right to know the bases of any decisions that affect their lives. The present position on the right to know is a change in policy that reflects current realities. Previously, guarding the security of tests was of paramount importance. The new position states that all precautions should be taken to protect test security but not at the expense of an individual's right to know the basis for detrimental or adverse decisions. Other human rights, some of which are only now being accepted on a widespread basis, are the right to know who will have access to test data and the right to have the confidentiality of test results protected. (This right to privacy is discussed below.)

Test users have a moral as well as an ethical obligation to protect human rights. Potential test takers have the responsibility of knowing and demanding their rights. The increasing awareness among test users and the public of the importance of human rights is an important factor currently shaping the testing field.

Labeling.   In standard medical practice, a person's disease or disorder is first identified (diagnosed). Once diagnosed, the disease can be labeled, and standard medical intervention procedures can be implemented. It is no embarrassment to be diagnosed as having gall-bladder or heart disease. No one will avoid you or think less of you if you are given these labels. However, it is well known that psychiatric labels can be extremely damaging (Smith, 1981). The public has little understanding of the label *schizophrenia*, for example. Therefore, someone with this label is vulnerable to being stigmatized, perhaps for life. These labels may also be detrimental in that many carry certain negative connotations. Chronic schizophrenia, for example, has no cure. Labeling someone a chronic schizophrenic may be a self-fulfilling prophecy. Because the disorder is incurable, nothing can be done. Because nothing can be done, why should one bother to help? Because no help is given, the person is a chronic case.

Still another problem with labels, which are unfortunately often justified by psychological tests as they are currently used, is a theoretical one. As Szasz (1961) and others note, a medical label such as schizophrenia implies that a person is ill or diseased. Because no one can be blamed for becoming ill, a medical or psychiatric label implies that the person is not responsible for the condition. However, it may very well be that those who are labeled as psychiatrically disturbed must take responsibility for their lives in order to get better.

When we take responsibility for our lives, we believe that we can exercise some degree of control over our fates (after all, what is intelligence?) rather than simply being the victims of uncontrollable external forces. Individuals who feel a sense of control or responsibility for themselves should be able to tolerate more stress, frustration, and pain than those who feel like passive victims of external forces. Certainly a person who feels responsible or in control makes a greater effort to alter negative conditions than one who does not.

Labels that imply a person is not responsible may therefore increase the risk that the person so labeled will feel like a passive victim. Thus, the labeling process may not only stigmatize the person but also lower tolerance for stress and make treatment more difficult. In view of the potentially negative effects of labels, APA (1974) states that a person has the right not to be labeled and suggests that rather than being labeled the person be described.

Invasion of privacy.   Still another moral issue concerns invasion of privacy. As we stated earlier, people have a right to privacy. When people respond to psychological tests, they have little idea what is being revealed, but they often feel that their privacy has been invaded and that this intrusion into their lives is not justified by the benefits. Public concern over this issue once became so strong that tests were investigated by the Senate Subcommittee on Constitutional Rights and the House Subcommittee on Invasion of Privacy. Neither of these subcommittees found evidence of deliberate and widespread misuse of tests (see Brayfield, 1965).

Again, there are two sides to the issue. Dahlstrom (1969b) argues that the issue of invasion of privacy is based on serious misunderstandings. He states that tests have been oversold and that the public doesn't realize their limitations. Psychological tests can't invade one's privacy because they are so limited that they are incapable of doing so. Another issue, according to Dahlstrom (1969b), is the ambiguity of the notion of invasion of privacy. It isn't necessarily wrong, evil, or detrimental to find out information about a person. The person's privacy is invaded when this information is used in inappropriate ways. But psychologists are morally, ethically, and often legally bound to maintain confidentiality and do not have to reveal any more information about a person than is necessary to accomplish the purpose for which testing was initiated. Furthermore, psychologists are bound to inform subjects of the limits of confidentiality, and subjects have the right not to be tested. As Dahlstrom (1969b) notes, subjects must cooperate in order to be tested. On the whole, those tested by today's procedures must be willing participants.

The ethical code of the APA (1981) includes the principle of confidentiality. This principle, which is guaranteed by law in most states that have laws governing the practice of psychology, means that personal information obtained by the psychologist from any source is communicated only with the person's consent. However, there are exceptions, such as circumstances in which there is danger to the person or society or when certain records, including tests, are subpoenaed by the courts. Therefore, included in a person's right to know is the right to know the limits of confidentiality and to know that test data can be subpoenaed and used as evidence in a court of law.

C. *Ethical issues*

Ethical issues are closely related to professional and moral issues and indeed often cannot be easily separated from these other issues. Two extremely important ethical issues are divided loyalties and the responsibilities of test users and test constructors.

Divided loyalties.   Jackson and Messick (1967, Chap. 69) argue that it has not been possible to formulate a coherent set of ethical principles that govern all legitimate uses of testing. These authors believe the core of the problem lies in divided loyalties—the often conflicting commitments of the psychologist who uses tests. One ethical principle is that the psychologist must protect the welfare and privacy of the client or consumer of tests. A conflict arises, however, when the welfare of the individual is at odds with the welfare of the institution that employs the psychologist. For example, a psychologist employed by an industrial firm to identify individuals who might break down under stress has a responsibility to the institution to identify such individuals as well as a responsibility to protect the rights and welfare of clients seeking employment with the firm. Thus, the psychologist's loyalty is divided. Similarly, the psychologist must maintain test security but also not violate the client's right to know the basis for an adverse decision. However, if the basis for an adverse decision is explained to one client, this information may leak out and others with the same problem can then outsmart the test. Again, the test user is trapped between two opposing forces and principles.

The conflict is presently being resolved in this way. Ethically, psychologists must inform all concerned where their loyalty lies. They must tell clients or subjects in advance how tests are to be used and describe the limits of confidentiality. To the institution, they provide only the minimum information possible, such as "This subject has a low probability of breaking down under stress, and the probability that this conclusion is accurate is 68/100." Unnecessary or irrelevant personal information remains private and confidential.

In addition, test security is not as important as the person's right to know the basis of an adverse decision. Either the results are explained to the client or they are given to a representative of the client who is qualified to explain them. A law in the state of New York prohibits the distributors of standardized tests used in selection procedures (for example the SAT, the GRE, the MCAT) from keeping the items confidential (see Chapter 21). The implication of the ruling is that the person has the right to see the items missed. In other words, the dilemma of test security versus client welfare has been decided by the courts, and the decision clearly favors the client.

Responsibilities of test users and test constructors.   A second ethical issue in testing concerns the responsibilities of test users. Because even the best test can be misused, the testing profession has become increasingly stringent and precise in outlining the ethics of responsible test use. According to APA (1974), almost any test can be useful in the right circumstances, but even the best test, when used inappropriately, can be damaging to the subject. To reduce potential damage, APA (1974) specifies that users of tests are responsible for knowing the reason for using the test, the consequences, and the procedures necessary to maximize effectiveness of the test and to minimize unfairness. Test users must thus possess sufficient knowledge to understand the underlying principles in the construction and supporting research of any test they administer. They must also know the psychometric qualities of the test being used as well as the literature relevant to the test. In addition, they are responsible for ensuring that interpretations based on the test are justified and that the test is properly used. In our judgment, a test user cannot claim ignorance ("I didn't realize normative data were not representative"). The test user is responsible for finding out all the necessary and pertinent information before using any test.

It is the test developer's responsibility to provide this information. The APA (1974) standards state that test constructors must provide a test manual with sufficient data to permit appropriate use of the test, including adequate validity and reliability data, clearly specified scoring and administration standards, and a clear description of the normative sample. The 1974 standards also state that the test manual should warn against possible misinterpretation and identify necessary qualifications for responsible test use. Despite these guidelines, some new tests are still being published that do not meet specified standards. It is not unusual for a researcher to receive requests from test designers to investigate a newly developed test. These designers hope that others will conduct the necessary research to provide adequate psychometric documentation.

However, a test user has no excuse for employing an inadequately documented instrument that has damaging consequences. The test user must know enough to tell the difference between a test that meets present standards and one that does not. Jackson and Messick (1967, Chap. 69) wisely suggest that the test user always ask two questions whenever a test is proposed for a particular use. First, "Is the test any good as a measure of the characteristics it purports to measure?" This is a technical question; the answer lies in the psychometric qualities of the test, such as reliability and validity documentation. Second, "Should the test be used for this purpose?" The answer to this second question is based on ethical and social values. It requires the test user to think about the effect of the test on the individual and on the individual's human rights. Thus, test constructors bear the responsibility for a poorly designed test or an inadequate test manual. However, the ultimate responsibility for ethical use of tests rests with the test user.

D. Social issues

In addition to professional issues, moral issues, and ethical issues, a number of social issues play an important role in the testing field. We discuss four of these social issues: dehumanization, the usefulness of tests, access to psychological testing sources, and bias in tests.

Dehumanization.   One social issue in the testing field concerns the dehumanizing tendencies that lurk in the testing process. For example, a number of corporations provide computerized analyses of MMPI test results (see Graham, 1977). Such technology tends to minimize individual freedom and uniqueness. With high-speed computers and centralized data banks, the risk that machines will some day make important decisions about our lives is an ever increasing one. Thus, society must weigh the risks against the benefits of adding modern technology to the testing field. This evaluation should be made now or a situation may develop that nobody likes but that cannot be changed. If psychologists or the public allow test results to be stored and analyzed by computers, it may become extremely difficult to reverse this trend. Our society is founded on principles of individual rights and freedom. Any potential threat to these principles—such as computerized test interpretations—must be evaluated, and decisions concerning such issues should be made with an awareness of the potential risks as well as of the benefits. Only when the benefits far outweigh the risks and the risks are minimized can the decision be socially acceptable.

Usefulness of tests.   From a social perspective, it is not necessary to demand that all tests be perfect in all ways. Society often finds uses for tools that are initially crude but that become precise with research and development. To gain a perspective of the testing field, you should discriminate between something that is useful (something that works) and something that is true or correct. When Western society believed the sun revolved around the earth, instead of the other way around, the available formulas and principles were useful in that they led to some accurate predictions, even though the underlying theories were incorrect. This may also be the situation of testing as it is currently practiced. Our underlying theories and assumptions may be fundamentally incorrect and the resulting test instruments far from perfect. However, the tests may still be useful as long as they provide information that leads to better predictions and understanding than can otherwise be obtained. The point is that a test may be useful to society even if all the principles that underlie tests are totally incorrect.

Thus, the crucial social issue in testing is not whether tests are perfect but whether they are useful to society. Obviously the answer to this question to date has been a strong but disputed "yes." However, as new knowledge is gained, society must continually weigh the risks of tests against the benefits. The risks, of course, include possible misuse of tests, which in turn may adversely affect the life of an individual or may discriminate systematically against a specific cultural group. The benefits include the potential for increased precision and fairness in the decision-making process. The issue is one that recurs, and the resolution will obviously have a profound effect on the field of testing.

Modern tests are and have been used by society on a wide scale. First the military, then the schools and psychiatric facilities, and finally business and industry found important uses for psychological tests. Indeed, there appears to be no end in sight to the proliferation of tests, despite criticisms and heated debates. If the pervasiveness of tests in our society is any indication of society's opinion of the usefulness of tests, then certainly society has found tests useful. Thus, tests are currently serving a function in society, and, as long as tests continue to serve a useful purpose, they will continue to be used.

Access to psychological testing services.   If tests are of value to society, who will have access to psychological testing services? Being tested can be quite an expense. It is not unusual for a practitioner in a large metropolitan area to command a fee of $600 or more to administer a full battery of individual tests, score and interpret the findings, and produce a written report. As with many other commodities, the cost of testing places these services beyond the reach of many members of society. Yet, if a person's well-being depends on information from a psychological test battery, how will it be decided who will have access to testing and who will not?

As it stands now, the expensive test batteries for neurological and psychiatric assessment are available to those who can afford them and to those who have insurance that covers all or most of the expense. In California, developmentally disabled persons (for example, the mentally retarded) or those with suspected developmental disabilities have access to psychological testing services through regional centers. Unless California laws are changed, anyone suspected of having a handicap that originated during the developmental years can request (or have someone request on his or her behalf) an evaluation that may include a medical examination and psychological testing. The service is free regardless of income or socioeconomic status, and, if the person is found developmentally disabled by a team of specialists, additional services are available.

Anyone with a developmental disability in California may be eligible to receive Medi-Cal, which provides free medical services, including the services of a psychologist for psychotherapy and psychological testing. The individual may also be eligible for federal assistance such as Medicare and SSI, which provide cash benefits. Thus, current California and federal laws and policies help ensure that certain disabled persons will have access to psychological testing services. However, such guarantees are not available in all states and only certain disabled persons are covered.

Some in our society have offered national health insurance as a possible solution to the general problem of providing adequate medical care to everyone. As of this writing, no program of national health insurance has been implemented, but talk about it continues. One of the controversies in proposals for national health insurance concerns the extent of mental health coverage and whether psychological services will be included. Presumably, if psychological testing services are included in a national health insurance program, then anyone needing such services will have access to them. If not, then availability of testing services may be substantially limited. In a sense, society will be making a judgment concerning the value of tests in its decision to include or not include psychological testing services in a national health insurance program. Resources are clearly limited, and testing services may have to be included at the expense of some other needed service or vice versa.

Bias in tests.   We discussed the issue of bias in psychological tests in Chapter 20, and we will not restate the issues here. However, it is worth noting at this point that test bias is an important social issue. It should be of concern to everyone in a society if devices such as psychological tests systematically discriminate against one segment of society at the expense of another. If one group or segment can be hurt by tests, nothing will prevent another group from being similarly affected at some other time.

In October 1979 a court ruled that standard intelligence tests could not be used as necessary and sufficient evidence of mental retardation in Black children (see Chapter 21). The judge in the case declared that the tests were biased against Blacks and should not be used to remove Black children from the regular classroom and place them in special classes. Whether or not the judge's evaluation concerning bias in tests is correct, the decision again illustrates how the future of testing will depend on decisions and factors that extend far beyond the level of psychometric adequacy acceptable to the testing profession at any given time.

II.   CURRENT TRENDS

Professional, moral, ethical, social, and even legal issues have interacted to produce today's trends in testing. These trends are discussed by Saccuzzo (1976), who argues that the most important one is the development of alternative approaches to traditional procedures based on the medical model. Using Saccuzzo's (1976) discussion as a starting point, we believe current trends in testing can be placed in three main categories: the proliferation of new tests; higher standards, improved technology, and increased objectivity; and greater public awareness and influence.

A.   *Proliferation of new tests*

The fact that new tests keep coming out all the time is clearly documented by Buros in the *Mental Measurements Yearbooks*. If we count revised and updated tests, we find hundreds of new tests being published each year. The impetus for the development of these new tests comes from professional disagreement over optimal strategies for measuring human characteristics, over the nature of these characteristics, and over theories about the causes of human behavior. The impetus also stems from public and professional pressure to employ only fair, accurate, unbiased instruments. Finally, if tests are used, then the authors and publishers of tests stand to profit financially. As long as it is profitable to publish tests, new tests will be developed and marketed.

An examination of the *Mental Measurements Yearbooks* indicates that most new tests are based on the same principles and underlying theories as are the more established tests. Indeed, most newly developed tests justify their existence either on the grounds that they are psychometrically superior to the existing tests or on the grounds that they are more specific and thus more appropriate for particular problems. However, as discussed by Saccuzzo (1976) and elaborated by us in Chapter 18, many of the newer tests, especially the most recent ones, are based on models, theories, and concepts that are fundamentally different from those on which the traditional, established tests are based. These nontraditional tests are based on modern concepts and theories from learning, social, physiological, and experimental psychology. Most of these newer tests are rooted in empirically derived data.

The proliferation of nontraditional tests is related to two other current trends in testing. First, the development of these nontraditional tests reflects the increasing application and role of the science of psychology in testing, as Anastasi (1967) has called for. Even critics of testing must admit that the testing field has been characterized by a responsiveness to criticism and an honest and persistent effort to improve the quality of tests. The application of insights and empirical findings from psychological laboratories is a current trend that reflects this responsiveness.

Second, efforts are being made to achieve an integration of tests and other aspects of applied psychology. Many psychologists, especially behaviorally oriented psychologists (for example, Kanfer & Saslow, 1969), have long been disillusioned by the poor relationship between clinical assessment, traditional tests, and subsequent treatment interventions. Of greatest desirability would be tests whose results not only have a direct relationship to treatment but can also be used to assess the effectiveness of treatment. Psychologists are presently making an effort to devise such procedures, and their products add to the list of the many new tests that are published each year.

B.   *Higher standards, improved technology, and increasing objectivity*

In addition to a proliferation of new tests, the various pressures and issues have led to still another current trend. The minimum acceptable standards for tests are becoming higher and more stringent. Before APA (1974) clearly and specifically defined their responsibilities, test constructors had neither a uniform nor a widely accepted set of guidelines. As a result, the quality of newly published tests was quite variable. Now that published standards are available, test constructors no longer have to work in the dark. Already it is possible to see that an increasing percentage of new tests provide the information necessary for test users to make a fully informed choice in test selection and for maximizing the probability that the tests will be used properly.

Higher standards of test construction are encouraging better and more appropriate use of tests. The APA (1974) standards have helped considerably by reemphasizing the critical importance of proper test use and by articulating the responsibilities of test users. Indeed, as we indicated earlier, the ethics of testing have been modified in an effort to encourage the proper use of tests and to avoid misuse. Now that test users have a specific published set of standards, there is no excuse for misusing a test. Naturally, misuse and even abuse will never be entirely eliminated. However, the trend toward better and more appropriate use of existing tests is a most desirable one.

Related to higher standards is the improved technology currently being applied in the testing field. Those in the testing field now have at their disposal the benefits of the remarkable technology that has developed during the previous few decades. Mostly because of advances in computer technology, statistical procedures such as factor analysis and item analysis can be performed with great ease. This technology contributes to the current trend toward better tests.

Also related to high standards is the trend toward increasing objectivity in test interpretation. Although we generally spoke in favor of projective tests such as the Rorschach, many practitioners have been displeased with the often subjective nature of the interpretation of projective tests. As a result, many practitioners have shown a tendency to rely heavily on objective data such as that provided by the MMPI and 16PF. This trend toward increased objectivity in testing can be readily seen by the shift in the number of references devoted to the Rorschach and MMPI in the *Mental Measurements Yearbooks*. For many years the Rorschach was first among personality tests in number of references in the *Mental Measurements Yearbooks*, and its supremacy in this regard almost seemed to be a tradition. However, the MMPI is the current leader in number of references for personality tests. Interest is shifting from projective to objective tests, and personality assessment has come full circle in this regard.

Also a reflection of the trend toward objectivity in testing is the continuing research interest in testing. In view of the many thousands, if not tens of thousands, of published studies directly or indirectly related to psychological tests, a casual observer might conclude that there is little else to be done. This conclusion is far from correct. Despite the thousands of published articles devoted to the MMPI, for example, hundreds more creative and scientifically rigorous articles are published each year on this test, not to mention the hundreds of other tests listed in the Buros publications. As long as tests are anything but perfect, and in this regard they are a long way off, psychological researchers will no doubt continue to conduct investigations to facilitate the objective use of tests.

C. *Greater public awareness and influence*

The current trend toward greater public awareness of the nature and use of psychological tests has led to the trend of increasing external influence on the practice of testing. This awareness and influence from outside of psychology has, furthermore, led to still other trends in psychological testing. At one time the public knew little about psychological tests; psychologists played an almost exclusive role in governing how tests were used. With the greater assertiveness on the part of the public during the 1970s, the days when psychologists alone called the shots are gone forever. In our opinion, this is a desirable trend that overall has had a positive effect on the field.

Public awareness has led to the current trend toward an increased demand for psychological services, including testing services. Balancing this increased demand is the tendency toward restrictive legislative and judicial regulations and policies such as the judicial decision restricting the use of standard intelligence tests in diagnosing mental retardation. These restrictions originate in real and imagined public fears. In short, the public seems to be ambivalent about psychological testing, simultaneously desiring the benefits yet fearing the power the general public attributes to tests.

Perhaps the greatest benefit of increased public awareness of tests has been the increased insistence on safeguarding human rights. As more individuals share the responsibility of encouraging the proper use of tests by becoming informed of their rights and insisting on receiving them, the probability of misuse and abuse of tests will be reduced. The commitment of the field of psychology to high standards in matters such as ethics, morals, and human rights can be easily seen in the published ethical guidelines, position papers, and debates that have evolved during the relatively short period beginning in 1947 with the development of formal standards for training in clinical psychology (Shakow, Hilgard, Kelly, Sanford, & Shaffer, 1947). Practitioners of psychology as well as their instructors and supervisors have a deep concern for social values and the dignity of the individual human being. However, the pressure of public interest in psychological tests has led psychological practitioners to even greater sensitivity to and awareness of their role and responsibility in safeguarding the rights and dignity of the individual human being. Increased concern for ensuring and protecting human rights is thus still another desirable current trend in the field.

Interrelated with all of these trends is the trend toward greater protection for the public. Although some states such as Florida have chosen not to renew legislation governing the practice of psychology (see Malcolm, 1981), nearly every state has such laws, including laws about the use of psychological tests (see Dörken, 1981). Limiting testing to reduce the chance that unqualified persons will use psychological tests, sensitivity among practitioners to the rights of the individual, relevant court decisions, and a clearly articulated set of ethical guidelines for proper test use give the public significant protection against the inherent risks involved in testing. Thus, yet another desirable current trend in the field is increasingly greater protection and safeguards for the consumer of tests, the public.

III. FUTURE TRENDS

Having analyzed the major relevant issues and forces in testing and identified current trends, we are now ready to venture a few guesses about what the future holds for the field. Certainly we are reasonably safe in stating that the trends identified above will continue and become established as realities of the field. However, our predictions for the future are educated guesses based on limited knowledge. In addition to this disclaimer, we are further reducing the risks inherent in any prediction by dividing our discussion into safe and speculative predictions.

A. Safe predictions

Future prospects for testing are promising.   Our studies lead us to feel safe in concluding that testing has a promising future. Our optimism in this regard is based on the integral role testing has played in the development and recognition of psychology in general and of professional psychology in particular. Psychology gained its first real status from its role in the development of screening tests for the military in World War I. Later, psychologists' creativity and skill in the testing field during World War II were no doubt among the factors that ultimately led to government funding through the Veterans Administration to encourage the development of professional psychology. Indeed, this federal funding, which was first earmarked for psychology in 1945, played an important role in the birth of clinical psychology and formal training standards.

The central role played by testing in the development and recognition of psychology, however, is certainly not enough to ensure for testing an important role in the future. Despite discontent and division within psychology concerning the role and value of testing, psychological testing in the general sense remains one of the few unique functions of the professional psychologist. When one sees psychological testing as encompassing not only traditional uses but also new and innovative uses, such as in behavioral assessment, psychophysiology, evaluation research, and investigations into the nature of human functioning, one can understand just how important tests are to psychologists (see Korchin & Schuldberg, 1981).

Thus, psychologists have a traditional and fundamental tie with psychological tests and are the undisputed leaders in the field. We do not believe that attacks on and dissatisfaction with traditional psychological tests will suddenly compel psychologists to totally abandon tests, which would likely lead to the demise of testing. Instead, we predict that psychologists will continue to take the lead in this field to produce better and better tests, and that such a direction will be of benefit to both psychologists and the field.

In addition, tests are used in most of our institutions—schools, colleges, hospitals, industry, business, the government, and so forth—and new applications and creative uses continue to emerge. It is inconceivable that tests will suddenly disappear with nothing to replace them. If anything, current tests will continue to be used until replaced by still better tests, which of course may be based on totally new ideas. Tests as we know them today may gradually fade from the scene, but we believe psychological testing will not simply survive but rather will flourish and thrive through the rest of this and the next century.

The proliferation of new and improved tests will continue unabated.   In conjunction with our prognostication of a promising future for psychological testing, we feel safe in predicting that the future will see the development of still more tests. In our evaluation of the status of *intelligence tests* (Chapters 11 and 12), we presented our belief that currently available intelligence tests are far from perfect and that we have a long way to go before the ultimate in such tests is seen. Consistent with this belief, we believe the dominant role of the Stanford-Binet and Wechsler tests is far from secure. These two major intelligence scales are probably about as technically adequate as they will ever be. They can, of course, be improved through minor revisions to update test stimuli and to provide larger and even more representative normative samples with special norms for particular groups and through additional research to extend and support validity documentation. However, the fundamental characteristics and underlying concepts of these tests are unlikely to change.

During the next few decades we will be most suprised if these two major intelligence scales are not challenged at least several times by similar tests whose justification will be superior standardization and normative data. However, if history is any indicator of what is to be, a true challenge can come only from a test based on original concepts and a more comprehensive theoretical rationale than that of the present scales. We believe that the development of such a test is inevitable and only a question of time (see, for example, Sternberg, 1981). Just how soon such a test appears will, of course, depend primarily on need. Should a compelling need for such an instrument arise, then we will see it sooner than later.

In *structured personality testing* we are also most likely to see new instruments. However, in this area we believe the quantum leap has already been taken by the Cattell personality tests, which we discussed in detail to illustrate the factor analytic model, with Jackson's Personality Research Form a close competitor (see Chapter 15). What we are saying here is that, despite the fact that all available indicators seem to reflect an almost unshakeable position of dominance for the MMPI, the MMPI is now at its zenith and will soon see a decline. The MMPI will, without doubt, remain in use for quite some time to come, but we do not believe this important test, which itself was a quantum leap from its predecessors, can maintain its dominant position for any more than another two decades or so.

Our evaluation of the MMPI is based on the fundamental weaknesses

delineated in Chapter 15. The MMPI has survived and flourished almost exclusively because of the creativity and determination of the many distinguished
psychologists who have devoted themselves to its continual improvement. Unfortunately, the MMPI has, in our judgment, too many fundamental weaknesses
that can never be corrected. As a result, it is just a question of time before the
major challengers come close enough in empirical support to justify their use in
place of the MMPI.

As with the major intelligence scales, the supremacy of the MMPI is also
vulnerable to theoretical and conceptual advances in measuring both normal
and abnormal personality. Such an advance is likely to originate from research
that leads to a better and perhaps more precise clarification of the fundamental
nature of human behavior than has been articulated to date.

In sum, whether the challenge comes from an existing procedure, such as
the family of personality tests stemming from Cattell's work, or comes from
inevitable theoretical and conceptual advances in scientific psychology, we make
the risky prediction that enthusiasm for and interest in the MMPI will soon
decline. A test can remain in use even after it has been revised or a clearly
superior alternative becomes available because practitioners get their best information from those tests with which they have the most experience. Nevertheless,
progress is inevitable.

Regarding *projective personality testing*, we've already stated our view that
the Rorschach will achieve a new level of acceptance and respectability as the
21st century dawns. Here, we do not see much threat from new tests. The
Holtzman Inkblot Test takes care of just about every psychometric criticism of
the Rorschach, yet it still has not found widespread clinical use. Our view of the
Rorschach is that it is fundamentally sound and will ultimately be vindicated
because of the work of psychologists such as J. Exner and I. B. Weiner. Most
likely the Rorschach will never achieve the prominence it enjoyed during its
heyday. In fact, relative to other personality tests, the Rorschach may show even
further declines. However, only when the mysteries of schizophrenia are better
understood and new ways to measure the pathology of schizophrenia perfected
will the Rorschach be seriously threatened.

The future of the TAT is more difficult to predict. The TAT is affixed to some
of the main arteries of psychological theory, has an incredibly extensive research
base, and is also a prominent clinical tool. Unfortunately, the TAT stimuli are
quite out of date. In a projective test, outdated stimuli are not a devastating
weakness because projective stimuli are by nature ambiguous. Nevertheless, the
TAT stimuli have been revised (Ritzler, Sharkey, & Chudy, 1980), and so, like the
Rorschach, the TAT may enjoy increased respectability as data are acquired on
the latest version.

Continued controversy, disagreements, and changes.   We feel
quite safe in predicting continued controversy and disagreements in the testing
field, which will no doubt produce further change. Disagreement and con-

troversy are second nature to psychologists; it doesn't matter whether the topic is testing or animal learning. Because of disagreements, however, new data are sought, found, and ultimately produce some clarification of old controversies along with brand new contradictions and battle lines. This is the way of psychology. Therefore, it's not likely psychologists will ever agree that any one test is perfect. As a consequence, change will be a constant characteristic of the field. Our optimism continues to run high because we see the change as ultimately resulting in more empirical data, better theories, continuing innovations and advances, and higher standards.

B. *Speculative predictions*

Increasingly narrow and specific tests. Lewandowski and Saccuzzo (1976) propose that as a primary long-range goal, the testing field should concentrate on developing more specific norms for tests rather than trying to use limited available norms for any and all types of subjects. They propose that the question should be something like "What test or test index should be used for this particular age group, sex, and race under what circumstances, with what kind of examiner, and for what specific purpose?" Sattler (1981) believes such a proposal goes too far in its demands for specificity, and he is probably correct. In any case, no one has, as yet, echoed Lewandowski and Saccuzzo's call for such specificity nor does there appear to be any rush to this position. However, tests as well as normative data are becoming more specific. Perhaps the future will see some compromise between today's general lack of specificity in normative data and the suggestion of Lewandowski and Saccuzzo. However, until we see more evidence of increased specificity than we see today, we consider this prediction of increasing specificity as only a 50-50 proposition.

Creative and expanded applications of tests. Today, the goals of testing are for the most part restricted to measurement of current functioning, ability, or potential for the purpose of diagnosis, evaluation, selection, and prediction of future behavior. Actually, these goals may be only a small part of what tests can potentially accomplish. For example, one relatively new idea is to attempt to devise psychological tests to aid in medical diagnosis. Such tests would be possible if medical disorders systematically covary with sources of variance that can be tapped by tests. Perhaps unlikely, this idea is not inconceivable in that certain forms of cancer and heart disease can be associated with personality variables that can be measured given the right set of test stimuli (for example, see Holroyd, 1979).

Still another example of new applications for tests can be found in the area of prevention. Many people talk about the importance of preventive techniques in the mental health field, but we have not seen any major developments to date. Why can't tests be developed to detect psychological disturbances in their earliest phases? Such early detection might provide an opportunity for constructive intervention before irreversible damage has occurred or maladaptive habits have become firmly established.

The feasibility of developing an instrument for the early detection of schizophrenia was noted by Saccuzzo and colleagues (for example, Saccuzzo, Hirt, & Spencer, 1974; Miller, Saccuzzo, & Braff, 1979), who, as we discussed in Chapter 18, found that schizophrenics could be discriminated from nonschizophrenics on the basis of processing speed as measured by the ability to detect a target stimulus that is followed by a noninformational stimulus at varying intervals. More recently, Saccuzzo and Schubert (1981) found that a group of subjects (commonly known as schizotypal personalities, or latent schizophrenics) known to be genetically related to schizophrenics but who had never shown a psychotic episode could also be identified by the same detection procedure. The implication is that the difficulty shown by actively psychotic schizophrenics (Saccuzzo et al., 1974; Saccuzzo & Miller, 1977), remitted schizophrenics (Miller et al., 1979), and latent schizophrenics (Saccuzzo & Schubert, 1981) is a weakness that precedes and perhaps plays a causative role in the pathology of schizophrenia. If this is so, the detection task can be used to diagnose the weakness prior to the onset of active schizophrenic episodes. However, work in this area is in its infancy and is presented here only as an example of the potential of tests for new applications.

In line with new uses for tests, the future might see an increasing emphasis on positive uses for tests. Tests are often used for what might be viewed as negative purposes such as identifying an intellectually limited human being so that he or she can be traumatized by removal from the normal classroom or diagnosing schizophrenia so that the person can be so labeled and placed on the locked unit of a psychiatric hospital. No wonder so many people dislike the whole idea of tests. Why can't tests be devised for positive purposes, such as isolating a person's greatest strengths or identifying hidden talents? Such tests couldn't hurt, could be useful, and would no doubt help to improve testing's presently poor reputation.

A complete revolution in the field.   Because, as we noted at the outset of this chapter, the underlying assumption of tests may some day prove to be less than correct, there is always the possibility that such a discovery may lead to a complete reconceptualization in testing. We don't see this possibility as too likely because violent changes are rare in psychology. Nevertheless, it's not out of the question.

IV. SUMMARY

Obviously anything is possible, especially in a field as new as testing, which originated in one of the youngest sciences. Psychology is better equipped now in technique, methodology, empirical data, and experience than ever before, and the members of this new and expanding field, as a group, are relatively young.

Therefore, it does not, on the one hand, seem unrealistic or overly optimistic to expect that the next 50 years will see advances equal to those of the last 50 years. On the other hand, psychology has come so far in the last 50 years that a comparable advance in the next 50 years could easily produce results unimaginable today. What happens to testing in the future will depend on the goals and objectives chosen by those in the field and by their persistence and creativity in accomplishing these goals.

Appendix 1
Areas of a Standard Normal Distribution

PART I   PERCENTILES ASSOCIATED WITH VARIOUS z SCORES

z	%Rank	z	%Rank
−3.0	.13	0	50.00
−2.9	.19	.1	53.98
−2.8	.26	.2	57.93
−2.7	.35	.3	61.79
−2.6	.47	.4	66.54
−2.5	.62	.5	69.15
−2.4	.82	.6	72.57
−2.3	1.07	.7	75.80
−2.2	1.39	.8	78.81
−2.1	1.79	.9	81.59
−2.0	2.28	1.0	84.13
−1.9	2.87	1.1	86.43
−1.8	3.59	1.2	88.49
−1.7	4.46	1.3	90.32
−1.6	5.48	1.4	91.92
−1.5	6.68	1.5	93.32
−1.4	8.08	1.6	94.52
−1.3	9.68	1.7	95.54
−1.2	11.51	1.8	96.41
−1.1	13.57	1.9	97.13
−1.0	15.87	2.0	97.72
− .9	18.41	2.1	98.21
− .8	21.19	2.2	98.61
− .7	24.20	2.3	98.93
− .6	27.43	2.4	99.18
− .5	30.58	2.5	99.38
− .4	34.46	2.6	99.53
− .3	38.21	2.7	99.65
− .2	42.07	2.8	99.74
− .1	46.02	2.9	99.81
0	50.00	3.0	99.87

PART II   AREAS BETWEEN MEAN AND VARIOUS *z* SCORES

z	.00	.01	.02	.03	.04	.05	.06	.07	.08	.09
0.0	.0000	.0040	.0080	.0120	.0160	.0199	.0239	.0279	.0319	.0359
0.1	.0398	.0438	.0478	.0517	.0557	.0596	.0636	.0675	.0714	.0753
0.2	.0793	.0832	.0871	.0910	.0948	.0987	.1026	.1064	.1103	.1141
0.3	.1179	.1217	.1255	.1293	.1331	.1368	.1406	.1443	.1480	.1517
0.4	.1554	.1591	.1628	.1664	.1700	.1736	.1772	.1808	.1844	.1879
0.5	.1915	.1950	.1985	.2019	.2054	.2088	.2123	.2157	.2190	.2224
0.6	.2257	.2291	.2324	.2357	.2389	.2422	.2454	.2486	.2517	.2549
0.7	.2580	.2611	.2642	.2673	.2704	.2734	.2764	.2794	.2823	.2852
0.8	.2881	.2910	.2939	.2967	.2995	.3023	.3051	.3078	.3106	.3133
0.9	.3159	.3186	.3212	.3238	.3264	.3289	.3315	.3340	.3365	.3389
1.0	.3413	.3438	.3461	.3485	.3508	.3531	.3554	.3577	.3599	.3621
1.1	.3643	.3665	.3686	.3708	.3729	.3749	.3770	.3790	.3810	.3830
1.2	.3849	.3869	.3888	.3907	.3925	.3944	.3962	.3980	.3997	.4015
1.3	.4032	.4049	.4066	.4082	.4099	.4115	.4131	.4147	.4162	.4177
1.4	.4192	.4207	.4222	.4236	.4251	.4265	.4279	.4292	.4306	.4319
1.5	.4332	.4345	.4357	.4370	.4382	.4394	.4406	.4418	.4429	.4441
1.6	.4452	.4463	.4474	.4484	.4495	.4505	.4515	.4525	.4535	.4545
1.7	.4554	.4564	.4573	.4582	.4591	.4599	.4608	.4616	.4625	.4633
1.8	.4641	.4649	.4656	.4664	.4671	.4678	.4686	.4693	.4699	.4706
1.9	.4713	.4719	.4726	.4732	.4738	.4744	.4750	.4756	.4761	.4767
2.0	.4772	.4778	.4783	.4788	.4793	.4798	.4803	.4808	.4812	.4817
2.1	.4821	.4826	.4830	.4834	.4838	.4842	.4846	.4850	.4854	.4857
2.2	.4861	.4864	.4868	.4871	.4875	.4878	.4881	.4884	.4887	.4890
2.3	.4893	.4896	.4898	.4901	.4904	.4906	.4909	.4911	.4913	.4916
2.4	.4918	.4920	.4922	.4925	.4927	.4929	.4931	.4932	.4934	.4936
2.5	.4938	.4940	.4941	.4943	.4945	.4946	.4948	.4949	.4951	.4952
2.6	.4953	.4955	.4956	.4957	.4959	.4960	.4961	.4962	.4963	.4964
2.7	.4965	.4966	.4967	.4968	.4969	.4970	.4971	.4972	.4973	.4974
2.8	.4974	.4975	.4976	.4977	.4977	.4978	.4979	.4979	.4980	.4981
2.9	.4981	.4982	.4982	.4983	.4984	.4984	.4985	.4985	.4986	.4986
3.0	.4987	.4987	.4987	.4988	.4988	.4989	.4989	.4989	.4990	.4990

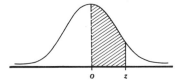

Standard score values are listed in the column headed "z." To find the proportion of the total area occurring between the mean and any given z-score, locate the entry indicated by the z-score. For example, a z-score of +1.85 is located by reading across to column 5 from the value of 1.8 in the "z" column. The value in the body of the table is .4678. Since the total area above the mean is equal to .5000, this means that only .0322 of the area is beyond the z-score of +1.85.

Appendix 2
Publishers of Major Tests

Below are the names and addresses of the publishers of major tests mentioned in this book.

Bayley Scales of Infant Development
Psychological Corporation
757 Third Avenue
New York, N.Y. 10017

Bender Visual Motor Gestalt Test
American Orthopsychiatric Association, Inc.
1790 Broadway
New York, N.Y. 10019

Bennett Mechanical Comprehension Test
Psychological Corporation
757 Third Avenue
New York, N.Y. 10017

Benton Visual Retention Test
Psychological Corporation
757 Third Avenue
New York, N.Y. 10017

California Psychological Inventory
Consulting Psychologists Press, Inc.
577 College Avenue
Palo Alto, Calif. 94306

Career Assessment Inventory
Interpretive Scoring Systems
4401 West 76th Street
Minneapolis, Minn. 55435

Cattell Infant Intelligence Scale
Psychological Corporation
757 Third Avenue
New York, N.Y. 10017

Children's Apperception Test
CPS, Inc.
P.O. Box 83
Larchmont, N.Y. 10538

Children's Personality Questionnaire
Institute for Personality and Ability Testing
1602 Coronado Drive
Champaign, Ill. 61820

Clinical Analysis Questionnaire (research edition)
Institute for Personality and Ability Testing
1602 Coronado Drive
Champaign, Ill. 61820

Cognitive Abilities Test
Houghton Mifflin
110 Tremont Street
Boston, Mass. 02107

Columbia Mental Maturity Scale
Harcourt Brace Jovanovich
757 Third Avenue
New York, N.Y. 10017

Cooperative School and College Ability Tests—Series II
Addison-Wesley Testing Service
2725 Sand Hill Road
Menlo Park, Calif. 94025

Culture Fair Intelligence Test
Institute for Personality and Ability Testing
1602 Coronado Drive
Champaign, Ill. 61820

Dental Admission Testing Program
Division of Educational Measurements
Council on Dental Education
American Dental Association
211 East Chicago Avenue
Chicago, Ill. 60611

Differential Aptitude Test
Psychological Corporation
757 Third Avenue
New York, N.Y. 10017

Edwards Personal Preference Schedule
Psychological Corporation
757 Third Avenue
New York, N.Y. 10017

Fear Survey Schedule
Educational and Industrial Testing Service
P.O. Box 7234
San Diego, Calif. 92107

General Aptitude Test Battery
U.S. Employment Service

Gerontological (Senior) Apperception Test
CPS, Inc.
P.O. Box 83
Larchmont, N.Y. 10538

Gesell Developmental Schedules
Psychological Corporation
757 Third Avenue
New York, N.Y. 10017

Goodenough-Harris Drawing Test
Harcourt Brace Jovanovich
757 Third Avenue
New York, N.Y. 10017

Graduate Record Examination Aptitude Test
Educational Testing Service
Princeton, N.J. 08540

Guilford-Zimmerman Temperament Survey
Sheridan Psychological Services
P.O. Box 6101
Orange, Calif. 92667

Henmon-Nelson Tests of Mental Ability (1973 revision)
Houghton Mifflin
110 Tremont Street
Boston, Mass. 02107

Holtzman Inkblot Test
Psychological Corporation
757 Third Avenue
New York, N.Y. 10017

Illinois Test of Psycholinguistic Abilities
University of Illinois Press
Urbana, Ill. 61801

Jr. Sr. High School Personality Questionnaire
Institute for Personality and Ability Testing
1602 Coronado Drive
Champaign, Ill. 61820

Kuder Occupational Interest Survey
Science Research Associates, Inc.
259 East Erie Street
Chicago, Ill. 60611

Kuhlmann-Anderson Test (seventh edition)
Personnel Press
191 Spring Street
Lexington, Mass. 02173

Law School Admission Test
Educational Testing Service
Princeton, N.J. 08540

Leiter International Performance Scale
C. H. Stoelting Company
1350 South Kostner Avenue
Chicago, Ill. 60623

McCarthy Scales of Children's Abilities
Psychological Corporation
757 Third Avenue
New York, N.Y. 10017

Memory-for-Designs Test
Psychological Test Specialists
Box 1441
Missoula, Mont. 59801

Miller Analogies Test
Psychological Corporation
757 Third Avenue
New York, N.Y. 10017

Minnesota Multiphasic Personality Inventory
Psychological Corporation
757 Third Avenue
New York, N.Y. 10017

Mooney Problem Checklist
Psychological Corporation
757 Third Avenue
New York, N.Y. 10017

Otis Self-Administering Tests of Mental Ability
Harcourt Brace Jovanovich
757 Third Avenue
New York, N.Y. 10017

Peabody Picture Vocabulary Test
American Guidance Service
Publisher's Building
Circle Pines, Minn. 55014

Personality Research Form
Research Psychologists Press
13 Greenwich Avenue
Goshen, N.Y. 10924

Pictorial Test of Intelligence
Houghton Mifflin
110 Tremont Street
Boston, Mass. 02107

Porteus Maze Test
Psychological Corporation
757 Third Avenue
New York, N.Y. 10017

Progressive Matrices
Psychological Corporation
757 Third Avenue
New York, N.Y. 10017

Quick Test
Psychological Test Specialists
Box 1441
Missoula, Mont. 59801

Revised Beta Examination
Psychological Corporation
757 Third Avenue
New York, N.Y. 10017

Revised Minnesota Paper Form Board Test
Psychological Corporation
757 Third Avenue
New York, N.Y. 10017

Rorschach Inkblot Test
Grune & Stratton, Inc.
757 Third Avenue
New York, N.Y. 10017

Scholastic Aptitude Test
Educational Testing Service
Princeton, N.J. 08540

Sixteen Personality Factor Questionnaire
Institute for Personality and Ability Testing
1602 Coronado Drive
Champaign, Ill. 61820

Stanford-Binet Intelligence Scale
Houghton Mifflin
110 Tremont Street
Boston, Mass. 02107

State-Trait Anxiety Inventory
Consulting Psychologists Press, Inc.
577 College Avenue
Palo Alto, Calif. 94306

Strong-Campbell Interest Inventory
Consulting Psychologists Press, Inc.
577 College Avenue
Palo Alto, Calif. 94306

System of Multicultural Pluralistic Assessment
Psychological Corporation
757 Third Avenue
New York, N.Y. 10017

Thematic Apperception Test
Harvard University Press
79 Garden Street
Cambridge, Mass. 02138

Torrance Tests of Creative Thinking
Personnel Press
191 Spring Street
Lexington, Mass. 02173

Wechsler Adult Intelligence Scale
Psychological Corporation
757 Third Avenue
New York, N.Y. 10017

Wechsler Intelligence Scale for Children—Revised
Psychological Corporation
757 Third Avenue
New York, N.Y. 10017

Wechsler Preschool and Primary Scale of Intelligence
Psychological Corporation
757 Third Avenue
New York, N.Y. 10017

Wide Range Achievement Test (revised edition)
Guidance Associates of Delaware
1526 Gilpin Avenue
Wilmington, Delaware 19806

Wonderlic Personnel Test
E. P. Wonderlic & Associates
P.O. Box 7
Northfield, Ill. 60093

Glossary

achievement   Previous learning.

acquiescence   The tendency to agree or to endorse a test item as true.

adverse impact   The effect of any test used for selection purposes if it systematically rejects substantially higher proportions of minority than majority job applicants.

age differentiation   Discrimination based on the fact that older children have greater capabilities than younger children.

age scale   A test in which items are grouped according to age level. (The Binet scale, for example, grouped into one age level items that two-thirds to three-quarters of a representative group of children a specific age could successfully pass.)

anxiety   An unpleasant emotional state marked by worry, apprehension, and tension.

aptitude   Potential for learning a specific skill (for example, musical aptitude).

assessment   A procedure used to evaluate an individual so that he or she can be described in terms of current functioning and also so that predictions can be made concerning future functioning. Tests are used in the assessment process.

basal age   In the Stanford-Binet intelligence scale, the highest year level at which the subject successfully passes all tests.

base rate   In decision analysis, the proportion of persons expected to succeed on a criterion if selected without a test.

biserial correlation   An index used to express the relationship between a continuous variable and an artificially dichotomous variable.

category format   A rating scale format that often uses the categories 1 to 10.

ceiling   In the Stanford-Binet intelligence scale, the year level at which all tests are failed.

class interval   The unit for the horizontal axis in a frequency distribution.

closed-ended question   In interviewing, a question that can be answered specifically (for example, "yes" or "no"). Such questions generally require the interviewee to recall something.

coefficient alpha   A generalized method for estimating reliability. Alpha is similar to the KR20 formula, except it allows items to take on values other than 0 and 1.

coefficient of alienation   In correlation and regression analysis, the index of nonassociation between two variables.

coefficient of determination   The correlation coefficient squared. Gives an estimate of the percentage of variation in Y that is known as a function of knowing X (and vice versa).

concurrent validity   A form of criterion validity in which the test and the criterion are administered at the same point in time.

confrontation   A statement that points out a discrepancy or inconsistency.

construct validity   A process used to establish the meaning of a test through a series of studies. To evaluate construct validity, a researcher simultaneously defines some construct and develops the instrumentation to measure it. In the studies, observed correlations between the test and other measures come to define the meaning of the test. See also *convergent validity* and *discriminant validity*.

content validity   The extent to which the content of a test is representative of the conceptual domain it is designed to cover.

convergent validity   A form of construct validity in which evidence is obtained to demonstrate that a test measures the same attribute as do other measures that purport to measure the same thing.

correction for attenuation   Correction of the reduction in the estimated correlation between a test and another measure caused by low reliability. The correction for attenuation formula is used to estimate what the correlation would have been if the variables had been perfectly reliable.

correlation coefficient   A mathematical index used to describe the direction and the magnitude of a relationship between two variables. The correlation coefficient ranges between -1.0 and 1.0.

criterion-referenced test   A test that describes the specific types of skills, tasks, or knowledge of an individual relative to a well-defined mastery criterion. The content of criterion-referenced tests is limited to certain well-defined objectives.

criterion validity   The extent to which a test score corresponds to an accurate measure of interest. The measure of interest is called the criterion.

cross validation   The process of evaluating a test or a regression equation for a sample other than the one used for the original studies.

deciles   Points that divide the frequency distribution into equal tenths.

descriptive statistics   Methods used to provide a concise description of a collection of quantitative information.

developmental quotient   In the Gesell Developmental Schedules, a test score that is obtained by assessing the presence or absence of behaviors associated with maturation.

diagnostic interview   An interview designed to elicit information concerning emotional functioning, including feelings, thoughts, and attitudes.

dichotomous format   A test-item format in which there are two alternatives for each item.

differential validity   The extent to which a test has different meanings for different groups of people. For example, a test may be a valid predictor of college success for White students but not for Black students.

discriminability   In item analysis, how well an item performs in relation to some criterion. For example, items may be compared according to how well they separate groups who score high and low on the test. The index of discrimination would then be the correlation between performance on an item and performance on the whole test.

discriminant analysis   A multivariate data analysis method for finding the linear combination of variables that best describes the classification of groups into discrete categories.

discriminant validity   A form of construct validity in which evidence is obtained to demonstrate that a test measures something unique and different from what other available tests measure.

distractor   An alternative on a multiple-choice exam that is not correct or for which no credit is given.

drift   The tendency for observers in behavioral studies to stray from the definitions they learned during training and to develop their own idiosyncratic definitions of behaviors.

EEOC guidelines   A set of procedures created by the Equal Employment Opportunity Commission (EEOC) to ensure fairness in employment practices. The EEOC guidelines discuss the minimum requirements for the validity and reliability of the psychological tests that are used for employee selection.

empathy response   In interviewing, a statement that communicates understanding. (Also called an *understanding response*.)

employment interview   An interview designed to elicit information pertaining to a person's qualifications and capabilities for particular employment duties.

Estimated Learning Potentials (ELPs)   In the SOMPA system, WISC-R scores adjusted for the socioeconomic background of the children. ELPs take the place of IQ scores.

evaluative statement   A statement in interviewing that judges or evaluates.

expectancy effect   The tendency for what an experimenter or a test administrator expects to find to influence the results. Also known as the Rosenthal effect for the psychologist who has studied this problem intensively.

face validity   The extent to which items on a test appear to be meaningful and relevant. Actually not a form of validity because face validity is not a basis for inference.

factor analysis   A set of multivariate data analysis methods for reducing large matrixes of correlations to fewer variables. The variables are linear combinations of the variables that were in the original correlation matrix.

false negative   In test decision theory, a case in which the test suggests a negative classification, yet the correct classification is in the positive category.

false positive   In test decision analysis, a case in which the test suggests a positive classification, yet the correct classification is in the negative category.

four-fifths rule   A rule used by federal agencies in deciding whether there is equal employment opportunity. Any procedure that results in a selection rate for any race, sex, or ethnic group that is less than four-fifths (or 80%) of the selection rate for the group with the highest rate is regarded as having an adverse impact.

frequency distribution   The systematic arrangement of scores on a measure to reflect how frequently each value on the measure occurred.

general cognitive index   In the McCarthy Scales of Children's Abilities, a standard score with a mean of 100 and standard deviation of 16.

group test   A test that can be given to more than one person at a time by a single test administrator.

hit rate   In test decision analysis, the proportion of cases in which a test accurately predicts success or failure.

hostile statement   A statement in interviewing that reflects anger.

human ability   Behaviors that reflect either what a person has learned or the person's capacity to emit a specific behavior. Includes *achievement*, *aptitude*, and *intelligence*.

individual test   A test that can be given to only one person at a time.

inference   A logical deduction (from evidence) about something we cannot observe directly.

inferential statistics   Methods used to make inferences from a small group of observations, called a sample. These inferences are then applied to a larger group of individuals, known as a population. Typically, the researcher wants to make statements about the larger group but cannot make all the necessary observations.

intelligence   General potential, independent of prior learning.

intelligence quotient   A unit for expressing the results of intelligence tests. The intelligence quotient is based on the ratio of the individual's mental age (MA) (as determined by the test) to actual or chronological age (CA): $IQ = MA/CA \times 100$.

intercept   The point on a two-dimensional graph on the y axis where x equals 0. In regression, this is the point at which the regression line intersects the y axis.

interquartile range   The interval of scores bounded by the 25th and the 75th percentiles.

interval scale   A scale that can be used to rank order objects and on which the units reflect equivalent magnitudes of the property being measured.

interview   A method of gathering information by talk, discussion, or direct questions.

ipsative scores   Test results presented in relative rather than absolute terms. Ipsative scores compare the individual against himself or herself. Each person thus provides his or her own frame of reference.

isodensity curve   An ellipse on a scatterplot (or two-dimensional scatter diagram) that encircles a specified proportion of the cases constituting particular groups.

item analysis   A set of methods used to evaluate test items. The most common techniques involve assessment of item difficulty and item discriminability.

item characteristic curve   A graph prepared as part of the process of item analysis. One graph is prepared for each test item and shows the total test score on the x axis and the proportion of test takers passing the item on the y axis.

item difficulty   A form of item analysis used to assess how difficult items are. The most common index of difficulty is the percentage of test takers responding with the correct choice.

item discriminability   See *discriminability*.

Kuder-Richardson 20   A formula for estimating the internal consistency of a test. The KR20 method is equivalent to the average split-half correlation obtained from all possible splits of the items. For the KR20 formula to be applied, all items must be scored either 0 or 1.

Likert format   A format for attitude-scale items in which subjects indicate their degree of agreement to statements using these categories: strongly disagree, disagree, neither disagree nor agree, agree, strongly agree.

McCall's *T*   A standardized score system with a mean of 50 and a standard deviation of 10. McCall's *T* can be obtained from a simple linear transformation of Z scores ($T = 10Z + 50$).

mean   The arithmetic average of a set of scores on a variable.

measurement error   The component of an observed test score that is not the true score or the quality you wish to measure.

median   The point on a frequency distribution marking the 50th percentile.

mental age   A unit for expressing the results of intelligence tests based on comparing the individual's performance on the test with the average performance of individuals in a specific chronological age group.

multiple regression   A multivariate data analysis method that considers the relationship between a continuous outcome variable and the linear combination of two or more predictor variables.

multivariate analysis   A set of methods for data analysis that consider the relationships between combinations of three or more variables.

nominal scale   A system of arbitrarily assigning numbers to objects. Mathematical manipulation of numbers from a nominal scale is not justified. For example, numbers on the backs of football players' uniforms are a nominal scale of measurement.

normative sample   A comparison group consisting of individuals who have been administered a test under standard conditions—that is, with the instructions, format, and general procedures outlined in the test manual for administering the test. (Also called a *standardization sample*.)

norm-referenced test   A test that evaluates each individual relative to a normative group.

norms   A summary of the performance of a group of individuals on which a test was standardized. The norms usually include the mean and the standard deviation for the reference group and information on how to translate a raw score into a percentile rank.

open-ended question   In interviewing, a question that usually cannot be answered specifically. Such questions require the interviewee to produce something spontaneously.

ordinal scale   A scale that can be used to rank order objects or individuals.

parallel forms reliability   The method of reliability assessment used to evaluate the error associated with the use of a particular set of items. Equivalent forms of a test are developed by generating two forms using the same rules. The correlation between the two forms is the estimate of parallel forms reliability.

Pearson product moment correlation   An index of correlation between two continuous variables.

percentile band   The range of percentiles that are likely to represent a subject's true score. It is created by forming an interval that is one standard error of measurement above and below the obtained score and converting the resulting values to percentiles.

percentile rank   The proportion of scores that fall below a particular score.

performance scale   A test that consists of tasks that require a subject to do something rather than to answer questions.

personality test   A test that measures overt and covert dispositions of the individual (the tendency that the individual will show a particular behavior or response in any given situation). Personality tests measure typical human behavior.

point scale   A test in which points (0, 1, or 2, for example) are assigned for each item. In a point scale all items with a particular content can be grouped together.

polychotomous format   A format for objective tests in which three or more alternative responses are given for each item. This format is popular for multiple-choice exams.

predictive validity   The extent to which a test forecasts scores on the criterion at some future point in time.

probing statement   A statement in interviewing that demands more information than the interviewee has been willing to provide of his or her own accord.

projective hypothesis   The proposal that when a person attempts to understand an ambiguous or vague stimulus, his or her interpretation reflects needs, feelings, experiences, prior conditioning, thought processes, and so forth.

projective test   A test in which the stimulus or the required response or both are ambiguous. The general idea behind projective tests is that a person's interpretation of an ambiguous stimulus reflects his or her unique characteristics.

prophecy formula   A formula developed by Spearman and Brown that can be used to correct for the loss of reliability that occurs when the split-half method is used and each half of the test is one half as long as the whole test. The method can also be used to estimate how much the test length must be increased to bring the test to a desired level of reliability.

psychological test   A device for measuring characteristics of human beings that pertain to overt (observable) and covert (intraindividual) behavior. A psychological test measures past, present, or future human behavior.

psychological testing   The use of psychological tests. Psychological testing refers to all the possible uses, applications, and underlying concepts of psychological tests.

quartiles   Points that divide the frequency distribution into equal fourths.

randomly parallel tests   Tests created by successive random sampling of items from a domain or universe of items.

ratio scale   An interval scale with an absolute zero, or point at which there is none of the property being measured.

reactivity   The phenomenon causing the reliability of a scale in behavioral studies to be higher when an observer knows that his or her work is being monitored.

reassuring statement   In interviewing, a statement that tries to comfort or support.

receptive vocabulary   In the Peabody Picture Vocabulary Test, a nonverbal estimate of verbal intelligence. Ability to understand language.

regression line   The best-fitting straight line through a set of points in a scatter diagram.

reliability   The extent to which a score or measure is free of measurement error. Theoretically, reliability is the ratio of true score variance to observed score variance. This ratio can be estimated using a variety of correlational methods, including *coefficient alpha*, *KR20*, *test-retest*, *parallel forms*.

representative sample   A sample (group) that is comprised of individuals whose characteristics are similar to those for whom the test is to be used.

residual   The difference between predicted and observed values from a regression equation.

response style   The tendency to mark a test item in a certain way irrespective of content.

Rosenthal effect   See *expectancy effect*.

scaled score   On the Wechsler tests, a standard score with a mean of 10 and a standard deviation of 3.

scatter diagram   A picture of the relationship between two variables. For each individual a pair of observations is obtained, and the values are plotted in a two-dimensional space created by variables X and Y.

selection ratio   In test decision analysis, the proportion of applicants who are selected.

self-report questionnaire   A questionnaire that provides a list of statements about an individual and requires the subject to respond in some way to each, such as "true" or "false."

shrinkage   Many times a regression equation is created on one group and used to predict the performance on another group of subjects. This procedure tends to overestimate the magnitude of the relationship for the second group. The amount of decrease in the strength of the relationship from the original sample to the sample on which the equation is employed is known as shrinkage.

social ecology   A relatively new field of study that deals with the relationship between environments and behavior, the description of behavioral settings, and other related topics.

social facilitation   Tendency of people to behave like the models around them.

Spearman's rho   A method for finding the correlation between two sets of ranks.

split-half reliability   A method for evaluating reliability in which a test is split into halves. The correlation between the halves of the test, corrected for the shortened length of the halves, is used as an estimate of reliability.

standard administration   The procedures outlined in the test manual for administering a test.

standard deviation   The square root of the average squared deviation around the mean (or the variance). It is used as a measure of variability in a distribution of scores.

standard error of estimate   An index of the accuracy of a regression equation. It is equivalent to the standard deviation of the residuals from a regression analysis. Prediction is most accurate when the standard error of estimate is small.

standard error of measurement   An index of the amount of error in a test or measure. The standard error of measurement is a standard deviation of a set of observations for the same test.

standardization sample   A comparison group consisting of individuals who have been administered a test under standard conditions—that is, with the instructions, format, and general procedures outlined in the test manual for administering the test. (Also called a *normative sample*.)

standardized interview   An interview conducted under standard conditions.

stanine distribution   A system for assigning the numbers 1 through 9 to a test score. The system was developed by the U.S. Air Force. The standardized stanine distribution has a mean of 5 and a standard deviation of approximately 2.

state anxiety   An emotional reaction to a situation. State anxiety varies from one situation to the next.

stress   A response to situations that pose demands, place constraints, or give opportunities.

structured personality test   A test that provides a statement, usually of the self-report variety ("I like rock and roll music"), and requires the subject to choose between two or more alternative responses ("true" or "false," for example). Also sometimes known as an objective personality test.

subtest scatter   On the Wechsler tests, the degree of subtest variability.

Taylor-Russell tables   A series of tables that can be used to evaluate the validity of a test in relation to the amount of information it contributes beyond what would be known by chance.

test   A measurement device.

test administration   The act of giving a test.

test administrator   Person giving a test.

test anxiety   Anxiety that occurs in test-taking situations.

test battery   A collection of tests whose scores are used together in appraising an individual.

test-retest reliability   A method for estimating how much measurement error is caused by time sampling, or administering the test at two different points in time. Test-retest reliability is usually estimated from the correlation between performances for two different administrations of the test.

third variable   A variable that may account for the observed relationship between two other variables.

tracking   The tendency to stay at about the same level of growth or performance relative to other peers who are the same age.

trait   An enduring or persistent characteristic of an individual that is independent of situations.

trait anxiety   A personality characteristic reflecting the differences among people in the intensity of their reaction to stressful situations.

true score   The score that would be obtained on a test or measure if there were no measurement error. In practice the true score can be estimated, but it is not directly observed.

T-score   On the MMPI, a standand score with a mean of 50 and a standard deviation of 10. (Also see McCall's T.)

understanding response   In interviewing, a statement that communicates understanding. (Also called an *empathy response*.)

unstructured interview   An interview conducted without any specific or particular questions or sequences of questions.

validity   The extent to which a test measures the quality it purports to measure. Types of validity include *content validity*, *criterion validity*, and *construct validity*.

variance   The average squared deviation around the mean. The standard deviation squared.

References

Aaronson, B. S. Age and sex influence on MMPI profile peak distributions in an abnormal population. *Journal of Consulting Psychology*, 1958, *22*, 203–206.

Abrahams, N. M., Neumann, I., & Gilthens, W. H. Faking vocational interests: Simulation versus real life motivation. *Personnel Psychology*, 1971, *24*, 5–12.

Abrams, E. W. Predictions of intelligence from certain Rorschach factors. *Journal of Clinical Psychology*, 1955, *11*, 81–84.

Abramson, L. U., Seligman, M. E. P., & Teasdale, J. D. Learned helplessness and reformulations. *Journal of Abnormal Psychology*, 1978, *87*, 49–74.

Abramson, T. The influence of examiner race on first-grade and kindergarten subjects' Peabody Picture Vocabulary Test scores. *Journal of Educational Measurement*, 1969, *6*, 241–246.

Adorno, I. W., Frenkel-Brunswik, E., Levinson, D. J., & Sanford, R. N. *The authoritarian personality*. New York: Harper & Row, 1950.

Akutagawa, D. A. *A study in construct validity of the psychoanalytic concept of latent anxiety and a test of projection distance hypothesis*. Unpublished doctoral dissertation, University of Pittsburgh, 1956.

Allen, G. J. The behavioral treatment of test anxiety: Recent research and future trends. *Behavior Therapy*, 1972, *3*, 253–262.

Allen, M. J., & Yen, W. M. *Introduction to measurement theory*. Monterey, Calif.: Brooks/Cole, 1979.

Allen, N. J. *A comparison of computer-interactive and paper-pencil methods of measuring individual time orientation*. Unpublished master's thesis, School of Business, San Diego State University, 1979.

Allison, J., Blatt, S. J., & Zimet, C. N. *The interpretation of psychological tests*. New York: Harper & Row, 1968.

Allport, G. W., & Odbert, H. S. Trait-names, a psycholexical study. *Psychological Monographs*, 1936, *47*, No. 1.

Alpert, R., & Haber, R. N. Anxiety in academic achievement situations. *Journal of Abnormal and Social Psychology*, 1960, *61*, 207–215.

Altman, I. *The environment and social behavior*. Monterey, Calif., Brooks/Cole, 1975.

American Psychological Association (APA). *Psychology and its relations with other professions*. Washington, D.C.: Author, 1954.

American Psychological Association (APA). *Standards for educational and psychological tests*. Washington, D.C.: Author, 1974.

American Psychological Association (APA). Ethical principles of psychologists. *American Psychologist*, 1981, *36*, 633–638.

Ames, L. B., Metraux, R. W., & Walker, R. N. *Adolescent Rorschach responses*. New York: Brunner/Mazel, 1971.

Ammons, R. B., & Ammons, C. H. The quick test (QT): Provisional manual. *Psychological Reports*, 1962, *11*: 111–161.

Ammons, R. B., & Ammons, C. H. Review of the McCarthy Scales of Children's Abilities. *Psychological Reports*, 1974, *34*, 1347.

Anastasi, A. Psychology, psychologists, and psychological testing. *American Psychologist*, 1967, *22*, 297–306.

Anastasi, A. Personality Research Form. In O. K. Buros (Ed.), *The seventh mental measurements yearbook* (Vol. 1). Highland Park, N.J.: Gryphon Press, 1972. (a)

Anastasi, A. Review of the Goodenough-Harris Drawing Test. In O. K. Buros (Ed.), *The seventh mental measurements yearbook* (Vol. 1). Highland Park, N.J.: Gryphon Press, 1972. (b)

Anastasi, A. *Psychological testing* (4th ed.). New York: Macmillan, 1976.

Anastasi, A. Abilities and the measurement of achievement. *New Directions for Testing and Measurement*, 1980, *5*, 1–10.

Anastasi, A. Coaching, test sophistication, and developed abilities. *American Psychologist*, 1981, *36*, 1086–1093.

Anderson, N. H. How functional measurement can yield validated interval scales for mental qualities. *Journal of Applied Psychology*, 1976, *61*, 677–692.

Angoff, W. H. Scales, norms and equivalent scores. In R. L. Thorndike (Ed.), *Educational measurement* (2nd ed.). Washington, D.C.: American Council on Education, 1971.

Anton, W. D. An evaluation of outcome variables in the systematic desensitization of test anxiety. *Behaviour Research and Therapy*, 1976, *14*, 217–224.

Aponte, J. F., & Aponte, C. E. Group preprogrammed systematic desensitization without the simultaneous presentation of aversive scenes with relaxation training. *Behaviour Research and Therapy*, 1971, *9*, 337–346.

Aronow, E., Reznikoff, M., & Rauchway, A. Some old and new directions in Rorschach testing. *Journal of Personality Assessment*, 1979, *43*, 227–234.

Arthur, G. *Arthur point scale of performance tests*. Chicago: Stoelting, 1930.

Asher, J. J., & Sciarrino, J. A. Realistic work sample tests: A review. *Personnel Psychology*, 1974, *27*, 519–533.

Astin, A. W., & Holland, J. L. The environmental assessment technique: A way to measure college environments. *Journal of Educational Psychology*, 1961, *52*, 308–316.

Atkinson, J. W. Studying personality in the context of an advanced motivational psychology. *American Psychologist*, 1981, *36*, 117–128.

Auerbach, A. H., & Luborsky, L. Accuracy of judgements of psychotherapy and the nature of the "good hour." In J. Shlien, H. Hunt, J. D. Matarazzo, & C. Savage (Eds.), *Research in psychotherapy* (Vol. 3). Washington, D.C.: American Psychological Association, 1968.

Auld, F. Vicissitudes of communication in psychotherapy. In J. Shlien, H. Hunt, J. D. Matarazzo, & C. Savage (Eds.), *Research in psychotherapy* (Vol. 3). Washington, D.C.: American Psychological Association 1968.

Ax, A. F. The physiological differentiation between fear and anger in humans. *Psychosomatic Medicine*, 1953, *15*, 433–442.

Azrin, N. H., Holz, W., Ulrich, R., & Goldiamond, I. The control of the content of conversation through reinforcement. *Journal of the Experimental Analysis of Behavior*, 1961, *4*, 25–30.

Azrin, N. H., & Powell, J. Behavioral engineering: The reduction of smoking behavior by a conditioning apparatus and procedure. *Journal of Applied Behavior Analysis*, 1968, *1*, 193–200.

Baglan, T. Effects of interpersonal attraction and type of behavior on attributions. *Psychological Reports*, 1981, *48*, 299–304.

Baird, L. L. Review of the Torrance Tests of Creative Thinking. In O. K. Buros (Ed.), *The seventh mental measurements yearbook* (Vol. 1). Highland Park, N.J.: Gryphon Press, 1972.

Bandura, A. Psychotherapy based upon modeling principles. In A. E. Bergin & S. L. Garfield (Eds.), *Handbook of psychotherapy and behavior change*. New York: Wiley, 1971.

Bandura, A. Self-efficacy: Toward a unifying theory of behavioral change. *Psychological Review*, 1977, *84*, 191–215.

Bandura, A., Ross, D., & Ross, S. A. A comparative test of status envy, social power, and secondary reinforcement theories of identification learning. *Journal of Abnormal and Social Psychology*, 1963, *67*, 527–534. (a)

Bandura, A., Ross, D., & Ross, S. A. Imitation of film-mediated aggressive models. *Journal of Abnormal and Social Psychology*, 1963, *66*, 3–11. (b)

Bandura, A., Ross, D., & Ross, S. A. Vicarious reinforcement and imitative learning. *Journal of Abnormal and Social Psychology*, 1963, *67*, 601–607. (c)

Barber, T. X., & Silver, M. J. Fact, fiction, and the experimenter bias effect. *Psychological Bulletin Monograph Supplement*, 1968, *70*, 1–29.

Barker, R. G. *Ecological psychology: Concepts and methods for studying the environment of human behavior*. Stanford, Calif.: Stanford University Press, 1968.

Barker, R. G. Settings of a professional lifetime. *Journal of Personality and Social Psychology*, 1979, *37*, 2137–2157.

Barker, R. G., & Schoggen, P. *Qualities of community life*. San Francisco: Jossey-Bass, 1973.

Baron, R. A. Aggression as a function of ambient temperature and prior anger arousal. *Journal of Personality and Social Psychology*, 1972, *21*, 183–189.

Bartlett, C. J., & O'Leary, B. S. A differential prediction model to moderate the effects of heterogeneous groups in personnel selection and classification. *Personnel Psychology*, 1969, *22*, 1–17.

Bayley, N. On the growth of intelligence. *American Psychologist*, 1955, *10*, 805–818.

Bayley, N. *Manual: Bayley Scales of Infant Development*. New York: Psychological Corporation, 1969.

Beck, R. A. The discriminative efficiency of the Bayley Scales of Infant Development. *Journal of Abnormal Child Psychology*, 1979, 7, 113–119.

Beck, S. J. Configurational tendencies in Rorschach responses. *American Journal of Psychology*, 1933, *45*, 433–443.

Beck, S. J. *Rorschach's test. I: Basic processes*. New York: Grune & Stratton, 1944.

Beck, S. J. *Rorschach's test. II: A variety of personality pictures*. New York: Grune & Stratton, 1945.

Beck, S. J. *Rorschach's test. III: Advances in interpretation*. New York: Grune & Stratton, 1952.

Bellak, L. *The T.A.T., C.A.T., and S.A.T. in clinical use* (3rd ed.). New York: Grune & Stratton, 1975.

Bellak, L., & Bellak, S. S. *Manual: Senior Apperception Technique*. Larchmont, N.Y.: CPS, Inc. 1973.

Bellows, R. M., & Estep, M. F. *Employment psychology: The interview*. New York: Holt, Rinehart & Winston, 1954.

Bem, D. J., & Allen, A. On predicting some of the people some of the time: The search for cross-situational consistencies in behavior. *Psychological Review*, 1974, *81*, 506–520.

Bem, D. J., & Funder, D. C. Predicting more of the people more of the time: Assessing the personality of situations. *Psychological Review*, 1978, *85*, 485–501.

Bennett, F., & Schubert, D. Use of local norms to improve configural reproducibility of an MMPI short form. *Journal of Personality Assessment*, 1981, *45*, 33–39.

Bergan, A., McManis, D. L., & Melchert, P. A. Effects of social and token reinforcement on WISC block design performance. *Perceptual and Motor Skills*, 1971, *32*, 871–880.

Bergan, J. R., & Parra, E. B. Variations in IQ testing and instruction and the letter learning and achievement of Anglo and bilingual Mexican-American children. *Journal of Educational Psychology*, 1979, *71*, 819–826.

Berger, M. The third version of the Stanford-Binet (Forms L-M): Some methodological limitations and their practical implications. *Bulletin of the British Psychological Society*, 1970, *23*, 17–26.

Bergin, A. E. The evaluation of therapeutic outcomes. In A. E. Bergin & S. L. Garfield (Eds.), *Handbook of psychotherapy and behavior change*. New York: Wiley, 1971.

Bernreuter, R. G. *The personality inventory*. Palo Alto, Calif.: Consulting Psychologists Press, 1931.

Bersoff, D. N. Regarding psychologists testily: Legal regulation of psychological assessment in the public schools. In B. Sales & M. Novick (Eds.), *Perspectives in law and psychology. III: Testing and evaluation*. New York: Plenum, 1979.

Bersoff, D. N. Testing and the law. *American Psychologist*, 1981, *36*, 1047–1057.

Bianchini, J. C. *Achievement tests and differentiated norms*. Paper presented at the U.S. Office of Education invitational conference on achievement testing of disadvantaged and minority students for educational program evaluation, Reston, Va., May 1976.

Bindman, A. J., & Spiegel, A. D. *Perspectives in community mental health*. Chicago: Aldine-Atherton, 1969.

Binet, A. Perceptions d'enfants. *La Révue Philosophique*, 1890, *30*, 582–611. (a)

Binet, A. Réchèrches sur les mouvements de quelques jeunes enfants. *La Révue Philosophique*, 1890, *29*, 297–309. (b)

Binet, A., & Henri, V. La psychologie individuelle. *L'Année Psychologique*, 1895, *2*, 411–463.

Binet, A., & Henri, V. La psychologie individuelle. *L'Année Psychologique*, 1896, *3*, 296–332.

Binet, A., & Simon, T. Méthodes nouvelles pour le diagnostic du niveau intéllectuel des anormaux. *L'Année Psychologique*, 1905, *11*, 191–244.

Birdwhistell, R. L. Paralanguage 25 years after Sapir. In H. W. Brosin (Ed.), *Lectures on experimental psychiatry*. Pittsburgh: University of Pittsburgh Press, 1961.

Birdwhistell, R. L. The kinesic level in the investigation of the emotions. In P. H. Knapp (Ed.), *Expression of the emotions in man*. New York: International Universities Press, 1963.

Birk, J. M. Interest inventories: A mixed blessing. *Vocational Guidance Quarterly*, 1974, *22*, 280–286.

Birney, R. C. Research on the achievement motive. In E. F. Borgatta & W. W. Lambert (Eds.), *Handbook of personality theory and research*. Chicago: Rand McNally, 1968.

Blatt, S. J. The validity of projective techniques and their clinical and research contributions. *Journal of Personality Assessment*, 1975, *39*, 327–343.

Block, J. *The Q-sort method in personality assessment and psychiatric research*. Springfield, Ill.: Charles C Thomas, 1961.

Block, J. *The challenge of response sets: Unconfounding meaning, acquiescence, and social desirability in the MMPI*. New York: Appleton-Century-Crofts, 1965.

Block, J. *Lives through time*. Berkeley, Calif.: Bancroft Books, 1971.

Block, J. Advancing the psychology of personality: Paradigmatic shift for improving the quality of research. In D. Magnusson & N. S. Endler (Eds.), *Personality at the crossroads: Current issues in interactional psychology*. Hillsdale, N.J.: Erlbaum, 1977.

Bloom, B. S. The new direction in educational research: Alterable variables. *New Directions for Testing and Measurement*, 1980, *5*, 17–30.

Blumenthal, J. A., Williams, R. B., Jr., Kong, Y., Thompson, L. W., Jenkins, C. D., & Rosenman, R. H. *Coronary-prone behavior and a geographically documented coronary disease*. Paper presented at the American Psychosomatic Society convention, 1975.

Boor, M., & Schill, T. Subtest performance on the WAIS as a function of anxiety and defensiveness. *Perceptual and Motor Skills*, 1968, *27*, 33–34.

Borgida, E., & Nisbett, R. The differential impact of abstract vs. concrete information on decisions. *Journal of Applied Social Psychology*, 1977, *7*, 258–271.

Boring, E. G. *A history of experimental psychology* (2nd ed.). New York: Appleton-Century-Crofts, 1950.

Bortner, M. Review of the Progressive Matrices test. In O. K. Buros (Ed.), *The sixth mental measurements yearbook*. Highland Park, N.J.: Gryphon Press, 1965.

Bowers, K. S. Situationalism in psychology: An analysis and critique. *Psychological Review*, 1973, *80*, 307–336.

Braun, P. R., & Reynolds, D. N. A factor analysis of a 100 item fear survey inventory. *Behaviour Research and Therapy*, 1969, *7*, 399–402.

Brayfield, A. H. (Ed.). Testing and public policy. *American Psychologist*, 1965, *20*, 857–1005.

Brazelton, T. B. *Neonatal behavioral assessment scale*. Philadelphia: Lippincott, 1973.

Brill, S. The secrecy behind the college boards. *New York Magazine*, 1973. (Reprinted by the NYG Corporation.)

Brittain, M. A comparative study of the use of the Wechsler Intelligence Scale for Children and the Stanford-Binet intelligence scale (Form L-M) with eight-year-old children. *British Journal of Educational Psychology*, 1968, *38*, 103–104.

Brogden, H. E. On the interpretation of the correlation coefficient as a measure of predictive efficiency. *Journal of Educational Psychology*, 1946, *37*, 65–76.

Brogden, H. E. When tests pay off. *Personnel Psychology*, 1949, *2*, 171–183.

Brown, F. G. The algebra works—but what does it mean? *School Psychology Digest*, 1979, *8*(2), 213–218. (a)

Brown, F. G. The SOMPA: A system of measuring potential abilities? *School Psychology Digest*, 1979, *8*(1), 37–46. (b)

Brown, J. S., & Burton, R. B. Diagnostic models for procedural bugs in basic mathematical skills. *Cognitive Science*, 1978, *2*, 155–192.

Bruvold, W. H. *Are beliefs and behavior consistent with attitudes?* Paper presented at the meeting of the Western Psychological Association, Los Angeles, April 1970.

Burgemeister, B. B., Blum, L. H., & Lorge, I. *Columbia Mental Maturity Scale* (3rd ed.). New York: Harcourt Brace Jovanovich, 1972.

Buros, O. K. (Ed.). *Personality tests and reviews*. Highland Park, N.J.: Gryphon Press, 1970.

Buros, O. K. (Ed.). *The seventh mental measurements yearbook* (2 vols.). Highland Park, N.J.: Gryphon Press, 1972.

Buros, O. K. *Tests in print II*. Highland Park, N.J.: Gryphon Press, 1974.

Buros, O. K. (Ed.). *Intelligence tests and reviews*. Highland Park, N.J.: Gryphon Press, 1975. (a)

Buros, O. K. (Ed.). *Personality tests and reviews* (Vol. 2). Highland Park, N.J.: Gryphon Press, 1975. (b)

Buros, O. K. (Ed.). *Vocational tests and reviews*. Highland Park, N.J.: Gryphon Press, 1975. (c)

Buros, O. K. Fifty years in testing: Some reminiscences, criticisms and suggestions. *Educational Researcher*, 1977, *6*, 9–15.

Buros, O. K. (Ed.). *The eighth mental measurements yearbook* (2 vols.). Highland Park, N.J.: Gryphon Press, 1978.

Burtt, H. E. *Principles of employment psychology*. Boston: Houghton Mifflin, 1926.

Butcher, H. L. Review of Cooperative School and College Ability Tests: Series 2. In O. K. Buros (Ed.), *The seventh mental measurements yearbook* (Vol. 1). Highland Park, N.J.: Gryphon Press, 1972.

Caldwell, M. B., & Knight, D. The effects of Negro and White examiners on Negro intelligence test performance. *Journal of Negro Education*, 1970, *39*, 177–179.

Campbell, D. P. *Handbook for the Strong Vocational Interest Blank*. Stanford, Calif.: Stanford University Press, 1971.

Campbell, D. P. *Manual for the SVIB-SCII Strong-Campbell Interest Inventory* (2nd ed.). Stanford, Calif.: Stanford University Press, 1974.

Campbell, D. P. *Manual for the Strong-Campbell Interest Inventory*. Stanford, Calif.: Stanford University Press, 1977.

Campbell, D. P., & Hansen, J. C. *Manual for the SVIB-SCII Strong-Campbell Interest Inventory* (3rd. ed.). Stanford, Calif.: Stanford University Press, 1981.

Campbell, D. T., & Fiske, D. W. Convergent and discriminant validation by the multitrait-multimethod matrix. *Psychological Bulletin*, 1959, *56*, 81–105.

Campbell, J. P. Psychometric theory. In M. D. Dunnette (Ed.), *Handbook of industrial and organizational psychology*. Chicago: Rand McNally, 1976.

Campion, J. E. Work sampling for personnel selection. *Journal of Applied Psychology*, 1972, *56*, 40–44.

Canfield, A. A. The "sten" scale—a modified C-scale. *Educational and Psychological Measurement*, 1951, *11*, 295–297.

Cannell, C. F., & Henson, R. Incentives, motives, and response bias. *Annals of Economic and Social Measurement*, 1974, *3*, 307–317.

Carkhuff, R. R. *Helping and human relations. I: Selection and training. II: Practice and research*. New York: Holt, Rinehart & Winston, 1969.

Carkhuff, R. R., & Berenson, B. C. *Beyond counseling and therapy*. New York: Holt, Rinehart & Winston, 1967.

Carlson, R. E., Thayer, P. W., Mayfield, E. C., & Peterson, D. A. Improvements in the selection interview. *Personnel Journal*, 1971, *50*, 268–275.

Carroll, J. B., & Horn, J. L. On the scientific basis of ability testing. *American Psychologist*, 1981, *36*, 1012–1020.

Carter, J. E., & Heath, B. Somatotype methodology and kinesiology research. *Kinesiology Review*, 1971, 10.

Castaneda, A., & Ramirez, M. *Cultural democracy, bicognitive development, and education*. New York: Academic Press, 1974.

Cattell, J. B. Mental tests and measurements. *Mind*, 1890, *15*, 373–380.

Cattell, J. M. Psychology in America. *Scientific Monthly*, 1930, *30*, 114–126.

Cattell, P. *The measurement of intelligence of infants and young children*. New York: Psychological Corporation, 1940.

Cattell, R. B. *Manual for forms A and B: Sixteen Personality Factor Questionnaire*. Champaign, Ill.: Institute for Personality and Ability Testing, 1949.

Cattell, R. B. *Personality and motivation, structure and measurement*. Yonkers, N.Y.: World Book, 1957.

Cattell, R. B. *The scientific analysis of personality*. Chicago: Aldine-Atherton, 1965.

Cattell, R. B., & Bolton, L. S. What pathological dimensions lie beyond the normal dimensions of the 16 PF? A comparison of MMPI and 16 PF factor domains. *Journal of Consulting and Clinical Psychology*, 1969, *33*, 18–29.

Cattell, R. B., Eber, H. W., & Tatsuoka, M. M. *Handbook for the Sixteen Personality Factor Questionnaire (16 PF)*. Champaign, Ill.: Institute for Personality and Ability Testing, 1970.

Cattell, R. B., & Scheier, I. H. *The meaning and measurement of neuroticism and anxiety*. New York: Ronald Press, 1961.

Cattell, R. B., & Scheier, I. H. *The IPAT Anxiety Scale Questionnaire: Manual* (2nd ed.). Champaign, Ill.: Institute for Personality and Ability Testing, 1963.

Cautela, J. R., & Upper, D. The behavioral inventory battery: The use of self-report measures in behavioral analyses and therapy. In M. Hersen & A. S. Bellack (Eds.), *Behavioral assessment*. New York: Pergamon Press, 1976.

Champney, H., & Marshall, H. Optimal refinement of the rating scale. *Journal of Applied Psychology*, 1939, *23*, 323–331.

Chase, C., & Sattler, J. M. Determining areas of strengths and weaknesses on the Stanford-Binet. *School Psychology Review*, 1980, *9*, 174–177.

Chun, K., & Campbell, J. B. Dimensionality of the Rotter Interpersonal Trust Scale. *Psychological Reports*, 1974, *35*, 1059–1070.

Chun, K., Cobb, S., & French, J. R. P., Jr. *Measures for psychological assessment*. Ann Arbor, Mich.: Survey Research Center of the Institute for Social Research, 1975.

Clarizio, H. F. In defense of the IQ test. *School Psychology Digest*, 1979, *8*(1), 79–88. (a)

Clarizio, H. F. SOMPA—A symposium continued: Commentaries. *School Psychology Digest*, 1979, *8*(2), 207–209. (b)

Clark, K. E. *The vocational interests of nonprofessional men*. Minneapolis: University of Minnesota Press, 1961.

Clark, K. E., & Campbell, D. P. *Manual for the Minnesota Vocational Interest Inventory*. New York: Psychological Corporation, 1965.

Cleary, T. A. Test bias: Prediction of grades of Negro and White students in integrated colleges. *Journal of Educational Measurement*, 1968, *5*, 115–124.

Cleary, T. A., Humphreys, L. G., Kendrick, S. A., & Wesman, A. Educational uses of tests with disadvantaged populations. *American Psychologist*, 1975, *30*, 15–41.

Clemans, W. V. Test administration. In R. L. Thorndike (Ed.), *Educational measurement* (2nd ed.). Washington, D.C.: American Council on Education, 1971.

Cohen, I. The effects of material and non-material reinforcement upon performance of the WISC block design subtest by children of different social classes: A follow-up study. *Psychology*, 1970, *7*(4), 41–47.

Cohen, J. The factorial structure of the WAIS between early adulthood and old age. *Journal of Consulting Psychology*, 1957, *21*, 283–290.

Cohen, J. A coefficient of agreement for nominal scales. *Educational and Psychological Measurement*, 1960, *20*, 37–46.

Cohen, J., & Cohen, P. *Applied multiple regression/correlation analysis for the behavioral sciences*. Hillsdale, N.J.: Erlbaum, 1975.

Cole, N. S. Bias in selection. *Journal of Educational Measurement*, 1973, *10*, 237–255.

Cole, N. S. Bias in testing. *American Psychologist*, 1981, *36*, 1067–1077.

Coleman, J. C. Life stress and maladaptive behavior. *American Journal of Occupational Therapy*, 1973, *27*, 169–180.

Coleman, W., & Cureton, E. E. Intelligence and achievement: The "jangle fallacy" again. *Educational and Psychological Measurement*, 1954, *14*, 347–351.

Comrey, A. L., Backer, T. E., & Glaser, E. M. *A sourcebook for mental health measures*. Los Angeles: Human Interaction Research Institute, 1973.

Condit, J. E., Lewandowski, D. G., & Saccuzzo, D. P. Efficiency of Peabody Picture Vocabulary for estimating WISC scores for delinquents. *Psychological Reports*, 1976, *38*, 359–362.

Conklin, E. S. The scale of values method for studies in genetic psychology. *University of Oregon Publications*, 1923, *2*, No. 1.

Conley, J. J. An MMPI typology of male alcoholics. *Journal of Personality Assessment*, 1981, *45*, 40–43.

Cooley, W. W., & Lohnes, P. R. *Multivariate data analysis*. New York: Wiley, 1971.

Coons, W. H., & Peacock, E. P. Inter-examiner reliability of the WAIS with mental hospital patients. *Ontario Psychological Association Quarterly*, 1959, *12*, 33–37.

Cooper, H. M., & Rosenthal, R. Statistical versus traditional procedures for summarizing research findings. *Psychological Bulletin*, 1980, *87*, 442–449.

Copple, C. E., & Succi, G. J. The comparative ease of processing standard English and Black nonstandard English by lower-class Black children. *Child Development*, 1974, *45*, 1048–1053.

Costello, J., & Dickie, J. Leiter and Stanford-Binet IQ's of preschool disadvantaged children. *Developmental Psychology*, 1970, *2*, 314.

Crites, J. O. *Career Maturity Inventory: Theory and research handbook and administration and use manual*. Monterey, Calif.: CTB/McGraw-Hill, 1973.

Crites, J. O. The Career Maturity Inventory. In D. E. Super (Ed.), *Measuring vocational maturity for counseling and evaluation*. Washington, D.C.: National Vocational Guidance Association, 1974.

Cronbach, L. J. Coefficient alpha and the internal structure of tests. *Psychometrika*, 1951, *16*, 297–334.

Cronbach, L. J. *Essentials of psychological testing* (3rd ed.). New York: Harper & Row, 1970.

Cronbach, L. J. Test validation. In R. L. Thorndike (Ed.), *Educational measurement* (2nd ed.). Washington, D.C.: American Council on Education, 1971.

Cronbach, L. J. Beyond the two disciplines of scientific psychology. *American Psychologist*, 1975, *30*, 116–127. (a)

Cronbach, L. J. Five decades of public controversy over mental testing. *American Psychologist*, 1975, *30*, 1–14. (b)

Cronbach, L. J. Black Intelligence Test of Cultural Homogeneity: A review. In O. K. Buros (Ed.), *The eighth mental measurements yearbook* (Vol. 1). Highland Park, N.J.: Gryphon Press, 1978.

Cronbach, L. J. Validity on parole: How can we go straight? *New Directions for Testing and Measurement*, 1980, *5*, 99–108.

Cronbach, L. J., & Furby, L. How we should measure "change"—or should we? *Psychological Bulletin*, 1970, *74*, 68–80.

Cronbach, L. J., & Gleser, G. C. *Psychological tests and personnel decisions*. Urbana: University of Illinois Press, 1965.

Cronbach, L. J., Gleser, G. C., Nanda, H., & Rajaratnam, N. *The dependability of behavioral measures: Theory of generalizability for scores and profiles*. New York: Wiley, 1972.

Cronbach, L. J., & Meehl, P. E. Construct validity in psychological tests. *Psychological Bulletin*, 1955, *52*, 281–302.

Dahlstrom, W. G. Invasion of privacy: How legitimate is the current concern over this issue? In J. N. Butcher (Ed.), *MMPI: Research developments and clinical applications*. New York: McGraw-Hill, 1969. (a)

Dahlstrom, W. G. Recurrent issues in the development of the MMPI. In J. N. Butcher (Ed.), *MMPI: Research developments and clinical applications*. New York: McGraw-Hill, 1969. (b)

Dahlstrom, W. G., & Welsh, G. S. *An MMPI handbook: A guide to use in clinical practice and research*. Minneapolis: University of Minnesota Press, 1960.

Dahlstrom, W. G., Welsh, G. S., & Dahlstrom, L. E. *An MMPI handbook. I: Clinical interpretation* (Rev. ed.). Minneapolis: University of Minnesota Press, 1972.

Dahlstrom, W. G., Welsh, G. S., & Dahlstrom, L. E. *An MMPI handbook. II: Research applications* (Rev. ed.). Minneapolis: University of Minnesota Press, 1975.

Damarin, F. Review of Bayley Scales of Infant Development. In O. K. Buros (Ed.), *The eighth mental measurements yearbook* (Vol. 1). Highland Park, N.J.: Gryphon Press, 1978. (a)

Damarin, F. Review of Cattell Infant Intelligence Scale. In O. K. Buros (Ed.), *The eighth mental measurements yearbook* (Vol. 1). Highland Park, N.J.: Gryphon Press, 1978. (b)

Dangel, H. L. *The biasing effect of pretest information on the WISC scores of mentally retarded children* (doctoral dissertation, Pennsylvania State University, 1970). (University Microfilms No. 71-16, 588)

Danish, S. J., & Smyer, M. A. Unintended consequences of requiring a license to help. *American Psychologist*, 1981, *36*, 13–21.

Darlington, R. B. Another look at "cultural fairness." *Journal of Educational Measurement*, 1971, *8*, 71–82.

Darlington, R. B. Cultural test bias: Comment on Hunter and Schmidt. *Psychological Bulletin*, 1978, *85*, 673–674.

Datta, L. Foreword. In E. E. Diamond (Ed.), *Issues of sex bias and sex fairness in career interest measurement*. Washington, D.C.: National Institutes of Education, 1975.

Davis, M. Spotlight on WISC-R: 1. A comparison of verbal scales on WISC and WISC-R. *Association of Educational Psychologists Journal*, 1978, *4*, 32–35.

Davis, R. B. *Error analysis in high school mathematics, conceived as information processing pathology*. Paper presented at the annual meeting of the American Educational Research Association, San Francisco, 1979.

Davis, R. B., Jockusch, E., & McKnight, C. Cognitive process in learning algebra. *Journal of Children's Mathematics Behavior*, 1978, *2*, 1–320.

Dearborn, G. Blots of ink in experimental psychology. *Psychological Review*, 1897, *4*, 390–391.

Dearborn, W. F., & Rothney, J. W. M. *Predicting the child's development*. New York: Sci-Art Publishers, 1941.

DeLeon, P. Synopsis of a speech. *The Professional Psychologist*, 1979, *3*, 20–21.

Delhees, K. H., & Cattell, R. B. The dimensions of pathology: Proof of their projection beyond the normal 16 PF source traits. *Personality*, 1971, *2*, 149–173. (a)

Delhees, K. H., & Cattell, R. B. *Manual for the Clinical Analysis Questionnaire (CAQ)*. Champaign, Ill.: Institute for Personality and Ability Testing, 1971. (b)

DeMoivre, A. *Approximatio ad summam terminorum binomii* $(a+b)^n$ *in seriem expansi*, 1733. (Cited in Stanley, 1971.)

Desiderato, O., & Koskinen, P. Anxiety, study habits, and academic achievement. *Journal of Counseling Psychology*, 1969, *16*, 162–165.

Diamond, E. E. Sex equality and measurement practices. *New Directions for Test and Measurement*, 1979, *3*, 61–78.

Dicken, C. F. Simulated patterns on the Edwards Personal Preference Schedule. *Journal of Applied Psychology*, 1959, *43*, 372–378.

DiMatteo, M. R. A socio-psychological analysis of physician-patient rapport: Toward a science of the art of medicine. *Journal of Social Issues*, 1979, *85*(1), 12–33.

Dittmann, A. T. The relationship between body movements and moods in interviews. *Journal of Consulting Psychology*, 1962, *26*, 480.

Dittmann, A. T., & Wynne, L. C. Linguistic techniques and the analysis of emotionality in interviews. *Journal of Abnormal and Social Psychology*, 1961, *63*, 201–204.

Doctor, R. Review of the Porteus Maze Test. In O. K. Buros (Ed.), *The seventh mental measurements yearbook* (Vol. 1). Highland Park, N.J.: Gryphon Press, 1972.

Doctor, R., & Altman, F. Worry and emotionality as components of test anxiety: Replication and further data. *Psychological Reports*, 1969, *24*, 563–568.

Doll, E. A. Review of developmental diagnosis: Normal and abnormal child development: Clinical methods and practical applications. *American Journal of Psychology*, 1942, *55*, 611–612.

Donahue, D., & Sattler, J. M. Personality variables affecting WAIS scores. *Journal of Consulting and Clinical Psychology*, 1971, *36*, 441.

Doppelt, J. E., & Wallace, W. L. Standardization of the Wechsler Adult Intelligence Scale for older persons. *Journal of Abnormal and Social Psychology*, 1955, *51*, 312–330.

Dorans, N. J., & Drasgow, F. A note on cross-validating prediction equations. *Journal of Applied Psychology*, 1980, *65*, 728–730.

Dörken, H. Coming of age legislatively in 21 steps. *American Psychologist*, 1981, *36*, 165–173.

Drake, L. E. A social I. E. scale for the MMPI. *Journal of Applied Psychology*, 1946, *30*, 51–54.

DuBois, P. H. A test-dominated society: China 115 B.C.–1905 A.D. In A. Anastasi (Ed.), *Testing problems in perspective*. Washington, D.C.: American Council on Education, 1966.

DuBois, P. H. *A history of psychological testing*. Boston: Allyn & Bacon, 1970.

DuBois, P. H. Increase in educational opportunity through measurement. In *Proceedings of the 1971 Invitational Conference on Testing Problems*. Princeton, N.J.: Educational Testing Service, 1972. (a)

DuBois, P. H. Review of the SAT. In O. K. Buros (Ed.), *The seventh mental measurements yearbook* (Vol. 1). Highland Park, N.J.: Gryphon Press, 1972. (b)

Duncan, S., Jr. Paralinguistic analysis of psychotherapy interviews. *Proceedings of the 74th Annual Convention of the American Psychological Association*, 1966, *1*, 191–192.

Dunn, J. A. Review of the Goodenough-Harris Drawing Test. In O. K. Buros (Ed.), *The seventh mental measurements yearbook* (Vol. 1). Highland Park, N.J.: Gryphon Press, 1972.

Dunn, L. M. *Peabody Picture Vocabulary Test manual*. Minneapolis: American Guidance Service, 1959.

Dunn, L. M. *Expanded manual for the Peabody Picture Vocabulary Test*. Minneapolis: American Guidance Service, 1965.

Dunnette, M. D. The assessment of managerial talent. In F. R. Wickert & D. E. McFarland (Eds.), *Measuring executive effectiveness*. New York: Appleton-Century-Crofts, 1967.

Dunnette, M. D. *Validity study results for jobs relevant to the petroleum refining industry*. Washington, D.C.: American Petroleum Institute, 1972.

Dunnette, M. D. Aptitudes, abilities, and skills. In M. D. Dunnette (Ed.), *Handbook of industrial and organizational psychology*. Chicago: Rand McNally, 1976.

Dunnette, M. D., & Borman, W. C. Personnel selection and classification systems. *Annual Review of Psychology*, 1979, *30*, 477–525.

Ebel, R. L. *Essentials of educational measurement*. Englewood Cliffs, N.J.: Prentice-Hall, 1972.

Ebel, R. L. Comments on some problems of employment testing. *Personnel Psychology*, 1977, *30*, 55–63.

Edwards, A. L. *Manual for the Edwards Personal Preference Schedule*. New York: Psychological Corporation, 1954.

Edwards, A. L. *Techniques of attitude scale construction*. New York: Appleton-Century-Crofts, 1957.

Edwards, A. L. *Edwards Personal Preference Schedule*. New York: Psychological Corporation, 1959.

Edwards, A. L. *The measurement of personality traits by scales and inventories*. New York: Holt, Rinehart & Winston, 1970.

Edwards, A. L., & Abbott, R. D. Relationships among the Edwards Personality Inventory Scales, the Edwards Personal Preference Schedule, and the Personality Research Form Scales. *Journal of Consulting and Clinical Psychology*, 1973, *10*, 27 32.

Edwards, G. A. Anxiety correlates of the WAIS. *California Journal of Educational Research*, 1966, *17*, 144–147.

Egeland, B. R. Examiner expectancy: Effects on the scoring of the WISC. *Psychology in the Schools*, 1969, *6*, 313–315.

Egeland, B. R. Review of Columbia Mental Maturity Scale. In O. K. Buros (Ed.), *The eighth mental measurements yearbook* (Vol. 1). Highland Park, N.J.: Gryphon Press, 1978.

Eichler, R. M. A comparison of the Rorschach and Behn-Rorschach inkblot tests. *Journal of Consulting Psychology*, 1951, *15*, 185–189.

Eisenberger, R. Is there a deprivation-satiation function for social approval? *Psychological Bulletin*, 1970, *74*, 255–275.

Eisenberger, R. Explanation of rewards that do not reduce tissue need. *Psychological Bulletin*, 1972, *77*, 319–339.

Eisenberger, R., Kaplan, R. M., & Singer, R. D. Decremental and nondecremental effects of noncontingent social approval. *Journal of Personality and Social Psychology*, 1974, *30*, 716–722.

Ekman, P. Communication through nonverbal behavior: A source of information about an interpersonal relationship. In S. S. Tomkins & C. E. Izard (Eds.), *Affect, cognition, and personality*. New York: Springer, 1965. (a)

Ekman, P. Differential communication of affect by head and body cues. *Journal of Personality and Social Psychology*, 1965, *2*, 725–735. (b)

Ekman, P., & Friesen, W. V. Nonverbal behavior in psychotherapy research. In J. Shlien, H. Hunt, J. D. Matarazzo, & C. Savage (Eds.), *Research in psychotherapy* (Vol. 3). Washington, D.C.: American Psychological Association, 1968.

Ekren, U. W. *The effect of experimenter knowledge of subjects' scholastic standing on the performance of a task*. Unpublished master's thesis, Marquette University, 1962.

Elashoff, J., & Snow, R. E. (Eds.), *Pygmalion revisited*. Worthington, Ohio: C. A. Jones, 1971.

Ellis, A. The validity of personality questionnaires. *Psychological Bulletin*, 1946, *43*, 385–440.

Ellis, B. *Basic concepts in measurement*. London: Cambridge University Press, 1966.

Endler, N. S. The person versus the situation—a pseudo issue? A response to Alker. *Journal of Personality*, 1973, *41*, 287–303.

Endler, N. S., & Hunt, J. McV. S-R Inventories of hostility and comparisons of the proportions of variance from persons, responses, and situations for hostility and anxiousness. *Journal of Personality and Social Psychology*, 1968, *9*, 309–315.

Endler, N. S., & Magnusson, D. *Interactional psychology and personality*. Washington, D.C.: Hemisphere, 1976.

Epstein, L. Psychophysiological measurement in assessment. In M. Hersen & A. S. Bellack (Eds.), *Behavioral assessment*. New York: Pergamon, 1976.

Epstein, S. The self-concept: A review and the proposal of an integrated theory of personality. In E. Stauk (Ed.), *Personality: Basic issues and current research*. Englewood Cliffs, N.J.: Prentice-Hall, 1979.

Erdberg, S. P. *MMPI differences associated with sex, race, and residence in a Southern sample*. Unpublished doctoral dissertation, University of Alabama, 1969.

Escalona, S. K., & Moriarty, A. Prediction of schoolage intelligence from infant tests. *Child Development*, 1961, *32*, 597–605.

Exner, J. E. *The Rorschach: A comprehensive system*. New York: Wiley, 1974.

Exner, J. E. Projective techniques. In I. B. Weiner (Ed.), *Clinical methods in psychology*. New York: Wiley, 1976.

Exner, J. E. But it's only an inkblot. *Journal of Personality Assessment*, 1980, *44*, 562–577.

Exner, J. E., Gillespie, R., Viglione, D., & Coleman, M. Some intercorrelational data concerning Rorschach structural variables. *Journal of Personality Assessment*, 1982, in press.

Exner, J. E., & Weiner, I. B. *The Rorschach: A comprehensive system. III: Assessment of children and adolescents*. New York: Wiley, 1981.

Eysenck, H. J. *The structure of human personality*. London: Methuen, 1952.

Eysenck, H. J. Review of the Rorschach. In O. K. Buros (Ed.), *The fifth mental measurements yearbook*. Highland Park, N.J.: Gryphon Press, 1959.

Eysenck, H. J. Intelligence assessment: A theoretical and experimental approach. *British Journal of Educational Psychology*, 1967, *37*, 81–98.

Eysenck, H. J., & Rochman, S. *The causes and cures of neurosis: An introduction to modern behavior therapy based on learning theory and the principles of conditioning*. San Diego: Knapp, 1965.

Feldman, M. J., & Corah, N. L. Social desirability and the forced choice method. *Journal of Consulting Psychology*, 1960, *24*, 480–482.

Feldman, S. E., & Sullivan, D. S. Factors mediating the effects of enhanced rapport on children's performance. *Journal of Consulting and Clinical Psychology*, 1971, *36*, 302.

Finger, R., & Galassi, J. P. Effects of modifying cognitive versus emotionality responses in the treatment of test anxiety. *Journal of Consulting and Clinical Psychology*, 1977, *45*, 280–287.

Firestone, M. H. Review of developmental diagnosis: Normal and abnormal child development: Clinical methods and practical applications. *American Journal of Psychiatry*, 1942, *99*, 470.

Flanagan, J. C. The critical incident technique. *Psychological Bulletin*, 1954, *51*, 327–358.

Flanagan, J. C. The PLAN system of individualizing education. *NCME Measurement in Education*, 1971, *2*(2), 1–8.

Flaugher, R. L. *Bias in testing: A review and discussion* (TM Rep. 36). Princeton, N.J.: ERIC Clearinghouse on Tests, Measurements, and Evaluation, 1974.

Flaugher, R. L. The many definitions of test bias. *American Psychologist*, 1978, *33*, 671–679.

Flaugher, R. L., & Schrader, W. B. *Eliminating differentially difficult items as an approach to test bias* (RB-78-4). Princeton, N.J.: Educational Testing Service, 1978.

Fleiss, J. L. Measuring nominal scale agreement among many raters. *Psychological Bulletin*, 1971, *76*, 378–382.

Foltz, D. Courts take psychologists' side in copyright, confidentiality fight. *APA Monitor*, 1981, June/July, 13.

Ford, M. *The application of the Rorschach test to young children*. Minneapolis: University of Minnesota Press, 1946.

Forrester, B. J., & Klaus, R. A. The effect of race of the examiner on intelligence test scores of Negro kindergarten children. *Peabody Papers in Human Development*, 1964, *2*, 1–7.

Fosberg, I. A. An experimental study of the reliability of the Rorschach psychodiagnostic technique. *Rorschach Research Exchange*, 1941, *5*, 72–84.

Fowler, R. D., & Coyle, F. A. Collegiate normative data on MMPI content scales. *Journal of Clinical Psychology*, 1969, *25*, 62–63.

Fox, L. H. Identification of the academically gifted. *American Psychologist*, 1981, *36*, 1103–1111.

Frank, G. H. The measurement of personality from the Wechsler tests. In B. A. Mahrer (Ed.), *Progress in experimental personality research*. New York: Academic Press, 1970.

Frank, G. H. Measures of intelligence and conceptual thinking. In I. B. Weiner (Ed.), *Clinical methods in psychology*. New York: Wiley, 1976.

Frank, L. K. Projective methods for the study of personality. *Journal of Psychology*, 1939, *8*, 343–389.

Fraser, E. D. Review of the Stanford-Binet intelligence scale, third revision. In O. K. Buros (Ed.), *The sixth mental measurements yearbook*. Highland Park, N.J.: Gryphon Press, 1965.

Frederiksen, C. Abilities transfer and information retrieval in verbal learning. *Multivariate Behavioral Research Monographs*, 1969, 1–82.

Freedman, J. L., Sears, D. O., & Carlsmith, J. M. *Social psychology* (2nd ed.). Englewood Cliffs, N.J.: Prentice-Hall, 1978.

French, J. L. *Manual: Pictorial Test of Intelligence*. Boston: Houghton Mifflin, 1964.

Freud, S. Fragment of an analysis of a case of hysteria. In *The standard edition of the complete psychological works of Sigmund Freud* (Vol. 7). London: Hogarth, 1953. (Originally published, 1905.)

Friedman, M., & Rosenman, R. H. *Type A behavior and your heart*. New York: Knopf, 1974.

Friedman, M., Rosenman, R. H., & Byers, S. O. Serum lipids and conjunctional circulation after fat ingestion in men exhibiting Type A behavior pattern. *Circulation*, 1964, *29*, 874–886.

Galton, F. *Inquiries into human faculty and its development*. London: Macmillan, 1883.

Gamble, K. R. The Holtzman Inkblot Technique: A review. *Psychological Bulletin*, 1972, *77*, 172–194.

Garcia, J. The logic and limits of mental aptitude testing. *American Psychologist*, 1981, *36*, 1172–1180.

Gardener, B. O., & Swiger, M. K. Developmental status of two groups of infants released for adoption. *Child Development*, 1958, *29*, 521–530.

Garfield, S. L., & Sineps, J. An appraisal of Taulbee and Sisson's "configurational analysis of MMPI profiles of psychiatric groups." *Journal of Consulting Psychology*, 1959, *23*, 333–335.

Garrett, E. S., Price, A. C., & Deabler, H. L. Diagnostic testing for cortical brain impairment. *American Medical Association Archives of Neurological Psychiatry*, 1957, *77*, 223–225.

Geer, J. H. The development of a scale to measure fear. *Behaviour Research and Therapy*, 1965, *3*, 45–53.

Gehman, I. H., & Matyas, R. P. Stability of the WISC and Binet tests. *Journal of Consulting Psychology*, 1956, *20*, 150–152.

Gendlin, E. T. Focusing ability in psychotherapy, personality, and creativity. In J. Shlien, H. Hunt, J. D. Matarazzo, & C. Savage (Eds.), *Research in psychotherapy* (Vol. 3). Washington, D.C.: American Psychological Association, 1968.

Gesell, A. Monthly increments of development in infancy. *Journal of Genetic Psychology*, 1925, *32*, 203–208.

Gesell, A., & Amatruda, C. S. *Developmental diagnosis: Normal and abnormal child development: Clinical methods and practical applications*. New York: Paul B. Hoebler, 1941.

Gesell, A., & Amatruda, C. S. *Developmental diagnosis: Normal and abnormal child development: Clinical methods and pediatric applications* (2nd ed.). New York: Paul B. Hoebler, 1947.

Gesell, A., Halverson, H. M., Thompson, H., Ilg, F. L., Castner, B. M., Ames, L. B., & Amatruda, C. S. *The first five years of life: A guide to the study of the preschool child*. New York: Harper & Row, 1940.

Gianetti, R. Z., Klinger, D. E., Johnson, J. H., & Williams, T. A. The potential for dynamic assessment systems using on-line computer technology. *Behavior Research Methods and Instrumentation*, 1976, *8*, 101–103.

Giannell, A. S., & Freeburne, C. M. The comparative validity of the WAIS and Stanford-Binet with college freshmen. *Educational and Psychological Measurement*, 1963, *23*, 557–567.

Gibby, R. G., Miller, D. R., & Walker, E. L. The examiner's influence on the Rorschach protocol. *Journal of Consulting Psychology*, 1953, *17*, 425–428.

Gilberstadt, H., & Duker, J. *A handbook for clinical and actuarial MMPI interpretation*. Philadelphia: Saunders, 1965.

Gillingham, W. H. *An investigation of examiner influence on Wechsler Intelligence Scale for Children scores* (doctoral dissertation, Michigan State University, 1970). (University Microfilms No. 70–20, 458)

Gilmore, S. K. *The counselor-in-training*. New York: Appleton-Century-Crofts, 1973.

Glass, D. C. *Behavior patterns, stress, and coronary disease*. Hillsdale, N.J.: Erlbaum, 1977.

Goddard, H. H. The Binet and Simon tests of intellectual capacity. *Training School*, 1908, *5*, 3–9.

Goddard, H. H. A revision of the Binet scale. *Training School*, 1911, *8*, 56–62.

Goetcheus, G. *The effects of instructions and examiners on the Rorschach*. Unpublished master's thesis, Bowling Green State University, 1967.

Gokhale, D. V., & Kullback, S. *The information in contingency tables*. New York: Marcel Dekker, 1978.

Goldberg, L. R. Man versus model of man: A rationale, plus some evidence for a method of improving on clinical inferences. *Psychological Bulletin*. 1970, *73*, 422–432.

Goldberg, L. R. California Psychological Inventory. In O. K. Buros (Ed.), *The seventh mental measurements yearbook* (Vol. 1). Highland Park, N.J.: Gryphon Press, 1972. (a)

Goldberg, L. R. Parameters of personality inventory construction and utilization: A comparison of prediction strategies and tactics. *Multivariate Behavioral Research Monographs*, 1972, *7*(2). (b)

Goldberg, L. R. Objective personality tests and measures. *Annual Review of Psychology*, 1974, *25*, 343–366.

Goldfried, M. R. Behavioral assessment. In I. B. Weiner (Ed.), *Clinical methods in psychology*. New York: Wiley-Interscience, 1976.

Goldfried, M. R., & Kent, R. N. Traditional versus behavioral personality assessment: A comparison of methodological and theoretical assumptions. *Psychological Bulletin*, 1972, *77*, 409–420.

Goldfried, M. R., & Sobocinski, D. Effect of irrational beliefs on emotional arousal. *Journal of Consulting and Clinical Psychology*, 1975, *43*, 504–510.

Goldman, R. D. Hidden opportunities in the prediction of college grades for different subgroups. *Journal of Educational Measurement*, 1973, *10*(3), 205–210.

Goldman, R. D., & Hartig, L. The WISC may not be a valid predictor of school performance for primary-grade minority children. *American Journal of Mental Deficiency*, 1976, *80*, 583–587.

Goldman, R. D., & Hewitt, B. *Culture-free selection of professional school students*. Unpublished manuscript, University of California, Riverside, 1976.

Goldstein, A. P., & Simonson, N. R. Social psychological approaches to psychotherapy research. In A. E. Bergin & S. L. Garfield (Eds.), *Handbook of psychotherapy and behavior change*. New York: Wiley, 1971.

Goodman, J. The diagnostic fallacy: A critique of Jane Mercer's concept of mental retardation. *Journal of School Psychology*, 1977, *15*, 197–206.

Goodman, J. "Ignorance" versus "stupidity"—the basic disagreement. *School Psychology Digest*, 1979, *8*(2), 218–223.

Goodman, L. A., & Kruskal, W. H. Measures of association for cross-classification. IV: Simplification of asymtotic variances. *Journal of the American Statistical Association*, 1972, *67*, 415–421.

Gordon, E. W., & Terrell, M. D. The changed social context of testing. *American Psychologist*, 1981, *36*, 1167–1171.

Gordon, L. V., & Stapleton, E. S. Fakability of a forced-choice personality test under realistic high school employment conditions. *Journal of Applied Psychology*, 1956, *40*, 258–262.

Gorsuch, R. L. *Factor analysis*. Philadelphia: Saunders, 1974.

Gottfredson, L. S. Construct validity of Holland's occupational typology in terms of prestige, census, Department of Labor, and other classification systems. *Journal of Applied Psychology*, 1980, *65*, 697–714.

Gough, H. G. *California Psychological Inventory manual*. Palo Alto, Calif.: Consulting Psychologists Press, 1957.

Gough, H. G. The adjective checklist as a personality assessment research technique. *Psychological Reports*, 1960, *6*, 107–122.

Gough, H. G. Conceptual analysis of psychological test scores and other diagnostic variables. *Journal of Abnormal Psychology*, 1965, *70*, 294–302.

Gough, H. G. An interpreter's syllabus for the California Psychological Inventory. In P. McReynolds (Ed.), *Advances in psychological assessment* (Vol. 1). Palo Alto, Calif.: Science and Behavior Books, 1968.

Gough, H. G. *California Psychological Inventory, revised manual*. Palo Alto, Calif.: Consulting Psychologists Press, 1969.

Graham, F. K., & Kendall, B. S. Performance of brain-damaged cases on a Memory-for-Designs test. *Journal of Abnormal Social Psychology*, 1946, *41*, 303–314.

Graham, F. K., & Kendall, B. S. Memory-for-Designs test: Revised general manual. *Perceptual Motor Skills*, 1960, *11*, 147–190.

Graham, J. R. *The MMPI: A practical guide*. New York: Oxford University Press, 1977.

Green, B. F. In defense of measurement. *American Psychologist*, 1978, *33*, 664–670.

Green, B. F. A primer of testing. *American Psychologist*, 1981, *36*, 1001–1011.

Guertin, W. H., Ladd, C. E., Frank, G. H., Rabin, A. I., & Hiester, D. S. Research with the Wechsler Intelligence Scales for Adults: 1960–1965. *Psychological Bulletin*, 1966, *66*, 385–409.

Guertin, W. H., Ladd, C. E., Frank, G. H., Rabin, A. I., & Hiester, D. S. Research with the Wechsler Intelligence Scales for Adults: 1965–1970. *Psychological Record*, 1971, *21*, 289–339.

Guertin, W. H., Rabin, A. I., Frank, G. H., & Ladd, C. E. Research with the Wechsler Intelligence Scales for Adults: 1955–1960. *Psychological Bulletin*, 1962, *59*, 1–26.

Guilford, J. P. *An inventory of factors*. Beverly Hills, Calif.: Sheridan Supply, 1940.

Guilford, J. P. *Psychometric methods* (2nd ed.). New York: McGraw-Hill, 1954.

Guilford, J. P. *Personality*. New York: McGraw-Hill, 1959.

Guilford, J. P., & Fruchter, B. *Fundamental statistics in psychology and education* (5th ed.). New York: McGraw-Hill, 1973.

Guilford, J. P., & Martin, H. G. *The Guilford-Martin inventory of factors: GAMIN: Manual of directions and norms*. Beverly Hills, Calif.: Sheridan Supply, 1943.

Guilford, J. P., & Zimmerman, W. S. *The Guilford Temperament Survey: Manual of instructions and interpretations*. Beverly Hills, Calif.: Sheridan Supply, 1949.

Guilford, J. P., & Zimmerman, W. S. Fourteen dimensions of temperament. *Psychological Monographs*, 1956, *70*, No. 10.

Guion, R. M. Recruiting, selection and job placement. In M. D. Dunnette (Ed.), *Handbook of industrial and organizational psychology*. Chicago: Rand McNally, 1976.

Guthrie, R. V. *Even the rat was white: A historical view of psychology*. New York: Harper & Row, 1976.

Guttman, L. Relation of scalogram analysis to other techniques. In S. A. Stouffer et al. (Eds.), *Measurement and prediction*. Princeton, N.J.: Princeton University Press, 1950.

Gynther, M. D. White norms and Black MMPIs: A prescription for discrimination? *Psychological Bulletin*, 1972, *78*, 386–402.

Gynther, M. D., Fowler, R. D., & Erdberg, P. False positives galore: The application of standard MMPI criteria to a rural, isolated, Negro sample. *Journal of Clinical Psychology*, 1971, *27*, 234–237.

Gynther, M. D., & Gynther, R. A. Personality inventories. In I. B. Weiner (Ed.), *Clinical methods in psychology*. New York: Wiley, 1976.

Gynther, M. D., & Shimkunas, A. M. Age, intelligence, and MMPI F scores. *Journal of Consulting Psychology*, 1965, *29*, 383–388.

Gynther, M. D., & Shimkunas, A. M. Age and MMPI performance. *Journal of Consulting Psychology*, 1966, *30*, 118–121.

Haber, R. H. Perception and thought: An information processing analysis. In J. I. Voss (Ed.), *Approaches to thought*. Columbus, Ohio: Charles E. Merrill, 1969.

Hall, C. S., & Lindzey, G. *Theories of personality* (2nd ed.). New York: Wiley, 1970.

Hall, J. C. Correlation of a modified form of Raven's Progressive Matrices (1938) with the Wechsler Adult Intelligence Scale. *Journal of Consulting Psychology*, 1957, *21*, 23–26.

Hall, V. C., Huppertz, J. W., & Levi, A. Attention and achievement exhibited by middle and lower-class Black and White elementary school boys. *Journal of Educational Psychology*, 1977, *69*, 115–120.

Hall, W. B., & MacKinnon, D. W. Personality inventories as predictors of creativity among architects. *Journal of Applied Psychology*, 1969, *53*, 322–326.

Hambleton, R. K. Validation of criterion-referenced test score interpretations and standard setting methods. In R. A. Berk (Ed.), *Criterion-referenced measurement: The state of the art*. Baltimore: Johns Hopkins University Press, 1980.

Haney, W. Validity, vaudeville, and values: A short history of social concerns over standardized testing. *American Psychologist*, 1981, *36*, 1021–1034.

Harari, H., & Kaplan, R. M. *Psychology: Personal and social adjustment*, New York: Harper & Row, 1977.

Hardy, J. B., Welcher, D. W., Mellits, E. D., & Kagan, J. Pitfalls in the measurement of intelligence: Are standardized intelligence tests valid for measuring the intellectual potential of urban children? *Journal of Psychology*, 1976, *94*, 43–51.

Hardyck, C. D., & Petrinovich, L. F. *Statistics for the behavioral sciences* (2nd ed.). Philadelphia: Saunders, 1976.

Hargadon, F. Test and college admissions. *American Psychologist*, 1981, *36*, 1112–1119.

Harman, H. H. *Modern factor analysis* (2nd ed.). Chicago: University of Chicago Press, 1967.

Harmon, L. W., Cole, N., Wysong, E., & Zytowski, D. G. AMEG commission report on sex bias in interest measurement. *Measurement and Evaluation in Guidance*, 1973, *6*, 171–177.

Harris, R. J. *A primer of multivariate statistics*. New York: Academic Press, 1975.

Harrison, R. Studies in the use and validity of the Thematic Apperception Test with mentally disordered patients. II: A quantitative validity study. III: Validation by blind analysis. *Character and Personality*, 1940, *9*, 122–133, 134–138.

Harrison, R. Thematic apperceptive methods. In B. Wolman (Ed.), *Handbook of clinical psychology*. New York: McGraw-Hill, 1965.

Harrison, R., & Rotter, J. B. A note on the reliability of the Thematic Apperception Test. *Journal of Abnormal and Social Psychology*, 1945, *40*, 97–99.

Harrower, M. R., & Steiner, M. E. *Psychodiagnostic inkblots*. New York: Grune & Stratton, 1945.

Hart, B., & Spearman, C. General ability, its existence and nature. *British Journal of Psychology*, 1912, *5*, 51–84.

Hartlage, L. C., & Steele, C. T. WISC and WISC-R correlates of academic achievement. *Psychology in the Schools*, 1977, *14*, 15–18.

Hartmann, D. P. Considerations in the choice of interobserver reliability estimates. *Journal of Applied Behavior Analysis*, 1977, *10*, 103–116.

Hase, H. D., & Goldberg, L. R. Comparative validity of different strategies of constructing personality inventory scales. *Psychological Bulletin*, 1967, *67*, 231–248.

Hathaway, S. R. A coding system for MMPI profiles. *Journal of Consulting Psychology*, 1947, *11*, 334–337.

Hathaway, S. R., & McKinley, J. C. A multiphasic personality schedule (Minnesota). I: Construction of the schedule. *Journal of Psychology*, 1940, *10*, 249–254.

Hathaway, S. R., & McKinley, J. C. *Manual for the Minnesota Multiphasic Personality Inventory*. New York: Psychological Corporation, 1943.

Hathaway, S. R., & McKinley, J. C. *Minnesota Multiphasic Personality Inventory* (Rev. ed.). New York: Psychological Corporation, 1951.

Hathaway, S. R., & McKinley, J. C. *Minnesota Multiphasic Personality Inventory, revised manual*. New York: Psychological Corporation, 1967.

Hattie, J. Should creativity tests be administered under test like conditions? An empirical study of three alternative conditions. *Journal of Educational Psychology*, 1980, *72*, 87–98.

Healy, W., & Fernald, G. M. Tests for practical mental classification. *Psychological Monographs*, 1911, *13*, No. 2.

Hebb, D. O. Reply irrelevant? *American Psychologist*, 1981, *36*, 423–424.

Heider, F. Social perception and phenomenal causation. *Psychological Review*, 1944, *51*, 358–374.

Heider, F. *The psychology of interpersonal relations*. New York: Wiley, 1958.

Heilbrun, A. B., Jr. Edwards Personal Preference Schedule. In O. K. Buros (Ed.), *The seventh mental measurements yearbook* (Vol. 1). Highland Park, N.J.: Gryphon Press, 1972.

Heller, K. Ambiguity in the interview interaction. In J. Shlien, H. Hunt, J. D. Matarazzo, & C. Savage (Eds.), *Research in psychotherapy* (Vol. 3). Washington, D.C.: American Psychological Association, 1968.

Heller, K. Laboratory interview research as an analogue to treatment. In A. E. Bergin & S. L. Garfield (Eds.), *Handbook of psychotherapy and behavior change*. New York: Wiley, 1971.

Heller, K., Davis, J. D., & Myers, R. A. The effects of interviewer style in a standardized interview. *Journal of Consulting Psychology*, 1966, *30*, 501–508.

Henderson, N. B., Fay, W. H., Lindemann, S. J., & Clarkson, Q. D. Will the IQ test ban decrease the effectiveness of reading prediction? *Journal of Educational Psychology*, 1973, *65*, 345–355.

Henrichs, T. Objective configural rules for discriminating MMPI profiles in a psychiatric population. *Journal of Clinical Psychology*, 1964, *20*, 157–159.

Herring, J. P. *Herring revision of the Binet-Simon tests*. Yonkers, N.Y.: World Book, 1922.

Hermstein, R. J. Try again Dr. Albee. *American Psychologist*, 1981, *36*, 424–425.

Hersen, M. Fear scale norms for an in-patient population. *Journal of Clinical Psychology*, 1971, *27*, 375–378.

Hersh, J. B. Effects of referral information on testers. *Journal of Consulting and Clinical Psychology*, 1971, *37*, 116–122.

Hertz, M. R. Discussion on "Some recent Rorschach problems." *Rorschach Research Exchange*, 1937, *2*, 53–65.

Hertz, M. R. Scoring the Rorschach inkblot test. *Journal of Genetic Psychology*, 1938, *52*, 16–64.

Hiscock, M. Imagery assessment through self report: What do imagery questionnaires measure? *Journal of Consulting and Clinical Psychology*, 1978, *46*, 223–230.

Hochreich, D. J., & Rotter, J. B. Have college students become less trusting? *Journal of Personality and Social Psychology*, 1970, *15*, 211–214.

Hodges, W., & Spielberger, C. Digit span: An indication of trait or state anxiety? *Journal of Consulting and Clinical Psychology*, 1969, *33*, 430–434.

Hodos, W., & Campbell, C. B. G. Scala naturae: Why there is no theory in comparative psychology. *Psychological Review*, 1969, *76*, 337–350.

Hoffman, H., Loper, R. G., & Kammeier, M. L. Identifying future alcoholics with MMPI alcoholism scales. *Quarterly Journal of Studies on Alcohol*, 1974, *35*, 490–498.

Hoffman, K. I., & Lundberg, G. D. A comparison of computer-monitored group tests with paper-and-pencil tests. *Educational and Psychological Measurement*, 1976, *36*, 791–809.

Hogan, R., DeSoto, C. B., & Solano, C. Traits, tests, and personality research. *American Psychologist*, 1977, *32*, 255–264.

Holland, J. L. *Making vocational choices: A theory of careers*. Englewood Cliffs, N.J.: Prentice-Hall, 1973.

Holland, J. L. *Manual for the Vocational Preference Inventory*. Palo Alto, Calif.: Consulting Psychologists Press, 1975.

Holland, J. L., & Gottfredson, G. D. Using a typology of persons and environments to explain careers: Some extensions and clarifications. *Counseling Psychologist*, 1976, *6*, 20–29.

Holland, J. L., & Nichols, R. C. Prediction of academic and extra-curricular achievements in college. *Journal of Educational Psychology*, 1964, 55, 55–65.

Hollingworth, H. L. *Judging human character*. New York: Appleton-Century-Crofts, 1922.

Holroyd, K. A. Stress, coping, and the treatment of stress-related illness. In J. R. McNamara (Ed.), *Behavioral approaches to medicine: Application and analysis*. New York: Plenum, 1979.

Holt, R. R. Diagnostic testing: Present status and future prospects. *Journal of Nervous and Mental Disease*. 1967, 141, 444–464.

Holt, R. R. Yet another look at clinical and statistical prediction: Or, is clinical psychology worthwhile? *American Psychologist*, 1970, 25, 337–349.

Holtzman, W. H., Thorpe, J. S., Swartz, J. D., & Herron, E. W. *Inkblot perception and personality*. Austin: University of Texas Press, 1961.

Holzberg, J. D., & Belmont, L. The relationship between factors on the Wechsler-Bellevue and Rorschach having a common psychological rationale. *Journal of Consulting Psychology*, 1952, 16, 23–30.

Holzberg, J. D., & Wexler, M. Predictability of performance and the Rorschach test. *Journal of Consulting Psychology*, 1950, 14, 395–399.

Hotelling, H. Analysis of a complex statistical variable into principal components. *Journal of Educational Psychology*, 1933, 24, 417–441, 498–520.

Howard, A., & Shoemaker, D. J. An evaluation of the Memory-for-Designs test. *Journal of Consulting Psychology*, 1954, 18, 266.

Howes, R. J. The Rorschach: Does it have a future. *Journal of Personality Assessment*, 1981, 45, 339–351.

Hunt, H. F. Testing for psychological deficit. In D. Brower & L. E. Abt (Eds.), *Progress in clinical psychology* (Vol. 1). New York: Grune & Stratton, 1952.

Hunt, T. V. Review of McCarthy Scales of Children's Abilities. In O. K. Buros (Ed.), *The eighth mental measurements yearbook* (Vol. 1). Highland Park, N.J.: Gryphon Press, 1978.

Hunter, J. E., & Schmidt, F. L. Critical analysis of statistical and ethical implications of various definitions of test bias. *Psychological Bulletin*, 1976, 83, 1053–1071.

Hunter, J. E., & Schmidt, F. L. Bias in defining test bias: Reply to Darlington. *Psychological Bulletin*, 1978, 85, 675–676.

Hyman, H. H., & Sheatsley, T. B. The authoritarian personality: A methodological critique. In R. Christie & M. Johoda (Eds.), *Studies in the scope and method of "The Authoritarian Personality."* New York: Free Press, 1954.

Ihli, K. K., & Garlington, W. K. A comparison of group vs. individual desensitization of test anxiety. *Behaviour Research and Therapy*, 1969, 7, 207–209.

Ingram, R. E. *The GREs: Are we weighing them too heavily in graduate psychology admissions?* Unpublished manuscript, University of Kansas, 1980.

Iscoe, I., & Spielberger, C. D. *Community psychology: Perspectives in training and research*. New York: Appleton-Century-Crofts, 1970.

Jackson, D. N. *Personality Research Form manual*. Goshen, N.Y.: Research Psychologists Press, 1967.

Jackson, D. N. A sequential system for personality scale development. In C. D. Spielberger (Ed.), *Current topics in clinical and community psychology* (Vol. 2). New York: Academic Press, 1970.

Jackson, D. N., & Messick, S. (Eds.). *Problems in human assessment*. New York: McGraw-Hill, 1967.

Jaffe, J. Computer assessment of dyadic interaction rules from chronographic data. In J. Shlien, H. Hunt, J. D. Matarazzo, & C. Savage (Eds.), *Research in psychotherapy* (Vol. 3). Washington, D.C.: American Psychological Association, 1968.

Jenkins, C. D., Rosenman, R. H., & Zyzanski, S. J. *The Jenkins activity survey for health prediction*. Boston: Authors, 1972.

Jenkins, C. D., Zyzanski, S. J., & Rosenman, R. H. Risk of new myocardial infarction in middle-aged men with manifest coronary heart disease. *Circulation*, 1976, 53, 342–347.

Jensen, A. R. Review of the Rorschach. In O. K. Buros (Ed.), *The sixth mental measurements yearbook*. Highland Park, N.J.: Gryphon Press, 1965.

Jensen, A. R. How much can we boost IQ and scholastic achievement? *Harvard Educational Review*, 1969, 39, 1–23.

Jensen, A. R. A theory of primary and secondary familial mental retardation. In N. R. Ellis (Ed.), *International review of research in mental retardation* (Vol. 4). New York: Academic Press, 1970.

Jensen, A. R. *Genetics and education*. New York: Harper & Row, 1972.

Jensen, A. R. *Bias in mental testing*. New York: Free Press, 1980.

Johansson, C. B. *Manual for the Career Assessment Inventory*. Minneapolis: National Computer Systems, 1976.

Johansson, C. B., & Johansson, J. C. *Manual supplement for the Career Assessment Inventory*. Minneapolis: National Computer Systems, 1978.

Johnson, O. G., & Bommarito, J. W. *Tests and measurements in child development: A handbook*. San Francisco: Jossey-Bass, 1971.

Jones, E. E. The rocky road from acts to dispositions. *American Psychologist*, 1979, *34*, 107–117.

Jones, E. E., & Davis, X. E. From acts to dispositions: The attribution process in person perception. In L. Berkowitz (Ed.), *Advances in experimental social psychology* (Vol. 2). New York: Academic Press, 1965.

Jones, E. E., & Nisbett, R. E. *The actor and observer: Divergent perceptions of the causes of behavior*. Morristown, N.J.: General Learning Press, 1971.

Jones, R. A. *A factored measure of Ellis' irrational belief system with personality and maladjustment correlates*. Unpublished doctoral dissertation, Texas Technological College, 1968.

Kagan, J., & Freeman, M. Relation of childhood intelligence, maternal behaviors, and social class to behavior during adolescence. *Child Development*, 1963, *34*, 899–911.

Kagan, J., Moss, H. A., & Siegel, I. E. Psychological significance of styles of conceptualization. *Monographs of the Society for Research in Child Development*, 1963, *28*(2, Serial No. 86), 73–124.

Kaiser, H. F. A modified stanine scale. *Journal of Experimental Education*, 1958, *26*, 261.

Kallingal, A. The prediction of grades for Black and White students at Michigan State University. *Journal of Educational Measurement*, 1971, *8*, 263–265.

Kallman, W. M., & Feuerstein, M. Psychophysiological procedures. In A. R. Ciminero, K. S. Calhoun, & H. E. Adams (Eds.), *Handbook of behavioral assessment*. New York: Wiley-Interscience, 1977.

Kamin, L. J. *The science and politics of IQ*. Hillsdale, N.J.: Erlbaum, 1974.

Kamiya, J. Conscious control of brain waves. *Psychology Today*, 1968, *1*, 57–60.

Kammeier, M. L., Hoffman, H., & Loper, R. G. Personality characteristics of alcoholics as college freshmen and at time of treatment. *Quarterly Journal of Studies on Alcohol*, 1973, *34*, 390–399.

Kanfer, F. H., & Saslow, G. Behavioral diagnosis. In C. M. Franks (Ed.), *Behavior therapy: Appraisal and status*. New York: McGraw-Hill, 1969.

Kangas, J., & Bradway, K. Intelligence at middle age. *Developmental Psychology*, 1971, *5*, 333–337.

Kaplan, O. J. Psychological testing in seniles. In O. J. Kaplan (Ed.), *Psychopathology and aging*. New York: Academic Press, 1979.

Kaplan, R. M. Components of trust: Note on use of Rotter's scale. *Psychological Reports*, 1973, *33*, 13–14.

Kaplan, R. M. Nader's raid on the Educational Testing Service. *American Psychologist*, 1982.

Kaplan, R. M., Bush, J. W., & Berry, C. C. Health status: Types of validity for an index of well-being. *Health Services Research*, 1976, *11*, 478–507.

Kaplan, R. M., & Ernst, J. *Are there distribution effects in category scaling?* Paper presented at the meeting of the American Society for the Advancement of Science, San Francisco, January 1980.

Kaplan, R. M., & Litrownik, A. J. Some statistical methods for the assessment of multiple outcome criteria in behavioral research. *Behavior Therapy*, 1977, *8*, 383–392.

Kaplan, R. M., McCordick, S., & Twitchell, M. Is it the cognitive or the behavioral component which makes cognitive behavior modification effective in test anxiety? *Journal of Counseling Psychology*, 1979, *26*, 371–377.

Kaplan, R. M., & Singer, R. D. Television violence and viewer aggression: A reevaluation of the evidence. *Journal of Social Issues*, 1976, *34*, 35–86.

Kaswan, J. Manifest and latent functions in psychological services. *American Psychologist*, 1981, *36*, 290–299.

Kaufman, A. S. Factor structure of the McCarthy Scales of Children's Abilities. *Educational and Psychological Measurement*, 1975, *35*, 641–656. (a)

Kaufman, A. S. Note on interpreting profiles of McCarthy scale indexes. *Perceptual and Motor Skills*, 1975, *41*, 262. (b)

Kaufman, A. S. Review of Columbia Mental Maturity Scale. In O. K. Buros (Ed.), *The eighth mental measurements yearbook* (Vol. 1). Highland Park, N.J.: Gryphon Press, 1978

Kaufman, A. S. *Intelligence testing with the WISC-R*. New York: Wiley, 1979.

Kazdin, A. E. Artifact, bias, and complexity of assessment: The ABC's of reliability. *Journal of Applied Behavior Analysis*, 1977, *10*, 141–150.

Keir, G. The Progressive Matrices as applied to school children. *British Journal of Psychology* (statistical section 2), 1949, 140–150.

Kelley, T. L. *Interpretation of educational measurements*. Yonkers, N.Y.: World Book, 1927.

Kelly, E. L. Personality Research Form. In O. K. Buros (Ed.), *The seventh mental measurements yearbook* (Vol. 1). Highland Park, N.J.: Gryphon Press, 1972.

Kelly, H. H. Attribution theory in social psychology. In D. Levine (Ed.), *Nebraska Symposium on Motivation*. Lincoln: University of Nebraska Press, 1967.

Kelly, J. G. Ecological constraints on mental health services. In A. J. Bindman & A. D. Spiegel (Eds.), *Perspectives in community mental health*. Chicago: Aldine-Atherton, 1969.

Kendall, B. S., & Graham, F. K. Further standardization of the Memory-for-Designs test on children and adults. *Journal of Consulting Psychology*, 1948, *12*, 349–354.

Kendall, P. C., & Korgeski, G. P. Assessment and cognitive-behavioral interventions. *Cognitive Therapy and Research*, 1979, *1*, 1–21.

Kendall, P. C., Williams, S., Pechacek, T. F., Graham, L. G., Shisslak, C. S., & Herzoff, N. Cognitive-behavioral and patient education interventions in cardiac catheterization procedures: The Palo Alto medical psychology project. *Journal of Consulting and Clinical Psychology*, 1979, *47*, 49–58.

Kennedy, W. A., Van de Riet, V., & White, J. C., Jr. A normative sample of intelligence and achievement of Negro elementary school children in the Southeast United States. *Monographs of the Society for Research in Child Development*, 1963, *28*(6, Serial No. 90).

Kent, R. N., Kanowitz, J., O'Leary, K. D., & Cheiken, M. Observer reliability as a function of circumstances of assessment. *Journal of Applied Behavior Analysis*, 1977, *10*, 317–324.

Kent, R. N., O'Leary, K. D., Diament, C., & Dietz, A. Expectation biases in observational evaluation of therapeutic change. *Journal of Consulting and Clinical Psychology*, 1974, *42*, 774–780.

Kerlinger, F. N., & Pedhazur, E. J. *Multiple regression in behavioral research*. New York: Holt, Rinehart & Winston, 1973.

Kerner, J. Klexographien (Pt. VI). In R. Pissin (Ed.), *Kerners Werke*. Berlin: Bong, 1857.

Kiersh, E. Testing is the name, power is the game. *The Village Voice*, January 15, 1979.

Kiesler, C. A. The status of psychology as a profession and a science. In C. A. Kiesler, N. A. Cummings, & G. R. VanderBos (Eds.), *Psychology and national health insurance: A sourcebook*. Washington, D.C.: American Psychological Association, 1979.

Kirkpatrick, E. A. Individual tests of school children. *Psychological Review*, 1900, *7*, 274–280.

Klein, D. C. The community and mental health: An attempt at a conceptual framework. In A. J. Bindman & A. D. Spiegel (Eds.), *Perspectives in community mental health*. Chicago: Aldine-Atherton, 1969.

Kleinbaum, D. G., & Kupper, L. L. *Applied multivariate analysis*. North Scituate, Mass.: Duxbury Press, 1978.

Klinger, E. Modes of normal conscious flow. In K. S. Pope & J. L. Singer (Eds.), *The stream of consciousness: Scientific investigations into the flow of human experience*. New York: Plenum, 1978.

Klinger, E., Barta, S., & Mahoney, T. Motivation, mood, and mental events: Patterns and implications for adaptive processes. In G. Serban (Ed.), *Psychopathology of human adaptation*. New York: Plenum, 1976.

Klopfer, B., & Davidson, H. H. Form level rating: A preliminary proposal for appraising mode and level of thinking as expressed in Rorschach records. *Rorschach Research Exchange*, 1944, *8*, 164–177.

Klopfer, B., & Kelley, D. *The Rorschach technique*. Yonkers, N.Y.: World Book, 1942.

Knapp, R. R., & Knapp, L. *The California Occupational Preference System, technical manual*. San Diego, Calif.: EDITS, 1976.

Knobloch, H. & Pasamanick, B. Environmental factors affecting human development, before and after birth. *Pediatrics*, 1960, *26*, 210–218.

Knox, H. A. A scale based on the work at Ellis Island for estimating mental defect. *Journal of the American Medical Association*, 1914, *62*, 741–747.

Knutson, J. F. Review of the Rorschach. In O. K. Buros (Ed.), *The seventh mental measurements yearbook* (Vol. 1). Highland Park, N.J.: Gryphon Press, 1972.

Koch, H. L. Review of developmental diagnosis: Normal and abnormal child development: Clinical methods and practical applications. *Journal of Consulting Psychology*, 1942, *6*, 272–273.

Kohs, S. C. *Intelligence measurement: A psychological and statistical study based upon the block-design tests*. New York: Macmillan, 1923.

Koller, P. S., & Kaplan, R. M. A two-process theory of learned helplessness. *Journal of Personality and Social Psychology*, 1978, *36*, 1077–1083.

Konecni, V. J. Annoyance, type and duration of postannoyance activity, and aggression: The "cathartic effect." *Journal of Experimental Psychology: General*, 1975, *104*, 76–102.

Koppitz, E. M. *The Bender Gestalt test for young children*. New York: Grune & Stratton, 1964.

Korchin, S. J., & Schuldberg, D. The future of clinical assessment. *American Psychologist*, 1981, *36*, 1147–1158.

Kraepelin, E. *Lehrbuch der psychiatrie*. Leipzig: Barth, 1912.

Kretschmer, E. *Physique and character*. New York: Harcourt Brace Jovanovich, 1926.

Kuder, G. F. *Manual, Kuder Occupational Interest Survey, Form DD*. Chicago: Science Research Associates, 1968.

Kuder, G. F. *Manual, Kuder Occupational Interest Survey, 1979 revision*. Chicago: Science Research Associates, 1979.

Kuder, G. F., & Richardson, M. W. The theory of the estimation of reliability. *Psychometrika*, 1937, *2*, 151–160.

Kuhlmann, F. A revision of the Binet-Simon system for measuring intelligence of children. *Journal of Psycho-Asthenics Monograph Supplement*, 1912, *1*(1), 1–41.

Kuhlmann, F. *A handbook of mental tests*. Baltimore: Warwick & York, 1922.

Kusyszyn, I. Comparison of judgmental methods with endorsements in the assessment of personality traits. *Journal of Applied Psychology*, 1968, *52*, 227–233.

Lake, D. G., Miles, M. B., & Earle, R. B., Jr. *Measuring human behavior*. New York: Teachers College Press, 1973.

Lamp, R. E., & Traxler, A. J. The validity of the Slosson Intelligence Test for use with disadvantaged Head Start and first grade children. *Journal of Community Psychology*, 1973, *1*, 27–30.

Landis, C. Questionnaires and the study of personality. *Journal of Nervous and Mental Disease*, 1936, *83*, 125–134.

Landis, C., Zubin, J., & Katz, S. E. Empirical evaluation of three personality adjustment inventories. *Journal of Educational Psychology*, 1935, *26*, 321–330.

Landy, F. J., Vance, R. J., Barnes-Farrell, J. L., and Steele, J. W. Statistical control of halo error in performance ratings. *Journal of Applied Psychology*, 1980, *65*, 501–506.

Lang, P. J. The application of psychophysiological methods to the study of psychotherapy and behavior modification. In A. E. Bergin & S. L. Garfield (Eds.), *Handbook of psychotherapy and behavior change*. New York: Wiley, 1971.

Lang, P. J., & Lazovik, A. D. Experimental desensitization of a phobia. *Journal of Abnormal and Social Psychology*, 1963, *66*, 519–525.

Larrabee, L. L., & Kleinsaser, L. D. *The effect of experimenter bias on WISC performance*. Unpublished manuscript. St. Louis, Mo.: Psychological Associates, 1967.

Lawlis, G. F. Response styles of a patient population on the Fear Survey Schedule. *Behaviour Research and Therapy*, 1971, *9*, 95–102.

Lefever, D. W. Review of the Henmon-Nelson Test of Mental Ability, revised edition. In O. K. Buros (Ed.), *The fifth mental measurements yearbook*. Highland Park, N.J.: Gryphon Press, 1959.

Lehman, C. H., & Witty, P. A. Faculty psychology and personality traits. *American Journal of Psychology*, 1934, *44*, 486–500.

Lerner, B. Tests and standards today: Attacks, counterattacks, and responses. *New Directions in Testing and Measurement*, 1979, *1*(3), 15–31.

Lerner, B. The minimum competence testing movement: Social, scientific, and legal implications. *American Psychologist*, 1981, *36*, 1057–1066.

Lesser, G. S., Fifer, G., & Clark, D. H. Mental abilities of children from different social-class and cultural groups. *Monographs of the Society for Research in Child Development*, 1965, *30*(4, Serial No. 102).

Levine, J., & Feirstein, A. Differences in test performance between brain-damaged, schizophrenic, and medical patients. *Journal of Consulting and Clinical Psychology*, 1972, *39*, 508–511.

Levy, S. E.T.S. and the "coaching" cover-up. *New Jersey Monthly*, 1979, *3*(5), 4–7.

Lewandowski, D. G., & Saccuzzo, D. P. Possible differential WISC patterns for retarded delinquents. *Psychological Reports*, 1975, *37*, 887–894.

Lewandowski, D. G., & Saccuzzo, D. P. The decline of psychological testing: Have traditional procedures been fairly evaluated? *Professional Psychology*, 1976, *7*, 177–184.

Lezak, M. D. *Neuropsychological assessment*. New York: Oxford University Press, 1976.

Liebert, R. M., & Morris, L. W. Cognitive and emotional components of test anxiety: A distinction and some initial data. *Psychological Reports*, 1967, *20*, 975–978.

Likert, R. A technique for the measurement of attitudes. *Archives of Psychology*, 1932, No. 40.

Lindzey, G. The Thematic Apperception Test: Interpretive assumptions and related empirical evidence. *Psychological Bulletin*, 1952, *49*, 1–25.

Linn, R. L. Test design and analysis for measurement of educational achievement. *New Directions for Testing and Measurement*, 1980, *5*, 81–92.

Lipsitz, S. *Effect of the race of the examiner on results of intelligence test performance of Negro and White children*. Unpublished master's thesis, Long Island University, 1969.

Littell, W. M. The Wechsler Intelligence Scale for Children: Review of a decade of research. *Psychological Bulletin*, 1960, *57*, 132–156.

Little, K. B., & Shneidman, E. S. Congruencies among interpretations of psychological test and anamnestic data. *Psychological Monographs*, 1959, *73*(6, Whole No. 476).

Long, P. A., & Anthony, J. J. The measurement of retardation by a culture-specific test. *Psychology in the Schools*, 1974, *11*, 310–312.

Loper, R. G., Kammeier, M. L., & Hoffman, H. MMPI characteristics of college freshman males who later became alcoholics. *Journal of Abnormal Psychology*, 1973, *82*, 159–162.

Lord, E. Experimentally induced variations in Rorschach performance. *Psychological Monographs*, 1950, *64*(10, Whole No. 316).

Lord, F. M. *Efficiency of prediction when a regression equation from one sample is used in a new sample* (Research Bulletin 50-40). Princeton, N.J.: Educational Testing Service, 1950.

Lord, F. M. On the statistical treatment of football numbers. *American Psychologist*, 1953, *8*, 750–751.

Lord, F. M. *A prediction interval for scores on a parallel test form* (Research Bulletin RB-78-5). Princeton, N.J.: Educational Testing Service, 1978.

Lotsoff, E. Intelligence, verbal fluency and the Rorschach test. *Journal of Consulting Psychology*, 1953, *17*, 21–24.

Loughmiller, G. C., Ellison, R. L., Taylor, C. W., & Price, P. B. Predicting career performances of physicians using the biographical inventory approach. *Proceedings of the American Psychological Association*, 1970, *5*, 153–154.

Loy, D. L. The validity of the Taulbee-Sisson MMPI scale pairs in female psychiatric groups. *Journal of Clinical Psychology*, 1959, *15*, 306–307.

Lubin, B., Wallis, H. R., & Paine, C. Patterns of psychological test usage in the United States: 1935–1969. *Professional Psychology*, 1971, *2*, 70–74.

Lubin, B. L. Adjective checklists for measurement of depression. *Archives of General Psychiatry*, 1965, *12*, 57–62.

Lumsden, J. Review of Illinois Test of Psycholinguistic Abilities. In O. K. Buros (Ed.), *The eighth mental measurements yearbook* (Vol. 1). Highland Park, N.J.: Gryphon Press, 1978.

Lunemann, A. The correlational validity of I.Q. as a function of ethnicity and desegregation. *Journal of School Psychology*, 1974, *12*, 263–268.

Lyman, B., Hatlelid, D., & Macundy, C. Stimulus-person cues in first-impression attraction. *Perceptual and Motor Skills*, 1981, *52*, 59–66.

Mackinnon, R. A., & Michels, R. *The psychiatric interview in clinical practice*. Philadelphia: Saunders, 1971.

Magnusson, D., & Endler, N. S. Interactional psychology: Present status and future prospects. In D. Magnusson & N. S. Endler (Eds.), *Personality at the crossroads: Current issues in interactional psychology*. Hillsdale, N.J.: Erlbaum, 1977.

Mahl, G. F. Gestures and body movements in interviews. In J. Shlien, H. Hunt, J. D. Matarazzo, & C. Savage (Eds.), *Research in psychotherapy* (Vol. 3). Washington, D.C.: American Psychological Association, 1968.

Mahoney, M. J. *Cognition and behavior modification*. Cambridge, Mass.: Ballinger, 1974.

Malcolm, K. The mythical oligarchy of clinical psychologists in Florida. *Clinical Psychologist*, 1981, *34*, 18–19.

Malgady, R., Barcher, P. R., Davis, J., & Towner, G. Validity of the vocational adaptation rating scale: Prediction of mentally retarded workers' placement in sheltered workshops. *American Journal of Mental Deficiency*, 1980, *84*, 633–640.

Maloney, M. P., & Ward, M. P. *Psychological assessment: A conceptual approach*. New York: Oxford University Press, 1976.

Mandler, G., & Sarason, S. B. A study of anxiety and learning. *Journal of Abnormal and Social Psychology*, 1952, *47*, 166–173.

Mannheim, K. *Ideology and utopia*. London: Kegan, Paul, Trench, Trubner, 1936.

Markel, N. N. The reliability of coding paralanguage: Pitch, loudness, and tempo. *Journal of Verbal Learning and Verbal Behavior*, 1965, *4*, 306–308.

Marks, P. A., Seeman, W., & Haller, D. L. *The actuarial use of the MMPI with adolescents and adults*. Baltimore: Williams & Wilkins, 1974.

Marlett, N. J., & Watson, D. Test anxiety and immediate or delayed feedback in a test-avoidance task. *Journal of Personality and Social Psychology*, 1968, *8*, 200–203.

Marsden, G. Content analysis studies of psychotherapy: 1954 through 1968. In A. E. Bergin & S. L. Garfield (Eds.), *Handbook of psychotherapy and behavior change*. New York: Wiley, 1971.

Masters, W., & Johnson, V. *Human sexual response*. Boston: Little, Brown, 1966.

Matarazzo, J. D. *Wechsler's measurement and appraisal of adult intelligence* (5th ed.). Baltimore: Williams & Wilkins, 1972.

Matarazzo, J. D., & Wiens, A. N. *The interview: Research on its anatomy and structure*. Chicago: Aldine-Atherton, 1972.

Matarazzo, J. D., Wiens, A. N., Matarazzo, R. G., & Saslow, G. Speech and silence behavior in clinical psychotherapy and its laboratory correlates. In J. Shlien, H. Hunt, J. D. Matarazzo, & C. Savage (Eds.), *Research in psychotherapy* (Vol. 3). Washington, D.C.: American Psychological Association, 1968.

Mayfield, E. C. The selection interview: A re-evaluation of published research. *Personnel Psychology*, 1964, *17*, 239–260.

Mayman, M., & Kutner, B. Reliability in analyzing TAT stories. *Journal of Abnormal and Social Psychology*, 1947, *42*, 365–368.

McCall, R. *Fundamental statistics for psychology* (3rd ed.). New York: Harcourt Brace Jovanovich, 1980.

McCall, W. A. *Measurement*. New York: Macmillan, 1939.

McCandless, B. B. The Rorschach as a predictor of academic success. *Journal of Applied Psychology*, 1949, *33*, 43–50.

McClelland, D. C. Measuring motivation in phantasy: The achievement motive. In H. Guetzkow (Ed.), *Groups, leadership, and men*. Pittsburgh: Carnegie University Press, 1951. (a)

McClelland, D. C. *Personality*. New York: William Sloane Associates, 1951. (b)

McClelland, D. C. Methods of measuring human motivation. In J. W. Atkinson (Ed.), *Motives in fantasy, action, and society*. New York: Van Nostrand Reinhold, 1958.

McClelland, D. C., & Atkinson, J. W. The projective expression of needs. I: The effect of different intensities of the hunger drive on perception. *Journal of Psychology*, 1948, *25*, 205–222.

McClelland, D. C., Atkinson, J. W., Clark, R. A., & Lowell, E. L. *The achievement motive*. New York: Appleton-Century-Crofts, 1953.

McCordick, S., Kaplan, R. M., Smith, S., & Finn, M. B. Variations in cognitive behavior modification for text anxiety. *Psychotherapy: Theory Research & Practice*, 1981, *18*, 170–178.

McCormick, E. J., & Ilgen, D. *Industrial psychology* (7th ed.). Englewood Cliffs, N.J.: Prentice-Hall, 1980.

McFall, R. M., & Lillesand, D. B. Behavior rehearsal with modeling and coaching in assertion training. *Journal of Abnormal Psychology*, 1971, *77*, 313–323.

McLeod, H. N., & Rubin, J. Correlation between Raven Progressive Matrices and the WAIS. *Journal of Consulting Psychology*, 1962, *26*, 190–191.

McNemar, O. W., & Landis, C. Childhood disease and emotional maturity in the psychopathic woman. *Journal of Abnormal and Social Psychology*, 1935, *30*, 314–319.

McNemar, Q. *The revision of the Stanford-Binet scale*. Boston: Houghton Mifflin, 1942.

McNemar, Q. *Psychological statistics*. New York: Wiley, 1962.

McNemar, Q. *Psychological statistics*. New York: Wiley, 1967.

McNemar, Q. *Psychological statistics* (4th ed.). New York: Wiley, 1969.

Meehl, P. E. *Research results for counselors*. St. Paul: State Department of Education, 1951.

Meehl, P. E. *Clinical versus statistical prediction: A theoretical analysis and a review of the evidence*. Minneapolis: University of Minnesota Press, 1954.

Meehl, P. E. Wanted—a good cookbook. *American Psychologist*, 1956, *11*, 263–272.

Meehl, P. E. When shall we use our heads instead of the formula? *Journal of Counseling Psychol ogy*, 1957, *4*, 268–273.

Meehl, P. E., & Dahlstrom, W. G. Objective configural rules for discriminating psychotic from neurotic MMPI profiles. *Journal of Consulting Psychology*, 1960, *24*, 375–387.

Meehl, P. E., & Rosen, A. Antecedent probability and the efficiency of psychometric signs, patterns or cutting scores. *Psychological Bulletin*, 1955, *52*, 194–216.

Megargee, E. I. *The California Psychological Inventory Handbook*. San Francisco: Jossey-Bass, 1972.

Meichenbaum, D. Cognitive modification of test-anxious college students. *Journal of Consulting and Clinical Psychology*, 1972, *39*, 370–380.

Meichenbaum, D. A cognitive-behavior modification approach to assessment. In M. Hersen & A. S. Bellack (Eds.), *Behavioral assessment*. New York: Pergamon Press, 1976.

Meichenbaum, D. *Cognitive-behavior modification*. New York: Plenum, 1977.

Meichenbaum, D., & Butler, L. Toward a conceptual model for the treatment of test anxiety: Implications for research and treatment. In I. G. Sarason (Ed.), *Test anxiety: Theory, research, and applications*. Hillsdale, N.J.: Erlbaum, 1980.

Meichenbaum, D., & Turk, D. The cognitive-behavioral management of anxiety, anger, and pain. In P. Davidson (Ed.), *Behavioral management of anxiety, depression and pain*. New York: Brunner/Mazel, 1976.

Meikle, S., & Gerritse, R. MMPI cookbook pattern frequencies in a psychiatric unit. *Journal of Clinical Psychology*, 1970, *26*, 82–84.

Meir, E. I., & Barak, A. A simple instrument for measuring vocational interests based on Roe's classification of occupations. *Journal of Vocational Behavior*, 1974, *4*, 33–42.

Melei, J. P., & Hilgard, E. R. Attitudes toward hypnosis, self predictions, and hypnotic susceptibility. *International Journal of Clinical and Experimental Hypnosis*, 1964, *12*, 99–108.

Meltzoff, J., & Kornreich, M. *Research in psychotherapy*. Chicago: Aldine-Atherton, 1970.

Mercer, J. R. Sociocultural factors in labeling mental retardates. *Peabody Journal of Education*, 1971, *48*, 188–203.

Mercer, J. R. *Anticipated achievement: Computerizing the self-fulfilling prophecy*. Paper presented at the meeting of the American Psychological Association, Honolulu, September 1972.

Mercer, J. R. *Labeling the mentally retarded: Clinical and social system perspective on mental retardation*. Berkeley: University of California Press, 1973.

Mercer, J. R. In defense of racially and culturally non-discriminatory assessment. *School Psychology Digest*, 1979, *8*(1), 89–115.

Mercer, J. R., & Lewis, J. F. *System of multi-cultural pluralistic assessment: Conceptual and technical manual*. New York: Psychological Corporation, 1979.

Messick, S. The standard problem: Meaning and values in measurement and evaluation. *American Psychologist*, 1975, *30*, 955–966.

Messick, S. Test validity and the ethics of assessment. *American Psychologist*, 1980, *35*, 1012–1037.

Messick, S., & Jungeblut, A. Time and method in coaching for the SAT. *Psychological Bulletin*, 1981, *89*, 191, 216.

Meunier, C., & Rule, B. G. Anxiety, confidence, and conformity. *Journal of Personality*, 1967, *35*, 498–504.

Miller, J. O., & Phillips, J. *A preliminary evaluation of the Head Start and other metropolitan Nashville kindergartens*. Unpublished manuscript, George Peabody College for Teachers, 1966.

Miller, S., Saccuzzo, D. P., & Braff, D. L. Information processing deficits in remitted schizophrenics. *Journal of Abnormal Psychology*, 1979, *88*, 446–449.

Millman, J. Criterion-referenced measurement. In W. J. Popham (Ed.), *Evaluation and education*. Berkeley, Calif.: McCutchan, 1974.

Millman, J. Reliability and validity of criterion-referenced test scores. *New Directions in Testing and Measurement*, 1979, *1*(4), 75–92.

Minton, H. L., & Schneider, F. W. *Differential psychology*. Monterey, Calif.: Brooks/Cole, 1980.

Mischel, W. *Personality and assessment*. New York: Wiley, 1968.

Mischel, W. Toward a cognitive social learning reconceptualization of personality. *Psychological Review*, 1973, *80*, 252–283.

Mischel, W. On the future of personality measurement. *American Psychologist*, 1977, *32*, 246–254.

Mischel, W. On the interface of cognition and personality: Beyond the person-situation debate. *American Psychologist*, 1979, *34*, 740–754.

Mitchell, S. K. Interobserver agreement, reliability, and generalizability of data collected in observational studies. *Psychological Bulletin*, 1979, *86*, 376–390.

Moos, R. H. Conceptualizations of human environment. *American Psychologist*, 1973, *28*, 652–665.

Moos, R. H. *Community Oriented Program Environment Scales manual*. Palo Alto, Calif.: Consulting Psychologists Press, 1976. (a)

Moos, R. H. *Correctional Institutions Environment Scale manual*. Palo Alto, Calif.: Consulting Psychologists Press, 1976. (b)

Moos, R. H. *Family Environment Scale manual*. Palo Alto, Calif.: Consulting Psychologists Press, 1976. (c)

Moos, R. H. *The human context*. New York: Wiley, 1976. (d)

Moos, R. H. *Ward Atmosphere Scale manual*. Palo Alto, Calif.: Consulting Psychologists Press, 1976. (e)

Moos, R. H., & Gerst, M. *University Residence Environment Scale manual*. Palo Alto, Calif.: Consulting Psychologists Press, 1976.

Moos, R. H., & Humphrey, B. *Group Environment Scale manual*. Palo Alto, Calif.: Consulting Psychologists Press, 1976.

Moos, R. H., & Insel, R. *Work Environment Scale manual*. Palo Alto, Calif.: Consulting Psychologists Press, 1976.

Moos, R. H., & Truckett, E. *Classroom Environment Scale manual*. Palo Alto, Calif.: Consulting Psychologists Press, 1976.

Morris, L. W., & Liebert, R. M. Relationship of cognitive and emotional components of test anxiety to physiological arousal and academic performance. *Journal of Consulting and Clinical Psychology*, 1970, *35*, 332–337.

Mullins, C. J., Weeks, J. L., & Wilbourn, J. M. *Ipsative rankings as an indicator of job-worker match* (Tech. Rep. 78-70). U.S. Air Force Human Relations Laboratory, 1978.

Munford, P. R., & Munoz, A. A comparison of the WISC and WISC-R on Hispanic children. *Journal of Clinical Psychology*, 1980, *36*, 452–457.

Munnsinger, H. The adopted child's I.Q.: A critical review. *Psychological Bulletin*, 1975, *82*, 623–659.

Murray, H. A. *Explorations in personality*. New York: Oxford University Press, 1938.

Murstein, B. I. *Theory and research in projective techniques*. New York: Wiley, 1963.

Museum of Modern Art. *The family of man*. New York: Maco Magazine Corporation, 1955.

Neisser, U. *Cognitive psychology*. New York: Appleton-Century-Crofts, 1967.

Nelson, R. E. Irrational beliefs and depression. *Journal of Consulting and Clinical Psychology*, 1977, *45*, 1190–1191.

Nelson, S. E. *The development of an indirect, objective measure of social status and its relationship to certain psychiatric syndromes*. Unpublished doctoral dissertation, University of Minnesota, 1952.

Nisbett, R., & Borgida, E. Attribution and the psychology of prediction. *Journal of Personality and Social Psychology*, 1975, *32*, 932–943.

Nisbett, R. E., & Ross, L. *Human inference: Strategies and shortcomings of social judgments*. Englewood Cliffs, N.J.: Prentice-Hall, 1980.

Norman, W. T. Toward an adequate taxonomy of personality attributes: Replicated factor structure in peer nomination personality ratings. *Journal of Abnormal and Social Psychology*, 1963, *66*, 574–583.

Norton, E. H. *The Bakke decision and the future of affirmative action*. Statement of the Chair, U.S. Equal Employment Opportunity Commission, at the National Association for the Advancement of Colored People convention, July 1978.

Novick, M. R. Federal guidelines and professional standards. *American Psychologist*, 1981, *36*, 1035–1046.

Nunnally, J. C. *Psychometric theory* (2nd ed.). New York: McGraw-Hill, 1978.

Oakland, T. Research on the ABIC and ELP: A revisit to an old topic. *School Psychology Digest*, 1979, *8*, 209–213.

Oakland, T., & Feigenbaum, D. Multiple sources of test bias on the WISC-R and the Bender-Gestalt test. *Journal of Consulting and Clinical Psychology*, 1979, *47*, 968–974.

O'Leary, K. D., & Kent, R. N. Behavior modification for social action: Research tactics and problems. In L. A. Hamerlynck, P. O. Davidson, & L. E. Acker (Eds.), *Critical issues in research and practice*. Champaign, Ill.: Research Press, 1973.

O'Leary, K. D., Kent, R. N., & Kanowitz, J. Shaping data collection congruent with experimental hypotheses. *Journal of Applied Behavior Analysis*, 1975, *8*, 43–51.

Olmedo, E. L. Testing linguistic minorities. *American Psychologist*, 1981, *36*, 1078–1085.

Olweus, D. Personality and aggression. In J. K. Cole & D. D. Jensen (Eds.), *Nebraska Symposium on Motivation* (Vol. 21). Lincoln: University of Nebraska Press, 1973.

Olweus, D. Personality factors and aggression: With special reference to violence within the peer group. In J. De Wit & W. W. Hartup (Eds.), *Determinants and origins of aggressive behavior*. The Hague: Mouton, 1974.

Olweus, D. Aggression and peer acceptance in preadolescent boys: Two short-term longitudinal studies of ratings. *Child Development*, 1977, *48*, 1301–1313. (a)

Olweus, D. A critical analysis of the "modern" interactionist position. In D. Magnusson & N. S. Endler (Eds.), *Personality at the crossroads: Current issues in interactional psychology*. Hillsdale, N.J.: Erlbaum, 1977. (b)

Opton, E. From California, two views. *APA Monitor*, April 1977, pp. 5; 18.

Opton, E. A psychologist takes a closer look at the recent landmark *Larry P.* opinion. *APA Monitor*, December 1979, pp. 1; 4.

Orlinsky, D., & Howard, B. The good therapy hour. *Archives of General Psychiatry*, 1967, *16*, 621–632.

Osipow, S. H. *Theories of career development* (2nd ed.). Englewood Cliffs, N.J.: Prentice-Hall, 1973.

Palmer, F. H. Socioeconomic status and intellectual performance among Negro preschool boys. *Developmental Psychology*, 1970, *3*, 1–9.

Parducci, A. The relativism of absolute judgments. *Scientific American*, 1968, *219*(6), 84–90.

Parducci, A. Category ratings: Still more contextual effects! In B. Wegener (Ed.), *Social attitudes in psychophysical measurements*. Hillsdale, N.J.: Erlbaum, 1982, in press.

Parkinson, C. N. The short list, or principles of selection. In C. N. Parkinson (Ed.), *Parkinson's law*. Boston: Houghton Mifflin, 1957.

Pasamanick, B. A., & Knobloch, H. Early language behavior in Negro children and the testing of intelligence. *Journal of Abnormal and Social Psychology*, 1955, *50*, 401–402.

Passini, F. T., & Norman, W. T. A universal conception of personality structure? *Journal of Personality and Social Psychology*, 1966, *4*, 44–49.

Patterson, C. H. *Relationship counseling and psychotherapy*. New York: Harper & Row, 1974.

Paul, G. L., & Eriksen, C. W. Effects of text anxiety on "real life" examinations. *Journal of Personality*, 1964, *32*, 480–494.

Pearson, K. Mathematical contributions to the theory of evolution. III: Regression, heredity and panmixia. *Philosophical Transactions, A*, 1896, *187*, 253–318.

Peoples, V. Y. Measuring the vocational interest of women. In S. H. Osipow (Ed.), *Emerging women: Career analysis and outlooks*. Columbus, Ohio: Charles E. Merrill, 1975.

Pettigrew, T. F. *A profile of the American Negro*. New York: Van Nostrand Reinhold, 1964.

Pfeifer, C., & Sedlacek, W. The validity of academic predictors for Black and White students at a predominantly White university. *Journal of Educational Measurement*, 1971, *8*, 253–261.

Piotrowski, Z. Rorschach compendium. *Psychiatric Quarterly*, 1947, *21*, 79–101.

Piotrowski, Z. Digital computer interpretation of inkblot test data. *Psychiatric Quarterly*, 1964, *38*, 1–26.

Polansky, N., Freeman, W., Horowitz, M., Irwin, L., Papanis, N., Rapaport, D., & Whaley, F. Problems of interpersonal relations in research on groups. *Human Relations*, 1949, *2*, 281–291.

Porter, E. H. *An introduction to therapeutic counseling*. Boston: Houghton Mifflin, 1950.

Porteus, S. D. *Guide to Porteus Maze Test*. Vineland, N.J.: The Training School, 1924.

Printner, R., & Paterson, D. G. *A scale of performance tests*. New York: Appleton-Century-Crofts, 1917.

Quay, L. C. Language dialect, reinforcement, and the intelligence-test performance of Negro children. *Child Development*, 1971, *42*, 5–15.

Radcliffe, J. A. Edwards Personal Preference Schedule. In O. K. Buros (Ed.), *The sixth mental measurements yearbook*. Highland Park, N.J.: Gryphon Press, 1965.

Ramirez, M., III, & Castaneda, A. *Cultural democracy, bicognitive development, and education*. New York: Academic Press, 1974.

Rapaport, D., Gill, M. M., & Schafer, R. *Diagnostic psychological testing* (2 vols). Chicago: Yearbook Publishers, 1945, 1946.

Rapaport, D., Gill, M. M., & Schafer, R. *Diagnostic psychological testing* (Rev. ed.) (R. R. Holt, Ed.). New York: International Universities Press, 1968.

Rathus, S. A. A thirty-item schedule for assessing assertive behavior. *Behavior Therapy*, 1973, *4*, 398–406.

Recase, M. D. Procedures for computerized testing. *Behavior Research Methods and Instrumentation*, 1977, *9*, 148–152.

Redfield, J., & Paul, G. L. Bias in behavioral observation as a function of observer familiarity with subjects and typicality of behavior. *Journal of Consulting and Clinical Psychology*, 1976, *44*, 156.

Reid, J. B. Reliability assessment of observation data: A possible methodological problem. *Child Development*, 1970, *41*, 1143–1150.

Reid, J. B., & DeMaster, B. The efficacy of the spot-check procedure in maintaining the reliability of data collected by observers in quasinatural settings: Two pilot studies. *Oregon Research Institute Research Bulletin*, 1972, *12*.

Reitan, R. M. Psychological deficit. *Annual Review of Psychology*, 1962, *13*, 415–444.

Reitan, R. M. Psychological assessment of deficits associated with brain lesions in subjects with normal and subnormal intelligence. In J. L. Khanna (Ed.), *Brain damage and mental retardation*. Springfield, Ill.: Charles C Thomas, 1968.

Reitan, R. M. Neurological and physiological bases of psychopathology. *Annual Review of Psychology*, 1976, *27*, 189–216.

Reschly, D. J. Psychological testing in educational classification and placement. *American Psychologist*, 1981, *36*, 1094–1102.

Reynell, J. Review of the Brazelton Neonatal Assessment Scale. *Journal of Child Psychology and Psychiatry*, 1975, *16*, 87–88.

Richardson, F. C., O'Neil, H. F., Whitmore, S., & Judd, W. A. Factor analysis of the test anxiety scale and evidence concerning components of test anxiety. *Journal of Consulting and Clinical Psychology*, 1977, *45*, 704–705.

Ritzler, B. A., Sharkey, K. J., & Chudy, J. F. A comprehensive projective alternative to the TAT. *Journal of Personality Assessment*, 1980, *44*, 358–362.

Robinson, J. P., & Shaver, P. R. *Measures of social psychological attitudes*. Ann Arbor: University of Michigan Press, 1973.

Rodgers, D. A. Minnesota Multiphasic Personality Inventory. In O. K. Buros (Ed.), *The seventh mental measurements yearbook* (Vol. 1). Highland Park, N.J.: Gryphon Press, 1972.

Roe, A. Early determinants of vocational choice. *Journal of Counseling Psychology*, 1957, *4*, 212–217.

Roe, A., & Klos, D. Occupational classification. *The Counseling Psychologist*, 1969, *1*, 84–92.

Roe, A., & Siegelman, M. *The origin of interests*. Washington, D.C.: American Personnel and Guidance Association, 1964.

Rogers, C. R. A tentative scale for the measurement of process in psychotherapy. In E. A. Rubinstein & M. B. Parloff (Eds.), *Research in psychotherapy*. Washington, D.C.: American Psychological Association, 1959.

Rogers, C. R. A process conception of psychotherapy. In C. R. Rogers (Ed.), *On becoming a person*. Boston: Houghton Mifflin, 1961.

Rorschach, H. *Psychodiagnostik*. Bern: Bircher, 1921. (Hans Huber Verlag, trans., 1942.)

Rosenman, R. H., Brand, R. J., Jenkins, C. D., Friedman, M., Straus, R., & Wurm, M. Coronary heart disease in the Western Collaborative Group Study: Final follow-up experience of $8\frac{1}{2}$ years. *Journal of the American Medical Association*, 1975, *233*, 872–877.

Rosenman, R. H., & Friedman, M. Neurogenic factors in pathogenesis of coronary heart disease. *Medical Clinics of North America*, 1974, *58*, 269–279.

Rosenthal, R. *Experimenter effects in behavioral research*. New York: Appleton-Century-Crofts, 1966.

Rosenthal, R., & Fode, K. L. The effects of experimenter bias on the performance of the albino rat. *Behavioral Science*, 1963, *8*, 183–189.

Rosenthal, R., Hall, J. A., DiMatteo, M. R., Rogers, P. L., and Archer, D. *Sensitivity to nonverbal communication: The PONS test*. Baltimore: Johns Hopkins University Press, 1980.

Rosenthal, R., & Jacobson, L. *Pygmalion in the classroom*. New York: Holt, Rinehart & Winston, 1968.

Ross, L. The intuitive psychologist and his shortcomings: Distortions in the attribution process. In L. Berkowitz (Ed.), *Advances in experimental social psychology* (Vol. 10). New York: Academic Press, 1977.

Rotter, J. B. Generalized expectancies for internal versus external control of reinforcement. *Psychological Monographs*, 1966, *80*(1, Whole No. 609).

Rotter, J. B. A new scale for the measurement of interpersonal trust. *Journal of Personality*, 1967, *35*, 651–665.

Rubin, Z. Measurement of romantic love. *Journal of Personality and Social Psychology*, 1970, *16*, 265–273.

Rubin, Z. *Liking and loving: An invitation to social psychology*. New York: Holt, Rinehart & Winston, 1973.

Rubin, Z. Los Angeles says it with love on a scale. *Los Angeles Times*, February 1979.

Rushmore, J. T. Fakability of the Gordon Personal Profile. *Journal of Applied Psychology*, 1956, *40*, 175–177.

Saccuzzo, D. P. Canonical correlation as a method of assessing the correlates of good and bad therapy hours. *Psychotherapy: Theory, Research and Practice*, 1975, *12*, 253–256.

Saccuzzo, D. P. *The practice of psychological testing in America: Issues and trends*. Paper presented at the meeting of the California Psychological Association, Los Angeles, April 1976.

Saccuzzo, D. P. Bridges between schizophrenia and gerontology: Generalized or specific deficits? *Psychological Bulletin*, 1977, *84*, 595–600. (a)

Saccuzzo, D. P. The practice of psychotherapy in America: Issues and trends. *Professional Psychology*, 1977, *8*, 297–306. (b)

Saccuzzo, D. P. Input capability and speed of processing in mental retardation: A reply to Stanovich and Purcell. *Journal of Abnormal Psychology*, 1981, *90*, 172–174.

Saccuzzo, D. P., & Braff, D. L. Associative cognitive dysfunction in schizophrenia and old age. *Journal of Nervous and Mental Disease*, 1980, *168*, 41–45.

Saccuzzo, D. P., & Braff, D. L. Early information processing deficits in schizophrenia: New findings using schizophrenic subgroups and manic controls. *Archives of General Psychiatry*, 1981, *38*, 175–179.

Saccuzzo, D. P., Braff, D. L., Shine, A., & Lewandowski, D. G. *A differential WISC pattern in the retarded as a function of sex and race*. Paper presented at the meeting of the Western Psychological Association, Los Angeles, April 1981.

Saccuzzo, D. P., Hirt, M., & Spencer, T. J. Backward masking as a measure of attention in schizophrenia. *Journal of Abnormal Psychology*, 1974, *83*, 512–522.

Saccuzzo, D. P., Kerr, M., Marcus, A., & Brown, R. Input capability and speed of information processing in mental retardation. *Journal of Abnormal Psychology*, 1979, *88*, 312–317.

Saccuzzo, D. P., & Lewandowski, D. G. The WISC as a diagnostic tool. *Journal of Clinical Psychology*, 1976, *32*, 115–124.

Saccuzzo, D. P., & Miller, S. Critical interstimulus interval in delusional schizophrenics and normals. *Journal of Abnormal Psychology*, 1977, *86*, 261–266.

Saccuzzo, D. P., & Schubert, D. Backward masking as a measure of slow processing in the schizophrenia spectrum of disorders. *Journal of Abnormal Psychology*, 1981, *90*, 305–312.

Saccuzzo, D. P., & Schulte, R. The value of a master's degree for the Ph.D. pursuing student in psychology. *American Psychologist*, 1978, *33*, 862–864.

Sarason, I. G. Effects on verbal learning of anxiety, reassurance, and meaningfulness of material. *Journal of Experimental Psychology*, 1958, *56*, 472–477.

Sarason, I. G. Intellectual and personality correlates of test anxiety. *Journal of Abnormal and Social Psychology*, 1959, *59*, 272–275.

Sarason, I. G. The effects of anxiety and threat on solution of a difficult task. *Journal of Abnormal and Social Psychology*, 1961, *62*, 165–168.

Sarason, I. G. Test anxiety, attention, and the general problem of anxiety. In C. D. Spielberger & I. G. Sarason (Eds.), *Stress and anxiety* (Vol. 1). New York: Halsted, 1975.

Sarason, I. G. (Ed.). *Test anxiety: Theory, research, and applications*. Hillsdale, N.J.: Erlbaum, 1980.

Sarason, I. G., & Palola, E. G. The relationship of test and general anxiety, difficulty of task, and experimental instructions to performance. *Journal of Experimental Psychology*, 1960, *59*, 185–191.

Sarason, I. G., & Sarason, B. R. *Abnormal psychology* (3rd ed.). Englewood Cliffs, N.J.: Prentice-Hall, 1980.

Sarason, I. G., Smith, R. E., & Diener, E. Personality research: Components of variance attributable to the person and the situation. *Journal of Personality and Social Psychology*, 1975, *3*, 199–204.

Sattler, J. M. Racial "experimenter effects" in experimentation, testing, interviewing, and psychotherapy. *Psychological Bulletin*, 1970, *73*, 137–160.

Sattler, J. M. Examiners' scoring style, accuracy, ability, and personality scores. *Journal of Clinical Psychology*, 1973, *29*, 38–39. (a)

Sattler, J. M. Intelligence testing of ethnic minority-group and culturally disadvantaged children. In L. Mann and D. Sabatino (Eds.), *The first review of special education* (Vol. 2). Philadelphia: JSE Press, 1973. (b)

Sattler, J. M. Racial experimenter effects. In K. S. Miller & R. M. Dreger (Eds.), *Comparative studies of Blacks and Whites in the United States*. New York: Seminar Press, 1973. (c)

Sattler, J. M. *Assessment of children's intelligence*. Philadelphia: Saunders, 1974.

Sattler, J. M. Personal communication, 1975.

Sattler, J. M. Review of McCarthy Scales of Children's Abilities. In O. K. Buros (Ed.), *The eighth mental measurements yearbook* (Vol. 1). Highland Park, N.J.: Gryphon Press, 1978.

Sattler, J. M. *Intelligence tests on trial; Larry P. et al. vs. Wilson Riles et al.* Paper presented at the meeting of the Western Psychological Association, San Diego, April 1979. (a)

Sattler, J. M. Standard intelligence tests are valid for measuring the intellectual potential of urban children: Comments on pitfalls in the measurement of intelligence. *Journal of Psychology*, 1979, *102*, 107–112. (b)

Sattler, J. M. Intelligence tests on trial: An interview with Judges Robert F. Peckham And John F. Grady. *APA Monitor*, November 1980, pp. 7–8.

Sattler, J. M. *Assessment of children's intelligence and special abilities*. Boston: Allyn & Bacon, 1982.

Sattler, J. M., & Gwynne, J. Ethnicity and Bender Visual Motor Test performance. *Journal of School Psychology*, 1982, in press.

Sattler, J. M., Hillix, W. A., & Neher, L. A. Halo effect in examiner scoring of intelligence test responses. *Journal of Consulting and Clinical Psychology*, 1970, *34*, 172–176.

Sattler, J. M., & Theye, F. Procedural, situational, and interpersonal variables in individual intelligence testing. *Psychological Bulletin*, 1967, *68*, 347–360.

Sattler, J. M., & Winget, B. M. Intelligence testing procedures as affected by expectancy and I.Q. *Journal of Clinical Psychology*, 1970, *26*, 446–448.

Saunders, B. T., & Vitro, F. T. Examiner expectancy and bias as a function of the referral process in cognitive assessment. *Psychology in the Schools*, 1971, *8*, 168–171.

Sawyer, J. Measurement and prediction, clinical and statistical. *Psychological Bulletin*, 1966, *66*, 178–200.

Sax, G. *Principles of educational and psychological measurement and evaluation*. Belmont, Calif.: Wadsworth, 1974.

Sax, G. *Principles of educational and psychological measurement and evaluation* (2nd ed.). Belmont, Calif.: Wadsworth, 1980.

Scarr, S. Testing for children: Assessment and the many determinants of intellectual compentence. *American Psychologist*, 1981, *36*, 1159–1166.

Scarr-Salapatek, S. Race, social class and I.Q. *Science*, 1971, *174*, 1285–1295.

Schact, T., & Nathan, P. But is it good for the psychologist? Appraisal and status of DSM-III. *American Psychologist*, 1977, *32*, 1017–1025.

Schmidt, F. L., Hunter, J. E., McKenzie, R. C., & Muldrow, T. W. Impact of valid selection procedures on work-force productivity. *Journal of Applied Psychology*, 1979, *64*, 609–626.

Schneider, D. J., Hastorf, A. H., & Ellsworth, P. C. *Person perception* (2nd ed.). Reading, Mass.: Addison-Wesley, 1979.

Schoggen, P. Roger G. Barker and behavioral settings: A commentary. *Journal of Personality and Social Psychology*, 1979, *37*, 2158–2160.

Schroeder, H. E., & Kleinsasser, L. D. Examiner bias: A determinant of children's verbal behavior on the WISC. *Journal of Consulting and Clinical Psychology*, 1972, *39*, 451–454.

Schultz, C. B., & Sherman, R. H. Social class, development, and differences in reinforcer effectiveness. *Review of Educational Research*, 1976, *46*, 25–59.

Schwartz, A. N., & Hawkins, H. L. Patient models and affect statements in group therapy. In *Proceedings of the 73rd Annual Convention of the American Psychological Association*. Washington, D.C.: American Psychological Association, 1965.

Schwartz, F., & Lazar, Z. The scientific status of the Rorschach. *Journal of Personality Assessment*, 1979, *43*, 3–11.

Schwartz, R., & Gottman, J. Toward a task analysis of assertive behavior. *Journal of Consulting and Clinical Psychology*, 1976, *44*, 910–920.

Scott, P., Burton, R. V., & Yarrow, M. Social reinforcement under natural conditions. *Child Development*, 1967, *38*, 53 63.

Seguin, E. *Idiocy: Its treatment by the physiological method*. New York: Bureau of Publications, Teachers College, Columbia University, 1907. (Originally published, 1866.)

Seligman, M. E. P. *Helplessness: On depression, development, and death*. San Francisco: W. H. Freeman, 1975.

Seligmann, J., Coppola, V., Howard, L., & Lee, E. D. A really final exam. *Newsweek*, May 28, 1979, pp. 97–98.

Selye, H. *The stress of life*. New York: McGraw-Hill, 1956.

Shaffer, L. Of whose reality I cannot doubt. *American Psychologist*, 1953, *8*, 608–623.

Shakow, D., Hilgard, E. R., Kelly, E. L., Sanford, R. N., & Shaffer, L. F. Recommended graduate training in clinical psychology. *American Psychologist*, 1947, *2*, 539–558.

Share, J. B., Webb, A., & Koch, R. A preliminary investigation of the early developmental status of mongoloid infants. *American Journal of Mental Deficiency*, 1961, *66*, 238–241.

Share, J. B., Webb, A., & Koch, R. The longitudinal development of infants and young children with Down's syndrome. *American Journal of Mental Deficiency*, 1964, *68*, 689–692.

Sheehan, G. *Running and being*. New York: Warner Books, 1978.

Sheldon, W. H. *Atlas of men*. New York: Harper & Row, 1954.

Shlien, J., Hunt, H., Matarazzo, J. D., & Savage, C. (Eds.). *Research in psychotherapy* (Vol. 3). Washington, D.C.: American Psychological Association, 1968.

Silverstein, A. B. Evaluation of a split-half short form of the WAIS. *American Journal of Mental Deficiency*, 1968, *72*, 839–840.

Silverstein, A. B. Review of McCarthy Scales of Children's Abilities. In O. K. Buros (Ed.), *The eighth mental measurements yearbook* (Vol. 1). Highland Park, N.J.: Gryphon Press, 1978.

Simon, W. E. Expectancy effects in the scoring of vocabulary items: A study of scorer bias. *Journal of Educational Measurement*, 1969, *6*, 159–164.

Sines, J. O. Actuarial versus clinical prediction in psychopathology. *British Journal of Psychiatry*, 1970, *116*, 129–144.

Slosson, R. L. *Slosson Intelligence Test (SIT) for children and adults*. New York: Slosson Educational Publications, 1963.

Smith, D. Unfinished business with informed consent procedures. *American Psychologist*, 1981, *36*, 22–26.

Smith, R. E., Ascough, J. C., Ettinger, R. F., & Nelson, D. A. Humor, anxiety, and task performance. *Journal of Personality and Social Psychology*, 1971, *19*, 243–246.

Smith, S. H. *Refining cognitive behavior modification treatments for test anxiety*. Unpublished master's thesis, San Diego State University, 1977.

Snow, R. E. Review of *Pygmalion in the Classroom* by R. Rosenthal and L. Jacobson. *Contemporary Psychology*, 1969, *14*, 197–199.

Snyder, C. R., Shenkel, R. J., & Lowery, C. R. Acceptance of personality interpretations: The "barnum effect" and beyond. *Journal of Consulting and Clinical Psychology*, 1977, *45*, 104–114.

Sommers, A. R. Violence, television, and the health of American youth. *New England Journal of Medicine*, 1976, *294*, 811–817.

Sostek, A. M. Review of the Brazelton Neonatal Assessment Scale. In O. K. Buros (Ed.), *The eighth mental measurements yearbook* (Vol. 1). Highland Park, N.J.: Gryphon Press, 1978.

Spearman, C. E. The proof and measurement of association between two things. *American Journal of Psychology*, 1904, *15*, 72–101.

Spearman, C. E. *The abilities of man*. New York: Macmillan, 1927.

Spiegler, M. D., Morris, L. W., & Liebert, R. M. Cognitive and emotional components of test anxiety: Temporal factors. *Psychological Reports*, 1968, *22*, 451–456.

Spielberger, C. D. Anxiety as an emotional state. In C. D. Spielberger (Ed.), *Anxiety: Current trends in theory and research*. New York: Academic Press, 1972.

Spielberger, C. D., Anton, W. B., & Bedell, J. The nature and treatment of test anxiety. In M. Zuckerman & C. D. Spielberger (Eds.), *Emotions and anxiety: New concepts, methods and applications*. Hillsdale, N.J.: Erlbaum, 1976.

Spielberger, C. D., Auerbach, S. M., Wadsworth, A. P., Dun, T. M., & Taulbee, E. S. Emotional reactions to surgery. *Journal of Consulting and Clinical Psychology*, 1975, *40*, 33–38.

Spielberger, C. D., Gorsuch, R. L., & Lushene, R. E. *Manual for the State-Trait Anxiety Inventory*. Palo Alto, Calif.: Consulting Psychologists Press, 1970.

Stanley, J. C. Reliability. In R. L. Thorndike (Ed.), *Educational measurement*. Washington, D.C.: American Council on Education, 1971.

Stanley, J. C., & Hopkins, K. D. *Educational and psychological measurement and evaluation*. Englewood Cliffs, N.J.: Prentice-Hall, 1972.

Stephenson, W. *The study of behavior*. Chicago: University of Chicago Press, 1953.

Stern, W. [The psychological methods of testing intelligence.] Die psychologische methoden der intelligenzprüfung. Leipzig: Barth, 1912. (Baltimore: Warwick & York, 1914.)

Sternberg, R. J. Testing and cognitive psychology. *American Psychologist*, 1981, *36*, 1181–1189.

Stevens, S. S. A metric for the social consensus. *Science*, 1966, *151*, 530–541.

Stevenson, I. *The diagnostic interview*. New York: Harper & Row, 1971.

Stokols, D. Environmental psychology. *Annual Review of Psychology*, 1978, *29*, 253–295.

Stormes, M. D. Videotape and the attribution process: Reversing actors' and observers' points of view. *Journal of Personality and Social Psychology*, 1973, *27*, 165–175.

Strauss, M. E., Gynther, M. D., & Wallhermfechtel, J. Differential misdiagnosis of Blacks and Whites by the MMPI. *Journal of Personality Assessment*, 1974, *38*, 55–60.

Stricker, L. J. Edwards Personal Preference Schedule. In O. K. Buros (Ed.), *The sixth mental measurements yearbook*. Highland Park, N.J.: Gryphon Press, 1965.

Strong, E. K., Jr., & Campbell, D. P. *Manual for Strong Vocational Interest Blank*. Stanford, Calif.: Stanford University Press, 1966.

Subkoviak, M. J. The reliability of mastery classification decisions. In R. A. Burk (Ed.), *Criterion-referenced measurement: The state of the art*. Baltimore: Johns Hopkins University Press, 1980.

Suinn, R. M. The relationship between fears and anxiety: A further study. *Behaviour Research and Therapy*, 1969, *7*, 317–318. (a)

Suinn, R. M. The STABS, a measure of test anxiety for behavior therapy: Normative data. *Behaviour Research and Therapy*, 1969, *7*, 335–339. (b)

Sundberg, N. D. The practice of psychological testing in clinical services in the United States. *American Psychologist*, 1961, *16*, 79–83.

Super, D. E. A theory of vocational development. *American Psychologist*, 1953, *8*, 185–190.

Super, D. E., & Hall, D. T. Career development: Exploitation and planning. *Annual Review of Psychology*, 1978, *29*, 333–372.

Svanum, S., & Dallas, C. L. Alcoholic MMPI types and their relationship to patient characteristics, Polydrug abuse, and abstinence following treatment. *Journal of Personality Assessment*, 1981, *45*, 278–287.

Sweet, R. C. *Variations in the intelligence test performance of lower-class children as a function of feedback or monetary reinforcement* (doctoral dissertation, University of Wisconsin, 1969). (University Microfilms No. 70-37,21)

Symonds, P. M. On the loss of reliability in ratings due to coarseness of the scale. *Journal of Experimental Psychology*, 1924, *7*, 456–461.

Szasz, T. S. *The myth of mental illness*. New York: Harper & Row, 1961.

Taking the Chitling Test. *Newsweek*, July 15, 1968, pp. 51–52, 72.

Tannenbaum, A. J. Review of the IPAT Culture Fair Intelligence Test. In O. K. Buros (Ed.), *The sixth mental measurements yearbook*. Highland Park, N.J.: Gryphon Press, 1968.

Taplin, P. S., & Reid, J. B. Effects of instructional set and experimenter influence on observer reliability. *Child Development*, 1973, *44*, 547–554.

Tasto, D. L. Self-report schedules and inventories. In A. R. Ciminero, K. D. Calhoun, & H. E. Adams (Eds.), *Handbook of behavioral assessment*. New York: Wiley-Interscience, 1977.

Taulbee, E. S., & Sisson, L. Configurational analysis of MMPI profiles of psychiatric groups. *Journal of Consulting Psychology*, 1957, *21*, 413–417.

Taylor, C. W., Price, P. B., Richards, Jr., J. M., & Jacobsen, T. L. An investigation of the criterion problem for a group of medical general practitioners. *Journal of Applied Psychology*, 1965, *49*, 399–406.

Taylor, H. C., & Russell, J. T. The relationship of validity coefficients to the practical effectiveness of tests in selection: Discussion and tables. *Journal of Applied Psychology*, 1939, *23*, 565–578.

Taylor, J. A. The relationship of anxiety to the conditioned eyelid response. *Journal of Experimental Psychology*, 1951, *41*, 81–92.

Taylor, J. A. A personality scale of manifest anxiety. *Journal of Abnormal Psychology*, 1953, *48*, 285–290.

Temp, G. Test bias: Validity of the SAT for blacks and whites in thirteen integrated institutions. *Journal of Educational Measurement*, 1971, *8*, 245–251.

Tenopyr, M. L. Content–construct confusion. *Personnel Psychology*, 1977, *30*, 47–54.

Torman, L. M. *The measurement of intelligence*. Boston: Houghton Mifflin, 1916.

Terman, L. M., & Merrill, M. A. *Measuring intelligence*. Boston: Houghton Mifflin, 1937.

Terman, L. M., & Merrill, M. A. Tests of intelligence. B. 1937 Stanford-Binet scales. In A. Weider (Ed.), *Contributions toward medical psychology* (Vol. 2). New York: Ronald Press, 1953.

Terman, L. M., & Merrill, M. A. *Stanford-Binet intelligence scale*. Boston: Houghton Mifflin, 1960.

Terrell, F., Taylor, J., & Terrell, S. L. Effects of type of social reinforcement on the intelligence test performance of lower-class Black children. *Journal of Consulting and Clinical Psychology*, 1978, *46*, 1538–1539.

Thorndike, E. L. *An introduction to the theory of mental and social measurements*. New York: Science Press, 1904.

Thorndike, E. L. *Principles of teaching*. New York: Seiler, 1906.

Thorndike, E. L. A constant error in psychological rating. *Journal of Applied Psychology*, 1920, *4*, 25–29.

Thorndike, E. L. Intelligence and its measurement: A symposium. *Journal of Educational Psychology*, 1921, *12*, 123–147, 195–216.

Thorndike, R. L. California Psychological Inventory. In O. K. Buros (Ed.), *The fifth mental measurements yearbook*. Highland Park, N.J.: Gryphon Press, 1959.

Thorndike, R. L. Review of *Pygmalion in the Classroom* by R. Rosenthal and L. Jacobson. *American Educational Research Journal*, 1968, *5*, 708–711.

Thorndike, R. L. Concepts of culture-fairness. *Journal of Educational Measurement*, 1971, *8*, 63–70.

Thorndike, R. L. Review of the Torrance Tests of Creative Thinking. In O. K. Buros (Ed.), *The seventh mental measurements yearbook* (Vol. 1). Highland Park, N.J.: Gryphon Press, 1972.

Thorndike, R. L. *Stanford-Binet intelligence scale, Form L-M, 1972 norms tables*. Boston: Houghton Mifflin, 1973.

Thumin, F. J. MMPI scores as related to age, education and intelligence among male job applicants. *Journal of Applied Psychology*, 1969, *53*, 404–407.

Thurstone, L. L., & Chave, E. J. *The measurement of attitude*. Chicago: University of Chicago Press, 1929.

Tiber, N., & Kennedy, W. A. The effects of incentives on the intelligence test performance of different social groups. *Journal of Consulting Psychology*, 1964, *28*, 187.

Timm, N. H. *Multivariate analysis with applications in education and psychology*. Monterey, Calif.: Brooks/Cole, 1975.

Titus, H. E., & Hollander, E. P. The California R Scale in psychological research: 1950–1955. *Psychological Bulletin*, 1957, *54*, 47–64.

Tomkins, S. S. *The Thematic Apperception Test: The theory and technique of interpretation*. New York: Grune & Stratton, 1947.

Torgerson, W. S. *Theory and methods of scaling*. New York: Wiley, 1958.

Traxler, A. E. Administering and scoring the objective test. In E. F. Linquist (Ed.), *Educational measurement*. Washington, D.C.: American Council on Education, 1951.

Trott, D. M., & Morf, M. E. A multimethod factor analysis of the Differential Personality Inventory, Personality Research Form, and Minnesota Multiphasic Personality Inventory. *Journal of Counseling Psychology*, 1972, *19*, 94–103.

Truax, C. B., & Carkhuff, R. R. *Toward effective counseling and psychotherapy: Training and practice*. Chicago: Aldine-Atherton, 1967.

Truax, C. B., & Mitchell, K. M. Research on certain therapist interpersonal skills in relation to process and outcome. In A. E. Bergin & S. L. Garfield (Eds.), *Handbook of psychotherapy and behavior change*. New York: Wiley, 1971.

Tukey, J. W. *Exploratory data analysis*. Reading, Mass.: Addison-Wesley, 1977.

Turner, J. H. Entrepreneurial environments and the emergence of achievement motivation in adolescent males. *Sociometry*, 1970, *33*, 147–165.

Tversky, A., & Kahneman, D. Belief in the law of small numbers. *Psychological Bulletin*, 1971, *76*, 105–110.

Tversky, A., & Kahneman, D. Causal schemas in judgments under uncertainty. In M. Fishbein (Ed.), *Progress in social psychology*. Hillsdale, N.J.: Erlbaum, in press.

Tyler, L. E. *The work of the counselor* (3rd ed.). New York: Appleton-Century-Crofts, 1969.

Tyler, L. E., & Walsh, W. B. *Tests and measurements* (3rd ed.). Englewood Cliffs, N.J.: Prentice-Hall, 1979.

Uhl, N., & Eisenberg, T. Predicting shrinkage in the multiple correlation coefficient. *Educational and Psychological Measurement*, 1970, *30*, 487–489.

Ulrich, L., & Trumbo, D. The selection interview since 1949. *Psychological Bulletin*, 1965, *63*, 100–116.

Uniform guidelines on employee selection procedures. *Federal Register*, 1978, *43*, 38296-38309.

Varble, D. L. Current status of the Thematic Apperception Test. In P. McReynolds (Ed.), *Advances in psychological assessment* (Vol. 2). Palo Alto, Calif.: Science and Behavior Books, 1971.

Vernon, P. E. *The structure of human abilities*. New York: Wiley, 1950.

Wade, T. C., & Baker, T. B. Opinions and uses of psychological tests: A survey of clinical psychologists. *American Psychologist*, 1977, *32*, 874–882.

Wagner, R. The employment interview: A critical review. *Personnel Psychology*, 1949, *2*, 17–46.

Walker, A. M., Rablen, R. A., & Rogers, C. R. Development of a scale to measure process changes in psychotherapy. *Journal of Clinical Psychology*, 1960, *16*, 79–85.

Wallace, W. L. Review of the SAT. In O. K. Buros (Ed.), *The seventh mental measurements yearbook* (Vol. 1). Highland Park, N.J.: Gryphon Press, 1972.

Walsh, J. A. California Psychological Inventory. In O. K. Buros (Ed.), *The seventh mental measurements yearbook* (Vol. 1). Highland Park, N.J.: Gryphon Press, 1972.

Watson, D., & Friend, R. Measurement of social-evaluative anxiety. *Journal of Consulting and Clinical Psychology*, 1969, *33*, 448–451.

Watson, R. I. *The clinical method in psychology*. New York: Harper & Row, 1951.

Webb, E. Character and intelligence. *British Journal of Psychology*, 1915. (Monograph Suppl. 3.)

Webb, J. T. *The relation of MMPI two-point codes to age, sex, and education level in a representative nationwide sample of psychiatric outpatients*. Paper presented at the meeting of the Southeastern Psychological Association, Louisville, Ky., April 1970.

Webster, E. C. *Decision making in the employment interview*. Montreal: Industrial Relations Center, McGill University, 1964.

Wechsler, D. *The measurement of adult intelligence*. Baltimore: Williams & Wilkins, 1939.

Wechsler, D. Non-intellective factors in general intelligence. *Journal of Abnormal and Social Psychology*, 1943, *38*, 101–103.

Wechsler, D. *Wechsler Intelligence Scale for Children*. New York: Psychological Corporation, 1949.

Wechsler, D. *Manual, Wechsler Adult Intelligence Scale*. New York: Psychological Corporation, 1955.

Wechsler, D. *The measurement and appraisal of adult intelligence* (4th ed.). Baltimore: Williams & Wilkins, 1958.

Wechsler, D. *Manual for the Wechsler Preschool and Primary Scale of Intelligence*. New York: Psychological Corporation, 1967.

Wechsler, D. *Wechsler Adult Intelligence Scale—Revised*. New York: Psychological Corporation, 1981.

Weiner, B., & Kukla, A. An attributional analysis of achievement motivation. *Journal of Personality and Social Psychology*, 1970, *15*, 1–20.

Welsh, G. S. An extension of Hathaway's MMPI profile coding system. *Journal of Consulting Psychology*, 1948, *12*, 343–344.

Welsh, G. S. Factor dimensions A and R. In G. S. Welsh & W. G. Dahlstrom (Eds.), *Basic readings on the MMPI in psychology and medicine*. Minneapolis: University of Minnesota Press, 1956.

Werner, E. E. Review of Gesell Developmental Schedules. In O. K. Buros (Ed.), *The sixth mental measurements yearbook*. Highland Park, N.J.: Gryphon Press, 1965.

Wesman, A. G. Writing the test item. In R. L. Thorndike (Ed.), *Educational measurement* (2nd ed.). Washington, D.C.: American Council on Education, 1971.

Whipple, G. M. *Manual of mental and physical tests*. Baltimore: Warwick & York, 1910.

Wicker, A. W. Ecological psychology: Some recent and prospective developments. *American Psychologist*, 1979, *34*, 755–765.

Wicker, A. W., & Kirmeyer, S. L. From church to laboratory to national park. In S. Wapner, S. B. Conen, & B. Kaplan (Eds.), *Experiencing the environment*. New York: Plenum Press, 1976.

Wickham, T. *WISC patterns in acting-out delinquents, poor readers, and normal controls*. Unpublished doctoral dissertation, United States International University, 1978.

Wiederholt, J. L. Review of Illinois Test of Psycholinguistic Abilities. In O. K. Buros (Ed.), *The eighth mental measurements yearbook* (Vol. 1). Highland Park, N.J.: Gryphon Press, 1978.

Wiener-Levy, D., & Exner, J. E. The Rorschach Ea-ep variable as related to persistence in a task frustration situation under feedback conditions. *Journal of Personality Assessment*, 1981, *45*, 118–124.

Wiens, A. N. The assessment interview. In I. B. Weiner (Ed.), *Clinical methods in psychology*. New York: Wiley, 1976.

Wiens, A. N., Matarazzo, J. D., & Saslow, G. The interaction recorder: An electronic punched paper tape unit for recording speech behavior during interviews. *Journal of Clinical Psychology*, 1965, *21*, 142–145.

Wiggins, J. S. *Personality and prediction: Principles of personality assessment*. Reading, Mass.: Addison-Wesley, 1973.

Wiggins, N. Individual viewpoints of social desirability. *Psychological Bulletin*, 1966, *66*, 68–77.

Wiggins, N., & Kohen, E. S. Man versus model of man revisited: The forecasting of graduate school success. *Journal of Personality and Social Psychology*, 1971, *19*, 100–106.

Wilder, J. The law of initial values. *Psychosomatic Medicine*, 1950, *12*, 392–401.

Williams, A., Heaton, R. K., & Lehman, R. A. An attempt to cross-validate two actuarial systems for neuropsychological test interpretation. *Journal of Consulting and Clinical Psychology*, 1980, *48*, 317–326.

Williams, R. L. Scientific racism and I.Q.: The silent mugging of the Black community. *Psychology Today*, 1974, *7*, 32–41.

Wilson, M. T. Review of developmental diagnosis: Normal and abnormal child development: Clinical methods and practical applications. *American Journal of Orthopsychiatry*, 1942, *12*, 372.

Wilson, R. S. Twins and siblings: Concordance for school-age mental development. *Child Development*, 1977, *48*, 211–216.

Wine, J. D. Cognitive-attentional theory of test anxiety. In I. G. Sarason (Ed.), *Test anxiety: Theory, research, and applications*. Hillsdale, N.J.: Erlbaum, 1980.

Wing, K. R. *The law and the public's health*. St. Louis: C. V. Mosby, 1976.

Wishner, J. Rorschach intellectual indicators in neurotics. *American Journal of Orthopsychiatry*, 1948, *18*, 265–279.

Wissler, C. The correlation of mental and physical tests. *Psychological Review*, 1901, *3*. (Monograph Suppl. 16.)

Witmer, J. M., Bornstein, A. V., & Dunham, R. M. The effects of verbal approval and disapproval upon the performance of third and fourth grade children of four subtests of the Wechsler Intelligence Scale for Children. *Journal of School Psychology*, 1971, *9*, 347–356.

Wolk, R. L., & Wolk, R. B. *Manual: Gerontological Apperception Test*. New York: Behavioral Publications, 1971.

Wolkind, S. Review of the Brazelton Neonatal Assessment Scale. *British Journal of Psychiatry*, 1974, *125*, 216–217.

Wolpe, J. *The practice of behavior therapy*. New York: Pergamon Press, 1969.

Wolpe, J., & Lang, P. J. A fear survey schedule for use in behavior therapy. *Behaviour Research and Therapy*, 1964, *2*, 27–30.

Woodring, P. Are intelligence tests unfair? *Saturday Review*, 1966, *49*, 79–80.

Woodworth, R. S. *Personal Data Sheet*. Chicago: Stoelting, 1917.

Woodworth, R. S. *Personal Data Sheet*. Chicago: Stoelting, 1920.

Wright, O. R., Jr. Summary of research on the selection interview since 1964. *Personnel Psychology*, 1969, *22*, 391–413.

Wright, T. L., & Tedeschi, R. G. Factor analysis of the interpersonal trust scale. *Journal of Consulting and Clinical Psychology*, 1975, *43*, 470–477.

Wrightsman, L. *Social psychology in the eighties*. Monterey, Calif.: Brooks/Cole, 1981.

Yerkes, R. M. The Binet versus the point scale method of measuring intelligence. *Journal of Applied Psychology*, 1917, *1*, 111–122.

Yerkes, R. M. (Ed.). Psychological examining in the United States Army. *Memoirs of the National Academy of Sciences*, 1921, *15*.

Yerkes, R. M., Bridges, J. W., & Hardwick, R. S. *A point scale for measuring mental ability*. Baltimore: Warwick & York, 1915.

Zajonc, R. B., & Bargh, J. Birth order, family size, and decline of SAT scores. *American Psychologist*, 1980, *35*, 662–668.

Zedeck, S., & Blood, M. R. *Foundations of behavioral science research in organizations*. Monterey, Calif.: Brooks/Cole, 1974.

Zimmerman, I. L., Woo-Sam, J. M., & Glasser, A. J. *Clinical interpretation of the Wechsler Adult Intelligence Scale*. New York: Grune & Stratton, 1973.

Zubin, J. Discussion of symposium on newer approaches to personality assessment. *Journal of Personality Assessment*, 1972, *36*, 427–434.

Zuckerman, M. The development of an affect adjective check list measure of anxiety. *Journal of Consulting Psychology*, 1960, *24*, 457–462.

Zuckerman, M. Physiological measures of sexual arousal in the human. *Psychological Bulletin*, 1971, *75*, 297–329.

Zytowski, D. G. Predictive validity of the Kuder Occupational Interest Survey: A 12–19 year follow-up. *Journal of Counseling Psychology*, 1976, *23*, 221–233.

Zytowski, D. G. The effects of being interest inventoried. *Journal of Vocational Behavior*, 1977, *11*, 153–158.

Zyzanski, S. J., Jenkins, C. D., Ryan, T. J., Flessas, A., & Everist, M. Psychological correlates of coronary angiographic findings. *Archives of Internal Medicine*, 1976, *136*, 1234–1237.

Author Index

Subject Index